Y0-EEL-740

Women and Politics in Chile

Women and Politics in Chile

Susan Franceschet

BOULDER
LONDON

Published in the United States of America in 2005 by
Lynne Rienner Publishers, Inc.
1800 30th Street, Boulder, Colorado 80301
www.rienner.com

and in the United Kingdom by
Lynne Rienner Publishers, Inc.
3 Henrietta Street, Covent Garden, London WC2E 8LU

Library of Congress Cataloging-in-Publication Data
Franceschet, Susan, 1965–
Women and politics in Chile / Susan Franceschet.
p. cm.
Includes bibliographical references and index.
ISBN 1-58826-316-9 (hardcover : alk. paper)
1. Women in politics—Chile—History. 2. Women and democracy—Chile.
3. Feminism—Chile. 4. Chile—Politics and government. I. Title.
HQ1236.5.C5F73 2005
323.3'4'0983—dc22

2004029655

British Cataloguing in Publication Data
A Cataloguing in Publication record for this book
is available from the British Library.

Printed and bound in the United States of America

The paper used in this publication meets the requirements of the American National Standard for Permanence of Paper for Printed Library Materials Z39.48-1992.

5 4 3 2 1

Contents

Tables

Acknowledgments

In the course of researching and writing this book, I encountered numerous people who gave generously of their time and knowledge to make completion of the project possible. The people to whom I owe the deepest gratitude are the Chilean women who agreed to be interviewed for this study. Many of these women invited me into their homes and offices, where they generously shared their experiences with me. Fabiola Oyarzún deserves particular mention because of the numerous times she invited me to accompany her to meetings and events organized by women both in her community and in Santiago. Ximena Velasco opened her home to me and provided endless advice and support during my research trips to Chile. I also wish to thank Magaly Ortiz for transcribing all of the interviews conducted in 1999; Ximena Velasco for transcribing those done in 2002; and Teresa Valdés and Mirta Monroy of the Facultad Latinoamericana de Ciencias Sociales (FLACSO-Chile) for providing a supportive environment during my work in Chile.

I would also like to thank some of the people who provided intellectual support and encouragement over the years. As a graduate student in political science at Carleton University (Ottawa), I was fortunate to work with two very inspiring scholars and exemplary role models, Laura Macdonald and Jill Vickers. Both provided me with intellectual stimulation and critical, thoughtful comments on my work. Other people, too, such as Patricia Richards, Julie Shayne, Marcela Ríos Tobar, and Magda Hinojosa, provided insightful comments on various chapters of this book. Patricia Richards and Julie Shayne read (and reread) earlier versions of many chapters, and I am immensely grateful to have had such careful, thoughtful, and encouraging critics. My colleagues in the Department of Political Science at Acadia University (Wolfville, Nova Scotia) are gratefully acknowledged for their good humor and intellectual encouragement. Finally, I would like to thank Lynne Rienner for her interest in and support for this project.

The research for this book was supported by the Social Sciences and Humanities Research Council of Canada, the International Development

Research Centre of Canada, and Acadia University. Some of the material in certain chapters of the book appeared in earlier form in journal articles, and I would like to thank the publishers for granting permission for their inclusion. Parts of Chapters 3 and 4 draw on "Explaining Social Movement Outcomes: Collective Action Frames and Strategic Choices in First- and Second-Wave Feminism in Chile," *Comparative Political Studies* 37 no. 5 (2004): 499–525 (© Sage Publications). Parts of Chapter 5 draw on "Women in Politics in Post-Transitional Democracies: The Chilean Case," *International Feminist Journal of Politics* 3, no. 2 (2001): 207–236, www.tandf.co.uk/journals (© Taylor and Francis). Parts of Chapter 7 draw on "State Feminism and Women's Movements: The Impact of Chile's Servicio Nacional de la Mujer on Women's Activism," *Latin American Research Review* 38, no. 1 (2003): 9–40 (© University of Texas Press).

My greatest debts are to my family. Ilse and George Meub and Sandi Weir always encouraged me, supported my pursuits, and helped sustain my confidence. But most of all, my husband, Antonio Franceschet, helped me through all stages of this project, encouraging and supporting me even when it meant long periods of separation while I did research in Chile. He was also a tireless and astute editor and critic, reading and rereading numerous versions of the manuscript. I thank him for the myriad ways in which he enriches my life.

Women and Politics in Chile

Women and Politics in Chile 1

A casual observer of Chilean politics today may be inclined to conclude that women have won their struggle for equality. As this book goes to press, two political women, Soledad Alvear of the Christian Democratic Party and Michelle Bachelet of the Socialist Party, are the frontrunners in the competition to become the presidential candidate for the governing Coalition of Parties for Democracy (Concertación de los Partidos por la Democracia) in the 2005 election. Both women held prominent posts in President Ricardo Lagos's cabinet. Alvear held the foreign affairs portfolio and Bachelet was minister of defense; significantly, both are posts that have historically been held by men.

The success of these political women notwithstanding, Chilean women's struggle for equality is far from over. Most women find the political arena inhospitable to their presence and to the issues that women in politics wish to pursue. Indeed, while women elsewhere in Latin America are making substantial gains in terms of their access to elected office, Chilean women hold a mere 12.5 percent of the seats in the Chamber of Deputies and only 4.1 percent of seats in the Senate (Inter-Parliamentary Union 2004).[1] Political parties in Chile have not yet undertaken the types of changes that would make it easier for women to compete for office. In fact, many women who participate in electoral politics suggest that political parties themselves are an important barrier to increasing the number of women in politics.

If Chilean politics is so sexist, or "machista" as they say in Latin America, then how is it possible that the next president may well be a woman? There are two answers to this question. First, political calculations within the governing Concertación favor the selection of a female candidate. The Concertación has formed the government since 1990, when democratic rule replaced the seventeen-year dictatorship of General Augusto Pinochet. If the coalition wins the 2005 presidential elections it would be the fourth consecutive Concertación government. According to President Lagos, a woman candidate would be a symbol of renovation after three consecutive governments led by the center-left Concertación: "The greatest indication of change would be to have the first female president in the country."[2]

The second answer is more revealing, and relates to many of the themes taken up in this book. That is, women face opportunities to enter politics when certain (gendered) characteristics and behaviors are deemed desirable. Arturo Barrio of the Socialist Party explained that among the reasons for the Chilean public's favorable view of women political leaders, such as Alvear and Bachelet, is women's different styles of doing politics. Barrio noted that people today believe that the political world needs "honesty, accountability, values and credibility," and that "women have these characteristics in high quantity."[3] This is particularly important today because a number of Concertación deputies were recently implicated in a series of bribery scandals. For this reason, pollster Marta Lagos claimed, "I think that both of these women have emerged not so much because they are women but because of a vacuum and a disenchantment with politics" (*New York Times,* December 20, 2004). In Chile, as elsewhere in Latin America, women are viewed as more honest and less corruptible. A 1995 public opinion survey revealed that Chileans are more likely to attribute moral qualities to women than to men (Busquet 1995, p. 210).

This view, along with the view that women bring something to politics that is distinct from their male counterparts, is a view that I address at length in this book. One of the women I interviewed explained that "women are needed to humanize politics."[4] Another noted that politics needs more women because they bring issues to the public's attention that are otherwise ignored.[5] Chile's most popular female politicians today use similar language to explain their high levels of support. Bachelet noted, "One reason we women have begun appearing as relevant figures is that we represent a type of humanization of politics, closer to how people see themselves." Alvear attributes the popularity of female political leaders to their "different style of leadership" (*New York Times,* December 20, 2004).

While this view can be used to justify women's entry into politics, it also reinforces perceptions and dichotomies that marginalize women from politics and inhibits the promotion of their issues in the political arena. This view can also lead to the perception that women's political roles are crisis-driven—that is, women are encouraged to enter the normally male-dominated political world only when their feminine characteristics are needed, particularly in times of crisis, change, or uncertainty.[6] When crises pass and politics-as-usual returns, women are expected to return to their social roles as mothers and community caretakers. Consequently, despite the highly visible activism of women during two of Chile's most turbulent and conflictual periods—the short-lived socialist government of Salvador Allende (1970–1973) and the lengthy and brutal Pinochet dictatorship (1973–1990)—politics has remained an inhospitable arena for women and many of their primary concerns.

In this book, I explore the various reasons for women's marginalization from politics. I argue that patterns of citizenship in Chile have taken deeply gendered forms that are primarily expressed in men's and women's different styles of political participation. These different styles of political activism are intricately related to the different social roles played by men and women and a gender ideology that reinforces a fairly rigid division of labor. While men tend to participate in party politics and government, women's activism is often directed toward the community or local arena, where they organize around issues that directly affect their families and their communities. For example, women hold only 16.2 percent of leadership posts in political parties, but hold 82 percent of leadership posts in *talleres solidarios* (solidarity and community workshops) and 95 percent of leadership posts in *ollas comunes* (community soup kitchens).[7] The problem for women is that participation in their communities is not normally perceived as "political" and therefore not normally perceived as an expression of citizenship. However, perceptions about what is political and what is not change over time. Consequently, there have been certain historical junctures when Chilean women confronted greater opportunities for reshaping the political arena to make it more open to their presence as women and to women's issues. These openings emerged out of Chile's process of democratization, which has proceeded through two distinct stages. The first period of democratization began in 1932, when the landowning elites lost their monopoly over political power, and ended in 1973 with a military coup that resulted in a lengthy dictatorship led by General Pinochet. The second period of democratization began in 1988, when in a plebiscite Chilean citizens voted against the continuation of Pinochet's rule. I address women's politics in both of these periods in this book, although I focus on the posttransition period in greater detail.

Throughout the book, I analyze women's politics in Chile through the lens of citizenship. Citizenship, at its most basic, is an institution that regulates membership in nation-states. Through the mutual rights and obligations that constitute citizenship, citizens are bound both to their state and to each other. Citizenship entails a set of rights that citizens may claim against the state, but also establishes less instrumental relationships through which common membership in a community "reinforces empathy and sustains solidarity by means of official statements of who is 'one of us'" (Cairns 1999, p. 4). Because citizenship is about membership in a political community, questions are raised about the criteria for membership as well as the benefits that membership brings. For many Chilean women who struggled for women's citizenship throughout the twentieth century, the main benefit sought was a political voice for women that would permit them to bring their issues and interests to the political arena. But citizenship is also about social rights or entitlements that are deserved or earned by virtue of one's membership in a political community. In the early part of the twentieth century women fought for the rights to vote and to hold elected political office, rights they achieved in 1949. But gaining formal political rights did not lead to a transformed political arena in which women and women's issues were accorded equal status to their male counterparts. As a result, in the later decades of the twentieth century, women's struggles for citizenship involved attempts to transform politics to make it more welcoming of both women and women's issues.

Studying women's politics through the lens of citizenship is a way of exploring women's struggles to construct a democracy that more fully includes them as equal citizens. While these struggles began around the turn of the twentieth century when women first organized around the goal of women's suffrage and social reform, and continued during the lengthy and brutal dictatorship, the main focus of the book is on women's roles in Chile's new democracy (1990 to the present). Since the return of democracy, Chilean women have been engaged in three different yet interconnected struggles to make democratic citizenship meaningful for women. First, they have tried to improve women's access to electoral politics, pressuring political parties to adopt gender quotas and to be more open to women's issues in politics. Second, women have taken their struggle into the state itself, particularly in the National Women's Service (Servicio Nacional de la Mujer, SERNAM), created in 1991 to promote gender equity through public policy. Third, women have continued to organize in women's movements and feminist movements in civil society, seeking both to lobby government for progressive reform and to target machismo and a variety of other forms of social inequality based on class, race, and ethnicity.[8]

Although there have been gains in each of these three areas since 1990, Chilean democracy remains incomplete when evaluated according to criteria of gender equality.[9] Chilean women remain woefully underrepresented in formal politics, despite some attempts by parties of the Concertación to address the issue. The creation of the state agency SERNAM has resulted in a number of gains for women, including the successful introduction of legislation that criminalizes domestic violence, legislation that improves the rights of married women and female workers, and policies that address the gendered sources of poverty. Nonetheless, women working in SERNAM frequently remark that the agency as a whole has too little influence within the Chilean state, and is constrained by a lack of political will on the part of successive governments to address controversial issues—for example, reproductive rights, sex education in school, and sexual harassment in the workplace. Finally, with respect to the women's movement in Chile's new democracy, numerous scholars have noted its decline or even disappearance following the end of the dictatorship (Matear 1997a; Schild 1998; Shayne 2004; Waylen 1997). Indeed, during the course of my research in Chile, many people told me that a women's movement no longer existed in the country. As I make clear throughout the book, however, women continue to organize in Chile's new democracy, but are facing immense challenges in making their activism more visible. The common thread among the problems that women face in each of the areas listed above is the negative impact that the shifting boundary between "formal" and "informal" politics has on women's citizenship.

Gendered Patterns of Citizenship

One of the problems identified by scholars of women's politics is that traditional conceptions of citizenship render women invisible as political actors. This is why so many earlier studies of women and politics have concluded that women have lower levels of engagement with politics than their male counterparts. While it is true that women are less likely than men to participate in formal political institutions, it is not necessarily true that they are less politically engaged.[10] Feminist scholars have warned that an accurate study of women's politics must avoid taking masculine models of politics as the norm, which will automatically lead to the conclusion that women are less active politically. Instead, as Jill Vickers argues, a feminist approach to political science must "start from where women are" (1997a, p. 56). For that reason, my study of women and politics in Chile includes analysis of women's incursions into electoral and bureaucratic politics as well as their community and social movement activism.

Scholars wishing to study women's politics face two challenges: first, to render women visible as political actors; and second, to make women's issues visible as political issues. Both concerns have led some scholars to reconceptualize politics so that it encompasses more than merely the sphere of government and political party competition. Thus, following the lead of other feminist scholars, I analyze women's politics in Chile employing a dichotomy that separates—at least conceptually—"formal" from "informal" political activity. This dichotomy is a gendered one, based primarily on the different social roles assigned to men and women, and the norms and ideas that underpin these roles. Women are the primary actors in informal politics while men tend to predominate in the formal political arena. According to feminist theorist Ruth Lister, the sphere of informal politics operates "at the interstices of the public and private, motivated often initially by personal, domestic concerns" (1997, p. 153). Because the sphere of informal politics is where family and community issues are more likely to be promoted, it has been constructed as feminine (p. 137). Thus it is not simply that informal politics is dominated by women, but that its attributes are those associated with feminine roles of caretaking rather than masculine roles of governing.

This is how gender is inscribed into constructions of the political while also shaping the very "spaces" in which politics is practiced.

In most contemporary political systems, the formal political arena includes all activity connected to governing, including partisan activities geared toward competing for office and influencing those who hold office. Thus the formal political arena includes the executive and legislative branches of government, the bureaucracy, political parties, and interest groups. The informal political arena, in contrast, includes community activism, movement politics, and all of those self-help or survival-oriented activities that are dominant in poor communities throughout Chile. In these latter activities, individuals are less likely to identify themselves as being engaged in politics, in large part because their activity is not directed by or associated with political parties, and they do not necessarily seek direct influence over government policy. In Chile, where partisan identification has traditionally been very strong, any activity that is not directed by political parties tends to be deemed nonpolitical. In brief, parties monopolize politics. Leaders of a women's organization in one of Santiago's poblaciones (shantytowns) noted that most of their members reject the idea that their activism is political precisely because it is not connected to any of the political parties.[11]

Women's greater likelihood to participate in the informal political arena of community and movement politics stems from their sexual difference and the roles, particularly the social and economic roles, associated with it. Because the sexual division of labor and the gender ideology in Chile assign women exclusive responsibility for the tasks of social reproduction, their political participation is conditioned by these roles. Hence women's activism often emerges out of struggles to fulfill their social roles—for example, organizing for better healthcare or community services. But women are also more likely to participate in the informal political arena because such activism is more flexible—that is, it can be adapted to women's schedules, and is normally less demanding in terms of time and material resources, both of which women often lack.[12] Of course, class and race also play critical roles. Women from marginalized class and race groups are even less likely to enter the formal sphere of politics, which is nearly universally monopolized by members from the dominant race group and the middle and upper classes. Consequently, the boundary between formal and informal politics produces not only gender privilege (for men) but also class and racial privileges for those with lighter skin from the middle and upper classes.

Like all conceptual distinctions, however, the distinction between formal and informal political arenas, when analyzed in practice, operates more as a continuum than as a dichotomy. This is especially true in Chile at the local level, where grassroots community organizations interact, often in pursuit of common goals, with municipal state agencies. Most significant, perceptions about the meaning of the formal versus informal politics distinction are not constant, but shift over time. Because the formal political arena was closed during the Pinochet dictatorship, activism in the informal arena was more likely to be perceived as political (especially by those carrying out the activities). Because citizenship has traditionally been bound up with acting politically rather than with fulfilling one's social (gendered) roles, women's activism may be considered an expression of citizenship in one context, when informal activities are perceived as political, and as a nonpolitical expression of women's private or social responsibilities in another, when only formal activities are deemed political. Seen this way, women's political participation does not necessarily decline following transitions to democracy simply because few of the women active in human rights or prodemocracy movements move into formal politics.[13] Rather, transitions to democracy result in a shift in the distinction between informal and formal political activities and the corresponding reemergence of perceptions that women's participation is not political because it is not necessarily geared toward holding political office.[14] Thus, in order to understand why struggles to expand women's citizenship succeed or not, we must pay attention to the discursive politics surrounding processes of political change (Beckwith 2000, p. 444). Understandings of what constitutes political activity are discursively constructed. Often, it is the political parties that seek to monopolize the political, because assertions of political activism by nonparty actors may be viewed as challenges to the parties' hegemony. This dynamic has proven especially strong in Chile, where, despite a seventeen-year dictatorship during which time partisan activity was repressed quite harshly, parties proved remarkably resilient and capable of reasserting their dominance in the posttransition political context (Scully 1995). The hegemony of parties leads organized women at the community level to view their participation as nonpolitical.

Throughout the book, I employ the dichotomy between the informal and formal political arenas as a conceptual tool to analyze gendered patterns of citizenship in Chile. A main argument I make is that the cultural practices and discursive politics that reinforce perceptions about the formal/informal dichotomy are a primary source of women's unequal citizenship, reflected in both women's scant presence in the political arena and the lack of attention to women's issues in national politics. Women's marginalized status as citizens flows from their *different* ways of participating politically, ways of participating that are not always perceived as political. Because of the importance of the formal/informal dichotomy to women's marginalization as citizens, the recent transition to democracy, which led to shifts in the perceptions of this dichotomy, is useful in studying changes to gendered patterns of citizenship. By exploring the process of democratization in Chile, we see in a very concrete way how perceptions about the boundary between formal and informal politics are constructed and reconstructed, and how, through these shifts, there are opportunities for expanding women's citizenship in one instance and obstacles in the next.

As the democratic transition unfolded in Chile, many observers optimistically believed that politics would subsequently be practiced differently in the new democracy, led by women's and other popular movements' styles of activism in civil society. Many believed that the politicization of the informal arena that took place during the dictatorship would be maintained after the transition to democracy. This did not happen, however. Once political parties resumed their central role, civil society organizations were marginalized. There are two main consequences of this. First, the monopolization of politics by political parties has rendered the activities of women's movements in civil society virtually invisible, leading many Chileans to conclude that there is no longer a women's movement in the country. Second, those women who do wish to enter formal politics face a dual challenge: an arena that is hostile to their presence as women; and relatedly, parties that are unwilling to promote issues that many women—whether self-declared feminists or not—wish to pursue. Only a handful of women who have succeeded in Chile's political world have identified themselves as champions of women's rights and equality.

With respect to the common view that the women's movement has disappeared in Chile's new democracy, I advance an alternative argument, emphasizing the ways in which women's movements in Chile have transformed themselves and their strategies to adapt to changing political conditions. During the dictatorship, women's movements organized to demand citizenship rights in all their forms—civil, political, and social—and often did so through mass movements that were multiclass in nature. After the transition, the movements divided, especially along class lines, as women were confronted with greater choices about where to focus their activism. While most women continued to play out their activism in the arena that is most hospitable, that is, the community or local arena, other women chose to enter the formal political arena. The new context also intensified the conflict among different segments of the women's movement as power relations within it shifted.

I argue that women's choices about where to participate and practice their citizenship identities are shaped by both gender and class factors. The transitions to democracy provided professional (normally middle-class) women with opportunities to move into formal politics, mainly into electoral or bureaucratic politics. These opportunities stemmed from the privileged social location of middle-class women and from women's roles in the opposition movements that brought about democracy. Many of the opposition parties that became the posttransition government perceived electoral gains from inviting (the very limited) representation of women and gender issues because of the success women's movements had in putting these issues on the transition's public agenda (see Baldez 2002; Frohmann and Valdés 1995; M. Valenzuela 1991; and Waylen 1997).

Even more significant, the posttransition government created a women's agency within the state (SERNAM) as a way to incorporate gender issues. But while this has given professional women greater opportunities to access arenas of formal politics, poor and working-class women do not enjoy such opportunities, and continue to carry out their activism in the informal arena. The issues around which most women organize in the informal political arena relate to the dismal material conditions in which Chile's popular sectors live. But in the currently ascendant neoliberal conception of citizenship, these issues are not to be resolved through the formal political process. Instead, it becomes the obligation of community members themselves to resolve their material hardships through collective self-help projects (see Schild 2000a, 2000b). This trend, predominant throughout much of Latin America, is related to the fiscal crises that most states confronted in the 1980s, Latin America's "lost decade." In Chile, economic restructuring has involved state withdrawal from the provision of social or welfare services. This process has led to the progressive depoliticization of welfare issues, a task that is accomplished through a discursive politics that valorizes civil society's active involvement in solving its problems collectively rather than expecting governments to solve them. These processes invite an analysis of the way patterns of citizenship are constructed not only through gender difference, but through class difference as well.[15]

In the end, the problem for women is not that citizenship patterns are gendered, but that the implications of this have been disadvantageous for women. What kind of citizenship patterns would be more beneficial for women? What would it take to improve women's citizenship in Chile? Two things come to mind. First, formal politics must be more accessible to women as individuals and to women's issues. Although women in Chile are less likely to seek elected office, those who do should not confront gendered obstacles to their participation (such as patronizing attitudes toward women or schedules that make it impossible to carry out their family responsibilities). Also, women who do succeed in accessing formal politics must be capable of placing women's gender interests on the public agenda. In other words, improving women's citizenship requires reversing the tendency to depoliticize social issues.[16] A second strategy for ameliorating the negative impact of Chile's gendered patterns of citizenship is to build linkages between the informal political arena, where many women are active, and the sphere of formal politics. Through such linkages, organized women in civil society could participate alongside members of the political class (both men and women) and play a more protagonistic role in setting the terms of public debate around social and political issues. The lack of linkages between formal and informal politics is a reflection of both gender and class dynamics. Women active in informal politics, particularly popular sector women, often carry out similar activities as gender policy experts in state bureaucracies. But the work of the former is normally deemed to be apolitical "volunteer" work in the sense that it is not paid and is frequently not heard when it is time to make policy decisions.[17]

Consequently, we cannot just look at indicators of women's participation in electoral politics to see if women's citizenship is improving. Put simply, we need to go beyond counting the number of women in political institutions. Rather, there must be ways for women to improve their political representation without having to actually be present in legislatures or decisionmaking arenas themselves. This distinction is normally described as the difference between "numerical representation" (how many members of any particular social group are present in decisionmaking bodies) and "substantive representation" (the extent to which the interests of a social group are represented in politics).[18] I take up this issue in later chapters in the book.

The Importance of Studying Women and Politics in Chile

There has been an impressive growth in the literature on women and politics in Latin America. Interestingly, much of this literature has focused on Chile (Baldez 2002; Haas 2000; Macaulay 1998; Matear 1995, 1997a, 1997b; Power 2002; Richards 2004; Rosemblatt 2000; Schild 1994, 1998, 2000a, 2000b; Waylen 1997, 2000). Why has the Chilean case attracted so much attention from students of gender politics in Latin America? In my view, the Chilean case contributes to four of the most relevant and hotly debated themes in the study of women and politics: (1) the "politics of difference" strategy, (2) the debate between "autonomy" and "double militancy," (3) women and electoral politics, and (4) women and states.

The Politics of Difference

What are the consequences of pursuing citizenship rights using a collective action frame that asserts women's difference from men, a difference that derives from their motherhood roles?[19] A number of scholars have argued that a difference or maternal collective action frame draws on the most conservative aspects of women's identity, and therefore makes any substantive changes to gender hierarchies unlikely (Feijoó 1989; Strange 1990). Others have argued that a maternal frame is by nature apolitical because the mother-child relationship is not based on autonomy or equality (Dietz 1998). As I show throughout the book, however, women's movements in Chile have emphasized women's differences from men as justifications for political and social rights and for the right to enter the political world as citizens. While first-wave feminists did not ultimately launch a strong challenge to the primacy of women's social roles as mothers, second-wave feminists drew on women's maternal identities while also making demands that challenged motherhood as women's primary role in society. In brief, maternal collective action frames are not inherently conservative.[20] Rather, the context in which they emerge will shape the content of the frame. The dictatorship-era women's movements drew on women's social roles to mobilize other women to action and to justify their political activism. At the same time, they attempted to subvert a strict gender hierarchy that entrenched a masculine ideal of citizenship. The radicalization of a maternal collective action frame partly owed to the politicization of the social and community arenas during the dictatorship and to the fact that much of what divides women's movements in times of "normal politics," for example, class, race, and ethnicity, was temporarily overcome during a period of severe crisis in Chile. Consequently, middle-class feminist ideas were quickly transmitted to women's movements in the popular sectors, and the discourses and demands of the movement as a whole were affected by this. For example, many popular sector women, normally skeptical of feminism, were proclaiming a "popular feminism," and middle-class feminists were involved in popular sector struggles for social justice.[21]

Autonomy Versus Double Militancy

Should movements seeking to promote women's equal citizenship defend their independence from other political actors or attempt to exert greater influence by bringing feminist politics to political parties, the state, or other political organizations? Autonomy is frequently valued by women's movements out of a fear of co-optation of movement goals by traditional political actors, especially parties. On the other hand, autonomy can leave women's movements without the necessary allies to promote their interests in the political world.[22]

Both autonomy and double militancy are valuable strategies for women's movements, but the advantages of either strategy are largely determined by the prevailing political context. In the Chilean case, the first-wave women's movement pursued an autonomy strategy, in part because their collective action frame drew a sharp boundary between the world of political parties and the world of women's organizations. But the autonomy strategy also helped them to appeal to women from all social classes in an era when political parties were very much class-based. In the end, however, the autonomy strategy failed to yield substantial successes because the women's movement was left without strong allies in politics and once the movement itself grew weaker, women entered the political parties without the strength to bring a feminist politics to them. The second-wave women's movement, in contrast, emerged in a context where political parties themselves were weak, and this relative autonomy gave the movement the necessary space to launch a gender-based critique of traditional politics in Chile. When the parties began to reconstitute themselves and play a larger role in the antidictatorship struggle, the women's movement had carved out a fairly important role for itself and activists who chose double militancy entered the parties from a position of greater strength. Additionally, women were an important electoral constituency, and thus feminists in the parties successfully influenced party leaders to address women's issues (Baldez 2002; Frohmann and Valdés 1995). Unfortunately, these favorable conditions were actually quite fleeting, and as the new democracy took shape it once again became difficult to pressure political parties to take up the theme of women's rights.

Since the return of democracy, the debate over movement autonomy and double militancy has shifted once again, due to a dramatically different political context.[23] In particular, the state grew relatively more open to a gender policy agenda, thus leading many feminists to view the state as a site for double militancy. This trend illustrates the importance of shifting political opportunity structures for shaping movement strategies. But the posttransition context in Chile also demands a more profound rethinking of the autonomy–double militancy debate. It is no longer clear what the references of these terms are. Patricia Richards writes, "many of the feminists who have remained outside the state are connected to it in some way (receiving state funds to conduct studies, implement programs, and so on), rendering the concept of autonomy extremely problematic" (2004, p. 57). Even more important, we need to make a distinction between autonomy as a *strategy* chosen by purposive agents and autonomy that is imposed on movement organizations because certain groups lack access—whether to political parties or the state. In the Chilean case, there are still a few feminist groups who refuse all forms of interaction with parties and state agencies. More common, however, are groups who seek input and interaction with state actors, while also retaining their autonomy to set their own goals and agendas. Where this strategy fits in the autonomy–double militancy scale is complex, and is rendered even more complicated by the fact that state actors are selective in terms of the level of access granted to civil society actors. In this context, scholars must take care to distinguish between movement strategy and state responses to movement demands (Beckwith 2001).

Women and Electoral Politics

Women are underrepresented in electoral politics in a majority of the world's countries. Indeed, despite substantial gains in gender equality in many parts of the world, most legislatures remain overwhelmingly male-dominated. Interestingly, a number of Latin American countries are at the forefront of attempts to improve women's access to electoral politics with the implementation of candidate gender quotas.[24] Chile, however, has not been part of this trend.

Transitions to democracy are interesting to those who study women and electoral politics, because it was believed by many that transitions would provide greater opportunities for women to compete in politics. In the Chilean case, relatively few of the women's activists who became involved in the struggle for democracy subsequently sought to enter the arena of formal politics. However, those who did faced gendered obstacles to their entry. Since the return of democracy, political parties in Chile have proven unwilling to adopt the type of strategies, particularly legislated gender quotas, that would improve women's numerical representation. Because access to decisionmaking positions, whether in legislatures, bureaucracies, or political executives, is tightly controlled by political parties, women's primary struggle is taking place in a domain whose norms have traditionally marginalized feminine styles of behavior. Women's access to electoral politics is also shaped by the electoral system, the procedures for candidate selection, and the strength of the women's movement in compelling parties to nominate women candidates. In the case of Chile, all of these factors work against the goal of improving women's numerical representation.

But a second problem for women is that those who do gain access to electoral politics often face difficulty promoting women's gender interests in that arena. This outcome is a result of more complex factors, including the dominance of a very conservative social and moral discourse in Chilean politics, the negative connotation of feminism, legacies of the dictatorship, including a fear of provoking conflict, and the lack of spaces for dialogue among organized women and women in formal politics. As a result of these factors, improving the substantive representation of women's interests in Chile requires much more than merely increasing the number of women in electoral politics.

Women and States

Should women view states as potential allies in the goal of expanding women's citizenship? Gender historians and feminist scholars have provided a great deal of insight into the ways that state power is often geared toward reinforcing unequal relations between genders, classes, and ethnic and race groups (Dore and Molyneux 2000). But it is also the case that state structures and power relations within them and between state and society are continually shifting (Banaszak, Beckwith, and Rucht 2003). As power shifts at the state level, opportunities are created for movements seeking inclusion. In the Chilean case, such an opportunity emerged out of the transition to democracy, when the influence of the women's movement translated into the creation of a space for the promotion of gender equality within the state.

Such a change at the state level, however, led to a corresponding shift in power relations among the various segments of the women's movement as some segments of the movement gained influence while others lost what little access they previously had to the political class. As noted, scholars need to separate out the effects on movements that result from changing state strategies and the strategies of either autonomy or double militancy that movements themselves choose. While movement choices are no doubt conditioned by changing state strategies, they must not be confused with them.

In Latin America today, the question of the state's relationship to women's equality struggles is the current formulation of the autonomy versus double militancy debate. On the one hand, feminist *autónomas* fiercely resist the idea that women's movement activists should work through state institutions to promote women's rights and equality. On the other hand, the *institucionales,* as they are termed in Latin America, believe that the state is a potentially promising arena in which to practice feminist politics. The division between the two segments of the women's movement in Latin America is complex and profound, and has led to bitter and divisive disputes (see Alvarez et al. 2002; Barrig 2001; Beckman 2001; and Ríos, Godoy, and Guerrero 2004). In the book, I show that the migration of many activists from civil society to the state has had both positive and negative consequences for women's movements. While it has clearly affected power relations among women and fragmented the movement, mainly along class lines, as professional and middle-class women with expertise in gender issues have opportunities to access the state while their popular sector and working-class counterparts do not, the existence of gender policy networks can also serve as a way of linking the formal and informal political arenas. Unfortunately, the nature of the links in the Chilean case is weak and unstable despite some well-intentioned steps by feminists within the state to construct more stable links with women's organizations outside the state.

Another problem is the status of the feminist segment of the women's movement. The self-exclusion of some feminist autónomas notwithstanding, feminist nongovernmental organizations (NGOs) and feminists working in SERNAM have not been successful in shaping public discourse on women's issues or on social issues in general in a more progressive way. Instead, as I show in the book, the Catholic Church and the political right have succeeded in reinforcing a conservative political discourse that denigrates feminism. Gains for women in general in posttransition Chile have not yet led to gains in the acceptance of feminism.

Overview of the Book

The findings of my research about Chile's gendered patterns of citizenship and how they have changed over time are developed in greater detail in the chapters that follow. In the early chapters I analyze the gendered patterns of citizenship in Chile's first period of democracy (1932–1973) and the Pinochet dictatorship (1973–1990); subsequently I analyze the posttransition context. Chapter 2 provides an overview of relevant Chilean political history, focusing especially on the gendered dimensions of Chile's democratization projects. In Chapters 3 and 4, I investigate in greater detail Chile's first- and second-wave women's movements and link their strategies, collective action frames, and successes and failures to the shifting political opportunity structures in each era. Chapters 5, 6, and 7 focus on women's politics in three arenas: electoral politics, "state feminism,"[25] and movement politics.

In Chapter 8, I return to the four themes discussed above, placing them in the context of attempts to deepen Chilean democracy in the current political environment. To a great extent, women's citizenship struggles today are inextricably linked to the nation's broader struggle to deepen democracy and to realize social justice.

Research and Methods

Studying the changing patterns of gendered citizenship in Chile over three distinct historical periods involved a variety of research strategies. There is already a vast and richly detailed literature on first-wave feminism in Chile and the emergence of feminist and pobladora movements during the Pinochet dictatorship (Gaviola et al. 1986; Lavrin 1995; Baldez 2002; Gaviola, Largo, and Palestro 1994; Rosemblatt 2000; Valdés and Weinstein 1993). Thus, research for the early chapters of the book primarily involved drawing on these and many other existing studies to assemble a comparison of women's organizing in the two periods that focused particularly on the similarities and differences with respect to women's discursive framing of their gender demands and to the strategies that movements devised to advance their goals.

Studying women's roles in posttransition politics involved research in Chile between June and November 1999 and again in July 2002. The research consisted primarily of open-ended interviews with women who participate in the three arenas that are a focus of the second half of the book: electoral politics, state feminism, and movement politics. In total, I conducted interviews with fifty-four women. Of these, sixteen were "informal" interviews (not tape-recorded) geared primarily toward gathering sufficient background information about the history of women's organizing, perceptions about Chile's state agency for women (SERNAM), and the status of women's organizing and feminism in posttransition Chile. The remaining (formal) interviews used a standard set of open-ended interview questions, varied according to whether the interview subject participated in electoral politics, SERNAM or another state agency, or NGOs and movement organizations.[26]

The interview questions were designed to allow women to "tell the story" of their participation, the challenges they face, and most important, their perceptions about politics and their relations with women active in other arenas.

Given the divisions and conflicts that currently exist among organized women in Chile, it is not surprising that the interviews depict a complex and often contradictory reality. For example, some political women, along with some feminist researchers in NGOs, note that there is no longer an active women's movement in Chile. However, women active in their communities who feel cut off from the world of professional NGOs and formal politics insist that, while numerous organizations lost members following the transition to democracy, many women remain committed to organizing around gender and class issues but no longer have the support of the middle-class and political women who supported them during the dictatorship. These sorts of conflicting perceptions of the nature of women's politics in posttransition politics in Chile are also evident in other studies (Ríos, Godoy, and Guerrero 2004; Richards 2004; Alvarez 1999). Likewise, women in community and base-level organizations have a different view of the state-NGO relationship than do women in the NGOs themselves. In assembling the story of women's politics since the return of democracy to Chile, my goal is to present the views and perceptions of the women I interviewed as faithfully and fairly as possible, while recognizing that contextual factors (such as class and location of participation) dramatically affect women's understandings of the role of their own activism in the broader context of a changing women's movement.

Notes

1. The number of women holding elected office elsewhere in Latin America has been growing significantly since the early 1990s due to the adoption of candidate gender quotas. Women hold 35.1 percent of the seats in Costa Rica's lower house and 33.6 percent in Argentina's (Inter-Parliamentary Union 2004).

2. Quoted in *El Mercurio,* February 3, 2004.

3. Quoted in *El Mercurio,* February 4, 2004.

4. Interview with María Ester Férez, August 25, 1999, Santiago.

5. Interview with Lily Pérez, October 1, 1999, Santiago.

6. This is a commonly documented trend in politics worldwide. See Jaquette 1989; Nelson and Chowdhury 1994; and West and Blumberg 1990.

7. Data taken from *Mujeres Latinoamericanas en Cifras,* www.eurosur.org/flacso/mujeres, retrieved February 28, 2004.

8. It is important to distinguish between a "women's movement" and a "feminist movement." Not all women's movements are feminist, although feminists are often an important segment of a women's movement. In this book, I am concerned

with women's activism in both feminist movements and women's movements that may not define themselves as feminist.

9. Indeed, Chilean democracy is lacking in ways that affect all citizens, but in this book I am primarily concerned with women's equality struggles.

10. In fact, in the case of Chile, women appear to take the civic (and legal) obligation to vote more seriously than do their male counterparts. Since being given the right to vote in presidential elections in 1949, women have consistently demonstrated lower rates of abstention from voting (CEPAL 2000, p. 145).

11. Interview with Myriam González and María Molina, October 20, 1999, Santiago.

12. One woman explained to me that being active in a community women's organization required careful balancing of her household responsibilities—for example, by ensuring that she prepared her family's meals in advance, especially when the organization's meetings were held late in the afternoon.

13. Although the literature on women and transitions to democracy is extremely diverse, many scholars have concluded that women's activism increases under authoritarianism and subsequently declines following a transition to democracy. See Waylen 1994, p. 353; Craske 1999, p. 3; Friedman 2000b, pp. 5–6; and Saint-Germain 1997, p. 75.

14. This is similar to the argument that Elisabeth Friedman puts forward in her studies of women and democratization in Venezuela (1998, 2000a, 2000b). She argues that political opportunities are *gendered,* and that women faced expanded opportunities to be politically active under authoritarianism due precisely to gender norms that cast women as nonpolitical.

15. See Richards 2004 for a discussion of how class and ethnic differences are reflected in the Chilean state's gender policies.

16. Of course, this is a problem that is not limited to women, but that affects many segments of the Chilean population, including the working class, the poor, indigenous peoples, and the elderly.

17. This tendency, and the feelings of exclusion that go along with it, were noted in interviews with Myriam González and María Molina, October 20, 1999, Santiago; Fabiola Oyarzún, November 18, 1999, Santiago; and Ana Pichulmán, July 15, 2002, Santiago.

18. Hanna Pitkin's classic text (1967) on political representation casts this as a distinction between representatives who "stand for" members of a social group and those who "act for" that group by promoting the group's interests.

19. In the social movement literature, a frame "refers to an interpretive schemata that simplifies and codifies the 'world out there' by selectively punctuating and encoding objects, situations, events, experiences, and sequences of actions within one's present or past environment" (Snow and Benford 1992, p. 137). All social movements construct and deploy collective action frames that identify situations of injustice according to fairly specific interpretive schema, and then specify remedies that correspond to this broader vision.

20. Temma Kaplan (1982), in her study of popular sector women in Barcelona, Spain, argues that "female consciousness," while emerging out of and perhaps even defending the gendered division of labor, also carries the seeds of radical political transformation.

21. Given that Chilean feminism has historically been associated with the political left, it was not unusual for middle-class feminists to be concerned with broader struggles for social justice and class equality.

22. For a discussion of these debates, see Beckwith 2000; Serrano 1990; and Waylen 1994.

23. For a discussion of the more recent debates and divisions among Latin American feminist movements over this issue, see Alvarez 1999; Barrig 2001; Beckman 2001; and Ríos, Godoy, and Guerrero 2004.

24. For a discussion of the trend toward candidate gender quotas, see Baldez 2004; Htun and Jones 2002; and Gray 2003.

25. For the purposes of this book, I employ Dorothy McBride Stetson and Amy Mazur's definition of state feminism as "activities of government structures that are formally charged with furthering women's status and rights" (1995, pp. 1–2).

26. See the Appendix for a complete list of names of interviews.

2 Gendered Citizenship in Chile: An Overview

Chilean women have played critical roles in their nation's history. They have organized in mass movements to pursue their own rights, most notably in the campaigns for female suffrage, and have led and participated in mobilizations to protect or defend the rights of others. Women on the left organized to defend Salvador Allende's socialist government (1970–1973) while conservative women mobilized on a massive scale to protest Allende and his policies. During the long years of General Augusto Pinochet's dictatorship (1973–1990) women were on the front lines of struggles for human rights, economic survival, and eventually the return of democracy. Despite the critical roles they have played throughout the course of Chilean history, women frequently remark that they are marginalized politically. Women's political marginalization derives from Chile's gendered patterns of citizenship.

Citizenship refers primarily to the rights and duties of all those considered to be members of a political community. In this chapter, I provide a historical overview of the ways in which Chile's processes of democratization have created profoundly gendered ways of being citizens. Men's and women's rights and responsibilities as members of the Chilean political community have differed according to the social and political roles that each gender is expected to play. Gendered patterns of citizenship have been evident for all three categories of citizenship rights—civil, political, and social—that T. H. Marshall delineated (1950). Civil citizenship rights (involving freedom of movement and control over one's person) have been gendered to the extent that dependent and married women lack the freedom to make basic choices that most men can make. All women lack full control over their bodies because abortion remains illegal under all circumstances (Blofield 2003; Htun 2003). Political citizenship rights (involving participation in governing) have been gendered to the extent that formal politics has been constructed as masculine, relegating women primarily to supporting roles. Finally, social citizenship rights (including rights to a level of welfare sufficient to allow one to participate in the national political community) are gendered to the extent that they have traditionally been accorded on the basis of one's identity as a productive worker, thereby excluding women, who were assumed to be engaged in tasks of social reproduction (Rosemblatt 2000). Because the "universe of political discourse" (Jenson 1986) in Chile was profoundly class-based, at least until the 1973 military coup, social reforms were largely conceived as class-based concessions. Thus, citizenship rights were linked to one's status as a worker, making it difficult for women to voice demands for rights as citizens. The general historical and political background provided in this chapter serves to ground the analysis of women's politics in the rest of the book.

Democratization in Chile, 1932–1973

Democratization began in earnest in Chile following the collapse of the oligarchic state in 1932. Although Chile gained independence from Spain in 1810–1818, the nation was largely dominated by an oligarchic elite led by landowners (*latifundistas*) and the mining sector until changes in the underlying social and economic structure produced a political crisis in the 1920s that ultimately led to more meaningful democratization (Oppenheim 1993; Oxhorn 1995b). Chile's victory over Bolivia and Peru in the War of the Pacific (1879–1883) led to the acquisition of the resource-rich Atacama Desert in the north of the country, and mineral (mainly nitrate) exports subsequently dominated the economy until the 1920s, when copper exports gained predominance. The growth of the mining economy produced two corresponding political changes: the expansion of the state, in terms of managing access to, and the rents from, these resources; and the growth of a middle class, largely employed by the state, and a working class, both of which challenged the hegemony exercised by the oligarchy.

The victory of Arturo Alessandri of the Radical Party reflected these underlying structural changes, and his presidency (1932–1938) "[laid] the foundations for four decades of widening democracy" (Collier and Sater 1996, p. 226). A new constitution took force, establishing a strong executive branch and a bicameral congress (a 100-member Chamber of Deputies and a 50-member Senate), but more important, Alessandri's victory represented the defeat of the oligarchy and the parties that traditionally represented their interests (the Liberals and the Conservatives).[1] The Radical Party emerged precisely to represent the interests of the growing middle- and working-class sectors. Hence, Alessandri's term saw the beginning of a welfare state in Chile, with the implementation of social security and the adoption of a labor code (Oppenheim 1993, pp. 12–13). Over the next two decades, the center and leftist parties built a series of "popular front" alliances through which middle-class reformists and working-class leaders promoted a highly nationalistic and fairly progressive style of politics (Rosemblatt 2000).

Scholars have characterized Chile's main problem as being political overdevelopment and economic underdevelopment (Oxhorn 1995b, p. 42; see also Garretón 1995, p. 182). From 1932 until 1973, the role of the state expanded, and it served as the main referent for the demands of social groups. Unlike elsewhere in Latin America, a strong and stable political party system emerged to mediate the relationships between social groups and the state. As political power became increasingly centralized in the national state, Chilean political parties responded by developing highly centralized party structures that linked social groups, through local political brokers, to centralized party structures (Valenzuela 1978; Oxhorn 1995b, p. 46). This led to what Manuel Garretón (1989) refers to as the "backbone" of Chilean politics: the overlap between party structures and social organizations. Class-based political parties penetrated all social organizations, even local sports clubs, and all demands expressed in the formal political arena were mediated through political parties. While this system contributed to an enviable level of stability, at least compared to other countries in the region, it also contributed to an underdeveloped civil society (Oxhorn 1995a). Also, the prevalence of a "workerist" discourse in leftist parties made it extremely difficult for women to raise any gender-based issues within them (Kirkwood 1986; Rosemblatt 2000).

The overdeveloped nature of the Chilean political system eventually led to a severe crisis because it was matched by an underdeveloped economic structure (Oxhorn 1995b, pp. 42, 59). The "compromise state" that replaced the oligarchic state after 1932 contained a number of internal contradictions (Garretón 1989; Oxhorn 1995b; Rosemblatt 2000; Valenzuela 1978). The "compromise" refers to the incorporation of the middle and working classes through the political party system and the satisfaction of their interests through the state as "benefactor" (Serrano 1992). The state provided employment as it increased its role in providing social services and welfare, but also as state-led industrialization replaced the emphasis on resource exports. According to Garretón, the Chilean political system in this era was defined by three tightly interrelated elements: "import-substituting industrialization with increasing state intervention in the economy; substantive democratization that was gradually incorporating diverse social sectors into the political system and improving their standards of living; and a democratic political regime" (1989, p. 3). But as noted, there were fundamental contradictions within the terms of the compromise: it rested upon maintaining a number of the oligarchy's key economic interests, which implied a lack of progressive social change in the countryside. Chilean peasants, therefore, were excluded from the terms of the compromise,[2] as was the urban marginal sector inhabiting the shantytowns that ringed the periphery of Santiago (Garretón 1989;

Oxhorn 1995b, p. 44). In brief, while democratization after 1932 included aspects of both political and social citizenship, the exclusion of key social groups (peasants and urban marginal sectors, and, as I discuss later, women) meant that the process was ultimately incomplete.

The internal contradictions within the compromise state began to undermine the project when the Christian Democratic Party (Partido Democrata Cristiana, PDC) replaced the Radical Party as the main center party. As part of the PDC's governing project (1964–1970), it began to incorporate formerly excluded social groups. Most of its attention was directed toward mobilizing the poor in the shantytowns (poblaciones). This was done through the creation of community organizations—the Juntas de Vecinos (Neighborhood Councils) linked to the PDC mandate of "Promoción Popular" (Popular Promotion).[3] Through citizens' participation in the Juntas de Vecinos they were tied to the PDC and mobilized around its ideology, a kind of Christian "communitarianism" that aimed at being neither left nor right (Oppenheim 1993, p. 16). The other main goal of PDC president Eduardo Frei Sr. was the incorporation of the peasants, largely within the framework of the U.S.-led Alliance for Progress. But agrarian reform and the extension of rights to rural workers were bitterly opposed by the political right, who had supported Frei in the 1964 elections.[4]

The growing class polarization and politicization of Chilean society produced an extremely close presidential race in 1970. Allende's coalition, Popular Unity (Unidad Popular, UP), won a bare plurality with 36.2 percent of the vote.[5] The UP coalition sought to expand the earlier reforms and bring about a complete socioeconomic transformation of Chilean society. They intended to do so, however, within the parameters of the country's constitution. But Allende ran into problems almost immediately, given the complete refusal of the opposition to support his reforms. Due to such intransigent opposition, Allende was forced more and more to employ executive actions, eroding established Chilean political traditions of negotiation with congress (Oxhorn 1995b, p. 61). The growing conflict at the elite level was reproduced at the societal level, which is unsurprising given the dominance of civil society by political elites. This led to open conflict among social groups outside the institutional arena of politics—something that was extremely rare in Chile. All political parties were mobilizing their social bases either to support or to protest the UP. This led to workers taking over factories, peasants seizing control of landed estates, trade associations (*gremios*), especially the truckers' associations, organizing crippling strikes, and women demonstrating against the lack of food through the famous "March of the Empty Pots" (Baldez 2002; Power 2002). Taken together, these mobilizations delegitimized the democratic regime and the normal channels of institutionalized political competition. Ultimately, support for a military solution grew. On September 11, 1973, Chile's process of democratization was brutally terminated by a military coup. According to some, the crisis that ended democracy grew out of the tensions between increasing political and social democratization in a developing economy ill-equipped to cope with expanding political and social demands (Oxhorn 1995b). Others emphasize the role of the political parties in escalating the levels of conflict (Valenzuela 1978).

Incomplete Democracy and Gendered Citizenship

Although not mentioned by authors such as Manuel Garretón, Philip Oxhorn, or Arturo Valenzuela, there were gendered dimensions to political and social democratization in the 1932–1973 period.[6] Women's citizenship was not exercised on the same terms as men's, and women were simply excluded in many ways. Political discourse in Chile was class-based and both left and right valorized the male-headed nuclear family and women's caring roles within it. Women's social benefits were linked to their relationship with male workers or delivered through charity. Women were not enfranchised as political citizens until 1949, after a lengthy and hard-fought campaign by women's movements. Even after women were granted formal political rights, they were incorporated and subsequently mobilized politically around their social roles as mothers, as I describe further in the next chapter. This translated into women's exclusion from positions of power and influence. A gender ideology that associated women exclusively with their maternal roles and cast citizenship in highly masculine terms made it difficult for women to participate in political parties in any capacity beyond a supportive role. Because access to arenas of influence was meditated through political parties, women's subordination in the parties resulted in few women in decisionmaking arenas. Between 1952 and 1992, only 7 women held executive office, compared to 509 men. Women's representation in the Chamber of Deputies and the Senate in the same period averaged only 4.5 percent and 2.2 percent respectively (Valdés and Gomariz 1992, pp. 101, 103). The absence of women in formal politics, combined with a class-based model of politics, meant that women lacked a political voice with which to promote their gender interests in politics (Kirkwood 1986).

Women as individuals did not benefit directly from Chile's expanding welfare state in the 1932–1973 period. Women received social citizenship rights through their relation to male workers. Likewise, the emphasis on women's caretaking responsibilities failed to recognize the productive labor (in both the formal and the informal sector) performed by poor, rural, and working-class women (Montecinos 1997, p. 226). According to Karin Rosemblatt, reformers of the era promoted a model of social reform that reinforced a strict gender division of labor. Male workers were to receive a decent wage that permitted wives and mothers to maintain healthy and stable homes. More significant, "political elites and labor activists together circumscribed women's rights by rejecting paid labor for women, downplaying the importance of informal forms of employment, and defining full-time homemaking as women's proper occupation" (2000, p. 51). Thus, while male workers received entitlements based on their contributions as (working) citizens, women without male providers received charity (p. 125).

Women's unequal status as citizens in this era is intricately linked to the dominant style of politics in Chile and the monopoly that political parties maintained over defining the political and social agenda. Claudia Serrano (1992, p. 199) notes that social security coverage was never universal largely because the extension of benefits depended on how much pressure a social group could bring to bear on the state through political parties. Women, the youth, and the elderly were largely left out because these groups were rarely organized by political parties. Even Allende's government (1970–1973) did not design programs to address the needs of working-class women until it had been in office for two full years (Power 2000, p. 290). Hence, women benefited from social policy only indirectly, according to Serrano, because the "state-as-benefactor" model in Chile was never designed to challenge gender inequality. When policies and programs were designed to integrate women, they also "permit[ed] the coexistence of a cultural patriarchal model and the egalitarian integrative spirit that characterized the era" (Serrano 1992, p. 199). This feature is best illustrated in the Centros de Madres (Mothers Centers), which served as the main vehicle for organizing and incorporating women as part of Eduardo Frei's Promoción Popular. Indeed, the Centros de Madres along with the Juntas de Vecinos were the main pillars of the PDC platform for incorporating the previously excluded popular sectors. In the Centros de Madres, women were mobilized around their caretaking roles, learning traditionally feminine skills to supplement family income, and gaining organizational capacities that would help them develop in their capacity as community caregivers, although community decisionmaking was to occur in the male-dominated Juntas de Vecinos. During Allende's presidency, the number of Centros de Madres increased significantly, and they again served as the main vehicle for mobilizing women around the revolution's goals. It has often been noted that Allende seemed unable to develop a coherent and effective strategy for integrating women in a more gender-egalitarian manner (Chaney 1974; Power 2002; Shayne 2004). In large part, the "workerist" discourse left little space to promote gender issues.

In 1972, the UP government established communal laundries in poor neighborhoods, set up childcare facilities in factories, and delivered hot meals for female workers to take home to their families (Power 2000, p. 291). Margaret Power explains that "the Allende government failed to challenge the belief that women were fundamentally mothers and housewives whose primary responsibility was to take care of their family" (2000, p. 291). The UP's inability to effectively incorporate women and to challenge the prevailing gender ideology led to their availability for mobilization in the conservative-led anti-Allende movement. Women, mostly from the middle and upper classes, but also from the popular sectors, participated in mass protests against the UP government (Baldez 2002; Bunster 1988; de los Angeles Crummet 1977; Mattelart 1976; Power 2002).

The authoritarian period (1973–1990) that followed the 1973 military coup had important consequences for women's citizenship. During military rule, certain aspects of the gender ideology were reinforced and manipulated to form part of the doctrine of national security, in which women were cast as the "'bearers' of the values of the Fatherland" (Bunster 1988, pp. 487–488). In speeches and in the writings of those associated with the military government, there was a constant analogy drawn between the family and the country as a whole. *Familia y patria* (family and fatherland) or *hogar y patria* (home and fatherland) were firmly linked through the roles that women played in inculcating Chilean values and tradition in their children (Molina 1989, p. 62). According to Natacha Molina, "government programs towards women show an almost perfect fit between the traditional role of women and the consolidation of authoritarianism" (1989, p. 61).

Following the coup, all Chileans were prevented from exercising their political citizenship. General Pinochet immediately closed congress and declared some political parties—those on the left—banned, and others to be "in recess." He also employed a rhetoric that was extremely antipolitical, declaring politics and those who engaged in politics responsible for the crisis, which the military was now "solving" (Garretón 1989, p. 71). Because of women's "private" identities, they were conceived as more "pure" and thus their nonpolitical nature was idealized, further undermining their capacities to exercise identities as citizens. A gender ideology that exclusively focused on women's maternal roles and that valorized women as apolitical was persistently reinforced through state discourse and policy (Munizaga and Letelier 1988).

Unlike other countries in Latin America where the authoritarian state transformed social and political relations but did not systematically reorient the economy, in Chile the economy underwent radical transformation after 1973. The incomplete social democratization that had accompanied political democratization between 1932 and 1973 was reversed. State-led industrialization ceased and the role of the market was given priority. The economy was reoriented around primary and natural resource sectors and emphasis on industry was basically abandoned (Garretón 1989, pp. 125, 135; Montecinos 1994, p. 162). The "shock therapy" policies that were implemented had severe effects: unemployment increased significantly due to privatization and public sector cutbacks; and the removal of price controls had a negative effect on the poor who had depended upon them to survive. Per capita consumption did not return to pre-1973 levels until 1981, only to decline again after the 1982–1983 economic collapse (Montecinos 1994, p. 163).

The social citizenship rights extended earlier were also dismantled through the project of social "modernizations" implemented by the Pinochet regime. Instead of conceiving of healthcare, education, and social security as universal entitlements of citizens, or at least male citizens, with women accessing these goods through their relationships with male workers, most aspects of the welfare state in Chile were privatized and transferred to the local (nonpolitical) level to be administered. According to Garretón, social modernization involved "attempting to transfer the principles of the market to new spheres" (1989, p. 134). The state would only act in those areas where the market was failing—that is, the state would provide services to those who were entirely excluded from the market. But in these instances, the state provided services or direct benefits to *individuals* who could not access services through the market, not to collective actors. This targeting of social welfare services led to a significant decline in state social spending, from 25 percent of gross domestic product (GDP) in 1971 to only 14 percent of GDP in 1981 (Serrano 1992, pp. 204–205).

Women's citizenship was affected in important ways by these changes, and a fuller description of these changes and their effects on women is contained in Chapter 4. Here it suffices to say that women of all classes were confronting fundamental contradictions that ultimately generated a women's movement in pursuit of democracy and citizenship. Popular sector women experienced the contradiction between the ideal of womanhood embedded in Chilean gender ideology and promoted through the dictatorship's social policies toward women,[7] and the daily realities of their lives. There was a fundamental tension here, because while the gender discourse emphasized a role for women that was limited to the family and community sphere, many women from the popular sectors were compelled to work outside this sphere given the prolonged male unemployment provoked by the regime's economic policies (Molina 1989; Munizaga and Letelier 1988). Middle- and upper-class women faced a contradiction that grew out of their high levels of education, which failed to translate into easy access to professional employment.[8] While women's participation in the labor force had grown in the 1960s, the discourse of Pinochet's regime reinforced the prevailing sexism in the (male-dominated) professional world by urging "the return of the woman to family life" (Munizaga and Letelier 1988, p. 533).[9] Finally, women from all classes experienced the contradiction between a public discourse that valorized both women and their nurturing roles, and the reality of a dictatorship that was daily violating these principles through its policies of terror, disappearances, and repression. Women, therefore, were the backbone of the human rights movements that emerged almost immediately, reclaiming political space and bringing to it "private" concerns.

The contradictions embedded in the total transformation of Chilean politics, economy, and society produced a multiclass women's movement that, although different segments began mobilizing for different reasons, ultimately came together with a single goal: the return of democracy. More important, the political and economic crises of the era created space for the redefinition of politics and citizenship. Within the Pinochet-era women's movement, feminists initiated the task of rethinking what democracy had meant for women and concluded that under the previous democracy, women's citizenship had been incomplete. Thus the women's movement demanded a democracy in which women would enjoy a more meaningful citizenship. The movement made creative use of slogans such as *¡Democracia en el país y en la casa!* (Democracy in the country and in the home!) and *¡Si la mujer no está, la democracia no va!* (If women aren't there, democracy won't go anywhere!). But because the movement was multiclass in nature, movement demands also focused on problems that emerged out of class inequality.

The women's movement that emerged under authoritarianism in Chile secured a number of its goals, as I show in later chapters. One of the reasons it enjoyed a degree of success, especially compared to women's movements in other countries that underwent transitions from authoritarianism, was due to women's participation in the wider movement to reestablish democracy in Chile. The Pinochet dictatorship completely destroyed existing political patterns, namely the relationship between the social and political aspects of democratization. Even since the restoration of democracy in 1989–1990, democratization has proceeded in the political arena, while the social and economic arenas continue to be governed primarily by market principles that are, to a large degree, inimical to a more robust sense of democratic citizenship, particularly one that recognizes social citizenship rights. This outcome, according to Garretón (1995), is linked to the fact that the economic crisis of 1982–1983, created by the global debt crisis, was not sufficient to dislodge the dictatorship. By the time a transition occurred, the economic crisis had been resolved and economic growth restored (see Haggard and Kaufman 1995). Consequently, the middle classes could not be counted on to support a strategy of sustained popular mobilization to defeat the dictatorship. Instead, prodemocracy political leaders clearly felt compelled to pursue a strategy of negotiation with the military regime, and a commitment not to alter the basic features of the promarket economic model that led to Chile being hailed as a Latin American "tiger."[10] This factor also narrowed the discursive politics of the transition, leading political elites to delink social rights from citizenship.

Nonetheless, the economic crisis of the early 1980s did produce the first mass protests against the regime, but these protests were not sufficient to cause its collapse largely because the opposition was still divided. The political crisis that ended democracy in 1973 and the brutality of the repression that followed were so severe as to practically incapacitate opposition political actors, especially the political parties. While other authoritarian regimes, notably Brazil, maintained the façade of functioning democracy by keeping parties running and congress open, the Chilean congress remained closed for seventeen years. The previously strong labor movement was effectively destroyed as a social and political force through the process of deindustrialization and labor code revisions that severely weakened the power of unions. Overall, the extensive relationships between civil and political society suffered major damage, although parties continued to operate underground. In addition to the severing of links between social organizations and parties, the bitterness and blame-laying surrounding the Allende years and the events of September 11, 1973, inhibited political parties from acting effectively in establishing the necessary alliances to defeat the dictatorship. It was not until 1986 that opposition parties began to work together to launch a serious challenge to the regime. Once working together, the opposition was successful in further delegitimizing the regime, although much of this work had already been carried out by the human rights and women's movements. What is most important for the purposes of analyzing women's citizenship in democratization processes is that the women's movement enjoyed important opportunities to influence the process because it could act as part of the wider prodemocracy movement, and, as an important public actor in the movement, it could insert gender-based demands into those of the broader movement. This process is described in fuller detail in Chapter 4.

Redemocratization and Gendered Citizenship

In 1988 Chileans voted to put an end to Pinochet's rule. They were afforded the opportunity to do so because the 1980 constitution, written by the military regime, contained a clause specifying that a plebiscite be held in 1988 on the continuation of Pinochet's rule for another eight years. The plebiscite was free and fair largely because of pressure from the prodemocratic opposition to make it so, and because Pinochet mistakenly believed that he would win. When the forces opposed to Pinochet's continued rule won the vote, it became clear there would be a transition to democracy, and elections for president and congress were scheduled for the following year. In the interim, negotiations took place between the outgoing military regime and the prodemocratic opposition. The 1980 constitution was made somewhat more democratic, while also maintaining certain "authoritarian enclaves."[11] The subsequent elections, both congressional and presidential, were won by the Coalition of Parties for Democracy (Concertación de los Partidos por la Democracia, CPD), the same alliance of center and left parties that had organized opposition against the dictatorship and campaigned for the "No" side in the plebiscite. In 1990, President Patricio Aylwin, a member of the Christian Democratic Party (which was the largest party in the Concertación), was inaugurated as Chile's first democratic president since Allende.

While Chile's democracy is today arguably one of Latin America's most stable, there are nonetheless several shortcomings that have important consequences for the goal of expanding women's citizenship in the country.[12] Most important, the incoming democratic government inherited a constitution written during the dictatorship that fails to establish full civilian control over the military, and that shapes electoral and legislative dynamics in nondemocratic ways. Since 1990, there have been numerous, yet largely unsuccessful, attempts at constitutional reform, particularly to remove the *designados* (nonelected senators) and to reform the binomial electoral system. More recently, however, a reform package was passed by the Senate that expands civilian control over the military, eliminates the *designados,* and reduces the presidential term from six to four years. Observers predict that it will be approved by the lower house by the end of 2005 (*El Mercurio,* December 31, 2004; *Economist,* October 21, 2004). The electoral system, designed by the outgoing military, gives an electoral advantage to the political right in two ways. First, districts were adjusted to overrepresent those areas where Pinochet's support was strongest in the 1988 plebiscite. Second, the electoral formula is such that "the second largest bloc can win one out of every two contested seats with only one third of the vote, which is the historic percentage of the vote for the right" (Silva 2002, pp. 461–462). Electoral reform was not part of the reform package recently approved in the Senate.

Other problems that plague Chile's democracy concern the failure to address adequately the legacy of the dictatorship's human rights violations. A 1978 amnesty law has prevented major prosecutions of military officials who violated human rights on a massive scale. In July 2002, Chile's Supreme Court upheld a verdict that suspended all charges against Pinochet on the grounds that he was mentally unfit to stand trial. It therefore came as a surprise to many that in May 2004 a court stripped Pinochet of his immunity from prosecution in another case, known as Operation Condor, involving the coordination of intelligence gathering and tracking down of leftists among the military regimes of Argentina, Brazil, Paraguay, Uruguay, and Chile. This opens the door to Pinochet eventually having to stand trial, although his advanced age makes that rather unlikely.

Another important consequence of Chile's path of transition is the commitment of each posttransition government to a promarket, outwardly oriented economic model. Far-reaching neoliberal reforms were put in place under Pinochet, but despite rhetoric of repaying the "social debt" of the dictatorship, no Concertación government has deviated very far from this model. As a consequence, social policies to address poverty and its gendered sources must fit within a market-friendly and fiscally prudent policy agenda. While Concertación governments deserve praise for their reduction of poverty from over 38.6 percent in 1990 to less than 21.7 percent in 1998, inequality in Chile has deepened since 1990 (MIDEPLAN n.d.[a]).[13] Also, while Chile's economy grew substantially in the first half of the 1990s, economic growth since has not been as strong, and high unemployment has become a serious problem. Chilean women have among the lowest rates of labor force participation in Latin America. While 72.9 percent of men participate in the work force, the corresponding figure for women is only 35 percent (MIDEPLAN n.d.[a]). More significant, women's unemployment figures are much higher than men's (see Table 2.1). Solutions to female poverty and unemployment have mainly taken the form of efforts to improve women's access to the market through job training and microenterprise projects (see Schild 2000b). However, as I discuss in Chapter 6, these programs are often poorly implemented and do little to address the variety of gendered sources of poverty and unemployment.

A final problem that confronts Chileans is the "fear of conflict" legacy created by seventeen years of dictatorship. Based on survey data that gathered citizens' views on politics and democracy, Louis Goodman concludes that "the data show a population that is divided, alienated from politics, and afraid to take political action" (2001, p. 213). Likewise, Marcela Ríos notes that the dictatorship profoundly affected Chilean political culture and has

Table 2.1 Rates of Unemployment by Sex, 1990–2000 (percentages)

	Men	Women
1990	6.6	9.2
1991	6.1	9.4
1992	5.0	8.9
1993	5.3	8.8
1994	6.5	10.3
1995	5.5	8.9
1996	4.8	6.7
1997	4.7	6.6
1998	7.0	7.6
1999	8.2	10.3
2000	8.0	9.0

Source: Adapted from MIDEPLAN n.d.(b).

created a "pathological search for consensus" (2003, p. 259). This has critical implications for women's politics in Chile. In a context where many gender equality issues are deeply contentious, political leaders have sought to avoid confrontation over issues that are likely to be divisive. As I show in Chapter 6, the desire to avoid confrontation led to the creation of a state agency for women with a weaker mandate than initially envisioned. Likewise, intense political and social divisions over the issue of divorce meant that it would take almost fourteen years and three legislative attempts before Chileans enjoyed the option of legal divorce. The political right and the Catholic Church maintain a nonnegotiable stance on abortion, which is a criminal offense in Chile, therefore no Concertación government has been willing to introduce the issue of reproductive freedom for women.

But the search for consensus and the fear of conflict also inhibit the emergence of a more assertive women's movement in Chile. Feminists, in particular, have had a hard time making their voices heard because of the negative connotation that the label "feminist" continues to have. In turn, women in electoral politics who support women's rights and equality avoid identifying as feminists and may even take measures to avoid such a perception on the part of voters and party leaders. The effect of this is to undermine further the creation of linkages between women's movements—whether self-declared feminist or not—and women in formal politics. As I argue throughout the book, it is only through the construction of such linkages that women's citizenship can be strengthened.

Conclusion

This chapter has offered a brief and general overview of Chilean political history and sketched out some of the ways that patterns of politics and citizenship are gendered. Throughout both periods of democratization in Chile, women's equal citizenship has been constrained by dominant political discourse and cultural practices that associate citizenship with masculine activities, either waged labor or participation in formal political institutions. Hence, both periods of democratization have been incomplete when assessed from the perspective of gender equality. Since the return of democracy, there are a number of factors, including the hegemony of political parties and a narrow neoliberal discourse, that make it difficult for women's movements to politicize gender issues.

In the next two chapters, I provide a more detailed analysis of first- and second-wave women's movements in Chile, linking their successes and failures to the shifting political opportunity structures and to the movements' own strategic responses to changing circumstances. In brief, first-wave feminists, drawing on a maternal collective action frame that deemed women to be "above politics," pursued autonomy from political parties. This stance, combined with a class-based language of politics, did not permit feminists to have much success with transforming the political arena to make it more accessible to women. The second-wave movement, in contrast, emerged in an era when politics was being opened up and challenged and when women's caretaking identities were being politicized. This context led many women's activists to pursue a double militancy strategy, taking feminist politics into political parties and gendering political discourse.

Notes

1. These two parties both moved to the right of the political spectrum after the emergence of the Radical Party, merging in 1967 to form the National Party, representing landowners, business and financial interests, parts of the middle class (mainly small business and entrepreneurs), and the peasants, whose votes were still controlled by landlords (Oppenheim 1993, p. 15).

2. For example, rural unionization remained illegal until 1967 (Valenzuela 1978, p. 26).

3. The term *popular* refers to the "popular sectors," a group much broader than the poor or the working class. In addition to implying a group that suffers some degree of material deprivation and lower life chances, it also has a normative basis—it is often deployed to refer to "the people," as the authentic inhabitants of a nation. According to Philip Oxhorn, "'popular' becomes associated with all that is indigenous to a society: traditional cultures, values, art forms and beliefs, and so forth. While not rejecting all that is 'foreign,' influences from the developed industrialized nations tend to be associated with the 'privileged' sectors and the popular sectors often see themselves as reservoirs of national identity" (1995b, p. 301).

4. Frei decisively defeated the leftist candidate Salvador Allende in the 1964 elections only because the right, fearful of splitting the anti-Allende vote, decided to withdraw their candidate and support Frei. When Frei began to implement reforms opposed by conservative elites, political conflict escalated and any alliance between center and right fell apart. The PDC itself became increasingly divided over reform issues—especially agrarian reform—as leftists in the party wanted reforms to go further. This led to the breakaway of a number of leftist members to form their own party in 1969—the Movement for United Popular Action, which in 1970 allied with the Allende forces (Oppenheim 1993, p. 20).

5. The rightist candidate received 34.9 percent and the Christian Democratic candidate received 27.8 percent (Oxhorn 1995b, p. 60).

6. See Rosemblatt 2000 for an excellent analysis of the gendered nature of the popular front projects between 1920 and 1950.

7. The military regime basically continued to utilize the Centros de Madres as the main vehicle for delivering goods and services to poor women.

8. Chilean women enjoyed considerable access to higher education compared to other countries in Latin America (Munizaga and Letelier 1988, p. 532).

9. The Brazilian case provides an interesting contrast, because unlike in Chile, the state under authoritarianism actually expanded, creating numerous professional jobs for women. When large numbers of educated working women confronted the blatant sexism in the labor force, the seeds were sown for the emergence of a feminist movement (Alvarez 1990).

10. The term *tiger* refers to the newly industrializing Asian economies such as South Korea and Taiwan.

11. Some of the authoritarian features include the lack of civilian control over the armed forces; measures to ensure that the civil service (staffed with Pinochet supporters) could not be removed by the incoming democratic government; nine "designated" senators (which ensured the political right an effective veto power); and a flurry of appointments (of Pinochet supporters) to the judiciary (Garretón 1995, p. 113).

12. Indeed, Felipe Agüero refers to Chile's "unfinished transition" due to the "lingering authoritarian enclaves that imposed constraints upon successor democratic administrations" (2003, p. 292).

13. Chile is one of the world's most unequal societies, "with the richest 20 percent of the population receiving 17 times more income than the poorest 20 percent" (Contreras 2003, p. 181).

From First-Wave Feminism to "Mobilized Mothers," 1932–1973

3

To understand the sources of Chile's gendered patterns of citizenship and women's initial incorporation into politics as "mobilized mothers," it is crucial to analyze first-wave feminism. Such an analysis also permits comparisons of the similarities and differences between the strategies women's movements employed in two different periods of democratization. Both first-wave feminists and the dictatorship-era women's movement used a politics of difference strategy to forward citizenship demands, but they did so with very different results, showing that a maternal mobilizing frame can lead women in various directions.

My analysis of first-wave feminism in Chile is situated in the context of an expanding state and party politics. As elsewhere in Latin America, and as with first-wave feminism more generally, first-wave women's movements in Chile organized to pursue social reform and female suffrage by appealing to women's maternal identities as a basis for political and social rights. In Ruth Lister's terms (1997), women pursued a "gender-differentiated" model of citizenship. In Chile, the politics of difference strategy was shaped by a gender ideology that valorized women's motherhood identities and by the prevailing political and economic context. The strategies and collective action frames of the first-wave movement also laid the groundwork for women's subsequent limited incorporation into Chile's political system. But the political and economic context, shaped by democratization, intensifying partisan and class competition, and state-led industrialization, also influenced the terms of women's incorporation into a political system dominated by male-led political parties organized around class identities, as well as their exercise of citizenship. The prevailing language of politics did not permit the politicization of women's "private" identities as mothers and community caretakers. Consequently, women's citizenship, once granted, was exercised according to the ideal of "mobilized mothers," an identity that kept women on the margins of Chile's class-based politics.

A discussion of first-wave feminism and its outcomes in Chile is important for understanding subsequent developments in the struggle for women's citizenship, as granting women formal citizenship rights did not produce major changes to the political system and produced only limited changes to gender relations. In the absence of substantive transformation following first-wave women's movements, the task fell to feminists in the 1970s and 1980s to launch gender-based critiques of Chilean political practice, and especially of the political parties, which monopolized political space. But perhaps even more important is the role of movement strategy: both the politics of difference and the autonomy strategy that first-wave movements employed contributed to the particular outcome, but also shaped subsequent movement strategy. Second-wave women's movements in Chile, unlike second-wave movements elsewhere (notably North America and parts of Europe), again appealed to women's maternal roles to justify their political activism. However, the meaning of the maternal frame had changed considerably due to a radically different political context. The shift in the meaning of the maternal frame, along with other aspects of the political opportunity structure during the dictatorship and the struggle for democracy, also led a significant number of second-wave feminists to pursue a double militancy strategy in favor of the autonomy strategy that dominated the first-wave movement.

Throughout this chapter, I argue that there are three central features of women's incorporation into politics in this period that are crucial for understanding later developments in Chile. First, because women demanded to enter politics based on their difference (i.e., they insisted that they would bring something to politics that was lacking), they had a difficult and complex relationship with the political parties, which dominated Chilean politics, right from the beginning. The parties initially could not merely incorporate women's issues into politics because women themselves framed their issues as being outside of, even above, the realm of class-based partisan politics. Most women's organizations in this early period sought autonomy from the world of traditional politics monopolized by the parties. While many groups clearly had allies within the progressive forces of the left, most women steadfastly refused to frame their issues in left-right terms.[1] Once women were given the vote, women's groups and women's political parties had a hard time maintaining their autonomous position, however, and found that it was impossible to practice their own style of nonpartisan politics. Women's parties and organizations soon collapsed and women who wanted to practice electoral politics joined the traditional parties. Once in the parties, women felt compelled to focus on the issues that dominated Chilean politics, that is, class and partisan issues.

Second, women's participation was institutionalized by the state in a way that reinforced collective identities rooted in women's caretaking roles.

Women's citizenship was expressed in their mobilization as mothers. As soon as the Chilean state started to take on a role in delivering social services, women became the link through which citizens were tied to the state as beneficiaries of state services. It should be noted, however, that the benefits that women received and passed along to their families were never the same as the welfare entitlements that male (worker) citizens received (Rosemblatt 2000). Instead, women's benefits were delivered though quasi-charitable and community-based institutions. By 1964 this role was institutionalized in the state-directed Centros de Madres (Mothers Centers). While women's social roles formed the basis around which they were organized and mobilized in the Centros de Madres, it was through these very roles that women were constructed by the state as a collective actor and were increasingly brought into Chile's intensifying partisan conflict. The party organizations that operated through community organizations such as the Centros de Madres appealed to women as mothers, and moreover, as mothers whose interests were above or outside of the narrow politics of class.

Finally, how women emerged as a collective actor and how they were incorporated into politics set up both the institutional infrastructure and certain "repertoires of collective action" that facilitated the emergence of the women's movement as a crucial actor in the anti-Pinochet movement of the 1980s. Moreover, the "mobilized mother" ideal of citizenship expressed in the Centros de Madres served as a basis for the mobilizing frame of "militant mothers" defending and protecting their families and communities from the dangers posed by the dictatorship.

Following a brief description of the political and historical context in which first-wave movements emerged in Chile, the chapter outlines the nature of women's mobilization for social and political reform, highlighting the relationship between women's organizations and traditional political parties. It then discusses the consequences of women's attainment of formal citizenship status (i.e., suffrage), and describes how women were incorporated into the intensifying partisan competition of the era as "mobilized mothers."

The Context for First-Wave Feminism in Chile

Feminism emerged in Chile as women pursued reforms to improve social conditions primarily for women, children, and the working class, and as women challenged their gender-based subordination and lack of civil and political rights. Women's subordination was reflected in the civil code, which converted married women into dependents of their husbands. *Patria potestad* (parental authority) gave fathers exclusive rights over their children, with the exception of children born outside of marriage. In such cases, the mother exercised parental rights unless the father recognized the child as his own (Lavrin 1995, p. 196). Chile's 1855 civil code established women as completely subordinate to their husbands (Fríes and Matus 1999, p. 78; González and Sabel 1989; Lavrin 1995, p. 193). The code was extremely patriarchal, and denied married women any control over their bodies, their assets, or their children, and further obliged wives to obey their husbands (Covarrubias 1978, p. 617). The husband determined the couple's residence, and held total administrative control over property owned before and acquired after marriage (Lavrin 1995, pp. 194–195). Married women, due to their subordination to their husbands, were deemed *incapaz* (incapable) of legal actions.

Women's subordination was of course linked to the prevailing gender ideology, which exclusively associated women with the private domain of the family. The social roles associated with motherhood came to form the basis of the gender ideology in Chile. Women, as mothers, were expected to act *for* others, mainly their children, but women's caring responsibilities often extended to their communities as well. The feature that was most closely bound up with the motherhood identity was women's supposed boundless capacity for self-sacrifice and for putting the needs of others before their own. According to Elsa Chaney, "the characterization of women as sacrificial mothers sums up what Latin Americans consider the most positive aspect of the image of woman" (1979, p. 47). A Chilean newspaper article in 1915 noted that "the greatest merit of the woman throughout the ages is her capacity to love and her maternal instinct, qualities which the Chilean woman greatly demonstrates" (cited in Gaviola et al. 1986, p. 21).

The emergence of women's activism in this period was also linked to the major social and political changes that were occurring, changes that had a significant impact on women and their subsequent organization in pursuit of progressive reform. The key change was the expansion of the state following the collapse of the oligarchy and the emergence of a reformist government under Arturo Alessandri in 1932. During this period, a (limited) welfare state emerged and the public sector took control of large portions of the economy. Women ceased to be restricted to the private realm in the first few decades of the twentieth century because the changing economic and social landscape increasingly necessitated their entrance into the labor force (Covarrubias 1978, p. 621). Despite many women being drawn into the work force, political discourse and social reformers emphasized waged work as a masculine activity and valorized the stable nuclear family with the woman as homemaker (Rosemblatt 2000). A mainly rural economy was gradually being transformed into an urban industrial economy, a transformation that resulted in a prolonged period of rural to urban migration.[2] In many of these displaced families, women played the main subsistence role, earning income through domestic service, selling food, drinks, and handicrafts, or renting out parts of their dwellings as shelter for other new migrants (Gaviola et al. 1986; Valdés and Weinstein 1993). Women from the middle classes began to see a professionalization of their social roles as caregivers as the state began to take a greater interest in the health, education, and well-being of its citizens. The emergence of the populist welfare state meant that the state took on the role of providing social services, at first in a limited way, but expanding over time. Previously, upper-class women delivered services through charity work, caring for the sick, the elderly, and the very young. When state social services displaced charity, women often continued to play the same roles, but subsequently did so as professionals—as teachers, nurses, and social workers (Lavrin 1995, p. 296). Thus, women's private social roles were being performed in the public domain. This did not lead to a public perception of women professionals or workers as acceptable or desirable, however. Instead, the image of woman as homemaker remained dominant.

Perhaps the key defining feature of the political system in this period was the exaggerated importance of the state, which according to Arturo Valenzuela "consisted of an awesome set of structures and institutions" (1978, p. 13). As the state expanded to play greater social and economic roles, middle classes and the bourgeoisie began to develop links to the state to pursue their economic interests. According to Manuel Garretón (1989, p. 12), this feature of Chilean politics is responsible for the type of party system that evolved in Chile, namely one wherein parties became the key vehicles for organizing civil society, in turn stifling the capacity of autonomous civil society organizations (see also Oxhorn 1995a). Consequently, "the dominant mode of political action consisted of organizing a social base in order to bind it to party structures and thus exert pressure on the state, at times demanding fulfillment of claims and at other times seeking to take control of the state" (Garretón 1989, p. 2).

The importance and strength of political parties to Chilean politics cannot be overstated. Political parties in Chile organize more than just formal politics; they also extend deep into local community and social organizations. One scholar has noted that prior to 1973, "Chile's party system was everywhere, not only determining the political recruitment process for important national posts but also structuring contests in such diverse institutions as government agencies, professional and industrial unions, neighborhood organizations, and even local high schools" (Valenzuela 1978, p. 3). As we shall see, this feature of Chilean politics has exerted a powerful influence over gendered patterns of citizenship.

The Emergence of Women's Movements

When women began to organize and pursue change, they appealed to women's "difference" as justification. Because of the importance of Chilean gender ideology, women asked for citizenship rights based on their identities as mothers. Asunción Lavrin describes Chilean feminism of this era as "compensatory feminism" because it did not challenge women's social roles but only challenged the deprivation of women's political rights based on their social functions. Compensatory feminism "created a gendered social space where the woman-mother's 'spiritual equality' was recognized and legal reforms repaired previous inequities" (1995, p. 40). The kind of equality sought by Chilean women was evident in leading feminist Amanda Labarca's comments in a magazine:

> We do not ask for our civil equality in a tragicomic effort to be exactly like you [men]. We know that our functions are different . . . but our spirit is equal, and our ideals for the redemption of humankind are identical. We only wish to reside harmoniously with you at the same level of spiritual equality. We dislike equally the man who feminizes himself and the woman who adopts the deportment of a man. (cited in Lavrin 1995, p. 38)

The Chilean gender ideology prescribes behavior that keeps women in the private sphere of the home and the family. This reinforces a sexual division of labor in which men are political or public actors and women are restricted to the tasks necessary to the reproduction of the private sphere. This is neatly captured in the popular Spanish saying *la mujer en la casa, el hombre en la calle* (the woman in the home, the man on the street) (cited in Chaney 1979, p. 49). By the end of the nineteenth century, however, this saying had ceased to hold literally, as the boundaries of *la casa* (private) and *la calle* (public) were more symbolic than real. Women had begun to undertake activities that, while clearly relating to the private realm—for example, children's education and health—required them to be more visible and often required them to act publicly. Importantly, in pursuing the interests that motivated them, women strategically drew on the images of woman-as-mother (Chaney 1979; Lavrin 1995; Miller 1994). Moreover, even when a coherent feminist identity began to emerge in Chile, it celebrated rather than rejected women's maternal roles. Chilean suffragists, for example, insisted that women "could never surrender the sense of motherhood that surrounds and penetrates our understanding of life" (cited in Lavrin 1995, p. 298).

The Suffrage Movement

In the 1870s, women undertook a variety of actions to challenge their exclusion and marginalization from politics. Initially, these were carried out by elite women from the educated middle and upper classes. Women from these classes were more likely to be familiar with the liberal political ideals that were spreading throughout Europe and North America. But it was not just women who began to note the contradictions between professing liberal and progressive values of a just social order while accepting precepts that severely limited their educational opportunities and maintained their subordinate and nearly childlike political status. Many leading male intellectuals of the era supported the idea that women should be educated and be granted, at least formally, the same equality conferred to men (Lavrin 1995). In 1877 the Amunátegui Decree granted women the right to enter the universities, making Chile the first Latin American country in which women had access to higher education. Chilean elites, however, were unwilling to extend any political rights to women. In 1884 a group of women from San Felipe, a small town just north of Santiago, challenged their exclusion by registering themselves to vote in the upcoming elections. They argued that they should have this right because there was nothing in the Chilean constitution that specifically denied suffrage to women. The government's response was to amend the constitution with a clause that did just that—it explicitly stated that the right to vote was specific to men (Covarrubias 1978; Gaviola et al. 1986, p. 19). It would be well over sixty years before suffrage was extended to women. But the issue was only on the agenda for a small segment of middle- and upper-class women.

In their detailed history of the Chilean suffrage movement, Edda Gaviola and colleagues (1986, p. 39) note that the period between 1913 and 1925 is characterized by the awakening of the "associative spirit" of women. During this period a number of explicitly feminist organizations were founded and women came to constitute themselves as a collective actor demanding social, political, and economic rights. The "pioneers" of Chilean feminism were the Centros Femeninos Belén de Sárrago (Belén de Sárrago Women's Centers), which took their name from a popular intellectual of the era who promoted ideals of free thinking and anticlericalism (Kirkwood 1986, pp. 96–97). These centers were established in the north of the country, first in Antofagasta and later in Iquique. According to Gaviola and colleagues, the north produced the early feminist movement because of women's important mobilizing roles in the broader popular movements of the region, especially those linked to labor conflicts in the mining area (1986, p. 32). Women's organizations were also flourishing among urban middle- and upper-class women as well. By 1915 in Santiago there were two women's organizations—the Club de Señoras (Women's Club) and the Círculo de Lectura (Reading Circle)—whose ends were mainly cultural. But in addition to discussing poetry, art, and literature, these groups organized discussions on women's political rights (Gaviola et al. 1986, p. 34). Most organized women wanted civil code reform, especially greater control over marital assets for married women.

Despite women's formal exclusion from exercising political citizenship, political parties were concerned with mobilizing women, and many of them established separate women's wings to that end. The Radical Party recruited women members as early as 1888 and set up a women's wing in 1934 (Chaney 1979, p. 93). Leading feminist Amanda Labarca was an active member of this party. Women were active in the Communist Party since its inception in 1911, but the party has never organized women into separate organizations. The Socialist Party, on the other hand, established a women's wing in 1933. The main parties on the right—the Conservative and Liberal Parties—both created separate women's wings. According to Gaviola and colleagues, because of assumptions about women's "natural" conservatism, the parties of the right made greater efforts to attract women members than did the leftist parties (1986, p. 47). The Conservative Party's women's wing (created in 1941) served mainly as a vehicle for women's charity work with the poor (Chaney 1979, p. 94). While women therefore had a presence in political parties, their separation into women's wings kept them marginalized and out of the parties' decisionmaking structures. The parties' main goals were to get women involved in supportive activities and to mobilize the vote. Teresa Valdés and Marisa Weinstein (1993, p. 45) note, however, that due to the emergence of feminism and women's activism around social issues, by the 1930s all political parties had some position on women's issues. Many parties were beginning to view women as future voters, and therefore sought to gain their allegiance. However, due to the profoundly class-based language of politics, women's gender issues remained unarticulated in the arena of partisan politics.

Although women activists and feminists often had links to political parties, many of them sought to portray themselves—and women overall—as *apolitical* and above partisan politics. Women's movements of this era opted for a strategy of autonomy rather than double militancy, but not always out of a fear of co-optation. Rather, they opted for autonomy because their politics of difference led many to draw a sharp distinction between masculine politics, which feminists viewed as a corrupt activity that was all about the pursuit of power for partisan or individual purposes, and feminine activism, which sought neither power nor prestige but the betterment of society. This position influenced the type of women's organizations that formed to pursue female suffrage.

Many feminists in Chile, as elsewhere in the region (Brazil and Argentina), shunned traditional politics by forming their own political parties. Lavrin explains that "within the female parties women felt comfortable and free from masculine influence in determining their course of action and their goals." Prior to achieving suffrage, female parties "were exercises in organization and mobilization to lobby for political rights and other causes" (1995, p. 46). In Chile, two women's parties were formed in the 1920s, the Feminine Civic Party and the Feminine Democratic Party. The women who formed these parties placed a high value on autonomy and believed that women needed to remain above traditional partisan conflicts. For example, the Feminine Civic Party declared its independence from any political or religious groupings in its statutes. María de la Cruz, the party's founder, believed that women must be able to pursue their aims independently of men and needed their own party to do so (Covarrubias 1978, pp. 628, 639).

In addition to the creation of female parties, the 1930s also saw the formation of a host of women's groups and networks that sought women's rights. The most important of these was the Chilean Women's Proemancipation Movement (Movimiento Pro-Emancipación de Mujeres de Chile, MEMCH), formed in 1935 mostly by women of the left who proposed radical social change to improve their situation. In its declaration of principles, MEMCH described itself as "a wide organization of national character that groups women of all ideological tendencies that are disposed to struggle for the social, economic, and juridical liberation of women" (cited in Gaviola et al. 1986, p. 43). MEMCH was the first organization to mobilize women massively through large rallies and public events. It linked women's political struggles to other issues of the day—peace, unemployment, and the high cost of living—and was also a strong promoter of the rights of working women.

Despite the influence of leftist ideology on MEMCH, it consciously avoided the prevailing language of politics—that is, the language of class struggle (Lavrin 1995, p. 310). Although MEMCH was founded mostly by women of the left, its members, like those in the women's parties, vigorously pursued their independence from the "corrupt" world of masculine politics. MEMCH's founder, Elena Caffarena, explains, "the fact of being apolitical doesn't deny that women be trained for and enter into the political parties, but it is an error to give to MEMCH a political tendency. Each group has its function: the class struggle is for the parties, and for the feminine struggles, the feminine organizations like MEMCH" (cited in Covarrubias 1978, p. 632). Caffarena's words indicate that women's struggles were not considered political, which was a concept monopolized exclusively by parties.

Their claims of autonomy notwithstanding, MEMCH worked closely with the parties of the left, especially those that came to form the Popular Front in 1936. In fact, according to Gaviola and colleagues, MEMCH eventually became the "feminine arm" of the Popular Front (1986, p. 44). MEMCH's preoccupation with issues of working-class women and their families ultimately generated tensions with middle-class women. Partisan tensions seriously undermined MEMCH by the late 1940s, when the Communist Party was outlawed by the Chilean government. When MEMCH and its members mobilized against this form of political exclusion, they came to be seen as too closely allied with the Communists, which then resulted in their own marginalization from Chilean politics (Gaviola et al. 1986, p. 45).[3]

The struggle for suffrage finally gained a mass following in 1944, when MEMCH, along with another umbrella group created that same year, the Chilean Federation of Feminine Institutions (Federación Chilena de Instituciones Femeninas, FECHIF), began to mobilize massively for women's political rights. According to Karin Rosemblatt, feminists in the suffrage movement "both used and subverted gender-specific understandings of citizenship" (2000, p. 243). While many activists drew on women's maternal identities to argue for political rights, others, notably women workers, argued that women's political rights should be granted by virtue of the fact that many women were essentially performing roles and labor similar to those of men (pp. 243–244). In the suffrage campaign, however, most organized women emphasized the special qualities that women would bring to politics because of their social functions—such as a "moral voice"—and emphasized that they would focus attention on day-to-day issues that were related to the difficulties so many families faced but that were not sufficiently addressed by the existing political class. Women argued that they would bring to politics values they naturally acquired in their roles as mothers. It is evident that Chilean feminists who argued for women's inclusion into formal politics believed women had a particular role to play. An activist within FECHIF stated, "we want women to vote not because she is like man, but because she is different" (cited in Rosemblatt 2000, p. 244).

Women had a number of allies within the male political elite in their struggle for female suffrage. In March 1934 a bill was finally passed to allow women to vote in municipal elections, which would serve as sort of a testing ground to determine if women were "ready" to vote in national elections. According to Gaviola and colleagues, the municipal arena was seen as little more than a *casa grande* (big house) and thus women would simply extend their traditional roles by participating in municipal affairs as both voters and candidates. Perhaps the most important outcome of the municipal elections of 1935 was the confirmation of what many male elites had suspected: women tended toward conservatism. While the number of women who voted was small, they tended to support the parties of the right, in large part because it was precisely these parties that made greater efforts to appeal to women in their campaigns. Likewise, most of the women candidates who won represented the Conservative Party: of the twenty-five women candidates in these elections who won (out of a total of ninety-eight), sixteen were Conservatives. Where women participated as candidates, the administration of the municipality was depicted as analogous to running a home. This election conditioned the subsequent behavior of Chilean political parties toward women. Since then, the right has tried actively to appeal to women by emphasizing their moral duties and appealing to women's "natural" desire for order, while the left, assuming women to be conservative, has very little to say to them (Gaviola et al. 1986, pp. 59, 61, 63; Lavrin 1995, p. 317).

A bill was finally passed granting women the right to vote and be elected nationally in 1948. The delayed timing had less to do with massive opposition to women's suffrage than with the fact that legislation on women's suffrage was continually put on the back-burner and was never considered a high priority by presidents or congress. One of the suffrage movement's biggest supporters was President Pedro Aguirre Cerda of the Popular Front, who introduced a bill on women's suffrage in 1941. Unfortunately, he died soon after, thus depriving the movement of one of its strongest supporters while the bill languished in the legislative process, not even to be discussed for another four years. Legislation often takes years to make its way through the congress and committee system in Chile. One of the executive's most important powers, however, is the capacity to declare certain bills "urgent," which requires their discussion within a specified time period. The Chilean executive, therefore, has important "agenda-setting" powers. Women's rights legislation, however, was seldom declared urgent. After a new bill on women's suffrage was introduced in 1945, it too languished in congress until it ultimately received a "simple urgency" classification from the president (Gaviola et al. 1986, p. 73).

By this time, the movement was becoming much more militant in demanding equal rights. In part, women were spurred on by international developments, especially the fact that, after World War II, women received the vote in a number of countries.[4] Additionally, Chile had signed on to a number of international agreements that dealt with equal rights for women. Thus, even one of Chile's Conservative senators, Horacio Walker, argued that the country's laws needed to be reformed to conform with international agreements and the laws of other Western democratic countries (Gaviola et al. 1986, p. 73).

Women's organizations, especially FECHIF and MEMCH, organized massive mobilization rallies for women's suffrage. Most significant, they continued to emphasize the importance of allowing women's "moral voice" to be heard, as women's activism was framed as fundamentally different from men's. In this spirit, the Feminine Civic Party insisted that women were needed to "purify" politics. It also declared itself to be neither left nor right: *los hombres se dividen por la idea, nosotras nos unificamos por el sentimiento* (men are divided over ideas, we women are unified by feelings) (cited in Gaviola et al. 1986, p. 73). Soon, all women's organizations were working together, pursuing a dual strategy of mobilizing women and pressuring political leaders in congress (Gaviola et al. 1986, p. 46). Finally, in December 1948, women's suffrage became law.

Women as Citizens: "Mobilized Mothers," 1950–1973

After women's formal political citizenship was granted, women were increasingly incorporated into the Chilean political process as actors with a particular set of interests and concerns deriving from their social roles as mothers. In part, this incorporation emerged from the strategies that women's movements employed to achieve their political rights, but these strategies themselves emerged from Chilean gender ideology and the prevailing political context. There are two important consequences of first-wave feminism that are relevant to explaining subsequent developments: first, women's relations with and in political parties; and second, the nature and role of the state- and party-linked organizations created to incorporate women as "mobilized mothers" acting primarily in the informal political arena.

As noted earlier, feminists and women's leaders created their own political parties as part of their politics of difference strategy for achieving citizenship. This insistence on autonomy from traditional political actors, however, led to a number of problems for women. Lavrin notes the ambiguous and contradictory nature of women's parties in this period. Female parties were clearly engaging in the political process, while claiming to be apolitical. This essential contradiction contributed to the problems women confronted after they were enfranchised. As Lavrin explains, "refusing to accept politics on the same premises as men perpetuated the idea of female political leaders as oddities and lessened their potential for exerting power in national politics" (1995, pp. 46–47). In a similar vein, Valdés and Weinstein explain that once women entered the messy world of politics, they "felt incapable of carrying forward their own form of doing politics" (1993, pp. 51–52). In framing their motivations as "morally pure," women were, in effect, putting themselves, and the issues they pursued, above politics. This strategy backfired, however, ultimately leading to the collapse of women's parties.

Prior to winning the vote, women's parties worked at mobilizing women and pressuring political leaders to pass female suffrage. After 1949, these parties participated in elections, and the leader of the Chilean Feminine Party (Partido Femenino Chileno, PFCH), María de la Cruz, was elected to the Senate. Through this party, Chilean feminists believed they could practice an autonomous form of politics, rooted in women's political nature—for example, more moral, less prone to corruption, and not limited to the left-right ideological divisions that organized traditional politics. When women were confronted with having to practice politics in the political arena, however, they opened themselves up to greater scrutiny and criticism because of the high standards they had set for themselves. As Julieta Kirkwood explains, "starting from the moment in which it began to act in 'politics' the PFCH had to confront adversaries, make alliances, endure internal divisions, [and] initiate ideological debates with other feminist groups and politicians" (1986, p. 153). Ultimately, the party fell apart after Cruz became embroiled in a scandal. Both the party and its leader were being attacked by the left and the right. Three women parliamentarians from outside the party presented charges of "dishonorable conduct" against Cruz, claiming that she was involved in an illicit and illegal business scheme. The leader of the only women's political party gave up her Senate seat in disgrace.

In Chile, as elsewhere, first-wave women's movements began to dissolve after achieving suffrage. The organizations composing the suffrage movement lost visibility and internal articulation (Covarrubias 1978; Gaviola et al. 1986; Kirkwood 1986; Valdés and Weinstein 1993). Especially after the failure of a women's political party, women began to enter the existing parties, where class and partisan issues took priority, and women's issues were increasingly marginalized (Kirkwood 1986, pp. 162–163). The movement as a whole fell prey to partisan divisions. MEMCH grew weaker, mainly as a result of internal disputes between those who wanted it to be primarily a working-class women's organization and those who wanted it to pursue a broader set of alliances. But after 1949, many of its members also departed for the political parties (Gaviola et al. 1986, p. 45). However, because women were entering political parties during a time in which the women's movement was weakening, they simply did not have any opportunities to promote women's issues through partisan militancy. Hence, once women moved into the traditional political parties, women's issues were ignored. Consequently, Edda Gaviola, Eliana Largo, and Sandra Palestro (1994, p. 21) refer to this period as the "illusion of integration," and Kirkwood (1986, p. 77) calls it the period of "feminist silence." As feminists increasingly moved into political parties, especially those on the left, they entered a masculine world where they were inhibited from discussing their particular concerns—that is, those arising from their social positions as women.

Spaces of Gendered Citizenship: The Centros de Madres

Another important effect of women's formal citizenship status emerged from their growing importance as voters. The nature of Chile's political process, centered as it was on the organization of various sectors of society by political parties, led to the parties' growing interest in organizing and mobilizing women. What is important is how this was done. Women were organized and mobilized around their social roles as reproducers of the social sphere of family and community through state-led organizations linked to political parties.[5] Thus, women's incorporation as citizens in this period was bound up with their social roles as reproducers of the private realm. Women's citizenship was expressed through their identity as "mobilized mothers" in organizations that were not autonomous, but firmly linked to the objectives of the government of the day.

Women's incorporation into politics occurred as the populist state was further expanding its role, especially in the sphere of social services. Populism in Chile differed from the type of populist corporatism that was common elsewhere in Latin America, particularly Brazil and Argentina, in the interwar years. Instead of arrangements whereby social groups—normally organized labor—were linked to the state and mobilized around a single populist leader like Brazil's Getúlio Vargas or Argentina's Juan Perón, Chilean politics continued to be dominated by political parties that competed for the allegiance of social groups such as organized labor, peasants, and the urban popular sectors. In the postwar period and until 1973, party competition in Chile intensified as these allegiances were used to bind social groups to the state, but more importantly, to whichever party occupied the state at a particular time.

In this context, women became an important link through which citizens were connected to the state. One of the most important means by which the state began to address poverty was by organizing popular sector women. This set in motion a pattern that would continue in Chile: the state delivered services to families, especially to poor families, through women who were organized around their caretaking responsibilities. It is important to note, however, that the services delivered through women were not the same as the welfare entitlements available to male workers (see Rosemblatt 2000). The social rights of citizenship remained masculine, while the charity and community services—delivered often by volunteers—were the feminine equivalents. The first program emerged in 1947, when the government created the Asociación de Dueñas de Casa (Housewives Association), under the direction of the First Lady. This program aimed at "preparing women of scarce resources to better fulfill their roles as housewives and as consumers, to prepare them to struggle against the high cost of living; on the other hand, to initiate their interest in other aspects of the institutional life of the country, such as labor and political participation" (Valdés and Weinstein 1993, p. 47). The program had both social and political aims: to address poverty through women's caretaking roles—for example, enabling them to stretch family budgets a little further—but also to mobilize women politically around the Radical Party's government of González Videla (Gaviola et al. 1986, p. 73).

A similar undertaking in the 1950s was the Ropero del Pueblo (People's Closet), also under the direction of the First Lady, in which middle- and upper-class women were organized through the state to participate in charity work aimed at providing clothing to popular sector women. During this period, the patterns of women's relationship to the state became more entrenched and formalized. Middle- and upper-class women were organized to act "charitably" toward women in the popular sectors, while the latter were increasingly becoming linked to the state through its provision of services to them as mothers in poor and working-class families.

During the Christian Democratic presidency of Eduardo Frei Sr. (1964–1970), social participation became even further institutionalized and mediated through state agencies with important consequences for women's citizenship.[6] This development, however, must be situated in the context of the intensifying partisan competition that accompanied the emergence of the Christian Democratic Party (Partido Democrata Cristiana, PDC) as the main center party, replacing the Radical Party. In this context, partisan competition among left, center, and right increased, as the PDC, unlike the Radical Party, was less pragmatic and therefore less likely to act as a pendulum to reduce ideological competition. Consequently, all parties increased their efforts to mobilize support among various social groups, with the PDC focusing its efforts on previously excluded groups—the urban poor and women. The PDC's strategy for incorporating marginalized groups involved the creation of community organizations through which citizen participation could be channeled and, more importantly, linked to the party. The programs and organizations that emerged (the Centros de Madres, youth centers, sports clubs, and the Juntas de Vecinos [Neighborhood Councils]) created networks that tied the community organization and its members to state bureaucrats and local party officials (Oxhorn 1995b, p. 52).

The main mechanism for mobilizing women was the Centros de Madres, the origins of which lay in the Catholic Church–affiliated charitable organizations created in 1935, in which mainly middle- and upper-class women worked with women in the poblaciones. Some of the organizations used the name "Centro de Madres." Their purposes included providing spaces for poor women to gather and learn "feminine" skills, but also imparting "moral learning" to "teach [the women] to be exemplary mothers and wives" (Valdés and Weinstein 1993, pp. 44–45).

The importance of the Centros de Madres to the construction of women as a collective actor cannot be overstated. Gaviola, Largo, and Palestro claim that they laid the groundwork for a popular women's movement (1994, p. 34). Valdés and Weinstein (1993) see them as crucial to the formation of a new collective consciousness among popular sector women that ultimately sowed the seeds for the massive organizational capacity displayed during Pinochet's dictatorship. Margaret Power, however, emphasizes that the Centros de Madres also laid the groundwork for the massive mobilization of women in opposition to Allende's government. Power's extensive research on women's activism during the 1964–1973 period shows that women's organization in the Centros de Madres helped to produce two ideologically distinct types of mobilizations: "one in solidarity with the UP [Allende's Popular Unity government], and one in opposition to it" (2002, p. 118).

In this context, patterns of women's citizenship were changing. Political parties viewed women's activities in community organizations as channels through which partisan support could be generated and reinforced. This indicates the often blurred and continually shifting boundary between the formal and informal political arenas. Women's community (informal) participation was not entirely separate from the arena of partisan politics, yet it was clearly "invisible" in the sense that it was primarily about supporting a male-led politics. Women were also seen as economically relevant—their participation in productive and reproductive activities was deemed necessary to Chile's development. But neither of these activities challenged women's exclusive association with the informal political arena or prevailing unequal and hierarchical gender relations. According to Power, "the Mothers' Centers improved women's lives, but did not radically transform them" (2002, p. 115). A woman did not have to abandon her traditional social role, but merely spend a few hours in a community center, where she received training in "productive" activities. The Centros de Madres established agreements with other state agencies through which women could acquire the necessary equipment or materials they needed, or alternatively, through which purchases of the women's products could be arranged. For example, women sewed school uniforms, which were in turn purchased by the state. During Frei's 1964 presidential campaign, he promised "to each Chilean woman, a sewing machine" (cited in Valdés and Weinstein 1993, p. 57).[7]

Between 1964 and 1970 the Centros de Madres grew substantially in number and importance. This process formed part of the state's growing control over social organizations. In 1968 the government created a ministry of community organizations to further direct and control local social organizations, including the Juntas de Vecinos and the Centros de Madres. The increasing institutionalization of these organizations and their links to the state structure led all parties to view them as sites for community mobilization around partisan goals. Consequently, community organizations were key to distilling the ideology of the governing party, in this case the Christian Democrats.

"Mobilized Mothers" and Political Crisis in Chile: The Allende Years

Chile experienced a profound political crisis between 1970 and 1973, during which women were further incorporated into an intensifying class conflict that culminated in a brutal military coup. In 1970 the coalition of leftist parties, the Popular Unity (Unidad Popular, UP), led by socialist Salvador

Allende, won the elections with a very slight plurality of the popular vote. The 1970–1973 period saw a massive increase in social organization, but one that continued to be directed by political parties. Women became more involved in the political and social struggles, as both left and right tried to win their support through appeals that drew on and reinforced women's maternal identities. Two recent detailed historical studies, one by Lisa Baldez (2002) and one by Margaret Power (2002), illustrate the extent to which the struggle between the left and the right in this period was a profoundly gendered one. In part, the success of the right in mobilizing women against Allende owes substantially to existing gendered patterns of citizenship in the country. Baldez explains that "women [opposed to Allende] portrayed themselves as uniquely capable of transcending party conflict, while men were mired in turf battles that impeded the progress [of the anti-Allende forces]" (2002, p. 95). Power explains that as conservative forces began the task of mobilizing opposition to Allende, "the right appealed to women based on their supposedly natural and politically disinterested concern for their homes and families" (2002, p. 135).

While in office, however, the UP government continued to organize women primarily through the Centros de Madres in the absence of any other strategy for addressing the "woman question." Kirkwood argues that the UP failed to recognize women's distinct political contributions, addressing women simply as wives, mothers, daughters, or sisters of the workers (1986, pp. 40–41). Likewise, Chaney (1974) argues that the left simply did not know how to mobilize women during this period, leaving women open to the eventual massive mobilization of the center and right-wing anti-UP forces. Julie Shayne (2004, chap. 3) notes that while the UP's major accomplishments for women were material, there were also significant cultural accomplishments that sowed the seeds of a feminist consciousness among some women. Part of the political left's ambivalence toward women owes to women's tendency to vote conservatively. In the 1964 elections, 63 percent of women voted for Frei, compared to only 49 percent of men. The gender gap continued in the 1970 elections, when 68 percent of women voted against Allende (38 percent for the rightist candidate and 30 percent for the Christian Democratic candidate), compared to 58 percent of men who voted against Allende (Power 2002, p. 138).

In this context, Allende knew that he had to try to win the allegiance of women for the project of social change promoted by his government. However, he did very little to involve women in the upper echelons of power. It was only after two full years in office that he appointed a woman to his cabinet. While he did send a bill to congress to create a family ministry to address women's and family issues, he subsequently allowed it to languish in the legislative process without ever declaring it urgent (Chaney 1974, p. 269). In 1972, through a presidential decree, Allende created a national women's secretariat, which was supposed to have aided the government in devising policy regarding women's issues and also propose changes that would promote women's equality. By the time of the coup, however, the bill was still in the process of being reworked (Valdés and Weinstein 1993, p. 66). And while Allende created a women's unit within the UP coalition, its main purpose was to mobilize women in support of the government, rather than to empower them as women (Shayne 2004). Ultimately, the UP relied on expanding the Centros de Madres, which were further institutionalized and placed under the purview of the National Ministry for Social Development (which replaced Frei's National Ministry for Popular Promotion).

By 1973 the number of Centros de Madres and the number of women participating in them had more than doubled from the 1970 figures. They became even more important to popular sector women due to the economic crises that emerged during the UP's time in office. Allende's economic and social policies seriously threatened the class interests of the conservative right. The right's response was to try to undermine the UP's project by, for example, hoarding and disrupting the internal transport of goods, which resulted in chronic shortages and a growing black market. Women were confronted with these crises on a daily basis because they were the ones who did the household shopping. Thus it was women who had to wait in line for hours, and find creative ways to replace items that could no longer be purchased. Women's "natural" honesty was also deployed by the UP government, which called on women to act as monitors of its price control policies, and to report any black market activity. Women were also recruited for other UP programs such as education, health, and literacy campaigns. Even though the activities of the women mobilized by the UP government did little to challenge traditional gender roles, and even reinforced them, the experiences women gained were significant (Shayne 2004). Women were participating in a transformative political project, and they clearly felt they were part of an important historical task.

The 1970–1973 period also witnessed the mass mobilization of women opposed to Allende. A number of conservative women's organizations were formed, such as the Frente Democrática de Mujeres (Women's Democratic Front), El Poder Femenino (Feminine Power), and the Organización Cívico-Familiar "Solidaridad, Orden y Libertad" (Civic-Family Organization for Solidarity, Order, and Liberty). Immediately following the election of Salvador Allende as president, small groups of women engaged in public acts indicating their opposition to a socialist government. One small group of women, dressed entirely in black, led a funeral procession around the presidential palace, La Moneda, to signify what it perceived as the death of democracy (Mattelart 1976, p. 282). But one of the most important mobilizations was the December 1, 1971, "March of the Empty Pots," in which over 5,000 anti-Allende women participated. This massive event was organized by the Women's Democratic Front, which brought together women from the National Party (of the right) and some of the Christian Democrats opposed to the UP government. The demonstration became a weekly event, in which anti-Allende women marched together, banging on empty pots and pans to signify the lack of food under Chile's socialist government. This was a mobilization that drew symbolically on women's traditional social roles as providers of food for their families. Their stated motivation for acting publicly was their inability to fulfill adequately their social responsibilities. Their citizenship was being expressed, therefore, as "mobilized mothers."

What is noteworthy about women's activism in this instance is that although many of these women were clearly defending their class interests, which were threatened by the UP government, their protests were framed as being above the narrow politics of class and partisan interests. According to Baldez, this was a strategic mechanism employed to mobilize greater numbers of women. Baldez points to the dual strategy that female anti-Allende activists used: "they claimed to be non-partisan in order to forge unity among the parties of the opposition, but they simultaneously mobilized voters on behalf of particular political parties" (2002, p. 96). Once again, women's activism as citizens was being cast as apolitical, given that any activity depicted as nonpartisan was assumed to be nonpolitical. In a period of intense class conflict, women were being deployed to represent the interests of all citizens, not just a narrow social base, whether of the left or the right. Michele Mattelart, like Baldez, argues that this was in fact a clear strategy of the right: "The right was able to camouflage the defense of its class interests behind the protests of women, behind demands that, since they have to do with subjects traditionally of marginal political interest (home, familial organization, care and education of children), . . . [appear unconnected to] a class strategy" (1976, p. 288). The right was more successful in mobilizing women, precisely because it called on them as nonpolitical actors. This image appealed to many women who considered politics a brutal, dirty, and corrupt business. The women themselves reinforced this image in their calls to mobilize other women to participate, and in trying to frame their activism as representing all Chileans and not just members of a particular class or political party. In a newspaper article that called on women to participate in the weekly "March of the Empty Pots," a woman wrote, "We are the people! Every child in this land has come from our wombs" (cited in Mattelart 1976, p. 288). Another woman, a PDC leader, reminded women in a newspaper that "you are the light and defense of your children, you must defend your home and your physical and spiritual liberty" (cited in Power 2000, p. 296).

The most important aspect of women's activism in opposition to the socialist project was its reinforcement of the nonpolitical identity of women and the notion that women act publicly only in crisis situations. Power notes that many women who organized anti-Allende marches were militants in the PDC and right-wing parties, but that "they took great pains to downplay the extent and depth of their political involvement. . . . They ignored their organizational ties and instead emphasized only that they were women" (2000, p. 296). The implication is that women's activism is necessarily temporary, and even something extreme and distasteful in itself. As Mattelart (1976) explains, the right was very careful in its strategy for mobilizing women to participate, because it wanted to ensure that in doing so, it did not overturn the gendered patterns of citizenship that normally left politics to men. The right did not want women's activism to challenge the traditional images of women, but rather to conform to them. Thus a commentator in a magazine explained, "by an 'historic crusade of the empty pots' women found a way of demonstrating to the government that . . . if it should prove necessary, she would leave her cozy kitchen in order to devote her energy to warfare" (cited in Mattelart 1976, p. 293). Women's activism, therefore, was something that women were pushed into by necessity. It was a response to a temporary situation and was not therefore viewed as a regular expression of political citizenship. This phenomenon stands out as a key feature of gendered citizenship in Chile.

Conclusion

This chapter has analyzed the sources of Chile's gendered patterns of citizenship through a focus on first-wave feminism and its outcomes. Like many other first-wave movements, women's movements in Chile demanded citizenship rights on the basis of their social roles as mothers. In Chile, this strategy emerged out of the prevailing gender ideology and the value it placed on women's motherhood identities. But the politics of difference strategy also shaped women's relationships with traditional political actors, namely political parties. First-wave feminists sought autonomy from the parties, not for fear of co-optation, but because women's difference led them to shun what they perceived to be the corrupt world of political parties. Most important, women's movements of the first half of the twentieth century in Chile did not cast themselves as political actors despite the fact that they elaborated political goals—for example, the right to vote and be elected, peace, improvements to social welfare, and improvements to women's status. Instead, women's movements in this period depicted women's activism as being above politics. The political opportunity structure that the first-wave women's movement confronted was not conducive to the politicization of women's gender identities. The language of politics was rigidly class-based and parties of the left remained deeply hostile to a "bourgeois" ideology such as feminism. Political parties monopolized the political arena, leaving no space for the public discussion of gender inequality that was not linked to class exploitation or capitalism.

Because most first-wave feminists drew on rather than challenged the importance of women's maternal identities, women as a social group were available for subsequent mobilization by political elites around their social roles as mothers. As democratization proceeded and as previously excluded segments were brought into the political process, greater political competition among parties and their social bases was unleashed. Women were drawn into these contests as "mobilized mothers" standing outside or above the narrow class and partisan politics that dominated the era. In this context, women were organized from above, primarily through the Centros de Madres.

It is important to note, however, that the limited successes of first-wave feminism were not merely due to the politics of difference strategy employed by activists. Equally important in terms of shaping political outcomes was the preferred strategy of movement autonomy over double militancy. While a number of female party militants played important roles in women's organizations such as MEMCH and FECHIF, they were less likely to bring their feminist politics to the parties. Political parties remained closed and hostile to feminism, preferring to mobilize women exclusively around partisan ideas and left-right ideologies.

In sum, in a context dominated by political parties and the language of class, women could not successfully politicize their gender interests. As a result, Chile's gendered patterns of citizenship remained relatively unchanged.

Notes

1. Many feminists avoided framing their issues in strictly class terms because their goal was to construct a multiclass movement (Rosemblatt 2000).

2. Urbanization actually began in the second half of the nineteenth century. In 1859, 20 percent of the population lived in cities, but by 1895 this figure had risen to 46 percent (Covarrubias 1978, p. 618).

3. See Rosemblatt 2000, pp. 99–121, for a discussion of MEMCH's troubled relationship with the Communist Party.

4. By 1947, women had been enfranchised in nine Latin American countries (Valdés and Gomariz 1995, p. 139).

5. The intensifying process of partisan competition in Chile during this period meant that the state-led social organizations of the era were never free from partisan control. Thus the aims of the state (and by extension the organizations it initiated) cannot be separated from the aims of the party that occupied it.

6. See Power 2002, chap. 4, for an excellent discussion of the relationship between the Christian Democratic Party and women.

7. Over 70,000 women received sewing machines through Frei's program, which allowed women to purchase the machines on very easy terms of credit (Power 2002, pp. 109–111).

4 Dictatorship and Women's Struggles for Democracy, 1973–1990

> In moments of crisis, women, with all their hearts and minds, put themselves into defending their communities against the situation that is occurring. In various moments, women go into the streets and take a protagonistic role, but the conflict ends and women return to the four walls of their house and continue to be relegated to their kitchen where they remain without rights. You ask what has happened with the women's movement during the dictatorship. That is a little of what happened.
>
> —Paulina Weber, MEMCH[1]

This chapter discusses the reemergence of women's movements in Chile during the period of authoritarianism (1973–1990), highlighting the relevant continuities and divergences from the first-wave movements.[2] In terms of continuities, it is significant that when women mobilized in the 1970s and 1980s, they retained a politics of difference collective action frame, drawing mainly on their motherhood roles as the basis for their public activism. However, the content of the difference frame had shifted considerably because of the dramatically changed context. Most significant, the meaning of the maternal identity that served to mobilize women in the 1970s and 1980s was politicized, in contrast to the claims of first-wave feminists that women were above politics. Within the context of a motherhood identity that was more political, the difference strategy could be put to radical purposes and used to make demands for gender equality in the political arena. The analysis in this chapter highlights the extent to which collective action frames are both contextual and constructed through movement activism itself (see Tarrow 1998). In the case of the dictatorship-era women's movement, existing meanings attached to women's maternal identities were challenged as the cultural symbols that valorized women's maternal identities were used to justify their public activism in response to the injustices of the dictatorship.

There were other important differences in the political contexts of the first- and second-wave movements that led to the greater impact of the latter movement. Most important, political parties were forced underground and the formal political arena was closed. In this context, the traditional dichotomy between formal and informal politics was blurred as the informal arena in which women's activism predominated became the main site for opposition politics. Women's activism, therefore, emerged in a context in which politics, as traditionally practiced, had ceased to exist and people had to invent other forms of collective action to pursue their goals. Women were the earliest collective actors in this context as they drew on both infrastructure that facilitated collective action (such as the Centros de Madres [Mothers Centers]) and a repertoire of collective action that was part of women's collective historical memory.

In contrast to the previous era, the women's movement in this period began to evaluate Chilean democracy more critically. This process was not undertaken during first-wave women's movements in which feminists first sought autonomy from traditional political actors, placing women and their concerns above politics, and later, when that strategy faltered after achieving female suffrage, feminists simply entered existing parties without asserting a feminist politics within them. In the Pinochet era, the feminist movement, emerging in an arena with few traditional political actors, began to critically assess the political process and the ways in which women's gender-based concerns were marginalized within it. When feminists began working with the opposition movement, they struggled not just for democracy, but also for a democracy that was more open to women's different styles of participation. Most important, when parties began to reconstitute themselves and rebuild their relationships with civil society, they needed the help of women's movements. As a result, feminists who opted to enter political parties could do so from a position of strength and practice a true double militancy.

In documenting the emergence of a women's movement under authoritarianism in Chile, this chapter shows that both movement autonomy and double militancy are useful strategies, but that they are useful at different points in time. Feminists' independence from parties in the early stages of their movement facilitated the emergence of a gender-based critique of traditional political practices and the elaboration of a set of demands that challenged a gendered citizenship that rendered women's interests invisible. However, once parties regained their strength and, after 1983, began to assume a more central role in the opposition to the dictatorship, women's movements confronted a dilemma. Georgina Waylen poses the question in the following way: "Should women's movements work with the new institutions and parties and risk being co-opted and losing autonomy, or should they remain outside, preserving their independence but risking marginalization and loss of influence as power shifts toward the political parties?" (1994, pp. 339–340).

In Chile, the autonomy versus double militancy dilemma led to partisan divisions that weakened and fragmented many organizations. What is significant, however, is that many leading feminists in this period made the choice to enter political parties to pursue a double militancy strategy—that is, to be part of both the feminist movement and a political party. This decision allowed feminists to place their gender-based demands on the public agenda of the transition to democracy. For example, women demanded the creation of national policy machinery to promote gender equality and programs to improve women's lives. In achieving these goals, women succeeded in gendering the transition.

Unfortunately, there were other, less positive outcomes of the transition for women's citizenship. The double militancy strategy was not an unqualified success because many feminist citizenship demands, such as quotas for women in decisionmaking and reproductive choice, were considered too radical by political parties and therefore were not adopted as part of the transition's agenda. Also, the women's movement grew increasingly divided, which meant that the feminists in the main opposition parties could not adequately represent the movement as a whole. Finally, as political parties reemerged and a formal political arena was reconstructed, women were once again marginalized within it because Chilean gender ideology had not been transformed. Hence, women's citizenship continued to be idealized as "mobilized mothers" acting primarily in the informal political arena unless extraordinary circumstances called for their activism in the formal political arena. The class- and gender-based divisions between formal and informal politics were not effectively undermined.

The events examined in this chapter are crucial to understanding the post-1990 struggles by women to exercise their citizenship. The limited access women have to formal politics and the difficulties they face in promoting feminist goals are rooted in the period analyzed here. Likewise, the difficulties women's movements face in the posttransition context in terms of mobilizing women and putting their goals on the public agenda are also linked to the ways in which the movements fragmented over partisan and strategic issues during the transition process.

The chapter begins with an outline of the key social, economic, and political features that generated women's mobilization following the 1973 military coup, followed by an outline of the emergence of women's activism and how various types of organizations came together to form a united movement with a common set of goals. It next discusses the demands of women's movements, emphasizing how they went beyond the limited citizenship demands of first-wave feminists in Chile. Finally, the role of women's movements in the transition to democracy is outlined, with a focus on how various women's organizations confronted the autonomy versus double militancy dilemma, and its consequences for promoting women's citizenship during the transition process.

Women Under Military Rule

The coup of September 11, 1973, put a swift end to the heightened climate of politicization and class confrontation that had been building steadily since the 1960s. While the initial goal of the four-man military junta was to restore order, General Augusto Pinochet eventually consolidated his own power and initiated a project of massive social, economic, and political change. The discourse of the regime, and of Pinochet in particular, illustrates that women had a crucial role to play in healing a society that had become "sick" due to an excess of politics. Women were depicted as models of apolitical passivity, one of the highest virtues in the national project of reconstruction. In a speech to the women of El Poder Femenino (Feminine Power) in April 1974, Pinochet stated, "women wanted the fall of the marxist government, which symbolized slavery for their children, but they also wanted a new order: [women] sought the protection of a strong and severe authority, that would restore order and the moral public sphere in our society" (cited in Molina 1989, p. 64). The ideals promoted by the military—apoliticism and an unwavering obedience to authority—were ideals that, according to the military's rhetoric, were embodied by women.

The activism of anti-Allende women in the 1970–1973 period led the military to see women as a crucial support base for their regime. To further increase their support among women and, more important, to control the organization and participation of women, the military government oversaw the reorganization of the Centros de Madres, and set up the National Women's Secretariat (Secretaría Nacional de la Mujer, SNM). The SNM was part of the state, and its role was to design and implement policy for women. According to Ximena Bunster, the SNM was explicitly "political" to the extent that its core purpose was to spread the values and ideals of the government regarding women's roles in society (1988, p. 487). The SNM relied upon a massive core of volunteers, mainly wives of military officers, to implement many of its programs, specifically its campaigns of civic awareness, literacy drives, and other education or awareness campaigns. The volunteers, many of whom were professional women from the middle and upper classes, gave talks and speeches to audiences of women in parent-teacher associations, the Juntas de Vecinos (Neighborhood Councils), and even women in the civil service. According to Bunster, "through this ideological process the woman volunteer becomes a public mother" (1988, p. 489).

While the SNM promoted the gender ideology of the military regime through its core of middle- and upper-class female volunteers, popular sector women continued to be organized through the Centros de Madres, but the role of the Centros changed a great deal under the Pinochet regime. Under both the Frei and Allende governments, the Centros aimed at integrating women into social and political processes and mobilized women around the partisan ends of government. Under Pinochet, however, they actively sought to demobilize and depoliticize women and became mechanisms for control, or even "disciplining" according to some authors (see Munizaga and Letelier 1988; Molina 1989; and Valdés and Weinstein 1993). The Centros, like all other social and community organizations, were purged of leaders with connections to the Popular Unity (Unidad Popular, UP) government. New directives were appointed for all social and community organizations (Valdés and Weinstein 1993, p. 75). While social and community organizations under Frei and Allende had clear links to the state, they also had formed part of broader social networks with links to church, party, or other social groupings. After the coup, the dismantling of these social networks was a key priority. Consequently, the Centros, like all remaining community organizations, were tightly controlled, and forced to sever links to other organized groups.[3]

There was some continuity in the Centros de Madres of the Pinochet era with the goals of the Frei and Allende governments—for example, women continued to receive training in activities revolving around their social roles, and could choose from courses in cooking, sewing, macramé, hairstyling, and handicraft production. Members could also join *talleres laborales y artesanales* (productive and handicraft workshops), through which they received a regular salary. The products made in the *talleres* were either sold to the state (e.g., school or hospital uniforms) or, in the case of handicrafts, sold through galleries, stores, or businesses that had agreed to sell such Centros-produced goods. These activities, and the benefits they brought to women members, did not differ significantly from those of the Centros in previous periods. What was different, however, was the "carrot and stick" approach used by the Centros under the dictatorship. Membership in the Centros brought certain concrete benefits to women beyond the skills they learned or the income they earned in the *talleres.* Women who were members of the Centros received identification cards that entitled them to claim benefits, including scholarships for themselves and their families, access to clinics and daycare spots, and the right to shop in special stores with reduced prices. These benefits or rewards, however, could be revoked for a number of reasons. For example, attendance at meetings or workshops in the Centros was mandatory, and if a woman missed a certain number of meetings, her identity card would be revoked, thereby depriving her of the benefits. Members were also required to attend events organized by the military, such as parades, celebrations, or visits by Pinochet or other high-ranking officers, supposedly to show the extent of popular support for the regime (Valdés and Weinstein 1993, p. 114).

The Centros de Madres contributed to the organizational infrastructure necessary for the reemergence of women's movements in Chile. But there are three other features of the Chilean context in this period that led to the mass mobilization of women: first, the repression involved in carrying out the project of depoliticizing society; second, the negative impact of the regime's project of neoliberal socioeconomic transformation; and third, the relative absence of political parties. The repression was at its most severe in the months immediately following the 1973 coup.[4] Anyone associated with politics was a target, but especially those associated with the UP coalition or the labor unions. Thousands of individuals were arrested, sent to concentration camps, tortured, and executed. Many more were exiled (or chose exile), either internally or abroad. According to Philip Oxhorn, the repression during this early period, lasting until June 1974, "was characterized by its arbitrary nature and lack of any moral or legal limitations" (1995b, p. 65). After 1974, the Directorate for National Intelligence (DINA) was created as a centralizing body of national security forces and its director maintained constant contact with General Pinochet. In this phase repression was less arbitrary and more selective, and also entirely secret and "hidden." "Disappearances" were common, spreading fear throughout the population (Oxhorn 1995b, p. 66). After August 1977 a new phase was initiated that corresponded to the regime's attempts to institutionalize and legalize itself. DINA was replaced by the National Center for Information and the latter no longer operated without legal limits. The main objective was to contain opposition (Oxhorn 1995b, p. 67). Repression remained quite severe, however, resulting in a population whose capacity to organize and act politically was severely undermined.

The imperfect welfare state that had accompanied democratization in Chile until 1973 was mostly dismantled by the military regime, leaving only a limited approach that targeted society's most vulnerable groups. The military's project of socioeconomic transformation has been referred to as a "radical conservative experiment" in neoconservative economics (Foxley 1983) and as "radical neoliberalism" (Silva 1991). The project's central architects have come to be known as the "Chicago Boys" due to their training at the University of Chicago. The project involved a dramatic reduction of the state's economic and social roles through privatization and a series of "social modernizations" that applied strict market principles to the delivery of social services in the areas of health, welfare, and education, eventually transferring responsibility for their delivery to the municipalities; an opening up of the economy to international competition by devaluing the peso, adopting a low and uniform tariff,[5] and abandoning the industrial strategy of import substitution; and a freeing up of the domestic economy by eliminating price controls, liberalizing capital markets, and revising the labor code to curtail the power of the unions (Oxhorn 1995b; Silva 1991; Montecinos 1994).[6]

The effects of this transformation were overwhelmingly negative for the popular sectors. Between 1975 and 1981, unemployment averaged 18 percent, and in 1983, during the height of the recession, it climbed to 31.3 percent.[7] The number of Chileans living in extreme poverty, defined as the inability to meet their minimum dietary needs, tripled between 1970 and 1985, and the consumption level of the poorest 20 percent of Chileans fell by over 30 percent (Oxhorn 1995b, pp. 69–71). Amid the growing unemployment and falling living standards brought about by economic restructuring, the state's welfare system was greatly reduced. The state was also increasingly decentralized, as more and more areas were turned over to the municipalities. Also, the number of municipalities, or *comunas,* more than doubled (Silva 1991). Starting in 1979, the *campamentos,* or squatter settlements, began to be eradicated by the government. Inhabitants were physically transferred to new places within the city. The most common pattern was to remove squatters from the "good" neighborhoods (the wealthier barrios) to the poor neighborhoods (the poblaciones). Approximately 30,000 families were relocated (Valdés and Weinstein 1993, p. 74). Municipal reform therefore resulted in the spatial segregation of poverty.

Processes of economic restructuring are seldom gender-neutral in their consequences. In Chile, women experienced the effects of this transformation more acutely than men. For example, women's unemployment increased more than did male unemployment.[8] Women were also particularly affected because during periods of economic crisis and high (male) unemployment, couples are more likely to separate, leaving women to struggle to cope as "heads of households." By the end of the 1980s, "more than 40 percent of poor families were headed by women" (Montecinos 1994, p. 164). This, combined with higher female unemployment, partially explains the greater participation of women in the government programs designed to alleviate the worst effects of the economic restructuring. The government developed the minimum-employment program to absorb some of the unemployed, but it paid only 40 to 60 percent of the minimum wage (Oxhorn 1995b, p. 73). The program ran from 1974 to 1988 and normally covered between 2 to 6 percent of the economically active population. In the crisis of 1982–1983 its coverage rose to 13 percent (Valdés and Weinstein 1993, p. 73). Women composed 75 percent of participants (Montecinos 1994, p. 169).

The third defining feature of the post-1973 context was the relative absence of political parties, primarily due to repression. Immediately following the military takeover, the UP was declared illegal and all other parties, including those of the right, were declared "in recess." By 1977 all parties had been disbanded. The repression of the parties of the left was the most severe: party leaders were tortured, killed, or both, and former UP government officials were rounded up and sent to Dawson Island, which was converted into a concentration camp (Oppenheim 1993, p. 174). Even members of the centrist Christian Democratic Party were targeted—for example, there was an assassination attempt on Bernardo Leighton (while in exile in Europe), a high-profile Christian Democrat who spoke out against the military regime. Ultimately, all parties were driven underground, and while they continued to exist, they were significantly weakened. Chilean parties, with the exception of the Communist Party, banned in 1948, had virtually no experience maintaining clandestine networks and party organization (Oppenheim 1993, p. 174). Because Chilean civil society was traditionally dominated by political parties, thereby possessing few autonomous capacities for mobilization, the intense repression severely undermined any organized opposition to the dictatorship in the early years.

Women Mobilize as "Militant Mothers" and Feminists

Women's activism emerged in this context, marked by extreme political repression, economic crisis, and the relative absence of partisan actors. The earliest groups formed to respond to the repression and extreme levels of human rights violations. Support from the Catholic Church was key: within a month of the coup, in October 1973, the Archbishop of Santiago set up the Cooperating Committee for Peace in Chile (Comité de Cooperación para la Paz de Chile, COPACHI) to initiate legal actions on the behalf of the thousands of political prisoners and workers fired for political reasons. Over the next two years, COPACHI also set up soup kitchens and health clinics in the poor neighborhoods.[9] In 1975, however, COPACHI was dissolved under pressure from the military regime. The archbishop responded by setting up the Vicaría de la Solidaridad (Vicariate of Solidarity), which would operate under his direct control and which therefore could not be interfered with by the military. Through this organization the church expanded its role in aiding human rights victims and those suffering the effects of the regime's economic policies.

The first group specifically for women was the Agrupación de Mujeres Democráticas (Democratic Women's Group), formed just months after the coup and consisting mainly of middle-class women, professionals or housewives, who wanted to do something in response to the repression and violation of human rights. Their work involved carrying out solidarity projects with the political prisoners and their families (Chuchryk 1989a, pp. 157–158; Valdés and Weinstein 1993, p. 131). As elsewhere in Latin America, women's human rights groups were the first actors to publicly denounce dictatorships and their actions. According to María Valenzuela, their rhetoric played on the inherent contradiction between the military's discourse and its actions: the military claimed to place the highest value on the family—the very foundation of the social order—yet their repression violated the integrity of the family in a very extreme manner. Women in the human rights groups, pointing to this contradiction, said they, not the military, were the real defenders of the value of the family (1991, p. 167).

Women's activism in the human rights groups clearly grew out of their role as mothers. As during the first-wave movements, women used the discourse of motherhood to justify their actions, and to mobilize other women to join in their efforts. According to Patricia Chuchryk, who interviewed numerous women from the Agrupación de Familiares de Detenidos-Desaparecidos (Group of Relatives of the Detained and Disappeared), women were motivated to act because they felt an obligation as wives, mothers, sisters, and daughters (1989b, p. 140). Their male family members were being targeted for repression, and despite their fear of getting involved in politics, they acted according to the norms defined by the gender ideology—they put their concern for their families over and above the concern for their own well-being, and they acted, at times publicly, in defense of their families.

In addition to women's involvement in the human rights movements, women organized in response to economic hardships. Again, in a pattern common throughout Latin America, women's maternal roles served as the main basis for activism in the subsistence organizations in poor neighborhoods (see Safa 1990). Subsistence organizations have been defined as groups of people inhabiting the same geographical area who contribute small amounts of resources but mostly their own labor to collectively fulfill unmet necessities (Valdés and Weinstein 1993, pp. 141–142). Subsistence organizations have come to be known as popular economic organizations (*organizaciones económicas populares,* OEPs). The OEPs emerged in the context of the economic crisis described above, which hit the inhabitants of the poblaciones the hardest. There were numerous types of OEPs, including *talleres productivos* (productive workshops), *ollas comunes* (collective kitchens), and *comprando juntas* (purchasing collectives). Many of these initiatives emerged and grew significantly in the months and years immediately following the coup, but decreased in the late 1970s when the economy began to recover. Their numbers dramatically increased again during the economic crisis of 1982–1983, when even official unemployment was over 30 percent (Chuchryk 1989a, p. 154). By 1990 there were 1,370 talleres productivos in Santiago alone and in 1989 there were 279 ollas comunes, which benefited around 30,000 people in the capital city (Valdés and Weinstein 1993, pp. 141–155). The membership of the OEPs was overwhelmingly female, in part because they emerged out of the previous organizational experiences of popular sector women in the Centros de Madres (Valdés and Weinstein 1993, p. 145).

Many argue that these organizations collectivized the problems of poverty created by the dictatorship's neoliberal economic model (Chuchryk

1989a, p. 155; Dandavati 1996, pp. 76–77; Schild 1990; Valdés and Weinstein 1993, p. 147). Collectivizing these issues was the first step in politicizing the members. Edda Gaviola, Eliana Largo, and Sandra Palestro interviewed one woman who explained that when she first started attending one of the talleres in her neighborhood, at the urging of her mother, she was not really sure what the group's purpose was. She went because "there was nothing else to do." Soon, however, she realized that "really the purpose of the group is to make us begin to feel like persons, to be able to show that we are capable, that there is a world out there where the woman has lots to say and lots to do." Most important, it was in this context that women learned that "the problems they have within their house are not just theirs, but are the problems of all women" (1994, p. 80).

The context created by the dictatorship was considerably different from previous instances in which popular sector women undertook collective action, however, because this time, women's goals expanded as they linked their daily problems with the dictatorship to a society that subordinated women. According to María Valenzuela, the women's groups based in the poblaciones, who were at first mainly concerned with survival issues, were also more autonomous than some of the other women's groups (human rights and political groups with links to parties), and hence more likely to be critical of traditional Chilean political practice. Many of the OEPs expanded their activities, developing workshops on sexuality, family relations, and personal development (1991, p. 170). This is partly because contributing collectively to confronting the crises in which these women were living gave them a sense of accomplishment and self-esteem. According to Natacha Molina, "the crisis transforms women into mothers-providers, which produces, as has occurred in many cases—a feeling of self-esteem and personal security that authorizes women to struggle for themselves in defense of their own" (1989, p. 75). Verónica Montecinos argues that gender relations in low-income groups were also changing in this period: "The hierarchy of the patriarchal family was challenged as women became more involved in community activities and their contributions as family providers increased" (1997, p. 228).

Another important source of women's changing consciousness in this period was the interaction that began to take place among women from different classes and with different partisan identities. With the political parties in a weakened state, and male leaders dead, in jail, or in exile, female militants created their own organizations, some with links to the underground parties and others more autonomous. In the groups with links to political parties, women enjoyed a degree of autonomy from the parties because the repression was hitting traditional political actors the hardest. These groups were not always formed at the behest of the parties, but in some cases emerged from the desire of the women to do something and not just accept the closure of political spaces.[10] Other women, who had never had the opportunity to be political leaders, stepped in to fill the leadership roles vacated by the men. Some examples of women's groups with links to political parties or actors are the Committee for the Defense of Women's Rights (Comité de Defensa de los Derechos de la Mujer, CODEM), created by women from the Movement of the Revolutionary Left (Movimiento de Izquierda Revolucionaria, MIR); the Women of Chile (Mujeres de Chile, MUDECHI), formed by women with links to the Communist Party; and the Chilean Women's Union (Unión Chilena de Mujer, UCHM), created by women from the Socialist Party.

In their early years, these groups served as a mechanism for reconstructing relationships between political leaders and their social bases. In this sense, women's groups were crucial in taking the first steps toward rebuilding a sense of active citizenship in a country where passivity was a virtue according to the military regime. The important role that women's organizations were playing in this context contributed to an expanding notion of politics in this period. Women's activity was politicized because the formal political arena traditionally occupied by political parties was closed. Hence, according to María Valenzuela, "under military rule, the organizations of civil society became a substitute political arena that contributed to the politicization of the private and social spheres" (1991, p. 170). Women's activism in this period was conceived as an expression of citizenship because the boundary between formal and informal politics, a boundary that normally undermines women's citizenship, was (temporarily) blurred.

In this context—the relative absence of political parties and women's increasing organization—it is not surprising that eventually women's groups emerged in the popular sectors that defined themselves as feminist. Popular sector women made a key distinction, however, between feminism in general and their particular kind of feminism—"popular feminism"—given that prevailing stereotypes depicted "feminism" as middle-class and anti-male. An important example is the Popular Women's Movement (Movimiento de Mujeres Populares, MOMUPO), which formed in the Santiago población of Renca in 1979. The women who initially formed the group had been participating in mixed organizations but started to feel that they were marginalized as women. While they began meeting to resolve economic issues, they soon started holding consciousness-raising and personal development workshops (Chuchryk 1989a, p. 164). The women of MOMUPO aimed at constructing an identity rooted in both their sex and class position (Valdés and Weinstein 1993, p. 167; Gaviola, Largo, and Palestro 1994, pp. 139–142). MOMUPO worked hard at remaining independent and autonomous from political parties and tried to relate only with other women's groups. Although some of the members of MOMUPO were party militants, others left the party because they wanted to avoid having parties interfere with MOMUPO's activities (Gaviola, Largo, and Palestro 1994, p. 140).

This period also witnessed the rebirth of a feminist movement in Chile. Many explanations have been offered for why feminism (re)emerged in such a presumably hostile setting. Teresa Valdés and Marisa Weinstein (1993) credit the initiation of the UN Decade for Women in 1975 with reigniting Chilean feminism by focusing attention on women's issues in development and making international funding available. The number of nongovernmental organizations (NGOs) in Chile expanded rapidly under authoritarianism as professionals in the government and in universities lost their jobs and responded by creating such entities. Given the concern with gender issues sparked by the UN Decade for Women, international aid agencies favored NGOs that devoted specific attention to women's concerns. This gave women academics the space and freedom needed to work on gender issues and to carry out projects specifically for women. By 1987 there were eighty-seven NGOs or other support agencies that had a gender focus (either academically or in terms of social services) (Valdés and Weinstein 1993, pp. 194–195). Others emphasized the importance of the exile experience, particularly for political women (Gaviola, Largo, and Palestro 1994; Serrano 1990; Shayne 2004; M. Valenzuela 1991). Many women who had been politically active in the Frei and Allende years were exiled in Europe, where they came into contact with feminist organizing and ideas. Another important explanation for the appearance of feminism in this period is the weakness of the political parties, which gave women activists the necessary space to initiate critical reflections on traditional political practice. Feminists such as Julieta Kirkwood began to argue that democracy had never really existed for women in Chile. Kirkwood explained that Chilean democracy's proclaimed values of equality, nondiscrimination, and liberty were never experienced by women, who, relegated to the private sphere, were subjected to the undisputed authority of the male head of household. Hence "the daily experience for women *is* authoritarianism" (1988, pp. 19–20, emphasis in original).

The Consolidation of a Women's Movement

We can speak of a united and multiclass women's movement at this point because organized women in this period shared an overarching common goal—the defeat of the dictatorship—but also because a common outlook was emerging among women about the particularities of their condition as women. Their common goal led women's groups to come together to form larger networks, and their common outlook led to the elaboration of a set of demands that went beyond merely the return of democracy to include the promotion of a women's rights agenda. Women began to think critically about Chile's gendered patterns of citizenship, and to argue that a more inclusive democracy be established. As we shall see, however, this period was not without significant conflict—conflict that ended up fragmenting the movement even as it was coming together. Both aspects are crucial to explaining what happened to the movement after the return of democracy.

During the first ten years of dictatorship, Chilean women organized collectively in response to the social, political, and economic dislocations the dictatorship was producing. After 1983, however, a more united women's movement developed and gained significant public visibility through its opposition to the dictatorship. In this section I discuss the nature of the movement, focusing specifically on its strategies and the conflicts that were generated between it and traditional political actors. It is significant that when confronted with the autonomy versus double militancy dilemma, many feminists in this period rejected the autonomy strategy and opted instead for double militancy as a means of placing gender issues on the agenda of the transition. Double militancy meant working with traditional political actors as feminists and trying to insert feminist aims into the partisan aims of traditional political actors.

While members of many social organizations had maintained links with the underground political parties, once parties could operate more or less freely again, greater tensions emerged between parties and movements. Although political activities were harshly repressed in the decade following the military coup, the repression became more selective by the 1980s. Indeed, the dictatorship tolerated some opposition activities, especially those organized by the centrist parties, as a way of regaining some of the legitimacy it was losing in the wake of the 1982–1983 economic crisis. By the mid-1980s, the bulk of the repression was falling on the popular sector movement, with many of the poblaciones becoming sites of violent conflict between regime forces and protesters.

In this context, movements were often weakened by partisan conflict among members, especially because leftist and centrist parties held competing views about how best to defeat the dictatorship and bring about democracy. By the mid-1980s the democratic opposition had firmly split into two factions: the more centrist Democratic Alliance (Alianza Democrática, AD) and the more leftist Popular Democratic Movement (Movimiento Democrático Popular, MDP). Both of these opposition networks wanted the support and mobilizing capacity of women's groups (M. Valenzuela 1991, p. 172), but were fundamentally divided over strategy. The AD felt that the best strategy was to negotiate with the dictatorship and utilize the small opening afforded by the 1980 constitution.[11] This strategy involved using social mobilization only to get the military to the negotiating table, after which political elites would arrange the terms of the transition. The

MDP, on the other hand, believed that only sustained popular mobilization would provoke the collapse of the dictatorship. As it became more clear that the defeat of the dictatorship was imminent, the AD took center stage, marginalizing the MDP, whose members refused to take part in the AD's strategy. Women's groups that sided with the MDP were consequently marginalized as well. Other women, upon seeing their political parties ally with the moderate opposition of the AD, dominated by the Christian Democrats, withdrew from women's groups and parties in protest.[12]

What was most significant about this period was the relationships and links forged among variously situated women. These relationships were initiated largely because middle-class and professional women working in the NGOs received international funding to carry out work (including consciousness-raising activities) with poor and working-class women in the poblaciones. Feminists organized *jornadas* (workshops) and various types of sessions for interchange and *conscientización* (consciousness-raising) with pobladora women. Through these interchanges, women's groups in the popular sectors began to expand their own activities, and most groups added workshops on sexuality, personal development, and family relations to their schedule of activities. In this way, according to Valdés and Weinstein, a "feminist curriculum" spread throughout women's organizations, a curriculum that addressed day-to-day issues from a feminist perspective that included an awareness of the gendered bases of the struggles of popular sector women (1993, p. 196).

Unlike in North America, where second-wave feminism abandoned a politics of difference, the Chilean women's movement in the 1980s displayed both similarities and striking differences from the first-wave movement. The most significant similarity was the maintenance of the maternal collective action frame. As we shall see, however, the significance attached to the maternal frame had shifted, leading women's groups to make fairly radical demands to restructure gender relations and reorganize political space to include women. The analysis here indicates that a maternal frame does not have a fixed content, but is shaped by the political context. Hence it can lead women to make a variety of citizenship claims. The emphasis on women's motherhood as the source for public activism was in fact an important element of the common outlook being forged among organized women in this period. Valdés and Weinstein explain that "maternity is located at the center of women's mobilization symbolized in the theme of 'Life'" and in this period "there is a resignification of maternity as a point of departure for collective action" (1993, p. 188). This resignification was taking place among pobladora women, organizing at first to provide for their families, as well as middle-class women, organizing in the human rights organizations and the feminist groups. The main differences between the Pinochet-era women's movement and the first-wave movement are revealed in the nature of the demands emanating from various women's organizations and in their relationships with political parties.

Some of the most important groups to emerge in or after 1983 were Women for Life (Mujeres por la Vida), the Chilean Women's Proemancipation Movement '83 (Movimiento Pro-Emancipación de Mujeres de Chile [MEMCH] '83), and the Feminist Movement (Movimiento Feminista, MF). Women for Life emerged primarily in response to human rights violations, yet it differed from other human rights groups because its members were political women who were not necessarily relatives of the victims, although some members had been victims of arrest and exile themselves due to their own political activities. The women who formed the group were also responding to the inability of the opposition to overcome partisan divisions and struggle effectively for democracy (Baldez 2002, p. 154; Gaviola, Largo, and Palestro 1994, p. 153). Throughout the 1970s, the military had been extremely successful at pacifying the population and thus there was very little public protest activity during the first ten years of dictatorship. This changed after the economic crisis of 1982–1983. The forces opposed to the dictatorship were extremely fragmented, however, and the political parties seemed incapable of overcoming partisan differences to work together for the common goal of democracy. A number of women militants from different parties united to reflect on the disarray of the opposition and to do something about it.[13] They organized a women-only event, with the aim of illustrating that it was possible to work collectively despite partisan differences. On December 29, 1983, at Caupolicán Theater in Santiago, 10,000 women joined together in an act of opposition to the dictatorship, despite the fact that a significant police presence was outside. The success of this event led the women who organized it to form Women for Life (Gaviola, Largo, and Palestro 1994, p. 154). The motivations for forming this group clearly emerged out of women's distinct way of practicing politics. They believed it important to transcend partisan differences and to act collectively in pursuit of an ideal—in this case, democracy. According to Lisa Baldez, "[Women for Life] perceived its agenda in gendered terms: its leaders saw the task of inspiring unity within the opposition as one that women were uniquely qualified to carry out" (2002, p. 156).

Women's Citizenship Demands

In 1986, Women for Life presented a statement of women's demands to the Asamblea de la Civilidad (Civil Assembly), an opposition event hosted by a prodemocracy network, and women's demands formed part of the "Pliego de Chile" (Chilean People's Charter). This was the first time that women's demands formed such an integral part of the public agenda. In the document, women insisted that "it is not possible to conceive of a truly democratic society without the real democratization of the condition of women."[14] Women's demands for democracy included respect for human rights, better wages, the creation of "dignified" jobs and an end to unemployment, and access to education, housing, and healthcare. They called for free contraception on demand, divorce legislation, and more equal relations within the family. Regarding access to the political arena, they called upon the state to promote women's participation in all social and political organizations and within the state itself. Moreover, they appealed to women's different styles of practicing politics as justification: "[women's] participation will generate a political renovation, with non-authoritarian styles of debate, organization, and direction."

MEMCH '83 was formed primarily by women from the leftist parties as an umbrella group, and at its highest point had twenty-six member organizations. MEMCH '83 also worked at elaborating women's demands, and in 1983 they prepared a document for the preparatory meeting of the 1985 Nairobi conference that ended the UN Decade for Women. The women's platform elaborated by MEMCH '83 was remarkably similar to that of Women for Life. They, too, argued that "[a] truly democratic society is not possible without the active incorporation and protagonism of women in the struggle to achieve it."[15] Specifically, they called for an end to gender discrimination in the labor force, in healthcare, and education. The platform included a section on sexuality, demanding respect and assurance for a woman's right "to know and decide about her own body." In terms of political participation, they demanded training for women to improve their access to decisionmaking and an increase in the number of women in public positions, but they stopped short of demanding specific institutional reforms to achieve the goal. It is evident from the demands of both Women for Life and MEMCH '83 that women's movements in this period, unlike those of the 1940s, were calling for significant changes to gender relations in order that women be able to exercise their political citizenship.

The Feminist Movement was formed in 1983 by women who wanted to participate in the democratic struggle and the "National Days of Protest" organized by the prodemocratic opposition specifically as feminists (Chuchryk 1989a, p. 166). The MF was responsible for the first public demonstration of feminists: in August 1983 the group gathered on the steps of the National Library in downtown Santiago under a large banner that demanded "Democracy Now" (Gaviola, Largo, and Palestro 1994, p. 131). Valdés and Weinstein claim that the demands of the MF were the most substantive in terms of containing a critique of traditional democratic practice in Chile and proposing measures to promote women's participation as citizens, mothers, and workers (1993, p. 229). In its manifesto, issued in 1983, the MF claimed: "Chilean feminism has shown that authoritarianism is more than a political problem, it has origins and deep roots in the whole social structure. Many elements and contents which have not been considered political due to their links to private daily life must be questioned and rejected."[16] Feminists in this group went much further in their critique, not just of politics, but also of the private sphere—a critique not developed by first-wave feminists: "We affirm that the family is authoritarian, that the socialization of children—the future—is authoritarian, rigid in the assigning of stereotypical sexual roles; that education is authoritarian and subject to censorship; that the factories, offices, intermediate organizations, political parties, have all been constituted in an authoritarian manner."

In terms of specific demands, however, those of the MF were similar to those of MEMCH '83 and Women for Life. Women demanded that the state improve the material conditions of life for women through the provision of social services and access to jobs and education. However, the MF manifesto made no concrete proposals for political reform. In 1988, around the time of the plebiscite on Pinochet's continued rule, the MF issued "Women's Demands of Democracy," calling on Chilean women to make their gender-based demands heard at a crucial juncture in their nation's history. In their statement, they asked that all Chilean women work together to pose "to political parties, social and labor organizations, religious institutions, and to the Chilean Commission of Human Rights, that women's demands acquire a commitment, that they be contained in the democratic system that all Chilean men and women are constructing."[17] The specific demands of the MF in this document went well beyond any earlier demands of women's organizations in terms of specificity and substantiveness. For the first time, feminists called for the creation of a state agency to devise policy for women and to ensure women's participation in all areas relevant to national life. They proposed quotas for women in government and parliament. Regarding motherhood, they claimed, "we value our maternal role and we exercise it with great commitment and responsibility, but our realization as persons is not exhausted by it." In perhaps the most radical departure yet, the document stated that "women's liberty to choose whether to be mothers or not must be respected." Unfortunately, the more radical demands of feminists, such as quotas and reproductive rights, were dropped from the transition's agenda by women's groups who pursued double militancy to placate the parties forming the prodemocracy opposition.

Women's Movements and Political Parties

After 1983, popular protest against the dictatorship exploded, ignited initially by the call of the Copper Workers Union for a "National Day of Protest." Eventually, the protests became regular, weekly events and political parties reemerged to take a leading role in organizing and directing the protest and opposition to the dictatorship. Hence the relative autonomy of social actors from political parties and organizations was short-lived. After 1983 and the emergence of a more visible and public democratic opposition, political parties began to intervene more directly and more forcefully in the workings of movements. Movement organizations, however, resented the erosion of their autonomy that came with the expansion of partisan activities. According to María Valenzuela: "Because political parties had no channels for expression during the first decade of military rule, they tended to function through social organizations. Once the parties began to reconstruct their own spaces for action after 1983, they tried to control and co-opt the social organizations—including women's groups—that had developed autonomously" (1991, p. 167). In this context, women's organizations became more divided over strategy (i.e., autonomy versus double militancy), and over partisan differences among members. MEMCH '83, for example, was plagued by partisan conflict among its members. Paulina Weber, MEMCH's current director, explained that because MEMCH '83 was formed by women drawn mostly from the leftist parties, those parties "sought in MEMCH a place for expression."[18] This period witnessed growing tensions between the more partisan aims of party members and the aims of other collective actors, especially pobladora actors. As traditional political actors began to reconstruct a formal political arena, the content of politics was once again monopolized by the political parties, with a resulting loss of public visibility for social organizations. Hence the struggles that were played out in MEMCH '83 and in the other organizations of this period illustrate the conflict between the women's movement and the political parties, and more profoundly, the conflict between formal political activism and informal political activism (as perceived by the actors themselves).

While many women wanted to participate in the political struggle for democracy, some were wary about allying too closely with the political parties. Other women believed that party militancy was key, and that there was no problem in participating in the parties as feminists. Yet other women wanted to avoid politics altogether, and focus on activities with and for other women, activities that emphasized first and foremost the socioeconomic problems they experienced as women. For these women, formal politics was an arena irrelevant to their daily problems, largely because partisan actors traditionally ignored such issues.

As political activity shifted back toward the parties, there were two main causes of conflict within women's organizations, similar to the conflicts experienced within the popular movement more generally (see Oxhorn 1995b). First, there were tensions within organizations between the grassroots members and the leaders. Many of the organizations in the popular sectors at this time were led by those with links to political parties.

Disputes often emerged over whether to prioritize the concrete material needs of the members, such as access to housing, healthcare, and employment, or to favor the political struggle against the dictatorship. The leaders, with links to the parties, often emphasized the political struggle, while the members were more concerned with the day-to-day material struggles that the policies of the dictatorship were creating (Valdés and Weinstein 1993, pp. 204–213). Additionally, many members of the community organizations in the poblaciones viewed politics in an unfavorable light.[19] According to Valdés and Weinstein, "there also existed the problem of 'eliticization' of political leaders in the measure that politics was transformed into a 'professional world' far removed from the concrete perceptions of the población" (1993, p. 213). These problems, which plagued the popular movement in general, were even more sharply felt within the women's movement, given the parties' traditional unwillingness to deal with the specificities of women's demands and situations.

The other main cause of conflict emerged more directly out of the partisan divisions within the opposition. After 1983, when women's activism became more public, the parties began to realize the power of women's mobilizing. This meant that the parties became more interested in women's groups. According to one feminist: "The women's movement pioneered the struggle, they organized before any other and had a strength not only numerically but a very strong moral force. Therefore the political parties were very nice, were very kind, instrumentalizing the women's movement. There was not a bad relation with them—on the contrary, they had to look after us."[20]

In a similar vein, one of the founders of Women for Life noted that the parties also sought to direct the mobilizational capacities of women. She explained that after the 1983 event, which drew over 10,000 women, "then began this difficult thing with the parties, the realization that we represented important social capital, tremendously strong, and they exerted pressure on us as a social organization so that we would do those things that they wanted as a party" (cited in Gaviola, Largo, and Palestro 1994, p. 155). Eventually, Women for Life became paralyzed by partisan conflict and tensions, especially after the 1986 assassination attempt on Pinochet, when the group's members sharply disagreed over strategy. They ceased acting shortly thereafter (Muñoz 1996, p. 9). A number of feminist activists with whom I spoke recalled the bitter and acrimonious divisions of the late 1980s, when a number of women stopped participating altogether in order to avoid such disputes. These kinds of tensions were occurring in almost all of the groups that composed the women's movement. MEMCH '83 lost most of its members over partisan tensions, which grew more intense throughout the 1980s, and the number of member organizations decreased from twenty-six to only seven (Gaviola, Largo, and Palestro 1994, p. 151).

These developments indicate the essential problem for women's politics: the dichotomy perceived between formal politics and informal politics. The actions of traditional actors such as political parties and new actors such as women's movements reinforced the dichotomy in this period, thereby maintaining the stereotypes about who acts in which realm and what types of issues can be raised in either. The dilemma for women was to try to convey their issues to those in the formal political arena, even if they themselves did not want to participate in partisan activities. This dilemma commonly figures into strategic debates over autonomy versus double militancy. The problem is how women's issues can be placed on the public agenda if women themselves do not enter the formal political arena to put them there. What sort of links can and should there be between autonomous women's movements and women party militants?

This dilemma is reflected in the nature of women's demands in this period, especially in the demands of popular sector women as compared to women from the political class. Valdés and Weinstein argue that popular sector women were making demands for citizenship (i.e., they were demanding access to education, housing, healthcare, and dignified jobs), but were also demanding that their motherhood roles be respected and valued. Most of their demands were directed at the state. Popular sector women believed the state should play a crucial role in expanding women's citizenship through the provision of services and resources for women, and through reinforcing laws that favor women. But it is significant, according to Valdés and Weinstein, that popular sector women were not demanding to be part of the political system (1993, pp. 231–232). Rather, women conceived their participation as occupying a space in between the formal political arena and the private sphere—that is, the informal political arena. Because women were demanding policies that favored women and improved their lives, rather than demanding to be part of the political system, the scant relevance of political parties to many women of this sector is entirely understandable. Valdés and Weinstein explain: "In this sense, it would seem that the pobladora groups did not propose a new form of linkage to the state; rather they continued to perceive it as a bureaucratic structure that delivered necessary benefits, without demanding mechanisms for channeling their concerns and demands" (1993, p. 232).

The absence of demands to enter the state, or to create mechanisms through which gender issues could enter the political arena, would become a problem for popular sector women in the post-1990 context, as I show in Chapter 7. After the return of democracy, popular sector women continued to express their citizenship primarily in the informal political arena. However, there are too few linkages between this arena and the formal political arena by which women's gender and class concerns can be raised, thereby creating gender- *and* class-based exclusion for popular sector women.

Not all women, however, were opposed to working with the political parties. Some activists believed the primary mistake of the feminist movement in the 1940s was that it had tried to remain above politics. When that strategy failed, women simply moved into the parties without trying to bring to them a feminist politics. This time, while some women continued to view party politics negatively and sought to maintain their autonomy from it, many others believed that pursuing women's interests required their presence in the parties. Kirkwood explains that the main difference between the *feministas* (autonomous feminists) and the *políticas* (political women) is that the políticas prioritized the democratic struggle, arguing that "there is no feminism without democracy," while the feministas placed a premium on the feminist struggle, insisting "there is no democracy without feminism" (1988, p. 19). What is important, however, is that there were a number of feminist party militants who believed they could pursue feminism within the parties, in other words, employ a strategy of double militancy.

The decision by many feminists to pursue double militancy had crucial consequences. On the one hand, women's presence in the parties clearly had positive consequences in terms of gendering the transition. This led some women to belatedly realize the value of engaging in the partisan processes of the period. For example, a woman whose group withdrew from MEMCH '83 over partisan conflict reflected: "I think we made a mistake in being very defensive of the professionals and the parties, we wanted to build a movement with its own direction, but it was a period in which the presence of external agents was so strong that one ended up disadvantaged before other groups that had more systematic support" (cited in Gaviola, Largo, and Palestro 1994, p. 142).

Adriana Delpiano, a former director of the National Women's Service (Servicio Nacional de la Mujer, SERNAM), was active in the Party for Democracy (Partido por la Democracia, PPD). She explained that the good thing about the women's movement in the 1980s was that it "was a movement that had a connotation of gender, but also was linked to the political struggle of the moment—it didn't marginalize itself from the political struggle."[21] Adriana Muñoz, when discussing women's roles in the debates about how to reform socialism,[22] explained that, at the time, women's roles in the opposition movement and their roles in "practicing politics" put them in a good position to exert influence on the debates about the future of socialism in Chile: "It was we women who were very linked to all of the social world and from there we could incorporate very strongly our gender demands."[23] Many of the "renovated" socialists currently participate in the PPD, which has had one of the highest number of women in positions of responsibility.

Two of the main parties composing the opposition (the Christian Democratic Party and the Núñez faction of the Socialist Party) had women working within them to elaborate proposals for women's issues. The Christian Democrats formed a "Technical Department," composed principally of professional women, to study and diagnose areas of concern to women—for example, the family, legislation, and health. Some of their proposals included democratizing family relations, more knowledge for women about their sexuality and their bodies, greater social value for domestic labor, and in terms of political participation, "greater access to and equality in political parties." The latter proposal did not specify a mechanism by which this goal would be achieved, however (Molina 1989, pp. 93–105). The proposals of the party that later became the PPD were initially elaborated by the Federation of Socialist Women (Federación de Mujeres Socialistas, FMS), from the Núñez faction of the Socialist Party. The feminists who formed the group pursued a double militancy strategy, believing that feminism must be practiced within the parties because parties were key actors in a democracy, making them a legitimate and necessary space for feminist politics (Molina 1989, p. 117). The gender-specific proposals of the FMS included increased participation of women in all major areas of decisionmaking that affect them, recognition of the value of domestic labor, nonsexist forms of education, and social justice and redistribution. They also called for greater reproductive freedoms for women and the decriminalization of abortion (Molina 1989, pp. 120–123). It is significant in both cases that women party militants made fairly radical proposals for equalizing gender relations. In the end, however, many proposals were not adopted by their political parties in the official election platforms. Women's roles in the parties and the prominence of the women's movement, nonetheless, led all political parties to express concern with women's gender issues during the 1989 election campaigns.

The National Coalition of Women for Democracy

In this period, women also used their public visibility to mobilize other women to vote against the continuation of Pinochet's rule in the 1988 plebiscite. During the opposition campaign, women were extremely active, and once again they were able to use their "moral voice" to persuade Chileans to vote to put an end to a regime that violated human rights, and therefore threatened the integrity of the family. In keeping with the dominant political discourse, women continued to be presented as entirely gendered actors during the campaign, and their support as voters was often sought by appealing to their traditional concern for the family. For example, a Christian Democratic campaign pamphlet said, "all Pinochet has to offer is that women will not have enough money to provide meals [for their families]. Thus they will have to take on work that leaves the family uncared for and destroys the home" (cited in M. Valenzuela 1991, p. 181).

Perhaps the most critical effort by women to place their particular demands at the center of the opposition's platform came after the 1988 referendum on Pinochet's rule. The opposition won the referendum with a vote of 54 percent against Pinochet. The opposition then had to prepare for presidential and parliamentary elections in 1989 and to this end they formed the Coalition of Parties for Democracy (Concertación de los Partidos por la Democracia, CPD). As candidate lists were prepared and platforms elaborated, women noted with growing concern that they were being marginalized in the process. Few women were being nominated as candidates. Their mobilizational capacities and their moral voice were employed strategically by the opposition in the plebiscite campaign, but it seemed that now that a more traditional style of party politics was returning, there was little space for women or their concerns. Women responded by creating the National Coalition of Women for Democracy (Concertación Nacional de las Mujeres por la Democracia, CNMD), formed by women militants of the CPD, feminists, and women from NGOs. Their main aim was to prepare a government program for women, and to support women candidates (Valdés 1994, p. 309). They were not, however, intended to be merely women supporters of the Concertación. According to Josefina Rossetti, executive secretary of the CNMD, "we did not aim to be the feminine arm of the Concertación."[24]

The CNMD was critically important because of the access that some of the leaders of the women's movement had to party elites (Frohmann and Valdés 1995, p. 288). As a result of pressure from women activists, the Concertación's program included a chapter on women, and most important, a commitment to promote women's equality through an executive-level agency (CPD 1989). Concertación presidential candidate Patricio Aylwin also integrated the women's movement's slogan of "democracy in the country and in the home" into his campaign. Alicia Frohmann and Teresa Valdés argue that this was "an important ideological breakthrough for the women's movement" because no presidential candidate had ever implicitly accepted the link "between oppression in the public sphere and oppression in the private sphere" (1995, p. 288). Unfortunately, due to the need to maintain opposition unity, any potentially divisive issues, such as abortion and divorce, were left off the agenda (Muñoz 1996, p. 13). The movement's most radical and substantive demands, encapsulated in the 1988 "Women's Demands of Democracy" presented by the Feminist Movement, were rejected by the prodemocracy opposition parties. The demands, which included quotas for women in government, the equal sharing of domestic work among men and women, and reproductive freedom, were not part of any opposition proclamation. In fact, political parties expressed their displeasure at this list of demands, saying that it would provoke controversy and disunity at a time when opposition unity was crucial (Frohmann and Valdés 1995, p. 286). Lisa Baldez explains that the Concertación party leaders were furious at the fact that the CNMD had generated a list of women from all shades of the political spectrum willing to be named as candidates in the upcoming elections. One of Baldez's interview respondents claimed that the party leadership viewed the process of candidate nomination as far too partisan an activity for women to be involved (2002, p. 176). This shows that the male political elite still viewed women's concerns as very much secondary to the overarching struggle for democracy. It also highlights their unwillingness to restructure politics to include women.

Radical demands were also absent from the CNMD's policy proposals. While the CNMD represented an enormous success for the women's movement by placing women's demands firmly on the agenda of the incoming government and showing the potential gains to be made from the strategy of double militancy, it cannot be considered an unqualified success. First, the CNMD's demands stopped short of a restructuring of political spaces to ensure women's access, and second, many women's groups were not represented. Women's organizations linked to parties outside of the Concertación, notably those linked to the Movement of the Revolutionary Left or the Communist Party, did not find expression in the CNMD (Matear 1997a, p. 89).

Conclusion

The period analyzed in this chapter is crucial to understanding how women's political participation changed after the transition to democracy in 1990. Under authoritarianism, the formal versus informal boundary was blurred so that women's activism was viewed as an expression of political citizenship. But as the transition proceeded, the boundary was reconstructed along both gender and class lines, with significant implications for how women's participation was viewed by traditional political actors and by women themselves.

This period also sheds light on two key themes in the study of women and politics: the politics of difference and autonomy versus double militancy strategies. Regarding the politics of difference, the first-wave movement's maternal collective action frame was maintained by the dictatorship-era movement, but with some key differences. While the latter movement displayed a similarity to the feminism of the first-wave movement in terms of retaining the maternal frame as a mobilizing referent, the feminist critiques undertaken and the challenge to existing political practice and gender relations diverged significantly. In a context defined by repression, economic crisis, the relative absence of political parties, and an extremely conservative gender ideology promoted by the dictatorship, Chilean women mobilized as "militant mothers" and as feminists to demand a return to democracy—but a democracy that included women. Through an analysis of the citizenship demands of various women's groups, I have shown that women used a difference frame to demand a reorganization of political space that would fully include them as citizens. The movement's citizenship model further recognized the important roles that women played as mothers, but also demanded that women's identities not be exhausted by these roles.

The reemergence of political parties, however, had a number of consequences for the movement. Most important, it raised the long-standing dilemma for feminists of autonomy versus double militancy. Maxine Molyneux explains that "from the earliest moments of women's political mobilization, women activists in political parties, trade unions and social movements have argued that they needed a place within which to elaborate their own programs of action, debate their own goals, tactics and strategies, free from outside influence" (1998, pp. 225–226). For the Chilean women's movement in the 1970s, autonomy was not entirely a strategic choice, but rather a conjunctural feature of the political context: parties were severely weakened by the political repression and were operating underground. When parties resumed their place at the center of Chilean politics, only then did movements face an important strategic choice. Debates about autonomy versus double militancy seriously fragmented the movement, leading a number of feminists to stop participating altogether. But as I have argued in this chapter, it is significant that a number of feminists sought to work closely with the parties, and endeavored to place feminist demands on the transition's agenda. The success of this strategy is most visible in terms of the platform of the prodemocracy parties: they included some of women's demands, most notably the demand to create women's policy machinery within the state. The Chilean case, in this sense, confirms the evidence from other cases of transition, such as Brazil, Spain, and South Africa, where feminists also gained in terms of policy changes by allying with prodemocracy forces that became the government following the transition. Hence, as Karen Beckwith notes, comparative evidence "suggests that there are circumstances where feminists, allied with progressive opposition parties, dramatically increase their policy influence under conditions where the political opportunity structure shifts" (such as transitions from authoritarian to democratic rule) (2000, p. 441).

However, it is also important to point out that double militancy was successful in this instance for two additional reasons: (1) the movement had developed in a context where they were fairly independent of partisan actors, thereby giving them the necessary space to forge fairly radical demands for change; and (2) when women entered the parties, party leaders needed women to help mobilize political support. Women were a very important electoral constituency given the substantial gender gap in the plebiscite: 47 percent of women voted in support of a continuation of

Pinochet's rule compared with only 40 percent of men (Baldez 2002, p. 174). All political parties were therefore very concerned with courting women voters. Thus the political opportunity structure facilitated the success of a double militancy strategy.

Once many women's movement activists began moving into political parties and a formal political arena was reconstructed, the movement itself underwent substantial change. According to one feminist:

> I think the movement divided into three major currents: one is the pobladora organizations that didn't have power, that didn't aspire to and never even took account of what to do with power. They returned to their base-level organizations and they carry out their work in the poblaciones. Another current is the nucleus of professionals—some feminist and others not—that entered into the institutionality of the state, with positions and public posts. A third group is the women political party militants who returned to their parties and practically canceled their organizations—their exclusively women's organizations.[25]

In each of these three arenas, the struggle for women's rights and equal citizenship continues.

Notes

1. Interview with Paulina Weber, October 21, 1999, Santiago.

2. It is somewhat unclear whether the movement that emerged in the 1980s is more accurately labeled a "women's movement" (*movimiento de mujeres*) or a "feminist movement" (*movimiento feminista*). While many of the women who became active in this period would have resisted the label "feminist," a number of the goals of women's organizations, and indeed much of their rhetoric, are decidedly feminist in content. This factor, in addition to the high levels of interaction among women from different organizations, means that the distinction often made between "feminist movements" and "women's movements" is difficult to apply to the Chilean movement in the 1980s.

3. One example of the forcible dismantling of existing social networks was the government's insistence that women volunteers in the Centros de Madres could not participate in any other group, including church groups. For years, the Centros had frequent association and links to Cáritas-Chile, a church-affiliated organization with which they coordinated many projects. In 1976, however, volunteers in the Centros were told they must choose one or the other. What many women did was to continue working secretly with Cáritas-Chile so that they could continue to share with other members of the Centros de Madres the goods and materials to which they had access through Cáritas-Chile (Valdés and Weinstein 1993, p. 77).

4. See Verdugo 2001 for a chilling account of the "Caravan of Death," organized by General Arellano Stark under the authorization of General Pinochet, in the month following the coup. It involved the extrajudicial execution of seventy-five political prisoners in five cities across the country. The magnitude of the transformation of Chilean state and society—from one where the rule of law prevailed to

one where it did not—is illustrated in Patricia Verdugo's book by the fact that the majority of the Caravan of Death's victims presented themselves voluntarily to military authorities after reading their names on the lists of individuals wanted for questioning or arrest.

5. Tariffs were 94 percent in 1973 and were cut to 10 percent by 1979 (Oxhorn 1995b, p. 72).

6. In 1979 the military replaced the labor code of 1931. The new code severely limited strikes and collective bargaining and made it far simpler to dismiss workers. Many of the protections in place for working women were eliminated, and consequently, pregnant workers could be dismissed. While union membership was at 41 percent of the population in 1972, it had dropped to just 10 percent by 1987 (Chuchryk 1989a, p. 154).

7. There are studies that put the unemployment rate at 80 percent in some of the poorest poblaciones (Chuchryk 1989a, p. 152).

8. Between 1980 and 1984, women's unemployment practically doubled, from 10.7 percent to 19 percent. Male unemployment increased by less than 4 percent, from 12.1 percent in 1980 to 15.9 percent in 1984 (Montecinos 1994, p. 168). Women workers were also particularly affected by the shrinking of the public sector. Over 130,000 public sector employees were dismissed; women represent a large portion of public sector employees. Also, when education was privatized and transferred to the municipalities in 1987, over 8,000 teachers lost their jobs; teaching is overwhelmingly a female occupation in Chile.

9. David Lehmann claims that over 300 lawyers, social workers, and medical personnel were engaged in the church's efforts in this regard (1990, p. 111).

10. Edda Gaviola and colleagues relate the story of one woman who argued with her husband over how to respond to the situation brought about by the coup and the repression. Both had been politically active during the Frei and Allende years, but he was now saying that "politics is over" (*la política se acabó*), and there was nothing more to be done. She argued back that the situation demanded action, especially by women who were not yet suspected of being politically active, and who therefore were not targets of repression. She argued that women were "safe" because "the men thought we women were all silly and if we were in a political party we obeyed the men and therefore we were not responsible nor capable of raising ourselves against them" (cited in Gaviola, Largo, and Palestro 1994, p. 54).

11. The constitution established a timetable for moving toward a very restricted form of democracy. There was to be a referendum in 1988 on whether Pinochet should continue in office for a further eight years. Then, rules were spelled out for (nominally) democratic elections, in which Pinochet (or a hand-chosen successor) was expected to win.

12. Many Socialists were opposed to the alliance with the Christian Democrats, who were still being blamed for the coup in 1973. One interview respondent explained to me that when the Socialist Party agreed to work with the Christian Democrats in the AD, she gave up her party membership in protest. But she went on to explain that this was an extremely painful time for her.

13. See Baldez 2002, pp. 154–158, for a detailed account of the formation of Mujeres por la Vida.

14. The document, "Pliego de la Mujeres" (Women's Charter), is reproduced in Gaviola, Largo, and Palestro 1994, pp. 244–247.

15. The document, "Prinicipios y Reivindicaciones que Configuran la Plataforma de la Mujer Chilena" (Principles and Demands That Compose the Chilean Women's Platform), is reproduced in Gaviola, Largo, and Palestro 1994, pp. 238–243.

16. The document is reproduced in Gaviola, Largo, and Palestro 1994, pp. 234–237.

17. The document is reproduced in Gaviola, Largo, and Palestro 1994, pp. 251–256.

18. Interview with Paulina Weber, October 21, 1999, Santiago.

19. It should be kept in mind that many of the women in the poblaciones had likely participated at some point in the Centros de Madres in the Pinochet era. As mentioned earlier in this chapter, the discourse promoted in the Centros depicted politics as an extremely negative activity, and moreover, one in which women should not participate.

20. Interview with Sandra Palestro, October 7, 1999, Santiago.

21. Interview with Adriana Delpiano, September 9, 1999, Santiago.

22. During the 1980s there were serious debates among socialists over their role in bringing about the coup. The debates were also influenced by the experiences of those who had been in exile in Europe, where debates were also taking place about how to renew socialist politics. Eventually, the party split into two factions—the Núñez faction and the Almeyda faction. The Núñez faction, otherwise known as the "Renovated" Socialists, were more moderate and participated in the centrist opposition strategy.

23. Interview with Adriana Muñoz, November 2, 1999, Santiago.

24. Speech at the Encuentro de la Concertación de las Mujeres por la Democracia, 1990, Santiago.

25. Interview with Sandra Palestro, October 7, 1999, Santiago.

5 Where Are the Women Now? Electoral Politics in Chile's New Democracy

Chile is out of step with current trends in Latin America. Women's participation in electoral politics has expanded dramatically elsewhere in the region—for example, in Argentina, Costa Rica, Peru, and Mexico—but has grown only slightly in Chile, from 7.5 percent in 1993 to 12.5 percent following the 2001 parliamentary elections. Indeed, considering Chile's other enviable social indicators relative to neighboring countries, the political underrepresentation of women stands out as a major shortcoming.

There are other interesting trends in terms of women's participation in formal politics in Chile. For example, women are doing far better in terms of their access to appointed positions in government than in their access to elected positions (see Tables 5.1 and 5.2). When Ricardo Lagos assumed the presidency in 2000, he named five women to his cabinet, composing 30 percent of executive posts. It is also notable that the Chilean electorate appears to be very willing to support female candidates. There is no evidence that female candidates are less likely to be elected than their male counterparts.[1] Rather, the evidence in Chile points to the political parties as the main barrier to women's greater involvement in electoral politics. Although there are substantially fewer women than men who seek to participate in the formal political arena, those women who do seek entry confront gendered obstacles to their involvement.

Political parties act as barriers to women's participation in a number of ways. First, most parties have resisted the implementation of mechanisms, such as legislated candidate gender quotas, that would increase the number of female candidates in electoral contests. However, the behavior of political parties must also be situated in the context of posttransition politics in Chile, most important being the impact of the electoral system designed by the outgoing military regime. The electoral system shapes candidate selection in a way that disadvantages women. A second way in which parties are a barrier to women involves the cultural practices and dynamics in a traditionally

Table 5.1 Women in Appointed Positions, 1995 and 2002

	1995			2002		
	Number of Women	Total	Percentage	Number of Women	Total	Percentage
Minister	2	19	11	5	17	29
Subsecretary	1	27	4	8	28	26

Source: www.sernam.gov.cl/basemujer, retrieved May 2, 2004.

Table 5.2 Women in Elected Positions, 1994–1997 and 2002–2005

	1994–1997			2002–2005		
	Number of Women	Total	Percentage	Number of Women	Total	Percentage
Deputy	9	120	8	15	120	13
Senator	3	38	8	2	38	5

Source: www.sernam.gov.cl/basemujer, retrieved May 2, 2004.

male-dominated environment. All of the women with whom I spoke described the atmosphere in parties and political meetings as "machista." This refers to a rather exaggerated aggressiveness and to a patronizing attitude toward women, especially toward young women. Third, political parties in posttransition Chile continue to monopolize formal politics, undermining any attempts by women who want to participate in the political process independently of partisan organizations.

This chapter begins with an outline of the main barriers to women's participation in electoral politics, focusing on the role of political parties, the electoral system, and a weakened women's movement. Next I look at the main strategies that have been pursued to try to improve women's underrepresentation in politics, focusing on the role of the National Women's Service (Servicio Nacional de la Mujer, SERNAM) and the debates over candidate gender quotas. Finally, I address the rather complex issue of why having more women in politics actually matters. Although it is commonly assumed that there is a causal relationship between women's numerical representation (the number of women elected) and the substantive representation of women's gender interests, there are a number of factors in Chile that actually undermine this relationship, including the absence of stronger links between women in formal politics and those active in the informal political arena (for example, women's movements), the weakness of the feminist movement in Chile, the dominance of a very conservative moral and social discourse, and the growing polarization of Chilean politics, which makes alliance building among women across political parties much more difficult.

Barriers to Women in Electoral Politics

The institutional features of political life, most notably electoral systems and candidate recruitment, exert a powerful influence over women's attempts to improve their numerical representation (Klausen and Maier 2001; Lovenduski 1993; Reynolds 1999; Rule 1987). Wilma Rule writes that "favorable societal conditions will not substitute for unfavorable electoral systems for women to reach their optimal representation in parliament and local legislatures. But unfavorable contextual conditions—including cultural biases and discriminatory practices—can be overcome to a great extent by alternate electoral systems" (cited in Reynolds 1999, pp. 554–555). According to Pippa Norris, three features of electoral systems are key: ballot structure (single candidate or party list), district magnitude (number of seats in each district), and degree of proportionality (allocation of votes to seats). Based on comparative research, she concludes that, "all other things being equal, women tend to do best under multi-member constituencies with a high number of seats per district" (1993, p. 313). Another important determinant of women's numerical representation in elected bodies is the process of candidate recruitment. According to Richard Matland (2000) women have more favorable chances at gaining their party's nomination where there are clear bureaucratic procedures for candidate selection and where a centralized body rather than the party base selects candidates. This second factor has been confirmed in a comparative study of women in municipal politics in Mexico and Chile (Hinojosa 2005, forthcoming).

The Chilean electoral system clearly undermines the goal of improving women's representation and also stacks the candidate selection process against women. The system established by the 1980 constitution replaced the country's traditional proportional representation system with a binominal majoritarian one. The electoral system establishes two-member voting districts. But in order for a party list to win both seats, it must double the amount of votes received by the second-largest vote getter. Where it does not, the second seat goes to the party receiving the second highest number of votes. The system was designed to overcome Chile's "three-thirds" historical tendency—where the electorate was more or less evenly divided among center, left, and right (Rabkin 1996, pp. 340–341; Siavelis 2002). The designers of this system wanted to foster coalition building, believing that it would moderate party platforms and make Chilean democracy more stable. But the system was also designed to favor the political right by giving an advantage to the party that garners the second highest number of votes.

An important consequence of this system for women is that it compels parties to put forth candidates that have a very high chance of winning majorities. Due to the need to double the amount of votes received by the opposition coalition in order to win both seats, women candidates are often passed over in favor of men, who are believed to be more appealing to voters (Araujo n.d., p. 12). In this context, it is not surprising that a large number of women who are named as candidates are *mujeres de* (women of), that is, wives or daughters of high-profile male politicians (Valdés 1998, p. 485). According to Peter Siavelis, "having the right *apellido* (surname) can help significantly in the quest for a parliamentary candidacy." Another dynamic that works against women is the importance of incumbency in Chile. Based on interviews with party leaders, Siavelis found strong perceptions that incumbent parliamentarians "are understood to have the right to re-nomination, barring extreme lack of party discipline." Hence, "for the 1993 and 1997 elections, 74 percent of deputies were re-nominated, either in their own district or in another district, or for the senate." And of those candidates, 81.5 percent were indeed reelected (2002, p. 426). Teresa Valdés, a feminist activist and researcher, explained that this leads to a vicious cycle for women, "who don't have the political capital to be nominated as candidates, but this keeps them from obtaining the political capital as well. Therefore, they never break into the system."[2]

Chile's electoral system also increases competition within and among the parties that compose the two main electoral coalitions (Siavelis 2002). Consequently, while each party has clear rules for candidate selection, bargaining inevitably occurs among coalition partners as they decide how many candidates each party can put forward and where they will be placed. It is at this stage where women are most disadvantaged. For example, even if a woman succeeds in winning her party's nomination—whether through a primary or a centralized process—the party may ultimately bargain away that candidacy as the various coalition partners negotiate each party's number of candidacies and, most important, the districts in which they will run.[3] As political competition between the two electoral coalitions intensified in the past few years, women faced even more difficulty being nominated. In the 1997 elections, women composed 19 percent of all candidates, a figure that dropped to 12 percent by the 2001 elections.[4] The highly competitive nature of Chile's system produces a zero-sum political game in which "to promote a woman [as a candidate] is to displace a man. In other words, one more woman is one less man."[5]

The unfavorable electoral system and competitive nomination process are compounded by the monopoly that political parties exercise in the formal political arena and intense competition for political posts, both seats in congress and appointed positions in government. This feature of Chilean politics, combined with certain electoral rules, makes it virtually impossible for any candidate to succeed who is not part of the two main coalitions—the center-left Concertación and the rightist Alianza por Chile (Alliance for Chile).[6] While parties outside of these coalitions continue to run candidates in elections, they do not win seats. Since the transition to democracy, political parties have again become the main barrier to women's participation in formal politics. Parties in Chile monopolize politics and control all access to spheres of decisionmaking. Due to the parties' monopolization of politics, there is a popular perception that any activity that is nonpartisan is also nonpolitical. For example, many locally active women with whom I spoke insist that they are not politically active since they are not party militants and their organizations are not linked to a party. Likewise, Gloria Marín, a union activist and militant in the Christian Democratic Party (Partido Democrata Cristiana, PDC), explained to me that she considers her union activities social rather than political, because "these are problems not only of Christian Democrats, but for all workers equally."[7]

Political parties determine access to spheres of power in Chile. They not only control national and local electoral slates, but also are key in determining decisionmaking posts within government, given the practice of allocating government posts according to party representation in congress. Parties normally submit to the president their list of recommendations for appointments to decisionmaking posts. Consequently, women who wish to be in the decisionmaking sphere must participate in and advance in the political parties.

When it comes to electoral contests and candidate selection, an extremely important barrier that women confront is the lack of access to support networks that male politicians enjoy, especially for financing electoral campaigns. In Chile there is no public financing of campaigns, making it difficult for candidates, especially those on the left, where most women candidates are found. Parties on the right may have links to business and thus more access to financing (Oppenheim 1998, p. 15). However, even the parties on the right are criticized for not helping women candidates. Lily Pérez, a parliamentarian from the rightist National Renovation Party (Renovación Nacional, RN), supports the idea of legislating campaign financing limits, because, as she insisted, access to funds for campaigns is one of the most insurmountable barriers to women's entry into politics.[8] Teresa Valdés (1998) argues that the parties of the center and left have also failed to support their female candidates financially. María Anonieta Saa explained to me that the lack of access to financing hits women harder than men because "men will take risks, they will sell the family house . . . but a woman is not going to put her family at risk."[9] According to Adriana Muñoz,

> Being a candidate is difficult for a woman because you need to have a lot of money. We have little help economically. Men have access to circles or

> networks where money is lent—they are friends with bank managers. But we are not supported this way. For us, it's pretty complicated, this arena of power and money. . . . Because even if the party accepts you and you are a candidate, how do you get elected if you have no money? How do you make a campaign? Where is the support of the party?[10]

Muñoz noted that without the economic resources to campaign effectively, women end up relying on the goodwill of the party to put them in districts where they have high chances of winning. In fact, Muñoz credited her own seat to the support of the party president, who placed her in a district where she was sure to win:

> If you don't have the party president supporting you, they are going to give a district that won't help you, that you'll never win, even if you invest ten million dollars you are not going to win. We [women] are very exposed to that, despite our advancement in public representation. [We will succeed] only if there is a conscious will in the party that they want, for example, seven women deputies—*deputies* not candidates—and the party supports you by giving you districts you can win.[11]

The second type of barrier that women face derives from cultural and discursive practices that associate women with the private sphere rather than the public arena of politics. These barriers ultimately reduce the supply of women willing to enter the political arena. Women are marginalized in the parties by a number of factors that emerge out of the sexual division of labor and the gender ideology that underpins it. One overwhelming factor that disadvantages women is that party activism—for example, attendance at meetings and campaign mobilization—involves double or even triple workdays for women. This is particularly problematic for women parliamentarians in Chile, because although Santiago remains the nation's capital (and houses all government activity), the congress is located in Valparaíso, a two-hour drive from Santiago. Political meetings have traditionally been held in the evenings, reflecting male preferences, schedules, and wifely or maternal supports. One woman explained to me that Chilean men love to go out at night and that attending political meetings is a good excuse to escape their homes. This presents difficult choices for women in a society that places a premium on women's roles in the family. Women often must choose between attending meetings or spending time with their families. Delia del Gato, of the PDC, explained that it was only when there was a large number of women present at a particular committee meeting that they were successful in pressuring the men to hold the next meeting over the lunch hour rather than in the evening.[12] Most women admit to experiencing guilt over the time they must spend away from their families. This is particularly problematic because even when women are motivated to public activism by concerns for their families' and communities' well-being, there remains a negative connotation associated with activity that takes them away from what they believe are their main responsibilities—looking after their families. For this reason, women's public activism continues to be viewed as a transgression; that is, women who spend too much time away from their families are considered to be acting selfishly by pursuing their individual interests over those of their families.[13]

These cultural expectations have the effect of dramatically reducing the supply of women willing to take on the heavy responsibilities of public life. According to Claudia Pascual, a candidate for the Communist Party in the 2001 parliamentary elections, women select themselves out of politics, leading to the phenomenon of numerous young women activists in the party's youth wing, but few women in other sections of the party. She noted: "In the youth wing there are many *dirigentas* (female leaders), but when they get older, they put brakes on their own development as dirigentas. This has to do with the culture, that is, having children will restrict you from public life for a number of years, and when you return, there are other leaders and you have to compete all over again."[14] Carolina Tohá, a parliamentarian for the Party for Democracy (Partido por la Democracia, PPD), echoed these thoughts, connecting them to the lack of women willing to take on the burdens of seeking public office: "For women, it's hard to remain politically active, so they leave, they take up other options. But this means there are fewer and fewer women entering political debate, offering their points of view. The lack of women makes all of this so much more difficult."[15]

In addition to setting out cultural norms, Chilean gender ideology places different expectations on men's and women's behavior. Therefore, another problem for women is the style of politics practiced in the parties. Women describe political practice as aggressive and conflictual and, more important, full of implicit rules and norms of which women, being relative newcomers, are unaware. Women's styles of speech and comportment appear out of place in this environment, which often means that they are "invisible" at meetings and cannot make their voices heard. María Rozas, formerly a parliamentarian of the PDC, and the first woman to head the Central Union of Workers, explained that at political meetings "there is a tendency not to see you when you ask to speak, not to look at you when you do speak, therefore they don't hear you and your proposals are not taken. In order that they do listen to you, women have to shout or swear, but that means adopting masculine behavior, and it should not be like that."[16]

Part of the problem is that women have been socialized to behave in ways at odds with current political practice, which is overwhelmingly masculine. Women frequently complain of machismo in the political parties. For example, Cristina Girardi, former mayor of Cerro Navia, one of Santiago's poorest municipalities, explained that many people think that a woman who participates in politics "must be treated as *pobrecita* [poor little thing!]," making women less likely to be treated as equals or taken seriously.[17] Adriana Muñoz added that, "if we want to do things as we are, to intervene in an assembly with our soft voices and our manner of analyzing concrete things, with few philosophical or doctrinaire theories, it is more difficult to have them listen than if we adopt a loud or strong voice and try to bang on the table and bring up more difficult concepts."[18]

All women agree that the parties are the most important barrier to women's representation in formal politics.[19] Adriana Delpiano claimed that "the parties are the main filter [and reason] for why women do not assume greater responsibilities in public decisions."[20] María Antonieta Saa, feminist and parliamentarian from the PPD, explained that many women who had been active in the women's movement have avoided formal politics due to the "power games" and intense competition that characterize the arena. Women, she explains, are neither prepared for, nor adept at, these kinds of struggles.[21]

This leads to both a "supply" and "demand" problem: some women simply leave the parties, not wanting to adapt their behavior—this is what María Antonieta Saa claimed is a key problem in attracting feminist activists to party politics. But on the other hand, those women who do want to compete for candidacies or leadership posts in the parties often face gender-based discrimination. Lily Pérez explained that internal competition in the parties is very tense and ends up "privileging men in the [decisionmaking] posts. It's something very cultural, where the codes and norms of power are still mostly masculine."[22] And this is precisely the problem for many young women, especially in the feminist movement, who become active in politics, but then withdraw because they feel uncomfortable with the masculine style of politics. Fanny Pollarrolo was active in the human rights movement and women's movement during the dictatorship and moved into party politics in the 1990s, serving as a parliamentarian for the Socialist Party. She explained: "We women have lots of trouble handling or managing power. That's been really a critical aspect. We've been learning that it's not just power, but how it's used, for what purposes. . . . But in politics, it's there, and it's used in a way that we women don't like, a way that we reject and criticize."[23]

These comments reflect a common perception in Chile that politics is all about power and the desire for power. This sentiment has grown stronger recently in Chile as corruption scandals undermine citizens' faith in the political class.[24] Not surprisingly perhaps, data reveal declining levels of trust in political parties, from 35 percent in 1997 to 12 percent in 2002 (Angell n.d., p. 4). Natacha Molina explained that feminists in Chile have traditionally resisted seeking power, viewing it as contrary to feminist ideals: "In relation to power in general, the women's movement still tends to say, 'No, that's not an issue that interests us,' or worse, 'Politics . . . how awful! Just look at how the political class goes around!'"[25]

The institutional factors and cultural stereotypes that inhibit women's entry into formal politics in Chile today are compounded by a third problem that political women face: the fragmentation and weakening of women's movements has undermined their capacity to mobilize support for women candidates. A weakened women's movement also reduces the pressure on the political parties to nominate female candidates to try to win the support of female voters. Adriana Muñoz and Scarlett Wojciechowski (1996) explained that organized women had no strategy for the 1989 elections. In part, they attributed this to the effects of the political parties' resurgence on the women's movement in the mid-1980s. The reemergence of political parties, as we saw in the previous chapter, fragmented the movement by introducing partisan divisions and also creating a division between the *feministas* (autonomous feminists) and the *políticas* (political women). This left the movement with no strategy for the first set of democratic elections in 1989. Consequently, "the few women who became candidates, and the fewer who were elected, did so through their own strength and personal risk, in the absence of effective support from the women's movement, which appeared divided before distinct political options" (Muñoz and Wojciechowski 1996, p. 32). The lack of support from organized women and lack of strategy among women party militants continued, and prior to the 1993 elections, competition for candidate selection was fierce and women again lacked a strategy for promoting other women as candidates. In the end, these contests even saw some women competing against each other for their party's nominations (Muñoz and Wojciechowski 1996, p. 34; Oppenheim 1998, p. 14). Women's movements in Chile have yet to play a stronger role in mobilizing support for female candidates.

Strategies for Promoting Women in Formal Politics

Joni Lovenduski identifies three main strategies that have been employed in advanced industrialized democracies to increase women's representation in political parties: first, "rhetorical" strategies on the part of political leaders that highlight the importance of women's participation at all levels of politics; second, "positive or affirmative action strategies" such as training female candidates or encouraging their participation by offering them financial support; and third, "positive discrimination" such as quotas for women in decisionmaking bodies or on candidate slates. Of these strategies, she concludes that rhetorical commitments invoking the importance of women's inclusion and representation are the least successful in improving the number of women in politics, while establishing quotas for women on candidate lists or decisionmaking posts is the most successful, but obviously the most contentious and controversial (1993, pp. 8–11).

In Chile, women believed that their role in bringing about the return of democracy would be sufficient to expand their presence in formal politics. Many women felt that their highly visible activism had overcome the stereotypes that women were not public actors and not suited to political life. By the time of the first elections in 1989, however, women realized that they needed more concrete strategies to increase their numbers in decisionmaking positions. Two of Chile's most prominent feminist parliamentarians, Adriana Muñoz and María Antonieta Saa, both of the PPD, argued that the women's movement committed a strategic error during the transition to democracy. Muñoz explained that not demanding political power "was our weakness at the moment when we were the strongest," while Saa noted that "we [the movement] lacked the strategies for bringing more women to posts of power, because, I think, we didn't recognize our own leadership."[26] Thus, although the movement was extremely successful in securing a commitment by the Concertación to promote women's equality, a commitment manifested in the creation of SERNAM, they lacked a strategy for acquiring more political power. According to Muñoz, "we achieved success with our program but we did not achieve the success of political power in representative positions, and now we no longer have the force or the unity [that we had before]. The political moment has passed."

There are two reasons for the absence of demands for institutional reform. First, the double militancy strategy reduced the autonomy of feminist party members and their demands stopped short of anything perceived by the parties as too divisive, such as quotas for women in decisionmaking and abortion. Second, the movement's politics of difference strategy—at least at that point—led women to be more concerned with proposing policy than with demanding power as individuals. It was only when women realized the extent to which they were being excluded that demands were made for institutional reform. But by then, as Muñoz noted, it was much harder to achieve these goals, because "the political moment has passed."

Political women are now aware of the need for new strategies to promote women's access to formal politics. In this section, I discuss the two main strategies women have employed to increase their political representation since 1990: (1) using SERNAM to promote women's participation, and (2) promoting policies of affirmative action, specifically candidate gender quotas.

SERNAM's Role

SERNAM has taken up the task of promoting women's political participation, but has not been very successful. SERNAM's objectives and priorities along with the strategies for achieving them are set out in the two Equal Opportunity Plans (1994–1999, 2000–2010).[27] Both plans identify increasing women's participation in decisionmaking positions as a crucial priority.[28] Significantly, SERNAM recognizes both "supply" and "demand" problems—that is, it is aware that many women choose to play out their activism in the informal political arena: "Women participate in [social, community, or religious] organizations, which they often initiate themselves, as a consequence of socialization processes that they have experienced, which lead them to identify their interests with areas linked to the needs of others" (SERNAM 2000, pp. 31–32). In terms of barriers to women in formal politics, SERNAM identifies cultural stereotypes that associate men with "politics" and women with the "private" sphere, and the *doble jornadas* (double days—full-time work and looking after families) that leave little or no time to participate politically, as key to explaining women's marginalization from politics (2000, p. 33).

SERNAM's proposals for promoting women's political participation demonstrate its awareness of the distinction between informal and formal political participation. Most of SERNAM's concrete proposals involve strengthening women's informal (social) participation, through, for example, a civil society fund that makes resources available to local women's groups to carry out projects that strengthen their organizations.[29] On the other hand, SERNAM's proposals are vague with respect to promoting women's access to formal political arenas. The current Equal Opportunity Plan's "objectives" and "lines of action" state that increasing the number of women in decisionmaking arenas will be promoted through "developing mechanisms of positive discrimination that increase women's effective participation in posts of popular election" (SERNAM 2000, p. 35). No mention is made of what these mechanisms are or how they will come into existence. To date, SERNAM has not proposed legislation to reform political institutions in such a way as to improve women's access.[30]

SERNAM is proving to be rather effective, however, in developing strategies to promote women's exercise of citizenship in the arena in which Chilean women have always been most active: the community or informal political arena. Even more significant is SERNAM's recognition of the need to create linkages between women active in their communities and women active in the formal political arena. SERNAM has done this through hosting workshops, roundtables, and regional parliaments (2000, p. 29). I discuss these initiatives (and their effects on women's organizing) in greater detail in subsequent chapters.

While SERNAM's initiatives are important, they tend to reinforce rather than challenge women's participation in the informal political arena and the gendered division of labor between formal and informal politics. For example, SERNAM has developed leadership training programs to increase women's participation in decisionmaking spheres. Yet these programs tend to strengthen women's activism in their communities more than in formal politics. Most of the women who participate in these workshops transfer the skills they learn to their activism at the community level. In 1998, almost 2,000 women participated in leadership training courses offered by SERNAM, but only 3.9 percent of these women identified themselves as "political leaders" while 4.1 percent described themselves as "union leaders." Most identified themselves as "social or community leaders" (34 percent) or leaders in "different arenas" (33 percent) (SERNAM n.d.[a]). To date, it does not appear that supporting or training women as political leaders has been a priority for SERNAM. A SERNAM official noted that the organization was considering implementing projects to help women candidates in elections.[31] It is quite likely that the lack of more concrete strategies for institutional reform results from SERNAM's lack of autonomy from the partisan aims of the government itself. Indeed, there have been criticisms that SERNAM officials have stronger links to the political class than to the feminist movement (Macaulay 1998; Matear 1995, 1997a; Waylen 1997). If so, SERNAM is unlikely to initiate proposals that call for restructuring political institutions along more gender-egalitarian lines if such reforms threaten male privileges in these institutions.

Gender Quotas

Candidate gender quotas have recently become the most popular mechanism for improving women's access to elected office. So far, thirty-five countries around the world have legislated some form of gender quota or reserved seats for women (Htun 2004, p. 452). In Latin America, ten countries have adopted legislation that requires parties to limit the percentage of candidates drawn from either sex. Table 5.3 contains a list of the Latin American countries that have adopted quotas and their impact on women's representation. Numerous explanations have been offered for the recent diffusion of gender quotas, such as the growth of transnational advocacy networks (Krook 2003), the role of partisan competition and electoral motivation (Caul 2001), and the existence of cross-partisan and societal mobilization (Baldez 2004; Htun and Jones 2002; Stevenson 1999; Waylen 2000). A close look at those countries where quota laws have been adopted reveals that the stories behind their adoption are often complex, and involve numerous political actors, both inside and outside the state. In some cases, powerful presidents played a key role in convincing legislators to support a quota law. This occurred in Peru, where former president Alberto Fujimori viewed women as a crucial electoral base, and to a lesser extent in Argentina, where the strong support of President Carlos Menem proved critical to the law's passage (Blondet 2001; Htun 1998; Waylen 2000). Elsewhere, pressure for quotas came from a women's state agency. This

Table 5.3 Gender Quota Laws in Latin America

	Legislation	Year Adopted	Percentage of Women in Parliament (lower house)
Argentina	30% quota for women on closed party lists (placement mandate)	1991	31
Bolivia	30% quota for women on closed party lists (placement mandate)	1997	19
Brazil	30% quota for women on open party lists (no placement mandate)	1997	9
Costa Rica	40% quota for women on closed party lists (placement mandate and sanctions as of 2002)	1997	35
Dominican Republic	25% quota for women on closed party lists (no placement mandate)	1997	17
Ecuador	33% quota for women on open party lists (no placement mandate)	1997	16
Mexico	30% quota for women on closed party lists (placement mandate)	1996 and 2002	23
Panama	30% quota for women on open party lists (no placement mandate)	1997	10
Paraguay	20% quota for women on closed party lists (placement mandate)	1996	3
Peru	30% quota for women on open party lists (no placement mandate)	1997	18

Sources: Htun and Jones 2002; Inter-American Commission of Women 2000; CEPAL n.d.
Note: For Mexico, the placement mandate and sanctions are part of the 2002 law.

happened in Costa Rica, where the Center for Women and Family (today called the National Women's Institute) led the campaign for gender quota legislation (see García 2003). In other cases, the adoption of quota mechanisms proceeded in distinct stages. In Mexico, a quota law was first adopted in 1996, but was largely ineffective given that it merely "recommended" that women receive at least 30 percent of nominations. It was not until 2002 that a more effective quota law was passed, a law that included a placement mandate and strict sanctions for noncompliance (Baldez 2004, p. 248).

Despite all the variation in the adoption of quota laws in Latin America, there are at least two things that all countries with successful quota laws have in common: (1) cross-partisan mobilization among women in the parties, and (2) some pressure from women outside the parties and the women's state agency. In Mexico, Argentina, and Costa Rica, women from across the party spectrum joined to support quotas and to pressure their male colleagues to support the initiative. Lisa Baldez argues that this factor was critical to the success of the law in Mexico. Based on interviews with party members, Baldez finds that resistant male legislators were more susceptible to lobbying from women outside their own party (2004, p. 247). In Argentina as well, women from both of the main parties organized across partisan lines to support the quota law (Gray 2003; Waylen 2000). In both Mexico and Argentina, support from women's organizations outside of the political parties also proved crucial. In both cases, segments of the feminist movement reconsidered their traditional skepticism about formal politics and mobilized around the goal of getting more women elected (Rodríguez 2003). Finally, the National Women's Council in Argentina and the National Women's Institute in Mexico launched public awareness campaigns to increase societal support for quota legislation (Baldez 2004; Waylen 2000). The absence of these and other factors explains why quota legislation has not yet been adopted in Chile.

Although lacking legislated gender quotas, a number of Chile's political parties use quotas for internal elections and for determining candidacies for popular elections. The PPD first applied a 20 percent quota for internal elections in 1989. In 1998 the quota was increased to 40 percent and was also extended to popular elections (Moltedo 1998, pp. 30–31). Although the quota increased women's representation in the national executive as well as in candidacies for external elections, both figures fall short of the 40 percent

Table 5.4 Women in National Party Executives, 2000

	Number of Men	Number of Women	Total Number of Positions	Percentage of Women
RN	6	1	7	14.2
UDI	8	2	10	20.0
PDC	5	1	6	16.6
PPD	5	2	7	28.5
PS	4	2	6	33.3

Source: Araujo n.d., p. 25.

Table 5.5 Female Candidates in the 2001 Parliamentary Elections

	Percentage of Female Candidates
PDC	10.7
PS	13.0
PPD	19.2
RN	10.0
UDI	8.0
Communist Party	17.0
Humanist Party	26.0

Source: www.mujereschile.cl/conocedoreas/articulos.php?articulo=325&area=ciudadania, retrieved June 12, 2003.

mark (see Tables 5.4 and 5.5). In the Socialist Party (Partido Socialista, PS), a 20 percent quota for internal posts was first established in 1989, and rose to 40 percent by 1996. With respect to selecting candidates for popular elections, the party's statutes state that quota criteria "will be taken into account as a goal to be achieved" (cited in Moltedo 1998, p. 43). This strategy has not proven effective, however. The PS nominates fewer female candidates than the PPD. The other party that uses quotas is the PDC, although it has been even less successful than its coalition partners.

While the application of internal quotas surely played a role in improving women's access to decisionmaking bodies within the parties, there is very little consensus—even among women—over the desirability of quotas. Some of the women I interviewed from the Socialist Party expressed doubts about whether the use of quotas, even for internal posts, would survive in the future. For example, Fanny Pollarrolo, former parliamentarian for the PS, noted that "the quota is continually under discussion, always at risk of being abolished." She went on to say that "it's generated a lot of dissatisfaction, not just for men, but for women too." Pollarrolo referred to the perception that quotas undermine women's dignity because women do not receive the votes they would otherwise: "people say to themselves, 'why vote for her if she'll get the post anyway because of the quota?'"[32] Cecilia Moltedo's study of quotas confirms this sentiment, noting that once gender quotas were applied, women began to receive fewer votes, thus leading many in the party to view the quota mechanism as producing paradoxical, even perverse, results (1998, p. 44). However, Pilar Armanet, member of the PPD, had a different view, explaining that, although in the early days of the quota, women got posts because of the quotas, "gradually the people understood that women could win, and so they started voting for women." She went on to say that "important female leaders have emerged as a product of positive discrimination."[33] Many of the women in the parties also acknowledged in interviews that increases in the number of women in party leadership structures had not led to any noticeable changes in the culture or style of politics, or to any changes in political schedules, such as holding meetings at times more consistent with women's schedules. Thus the argument that quotas are needed because more women in leadership posts will make the political arena more welcoming for women is hard to sustain.

Although there is some debate over the desirability of internal gender quotas in the parties of the Concertación, there is even less consensus over their use for popular election. A SERNAM study cites a senator from the Socialist Party who said, "we applied the quota in the PPD and PS and it was a disaster" (2002b, p. 33). Among the parties of the Concertación, the Party for Democracy has made the greatest efforts to implement the quota. But according to María Antonieta Saa, increasing women's nominations has not been without tension: "there is a generation of young men who want to be deputies and perceive that women are blocking them, therefore, it's very vicious, very strong, this struggle with the quota."[34] However, Carolina Tohá, also of the PPD, saw it differently, noting that it is not so much a problem that men are undermining women's candidacies, but that there are too few women willing to put themselves forward as candidates. Tohá explained:

> The PPD policy of seeking out women candidates is very difficult because the biggest problem today in the parties in general is more than having so much discrimination against women, what's happening is that there are few women who are publicly active militants. Therefore, when you want to place women in districts, it's really hard to find them, you have to really try. Usually, there's a whole bunch of men interested, but few or no women.[35]

Pilar Armanet, also of the PPD, noted the further problem posed by Chile's binomial electoral system. She asked, "How would you determine where to apply the quota?"[36]

These comments point to just one of the reasons why successful quota legislation is unlikely in Chile at this point. A number of women pointed out in interviews that without more women seeking involvement in electoral politics, candidate gender quotas would be counterproductive. That is, the absence of women willing to compete for nominations might make it difficult to fulfill the quota. According to Moltedo (1998), there is a perception among party leaders that, due to the binomial electoral system, candidates need to have well-recognized leadership potential, and there are fewer women who meet this criterion. Not only are quotas not supported enthusiastically by women within the parties of the Concertación, but quotas also have even less support within the parties of the right. Lily Pérez noted that most women in her party, the RN, along with those in the rightist Independent Democratic Union (Unión Democrática Independiente, UDI), are resolutely against legislated gender quotas.[37] This makes it unlikely that a cross-partisan coalition of women will mobilize around quota legislation, as happened in Argentina and Mexico. Chile also seems to lack the other crucial factor that led to the successful adoption of quotas elsewhere, that is, mobilization of feminist and women's organizations around the issue. At this point, the quota issue does not appear to be a high priority among women's movement organizations.

Further evidence of the weak support for gender quotas in Chile is the lack of mobilization around the two legislative initiatives on quotas to date. There have been two attempts to legislate gender quotas. A bill was introduced by ten parliamentarians from the Concertación in 1997, but the initiative failed to win any support from the executive or broad support from parliamentarians. Women's movement organizations also did not mobilize around the legislation. More recently, ten parliamentarians introduced a bill on March 13, 2003, specifying that parties must not draw more than 60 percent of their candidates from the same sex. However, the bill was not introduced by a broad cross-partisan group of parliamentarians. Instead, of the bill's sponsors, only two are from parties outside of the Concertación (one from the RN and one from the UDI). And only two of the sponsors are male. The legislative initiative is unlikely to succeed in the near future. One of the bill's sponsors, PDC parliamentarian Alejandra Sepúlveda, is also on the parliamentary Family Committee, in which the bill was under discussion. She explained that when the committee voted to prioritize the bills before it, the quota bill ended up last on the list.[38] Although the bill has the support of SERNAM's minister, Cecilia Pérez,[39] it was not declared "urgent" by the executive and was therefore not included in the "extraordinary" legislative session.[40] In July 2004, discussion of the bill was moved from the Family Committee to the parliamentary committee for the Ministry of Interior.[41]

The quota bill is unlikely to move forward unless more women inside and outside of the parties mobilize around the issue. However, no such support appears on the horizon. A study commissioned by SERNAM reveals that while political leaders all voice support for quotas—in part because, in the words of one male leader, it appears wrong to be against them—the support is actually quite superficial. For example, many of the party leaders who were interviewed by the report's authors ultimately qualified their support for quotas, saying that quotas should only be applied to municipal elections or to internal positions in the parties (2002b, p. 38).

SERNAM's study reveals other discouraging tendencies that undermine the likely success of quota legislation. First, there is a strong perception among political leaders—both male and female—that public support for quota legislation is quite low and that even within the political class, quotas are a low priority (2002b, pp. 41–42). Significantly, candidate gender quotas are not being discursively depicted as part and parcel of the democratization process in the country (as they were, for example, in Argentina). Rather, the party leaders interviewed for SERNAM's study explain that there are so many pressing issues related to democratization, such as the elimination of the *designados* (nonelected senators), electoral reform, and labor law reform, that gender quotas are simply not on the agenda (p. 42).

Second, the study's authors conclude that "women with a gender consciousness are a minority within the parties of the Concertación" (p. 58). More important, the authors note the absence of a new generation of women entering the parties from the women's movement (p. 36). Consequently, there is virtually no "turnover" of feminist leaders within the parties of the Concertación.[42] This has produced a certain level of "exhaustion" among those women who have struggled for women's equality, with little support from inside the parties and little support from a women's movement outside the parties (p. 58).

Given this context, Chile is unlikely to follow the regional trend toward the adoption of quota legislation in the near future. The two crucial features that produced successful quota laws elsewhere—cross-partisan support among women and mobilization by organized women outside the parties—do not currently exist in Chile.

Do Women in Politics Make a Difference?

When claims are made about women's underrepresentation in politics, two rather distinct things are actually meant: (1) that there are too few women in politics relative to their presence in the population (numerical representation), and (2) that women's issues and women's interests receive insufficient attention in politics (substantive representation). It is frequently assumed that there is a causal relationship between the two issues. That is, the more women there are holding elected office, the more women's interests will be reflected in politics. In the Chilean case, however, the relationship is rather ambiguous. In fact, there are at least three factors that undermine a positive relationship between women's numerical and substantive representation: a weakening women's movement, an executive-dominated political system, and a conservative moral and social climate.

At issue in any discussion of whether increasing women's numerical representation will increase the representation of women's interests is the thorny question of what "women's interests" actually are, an issue that feminist scholars have vigorously debated (Jónasdóttir 1988; Molyneux 1985; Phillips 1995; Sapiro 1998). The most obvious problem is that women are not a homogeneous group, making the notion of women's interests vague and perhaps even meaningless. To solve this problem Maxine Molyneux proposes the use of the term "gender interests" rather than "women's interests" and further distinguishes women's "practical" gender interests from their "strategic" gender interests. According to Molyneux, practical gender interests "arise from the concrete conditions of women's positioning within the gender division of labor," but pursuing those interests "do[es] not in [itself] challenge the prevailing forms of gender subordination, even though they arise directly out of them" (1985, p. 232). Strategic interests, on the other hand, are more closely bound up with "feminist" politics that arise "from the analysis of women's subordination and from the formulation of an alternative, more satisfactory form of arrangements," which would include, for example, abolishing the sexual division of labor (pp. 232–233). Others (Alvarez 1990; Kampwirth 1998) make a similar distinction between "feminine" and "feminist" interest. Feminine interests, such as demands for school lunch programs or better maternal healthcare, like practical interests, do not necessarily challenge women's sex/gender roles, although they clearly emerge out of them. Feminist interests, in contrast, represent a challenge to the unequal power relations between men and women. These distinctions, while conceptually useful, have been criticized for prioritizing the demands of feminist organizations over those of poor and working-class women's organizations. Moreover, some demands normally categorized as "practical" interests—for example, publicly funded childcare—are not entirely separable from "strategic" interests. Demanding that the state take some responsibility for caring for children challenges a gendered division of labor in which childcare is the exclusive responsibility of women. Thus, when poor and working-class women demand publicly funded childcare facilities, or that employers provide more adequate childcare services, these may be viewed as feminist demands even if the women making them do not explicitly organize under that label.

Even with a more clearly—although still not entirely uncontroversial—idea of women's gender interests, a recognition of women's heterogeneity makes the task of improving their substantive representation much more complicated. Above all, substantively representing women would seem to demand some process or strategy for establishing dialogue and linkages between women involved in formal and informal politics. If the task of women in formal politics is to be representatives for (women) constituents organized in the informal political arena, then there must be spaces in which the content of women's interests can be democratically debated. These spaces do not exist in Chile today, leading organized women to feel that women in the political class do not represent them.

This dynamic is partially a result of the weakened links among different segments of the women's movement since the return of democracy. During the antidictatorship struggle, as shown in Chapter 4, feminist nongovernmental organizations worked with a diverse array of women's organizations while also maintaining linkages with women in the political parties. Hence there was space for dialogue among variously situated women with a diverse set of gender, race, and ethnic interests. Due to this interaction, women parliamentarians of the Concertación parties had a sense of what women's gender interests actually were. Adriana Muñoz explained that in her first term as deputy she had a legislative agenda to promote twelve bills "that came directly from the women's movement. I had it very clear." She went on to say, however, that in her subsequent terms, "I have not proposed any bills [on these issues] because I don't have [a] clear [idea] what is important for women today. . . . I know that the question I have to ask myself is, 'For which group of women do I want to legislate? The *temporeras* [female temporary agricultural workers] or middle-class women?'"[43] Muñoz's comments are an acknowledgment that instead of being a homogeneous group, different groups of women have competing interests. More significant, her comments also indicate that without more meaningful and ongoing communication among political women and organized women in civil society, it is difficult to substantively represent women. During my conversations with organized women in Chile, I often heard remarks that women from the parties rarely attend events hosted by organized women, leading some women's organizations to feel abandoned by the political women alongside whom they had struggled for the return of democracy.

The relative weakness of women's movements in Chile, along with the weakness of feminism, undermines the link between numerical and substantive representation in other ways too. Above all, the negative connotation that the label "feminist" has in Chile reduces the likelihood that women party members who want to be candidates or occupy internal posts will identify publicly with the women's movement. Natacha Molina, a feminist researcher at the Instituto de la Mujer (Women's Institute) and a former subsecretary in SERNAM, noted that "what's happening [in the parties] is that there's a much greater acceptance of women who don't have a feminist discourse. . . . The parties recognize that there have to be more women, but it's much more acceptable to them that those women follow a masculine model of behavior." As a result, many political women pursue a strategy of "lowering the tone of their demands on behalf of women and instead showing concern with the themes of the party."[44]

This tendency creates a vicious cycle where the weakness of feminism in civil society reinforces its weakness in the political class, because there is insufficient societal pressure on political leaders to adopt feminist issues. In turn, the weakness of feminism in the political class reinforces its weakness in society, because feminist issues are not on the public agenda and have little official support. Carolina Tohá explained that while feminists in Chile have some access to the political leaders of the Concertación, "they are not strong as a social movement, not as a social movement that puts themes on the public agenda and shapes public opinion."[45] Without societal pressure for parties to promote feminist issues, it will continue to be difficult for women who want to advance in the parties to be aggressive advocates for gender equality.

A second factor that weakens the relationship between women's numerical and substantive representation involves the institutional constraints on women parliamentarians that emerge out of Chile's executive-dominated political system. The Chilean presidential system is one in which the executive determines the legislative agenda (Bickford and Noé 1997; Haas 2000; Siavelis 2000). The executive can declare bills "urgent" to expedite their discussion and passage, and the president can call "extraordinary sessions during which time the congress can consider only proposals put forth by the executive" (Bickford and Noé 1997, p. 32; Siavelis 2000, pp. 16–19). In addition to the congress's relative weakness in setting the legislative agenda, it is also severely underresourced. Relative to the executive branch, parliamentarians have very few resources, such as researchers, assistants, or advisers who could assist them in preparing legislation (Siavelis 2000; see also Valdés 1998). Furthermore, as Peter Siavelis notes, "unlike ministerial staff, members of the Chamber and the Senate must also concern themselves with the demands of their constituency and reelection (with the exception of designated Senators), which limit the time and resources that can be devoted to the study and formulation of legislative proposals" (2000, p. 22). The situation improved somewhat after the creation of the Family Committee in the Chamber of Deputies at the urging of women parliamentarians. This has allowed greater attention to and resources for studying (and strengthening) bills related to women's family issues, including divorce, domestic violence, and the distribution of parental authority and marital assets (Valdés 1998). But there is still no equivalent committee in the Senate, which means bills often get slowed down there. What this means, ultimately, is that without strong support from the executive branch, bills that promote women's gender interests are not likely to be successful, often languishing in congress for years without being discussed. This will likely be the fate of the quota bill discussed in the previous section.

The third factor that shapes the relationship between women's numerical and substantive representation is the conservative moral and social climate in Chile since the return of democracy. This factor not only reinforces the negative image of feminism but also makes it difficult for women parliamentarians to introduce or support legislation that improves women's rights but clashes with Chile's conservative gender ideology. For example, in 1991, Adriana Muñoz proposed a bill that would once again permit therapeutic abortion in Chile.[46] Muñoz subsequently faced vilification as a "baby-killer" by both the media and the political right. The bill had no government support, yet the political right still "called on the governing coalition to assume an actively pro-life stance or be exposed as pro-abortionists" (Blofield 2003, p. 118). The prevailing political discourse on many moral and social issues in Chile remains hostile to any attempts by women's movements and progressive women in parliament to transform the terms of debate.

Chile's conservative moral climate is a result of many factors. The Catholic Church earned enormous respect among citizens for its vocal and courageous role in the human rights struggle during the dictatorship. Since the return of democracy, the church has staked out an extremely hard-line position on moral and social issues, even though the attitudes of most Chileans on these same issues are more liberal.[47] Lily Pérez, of the RN, noted that while the base of her party is quite liberal on social issues such as divorce, the party leadership is very much linked to the Catholic Church.[48] Indeed, the conservative stance on issues such as divorce found within the political right appears to be at odds with societal attitudes. A

2002 opinion poll conducted by the Centro de Estudios Públicos (Center for Public Studies) found that 76.5 percent of Chileans agreed that divorce was the best option for couples with irresolvable marital problems.

The willingness of the church to speak out so forcefully against reform on issues such as divorce, sex education, and abortion is matched by the willingness of Chile's overwhelmingly conservative media to convey the church's views to the public. Moreover, as Merike Blofield (2003, p. 129) notes, Chile's two largest media giants—Edwards and Copesa—control over 70 percent of the country's print media. The church, the conservative media, and a host of Catholic lobby groups and organizations have all engaged in heavy lobbying of government officials and public opinion to reinforce a social order based on a nuclear family wherein women occupy a primarily maternal support role. Blofield argues that these groups have successfully framed discourse on moral issues in such a way as to put more progressive groups on the defensive rather than being able to set the agenda discursively themselves.

Despite a vigorous Catholic Church campaign against divorce legislation, reform of Chile's marriage law finally succeeded in 2004—nearly fourteen years after the Concertación initially indicated a desire to change legislation that prohibited the option of legal divorce for couples who wished to separate. In the absence of legal divorce, most couples who separated relied upon the practice of fraudulent annulments.[49] Because the issue of legal divorce was so divisive within the political class, the Concertación government did not come out in support of a parliamentary bill to legalize divorce introduced in 1991. Without executive support, this bill, along with two subsequent ones, introduced in 1993 and 1994, languished (Blofield 2003, p. 115). It was not until September 2001 that the bill introduced in 1994 received an "urgency" declaration from the executive.[50] The bill was subsequently debated in the Senate in 2002, but not passed until January 2004.[51] The new "civil marriage" law finally came into effect in November 2004.

Political women note that, given Chile's conservative political climate, it is easier to gain support for issues that are feminine rather than feminist. Valeria Ambrosio of SERNAM explained, "It is easier when you raise issues that have to do with pretty extreme situations [such as domestic violence] or that have to do with poverty. These are easier to put on the public agenda. The problem is in placing other issues on the public agenda."[52] Unfortunately, the Chilean political class remains quite polarized on social issues and consequently, political consensus on women's rights issues in Chile is becoming even more elusive. Lily Pérez explained that the era in which women from different parties could support each other is over: "I think that Chile has become more polarized and that six years ago it was easier to get women together. . . . Because first was the theme of women, and then themes of the party. But today, it's much more polarized." Pérez added that this has negative consequences for promoting many of the goals of the women's movement, because it is precisely women's rights issues—labor code reform, divorce, reproduction—that generate so much disagreement: "Because the country is so polarized, I see that the relations among women from the different sectors are no longer so good. There used to be more cross-party cooperation, but today, it's just too polarized for that."[53] As long as this situation continues, then a quota law is also unlikely.

Conclusion

This chapter has addressed the problem of women's underrepresentation in Chilean politics since the return of democracy. As a consequence of the democratic transition, perceptions about the boundary between formal and informal politics reemerged and political parties once again monopolized all activities that are perceived as political. This dynamic undermines women's citizenship because political parties have once again become a major barrier to improving women's access to politics. But constructing a more gender-egalitarian citizenship in posttransition Chile is further undermined by the growing divisions between women who have entered formal politics and those who continue to be active in informal political arenas. As I have argued in this chapter, the relative weakness of women's movements and the growing distance between women parliamentarians and women's organizations in civil society reduces the pressure that could otherwise be brought to bear on political parties both to increase women's candidacies and to address women's issues.

Similarly, women parliamentarians in Chile today rarely identify themselves as part of the women's movement. With the exception of well-known feminists such as María Antonieta Saa and Adriana Muñoz, who emerged out of the democratic transition, none of the younger generation of women parliamentarians is making a career out of taking up women's rights issues. While this is partly a result of the weakness of the feminist movement in Chile (to be further discussed in Chapter 7), it also reinforces the lack of public support for feminist issues and ideas, because such ideas are not vigorously promoted by the political class. Ultimately, this undermines a more positive relationship between women's numerical representation and the substantive representation of women's gender interests.

Notes

1. In the 2001 parliamentary elections, 36 percent of female candidates won their seats, compared with 37 percent of men (www.sernam.gov.cl/basemujer, retrieved May 2, 2004). Magda Hinojosa (2005, forthcoming) analyzed municipal

elections results from 1996 and 2000, finding that "the difference between female and male candidates winning office is 49 percent to 53.5 percent when controlling for both incumbency and major party."

2. Quoted in *Santiago Times,* December 21, 2001.

3. Interview with Natacha Molina, July 16, 2002, Santiago.

4. www.sernam.gov.cl/basemujer, retrieved May 7, 2004.

5. Interview with Fanny Pollarrolo, July 29, 2002, Santiago.

6. The Concertación comprises the Christian Democrats, the Party for Democracy, the Socialist Party, and the Radical Social Democrats. The Alianza por Chile comprises the National Renovation Party and the Independent Democratic Union.

7. Interview with Gloria Marín, August 23, 1999, Santiago.

8. Interview with Lily Pérez, July 24, 2002, Santiago.

9. Interview with María Anonieta Saa, September 29, 1999, Santiago.

10. Interview with Adriana Muñoz, November 2, 1999, Santiago.

11. Ibid.

12. Interview with Delia del Gato, August 20, 1999, Santiago.

13. Victoria Hurtado (1997) writes about women's attitudes toward public activism based on her work with women in leadership training workshops in Santiago. She notes that women take immense pride in the fact that they do things *for* others: *todo por los demás, nada por una misma* (everything for others, nothing for oneself). Given this predisposition, any activity that undermines a woman's commitments to others—especially to her family—is seen as selfish and therefore negative.

14. Interview with Claudia Pascual, July 15, 2002, Santiago.

15. Interview with Carolina Tohá, July 19, 2002, Santiago.

16. Cited in *La Tercera,* October 23, 1999.

17. Interview with Cristina Girardi, October 27, 1999, Santiago. Claudia Pascual made the same point, noting that it is especially difficult for young women, such as herself, to be taken seriously by the men in the party. Interview with Claudia Pascual, July 15, 2002, Santiago.

18. Interview with Adriana Muñoz, November 2, 1999, Santiago. Many women note that female political leaders have a more concrete style of speech than men, and that women use concise language while men tend to frame issues in a more abstract and theoretical manner.

19. All of the women with whom I spoke cited the parties as the main cause of women's low presence in politics. Lois Oppenheim's study (1998) of women in politics since the return of democracy in Chile reports similar findings.

20. Interview with Adriana Delpiano, September 9, 1999, Santiago.

21. Interview with María Antonieta Saa, September 29, 1999, Santiago.

22. Interview with Lily Pérez, September 29, 1999, Santiago.

23. Interview with Fanny Pollarrolo, July 29, 2002, Santiago.

24. A bribery scandal in 2002 involving a number of deputies from the Concertación shattered some of the myths that there is no corruption in Chile. The most important consequence of the "Caso Coimas" bribery scandal is that it is likely to lead to even more negative views of the political class as a whole.

25. Interview with Natacha Molina, July 16, 2002, Santiago. Former Socialist Party deputy Fanny Pollarrolo also noted that the political class in Chile is increasingly held in very low esteem and that "the parties are no longer prestigious." Interview with Fanny Pollarrolo, July 29, 2002, Santiago.

26. Interviews with Adriana Muñoz, November 2, 1999, Santiago; and María Antonieta Saa, September 29, 1999, Santiago.

27. The Equal Opportunity Plans for Women have been SERNAM's main vehicle for promoting gender equality in posttransition Chile. The first plan was incorporated into the mandate of President Frei's government, and the current plan forms part of Lagos's government program.

28. Another document, "Informe Comisión Participación" (Report of the Participation Commission) (SERNAM 1998b), also sets out the problem of and proposed solutions to women's low participation rates in formal politics.

29. Interview with Valeria Ambrosio, October 5, 1999, Santiago. When explaining the purpose of the fund, Ambrosio described it as "one of the strategies for greater social participation of women."

30. Legislation on candidate gender quotas, discussed in the next section, has been introduced by parliamentarians rather than by SERNAM.

31. Interview with Cecilia Peñaloza, August 11, 1999, Santiago.

32. Interview with Fanny Pollarrolo, July 29, 2002, Santiago.

33. Interview with Pilar Armanet, September 1, 1999, Santiago.

34. Interview with María Antonieta Saa, September 29, 1999, Santiago.

35. Interview with Carolina Tohá, July 19, 2002, Santiago.

36. Interview with Pilar Armanet, September 1, 1999, Santiago.

37. Interview with Lily Pérez, July 24, 2002, Santiago.

38. www.camara.cl/diario/noticia.asp?vid=9428, retrieved May 7, 2004.

39. SERNAM, "Noticias," March 17, 2003, www.sernam/gov.cl, retrieved May 7, 2004.

40. www.camara.cl/legis/legle.htm, retrieved May 10, 2004. Each year, the Chilean congress meets in an "ordinary" session where both legislative and executive branches can introduce bills, and an "extraordinary" session where only executive bills or those receiving an executive "urgency" are discussed. The ability of the executive to determine the legislative agenda—for example, which bills are discussed and which ones languish—is further discussed in the next section of the chapter.

41. "Tramites Proyecto de Ley, Boletín '3206-18,'" www.camara.cl, retrieved October 12, 2004.

42. This point was also made by Natacha Molina, who noted that it was the parties of the political right, rather than the Concertación, that seemed capable of attracting a new generation of young women (not necessarily feminists) into the party. Interview with Natacha Molina, July 16, 2002, Santiago.

43. Interview with Adriana Muñoz, November 2, 1999, Santiago.

44. Interview with Natacha Molina, July 16, 2002, Santiago.

45. Interview with Carolina Tohá, July 19, 2002, Santiago.

46. Therapeutic abortions were criminalized just prior to the exit of the military regime.

47. See Mala Htun's comparative study (2003) of Argentina, Brazil, and Chile for an excellent account of the factors that led to liberalization of divorce law in Brazil and Argentina and failure to reform in Chile. Merike Blofield (2003) also provides a compelling argument that focuses on levels of societal inequality as a key variable explaining lack of reform in Chile, compared with liberalization in Argentina and Spain.

48. Interview with Lily Pérez, July 24, 2002, Santiago.

49. The most common strategy was to have witnesses testify that at least one member of the couple had given false information, such as an incorrect address, on the marriage certificate. According to Htun, the widespread use of fraudulent annulments, amounting to thousands each year, worked to prevent greater societal pressure for legal divorce (2003, pp. 102–103).

50. *El Mercurio,* September 28, 2001.
51. *Santiago Times,* January 26, 2004.
52. Interview with Valeria Ambrosio, October 5, 1999, Santiago.
53. Interview with Lily Pérez, July 24, 2002, Santiago.

"State Feminism" in Posttransition Chile 6

One of the most interesting features of transitions to democracy is the potential opportunity they create for restructuring gender and, in some cases, class and race relationships. In the previous chapter we saw that Chilean women have made relatively few gains in improving their access to electoral politics; access is still controlled by political parties unwilling to open up more space for women. In this and the next chapter I turn to another area in which opportunities have been generated by democratic transitions: the opening of states to a gender-equality agenda.

States, according to Maxine Molyneux, "are saturated by gender in that they both influence gender relations and are influenced by them" (2000, p. 39). Most important though, the relationship between gender and the state is shifting, as both women's movements and state actors contest its form. While feminists have historically seen state power as a crucial element in reproducing patriarchy, most feminist scholars today argue that states are not monolithic agents that act solely in the interests of a particular social group, whether male elites or the capitalist class. Instead, states are viewed as a series of arenas that are both the product of earlier social struggle and appropriate sites for the continued contestation of gender, class, and racial hierarchies (see Pringle and Watson 1998). According to this view, there may well be instances in which states are potentially more open to the transformative agendas of women's movements.

In Latin America, such instances were the transitions to democracy that altered the relationship between states and women's movements. Above all, the state was no longer the unambiguous "enemy" of women that it was during the dictatorships. Instead, the prodemocracy parties that brought about transitions in countries such as Argentina, Brazil, and Chile incorporated a number of gender-based demands promoted by women's movements, one of which was the creation of women's policy machineries to promote women's interests through the state.[1] In Chile, the National Women's Service (Servicio Nacional de la Mujer, SERNAM) can contribute to improving women's citizenship in two ways: first, by introducing legislation aimed at gender equality; and second, by serving as a bridge between women who participate in the informal political arena and those who make policy in the formal political arena. My main goal in this chapter is to analyze the opportunities and obstacles SERNAM faces in fulfilling these roles.

There are two separate questions to be addressed. First, I explore the opportunities and obstacles to pursuing women's gender interests through the state, an arena frequently assumed to be inimical to a feminist agenda. Second, I explore the effects on women's movements, and their citizenship goals, of women's policy machineries. In many ways, these two questions are inextricably linked, because there is clear evidence that strong and relatively autonomous women's movements create greater pressure on women's policy machineries to pursue feminist goals—for example, by mobilizing displays of civil society support for women's issues (Alvarez 1997, p. 82; Friedman 2000a, p. 74). Likewise, it is very difficult to understand the changes in women's movements without taking into consideration the effects on the movement of the "institutionalization" of gender politics represented by the creation of women's policy machineries (Alvarez 1999; Matear 1997a; Ríos, Godoy, and Guerrero 2004; Schild 1997, 2000a, 2000b). But it is also helpful to separate the two questions, at least analytically, in order to examine each issue in its specificity. I do this by dividing the discussion into two separate chapters, one chapter focusing on SERNAM, and the other on the women's movement. In the present chapter, my main purpose is to analyze SERNAM and its role in expanding women's citizenship through legislative initiatives that expand women's rights and policy initiatives aimed particularly at the gendered sources of women's marginalization (for example, poverty alleviation measures targeted at certain groups of women). I also assess SERNAM's successes and failures in creating linkages between women within the state and organized women outside of state arenas.

The chapter begins with an outline of the conceptual framework of "state feminism" in Chile. The state feminism framework, borrowed from Dorothy Stetson and Amy Mazur (1995), identifies a series of variables for analyzing women's policy machineries. In the remainder of the chapter I employ three of these variables for assessing Chile's SERNAM: the politics surrounding its establishment, the organizational forms it takes, and society's attitudes toward the state's role in ameliorating inequality.

SERNAM and State Feminism in Chile

Stetson and Mazur's comparative investigation of state feminism elaborates useful definitions and variables for evaluating whether policy machineries are indeed state feminist. Agencies can be comparatively assessed as state feminist according to two features: (1) policy influence—the extent to which they influence feminist policy; and (2) policy access—the extent to which they open up access to societal actors such as women's movements (1995, pp. 14, 274). The framework is flexible because it avoids predetermining the meaning of "feminism" to recognize cross-national differences. Stetson and Mazur's definition specifies that "an ideology, policy, organization, or activity is feminist to the extent that it has the purpose of improving the status of women as a group and undermining patterns of gender hierarchy" (1995, p. 16).

In this section, I investigate SERNAM's overall influence on feminist policy goals, that is, policies that seek to improve the status of women and equalize gender relations, and its attempts to create access points for women's movements in civil society. Both of these goals are key to women's citizenship. By opening access to women's movements in civil society, SERNAM can link the formal and informal political arenas, allowing women who participate primarily in the informal arena to convey their issues to those in the formal arena. Both increasing gender equality and enhancing women's access to formal politics are stated goals of SERNAM. For example, SERNAM's recent Equal Opportunity Plan states that,

> with the creation of the Servicio Nacional de la Mujer in 1991 and the formulation of the first Equal Opportunity Plan 1994–1999, the Concertación governments have sent to society a clear signal regarding the role of the State in the construction of more equitable gender relations, through policies, programs, and legislative reforms, that specifically consider the situation of women and their differences with men in the distribution of social benefits and responsibilities. (2000, pp. 6–7)

SERNAM further emphasizes that the purposes of the Equal Opportunity Plans are "to produce a substantive change in the relations between men and women" (pp. 6–7). SERNAM has also declared its intentions "to favor the citizen participation of women in the process of elaborating public policies" by, for example, "fostering dialogue between State and civil society and creating possibilities for citizen control of gender policies and programs" (p. 64).

To what extent has SERNAM met these goals? Other scholars have deemed it unsuccessful in terms of policy influence (Craske 1999, pp. 185–186; Matear 1995; Waylen 1996), and my research confirms that it faces profound obstacles to exerting influence within the state apparatus as a whole. I also believe, however, that previous researchers have overlooked the extent to which SERNAM is well-placed, especially vis-à-vis feminists in parliament, to initiate gender-egalitarian legislation.[2] This is due to the dominance that the executive (of which SERNAM is a part) exerts over the political system as a whole in Chile. In terms of opening policy access to societal actors, principally to women's movements, Nikki Craske categorizes

SERNAM as a case of "high access" (1999, pp. 185–186). Others (most notably Patricia Richards [2004] and Verónica Schild [1997, 2000a, 2000b]) are more skeptical about the type of access being created for nonstate actors. In this chapter and the next I argue that while SERNAM is undertaking a number of well-intentioned steps to involve women's movements in the policy process, the success of these endeavors has been very limited. While feminists in some nongovernmental organizations (NGOs) have relatively greater access to the state, many note that their autonomy to press for feminist goals is being compromised in the process. Class-based forms of exclusion are also becoming more relevant. Base-level women's groups in the popular sectors are being left out of the process, or are being invited to participate as "clients" in such a way as to limit their real impact on the policymaking process. Schild, for example, describes the "clientelization" of poor and working-class women who participate in SERNAM's programs. She argues that "the clientelization of some poor and working-class women carried out by others in the name of advancing the causes of women, is in effect undermining the possibility of poor and working-class women coming together to articulate their own needs" (1997, p. 614).

Richards insists that class difference is a crucial factor shaping the relationship between "femocrats" and pobladora women. She argues that while SERNAM does invite the participation of women from base-level organizations, each group has a very different understanding of participation: "women with power in the state construct pobladoras as invalid participants, fail to communicate with them, and require that the major participants in the formulation of policy around women's rights have formal academic credentials" (2004, p. 95). On the other hand, for pobladora women, citizen participation involves real input into not only how policies are implemented but also input into the content of gender policy. Richards (2003) also points to a number of tensions between SERNAM and indigenous women over the meaning of citizenship and the types of policies the agency promotes to improve indigenous women's citizenship.

In the remainder of this chapter I explain some of the sources of outcomes such as these by applying Stetson and Mazur's comparative framework for the analysis of state feminism. The relevant variables they identify include: (1) the politics of establishment, (2) organizational form, and (3) conception of the state. Their fourth variable, form of women's movements, is only briefly addressed in this chapter; a full discussion is taken up in the next. With respect to the politics of SERNAM's establishment in Chile, a number of the agency's current obstacles stem from the political controversy surrounding its creation. While there was widespread support for women's equality within government circles, important and vocal opposition to the establishment of SERNAM came from the political right and the Catholic Church. This controversy led the government to water down SERNAM's earlier mandate and disassociate the agency's creation from a feminist political agenda. It also precluded the creation of an agency with a mandate to work closely with women's organizations in civil society.

SERNAM's organizational form has advantages and disadvantages. While SERNAM's director has ministerial status, the agency itself is embedded within another ministry—the Ministry of Cooperation and Planning (MIDEPLAN), which houses many of the government's social programs. While this significantly weakens its influence over state policy in general, the fact that SERNAM is part of the executive also affords it greater opportunities for legislating on women's issues. This is due to executive dominance of the legislative agenda in the Chilean political system, and the greater resources that the executive commands relative to legislators. What is most important in terms of effects of policy on women, however, is that SERNAM is itself part of a state that is in the process of "modernization," which in Chile means decentralization, turning over service provision to municipal governments, and contracting out to third parties. This makes the delivery of SERNAM's programs highly uneven. The extent to which women benefit from SERNAM's efforts depends, in large measure, on where they live, because many programs are administered through municipal governments, which vary too considerably in levels of commitment to gender equality and access to resources to effectively deliver gender policy.

In Chilean political culture, public attitudes regarding the state's role in ameliorating inequality contain conflicting views. Postdictatorship governments have consistently sought to discursively construct social issues as problems that communities themselves need to solve, thereby delegitimizing the notion that the state should contribute to equality. At the same time, however, the discourse of successive governments has supported the idea that the state has an important role to play in fostering a more participatory civil society, especially regarding women's participation and women's capacity to organize themselves. This factor is precisely what has allowed SERNAM to generate access to the state for women's movements. For example, SERNAM has added participatory aspects to various social programs that seek to gather input from the targeted group in policy design. While these goals are important, they have not been unambiguously successful.

The extent to which women's machineries generate access for women's movements to state institutions is bound up with the form of women's movements, as Stetson and Mazur's fourth variable posits. In the new democracies, however, this question is much more complex than in the established democracies. Transitions to democracy, especially in Latin America, affected the form of women's movements because in the period leading up to the transition, movements were united around a common goal—democracy—and displayed considerable cross-class linkages. Movements fragmented considerably during and after the transition because, on the one hand, the main goal was achieved, but also because the political context changed so dramatically. Perhaps the most significant change has been the creation of women's national policy machineries, which have taken feminist politics into the state.

The Politics of Establishing SERNAM

The creation of SERNAM was one of the main demands of the women's movement in the late 1980s. Not surprisingly, then, many feminists in Chile viewed the agency's creation as "their own conquest" (Ríos, Godoy, and Guerrero 2004, p. 61), a concrete indication of their successful strategy during Chile's transition to democracy. When the National Coalition of Women for Democracy (Concertación Nacional de las Mujeres por la Democracia, CNMD) formed in 1989 to formulate gender-specific policies for the incoming democratic government, one of its main recommendations was the creation of national policy machinery to promote women's equality goals (Alvear 1990, p. 19; Matear 1995, p. 93). The establishment of SERNAM, therefore, responded to a bottom-up or societal demand, thereby giving the institution much greater legitimacy than where policy machinery is created at the urging of external actors or governing elites in the absence of societal pressure (see Friedman 2000a). This particular demand of the CNMD was given further legitimacy because it was one of the recommendations of the UN Convention on the Elimination of All Forms of Discrimination Against Women (CEDAW), which Chile ratified in 1989. Additionally, similar agencies had been created in neighboring Latin American countries that had also undergone democratic transitions, such as Brazil and Argentina.

The demand to create a state agency responsible for promoting women's interests was not a new one, but fit within the larger historical legacy of Chilean women's movements. The demand had in fact been a part of women's movements' demands in earlier historical periods. Indeed, as mentioned in Chapter 3, during Salvador Allende's presidency (1970–1973), legislation to create such an agency had been introduced, but had not been passed by the time of the military coup that ended his presidency. The creation of SERNAM, however, indicates a crucial shift in the way that women's citizenship was conceived both by the women who demanded its creation and by the government that brought it into existence. As explained in Chapter 3, women's citizenship during the Frei and Allende periods was promoted by mobilizing women around their social roles, most notably in the Centros de Madres (Mothers Centers). There was little attention paid to how these very roles constrained women's capacities to exercise political citizenship and to fully participate in setting and achieving the goals of development.

The creation of SERNAM and its mandate to bring about gender equality thus reflects a considerable shift in the way the Chilean state tries to include women as citizens. It is important to note, however, that the demands of the women's movements regarding the creation of SERNAM were not translated directly into an agency with a mandate that reflected the women's movements' vision. Because the changes within women's movements about the role of women in Chilean society and politics were not matched with broader societal changes in the prevailing gender ideology, the government's intention to create a national state agency to promote women's equality generated widespread controversy, with the political right and the Catholic Church explicitly opposing SERNAM's creation. Although there was significant political will within the center-left political class to respond to women's concerns, political elites were not willing to address women's demands in those cases in which they perceived their own hold on power to be threatened. Hence the opposition from conservative social forces led to a watered-down mandate for SERNAM.

The creation of SERNAM must be placed in the wider context of the transition to democracy in Chile. Terry Lynn Karl (1990) refers to Chile as a "pacted" or "negotiated" transition. General Pinochet and the conservative political right maintained considerable power—for example, through the constitutional provision for nine "designated" senators, ensuring that the right held the balance of power in the upper chamber. The overrepresentation of the political right in Chile has created a situation in which the demands of other social groups—for example, indigenous peoples and organized labor—remain unmet as well. While the first posttransition president, a Christian Democrat, was committed to responding to the concerns of women that had been raised by the CNMD, he was also committed to a path of peaceful transition that emphasized reconciliation and moderation. When the bill to create SERNAM was introduced into congress on May 14, 1990, it generated opposition from parties on the right who did not favor state promotion of gender equality. The two main parties of the right, the National Renovation Party (Renovación Nacional, RN) and the Independent Democratic Union (Unión Democrática Independiente, UDI), are skeptical about the concept of women's equality. A parliamentarian from the RN stated that while men and women are equal insofar as they are both children of God, "our biology, psychology, and emotional particularities derive from each different gender. These differences explain why the same qualities are not given in a completely equal manner [to men and women]. [These differences] are distinct and complementary" (cited in Grau et al. 1997, p. 85). For the political right, women's most important roles are those of *madre y dueña de casa* (mother and homemaker).

Given the controversy that the bill to create SERNAM unleashed, President Patricio Aylwin compromised by limiting the agency's scope and inserting language into the bill that gave SERNAM a potentially contradictory mandate: to promote women's equality while also protecting and strengthening the traditional family. Thus the law creating SERNAM states that the purpose of the agency is "to collaborate with the executive in studying and proposing general plans and measures intended to ensure equality of rights and opportunities for women, . . . respecting the nature and particularities of women that derive from natural differences between the sexes, including adequate concern for family relations" (cited in Loveman 1995, p. 325). SERNAM's first minister, Soledad Alvear, publicly stated that SERNAM would not concern itself with issues such as divorce or abortion (which would threaten the traditional family), but instead would be concerned with protecting and strengthening the Chilean family (Grau et al. 1997).

There are two reasons why the first Concertación government was unwilling to push harder for a women's rights agenda that generated opposition from both the Catholic Church and the political right. First, one of the most important legacies of the seventeen-year dictatorship was psychological: a fear of confrontation in the public realm that could potentially lead to heightened political tensions and a repeat of September 11, 1973. This fear led Concertación political leaders to chart an extremely moderate course of transition. Consequently, the 1989 electoral campaign focused on "social peace, tolerance, and rebuilding consensus" (Loveman 1995, p. 305). President Aylwin's top adviser stated that "as long as severe polarization is avoided, the risk of authoritarian regression or a military coup is slight" (cited in Loveman 1995, p. 305).

The second reason for the conciliatory approach to a women's rights agenda is the power of the Catholic Church following the transition (discussed in the previous chapter) and the fact that the Christian Democratic Party was the largest party in the governing coalition. While the church acted in progressive ways during the long years of dictatorship, in the post-transition period it reverted to its former role of being Chile's moral voice on personal and social issues (Blofield 2001; Htun 2003, p. 80). As Michael Fleet and Brian Smith explain in their study of the Catholic Church in the transition and consolidation of democracy in Chile, "since 1990, the Chilean bishops have devoted much of their attention to personal and social moral issues. These include divorce, abortion, premarital sex, educational reform, and the growth of evangelical Protestantism" (1997, p. 172). The church has been outspoken in its opposition, first to SERNAM's existence, and later to many of its projects. At one point, when SERNAM's first sub-director, Soledad Larraín, became involved in a public debate with the church over the issue of whether a "moral crisis" existed in Chile (she denied that such a crisis existed), she became an unacceptable figure to the government and was compelled to resign from her position (Grau et al. 1997, p. 87).

What is most clear about the politics surrounding SERNAM's establishment is that Concertación leaders took great pains to disassociate the agency's creation from any sort of feminist political agenda. In a speech made upon signing into law the creation of SERNAM, President Aylwin (1990) explained, "I want to expressly state that this project is not determined by ideological considerations, it does not respond to a philosophy about woman's role in society. It responds to the necessity of considering the problems that are affecting women in modern society and of listening to, preferably, the voice of women themselves to solve these problems."

Given the Concertación's unwillingness to pursue policies that it knew would be divisive, SERNAM came into existence with a potentially irresolvable tension at its core: to pursue women's equality while strengthening the (traditional) family. The support for SERNAM by key political leaders allowed it to embark on a fairly ambitious policy agenda, but the nature of the negotiated transition and the potential for conflict with the political right meant that women's rights policies have to "fit" within the broad outlines of social policy. This is why a number of programs are situated within a social welfare or poverty alleviation framework that, unlike previous social policy aimed at reducing poverty, takes into account the gendered sources of poverty.

SERNAM's timidity regarding potentially controversial issues has yet to disappear. At both the 1995 Beijing World Conference on Women and the 2000 Beijing Plus Five Conference, SERNAM's directors committed Chile to a conservative stance, much to the dissatisfaction of feminists in the country. Prior to attending the 1995 conference, Josefina Bilbao, SERNAM's director, explained: "I have been in permanent contact with our ambassador at the Vatican to know the official position of the Holy See regarding the conference. As it happens, we agree with the issues the Vatican has assigned the highest priority."[3] However, this occurred after a successful motion of censure in the Senate forced SERNAM to reformulate its platform for Beijing. Significantly, ten senators from the Concertación supported the motion introduced by the political right. As a result, "the introduction to the final document was re-written to affirm the family as the central unit of society, explicitly oppose abortion, and eliminate the word 'gender'" (Baldez 2001, p. 19).

In 2000 the newly elected government of Ricardo Lagos named Adriana Delpiano as SERNAM's director, creating a great deal of optimism among Chile's feminists.[4] Nonetheless, partly due to heavy lobbying by the political right and conservative NGOs, and partly because the Concertación had narrowly avoided defeat in the recent presidential elections, Delpiano chose to avoid further conflict in Chile by taking a conservative stance at an international conference on women's rights. Chile's official position at the Beijing Plus Five Conference in New York disappointed feminists. Parliamentarians from the political right met with Delpiano just days before the conference and reported that Delpiano had promised them that Chile would publicly insist that any recognition of women's sexual and reproductive rights would not imply any commitment to legalize abortion in Chile.[5]

The politics of SERNAM's establishment limit both its policy influence and the policy access it affords organized women's movements. The mandate of the agency undermined its capacity to serve as a mechanism to strengthen women's movements in Chile. Instead, SERNAM was designed to be a policy coordinating agency rather than an agency that would work directly with women.[6] The Foundation for the Promotion and Development of Women (PRODEMU), under the direction of the First Lady, would be the agency charged with working directly with women in their communities, offering them workshops in *desarrollo personal* (personal development), handicraft making, sewing, and other skills. But PRODEMU has a much lower profile (and less prestige) than SERNAM, and while it does carry out important work, it does not have an explicit mandate to promote gender equality as does SERNAM. As I discuss in more detail later, the absence of a mandate to work directly with women would complicate SERNAM's relationship with certain segments of the women's movement, particularly with popular sector women's organizations. Likewise, the moderate stance of SERNAM (especially regarding sexuality and reproduction) also undermined its status in the eyes of many feminists. The controversy surrounding SERNAM's creation affected its organizational features as well.

SERNAM's Organizational Form

SERNAM was established by law "as the body responsible for working with the Executive to devise and propose general plans and measures designed to ensure that women enjoy the same rights and opportunities as men."[7] This mandate is achieved through intersectoral coordination, legal reforms, training public servants in a gendered perspective on public policy, designing social policy, increasing women's social and political participation, international cooperation, research aimed at producing knowledge and statistics that reveal women's situation, and strengthening equal opportunities at the community level.[8] In keeping with the targeted social policy approach of posttransition governments, SERNAM has focused most of its attention on particular segments of women. Its main programs are Mujeres Jefas de Hogar de Escasos Recursos (Low-Income Women Heads of Households), Mujeres Trabajadoras Temporeras (Women Seasonal Workers), Prevención Violencia Interfamiliar (Domestic Violence Prevention), and Prevención Embarazo Adolescente (Teen Pregnancy Prevention). The only major program not targeted at a specific group of women is the Women's Rights Informations Centers (Centros de Información de los Derechos de la Mujer,

CIDEMs), with an office in each of Chile's thirteen regions. Most of the programs (with the obvious exception of CIDEMs) involve cross-ministerial coordination, often through the creation of interministerial committees such as the Interministerial Committee for the Prevention of Family Violence and the Coordinating Committee for the Women Heads of Household. SERNAM also has agreements with other ministries, including agriculture, education, and health, to initiate programs with attention to gender equity.[9]

SERNAM was created by law rather than by presidential decree. This is significant because it makes SERNAM a permanent part of the state structure in Chile, therefore making it more difficult to reduce its role should a more conservative government come to power. In contrast, Argentina's National Women's Council was established through presidential decree. President Carlos Menem's early support for women's rights meant that the agency had a broad mandate and generous funding. When controversy over women's rights emerged in Argentina surrounding the 1995 Beijing Conference, President Menem sided with conservative forces and drastically curtailed the Council's activities and its budget (Waylen 2000). A true test of SERNAM's durability, however, would be a change in government from the center-left coalition, which has governed Chile since the transition, to a more conservative government opposed to a gender equity agenda.

It is also significant that SERNAM is not a ministry in its own right, but is housed within the Ministry of Cooperation and Planning, which is responsible for the majority of Chile's social programs. The nature of MIDEPLAN itself, a posttransition creation, tells us something about the underlying organizational philosophy guiding SERNAM. The Ministry of Cooperation and Planning embodies the posttransition government's approach to addressing poverty and social exclusion in Chile. The agencies within MIDEPLAN are those dealing with Chile's socially marginalized groups—women, indigenous peoples, youth, and the urban and rural poor. The latter group's exclusion and poverty are addressed through the Solidarity and Social Investment Fund (Fondo de Solidaridad e Inversión Social, FOSIS). What is significant about all of MIDEPLAN's agencies is that they are not intended to execute policy, but rather to design and fund projects executed by other state ministries and agencies, or by private entities like NGOs or social organizations (Hardy 1997). Clarisa Hardy notes a fundamental problem at the heart of MIDEPLAN's mandate: these crucial social programs are implemented by ministries far more powerful and autonomous, hence they have their own interests to pursue and may be less interested in devoting their energies to programs that originate elsewhere in the state (1997, p. 123). Virginia Guzmán explains that in implementing gender equity policy, the original aims of policies can be blocked or diluted because many different state actors are involved, not all of whom are working toward similar goals (1998, p. 66).

While some have argued that being embedded within another ministry weakens SERNAM's potential to promote gender equality and programs that improve women's status, according to Soledad Alvear, a member of the CNMD and the first director of SERNAM, there were strategic reasons for creating SERNAM in this manner. She explains:

> In the working group [of the CNMD] where the project [of creating SERNAM] was conceived, it was concluded that the creation of a Ministry would make it more difficult to execute actions. We didn't want to create a ghetto or separate entity. . . . We wanted the creation of an entity that crosses various ministries, enabling us to act in each of them, and in this form women would be integrated into the development process. (1990, p. 19)

Although SERNAM does not have status as a ministry, its director has the rank of minister of state and therefore can participate in cabinet meetings (Matear 1995, p. 95). The director, the deputy director, and all of the regional directors are appointed by the president (Alvear 1990). SERNAM has a somewhat decentralized structure; along with the national office, it has offices in each of Chile's thirteen regional administrations. SERNAM's staff participates in regional coordinating bodies to insert gendered perspectives into regional development policy planning. As part of the wider state project of decentralization, SERNAM has also been transferring more aspects of its programs to the municipal level. Most municipal governments currently have a Women's Office; these offices are technically dependent on the municipal governments, although they maintain some links with SERNAM. But they are entirely financed with resources from the municipal government (Matear 1995, p. 96), which of course results in extremely disproportional capacities between the offices in the wealthy communities and those in the poblaciones.

Stetson and Mazur find that a centralized cross-sectoral approach to gender equity in public policy is most successful, but to be effective in terms of policy influence, agencies must be powerful in their own right and capable of coordinating gender policy with other institutions for an integrative approach. Centralized agencies that lack the ability and the authority to work across other agencies are less effective, as are dispersed agencies without "a respected and influential central coordinating office" (1995, p. 288). The Chilean case confirms this finding: neither is it powerful in its own right nor does it have the authority to influence the agendas of other state agencies. One of the consequences of SERNAM not being its own ministry is that it is prohibited by law from implementing its own programs. Instead, SERNAM is charged with proposing and designing policy for other ministries or agencies to implement. The only projects SERNAM can directly carry out are pilot projects, which, once proven effective, are turned over to the relevant ministry or agency for future implementation. The stated advantage of this institutional design is that SERNAM is supposed to be able to coordinate gender policy planning and promote a gender perspective throughout the state. However, this has not happened. According to Ann Matear, "the [cross-]sectoral area within SERNAM has been largely underdeveloped, despite being the essence of SERNAM's functions within the state apparatus" (1995, p. 96). Georgina Waylen explains that the key problem is the lack of concrete mechanisms for intersectoral cooperation. SERNAM does not have a sufficiently high profile or influence within the state to ensure that high-ranking officials in other ministries will be predisposed to cooperating or giving sufficient attention to gender policy issues (1996, pp. 110–111). One of the consequences of the lack of formal mechanisms of coordination is that such coordination that takes place owes to the personal relationships or connections between SERNAM officials and officials in other parts of the state. According to Fiona Macaulay, SERNAM's influence on the work of other ministries—which must execute gender policy—"is still dependent on the strategic location of feminist sympathizers who act as gatekeepers to facilitate access" (1998, p. 102).

Personal relationships have been quite crucial, therefore, much as they are in party politics, discussed in the previous chapter. For example, SERNAM's first director and deputy director were spouses of the leaders of the Christian Democratic Party and the Socialist Party respectively (Macaulay 1998). That being said, however, the deputy director was also a known feminist, who was ultimately compelled to resign due to some of her more outspoken views. And of course, as in other agencies of the state, high-ranking officials in SERNAM are appointed based on party affiliation (i.e., to balance the representation among the parties of the Concertación). Links to the wider women's movement are not a key factor in making appointments (Macaulay 1998; Waylen 1996, p. 113). This means that SERNAM policy cannot be separated from the partisan ends of the ruling party. Indeed, the second Equal Opportunity Plan was released to coincide with the launching of Ricardo Lagos's presidential campaign.[10] The partisan nature of SERNAM's priorities also accounts for the absence of attention to issues that could potentially threaten coalition unity. In fact, abortion has not been raised by SERNAM at all because, according to one SERNAM official, "as we are part of the government, in that sense we have to be within the framework of the government's program."[11]

Due to the controversies surrounding SERNAM's creation, its budget, scope, and size were reduced.[12] As a consequence, despite the drive toward decentralization in Chile, budget constraints led to a centralized institution rather than one with large staffs and resources at the municipal, regional, and national levels. This contrasts with Brazil's three-tiered Women's

Councils (with separate municipal, state, and national structures), which according to Macaulay (1998) allow for greater "feedback" from women at each level. Chile's SERNAM has a regional structure, but no municipal structure. At the municipal level, SERNAM relies on local governments and NGOs to carry out its mandate. A further consequence of SERNAM's reduced budget, especially at the outset, was that it affected the design of key programs and their ultimate effectiveness. Because of a reduced staff and budget, when SERNAM's main programs were being designed, there was only one person to act as coordinator with each relevant ministry (Valenzuela 1994, p. 196). This person was supposed to have expertise in the corresponding policy area as well as knowledge in gender policy planning (Matear 1995, p. 96). But their counterparts in the corresponding ministry do not necessarily have any expertise, nor interest, in a gendered approach to policy. Hence the success of an initiative hinges on the interest or commitment of the staff in the ministry that is working with SERNAM (Valenzuela 1994, p. 196). While part of SERNAM's mandate is training civil servants in a gender policy perspective, participation is voluntary. Consequently, of the 2,000 civil servants trained in 1998, the overwhelming majority were women; only 452 men voluntarily attended workshops (Salinas 1998, p. 90).

Consequently, while the idea of mainstreaming gender policy through an agency charged with coordinating public policy with the ministries is a good one, the absence of formal and authoritative mechanisms to structure coordination undermines its effectiveness. Natacha Molina, a committed feminist and former subdirector of SERNAM, explains that the overall structure and organization of the Chilean state is not conducive to cross-sectoral coordination and that this is an important reason why SERNAM "has yet to establish an easy working relationship with the rest of the state apparatus" (1998, p. 132).

In sum, SERNAM's organizational features undermine its political influence within the overall Chilean state. This could be improved through the development of more stable and authoritative mechanisms for coordination between SERNAM and other ministries. With such mechanisms in place, the importance of personal, and often highly partisan, relationships would decline, and the policy influence of SERNAM would be less dependent on the existence of well-placed individual sympathizers. The opportunities and obstacles to expanding women's citizenship in Chile through SERNAM are evident in the three main strategies that have been pursued since 1990: social programs, legislative reform, and the Equal Opportunity Plans.

SERNAM's Programs

Some of the problems SERNAM has faced in cross-sectoral cooperation are evident in what is perhaps SERNAM's most ambitious program, the Mujeres

Jefas de Hogar (Women Heads of Household) program, which itself emerged out of the recommendations of the CNMD and is based on the view that the causes of poverty are gendered (Valenzuela 1994). There is clear evidence to support the claim that women suffer more poverty and greater obstacles to entering the formal labor market to overcome poverty.[13] The Jefas de Hogar program is contained within a larger national support plan involving actions that target the multiple sources of female poverty. The national plan focuses on legal reforms to establish the full legal capacity of married women to access and manage family resources,[14] and legal reforms surrounding paternity, to make men responsible for all the children they father. Additionally, the national plan involves programs and intersectoral coordination across many ministries, including education, housing, health, labor, and welfare. For example, the Ministry of Labor is charged with designing training programs for women heads of household to gain the skills to compete in the labor market; the Ministry of Housing assists women in accessing affordable housing; and the Ministry of Education devises childcare assistance programs. María Elena Valenzuela, who has carried out extensive studies of the national plan and its implementation, explains that the scope of the plan and the need for cooperation across so many ministries have caused problems. She points to "the absence of stable linkages between SERNAM and the rest of the ministries," the fact that there are no precedents at the executive level for an approach that spans numerous ministries and sectors, and finally, the absence of knowledge of women's issues and a gender policy perspective outside of SERNAM (1994, p. 195).

More recent studies conducted by SERNAM on the Jefas de Hogar program reveal a number of shortcomings. One study (SERNAM 1999) explored the intersectoral coordination in carrying out the labor-training aspect of the program, key because the entire philosophy guiding the Concertación's approach to poverty alleviation assumes that poverty results from insufficient integration into the market (Revilla 1995; Roberts 1997; Schild 2000b, p. 27). Consequently, the answer to alleviating female poverty is seen as facilitating women's entry to the formal labor market. As part of the Jefas de Hogar program, SERNAM has worked with smaller agencies in the Ministry of Labor, the most important of which is the Employment and Training Service (Servicio Nacional de Capacitación y Empleo, SENCE). The main responsibility for training women now rests with SENCE.[15] But the study conducted by SERNAM reveals that within SENCE, commitment to taking into account the gendered obstacles to women's employment varies greatly (1999, p. 8).

A further problem is that SENCE itself divides up its tasks and contracts out aspects of labor training. For example, SENCE does not design or propose the courses and training programs it offers. This is carried out by the Technical Training Agencies (Organismos Técnicos de Capacitación, OTECs) at the municipal level. SENCE, therefore, can only select courses from those proposed by the OTECs in a given community, and at this level there is little consideration of the needs of women heads of households (SERNAM 1999). Furthermore, as Patricia Provoste notes, the problem with the state's contracting of program implementation to third parties like the OTECs is that these agencies cannot be forced to adopt as their own the gender-equity goals that inform SERNAM's perspective. She explains that women are often excluded from certain training programs because there may not be a women's washroom on site, or because there is no place for women to leave their children while attending (1997, p. 54).

A further problem is that none of the programs were designed to combat the gender discrimination that pervades the private sector. Women will continue to face gendered obstacles to employment as long as employers can legally ask applicants to supply information concerning their sex, age, and marital status. In demanding such information, employers simply continue the practice of not hiring married women in their fertile years. Even more problematic, many job applications ask the applicant to attach a photograph, and advertisements for jobs often call for persons *de buena presencia* (presentable), which for women usually means young, white, and attractive. The discrimination women face in the job market is evidenced in the figures from a job placement program (part of the Jefas de Hogar program) in 1993: in the 18–25 age group, there were 116 women registered in the job placement program and 33 of them found jobs; for men, 161 were registered and all were placed in jobs (Provoste 1997, p. 48).

Training courses are also offered at the local level through the Women's Offices. However, according to some of the women with whom I spoke, these programs are ineffective because they teach women traditionally "feminine" skills such as hairstyling, sewing, or macramé. According to Rosana Ceorino of Tierra Nuestra, an NGO that works with popular sector women, training courses such as these do not lead to dignified jobs for poor women, but rather to more women participating in Chile's growing informal economy, where women work out of their home as hairdressers or seamstresses.[16] Myriam González and María Molina, leaders of a popular sector women's organization in one of Santiago's southern poblaciones, noted that such training workshops "don't help you at all to get a job and earn a salary."[17]

As mentioned earlier, a crucial feature of SERNAM's organizational structure is that it is embedded within a state in the process of decentralizing. Indeed, decentralization in Chile is portrayed as a fundamental aspect of state modernization and democratization (Garretón 1995). In this context, SERNAM has been progressively decentralized as well, and is increasingly transferring aspects of its programs to the municipal level. One of the justifications for this is that women are the primary users of municipal services and hence it should be at this level that gender policy is executed.

Research carried out by SERNAM into the implementation of the Jefas de Hogar program at the municipal levels reveals a number of problems. A main problem is that the effectiveness of the program at the local level depends greatly on the level of commitment exhibited by the mayor and other high-ranking local officials. Rosana Ceorino noted vast differences in the sorts of programs available to women through the Women's Offices in the communities with whom Tierra Nuestra works. In her view, the level of service and attention to women's issues varies according to the political commitment of the mayor.[18] Fabiola Oyarzún, a training monitor for PRODEMU as well as an activist on women's issues in her community of La Florida, noted that her experience with different municipal governments in Santiago has taught her that where the mayor is not committed to women's issues, they do not bother informing local women's organizations of their rights and the services available to them. She explained that, by law, municipalities must give some funding to registered local organizations, but that few organizations, with the exception of the Juntas de Vecinos (Neighborhood Councils), really know their rights.[19] With respect to the Jefas de Hogar program, without strong support, the resources budgeted to the program are easily diverted to other "emergency" areas, and municipal officials will not feel compelled to give adequate attention to implementation or monitoring of the program (SERNAM 1996b, p. 14). This problem is obviously more pressing in poorer communities, which have fewer resources, smaller staffs, and smaller budgets. Another problem is related to the level of intersectoral coordination demanded by the program. Officials complain that maintaining contact and a working relationship with so many other departments—health, labor, education—is far too time-consuming given their already hectic schedules (SERNAM 1996b, p. 21). There is a sense among local officials that the program (together with all the extra work that goes along with it) is externally imposed. As Patricia Provoste explains, "the civil servants always see it [promoting gender equity] more as SERNAM's problem rather than something essential to their own task" (1997, p. 49). Consequently, without very firm support from the mayor and strict directives from the mayor's office to adequately implement and monitor the program, these tasks will be ignored or carried out in a halfhearted manner (SERNAM 1996b, p. 40). According to SERNAM's study, the most important weakness "has to do with the characteristics of the design of the program. The focus on horizontal coordination (inter-disciplinary, inter-departmental, and of an integral character) is the exact opposite of the traditional functioning of the municipios [municipal governments]: sectoral, vertical, and self-referential" (1996b, p. 40).

Perhaps the greatest problem with increasingly decentralizing social programs is the unevenness of result engendered. Decentralization in Chile (as elsewhere in Latin America) essentially involves off-loading service delivery to municipal governments whether or not these governments have the resources to deliver services effectively. It is not just that effective program implementation depends on the commitment of the mayor and other key officials, but also that the resources of communities vary considerably. Women do not ultimately benefit equally from SERNAM's initiatives due to the massive inequalities between the wealthy and poor communities.

Legal Reforms and Executive-Legislative Relations

One area where SERNAM has been fairly successful is in bringing about legislative changes, which is a crucial aspect of its mandate and in which its organizational form as part of the executive gives it an advantage. SERNAM has introduced numerous bills that expand women's rights (Blofield and Haas 2003). Labor code reforms include removing the prohibition on women taking certain jobs, providing time away from work to care for sick children (a benefit that can be claimed by either parent), protecting women from being dismissed for becoming pregnant, and prohibiting the administration of pregnancy tests as a condition of employment. Other legal reforms introduced by SERNAM include the criminalization of intrafamily violence, and constitutional change that explicitly establishes women's and men's equality before the law (SERNAM n.d.[a]). It should be noted that while progressive legislative reforms have occurred in Chile, women's movement activists remain unimpressed by the lack of enforcement of new laws. Ana Pichulmán, leader of a popular sector women's network, noted that "there are laws, but there are no resources to enforce or monitor them."[20] Felisa Garay, active in the labor movement around women's issues, noted the same thing: "there's very little political will to ensure compliance with the legislation."[21]

Both SERNAM and a number of women parliamentarians have taken up the task of legislating women's equality, but SERNAM clearly enjoys the lead role. As indicated in the previous chapter, the posttransition Chilean political system is one in which the executive dominates the legislative agenda through its capacity to prioritize bills by attaching varying levels of "urgency" to a bill in congress and through the president's capacity to call extra sessions of parliament, during which time the executive entirely determines the priorities of the legislature (Bickford and Noé 1997, p. 32; Siavelis 2000, pp. 17–19). A second source of executive dominance is the ample access to resources, such as advisory staff and crucial information, enjoyed by executive agencies. According to Peter Siavelis, "the executive branch can rely on a vast network of attorneys, experts, and advisors within each of its ministries who are charged with particular subject areas, enabling it to elaborate proposals of a much higher quality than the legislative branch" (2000, p. 21). Another source of power is the executive's access to parliamentary committees in which bills are being debated. Parliamentarians who are not on a particular committee do not enjoy such access, nor do organized groups in civil society (Haas 2000; see also Bickford and Noé 1997).

These institutional biases in favor of the executive mean that executive bills are much more likely to succeed than are bills introduced by parliamentarians. During Aylwin's administration (1990–1994), only 8.2 percent of the legislation that was passed had originated in the legislative branch. Under Frei's term (1994–2000), the percentage rose to 24.9 percent, still reflecting considerable executive dominance (Siavelis 2000, p. 24). This tendency is also evident in the area of women's rights legislation. Between 1990 and 1995, twenty-four bills concerning women's issues were introduced—fifteen by the legislative branch and nine by the executive. Only one-third of legislative bills were successful, compared to over two-thirds of executive bills (Baldez 2001, p. 20). Thus the institutional structure of executive dominance in the Chilean system gives SERNAM the upper hand in terms of legislating women's equality. However, Liesl Haas (2000) points out the potential problem inherent in these arrangements. That is, SERNAM has, to date, been part of a government that supports the expansion of women's rights, but if a more conservative government assumed office in Chile, SERNAM, as part of a powerful executive, could be used to weaken parliamentary initiatives to promote women's rights.

Equal Opportunity Plans

Since 1994, the main tools for promoting gender equality in Chile are the two Equal Opportunity Plans: *Plan de Igualdad de Oportunidades Para la Mujer, 1994–1999* ("for women"), and *Plan de Igualdad de Oportunidades Entre Mujeres y Hombres, 2000–2010* ("between women and men"). The extended time period of the second plan was a conscious strategy to try to embed the promotion of gender equality in the state rather than making it merely a mandate of the current government.[22] According to SERNAM, the second Equal Opportunity Plan represented the third stage in SERNAM's history: during the first stage (1991–1994), "SERNAM legitimated before the state and society some of the themes associated with overcoming the problems that women face" (SERNAM 2000, p. 8). The second stage coincided with the launching of the first Equal Opportunity Plan, which formed part of the mandate of Chile's second posttransition government. With the first plan forming part of the government's agenda, "the importance of incorporating equal opportunities into the whole set of government policies was confirmed" (SERNAM 2000, p. 8). The third stage began in 1999 with the work of elaborating a second plan that would not only build upon and consolidate the advances made to date, but also take into account the ways in which the institutionalization of gender equity concerns in policy formulation were still weak and fragile.

Both plans aim to identify priorities and goals that the relevant ministries can then be encouraged to incorporate into their own goals, practices, and frameworks: "SERNAM, in its role of public policy co-ordinator, is responsible for the evaluation of the Plan's measures, but it will be the task of each one of the respective ministries to include the measures in their annual goals, and to achieve these targets" (SERNAM 1994, p. 1). The first plan identified the following priority areas: legal reforms, families, education, culture and communication, women's access to the labor market, women's health, social and political participation, and strengthening public institutions for gender equity implementation and evaluation. The second plan narrowed these eight areas into six overarching themes: culture, promoting women's rights and their capacity to exercise them, participation in decisionmaking arenas, economic autonomy and poverty alleviation, quality of life, and gender in public policy. Both plans are fairly similar in style and content. Both set out goals and objectives for achieving gender equity in a particular area, and identify some methods for realizing these goals.

There are a number of problems with the plans, however. First, the recommendations are rather vague, often merely pointing to the need for more research, or specifying that SERNAM will make proposals in certain areas. For example, in the chapter devoted to women's economic autonomy and poverty alleviation, one of the stated objectives is the elimination of obstacles to women's access to economic resources. The recommendations for achieving the objective include "initiating measures to reduce the current salary gap between men and women" (SERNAM 2000, p. 43). It is not clear, however, how SERNAM would accomplish this.

Second, and even more serious, is the sense among many women, particularly poor, working-class, and indigenous women, that because the plans were written without adequate input from diverse groups of women, they do not truly represent women's interests in all their diversity. Mercedes Montoya, leader of the Network of Women's Social Organizations (Red de Mujeres de Organizaciones Sociales, REMOS), a popular sector women's network, told me that "the plan was written by other people, the base did not take part, was not a part, was not consulted, not asked at all."[23] Patricia Richards (2004) conducted extensive interviews with popular sector and indigenous women, who argued that, as a result of the lack of consultation, they simply did not see themselves or their communities' interests addressed in the documents. This sentiment was noted by the women I talked to as well. Where they did know of the plans (and many women did not), they ultimately viewed them as "very far from their own reality" to the extent that they failed to address the real social problems confronted daily by Chile's poor.[24]

SERNAM is making efforts, however, to disseminate information to women concerning their rights, believing knowledge about women's rights is the first step to "empowerment" (Weinstein 1997). SERNAM has established

Women's Rights Information Centers, and more recently, in May 2000, launched an information campaign called "Mujer con Derechos, Mujer Ciudadana" (Woman with Rights, Woman Citizen). Administered through SERNAM's thirteen regional offices, the information centers are intended to help women learn about their rights and how to fully exercise them.[25] The aim of the information campaign is to increase women's knowledge of their rights through information workshops held around the country. Workshops are organized jointly through SERNAM's regional offices, the Family Foundation, PRODEMU, the Ministry of Justice, police, and municipal governments.[26] The workshops address themes such as family law, labor law, and information on programs to support community and social organizations.[27]

In sum, the organizational structure of SERNAM has burdened it with a number of weaknesses that emerge principally from the lack of formal mechanisms for intersectoral cooperation. Nonetheless, SERNAM has succeeded in legitimating itself and introducing gender equality in public policy. This has enabled it to elaborate fairly ambitious Equal Opportunity Plans. While the plans would be stronger if they contained more concrete measures for promoting women's rights, they have achieved one important goal—putting women's rights squarely on the public agenda and incorporating their promotion into the state structure. The extent to which women's movements have mobilized around this agenda is taken up in the next chapter.

Conceptions of the State's Role in Promoting Equality

Stetson and Mazur argue that the most successful cases of state feminism exist where the state is viewed as the proper vehicle for addressing social inequality (1995, p. 288). In the Chilean case, there are two relevant trends with respect to this variable. First, the extent to which the state is viewed as responsible for ameliorating inequality is undergoing significant transformation. Current political discourse stresses the importance of societal rather than state solutions to poverty and inequality. Second, both state and societal actors see it as entirely legitimate that the state facilitate the strengthening of civil society organizations in the pursuit of greater equality and democracy. According to a study of women's organizations in Chile, civil society actors do expect the state to facilitate their organization and participation (Guzmán, Hola, and Ríos 1999). Political discourse, however, currently depicts poverty and social inequality as stemming from a lack of organization on the part of civil society. Consequently, a number of government programs involve participatory components, with the justification that this is the way to foster a society more oriented toward self-help. Regarding poverty alleviation, the Concertación's view is that "the alleviation of poverty is a responsibility of the country. It requires the mobilization of the poor themselves in the process of improving their quality of life, to which must be added the support of civil society plus the contribution of those who have more" (CPD 1999). While there are a number of problems with this approach, particularly the way it depoliticizes social problems relating to poverty, it clearly creates opportunities for feminists in SERNAM to foster women's organizing in civil society and potentially generate policy networks around women's equality issues, despite the fact that the agency's mandate limits its actions in this regard. There are two problems, however. First, SERNAM can only invite participation of civil society groups if they are program beneficiaries. For example, SERNAM initiated Mesas Rurales (Rural Roundtables), at which *temporeras* (female temporary agricultural workers)—as program beneficiaries—got together with NGOs and SERNAM officials to exchange ideas about how the program was working.[28] But not all women fit into the categories of SERNAM's programs. Second, most of SERNAM's contact with nonstate actors is with NGOs, often on the basis of personal relations.

With respect to equality, the Chilean state clearly views promoting gender equality as part of its role: "in countries with democratic institutions, the State can and must assume an active role in the promotion of rights . . . making more equitable the relations of power between men and women" (SERNAM n.d.[b], pp. 1–2). But in Chile, as elsewhere in Latin America, gender equality has been pursued as part and parcel of attempts to reduce poverty by expanding employment opportunities. In other words, addressing the gendered sources of poverty—for example, by incorporating women into the labor market—is considered key to reducing the number of households living in poverty. Consequently, achieving women's equality in Chile is often synonymous with expanding their labor force participation rates. This contributes simultaneously to two of Chile's goals: women's equality and greater economic competitiveness. In President Lagos's first annual presidential address, in May 2000, he took up the theme of gender inequality by highlighting the fact that the country lags behind others in terms of women's labor force participation. Lagos insisted, "we have to confront this form of backwardness."[29]

Poverty alleviation in Chile today, however, is being attempted in a manner that differs fundamentally from previous (pre-1973) periods, when both state and societal actors viewed the state as the appropriate agent to direct the economy and pursue development as well as the redistribution of the benefits of economic growth. Today, while there are subtle differences among the parties in the governing coalition regarding the appropriate scope of the state's role, there is consensus that the market should play the primary role in allocating resources. Even the Socialist Party agrees: "the [Socialist] Party's strategy for alleviating poverty in Chile relies more heavily upon the employment-generating effects of economic growth than governmental redistribution of income or assets" (Roberts 1997, p. 331). Even more important, most of Chile's posttransition social programs depart from earlier programs by focusing on specific target groups such as women, indigenous peoples, and youth. Since 1996, over two-thirds of Chile's social programs have been of this type. Moreover, almost all of these programs have contained an emphasis on incorporating their beneficiaries as active participants (Hardy 1997, pp. 125–126; Raczynski 1999).

The focus on citizen participation began near the end of President Aylwin's term (1990–1994) and was a key feature of President Frei's mandate (1994–2000). The Concertación's main goal has been to promote equality through the "modernization" of the state, a component of which is fostering citizen participation. The Concertación's program for its third term claimed that "citizen participation must be a central basis in the new State that modernization aims at constructing" (CPD 1999).

How is SERNAM attempting to increase citizen participation? Since 1997, increasing women's participation and their "associative capacities" has been an important priority, manifested in the creation of the Participation Program within SERNAM.[30] According to a study of SERNAM's efforts at initiating greater state-society interlocution, SERNAM officials believe that it is their duty to create networks between the institution and women's groups in civil society (Guzmán, Hola, and Ríos 1999, p. 33). It appears, however, that while there have been some successes, the links between women inside and outside SERNAM are still weak and fragile and, more importantly, only extend to one segment of the movement. To date, the links between SERNAM and the NGO community are the most solid, with a number of women moving between the two realms. But few links have emerged between SERNAM and grassroots women's groups. According to a popular sector activist, "the relations between SERNAM and the women's movement only go so far. They go to NGOs but not any further."[31] Seventy percent of SERNAM's links to nonstate actors are to NGOs or educational institutions, but less than 10 percent are to grassroots women's organizations (Guzmán, Hola, and Ríos 1999, p. 51). Thus the policy access being generated by state feminism is limited largely to one segment of the movement. More important, these links emerge because NGO feminists and SERNAM officials are likely to know each other personally. Many went to university together, participated in partisan or feminist organizations in the 1980s, or have worked in SERNAM or NGOs at the same time.[32] The biographies of feminist activists gathered by Marcela Ríos, Lorena Godoy, and Elizabeth Guerrero (2004) indicate that moving back and forth between state agencies (like SERNAM) and NGOs is very common in Chile.

On the other hand, links between SERNAM and grassroots women's groups are sporadic and have not yet produced regular patterns of interaction. SERNAM officials themselves recognize that there is still a long way to go in fostering links between organized women and SERNAM. Delia del Gato, for example, admitted that despite SERNAM's expanded efforts in this area, most of the contact has been with NGOs and not with base-level women's movements. As she explained: "In the last two or three years there's been a little more emphasis on how to build relationships [with women's movements]. I think it's been insufficient, and I think it's one of the self-criticisms we make of ourselves as an institution, that is, the absence of spaces being opened."[33] Another SERNAM official, Valeria Ambrosio, said much the same thing: "We should create more mechanisms [for interaction], make it a permanent policy. What happens now, rather, is that in certain moments we call on people, but they don't come because they feel instrumentalized or used. Although I think that the truth is that there is always a good attitude on SERNAM's part."[34]

Leaders of base-level women's groups and women in the NGO community have a good deal more to say about this, and their perceptions and strategies are explored in the next chapter. In sum, the conception of the state's role in promoting equality in Chile is rather contradictory. On the one hand, the prevailing view is that poverty and socioeconomic inequality are best left to the market and the private sector to resolve, thereby preventing policies that substantively address the variety of sources of women's inequality. On the other hand, current political discourse stresses "citizen participation," thereby opening up opportunities to feminists in SERNAM to generate access to policymaking channels for women's movements outside the state. If such access were created, it could improve women's citizenship by linking the formal and informal political arenas in such a way as to facilitate the transmission of women's gender interests from societal groups to decisionmakers in the state. Unfortunately, as I show in the next chapter, this process remains very much incomplete.

Conclusion

This chapter has addressed the role of the state in promoting women's citizenship using Stetson and Mazur's state feminism framework (1995). The comparative framework assesses state feminism according to two main features: policy influence and policy access. In the case of Chile's SERNAM, I have shown that its policy influence is limited—both the politics of its establishment and the politics of its organizational form reduce its capacity to coordinate gender policy across state institutions. But I have also argued that SERNAM enjoys greater opportunities than feminist parliamentarians to introduce legislation that improves women's ability to exercise citizenship and to make claims as citizens. SERNAM's location in the executive affords it greater resources and influence to promote women's rights through legislative reform.

In terms of policy access, I have shown that, due to a political culture that views the state as key to fostering citizen participation, SERNAM has been able to devise mechanisms for improving women's movements' access to arenas of policymaking. To date, however, access exists for organized women in the NGOs, but not for grassroots activists, further fragmenting an already divided women's movement.

What does this analysis of SERNAM tell us about the relationship between gender, states, and citizenship more generally? The Chilean case demonstrates how dramatically the relationship can alter in certain instances, especially in periods of state restructuring (see Banaszak, Beckwith, and Rucht 2003; and Walby 1997). In the 1970s and 1980s, various state arenas in Chile undermined women's equality, and the women's movement depicted the state, through its social and economic policies, as an important cause of their marginalization. Since 1990, important segments of the women's movement have looked to the state as an ally and have worked through the state to expand women's citizenship. Most important, since 1990 gender equality has been pursued with some success through various state arenas. The successes of Chile's SERNAM show that it is possible and desirable that movements focus their attention on state institutions and seize the opportunities these institutions pose at certain political conjunctures. Despite some failures, SERNAM has produced legislation that improves women's status as equal citizens.

The case of SERNAM also shows the limits to this strategy, however, limits that are especially pressing in the new democracies. SERNAM has not succeeded in overcoming Chile's deeply gendered patterns of citizenship by serving as a link between the formal and informal political arenas. The potential weakness of state feminism in new democracies emerges out of the nature of women's movements in countries that have undergone transitions. Movements tend to be weaker precisely due to transition processes that fragment and institutionalize segments of the movement in a period of rapid and far-reaching political change. New democracies, therefore, normally contain women's movements that have undergone divisions over strategies—for example, whether to ally with political parties or remain autonomous—and have lost an important unifying goal (i.e., democracy). In this context, the institutionalization of gender politics within state agencies can have a further fragmenting effect as the various segments of the movement respond to the changing context.

Notes

1. The creation of state policy machinery to promote women's interests was also promoted by the United Nations and formed a part of the 1979 Convention on the Elimination of All Forms of Discrimination Against Women (CEDAW).

2. Liesl Haas (2000) highlights SERNAM's institutional resources, especially compared to those of parliamentarians.

3. *Chip News,* July 7, 1995.

4. Although Delpiano had not been active in the feminist movement, she had been active in the struggle for the return of democracy, and was considered to be very sympathetic to the goals of the women's movement.

5. *El Mercurio,* June 4, 2000.

6. Interview with Delia del Gato, August 20, 1999, Santiago.

7. www.eclac.cl.espanol.investigacion.series.mujer.directorio.htm, retrieved February 4, 2000.

8. www.sernam.cl/linea.htm, retrieved May 31, 1999.

9. www.eclac.cl.espanol.investigacion.series.mujer.directorio.htm, retrieved February 4, 2000.

10. Interview with Delia del Gato, August 20, 1999, Santiago.

11. Interview with Valeria Ambrosio, October 5, 1999, Santiago.

12. It should be noted that compared to other Latin American countries, Chile's SERNAM is well-financed, despite relying on international donors to "top up" its financing each year. Significantly, SERNAM is one of the few women's state agencies in the region with the authority to negotiate its own budget each year (ECLAC 1998).

13. While poverty has declined in Chile, the effects of the decrease have not been spread out evenly. Currently, the most persistent poverty is to be found in rural areas and among women heads of households. Additionally, women's unemployment is consistently higher than men's, especially among those in the lower-income segments (SERNAM 1996a).

14. The absence of legal divorce in Chile until 2004 meant that many couples were separated "in fact" (that is, living apart) while remaining legally married. This left many women as heads of households who did not have control over marital property or their children, at least until changes to Chile's civil code in the mid-1990s—changes recommended by SERNAM—created shared parental authority and gave married women the option of greater control over family assets.

15. In fact, the funding for this aspect of the program, since 1998, also rests with SENCE. The goal of many of SERNAM's programs is to increasingly transfer both the funding and the implementation of the programs to the agencies that will be directly responsible for them.

16. Interview with Rosana Ceorino, October 6, 1999, Santiago.

17. Interview with Myriam González and María Molina, October 20, 1999, Santiago.

18. Interview with Rosana Ceorino, October 6, 1999, Santiago.

19. Interview with Fabiola Oyarzún, November 18, 1999, Santiago.

20. Interview with Ana Pichulmán, July 15, 2002, Santiago.

21. Interview with Felisa Garay, August 26, 1999, Santiago.

22. Interview with Delia del Gato, August 20, 1999, Santiago. According to del Gato, this idea came from Spain, where having a longer-term plan in place meant that when a center-right government came to power, replacing the center-left government, the previous government's plan for promoting gender equality continued to be implemented.

23. Interview with Mercedes Montoya, October 4, 1999, Santiago.

24. Interview with Laura del Carmen Veloso and Tatiana Escalera, November 9, 1999, Santiago.

25. SERNAM website, www.sernam.cl/linea2.htm, retrieved May 31, 1999.

26. The Family Foundation and the Foundation for the Promotion and Development of Women (PRODEMU) are semiprivate organizations that are dependent on the First Lady.

27. SERNAM website, www.sernam.cl/noticias01.htm, retrieved May 14, 2000.

28. Interview with Delia del Gato, August 20, 1999, Santiago.

29. "Mensaje Presidencial," reproduced in *El Mercurio,* May 22, 2000.

30. Interviews with Delia del Gato, August 20, 1999, Santiago; and Valeria Ambrosio, October 5, 1999, Santiago.

31. Interview with Mercedes Montoya, October 4, 1999, Santiago.

32. Interview with Lorena Fríes, July 19, 2002, Santiago.

33. Interview with Delia del Gato, August 20, 1999, Santiago.

34. Interview with Valeria Ambrosio, October 5, 1999, Santiago.

7 Women's Movements: Confronting New Challenges

Women's movements seek improvements to citizenship in a number of ways. They organize around issues important to women and their communities and seek to raise public awareness about these issues—for example, inadequate healthcare, community safety, childcare, sexism, and violence against women. Women's movements also seek to have an impact on public policy, either by directly lobbying elected or bureaucratic officials or by mobilizing societal support for policy goals, which in turn may compel political parties to put those issues on the public agenda. Finally, individual participants in women's movements often undergo personal transformations through which they become more aware of the gendered sources of their problems, but also how class and race inequalities are implicated in political and social power structures. Through this process, groups that form to address particular problems—for example, lack of childcare facilities—may eventually forge alliances with other groups, creating broader struggles for social change.

Since the return of democracy to Chile, many observers have commented on the disappearance of the women's movement. Indeed, many Chileans were puzzled when I told them that I had come to their country to study the women's movement since the transition to democracy. In their view, there had been a women's movement under the dictatorship, but many felt that it had disappeared under democracy. My own view, however, is that we must beware of taking the dictatorship-era movement as the norm. While the movement throughout much of the 1980s was marked by cross-class, cross-partisan alliances and common objectives, in most other countries women's movements are characterized by internal conflicts and divisions among different segments, and often face hurdles in grabbing media headlines or the public spotlight.[1] That being said, however, a main challenge for organized women in Chile today is to find ways to create strategic linkages across different segments of the movement—especially among those feminists who have access to gender policy networks and women's organizations that do not. Another challenge is to gain greater public attention and societal support for feminism.

In this chapter, I outline the main strands or currents in the women's movement since the transition to democracy. I argue that the posttransition movement has been shaped by the shifting power dynamics brought about by the negotiated transition to democracy, state feminism, and the dictatorship's legacy. Essentially, the posttransition movement is composed of three currents: middle-class and professional women working in feminist nongovernmental organizations (NGOs) or in the National Women's Service (Servicio Nacional de la Mujer, SERNAM); grassroots women's organizations; and autonomous feminists. The autonomous feminists have lost much of their capacity to influence the direction of the movement, in large part because they have chosen to exclude themselves from arenas in which they could be more visible. Feminists who work in NGOs and SERNAM have access to decisionmaking arenas, but lack the power to mobilize civil society around their ideals for progressive change. Women organized at the base have lost much of the access they used to have to NGOs or agencies with external funding, and hence their most pressing concern is the sheer survival of their organizations. The relationship among the three segments of the movement has been marked by conflict. This conflict is a product of strategic and ideological differences, but also of class and race inequalities that are no longer subsumed under the common objective of defeating the dictatorship.

Another pressing problem for the women's movement is the resurgent boundary between formal and informal politics, a boundary that, as I argued in Chapter 1, has both gender and class dimensions. Not only do women's movements face enormous challenges in gaining public visibility in an environment dominated by political parties, but it is also difficult for many women themselves to view their activism as political. Without a greater sense among women themselves—especially popular sector women—that they are engaged in politics even if they are not party militants, it becomes more difficult to make political citizenship demands of the state or to connect one's activism to a larger political project for progressive change.

This chapter begins with a brief overview of the impact of the transition to democracy on Chilean social movements in general, emphasizing the essentially demobilizing consequences of transition politics. Next I outline the major strands or currents in the contemporary women's movement—grassroots organizations, feminist autónomas, and feminist NGOs—and the power relations among them that are produced by the current environment. Finally, I offer evidence that some of the fragmentation that characterized the women's movement for much of the 1990s is starting to be overcome by recent initiatives that link up dispersed organizations.

However, it remains too early to predict the likely success of these endeavors. Most important, a number of network organizations have recently emerged to challenge the more limited "official" women's rights agenda of SERNAM, while also seeking to develop channels of participation through SERNAM to expand women's gender-based demands. These women, mainly from the popular, campesino (rural), and indigenous sectors, reinsert socioeconomic issues into debates about citizenship. This is critical because, historically, patterns of citizenship in Chile have reinforced inequalities based on class and ethnicity as well as gender. Unfortunately, the process of rearticulating links and remobilizing around explicitly feminist themes has not yet occurred.

Movement Politics and the Chilean Transition to Democracy

Most people who have studied Chilean politics note the decline of social movements and the demobilization of civil society after the return of democracy (de la Maza 1999; Garretón 1995; Oxhorn 1995b; Ríos 2003; Schild 1997). This dynamic is a result of a number of factors. First, the resurgence of political parties—parties that had previously acted through social movements in the 1970s and 1980s—led to the subordination of many social movement organizations to partisan structures (see Oxhorn 1995b, chaps. 6–7). Political party monopolization of public space has also suited the interests of posttransition governments to the extent that parties are more likely to moderate social demands. Part of Chile's negotiated or "pacted" transition involved the prodemocracy parties' acceptance of the market reforms initiated by the military regime. According to Kurt Weyland, leaders in President Aylwin's government "feared that inequality and poverty would prompt a wave of demands for immediate benefits that would endanger sound economic policy" (1997, p. 40). Fourteen years later, this perception still lingers. While Concertación leaders frequently pay lip service to the need to expand citizen participation, observers also point out that "the Concertación has maintained democratic stability at the expense of the active participation of civil society" (Drake 2000, p. 112). Paulina Weber of the Chilean Women's Proemancipation Movement (Movimiento Pro-Emancipación de Mujeres de Chile, MEMCH) noted in an interview that despite government rhetoric that values citizen participation, "the government is afraid that there will be too much participation."[2] Other observers argue that the deactivation of the social movements that had mobilized in the struggle for democracy was a prerequisite of the transition (de la Maza 1999, p. 377; Silva 2004).

Posttransition governments in Chile have devised a variety of mechanisms to demobilize popular movements. Philip Oxhorn explains that

Aylwin's government created the División de Organizaciones Sociales (Division of Social Organizations) to serve as a channel between government and community organizations to transmit a message of patience and to lower society's expectations concerning economic justice (1994a, p. 743). Citizens were encouraged to organize at the community level and to turn their attention toward community solutions to poverty rather than expect the state to provide solutions. What this meant, ultimately, is that community organizations—often the very same ones that had participated in the popular movement against Pinochet—were encouraged to lower their social and economic expectations of democracy by moderating their demands of the new democratic government. But there are other factors at work that have kept civil society organizations fairly passive since the transition. Because at least two of the parties that compose the governing Concertación are from the left, and all parties in the coalition were part of the struggle for the return of democracy, there is a certain amount of reticence among some civil society organizations to criticize the government too harshly. Felisa Garay noted that this problem plagues the posttransition labor movement because any form of protest is viewed "as being against the government."[3] Likewise, some feminists in NGOs reported being made to feel like traitors if they do not support the government, especially SERNAM.[4]

Finally, the discursive politics of the democratic transition in Chile have drawn a sharp boundary between political and social issues in an effort to limit the kinds of issues and demands that can be voiced in the formal political arena. Resolving the material concerns of citizens is viewed as best left to the market. While President Aylwin did promise to repay the "social debt" of the dictatorship by developing specific antipoverty programs, the nature of these programs limits government involvement to coordinating the activities of program recipients and civil society organizations or NGOs contracted to execute program delivery. Government discourse also asserted that the main bases of the demands of popular sector groups—poverty and inequality—were social (community) problems and not political (government) problems. Today, "modernization" of the state means increasing citizen participation, but not necessarily in broad-based movements that make political demands of government. Instead, citizens are encouraged to participate in their communities—arenas that are increasingly constructed as nonpolitical (see Taylor 1998).

In accounting for the relative absence of social movement activity in posttransition Chile, Gustavo Rayo and Gonzalo de la Maza point to the role of the state in organizing communities and providing groups with opportunities to participate at the local level in competing for self-help project funding. This shifts the emphasis to activity that yields concrete results, rather than activity aimed at constructing a collective actor capable of mobilizing to challenge existing power relations. Consciousness-raising activities are abandoned in favor of technical projects of community improvement. The authors explain, "their [community organizations'] principal concern is rooted in *doing* something, and not in *representing* anything . . . none of the organizations seek to represent increasingly large territorial spaces; they are more interested in constructing networks focusing on specific topics" (2000, pp. 449–450). While during the years of dictatorship neighborhood groups initially emerged with material or survival concerns, they were ultimately drawn into larger popular movement networks making political demands—not only for democracy but for social justice and equality as well. In this environment, a collective identity was forged that served as the basis for political mobilization (see Oxhorn 1995b), and among women a feminist consciousness emerged (see Gaviola, Largo, and Palestro 1994). The feminist consciousness that permeated the women's movement of the 1980s is increasingly being challenged today as movement organizations divide, disappear, and react to the "official" women's rights agenda emanating from SERNAM, and to the reduced ability of feminist segments of the movement to set the public agenda and to gain greater public acceptance of feminist ideas in Chile. However, as I show later in the chapter, some of these tendencies are starting to be addressed by movement actors, although it is not yet clear how successful they will be.

Women's Movements, Feminists, and Democracy

Since the return of democracy, women's movements and feminists are operating in an entirely different context than the one in which their activism first emerged. Women's movements in Chile today face enormous challenges, the most important of which are to forge strategic linkages among groups divided by class and ethnic inequality and to regain a more proactive role in setting the public agenda with respect to feminist issues. During the dictatorship, the various segments of the women's movement, human rights groups, economic survival organizations, and feminists ultimately worked together (albeit not without certain conflicts) in pursuit of the broader goal of democracy. Today, there is no longer an overarching goal to unite the disparate segments of the women's movement, which is characterized by three general currents. The first segment is composed of women's organizations working at the grassroots level that may or may not self-identify as "feminist." This segment of the movement includes organizations created under the dictatorship to resolve material issues that continue to be a priority for poor and working-class women. There are also newer organizations that emerged at the local level to address mainly material and community issues. But the ultimate goals of many of these groups are in fact much broader, due in large part to the greater awareness of gender issues introduced by SERNAM and other state agencies. In this context, many grassroots organizations seek to mobilize their members around both gender and class issues, although they are sometimes uncertain of how best to accomplish the task. These groups also seek ways to make connections with or gain access to gender policy networks and wider women's movement networks, but again, are often uncertain of how to meet these goals.

While grassroots organizing among women has feminist goals in many cases, these women may not always self-identify as feminists, especially given the negative connotation of feminism in Chile. Many of the women with whom I spoke explained that feminism is perceived as being opposed to men or rejecting marriage and family life. Mercedes Montoya noted that "[talking about] feminism is like talking about the worst thing. Because, I believe, the word 'feminism' in Chile today is very much manipulated."[5] So, while many organized women readily admit to being in favor of greater equality for women, they continue to reject the label "feminist." The second and third segments of the movement today do embrace a feminist identity, and also seek to shed the term of its negative connotation. The second segment is the self-designated autónomas and the third, initially given their label by the autónomas, is the institucionales. This latter label is normally applied to feminists both in SERNAM and in NGOs.

The relations among the three currents of the women's movement today are complex and greatly complicated by class, race, and ideological differences. Class and race inequality have been translated into unequal access to the state and to other resources, a dynamic that is generating substantial resentment among grassroots organizations, feminist NGOs, and SERNAM. Women in each of these locations have competing conceptions of their roles in the broader women's movement. For example, leaders of grassroots women's organizations expressed a sense of resentment over the fact that NGOs have access to resources that are simply unavailable to grassroots organizations.[6] However, Teresa Valdés, who works in the Latin American Faculty of Social Sciences (Facultad Latinoamericana de Ciencias Sociales, FLACSO), a research-oriented NGO, complained that there is a very strong misperception in Chile that NGOs are replete with financial resources, which, she insists, they are not.[7] Base-level organizations also believe that all NGOs enjoy easy access to SERNAM, whereas women in the NGOs report that SERNAM is only open to a select group of NGOs. Rosana Ceorino remarked: "In SERNAM there are competitions [for projects] behind closed doors, I'm sure of it. They'll call three NGOs and then those three are assigned the project."[8] Likewise, Lorena Fríes said, "I believe that in general, the government is closed to NGOs, although it has a discourse that is more open than previous [Concertación] governments."[9]

There are also competing conceptions about what role feminist NGOs,

SERNAM, and grassroots organizations should be playing, and the extent to which any of these segments can or should be "representing" the other, or "facilitating" their participation. For example, women in the NGOs expressed a certain ambivalence about whether they should be agents or representatives of grassroots women's organizations simply because they have greater access to the state. According to Rosana Ceorino, SERNAM wants to convert NGOs into intermediaries between the state and civil society. But she argued that this is problematic because NGOs cannot represent or lead popular sector movements.[10] Lorena Fríes of Casa de la Mujer–La Morada (La Morada Women's Center), a feminist NGO, said much the same thing, noting that "pobladora women must represent their own interests."[11] Nonetheless, women in the grassroots organizations complained of the NGOs "appropriating" the social spaces available and speaking for popular sector and indigenous women.[12]

Similar tensions exist between grassroots women's organizations, especially popular sector ones, and SERNAM. Patricia Richards (2004, pp. 95–119) shows that women in each location attach different meanings to "participation." While popular sector women argue that they should have a role in setting the policy agenda for issues that concern them, SERNAM officials argue that these organizations are often too weak or insufficiently organized to be engaged in the policy process. According to Richards, "speaking from a position of greater (albeit contested) social authority, femocrats are able to discursively construct pobladoras as invalid participants by pointing out the shortcomings in their political skills" (p. 119). SERNAM officials, when asked about their responsibilities to open up political space for women's movements, often remark that civil society in Chile is too weak and thus there is only so much SERNAM can do. For example, Valeria Ambrosio emphasized that "there is one part that corresponds to the state and another to civil society. We [SERNAM] can be facilitators but civil society itself has to change, has to organize itself and take its initiatives too. It goes both ways."[13]

Another set of tensions exists among middle-class and professional women who self-identify as feminists. Feminists in Chile today can be found in a host of locations, including SERNAM, NGOs, and autonomous feminist collectives, with many women occupying more than one space simultaneously. It is important to note, however, that many feminists today differentiate between their political commitment to feminism and their professional roles as gender policy experts in the state or NGO sector.[14] Significantly, though, many of Chile's self-identified feminists work in NGOs or as gender policy experts in state agencies, particularly in SERNAM. According to a recent study, "the high concentration of feminists in NGOs and the state constitutes a predominant trait of Chilean feminism" (Ríos, Godoy, and Guerrero 2004, p. 192). The relations among women in these three arenas are complicated by ideological and strategic differences. The early posttransition years were marked by excessive conflict among feminists as the movement reacted to the shifting political context. While those who moved into state arenas clearly enjoyed more power than those who were excluded (by choice for the autonomous feminists, and by class and ethnic inequalities for other grassroots organizations), their power was constrained by a number of factors, including the limits imposed by a negotiated transition, the dominance of social conservatism in the political class, and the weakness of feminism as a visible social movement. According to Lorena Fríes of La Morada, "feminist NGOs are not capable of generating public opinion," in large part because the media is in the hands of conservatives in Chile.[15] More important, all the women with whom I spoke, whether in SERNAM, NGOs, or grassroots organizations, emphasized the importance of building a stronger movement with more linkages among groups. Francisca Rodríguez of the National Association of Rural and Indigenous Women (Asociación Nacional de Mujeres Rurales e Indígenas, ANAMURI) argued, "to make change, to make improvements, we need a women's movement that is coordinated, with strength, with negotiating capacity. Not like now, with each one in our little parcel."[16] As I show in the final section of this chapter, some of the steps needed to strengthen the movement are being taken.

Grassroots Organizing Among Women

Despite perceptions that women in Chile have ceased to be active following the transition to democracy, they remain remarkably active within their communities. Indeed, Mercedes Montoya argued that "for us [popular sector women], we can't talk about an absence of participation, we speak about an excess of participation. This is because here [in the poblaciones] we feel that women don't have any other space."[17] Montoya was referring to the fact that popular sector organizations no longer have the support of access to other spheres of participation that they had in the 1980s. While in earlier decades women's activism was motivated by material deprivations associated with the dictatorship's economic policies and the repression required to maintain them, women could also draw strength from many support networks to sustain their organizations and their activities. As shown in Chapter 4, the Catholic Church was key to the maintenance of popular sector social organizations in the dictatorship era, as was the work of middle-class and professional feminists whose activities were funded by international aid agencies.

Today, women's organizations have little support. The church has returned to its more traditional concerns of spirituality and morality. Likewise, the funding from international donors has been diverted, either to state agencies like SERNAM or to countries deemed needier than Chile.

The loss of international funding was a constant theme in my conversations with organized women in Chile, especially among those also active during the dictatorship who remember the (relative) ease with which resources from abroad were obtained for the struggle for democracy, freedom, and gender equality. But the social context in Chile has changed in other ways, too. At one gathering I attended, over fifty women from communities within one of the poorer municipalities in Santiago had met for a weekend retreat in Cartagena, a traditionally working-class vacation spot. There, a number of women who had been extremely active during the dictatorship began to reminisce about those years and to comment on the different challenges they face today. Some of the women insisted that the high levels of social solidarity forged during the antidictatorship struggle and the economic crisis of the early 1980s have disappeared. In those years, they explained, people would share everything they had with their neighbors, and everyone could be expected to participate in some form of community activity. With the current neoliberal model, they argued, people are less willing to share, and less willing to participate, even though poverty has not diminished that much from their point of view. They placed much of the blame for this on a changing political culture fostered by neoliberalism, which stresses values of individualism and consumerism, values that undermine the ideals of solidarity and concern for one's community. Women also noted that today there is greater shame in being poor rather than pride in sharing a collective identity as "poblador."

One of the popular sector women's organizations that illustrates the particular problems faced by poor and working-class women's organizations is the Coordinación de Mujeres Luisa Toledo (Luisa Toledo Coordination of Women), a network of four women's workshops from La Pintana, a poor neighborhood in the south of Santiago.[18] The organization initially formed in 1973–1974 to work with popular sector organizations suffering from repression and the economic downturn, and their activities were at their highest point during the campaign against the continuation of Pinochet's rule in the 1988 plebiscite. Throughout this period, their activities were heavily supported by the Catholic Church, especially through the Vicaría de la Solidaridad (Vicariate of Solidarity). Each week the church distributed packages to participants containing cooking oil, milk, sugar, and cheese. After the plebiscite was won and a transition to democracy took place, the Coordinación lost the material support of the church and many of the member groups dropped out. One of the group's leaders explained to me that because of the practice in those years of members receiving food packages, women continue to expect material benefits for attending meetings. At its largest, the Coordinación had twenty-eight groups, with about twenty-five members each. Today, only four groups remain, with about fifteen to twenty members each. The group's leaders attribute the decline to the fact that "we achieved the triumph—we got democracy which was what we wanted."

Since the return of democracy the organization faces two overwhelming challenges: first, finding the resources to continue meeting; and second, setting out broad goals and objectives around which to mobilize. In terms of resources, the organization's leaders explained that while they used to rent a small house in which they both held meetings and conducted workshops and other activities, they no longer have meeting space due to their losing a key source of funding. Indeed, they told me that this was the main problem they confronted. They explained that while they have many good ideas for projects, they lack the physical space in which to carry them out. In terms of their other main challenge, setting out goals and objectives, the leaders explained:

> In women's organizations right now, we don't have the objectives so clear. At best, they're clear to us—the leaders—but not so much for the other women. Many come simply to take tea because it's the afternoon and they get together to chat because it's the only break [in their days] for them. . . . Before, in the "No" campaign [for the 1988 plebiscite] our objective was clear—to defeat the government of Pinochet, that's why there were so many women, so many workshops. But once that was achieved, women said, "mission accomplished" and they left. Therefore, the objective was lost.

Similar problems exist in another popular sector women's group that I visited, this one much newer. Mujeres de Hoy (Women of Today) was formed in 1997 in the community of Renca, after a number of women from the neighborhood had participated in a workshop in *desarrollo personal* (personal development) conducted by the Foundation for the Promotion and Development of Women (PRODEMU).[19] This group faces the same problems as the Coordinación de Mujeres Luisa Toledo: a lack of resources, most notably the lack of meeting space; and a lack of clear goals and objectives to ensure the group's continued functioning. The lack of meeting space was a crucial obstacle and at the meeting I attended, a full half-hour was spent discussing the issue. Indeed, on that day, the meeting was held in a small local church, a last-minute arrangement because they were having problems with the (male) president of the Junta de Vecinos (Neighborhood Council) over access to the local community center. The group's members complained about their treatment by the president, who had refused to recognize their right to utilize the community center for meetings, a right granted to all community groups with *personalidad jurídica* (legal status). Indeed, the group dutifully applied for their legal status in order to be able to use the community center in addition to being eligible to apply for community projects from the municipal government.

Another problem the group faced, according to Tatiana Escalera, was to move beyond the economic and social incentives for women to participate. The main economic incentive for members was the funds the group had won from the municipal government to carry out an income-generating project. They applied for and won financing to purchase a large oven to bake *pan amasado* (homemade bread); the earnings from selling the bread were distributed among the group's members. Escalera explained that the other main motivation for women was social: attending meetings provides women, who are mainly homemakers, with the opportunity to leave their houses and get together to have tea with their neighbors. Escalera insisted that the group must move beyond these concerns and begin to mobilize around themes relating to gender equality. Significantly, she employed the language learned in PRODEMU's and SERNAM's workshops. She explained that the most important issue for women today is "the right to have rights. Everything else, education, health, family, reducing poverty, basically begins from one's having rights."

Women's resistance to perceiving their activism as political was another issue raised by Myriam Gonzáles and María Molina. Their comments illustrate a common problem for expanding women's political citizenship:

> Some women are really afraid of the word "politics." Because really, in Chile we don't have a sense of what politics is anymore. If you say to women, "But you practice politics every day in your home," they say to you, "No. It's only politics if it's got to do with political parties, that is, if you're Socialist or UDI." But they don't take the other, broader understanding. That's the main problem. For us, politics is what we do all the time. But for the majority of those [in the groups] politics is partisan activity.[20]

The final problem for women's groups at the base is their sense of exclusion, particularly their marginalization within a movement dominated by feminist NGOs. As shown in the previous chapter, SERNAM has recently been trying to expand the role of grassroots women's groups in the policymaking process—for example, by inviting their participation in town-hall meetings and workshops. To date, however, there have been shortcomings with respect to these initiatives. For example, Ana María Órdenes of the Solidarity and Social Organization (Solidaridad y Organización Social, SOL), an NGO that worked with popular sector women's groups, explained that "there was no relationship [between SERNAM and grassroots groups]. SERNAM wasn't going to the organizations and that was a very great frustration for these women."[21] However, according to Lorena Fríes, the distance that has emerged between movement organizations and SERNAM is not entirely surprising. She explains that "because you have to show effectively that you're an authority of government and not of civil society, therefore, there's a necessity to distance yourself [from the movement]."[22] On the other hand, organized women note that there are relations between one segment of the movement, NGOs, and SERNAM, but no relations between SERNAM and base-level organizations.[23] For example, SERNAM had come under heavy criticism because the first Equal Opportunity Plan had been entirely written by one women's NGO—the Center for Women's Studies (Centro de Estudios de la Mujer, CEM) (Matear 1997a). Consequently, SERNAM wanted to make the elaboration of the second plan more "participatory."[24] But the participatory process that SERNAM initiated did not satisfy women's groups. First, SERNAM held town-hall meetings and invited representatives of women's movements to voice their concerns and demands. In an informal discussion with one woman who attended, I was told that SERNAM officials simply heard the issues raised by participants, then closed the meeting and left. The women who had attended expected a more meaningful dialogue and hence were quite disappointed by SERNAM's actions. Second, many groups were excluded from the process. Mostly it was women's NGOs that were invited to give their input in face-to-face meetings, while grassroots and popular sector groups were merely sent questionnaires. The questionnaires were sent to municipal governments, which in turn distributed them to women's groups registered with them. González and Molina explained, "We didn't even know about the plan, we found out the moment the questionnaire arrived."[25] Mercedes Montoya was critical of the fact that the Network of Women's Social Organizations (Red de Mujeres de Organizaciones Sociales, REMOS), an organization that represented over 5,000 popular sector women, was not asked to send a representative to the meeting. However, in addition to being a leader of REMOS, Montoya also works for a human rights NGO, the Service for Peace and Justice (Servicio Paz y Justicia, SERPAJ), and was invited to attend the meeting in that capacity. She noted that this was very common, and that it indicated the discrimination that exists against popular sector women's organizations. She further pointed out that whenever she gets invited as a representative of SERPAJ, she makes a point of letting everyone know that REMOS has not been invited, but that, as a representative of REMOS, she will speak on its behalf as well.[26]

The fact that popular sector women feel this way indicates the problem SERNAM faces in adequately representing women where there are too few linkages among the variously situated organizations that make up the broader women's movement in Chile. González and Molina explained that they do not feel represented by the current Equal Opportunity Plan: "What happens is that this plan is composed of all that is, shall we say, government, and a government that [employs women to write it] who have not a single idea of what happens in the community or what happens in the organizations, and it is they who make [policy]."[27] Of even greater concern is that popular sector women's sense of being on the "outside" is reinforced through their interactions with professional women, whether in the NGOs or in the state. For example, González and Molina explained that when popular sector women participate in workshops offered by NGOs or the state (mostly through the municipal government), they are given certificates for their participation. But these certificates are worthless because they do nothing to enhance the chances of finding jobs. They complained that not even the municipal government that offers the courses will hire the women afterward. Worse, even if a women's organization applies for funding to carry out a project, most popular sector women cannot use the funding to draw a salary for themselves even though the work they do is considerable. This is because the rules are structured so that only women with professional accreditation—for example, social workers and educators—can be paid a salary.[28] This practice, according to González and Molina, "has led community women to quit the workshops and withdraw." In effect, this practice reinforces the class-based exclusion of popular sector women, thereby adding to the divisions within the movement between professional women and women activists without professional credentials.[29]

This phenomenon indicates that citizenship is exercised differently according to both gender and class. Women from the popular sectors are frequently engaged in very similar activities as women in the NGOs, yet their roles are not accorded the same value. Ana Pichulmán of REMOS explained that the work of community organizations is viewed as "volunteer work." This is evidenced by the fact that in their applications or project bids, they can only use the funds they apply for to pay for materials needed for the project, not to pay themselves a salary, or pay for the infrastructure needed to maintain themselves as organizations, such as paying the phone bill.[30] This affects the sense of citizenship experienced by popular sector women. They do not feel that their activities are accorded the same status as the activities of their "professional" counterparts in the NGOs, and more significant, they feel that their voices are therefore less likely to be heard when it comes to designing policy. Mercedes Montoya noted that, in order to be taken into account by government officials, "you need a little title."[31] Pichulmán explained that popular sector women remain marginalized as citizens precisely because there is still no "meaningful interchange between the state and civil society"; her comment points to the importance of establishing spaces for dialogue between state and civil society actors in Chile's new democracy.

Feminist Organizing in Posttransition Chile

It is widely acknowledged that the feminist movement in Chile has grown weaker since the return of democracy. While browsing in a feminist bookstore in downtown Santiago in July 2002, I had an interesting conversation with a woman who worked there. When she overheard me speaking English with a friend, she asked me why I had come to Chile, and why I was shopping in a feminist bookstore. I explained that I was working on a project about women's movements in Chile, and she became very interested. She told me that the story of feminism in Chile was quite sad because they had such a strong movement in the 1980s and were such a big part of the prodemocracy movement. She explained that although she had been extremely active herself in the early period of La Morada, one of the earliest second-wave feminist organizations in Santiago, she no longer kept in touch with any of the women involved. Significantly, she recalled that some of the Spanish feminists who had come to Chile to work with the Chilean movement had warned them of the demobilizing tendencies of democratic transitions based on their own experiences a few years earlier. So, what happened to Chilean feminism?

The Chilean feminist movement grew weaker throughout the 1990s as a result of a number of factors. The growing assertiveness of the Catholic Church and conservative NGOs have played an important role in reinforcing the negative stereotypes of feminism, depicting feminist issues such as reproductive freedom and women's autonomy as going against deeply engrained family values. Likewise, the parties of the Concertación have not proven themselves willing to take on the political right on these issues, in large part because of the fear of endangering coalition unity, especially as electoral politics becomes more competitive. Another factor, according to Marcela Ríos (2003, p. 259), is Chileans' fear of provoking political or social conflict, a fear that is linked to the dictatorship's legacy. As a result, feminists in Chile engage in a great deal of self-censorship, which also grows out of the hesitancy within the NGO community to be too critical of a government composed of former friends and allies. According to one feminist I interviewed, there is a marked informality of relations between state and civil society actors precisely because those in each sphere have a shared history of activism, education, and friendship. This informality makes it hard sometimes to criticize the government for fear of being labeled a "traitor."

Another crucial factor contributing to the weakness of feminism in Chile is the "institutionalization" of gender policy in the state and what Sonia Alvarez has termed the "NGO-ization" of feminism. This has created profound divisions among feminists while also undermining feminists' capacity to take a more protagonistic role in setting the terms of public debate on many social issues. As well, there is a common perception that the movement lost many of its leaders when gender policy experts were invited into the state (see Matear 1997a; and Waylen 1997). According to Rosana Ceorino, "the co-optation of women's movement leaders by the state is something very real in Chile. It is very effective in disarticulating the movement."[32] Fanny Pollarrolo, former parliamentarian for the Socialist Party, noted that "important sectors of the movement have been absorbed into the state machinery. . . . This has put a brake on the movement's protagonism."[33] Despite this perception, Marcela Ríos, Lorena Godoy, and Elizabeth Guerrero's study (2004) found that it was more common for women from the political parties to move into the state and very rare for feminist leaders to do so. And as noted earlier, many of the feminists who ended up working in state agencies such as SERNAM continued to participate in feminist groups.

A more profound problem that emerged in Chile by the mid-1990s was the intense acrimony between the two strands of the feminist movement: the autónomas, who, in large part due to their visceral condemnation of all activities and activists linked to NGOs or the state, have relegated themselves to virtual irrelevance in Chile, and the institucionales, feminists who believe that working through NGOs or state agencies can be productive. The division between these two groups began taking form by 1993, when a national feminist *encuentro* (encounter or meeting) was held in Concepción. Feminist encuentros have been crucial to Latin American feminism, serving as "critical transnational sites in which local activists have refashioned and renegotiated identities, discourses, and practices distinctive of the region's feminists" (Alvarez et al. 2002, p. 537). At the Latin American level, feminist encuentros have been held every three years since 1981. For Chilean feminists, the central debates and shape of their movement have been fashioned through their participation in both the regional encuentros and their own national encuentros. What happened, unfortunately, was that at both the encuentros and other *foros feministas* (feminist forums) held in the country in the first half of the 1990s, Chile's self-declared autónomas increasingly dominated these spaces and used them to denounce the actions of feminists who chose to work in NGOs, political parties, or state agencies (Godoy and Guerrero 2001, p. 11). However, the terms of this debate, cast as one between autónomas and institucionales, also had the effect of ignoring an important segment of the women's movement that had emerged under the dictatorship—the "popular feminists." Godoy and Guerrero note that this segment of the movement "carried out different encuentros in which they discussed the existence of a popular feminism based on the reaffirmation of a class identity and the necessity of elaborating a feminist project that was Latin American, popular, and anti-capitalist" (Godoy and Guerrero 2001, p. 11). Throughout the 1990s, however, the presence of these organizations in the broader debates about feminism began to decrease. This further reinforces the class nature of the debates within contemporary feminism. Some middle-class feminists do not recognize the extent to which their framing of feminist debates excludes popular sector women. For example, despite the fairly strong assertions of a class identity that I was hearing from pobladora activists, at least one middle-class feminist noted in an interview that "popular sector women do not always establish the theme of class as a theme of identity."

With respect to the autónomas-institucionales debate, two events in the mid-1990s, the preparations for the 1995 Beijing World Conference on Women and the 1996 Latin American Encuentro, further intensified the distance between the two currents of the movement, closing off the possibility of fruitful dialogue or cooperation between them. The preparations for the 1995 Beijing Conference involved NGOs working with SERNAM and international funding agencies to hold consultations and gather ideas from women in all of Chile's thirteen regions.[34] According to Godoy and Guerrero, while this process reignited feminist mobilization, it did so in such a way as to deepen tensions among women. As the autónomas increasingly took over the preparations for the upcoming Latin American feminist encuentro to be held in Cartagena, their vocal criticisms of the institucionales led many women from the latter group to stay away from the Cartagena meeting (2001, p. 13). Sonia Alvarez and colleagues report that the 1996 Latin American Encuentro involved "an angry display of insults, accusations, recriminations, and vicious attacks, a behavior never seen before in an Encuentro and painful for all to watch" (2002, pp. 556–557).

As a result of the acrimony displayed at the 1996 Latin American Encuentro, Chile's autonomous feminists have rendered themselves even more isolated, and, according to many of the people with whom I spoke, irrelevant to women's movement politics today. Whenever a social movement undergoes such intense conflict, the complete withdrawal of some activists is common, as is the fragmentation of broader organizations into a host of smaller ones. The Chilean feminist movement has been subject to both tendencies. I spoke to some women who reported that their disgust over the level of conflict led them to stop participating completely, and others reported a proliferation of smaller and smaller collectives, working in relative isolation (see also Godoy and Guerrero 2001; Ríos 2003; and Ríos, Godoy, and Guerrero 2004).

The conflict between the autónomas and the institucionales is similar in some ways to the disagreements that emerged during the prodemocracy struggle between the *feministas* (autonomous feminists) and the *políticas* (political women) (discussed in Chapter 4). While the políticas believed that double militancy involved bringing feminist politics into the political parties, some of today's institucionales believe that feminist politics can be brought into state agencies, whether by working directly in SERNAM or other agencies or in NGOs that carry out work for state agencies. Thus the debate between autonomy and double militancy has shifted its terms of reference since the state has opened itself up to gender politics. This indicates the importance of state-level changes for social movement strategies. One major difference today, however, is that unlike the earlier debates between the feministas and the políticas, the two sides of the current conflict do not engage in any dialogue or debate, thus closing off the possibility that the movement will actually be strengthened by conflict. According to one woman I interviewed, "autonomous feminism in Chile has been a failure. I would say that it hasn't succeeded in convincing anyone."[35]

More significant, though, is the fact that the "institutional" label is rejected by many feminists today, even those who work in NGOs or state agencies. Rosana Ceorino, for example, noted that she makes a distinction between her job in an NGO working with women, and her commitment to feminism.[36] Her comments indicate the extent to which the autónoma-institucional distinction may be irrelevant to the self-understanding that feminists hold of their own activism. As a result of the absence of fruitful exchange, the autónomas continue to self-exclude themselves from activism linked to what is today the most visible face of feminism in Chile—feminist NGOs. According to Ríos, Godoy, and Guerrero (2004, pp. 188–192), the vast majority of Chile's feminists have worked at one time or another in NGOs. Feminists working through NGOs, however, face the dilemma of being institutionally oriented while also trying to regain the capacity to set a more radical agenda for social and political change. This owes in part to their complicated relationship with Concertación governments. Significantly, the Concertación includes leftist parties with whom many feminists had a history of either militancy or collaboration during the dictatorship (Ríos, Godoy, and Guerrero 2004, p. 259). This initially generated substantial optimism among feminists, while also making it harder to criticize government policy.

Feminist NGOs in Chile, staffed mainly by professionals, confront the challenge of maintaining their autonomy from SERNAM and the Concertación while trying to serve as channels for interlocution between grassroots women's groups and the state—to which NGOs have somewhat greater access. NGOs in Chile today are particularly hard-hit by the drastic reduction in international funding. According to Teresa Valdés, the reduction in international funding has generated significant conflict within the women's movement as a whole and especially between organizations with access to scarce resources and those without such access.[37] Valdés concluded that, partly owing to the struggle to obtain funding, the "NGO-ization" of feminism contributes to its moderation:

> When you have an NGO that has cost you so much time to maintain and everything, the protection, sustainability, and maintenance of the NGO takes up much energy in acquiring resources, versus a logic of "movement" which is much more confrontational, with its own agenda. That's how something as concrete as financing generates such great tensions.

Valdés also pointed out that the autonomy of NGOs in Chile was being lost because of their need for state contracts simply to survive: "If NGOs had their own resources, the discussions around autonomy would be totally different than when you have to go presenting bids to SERNAM." She noted that NGOs that have been too critical of SERNAM or the government have been marginalized. Lorena Fríes of La Morada similarly commented on the difficulties inherent in the relationship between NGOs and the state in Chile today:

> It's not easy. There's a certain tendency toward informality and to lose respect for the different roles that each one has. For example, it may happen that SERNAM feels that Grupo Iniciativa [an NGO network] is a traitor because we haven't supported them. Or, it can be thought that Adriana Delpiano [then SERNAM's minister] is not fulfilling what she ought to be from the perspective of NGOs.[38]

Fríes's comments relate to another problem for feminist NGOs, one that involves the nature of the relationship among NGOs, Concertación governments, and state agencies like SERNAM. The tendency in recent years has been for feminists to move frequently among the different arenas, working for a time in SERNAM and then in an NGO, while also being a member of a leftist party.[39] Natacha Molina, for example, is currently a researcher at the Instituto de la Mujer (Women's Institute), an NGO, but was formerly a subdirector of SERNAM.[40] Ríos, Godoy, and Guerrero note that the work and professional links among Chile's feminists "generate a complex and many times promiscuous network of relationships" (2004, p. 259). The problem with this, according to Fríes, is that it has been extremely difficult for feminist NGOs to interact with the government on a *political* level. The fact that many of the links among the Concertación government, state agencies, and NGOs are based on personal relationships undermines the construction of more formalized political relationships whereby movement actors retain more independence. Fríes explained, "the access to the state that [feminist NGOs] enjoy is, because, for example, the sub-secretary of the presidency was a friend of someone who was here, or because they had participated earlier in a political party together."[41] This type of informal/personal relationship is a problem, however, because it seriously complicates the role of feminist NGOs as critics of government policy. The less feminist NGOs are willing or able to act as critics of state policy, the more the autónomas are likely to feel vindicated in their criticism of a double militancy strategy.

Others criticize state agencies and SERNAM in particular for trying to co-opt NGOs and grassroots organizations. ANAMURI (discussed further in the next section) takes immense pride in its autonomy from the state, despite the fact that, according to Francisca Rodríguez, one of the organization's leaders, "it is a constant struggle to seek financing for our activities."[42] But as Rodríguez also explained, while ANAMURI may seek funding from SERNAM, it will not carry out projects for SERNAM:

> We are not going to run behind this merry-go-round of being summoned for projects, because that is the characteristic of the subsidiary state, which every day is summoning for different projects and the whole world chases after these projects because of a problem of resources and ends up applying the policies of the state and abandoning the political proposals and the plans of their organization.

Rodríguez's comments raise an extremely important point: women's organizations and NGOs are in danger of depoliticizing their goals if they become too engaged in carrying out government projects. Although a women's movement may include actors located both within and outside the state, the nonstate aspect of the movement must have the necessary autonomy and organizational strength to continue to make the political demands deemed necessary to expanding citizenship for women from diverse social locations. Indeed, for many women the ability to make political demands, to have a political voice, is a key aspect of exercising citizenship. This is precisely why grassroots leaders are so critical of the ways in which the Concertación's rhetoric of citizen participation fails to be turned into reality. Ana Pichulmán, for example, explained to me that state agencies are only open to grassroots organizations if the organization fits precisely the theme or issue that the state agency has defined as a priority. She argues, however, that there needs to be more room for organizations to define the relevant issues and themes themselves, rather than having to fit what the state wants to do.[43]

New Directions in Women's Activism

The fragmentation of women's movements is problematic because it has undermined the possibility of publicizing women's issues through, for example, mass events to raise awareness and put pressure on governments. During my time in Chile, on the few occasions where events were held—for example, an event to celebrate rural women and another to protest an extremely sexist ad campaign for a Santiago radio station—they were poorly attended and received scant media attention. Likewise, Marcela Ríos notes that each year on March 8, International Women's Day, there are more and more separate events being held, with no single event attracting more than a couple hundred women (2003, p. 263). Others note that on these occasions, the divisions in the movement become very clear, as each current organizes its own separate event.[44] This trend is problematic, according to Paulina Weber, of MEMCH, because "if you don't have a strong social force of women, they [the government] are not going to pay any attention to you."[45] Lorena Fríes told me much the same thing. Because feminists are unable to influence public opinion, the government does not feel the need to rely on them as bases of political support.[46]

Many organized women realize this, and consequently there are a number of NGOs and grassroots organizations that identify as their main goal the fostering of a broader-based women's movement capable of pushing forward the public agenda on women's rights and equality. In terms of rebuilding a broader women's movement with more linkages among disparate groups, an important development at the grassroots level of civil society is the formation of two umbrella organizations: REMOS and ANAMURI. REMOS emerged precisely because a number of organized women were concerned that while popular sector women remained active, they did so in small, isolated groups with little awareness of each other's activities.[47] Thus there was little capacity for large-scale mobilizations that could bring government and societal attention to their problems, most notably lack of adequate housing, decent employment opportunities, and poor access to healthcare. REMOS formed initially in 1996 with thirty member groups; it grew to over fifty. The main goal of REMOS, according to Mercedes Montoya, was "to strengthen ourselves as an organization, or, rather, not that one [group] would be over here, the other over there, and the other way over there. We have to know how to find each other and strengthen ourselves. Interchange was what was needed."[48]

While the emergence of REMOS was linked to the desire to overcome the fragmentation of the popular sector women's movement, its current strategies are clearly linked to the context provided by SERNAM. REMOS describes its aims as "serv[ing] as a channel for interlocution with public and private institutions" and "promot[ing] popular sector women's participation in public spaces."[49] Ana Pichulmán explained that REMOS aimed "to prepare popular sector women to have a voice so that the government will consider their interests."[50] This means that members of REMOS are aware of and making very real use of the institutional and discursive transformations that have occurred over the past decade, most notably the existence of SERNAM and the discourse of women's rights and equality that it has promoted. Members of REMOS believe that in order to yield further results, they need to pressure the state to fulfill its commitments. When asked what the relationship between the state and REMOS should be like, Montoya explained that "we have to take part in actions that the government carries out and we have to follow and watch. In other words, we'll be saying to them, 'Listen, what's happening with this, or what's happening with that law?' . . . Here, we as an organization are carrying out our goals of being an organization that concerns itself with the government's plans."[51] To carry this out, REMOS holds monthly or bimonthly meetings where the member groups select issues relevant to their communities, such as health, education, or other municipal services. The constituent groups then monitor their municipalities' compliance with aspects of the Equal Opportunity Plan or other programs that relate to these issues. In this way, members generate increased awareness of the state's gender policy and the extent to which it is being implemented effectively. This means that the equality goals established by SERNAM become priorities for REMOS—an important segment of the broader women's movement. This contributes significantly to the movement's remobilization around a clearer set of purposes.

There are two additional reasons why REMOS is significant. First, the mere process of linking up dispersed organizations is crucial to the reconstitution of the women's movement as a collective actor seeking a more inclusive citizenship. While it is still too early to measure the success of REMOS in terms of policy outcomes, it is significant that nearly all of the popular sector women with whom I spoke—women from at least six different communities in Santiago—emphasized the importance of this network to the women's movement in Chile. While women could say little at this point about concrete policy successes, they all acknowledged that the network was recapturing something that had been lost in the immediate aftermath of the transition to democracy, namely a strong sense of their collective identity as *popular sector women* and their critical role in the nation's democratic political project. As Montoya explained to me, "we are not just any women—we are women from the popular sectors."

The second reason that REMOS is significant is revealed in Montoya's comment. The network reminds us that women are not a homogeneous group. Instead, members of REMOS insist that women have different interests depending upon their social location, and therefore priority must be given to both class and gender issues. To a certain extent, the emphasis on both class and gender issues recalls the discourse of the women's movement during the dictatorship, when there was more interchange between popular sector organizations and middle-class activists. In part, greater attention to the interconnectedness of class and gender issues could be expected due to the cross-class nature of the prodemocracy movement as a whole, but it was also related to the existence of the profound economic crisis of the early 1980s, when it was impossible to ignore the overwhelming problems created by poverty and social marginalization. In the late 1980s and early 1990s, economic recovery, the return to democracy, and the focus on SERNAM as the agency for dealing with gender equality issues all shifted attention away from the needs of Chile's poor. REMOS is significant for its efforts to draw attention back to the very real problems of poverty, unemployment, and continued social marginalization, and to insist that gender policy address these problems. However, the extent to which some middle-class feminists in Chile do not consider "popular feminism" a contributor to the key debates in feminism indicates that networks like REMOS still have a long way to go in gaining greater recognition.

ANAMURI, the other network that focuses attention on class and ethnicity in Chile, is rooted in rural women's organizing, and also emerged due to concerns over the lack of linkages among organized women, and a frustration that even though the state employed a discourse of women's equality, it was paying little attention to the particular needs of rural and indigenous women. ANAMURI formed in June 1998, initially representing fifty base organizations and regional networks of rural or indigenous women. It is firmly rooted in both the campesino (rural) movement and the women's movement. Consequently, its objectives are to incorporate gender issues into the world of rural organizing and to ensure that the particularities of rural and indigenous women are addressed when discussing women's issues, especially in state institutions.[52]

Like REMOS, ANAMURI prizes its independence, yet sees interaction with the state as crucial to realizing its aims. Francisca Rodríguez insists that autonomy from both the state and political parties is a key objective of ANAMURI.[53] With respect to SERNAM, ANAMURI is critical of the extent to which the specific needs of rural and indigenous women have been ignored, a lack of concern evident in their complete absence in the first Equal Opportunity Plan. At the same time, however, ANAMURI recognizes the advantage of having an agency such as SERNAM. For example, Rodríguez explains that SERNAM is important because women "now have a point of departure that is different." She adds that women must now use this institutional space to push for greater attention to their particular concerns and to ensure that SERNAM considers class and ethnicity in addition to gender as sources of inequality and discrimination.

ANAMURI has attracted a great deal of attention recently because of its aim to remobilize a segment of the women's movement that was both highly visible and highly mobilized during the dictatorship.[54] Both AMAMURI and REMOS formed out of a sense of frustration that SERNAM was giving insufficient attention to issues relevant to particular sectors of women, while also admitting that SERNAM's existence was crucial to the overall struggle for women's equality in Chile. Thus, while SERNAM provides these groups with a discourse of women's rights and equality around which to mobilize, both groups are motivated by a sense that a discourse of *women's* rights is insufficient if it ignores the variety of sources of marginalization that women experience.[55]

Both networks expressly view SERNAM and other state agencies as targets for pressure from civil society to ensure that state commitments to women are fulfilled. Hence their strategies are inextricably linked to the new institutional context that SERNAM provides. Both networks represent societal responses to state-level changes that provide opportunities for movements to mobilize. However, these state-level changes have also altered the power relations among segments of the movement in such a way as to privilege some while excluding others. Leaders of REMOS and ANAMURI feel that the relationship between the NGO sector and SERNAM privileges the concerns of middle-class women while weakening policy goals that take into account the needs of poor, working-class, rural, and indigenous women. At the same time, the responses of REMOS and ANAMURI to focus attention on the multiplicity of sources of women's inequality restore the class and indigenous issues that had been central to the women's movement in the 1970s and 1980s.

Another development of considerable significance is the formation of Grupo Iniciativa (Initiative Group), an umbrella network composed of eleven NGOs, most of which are feminist oriented. The group sees its role as gathering the demands of women within civil society and presenting them to the state. The initial motivation to form Grupo Iniciativa emerged during the preparations for the 1995 Beijing World Conference on Women, when it coordinated the activities of Chilean NGOs. After the conference, however, the group decided to maintain its organization and expand its activities.[56] Grupo Iniciativa was aware of and concerned about the lack of spaces for women to participate in the formulation of the policy agenda of the government. It sees its current role as being a facilitator and bridge for such contact. Grupo Iniciativa argues that the Chilean women's movement needs a multifaceted strategy for pursuing gender equality in which women's organizations in civil society play a much bigger role. One of its documents explains that, "today, many of the actions carried out have been focused on elaborating and presenting demands to the state, neglecting both the strengthening of the women's movement, and the construction of its own discourse which could permeate all of society" (Grupo Iniciativa Chile 1994, p. 29). Moreover, as Paulina Weber of MEMCH (an NGO member of Grupo Iniciativa) explains, "we are convinced that SERNAM cannot be a substitute for civil society," especially because there are many issues (like abortion) that SERNAM will not raise.[57]

Grupo Iniciativa is perhaps the first women's lobby group that has emerged since the transition to democracy. Its main strategy is to monitor state actions and to lobby the state to fulfill commitments to women that are embodied in international agreements such as the UN Convention on the Elimination of All Forms of Discrimination Against Women (CEDAW) and Chile's own Equal Opportunity Plans. To this end, in 1997, Grupo Iniciativa successfully lobbied the government of Eduardo Frei to sign an "act of commitment" to implement and to follow through on the commitments made at Beijing, especially to expanding the presence of women in spheres of decisionmaking. The public signing of this act in the presence of key government officials was the first part of Grupo Iniciativa's National Forum for the Following of the Beijing Accords. In signing the act, the government committed itself both to abstract goals, such as eliminating discrimination against women in their access to the state, as well as to concrete measures, such as assigning resources to women, and especially to maintaining the Civil Society Fund (Grupo Iniciativa 1997, pp. 6–7).

More recently, Grupo Iniciativa has developed concrete tools for carrying out "citizen control." One of the key criticisms of SERNAM has been the difficulty of actually measuring or evaluating the extent to which it is effective.[58] Thus, Grupo Iniciativa—which is composed of many research-oriented NGOs like FLACSO and CEM—elaborated the "Indice de Compromiso Cumplido" (Index of Fulfilled Commitments), which includes a system of indicators through which the group can measure the state's compliance with various international agreements and SERNAM's Equal Opportunity Plan (Grupo Iniciativa 1999c). One of the benefits of this system is that evaluations of government initiatives can be somewhat more objective than previous evaluations, which relied on subjective indicators such as interviews with program beneficiaries and opinion polls of citizens. Teresa Valdés explains that increased objectivity can also lead to greater autonomy for Grupo Iniciativa in its dealings with the state.[59]

Perhaps the most important priority of Grupo Iniciativa is to articulate the demands of the women's movement as a whole, using public spaces such as the media. To that end, the group elaborated the "Nueva Agenda" (New Agenda) of the women's movement for the new millennium and published it as a supplement in one of Chile's newspapers, "hop[ing] to contribute to the strengthening of civil society's role in the construction of democracy" (Grupo Iniciativa 1999a, p. 2). This document is important because it emanates from civil society, and hence the demands for women's equality are more radical than those made from within the state, either in the Equal Opportunity Plan or in legislation proposed by SERNAM or women parliamentarians. The "Nueva Agenda," therefore, could and did raise the issue that women's sexual and reproductive rights are key to women's equality. It could also highlight the growing inequality among women produced by the state's neoliberal policies, and strongly denounce the massive inequality suffered by indigenous, rural, and popular sector women.

Despite Grupo Iniciativa's reference to class and ethnic inequality in Chile today, there are those who criticize its leaders for trying to speak for or represent popular sector and indigenous women rather than giving women from these groups the space to represent their own interests. According to Rosana Ceorino, some NGOs (she did not say which ones) still believe that they should be leaders of the women's movement as a whole. In her view, such a position is problematic because it fails to make a separation between working in a feminist NGO (as a job) and being an activist in the feminist movement (a political and social commitment).[60] While she was clearly not saying that one's political commitments have no place in one's work, she seemed to be implying that representing interests is something that should grow out of one's political and social location, not one's professional location. Other NGO feminists whom I interviewed made a point of insisting that they have never claimed to represent women from other class positions, and that popular sector women must represent their own interests.[61]

Whatever the conflict among them, REMOS, ANAMURI, and Grupo Iniciativa are indicators of the movement's reconstitution. Their existence, together with the strategies they employ, indicates that earlier pronouncements that the institutionalization of gender politics in the state weakens women's movements are no longer entirely accurate in the case of Chile. The isolation of smaller women's groups is slowly being overcome, and network organizations are employing SERNAM's own discourses to mobilize women and to pressure the state to fulfill its commitments to women. Even more important, these networks go beyond SERNAM's priorities and refocus attention on class and ethnicity as bases of women's marginalization that need to be addressed at the same time as gender. What is less clear is whether a reconstituted women's movement in Chile can successfully put feminist ideas on the public agenda and begin to challenge the negative stereotypes that feminism continues to have in the country.

Conclusion

In this chapter I have argued that the women's movement has been affected in important ways by the transition to democracy, the discourse of neoliberalism, and state feminism. These trends have created a number of obstacles for the women's movement, and for feminists in particular, to the extent that the movement appears to have lost much of its capacity to mobilize around a political agenda for women's citizenship—especially a citizenship that includes socioeconomic rights. The transition to democracy left the movement without an overarching goal that could strategically link its diverse segments, and state feminism has created profound divisions among feminists. Therefore, a major challenge today for organized women is to find themes and issues to bring together diversely situated women in mobilizations or campaigns around women's issues. Although SERNAM is clearly contributing to this process, its role is not without complications, as shown in the previous chapter.

Another problem for the movement is the emphasis on stability and the neoliberal socioeconomic model, which has a demobilizing effect on all social movements in Chile. The loss of funding from the Catholic Church and international agencies has led community organizations and women's movements to look to the state for resources. This has induced competition among groups, further undermining solidarity, especially between activists with professional credentials and those without. It has also renewed debates about movement autonomy, this time not from political parties but from the state. NGOs that rely heavily on income from government contracts fear that they are losing their capacity to be critical advocates for feminist policy goals (Alvarez 1999). The profound disagreement between the autonomous and institutionalist segments of the movement further erodes the possibility of building a stronger movement capable of putting feminist issues on the public agenda.

Changes at the state level in Chile have therefore profoundly reshaped the terrain on which the women's movement and feminist politics are carried out. In order for the women's movement to improve women's capacities to exercise citizenship, at least two things must occur. First, more enduring and bottom-up linkages need to be forged between women's organizations with access to the state and those without. This would be one way of mitigating the negative impact of the informal-formal politics dichotomy. Women's organizations must be able to transmit their interests to those who participate in formal politics. Second, feminists in Chile must find ways to challenge more successfully the negative image of feminism and the overall invisibility of feminist activism. While the first of these processes appears to have begun, signified by the emergence of REMOS, ANAMURI, and Grupo Iniciativa, the second process has yet to begin. While it is not entirely clear what might provoke a remobilized feminist movement in Chile, I recall a conversation I had with one feminist during the 1999 electoral campaign after an opinion poll indicated that Socialist Party candidate Ricardo Lagos and Independent Democratic Union candidate Joaquín Lavín were virtually tied in their popular support. She ironically commented that nothing would reignite the feminist movement more quickly than a victory by a conservative political leader such as Lavín. Although this comment was offered in an offhand manner, it is nonetheless quite revealing. It implies that feminists have become too complacent and may require a more unambiguous "enemy" against which to organize.

Notes

1. The extent of unity in the dictatorship-era movement must also not be overstated. As I showed in Chapter 4, there were numerous conflicts over both strategy and goals.
2. Interview with Paulina Weber, October 21, 1999, Santiago.

3. Interview with Felisa Garay, August 26, 1999, Santiago.

4. This perception was mentioned in interviews with Rosana Ceorino, October 6, 1999, Santiago; Lorena Fríes, July 19, 2002, Santiago; and Teresa Valdés, November 3, 1999, and July 26, 2002, Santiago.

5. Interview with Mercedes Montoya, October 4, 1999, Santiago.

6. Interviews with Ana Pichulmán, July 15, 2002, Santiago; Mercedes Montoya, October 4, 1999, Santiago; Francisca Rodríguez, August 31, 1999, Santiago; and Felisa Garay, August 26, 1999, Santiago.

7. Interview with Teresa Valdés, July 26, 2002.

8. Interview with Rosana Ceorino, October 6, 1999, Santiago.

9. Interview with Lorena Fríes, July 19, 2002, Santiago.

10. Interview with Rosana Ceorino, October 6, 1999, Santiago.

11. Interview with Lorena Fríes, July 19, 2002, Santiago.

12. Interview with Francisca Rodríguez, August 31, 1999, Santiago.

13. Interview with Valeria Ambrosio, October 5, 1999, Santiago.

14. This point was made to me by Marcela Ríos, based on her recent study of feminism in the postdictatorship era. Personal communication with Marcela Ríos, November 7, 2004. Rosana Ceorino of Tierra Nuestra made a similar comment in an interview. Interview with Rosana Ceorino, October 6, 1999, Santiago.

15. Interview with Lorena Fríes, July 19, 2002, Santiago.

16. Interview with Francisca Rodríguez, August 31, 1999, Santiago.

17. Interview with Mercedes Montoya, October 4, 1999, Santiago.

18. The following information is drawn from an interview with two of the group's leaders, Myriam Gonzáles and María Molina, October 20, 1999, Santiago.

19. The following information is drawn from observations from my attendance at a meeting of the group on October 21, 1999, and an interview with two of the group's leaders, Laura del Carmen Veloso and Tatania Escalera, November 8, 1999, Santiago.

20. Interview with Myriam Gonzáles and María Molina, October 20, 1999, Santiago.

21. Interview with Ana María Órdenes, August 23, 1999, Santiago. Of course, as I noted in Chapter 6, fostering links between civil society organizations and the state was never part of SERNAM's mandate. Instead, it was designed to be a policy coordinating body.

22. Interview with Lorena Fríes, July 19, 2002, Santiago.

23. Interview with Mercedes Montoya, October 4, 1999, Santiago.

24. Interviews with Delia del Gato, August 20, 1999, Santiago; and Valeria Ambrosio, October 5, 1999, Santiago.

25. Interview with Myriam González and María Molina, October 20, 1999, Santiago.

26. Interview with Mercedes Montoya, October 4, 1999, Santiago.

27. Interview with Myriam González and María Molina, October 20, 1999, Santiago.

28. Ana Pichulmán also made this point in an interview, July 15, 2002, Santiago.

29. See Richards (2004) for a fuller elaboration of this phenomenon and how it is viewed by popular sector and indigenous women.

30. Interview with Ana Pichulmán, July 15, 2002, Santiago.

31. Interview with Mercedes Montoya, October 4, 1999, Santiago.

32. Interview with Rosana Ceorino, October 6, 1999, Santiago.

33. Interview with Fanny Pollarrolo, July 29, 2002, Santiago.

34. Interview with Teresa Valdés, November 3, 1999, Santiago.

35. Interview with Mercedes Montoya, October 4, 1999, Santiago.
36. Interview with Rosana Ceorino, October 6, 1999, Santiago.
37. Interview with Teresa Valdés, November 3, 1999, Santiago.
38. Interview with Lorena Fríes, July 19, 2002, Santiago.
39. According to the study by Ríos, Godoy, and Guerrero (2004), party militancy is less typical for younger feminists, but very common among the older generation.
40. Interview with Natacha Molina, July 16, 2002, Santiago.
41. Interview with Lorena Fríes, July 19, 2002, Santiago.
42. Interview with Francisca Rodríguez, August 31, 1999, Santiago.
43. Interview with Ana Pichulmán, July 15, 2002, Santiago.
44. Interview with Rosana Ceorino, October 6, 1999, Santiago.
45. Interview with Paulina Weber, October 21, 1999, Santiago.
46. Interview with Lorena Fríes, July 19, 2002, Santiago.
47. Most of the information that follows comes from interviews with Mercedes Montoya, then director of REMOS, October 4, 1999, Santiago; Ana María Órdenes, of SOL, August 23, 1999, Santiago; and Ana Pichulmán, president of REMOS, July 15, 2002, Santiago. Additional information was drawn from numerous informal conversations with women whose smaller organizations were members of REMOS.
48. Interview with Mercedes Montoya, October 4, 1999, Santiago.
49. These aims are stated in a pamphlet inviting popular sector women's groups to join REMOS.
50. Interview with Ana Pichulmán, July 15, 2002, Santiago.
51. Interview with Mercedes Montoya, October 4, 1999, Santiago.
52. A statement of these objectives is found on the program for their first meeting, held June 11–13, 1998, Santiago.
53. Interview with Francisca Rodríguez, July 19, 2002, Santiago.
54. The women's department of the rural labor movement was critical to the emergence of a women's movement in Chile in the late 1970s, and most important, a movement that was firmly committed to struggling for *both* gender and class emancipation (Gaviola, Largo, and Palestro 1994, pp. 87–88).
55. See Richards (2004) for a detailed analysis of the way SERNAM has addressed the problems of women's difference in Chile.
56. Interview with Teresa Valdés, July 26, 2002, Santiago.
57. Interview with Paulina Weber, October 21, 1999, Santiago.
58. Ibid.
59. Interview with Teresa Valdés, November 3, 1999, Santiago.
60. Interview with Rosana Ceorino, October 6, 1999, Santiago.
61. Interview with Lorena Fríes, July 19, 2002, Santiago.

8 Gendered Citizenship and the Future of Chilean Democracy

Chilean citizens, both women and men, struggled throughout the twentieth century to make democracy and citizenship more meaningful. These struggles continue. As I have shown throughout this book, there are numerous shortcomings in Chile's new democracy, shortcomings that undermine citizenship for women, the poor, the working class, and indigenous peoples. To a very great extent, therefore, women's efforts to improve their citizenship cannot be separated from the task of deepening Chile's democracy. This is especially true once we acknowledge differences among women. Women's movements in Chile, both historically and today, do not just advance the interests of women as a group, but often voice the demands of particular groups of women, with some focusing on class inequality, others on ethnic inequality, while others claim to be acting in the interests of all women, despite differences that produce gendered experiences that are mediated by class, ethnicity, generation, and sexual orientation.

In this final chapter, I conclude by returning to the four themes raised in Chapter 1: the politics of difference, movement autonomy versus double militancy, women and electoral politics, and women and states. I address these four issues by asking what each one means for women's citizenship in Chile today, while also trying to draw out some of the comparative lessons from studying the Chilean case. Revisiting these four themes also shows the extent to which struggles for women's citizenship in each of the arenas that I explored in the book—electoral politics, bureaucratic politics, and movement politics—are interconnected.

Politics of Difference

While feminist theorists have long debated the question of whether women should demand citizenship rights based on their fundamental equality with men or on their difference, my study of women's politics in Chile reveals that movement strategies and collective action frames emerge out of the legacies of earlier social struggles and from the prevailing political context. What this means is that difference frames will carry different meanings as political contexts change. The main "difference" that sets women apart is, of course, their capacity to be mothers. According to Carole Pateman, "childbirth and motherhood have symbolized the natural capacities that set women apart from politics and citizenship; motherhood and citizenship in this perspective, like difference and equality, are mutually exclusive" (1992, p. 18).

Yet women's movements in Chile have demanded both political and social citizenship rights on the basis of women's maternal identities. Significantly though, the meanings attached to motherhood, particularly its relevance for defining other aspects of social relations, have changed quite dramatically. While first-wave feminists in Chile emphasized the fundamentally apolitical aspect of motherhood, arguing that it transcended the political world, albeit a political world that was viewed as entirely constituted by partisan activities and identities, second-wave activists operated in an environment where maternal roles had been politicized. Moreover, politics was viewed as much broader than simply the activities of political parties.

Now that democracy has returned to Chile and politics has again been discursively restricted to partisan activities, what place does motherhood have for women's movements? As Nikki Craske points out, while motherhood has been a strategically useful mobilizer for Latin American women, "motherhood is not a biological function. Rather, its characteristics are culturally defined, and mutate across class, generation, race, and ethnicity" (1999, p. 196). So, in the present context, what sort of collective action frame for demanding rights and equality is likely to emerge? Unfortunately, there is no clear answer to this question yet. However, the legacy of the "mobilized mother" still exists in Chile's collective historical memory. Many people with whom I spoke, both women and men, recounted with pride the role of previously unorganized women, mostly housewives and mothers, in helping to defeat the dictatorship. This legacy, combined with the dominance of conservative views and traditional images of families and women's roles within them, means that we are unlikely to see a successful women's movement that does not somehow acknowledge the importance of women's caretaking roles. Chile remains one of the countries with the lowest portion of women in the work force. Societal attitudes reinforce this: a 2002 public opinion survey showed 66.7 percent of Chileans agreeing that, while having a job is okay, most women "want a home and children." More significant, 83 percent of respondents believed that preschool-aged children "suffer if their mother works" (Centros de Estudios Públicos 2002). In this context, women's movements that do not appeal to the importance of motherhood will find it harder to mobilize and attract new activists. However, it is also clear that as Chile's society is increasingly transformed through neoliberalism and its culture of modern consumerism, the image of traditional motherhood is likewise undergoing change. Unfortunately, this change appears to be led by the political right, who have been quite successful in giving new content to the meaning of modern womanhood.

According to some of the women I interviewed, the rightist parties, namely the RN and the UDI, have realized that young female candidates are attractive to voters. Thus, parties on the right rather than the left are experiencing relatively more "turnover" in terms of attracting a new generation of young female leaders. Similarly, a large part of the "Lavín phenomenon" in the second round of the 1999 presidential campaign was the role played by Lavín's wife, María Estela León. According to one observer, "young, modest, and attractive, her involvement was that of wife and mother. . . . Feminist discourse has a following in Chile, of course, but this family-centered mother of seven seemed to speak to the legions of women who are 'housewives' or who work only for money, and who were crying out for validation" (Fontaine 2000, p. 73).

Indeed, in the run-off election between Lavín and Lagos, Chilean women continued the tradition of supporting the conservative candidate: 51.3 percent of women voted for Lavín compared to only 45.7 percent of men. On the other hand, 54.2 percent of men voted for Lagos, compared to 48.6 percent of women.[1] This phenomenon needs further research in Chile. What will happen to women's equality struggles if political conservatives take the initiative in transforming the image of what it means to be a modern woman in Chile? While their vision rests on motherhood, it also rests on a subservient role for women, one that does not challenge a gendered model of citizenship whereby men lead and women's primary role is motherhood. This is not the vision that feminists in Chile have, which is that, while motherhood is valued, responsibility for caretaking must be shared more equally between men and women, and must also be publicly supported. Most important, women must have the capacity to choose whether or not to be mothers.

Even more significant, the image of the young modern mother that is deployed by the political right does not recognize differences among women, namely class and ethnic differences, but rather puts forth the ideal of a light-skinned middle-class woman. In today's Chile, where social inequality is worsening despite overall growth in the economy, the interaction of gender, class, and ethnic inequalities is more likely to shape the future of the women's movement. The language of difference in the current context, therefore, is more likely to involve debates over the relevant bases of difference and how public policy and social movement activism should address them. Given the extent of class and ethnic inequality in Chile, these debates are likely to remain quite contentious.

Autonomy Versus Double Militancy

Debates over whether to pursue "insider" versus "outsider" strategies confront all social movements at some point in time. For women's movements, autonomy is taken to mean exclusive participation in women's organizations and a conscious rejection of working through existing institutions and political parties. Double militancy, according to Karen Beckwith, is defined as "the location of activist women in two political venues, with participatory, collective identity, and ideological commitments to both" (2000, p. 442). However, both strategies are also influenced by the prevailing political context. Most important, because double militancy involves participation in two locations (women's movements and political parties or political institutions) and the promotion of women's gender-based interests in the latter, it assumes the existence of a fairly strong women's movement as well as parties or political institutions that at least permit, and perhaps even encourage, feminists to pursue some of their goals beyond movement organizations. The latter is likely to occur only when political parties or government leaders perceive some advantages (electoral or otherwise) from addressing women's equality demands. Hence the political opportunity structure will determine the potential for feminist alliances with parties and the very possibility of a double militancy strategy.

The Chilean case provides several valuable insights about the advantages and disadvantages of either strategy. First, the choice of autonomy or double militancy in both feminist and partisan politics cannot be separated from the nature of the women's movement overall and the broader political context in which it emerges. As I argued in Chapter 3, first-wave feminists' choice of autonomy stemmed from their difference politics and their belief that women's organizations were not political in the same way parties were. In the 1980s, in contrast, women's movements reemerged in Chile in the relative absence of political parties, thereby reducing any immediate need for activists to make the choice of autonomy or double militancy. It was not until political parties regained their historical dominance that women's organizations were confronted with the very serious dilemma of whether to remain autonomous or work through parties to achieve their goals. In brief, the Chilean case shows that the very nature of the autonomy versus double militancy issue is determined by the political context, especially the role of traditional political actors and the type of movement that exists—that is, whether it is pursuing a gender-differentiated or gender-neutral model of citizenship.

Second, the Chilean case shows that the strategies of autonomy versus double militancy are both useful, but *at different points* in the emergence of movements and the elaboration of movement demands. In Chapter 4, I argued that it was in large part the relative autonomy of the women's movement from political parties that allowed women to assemble a feminist critique of traditional Chilean political practice for its marginalization of women. This critique was crucial to the elaboration of a set of feminist demands of democracy. But for feminist demands to form part of the public agenda, women's movements need to adopt a double militancy strategy. If key segments of the Chilean women's movement had not chosen to work within the broader prodemocracy movement, it is highly unlikely that feminist goals would have formed part of the agenda for the transition to democracy. Movement autonomy, therefore, is a crucial resource when movement demands are being formulated. In the absence of pressure from male-dominated organizations, feminists are more free to challenge practices that reinforce masculine monopolization of political space. But if movements remain autonomous, their very autonomy can mean that the issues they raise also remain marginalized and absent from the public arena. Thus a double militancy strategy through which feminists insert their goals into party policy is more likely to realize the goal of putting feminist issues on the public agenda.

In the current posttransition environment, however, the terms of the debate over autonomy and double militancy shifted dramatically as the state itself opened up to gender politics. This created a new division between the self-designated autónomas and the institucionales. However, as the study of feminists conducted by Marcela Ríos, Lorena Godoy, and Elizabeth Guerrero (2004) finds, with the exception of a small segment of rigidly "anti-institutional" autónomas, many feminists in Chile move quite effortlessly among different arenas, whether women's consciousness-raising groups, NGOs, or state agencies like SERNAM. But it is important to note that women who do this, mainly middle-class and professional feminists, have the capacity to move in and out of institutional arenas because of their relatively privileged social position. The other important segment of today's women's movement, the popular sector and indigenous women's organizations, cannot move freely between state and nonstate arenas because they simply do not enjoy such access to formal politics. Thus, power differences among women that are shaped by class and ethnic inequality play a crucial role in shaping the terms of debate over autonomy versus double militancy. In brief, double militancy may be desirable for movement actors, but it is not always an option that is available. Instead, the Chilean case shows that power relations shape the kind of opportunities that are available to social movements and the various segments that compose them.

Women and Electoral Politics

Despite optimism that the protagonism of women's movements during the prodemocracy struggle would reduce the barriers to women's entry into formal politics, Chilean politics continues to be an inhospitable realm for women. As I argued in Chapter 5, political parties continue to resist the types of reforms, particularly candidate gender quotas, that would increase women's participation in electoral politics. This represents a major shortcoming in deepening Chile's democracy, because equal access to arenas of influence and power is an important aspect of political citizenship. More significant, improving women's citizenship requires improving women's sense that they are effectively represented in politics. Legislatures that predominantly contain men do not improve women's sense of being represented. However, merely increasing the number of women elected (numerical representation) does not automatically improve the promotion of women's gender interests in politics (substantive representation).

Given that increasing women's numerical representation is an important goal of women's movements, feminists, and even SERNAM, it is important to probe deeper and investigate the extent to which meeting this goal can actually improve the substantive representation of women's interests. The Chilean case shows that there are numerous factors that undermine a more positive link between numerical and substantive representation. First, the dominance of moral and social conservatism in the political class, combined with the weakness of the feminist movement, makes it difficult for women in politics to be aggressive advocates for women's gender interests. The parties of the right have successfully defined the political agenda on many moral issues, particularly the issue of reproductive rights. While they lost the battle on divorce, it is significant that it took fourteen years to bring about legislation that permits Chileans to legally dissolve their marriages. In a context where feminists have little capacity to set the public agenda on women's issues, political parties do not feel the need to respond to feminist issues to win votes. Hence, women who aspire to elected office cannot use their links to women's movements as a support base to enter politics. Instead, according to some of the women I interviewed, women prefer to downplay their support for feminist issues in order to gain support from party leaders. Thus, while the goal of increasing the number of women in elected office remains important, for political women to be effective in promoting women's gender interests, women's movements and feminists must regain some degree of public visibility and electoral influence.

A second factor that undermines a positive relationship between numerical and substantive representation is the heterogeneity of women and the absence of linkages between the different segments of the women's movement in Chile today. In this context, it is difficult for women in politics to promote women's gender interests, because the content of those interests is unclear. As Jill Vickers argues, we need to be careful about making a claim for representation based on women's difference while repressing differences among women by emphasizing "sisterhood" (1997b, p. 28). Women's interests are not determined solely by their gender, but are given further content by class, race, generational, and ethnic identities. In Chile, class and ethnic inequalities have not been substantially reduced, despite repeated commitments by Concertación leaders to "growth with equality" and to repaying the "social debt" of the dictatorship. Consequently, popular sector and indigenous women in Chile, even when organizing primarily in women's groups, remain adamant that their class and ethnic identities are every bit as important to shaping their daily lives as is their gender (Richards 2004). However, because the arena of formal politics is dominated by those from the middle and professional classes, popular sector and indigenous women do not feel that their gender, ethnic, and class interests are being adequately represented. Thus, without more space for dialogue among the various segments of the women's movement, particularly between women with access to the state and those without, increasing the number of women in politics is not likely to improve the substantive representation of women's interests.

Despite the current limitations that women in politics face in promoting women's gender interests effectively, the goal of increasing women's involvement in formal politics remains important. Above all, having more women in politics breaks down stereotypes that women are primarily private actors and that feminine characteristics are ill suited to the formal political arena. In brief, nominating and electing more women is a step toward breaking down the gendered patterns of citizenship that disadvantage women. However, as Vickers warns, "one conclusion about the electoral project as a strategy for achieving feminist goals . . . is that it can be only part of an overall strategy" (1997b, p. 32).

Women and States

Although political scientists often focus on the coercive aspects of state power, states must also generate societal consent in order to retain legitimacy. The need to generate consent frequently involves state strategies that aim to include segments of the population who have historically perceived themselves marginalized or excluded. For women, the transition to democracy produced important opportunities to reshape women's citizenship because the new democracy sought legitimacy partly by opening up access to groups who had helped to defeat the dictatorship. Thus the posttransition government created SERNAM as a mechanism to promote gender equality. This state-level change had important implications for the women's movement, leading to demobilization, fragmentation, and important shifts in the power relations among the movement's various segments. Since the transition to democracy, women's movements in Chile have been struggling to adapt to the new context, trying to find ways to create linkages among dispersed groups and, more important, trying to regain some of the protagonism they enjoyed in earlier decades. As I showed in Chapter 7, while there have been some successes in terms of reestablishing linkages among movement organizations, the movement as a whole has yet to attract much public attention.

The Chilean case shows the importance of state-level changes for movement politics. As the state in Chile opened itself up to gender policy, it invited the participation of "gender policy experts," many of whom came from the women's movement itself, particularly from the feminist segment. This had a number of consequences. First, the migration of activists into the state deprived a number of organizations of leadership. But because the governing coalition that occupied the state was composed of political parties that were formerly allies of the feminist movement, it was difficult for feminists who moved into the state to be critical of government policy without being viewed as "traitors" to their former allies. But the lack of a critical stance vis-à-vis state policy also meant that feminists and women's movements outside the state viewed these same women as "traitors" to the movement's equality goals. Thus, state feminism created strategic and ideological divisions within the movement.

State feminism also exacerbated inequalities among women and created growing divisions among women with access to the state and those without. Middle-class and professional women, both in the state and in NGOs, enjoyed relatively greater access to those with power on the basis of their social location. Popular sector women and indigenous women were excluded from these networks, also on the basis of their marginalized social location. Thus the division between women active in formal and women active in informal politics grew more profound, further undermining women's citizenship. Fortunately, there appears to be a general sense among organized women—both within and outside the state—that more meaningful linkages among women are a crucial step in the process of rebuilding a stronger movement.

A problem that does not appear to have a solution in the near future is the weakness of feminism in Chile. While feminist organizing certainly exists, and while feminists can be found in a variety of spaces—in NGOs, in state agencies, in political parties, and in autonomous organizations—the movement lacks a strategy for gaining public visibility and for orienting public debate on social issues in a more progressive way. In part, this could be a function of the state's own rhetoric of gender equality. Many women in Chile may believe that their battles have been won because successive posttransition governments have employed a discourse of equality. But as I have argued in the book, the policies for promoting women's equality adopted by the state are limited. They are often watered down in an effort to maintain coalition unity and to appease conservatives. More significant, important segments of the women's movement—namely popular sector and indigenous women—do not feel that state policies adequately reflect the differences among women based on race, class, and ethnicity. Thus the current movement is composed of three segments, each with competing conceptions of the others' roles and responsibilities. Autonomous feminists reject working through existing institutions and have been harsh critics of feminists in NGOs and SERNAM. Feminists who do work in state agencies like SERNAM or in NGOs are a fairly heterogeneous group themselves. Many see no contradiction in their choice of both working in state structures and joining "autonomous" feminist groups that engage in discussion and consciousness-raising (Ríos, Godoy, and Guerrero 2004). Thus the sharp division between autónomas and institucionales may be breaking down as feminist practices involve moving among different locations, whether in the state or in civil society. However, this also means that a clear division between state and nonstate segments of the women's movement no longer exists as activists move more seamlessly between the two realms. This further complicates the relationship between women's movements and the state and is a feature of Chile's politics that warrants more attention in future research.

I think that it is here, on the question of women's movements and the state, that further study of the Chilean case is warranted in order to make future contributions to the comparative study of women and politics. More work is needed on the evolving relationship of SERNAM to movement actors and to other institutions within the state. Are the relationships that have been forged since SERNAM's creation now frozen or are they open to further transformation? Specifically, can grassroots organizations, especially as represented by networks like ANAMURI and REMOS, make their voices heard by SERNAM and achieve their goals of opening up more space for currently excluded movement actors? Can adequate spaces for debate be created to act as bridges between formal and informal politics?

As Chilean democracy consolidates and political practice normalizes, a number of other interesting questions about gendered patterns of citizenship emerge. To date, each posttransition election has been won by the same center-left coalition of parties, and governments have been relatively open to a gender-equality agenda. What will be the fate of SERNAM and women's movements in Chile when (and surely it is a question of when, not whether) a coalition of rightist parties assumes power?[2] Will the gains made by Chilean women's movements be maintained? What will be the fate of the numerous feminist NGOs that rely on the state for contracts to carry out research or gender policy implementation? Will a more conservative orientation at the state level lead to a remobilization of women's movements in civil society? Chile will continue to offer crucial questions for researchers interested in women's citizenship in Latin America and elsewhere.

Notes

1. www.elecciones.gov.cl, retrieved June 2, 2004.

2. Some observers predict that the next government in Chile will be composed of the two main rightist parties, the moderate RN and the more conservative UDI. In fact, current socialist president Ricardo Lagos barely defeated UDI candidate Joaquín Lavín for the presidency in the 2000 elections. Over the past few years, the right has been making impressive gains, and in the parliamentary elections of December 16, 2001, the UDI made the greatest electoral gains, improving its share of the popular vote from 14.45 percent in 1997 to 25.19 percent (*El Mercurio,* December 20, 2001). In the 2004 municipal elections, the rightist Alliance for Chile received 39 percent of the popular vote, compared to 45 percent for the center-left Concertación (www.electoral.cl/muni2004/inicio.html, retrieved January 19, 2005).

Appendix: List of Interviews

Formal (recorded)

Sofía Prats, former mayor of Huechuraba	August 10, 1999
Denise Pascal, former regional governor, Melipilla[a]	August 18, 1999
Delia del Gato, SERNAM	August 20, 1999
Gloria Marín, CONTEVECH (labor union)	August 23, 1999
Ana María Ordenes, SOL (NGO)	August 23, 1999
Ximena Rincón, PRODEMU	August 24, 1999
María Ester Férez, Directorate of Labor	August 25, 1999
María Elena Ovalle, councilor, Central Bank of Chile	August 25, 1999
Felisa Garay and Raquel Romo, CODEMU (NGO)	August 26, 1999
Pilar Armanet, president, National Council for Television	September 1, 1999
Rosa González, deputy, independent[b]	September 2, 1999
Francisca Rodríguez, ANAMURI	August 31, 1999; July 19, 2002
Adriana Delpiano, vice president in charge of presidential campaign for Ricardo Lagos, 1999, minister of SERNAM (2000–2002)	September 9, 1999
María Antonieta Saa, deputy, Party for Democracy	September 29, 1999
Lily Pérez, deputy, National Renovation Party	October 1, 1999; July 24, 2002
Mercedes Montoya, REMOS	October 4, 1999
Valeria Ambrosio, SERNAM	October 5, 1999
Rosana Ceorino, Tierra Nuestra (NGO)	October 6, 1999
Sandra Palestro, feminist	October 7, 1999
Myriam González and María Molina, pobladora women's organization	October 20, 1999
Paulina Weber, MEMCH	October 21, 1999
Cristina Girardi, former mayor of Cerro Navia	October 27, 1999
Adriana Muñoz, deputy, Party for Democracy[b]	November 2, 1999

Teresa Valdés, sociologist, FLACSO, Grupo Iniciativa Mujeres	November 3, 1999; July 26, 2002
Tatiana Escalera and Laura del Carmen Veloso, pobladora women's organization	November 8, 1999
Eliana Largo, feminist	November 11, 1999
Fabiola Oyarzún, PRODEMU, REMOS	November 18, 1999
Ana Pichulmán, REMOS	July 15, 2002
Claudia Pascual, candidate for deputy in 2001, Communist Party	July 15, 2002
Natacha Molina, Instituto de la Mujer	July 16, 2002
Macarena Carvallo, regional governor of the Sector Cordillera, candidate for deputy, 1997 and 2002, Radical Party	July 17, 2002
Violeta Reyes, youth wing, Socialist Party	July 17, 2002
Lorena Fríes, Casa de la Mujer "La Morada" (NGO), Grupo Iniciativa	July 19, 2002
Carolina Tohá, deputy, Party for Democracy	July 19, 2002
Paula Fortes, Intendencia	July 29, 2002
Fanny Pollarrolo, former deputy, Socialist Party	July 29, 2002

Notes: All interviews took place in Santiago except as indicated.
a. Interview took place in Melipilla.
b. Interviews took place in Valparaíso.

Informal (not recorded)

Eugenia Hola, researcher at CEM	July 27, 1999
Claudia Núñez, Fundación Ideas (NGO)	July 28, 1999
Lisette García, SERNAM	July 29, 1999
Verónica Matus, Casa de la Mujer "La Morada" (NGO)	July 29, 1999
Sandra Palestro, sociologist, feminist	July 29, 1999
Carmen Delia and María Angelica Garrido, PRODEMU	August 2, 1999
Maricel Sauterel, Fundación Ideas (NGO)	August 3, 1999
Eliana Largo, feminist	August 4, 1999
Julia Medel, researcher at CEM	August 4, 1999
Caty Orellano, PRODEMU	August 5, 1999
Alejandra Valdés and Victoria Hurtado, organizers for women's leadership training workshops	August 6, 1999
Angélica Marín, SERNAM	August 11, 1999
Cecilia Peñaloza, SERNAM	August 11, 1999

Rosana Ceorino, Tierra Nuestra (women's NGO)	August 18, 1999
Nuria Núñez, director, Instituto de la Mujer (feminist research NGO)	August 19, 1999
Aída Moreno, Casa de la Mujer, Huamachuco	August 27, 1999

Note: All interviews took place in Santiago.

Acronyms

AD	Democratic Alliance (Alianza Democrática)
ANAMURI	National Association of Rural and Indigenous Women (Asociación Nacional de Mujeres Rurales e Indígenas)
CEDAW	UN Convention on the Elimination of All Forms of Discrimination Against Women
CEM	Center for Women's Studies (Centro de Estudios de la Mujer)
CIDEM	Women's Rights Information Center (Centro de Información de los Derechos de la Mujer)
CNMD	National Coalition of Women for Democracy (Concertación Nacional de las Mujeres por la Democracia)
CODEM	Committee for the Defense of Women's Rights (Comité de Defensa de los Derechos de la Mujer)
CODEMU	Welcome Space for Women Workers (Corporación Comedor Acogedor de la Mujer Trabajadora)
CONTEVECH	Textile Workers Confederation (Confederación del Trabajador Textil)
COPACHI	Cooperating Committee for Peace in Chile (Comité de Cooperación para la Paz de Chile)
CPD	Coalition of Parties for Democracy (Concertación de los Partidos por la Democracia)
DINA	Directorate for National Intelligence
FECHIF	Chilean Federation of Feminine Institutions (Federación Chilena de Instituciones Femeninas)
FLACSO	Latin American Faculty of Social Sciences (Facultad Latinoamericana de Ciencias Sociales)
FMS	Federation of Socialist Women (Federación de Mujeres Socialistas)
FOSIS	Solidarity and Social Investment Fund (Fondo de Solidaridad e Inversión Social)

GDP	gross domestic product
MDP	Popular Democratic Movement (Movimiento Democrático Popular)
MEMCH	Chilean Women's Proemancipation Movement (Movimiento Pro-Emancipación de Mujeres de Chile)
MF	Feminist Movement (Movimiento Feminista)
MIDEPLAN	Ministry of Cooperation and Planning
MIR	Movement of the Revolutionary Left (Movimiento de Izquierda Revolucionaria)
MOMUPO	Popular Women's Movement (Movimiento de Mujeres Populares)
MUDECHI	Women of Chile (Mujeres de Chile)
NGO	nongovernmental organization
OEP	popular economic organization (*organización económica popular*)
OTEC	Technical Training Agency (Organismo Técnico de Capacitación)
PDC	Christian Democratic Party (Partido Democrata Cristiana)
PFCH	Chilean Feminine Party (Partido Femenino Chileno)
PPD	Party for Democracy (Partido por la Democracia)
PRODEMU	Foundation for the Promotion and Development of Women
PS	Socialist Party (Partido Socialista)
REMOS	Network of Women's Social Organizations (Red de Mujeres de Organizaciones Sociales)
RN	National Renovation Party (Renovación Nacional)
SENCE	Employment and Training Service (Servicio Nacional de Capacitación y Empleo)
SERNAM	National Women's Service (Servicio Nacional de la Mujer)
SERPAJ	Service for Peace and Justice (Servicio Paz y Justicia)
SNM	National Women's Secretariat (Secretaría Nacional de la Mujer)
SOL	Solidarity and Social Organization (Solidaridad y Organización Social)
UCHM	Chilean Women's Union (Unión Chilena de Mujer)
UDI	Independent Democratic Union (Unión Democrática Independiente)
UN	United Nations
UP	Popular Unity (Unidad Popular)

Bibliography

Agüero, Felipe. 2003. "Chile: Unfinished Transition and Increased Political Competition." In Jorge I. Domínguez and Michael Shifter (eds.), *Constructing Democratic Governance in Latin America,* 2nd ed., pp. 292–320. Baltimore: Johns Hopkins University Press.

Alvarez, Sonia E. 1989. "Women's Movements and Gender Politics in the Brazilian Transition." In Jane S. Jaquette (ed.), *The Women's Movement in Latin America: Feminism and the Transition to Democracy,* pp. 18–71. Boston: Unwin Hyman.

———. 1990. *Engendering Democracy in Brazil: Women's Movements in Transition Politics.* Princeton: Princeton University Press.

———. 1997. "Contradictions of a 'Women's Space' in a Male-Dominant State: The Political Role of the Commissions on the Status of Women in Postauthoritarian Brazil." In Kathleen Staudt (ed.), *Women, International Development, and Politics: The Bureaucratic Mire,* 2nd ed., pp. 59–100. Philadelphia: Temple University Press.

———. 1999. "Advocating Feminism: The Latin American Feminist NGO 'Boom.'" *International Feminist Journal of Politics* 1 (2): 181–209.

Alvarez, Sonia, Elisabeth Jay Friedman, Ericka Beckman, Maylei Blackwell, Norma Stolz Chinchilla, Nathalie Lebon, Marysa Navarra, and Marcela Ríos Tobar. 2002. "Encountering Latin American and Caribbean Feminisms." *Signs: Journal of Women in Culture and Society* 28 (2): 537–579.

Alvear, Soledad. 1990. "Qué es el SERNAM." In *Ideas para la Acción: Informe Final de la Concertación de Mujeres por la Democracia,* pp. 19–20. Santiago: El Canelo do Nos.

ANAMURI (Asociación Nacional de Mujeres Rurales e Indígenas). 2000. *Mujeres Rurales e Indígenas en Marcha hacia un Nuevo Milenio.* Santiago.

Angell, Alan. N.d. "Party Change in Chile in Comparative Perspective." www.lac.ox.ac.uk/parties-ips.pdf. Retrieved October 14, 2004.

Araujo, Kathya. N.d. "Mujeres y Representación Política: El Caso de Chile." Unpublished manuscript.

Aylwin Azócar, Patricio. 1990. "Discurso del Presidente de la República." In *Transiciones: Mujeres en los Procesos Democráticos,* pp. 146–147. Santiago: ISIS Internacional.

Baldez, Lisa. 2001. "Coalition Politics and the Limits of State Feminism in Chile." *Women and Politics* 22 (4): 1–28.

———. 2002. *Why Women Protest: Women's Movements in Chile.* New York: Cambridge University Press.

———. 2004. "Elected Bodies: The Adoption of Gender Quota Laws for Legislative Candidates in Mexico." *Legislative Studies Quarterly* 29 (2): 231–258.

Banaszak, Lee Ann, Karen Beckwith, and Dieter Rucht (eds.). 2003. *Women's Movements Facing the Reconfigured State*. New York: Cambridge University Press.

Barrig, Maruja. 2001. "Latin American Feminism: Gains, Losses, and Hard Times." *NACLA Report on the Americas* 34 (5): 29–35.

Beckman, Ericka. 2001. "The Eighth *Encuentro*." *NACLA Report on the Americas* 34 (5): 32–33.

Beckwith, Karen. 2000. "Beyond Compare? Women's Movements in Comparative Perspective." *European Journal of Political Research* 37 (4): 431–468.

———. 2001. "Women's Movements at Century's End: Excavation and Advances in Political Science." *Annual Review of Political Science* 4: 371–390.

Bickford, Louis, and Marcela Noé. 1997. "Public Participation, Political Institutions, and Democracy in Chile." Santiago: FLACSO-Chile.

Blofield, Merike. 2001. "The Politics of 'Moral Sin': A Study of Abortion and Divorce in Catholic Chile Since 1990." Santiago: FLACSO-Chile.

———. 2003. "Inequality and Democratic Politics: The Catholic Church, Feminists, and Policy Reform on Abortion and Divorce in Argentina, Chile, and Spain." Ph.D. diss., University of North Carolina at Chapel Hill.

Blofield, Merike, and Liesl Haas. 2003. "Religion, Political Institutions, and Coalition Politics: Reforming Laws on Women's Rights in Chile." Paper presented at the annual meeting of the Latin American Studies Association, Dallas, TX, March 29–31.

Blondet, Cecilia. 2001. "Lecciones de la Participación Política de las Mujeres." Lima: Instituto de Estudios Peruanos.

Bunster, Ximena. 1988. "Watch Out for That Little Nazi Man That All of Us Have Inside: The Mobilization and Demobilization of Women in Militarized Chile." *Women's Studies International Forum* 11 (5): 485–491.

Busquet, Maritza. 1995. "Comentarios a la Encuesta CEP Sobre la Mujer en Chile." *Estudios Públicos* 60 (Spring): 204–211.

Cairns, Alan C. 1999. Introduction to Alan C. Cairns, John C. Courtney, Peter MacKinnon, Hans J. Michelmann, and David E. Smith (eds.), *Citizenship, Pluralism, and Diversity: Canadian and Comparative Perspectives*, pp. 3–22. Montreal: McGill-Queen's University Press.

Caldeira, Teresa P. 1998. "Justice and Individual Rights: Challenges for Women's Movements and Democratization in Brazil." In Jane S. Jaquette and Sharon L. Wolchik (eds.), *Women and Democracy: Latin America and Central and Eastern Europe*, pp. 75–103. Baltimore: Johns Hopkins University Press.

Carrasco Gutiérrez, Maritza, and Consuelo Figueroa Goravagno. 1998. "Mujeres y Acción Coletiva: Participación Social y Espacio Local." In *Proposiciones 28: Sociedad Civil, Participación y Ciudadanía Emergente*, pp. 37–60. Santiago: SUR Ediciones.

Caul, Miki. 2001. "Political Parties and the Adoption of Candidate Gender Quotas: A Cross-National Analysis." *Journal of Politics* 63 (4): 1214–1229.

Centros de Estudios Públicos. 2002. "Estudio Nacional de Opinión Pública." December.

CEPAL (Comisión Económica para America Latina). N.d. "Estadísticas de Género." www.eclac.cl/mujer/proyectos/perfiles/comparados/participacion2/htm. Retrieved August 3, 2003.

———. 2000. *Las Mujeres Chilenas en los Noventa: Hablan las Cifras*. Santiago: CEPAL.

Chaney, Elsa M. 1974. "The Mobilization of Women in Allende's Chile." In Jane Jaquette (ed.), *Women in Politics,* pp. 267–280. New York: Wiley.

———. 1979. *Supermadre: Women in Politics in Latin America.* Austin: University of Texas Press.

Chuchryk, Patricia M. 1989a. "Feminist Anti-Authoritarian Politics: The Role of Women's Organizations in the Chilean Transition to Democracy." In Jane Jaquette (ed.), *The Women's Movement in Latin America: Feminism and the Transition to Democracy,* pp. 149–184. Boston: Unwin Hyman.

———. 1989b. "Subversive Mothers: The Women's Opposition to the Military Regime in Chile." In Sue Ellen M. Charlton, Jana Everett, and Kathleen Staudt (eds.), *Women, the State, and Development,* pp. 130–151. New York: State University of New York Press.

Collier, Simon, and William F. Sater. 1996. *A History of Chile, 1808–1994.* Cambridge: Cambridge University Press.

Contreras, Dante. 2003. "Poverty and Inequality in a Rapid Growth Economy: Chile 1990–1996." *Journal of Development Studies* 39 (3): 181–200.

Covarrubias, Paz. 1978. "El Movimiento Feminista Chileno." In Paz Covarrubias and Rolando Franco (eds.), *Chile: Mujer y Sociedad,* pp. 615–648. Santiago: Fondo de las Naciones Unidas para la Infancia.

CPD (Concertación de los Partidos por la Democracia). 1989. *Programa de Gobierno.* Santiago.

———. 1999. "Iniciar el Siglo XXI con más Democracia y más Derechos." Bases Programáticos de la Concertación, June.

Craske, Nikki. 1998. "Remasculinization and the Neoliberal State in Latin America." In Vicky Randall and Georgina Waylen (eds.), *Gender, Politics, and the State,* pp. 100–120. London: Routledge.

———. 1999. *Women and Politics in Latin America.* New Brunswick, NJ: Rutgers University Press.

Dandavati, Annie G. 1996. *The Women's Movement and the Transition to Democracy in Chile.* New York: Peter Lang.

de la Maza, Gonzálo. 1999. "Los Movimientos Sociales en la Democratización de Chile." In Paul Drake and Iván Jaksic (eds.), *El Modelo Chileno: Democracia y Desarrollo en los Noventa,* pp. 377–405. Santiago: LOM Ediciones.

de los Angeles Crummet, María. 1977. "El Poder Femenino: The Mobilization of Women Against Socialism in Chile." *Latin American Perspectives* 4 (4): 103–113.

Dietz, Mary G. 1998. "Context Is All: Feminism and Theories of Citizenship." In Anne Phillips (ed.), *Feminism and Politics,* pp. 378–400. London: Oxford University Press.

Dore, Elizabeth, and Maxine Molyneux (eds.). 2000. *Hidden Histories of Gender and the State in Latin America.* Durham: Duke University Press.

Drake, Paul. 2000. "El Nuevo Escenario Político." In *Nuevo Gobierno: Desafíos de la Reconciliación, Chile 1999–2000,* pp. 109–117. Santiago: FLACSO-Chile.

ECLAC (Economic Commission for Latin America and the Caribbean). 1998. "The Institutionality of Gender Equity in the State: A Diagnosis for Latin America and the Caribbean." Document prepared by the Women and Development Unit of ECLAC.

Edwards, Sebastian. 1985. "Stabilization with Liberalization: An Evaluation of Ten Years of Chile's Experiment with Free-Market Policies, 1973–1983." *Economic Development and Cultural Change* 33 (2): 223–254.

Feijoó, María del Carmen. 1989. "The Challenge of Constructing Civilian Peace: Women and Democracy in Argentina." In Jane Jaquette (ed.), *The Women's*

Movement in Latin America: Feminism and the Transition to Democracy, pp. 72–94. Boston: Unwin Hyman.

Fleet, Michael, and Brian H. Smith. 1997. *The Catholic Church and Democracy in Chile and Peru.* Notre Dame: University of Notre Dame Press.

Fontaine Talavera, Arturo. 2000. "Chile's Elections: The New Face of the Right." *Journal of Democracy* 11 (2): 70–77.

Foxley, Alejandro. 1983. *Latin American Experiments in Neoconservative Economics.* Berkeley: University of California Press.

Friedman, Elisabeth J. 1998. "Paradoxes of Gendered Political Opportunity in the Venezuelan Transition to Democracy." *Latin American Research Review* 33 (3): 87–135.

———. 2000a. "State-Based Advocacy for Gender Equality in the Developing World: Assessing the Venezuelan National Women's Agency." *Women and Politics* 21 (2): 47–80.

———. 2000b. *Unfinished Transitions: Women and the Gendered Development of Democracy in Venezuela, 1936–1996.* University Park: Pennsylvania State University Press.

Fríes, Lorena, and Verónica Matus. 1999. *El Derecho: Trama y Conjura Patriarcal.* Santiago: LOM Ediciones/La Morada.

Frohmann, Alicia, and Teresa Valdés. 1995. "Democracy in the Country and in the Home: The Women's Movement in Chile." In Amrita Basu (ed.), *The Challenge of Local Feminisms: Women's Movements in Global Perspective,* pp. 276–301. Boulder: Westview.

García Quesada, Ana Isabel. 2003. "Putting the Mandate into Practice: Legal Reform in Costa Rica." Paper presented at International Idea Workshop, Lima, February 23–24.

Garretón, Manuel Antonio. 1989. *The Chilean Political Process.* Translated by Sharon Kellum in collaboration with Gilbert W. Merkx. Boston: Unwin Hyman.

———. 1995. *Hacia una Nueva Era Política: Estudio Sobre las Democratizaciones.* Mexico, D.F.: Fondo de Cultura Económica.

Gaviola, Edda, Ximena Jiles, Lorella Lopresti, and Claudia Rojas. 1986. *Queremos Votar en las Próximas Elecciones: Historia del Movimiento Femenino Chileno, 1913–1952.* Santiago: Co-edición de La Morada, Fempress, ILET, ISIS, Librería Lila, PEMCI, CEM.

Gaviola Edda, Eliana Largo, and Sandra Palestro. 1994. *Una Historia Necesaria: Mujeres en Chile, 1973–1990.* Santiago: Akí y Aora.

Godoy, Lorena, and Elizabeth Guerrero. 2001. "Trayectoria del Movimiento Feminista en Chile en la Década de los Noventa." Paper presented at a meeting of the Latin American Studies Association, Washington, DC, September 6–8.

González, Sandra, and María Sabel Norero. 1989. *Los Derechos de la Mujer en las Leyes Chilenas.* Santiago: CESOC Ediciones.

Goodman, Louis W. 2001. "Chilean Citizens and Chilean Democracy: The Management of Fear, Division, and Alienation." In Roderic Ai Camp (ed.), *Citizen Views of Democracy in Latin America,* pp. 206–219. Pittsburgh: University of Pittsburgh Press.

Grau, Olga, Riet Delsing, Eugenia Brito, and Alejandra Farías. 1997. *Discurso, Género, Poder: Discursos Públicos: Chile, 1978–1993.* Santiago: La Morada, Universidad ARCIS, Lom Ediciones.

Gray, Tricia. 2003. "Electoral Gender Quotas: Lessons from Argentina and Chile." *Bulletin of Latin American Research* 22 (1): 52–78.

Grupo Iniciativa Chile. 1994. "Mujeres: Ciudadanía, Cultura y Desarrollo en el Chile de los Noventa." Santiago.

———. 1997. "Acta de la Primera Sesión: Las Mujeres en el Ejercicio del Poder y la Toma de Decisiones." Foro Nacional Para el Seguimiento de Los Acuerdos de Beijing. Santiago.

———. 1999a. "Encuesta Nacional Opinión y Actitudes de las Mujeres Chilenas Sobre la Condición de Género." Santiago.

———. 1999b. "Indice de Compromiso Cumplido: Un Instrumento de Control Ciudadano para las Mujeres." Santiago.

———. 1999c. "Propuesta Política de las Mujeres para el Tercer Milenio." *La Nación,* November 12. Santiago.

Guzmán, Virginia. 1998. "La Equidad de Género como Tema de Debate y de Políticas Públicas." In Eliana Largo (ed.), *Género en el Estado, Estado del Género,* pp. 55–70. Santiago: ISIS Internacional.

Guzmán, Virginia, Eugenia Hola, and Marcela Ríos. 1999. "Interlocución Estado y Sociedad en la Implementación del Plan de Igualdad de Oportunidades para las Mujeres." Santiago: CEM.

Haas, Liesl. 2000. "Legislating Equality: Institutional Politics and the Expansion of Women's Rights in Chile." Ph.D. diss., University of North Carolina at Chapel Hill.

Haggard, Stephan, and Robert Kaufman (eds.). 1995. *The Political Economy of Democratic Transitions.* Princeton: Princeton University Press.

Hardy, Clarisa. 1997. "Las Políticas Sociales en Chile." In *Chile '96: Análisis y Opiniones,* pp. 119–135. Santiago: FLACSO-Chile.

Hinojosa, Magda. 2005, forthcoming. "Sex and the Cities: Candidate Selection and Women's Representation in Municipal Politics in Chile and Mexico." Ph.D. diss., Harvard University.

Hipsher, Patricia L. 1998. "Democratic Transitions and Social Movement Outcomes: The Chilean Shantytown Dwellers' Movement in Comparative Perspective." In Marco C. Giugni, Doug McAdam, and Charles Tilly (eds.), *From Contention to Democracy,* pp. 149–167. Boulder: Rowman and Littlefield.

Hojman, David E. 1996. "Poverty and Inequality in Chile: Are Democratic Politics and Neoliberal Economics Good for You?" *Journal of Interamerican Studies and World Affairs* 38 (2–3): 73–96.

Htun, Mala. 1998. "Participación, Representación y Liderazgo Político de la Mujer en América Latina." Report prepared for the Inter-American Dialogue.

———. 2003. *Sex and the State: Abortion, Divorce, and the Family Under Latin American Dictatorships and Democracies.* New York: Cambridge University Press.

———. 2004. "Is Gender Like Ethnicity? The Political Representation of Identity Groups." *Perspectives on Politics* 2 (3): 439–458.

Htun, Mala, and Mark P. Jones. 2002. "Engendering the Right to Participate in Decision-Making: Electoral Quotas and Women's Leadership in Latin America." In Nikki Craske and Maxine Molyneux (eds.), *Gender and the Politics of Rights and Democracy in Latin America,* pp. 32–56. New York: Palgrave.

Hurtado, Victoria. 1997. "Identidad Femenina, Liderazgo y Conflicto." In Guadalupe Santa Cruz (ed.), *Veredas por Cruzar,* pp. 139–148. Santiago: Instituto de la Mujer.

Inter-American Commission of Women. 2000. "Quota Laws." www.oas.org/cim/english/laws-cuota.htm. Retrieved August 2, 2003.

Inter-Parliamentary Union. 2004. "Women in National Parliaments." www.ipu.org/wmn-e/classif.htm. Retrieved January 5, 2005.

ISIS Internacional. 1996. "Evaluación Cualitativa del Plan de Igualdad de Oportunidades Para las Mujeres 1994–1999: Percepciones de Mujeres Líderes de

Opinión y Beneficiarias del Plan Región Metropolitana y Región del Maule." Santiago.

Jaquette, Jane. 1976. "Female Political Participation in Latin America." In June Nash and Helen Icken Safa (eds.), *Sex and Class in Latin America,* pp. 221–244. New York: Praeger.

———. (ed.). 1989. *The Women's Movement in Latin America: Feminism and the Transition to Democracy.* Boston: Unwin Hyman.

———. 1994. "Women's Movements and the Challenge of Democratic Politics in Latin America." *Social Politics* 1 (3): 335–340.

Jaquette, Jane S., and Sharon L. Wolchik (eds.). 1998. *Women and Democracy: Latin America and Central and Eastern Europe.* Baltimore: Johns Hopkins University Press.

Jelín, Elizabeth. 1997. "Emergent Citizenship or Exclusion? Social Movements and Non-Governmental Organizations in the 1990s." In William C. Smith and Roberto Patricio Korzeniewicz (eds.), *Politics, Social Change, and Economic Restructuring in Latin America,* pp. 79–101. Miami: North-South Center Press.

Jenson, Jane. 1986. "Gender and Reproduction; or, Babies and the State." *Studies in Political Economy* 20 (Summer): 9–46.

Jónasdóttir, Anna G. 1988. "On the Concept of Interest, Women's Interests, and the Limitations of Interest Theory." In Kathleen B. Jones and Anna G. Jónasdóttir (eds.), *The Political Interests of Gender: Developing Theory and Research with a Feminist Face,* pp. 33–65. London: Sage.

Jones, Kathleen B. 1990. "Citizenship in a 'Woman-Friendly' Polity." *Signs: Journal of Women in Culture and Society* 15 (4): 781–812.

Jones, Mark P. 1996. "Increasing Women's Representation Via Gender Quotas: The Argentine Ley de Cupos." *Women and Politics* 16 (4): 75–98.

Kampwirth, Karen. 1998. "Feminism, Antifeminism, and Electoral Politics in Postwar Nicaragua and El Salvador." *Political Science Quarterly* 113 (2): 259–279.

Kaplan, Temma. 1982. "Female Consciousness and Collective Action: The Case of Barcelona, 1910–1918." *Signs: Journal of Women in Culture and Society* 7 (3): 545–566.

Karl, Terry Lynn. 1990. "Dilemmas of Democratization in Latin America" *Comparative Politics* 23 (1): 1–21.

Kirkwood, Julieta. 1986. *Ser Política en Chile: Las Feministas y los Partidos.* Santiago: FLACSO-Chile.

———. 1988. "Feministas y Políticas." In *Mujeres Latinoamericanas: Diez Ensayos y Una Historia Colectiva,* pp. 17–27. Lima: Flora Tristán, Centro de la Mujer Peruana.

Klausen, Jytte, and Charles S. Maier (eds.). 2001. *Has Liberalism Failed Women? Assuring Equal Representation in Europe and the United States.* New York: Palgrave.

Krook, Mona Lena. 2003. "Get the Balance Right! Global and Transnational Campaigns to Promote Gender-Balanced Decision-Making." Paper presented at the International Studies Association annual convention, Portland, February 25–March 1.

Lagos, Ricardo. 2000. "Mensaje Presidencial." Reproduced in *El Mercurio,* May 22.

Lavrin, Asunción. 1995. *Women, Feminism, and Social Change in Argentina, Chile, and Uruguay, 1890–1940.* Lincoln: University of Nebraska Press.

Lehmann, David. 1990. *Democracy and Development in Latin America: Economics, Politics, and Religion in the Post-War Period.* Philadelphia: Temple University Press.

Lister, Ruth. 1997. *Citizenship: Feminist Perspectives.* London: Macmillan.

Loveman, Brian. 1995. "The Transition to Civilian Government in Chile." In Paul W. Drake and Iván Jaksic (eds.), *The Struggle for Democracy in Chile,* pp. 305–337. Lincoln: University of Nebraska Press.

Lovenduski, Joni. 1993. "Introduction: The Dynamics of Gender and Party." In Joni Lovenduski and Pippa Norris (eds.), *Gender and Party Politics,* pp. 1–15. London: Sage.

Macaulay, Fiona. 1998. "Localities of Power: Gender, Parties, and Democracy in Chile and Brazil." In Haleh Afshar (ed.), *Women and Empowerment: Illustrations from the Third World,* pp. 86–109. New York: St. Martin's Press.

Marshall, T. H. 1950. *Citizenship and Social Class.* Cambridge: Cambridge University Press.

Matear, Ann. 1995. "The Servicio Nacional de la Mujer (SERNAM): Women and the Process of Democratic Transition in Chile 1990–1994." In David E. Hojman (ed.), *Neo-Liberalism with a Human Face? The Politics and Economics of the Chilean Model,* pp. 93–117. Liverpool: Institute of Latin American Studies.

———. 1997a. "Desde la Protesta a la Propuesta: The Institutionalization of the Women's Movement in Chile." In Elizabeth Dore (ed.), *Gender Politics in Latin America,* pp. 84–100. New York: Monthly Review Press.

———. 1997b. "Gender and the State in Rural Chile." *Bulletin of Latin American Research* 16 (1): 97–105.

Matland, Richard E. 2000. "Enhancing Women's Political Participation: Legislative Recruitment and Electoral Systems." In Azza Karam (ed.), *Women in Parliament: Beyond Numbers.* www.idea.int/women/parl/ch3b.htm. Retrieved May 12, 2002.

Mattelart, Michele. 1976. "Chile: The Feminine Version of the Coup d'État." In June Nash and Helen Icken Safa (eds.), *Sex and Class in Latin America,* pp. 279–301. New York: Praeger.

MEMCH '83 (Movimento Pro-Emancipatión de Mujeres de Chile '83). 1985. "Principios y Reivindicaciones que Configuran la Plataforma de la Mujer Chilena." Reproduced in Edda Gaviola, Eliana Largo and Sandra Palestro, *Una Historia Necesaria: Mujeres en Chile, 1973–1990,* pp. 238–243. Santiago: Akí y Aora.

MIDEPLAN (Ministry of Cooperation and Planning). N.d.(a). "Indicadores Económicos y Sociales 1990–2000." www.mideplan.cl/sito/sitio/indicadores/htm/indicadores_indicadores. Retrieved April 20, 2004.

———. N.d.(b). "Tasa de Desocupación por Sexo, 1986–2000." www.mideplan.cl/estudios/empleo.pdf. Retrieved April 20, 2004.

Miller, Francesca. 1994. "The Suffrage Movement in Latin America." In Gertrude M. Yaeger (ed.), *Confronting Change, Challenging Tradition: Women in Latin America,* pp. 157–176. Wilmington: Scholarly Resources.

———. 1995. "Latin American Women and the Search for Social, Political, and Economic Transformation." In Sandor Halebsky and Richard L. Harris (eds.), *Capital, Power, and Inequality in Latin America,* pp. 185–206. Boulder: Westview.

Molina, Natacha. 1989. "Propuestas Políticas y Orientaciones de Cambio en la Situación de la Mujer." In Manuel Antonio Garretón (ed.), *Propuestas Políticas y Demandas Sociales,* vol. 3, pp. 33–171. Santiago: FLACSO-Chile.

———. 1997. "De la Denuncia a la Construcción de la Igualdad: Nuevas Articulaciones Entre Ciudadanía y Género." In Guadalupe Santa Cruz (ed.), *Veredas por Cruzar,* pp. 181–202. Santiago: Instituto de la Mujer.

———. 1998. "Women's Struggle for Equality and Citizenship in Chile." In Geertje Lycklama à Nijeholt, Virginia Vargas, and Saskia Wieringa (eds.), *Women's*

Movements and Public Policy in Europe, Latin America, and the Caribbean. pp. 126–142. New York: Garland.

———. 2000. "El Derecho a Elegir y a Ser Elegido." *Perspectivas* 20 (October–December): 33–37.

Molina, Natacha, and Patricia Provoste. 1997. "Igualdad de Oportunidades para las Mujeres: Condición de la Democracia." In Guadalupe Santa Cruz (ed.), *Veredas por Cruzar,* pp. 151–173. Santiago: Instituto de la Mujer.

Moltedo, Cecilia. 1998. "Experiencias de Participación de las Mujeres Chilenas en los Partidos Políticos: 1990 a 1998." Santiago: Instituto de la Mujer.

Molyneux, Maxine. 1985. "Mobilization Without Emancipation? Women's Interests, the State, and Revolution." *Feminist Studies* 11 (2): 227–254.

———. 1998. "Analyzing Women's Movements." *Development and Change* 29 (2): 219–245.

———. 2000. "Twentieth Century State Formations in Latin America." In Elizabeth Dore and Maxine Molyneux (eds.), *Hidden Histories of Gender and the State in Latin America,* pp. 33–81. Durham: Duke University Press.

Montecino, Sonia, and Josefina Rossetti (eds.). 1990. *Tramas para un Nuevo Destino: Propuestas de la Concertación de Mujeres por la Democracia.* Santiago: Concertación de Mujeres por la Democracia.

Montecinos, Verónica. 1994. "Neo-Liberal Economic Reforms and Women in Chile." In Nahid Aslanbeigui, Steven Pressman, and Gale Summerfield (eds.), *Women in the Age of Economic Transformation,* pp. 160–177. London: Routledge.

———. 1997. "Economic Reforms, Social Policy, and the Family Economy in Chile." *Review of Social Economy* 55 (2): 224–234.

Moulian, Tomás. 1997. "El Chile Actual y su Secreto." In *Chile '96: Análisis y Opiniones.* Santiago: FLACSO-Chile.

Movimiento Feminista. 1983. "Demandas Femenistas a la Democracia." Reproduced in Edda Gaviola, Eliana Largo, and Sandra Palestro, *Una Historia Necesaria: Mujeres en Chile, 1973–1990,* pp. 234–237. Santiago: Akí y Aora.

———. 1988. "Demandas de las Mujeres a la Democracia." Reproduced in Edda Gaviola, Eliana Largo, and Sandra Palestro, *Una Historia Necesaria: Mujeres en Chile, 1973–1990,* pp. 251–256. Santiago: Akí y Aora.

Munizaga, Giselle, and Lilian Letelier. 1988. "Mujer y Régimen Militar." *Mundo de Mujer: Cambio y Continuidad.* Santiago: Centros de Estudios de la Mujer.

Muñoz, Adriana. 1996. "Mujer y Política: Complejidades y Ambivalencias." Santiago: CEPAL.

Muñoz d'Albora, Adriana, and Scarlett Wojciechowski Levine. 1996. "Importancia de Una Ley de Cuotas en Chile." Santiago: Fundación Ideas.

Navarro, Marysa. 1989. "The Personal Is Political: Las Madres de Plaza de Mayo." In Susan Eckstein (ed.), *Power and Popular Protest: Latin American Social Movements,* pp. 241–258. Berkeley: University of California Press.

Nelson, Barbara J., and Najma Chowdhury (eds.). 1994. *Women and Politics Worldwide.* New Haven: Yale University Press.

Norris, Pippa. 1993. "Conclusions: Comparing Legislative Recruitment." In Joni Lovenduski and Pippa Norris (eds.), *Gender and Party Politics.* pp. 309–330. London: Sage.

O'Donnell, Guillermo, and Phillipe C. Schmitter. 1986. *Transitions from Authoritarian Rule: Tentative Conclusions About Uncertain Democracies.* Baltimore: Johns Hopkins University Press.

Oppenheim, Lois Hecht. 1993. *Politics in Chile: Democracy, Authoritarianism, and the Search for Development.* Boulder: Westview.

———. 1998. "Democratic Theory and Women's Participation in Politics: The Chilean Case." Santiago: ECLAC.

———. 1999. *Politics in Chile: Democracy, Authoritarianism, and the Search for Development.* 2nd ed. Boulder: Westview.

Órdenes, Ana María. 1998. "Nuevas Formas de Organización." In "Barreras y Potencialidades del Movimiento de Mujeres en Chile." Seminar, Santiago, November 27.

Oxhorn, Philip. 1994a. "Understanding Political Change After Authoritarian Rule: The Popular Sectors and Chile's New Democratic Regime." *Journal of Latin American Studies* 26 (3): 737–759.

———. 1994b. "Where Did All the Protestors Go? Popular Mobilization and the Transition to Democracy in Chile." *Latin American Perspectives* 21 (3): 49–68.

———. 1995a. "From Controlled Inclusion to Coerced Marginalization: The Struggle for Civil Society in Latin America." In John A. Hall (ed.), *Civil Society: Theory, History, Comparison,* pp. 250–277. London: Polity Press.

———. 1995b. *Organizing Civil Society: The Popular Sectors and the Struggle for Democracy in Chile.* University Park: Pennsylvania State University Press.

Palacios, Indira, and Teresa Valdés. 2000. "Las Mujeres en las Ultimas Elecciones Presidenciales." In *Nuevo Gobierno: Desafíos de la Reconciliación, Chile 1999–2000,* pp. 145–158. Santiago: FLACSO-Chile.

Pateman, Carole. 1992. "Equality, Difference, Subordination: The Politics of Motherhood and Women's Citizenship." In Gisela Block and Susan James (eds.), *Beyond Equality and Difference: Citizenship, Feminist Politics, and Female Subjectivity,* pp. 18–31. London: Routledge.

Phillips, Anne. 1995. *The Politics of Presence.* Oxford: Clarendon Press.

Pitkin, Hanna. 1967. *The Concept of Representation.* Berkeley: University of California Press.

Power, Margaret. 2000. "Class and Gender in the Anti-Allende Women's Movement: Chile 1970–1973." *Social Politics* 7 (3): 289–308.

———. 2002. *Right-Wing Women in Chile: Feminine Power and the Struggle Against Allende, 1964–1973.* University Park: Pennsylvania State University Press.

Pringle, Rosemary, and Sophie Watson. 1998. "'Women's Interests' and the Poststructuralist State." In Anne Phillips (ed.), *Feminism and Politics,* pp. 203–223. Oxford: Oxford University Press.

Provoste, Patricia. 1994. "¿Cómo Llegan las Políticas Sociales a las Mujeres?" Santiago: Instituto de la Mujer.

———. 1997. "Los Servicios Públicos y los Derechos de las Mujeres: Hacia una Modernización Democrática de la Gestión Pública." In *Veredas por Cruzar: 10 Años/Instituto de la Mujer,* pp. 43–64. Santiago: Instituto de la Mujer.

Rabkin, Rhoda. 1996. "Redemocratization, Electoral Engineering, and Party Strategies in Chile, 1989–1995." *Comparative Political Studies* 29 (3): 335–356.

Raczynski, Dagmar. 1999. "Políticas Sociales en los Años Noventa en Chile: Balance y Desafíos." In Paul Drake and Iván Jaksic (eds.), *El Modelo Chileno: Democracia y Desarrollo en los Noventa,* pp. 125–153. Santiago: LOM Ediciones.

Rai, Shirin M. 1996. "Women and the State in the Third World: Some Issues for Debate." In Shirin Rai and Geraldine Lievesley (eds.), *Women and the State: International Perspectives,* pp. 5–22. London: Taylor and Francis.

Rayo, Gustavo, and Gonzalo de la Maza. 2000. "Urban Action: Collective Efforts at the Grassroots Level." In Cristián Toloza and Eugenio Lahera (eds.), *Chile in the Nineties,* pp. 409–454. Stanford: Stanford University Libraries.

REMOS (Red de Mujeres de Organizaciones Sociales). N.d. Information pamphlet (mission, objectives, and member groups).

Revilla Blanca, Marisa. 1995. "Las Organizaciones de Mujeres en Chile: Participación e Integración en el Marco de las Políticas Sociales Neoliberales." *Síntesis* 23 (January–July): 109–132.

Reynolds, Andrew. 1999. "Women in the Legislatures and Executives of the World: Knocking at the Highest Glass Ceiling." *World Politics* 51 (4): 547–572.

Richards, Patricia. 2000. "Reviving Social Rights in Latin America: The Potential Role of International Human Rights Documents." *Citizenship Studies* 4 (2): 189–206.

———. 2003. "Expanding Women's Citizenship? Mapuche Women and Chile's National Women's Service." *Latin American Perspectives* 30 (2): 41–65.

———. 2004. *Pobladoras, Indígenas, and the State: Difference, Equality, and Women's Rights in Chile.* New Brunswick, NJ: Rutgers University Press.

Ríos Tobar, Marcela. 2003. "Chilean Feminism(s) in the 1990s: Paradoxes of an Unfinished Transition." *International Feminist Journal of Politics* 5 (2): 256–280.

Ríos Tobar, Marcela, Lorena Godoy Catalán, and Elizabeth Guerrero Caviedes. 2004. *¿Un Nuevo Silencio Feminista? La Transformación de un Movimiento Social en el Chile Posdictadura.* Sangiago: CEM, Editorial Cuarto Propio.

Roberts, Kenneth M. 1995. "From the Barricades to the Ballot Box: Redemocratization and Political Realignment in the Chilean Left." *Politics and Society* 23 (4): 495–519.

———. 1997. "Rethinking Economic Alternatives: Left Parties and the Articulation of Popular Demands in Chile and Peru." In Douglas A. Chalmers, Carlos M. Vila, Katherine Hite, Scott B. Martin, Kerianne Piester, and Monique Segarra (eds.), *The New Politics of Inequality in Latin America: Rethinking Participation and Representation,* pp. 313–336. Oxford: Oxford University Press.

Rodríguez, Victoria E. 2003. *Women in Contemporary Mexican Politics.* Austin: University of Texas Press.

Rosemblatt, Karin Alejandra. 2000. *Gendered Compromises: Political Cultures and the State in Chile, 1920–1950.* Chapel Hill: University of North Carolina Press.

Rule, Wilma. 1987. "Electoral Systems, Contextual Factors, and Women's Opportunity for Election to Parliament in Twenty-three Democracies." *Western Political Quarterly* 40 (3): 477–486.

Safa, Helen Icken. 1990. "Women's Social Movements in Latin America." *Gender and Society* 4 (3): 354–369.

Saint-Germain, Michelle A. 1997. "Mujeres '94: Democratic Transition and the Women's Movement in El Salvador." *Women and Politics* 18 (2): 75–99.

Salinas Alvarez, Raquel. 1998. "Chile: Una Experiencia de Aprendizaje en el Sector Público." In Eliana Largo (ed.), *Género en el Estado, Estado del Género,* pp. 84–94. Santiago: ISIS Internacional.

Sapiro, Virginia. 1998. "When Are Interests Interesting? The Problem of Political Representation." In Anne Phillips (ed.), *Feminism and Politics,* pp. 161–192. Oxford: Oxford University Press.

Schild, Verónica. 1990. "The Hidden Politics of Neighborhood Organizations: Women and Local Level Participation in the Poblaciones of Chile." *Canadian Journal of Latin American and Caribbean Studies* 15 (30): 137–158.

———. 1994. "Recasting 'Popular' Movements: Gender and Political Learning in Neighborhood Organizations in Chile." *Latin American Perspectives* 21 (2): 59–80.

———. 1997. "New Subjects of Rights? Gendered Citizenship and the Contradictory Legacies of Social Movements in Latin America." *Organization* 44 (4): 604–609.
———. 1998. "Market Citizenship and the 'New Democracies': The Ambiguous Legacies of the Contemporary Chilean Women's Movement." *Social Politics* 5 (2): 232–249.
———. 2000a. "'Gender Equity' Without Social Justice: Women's Rights in the Neoliberal Age." *NACLA Report on the Americas* 34 (1): 25–28.
———. 2000b. "Neo-liberalism's New Gendered Market Citizens: The 'Civilizing' Dimension of Social Programs in Chile." *Citizenship Studies* 4 (3): 275–305.
Scully, Timothy R. 1995. "Reconstituting Party Politics in Chile." In Scott Mainwaring and Timothy R. Scully (eds.), *Building Democratic Institutions: Party Systems in Latin America,* pp. 100–137. Stanford: Stanford University Press.
SERNAM (Servicio Nacional de la Mujer). N.d.(a). Cuadro 1, "Inserción Organizacional de Mujeres Líderes por Región." Santiago.
———. N.d.(b). *Planificación—Programa CIDEM, 1999.* Santiago.
———. N.d.(c). "Reformas Legales a Favor de la Mujer y la Familia." www. sernam.cl. Retrieved May 31, 1999.
———. 1994. *Plan de Igualdad de Oportunidades Para las Mujeres.* Santiago.
———. 1996a. "Pobreza, Género y Exclusión Social en Chile." Working Document no. 54. Santiago.
———. 1996b. "Seguimiento Evaluativo de la Implementación Municipal del Programa de Apoyo a Mujeres Jefas de Hogar." Working Document no. 43. Santiago.
———. 1998a. *Desigualdad en Cifras.* Santiago.
———. 1998b. "Informe Comisión Participación." Santiago.
———. 1998c. "Participar es un Derecho de las Mujeres y una Responsibilidad Ciudadana: Estadísticas, Argumentos, y Propuestas." Santiago.
———. 1999. "Evaluación y Seguimiento del Programa de Habilitación Laboral para Mujeres de Escasos Recursos Preferentemente Jefas de Hogar." Working Document no. 65. Santiago.
———. 2000. *Plan de Igualdad de Oportunidades Entre Mujeres y Hombres, 2000–2010.* Santiago.
———. 2002a. "Las Mujeres en la Toma de Decisiones." Departamento de Estudios y Estadísticas, January.
———. 2002b. "Percepción de los Líderes Políticos y Sociales Sobre la Ley de Cuotas: Contenidos y Factibilidad." Working Document no. 79. Santiago.
Serrano, Claudia. 1990. "Entre la Autonomía y la Integración." In *Transiciones: Mujeres en los Procesos Democráticos,* pp. 99–105. Santiago: ISIS Internacional.
———. 1992. "Estado, Mujer y Política Social en Chile." In Claudia Serrano and Dagmar Raczynski (eds.), *Políticas Sociales, Mujeres, y Gobiernos Locales,* pp. 195–216. Santiago: CIEPLAN.
Shayne, Julie. 2004. *The "Revolution Question": Feminisms in El Salvador, Chile, and Cuba.* New Brunswick, NJ: Rutgers University Press.
Siavelis, Peter M. 1997. "Executive-Legislative Relations in Post-Pinochet Chile: A Preliminary Assessment." In Scott Mainwaring and Matthew Soberg Shugart (eds.), *Presidentialism and Democracy in Latin America,* pp. 321–362. Cambridge: Cambridge University Press.
———. 2000. *The President and Congress in Post-Authoritarian Chile: Institutional Constraints to Democratic Consolidation.* University Park: Pennsylvania State University Press.
———. 2002 "The Hidden Logic of Candidate Selection for Chilean Parliamentary Elections." *Comparative Politics* 34 (4): 419–438.

Silva, Eduardo. 1991. "The Political Economy of Chile's Regime Transition: From Radical to 'Pragmatic' Neo-Liberal Policies." In Paul Drake and Iván Jaksic (eds.), *The Struggle for Democracy in Chile, 1982–1990,* pp. 98–127. Lincoln: University of Nebraska Press.

———. 2002. "Chile." In Harry E. Vanden and Gary Prevost (eds.), *Politics of Latin America: The Power Game,* pp. 437–481. New York: Oxford University Press.

Silva, Patricio. 2004. "Doing Politics in a Depoliticized Society: Social Change and Political Deactivation in Chile." *Bulletin of Latin American Research* 23 (1): 63–78.

Snow, David A., and Robert D. Benford. 1992. "Master Frames and Cycles of Protest." In Aldon D. Morris and Carol McClurg Mueller (eds.), *Frontiers in Social Movement Theory,* pp. 133–155. New Haven: Yale University Press.

Squires, Judith. 2000. *Gender in Political Theory.* Cambridge: Polity Press.

Stetson, Dorothy McBride, and Amy G. Mazur (eds.). 1995. *Comparative State Feminism.* London: Sage.

Stevenson, Linda S. 1999. "Gender Politics in the Mexican Democratization Process: Electing Women and Legislating Sex Crimes and Affirmative Action, 1988–97." In Jorge I. Domínguez and Alejandro Poiré (eds.), *Towards Mexico's Democratization: Parties, Campaigns, Elections, and Public Opinion,* pp. 57–87. New York: Routledge.

Strange, Carolyn. 1990. "Mothers on the March: Maternalism in Women's Protests for Peace in North America and Western Europe, 1900–1985." In Guida West and Rhoda Lois Blumberg (eds.), *Women and Social Protest,* pp. 209–224. New York: Oxford University Press.

Tarrow, Sidney. 1998. *Power in Movement: Social Movements and Contentious Politics.* 2nd ed. Cambridge: Cambridge University Press.

Taylor, Lucy. 1998. *Citizenship, Participation, and Democracy: Changing Dynamics in Chile and Argentina.* London: Macmillan.

Thelen, Kathleen, and Sven Steinmo. 1992. "Historical Institutionalism in Comparative Politics." In Sven Steinmo et al. (eds.), *Structuring Politics: Historical Institutionalism in Comparative Analysis,* pp. 1–32. New York: Cambridge University Press.

Tierra Nuestra. N.d. Information pamphlet (history and objectives).

———. 1999. "Escuela de Capacitación para Mujeres Líderes." Oficina de la Mujer, San Ramón.

Valdés, Teresa. 1994. "Movimiento de Mujers y Producción de Conocimiento de Género: Chile 1978–1989." In Magdalena León (ed.), *Mujeres y Participación Política: Avances y Desafíos en América Latina,* pp. 291–318. Bogota: Tercer Mundo Editores.

———. 1998. "Entre la Modernización y la Equidad: Mujeres, Mundo Privado y Familias." In Cristian Toloza and Eugenio Lahera (eds.), *Chile en los Noventa.* Santiago: LOM Ediciones.

Valdés, Teresa, and Enrique Gomariz. 1992. *Mujeres Latinoamericanas en Cifras: Tomo Chile.* Madrid: Instituto de la Mujer.

———. 1995. *Mujeres Latinoamericanas en Cifras: Tomo Comparativo.* Madrid: Instituto de la Mujer.

Valdés, Teresa, and Marisa Weinstein. 1993. *Mujeres que Sueñan: Las Organizaciones de Pobladoras en Chile 1973–1990.* Santiago: FLACSO-Chile.

Valenzuela, Arturo. 1978. *The Breakdown of Democratic Regimes: Chile.* Baltimore: Johns Hopkins University Press.

———. 1991. "The Military in Power: The Consolidation of One-Man Rule." In Paul Drake and Iván Jaksic (eds.), *The Struggle for Democracy in Chile, 1982–1990,* pp. 21–72. Lincoln: University of Nebraska Press.

Valenzuela, María Elena. 1991. "The Evolving Roles of Women Under Military Rule." In Paul Drake and Iván Jaksic (eds.), *The Struggle for Democracy in Chile: 1982–1990,* pp. 161–187. Lincoln: University of Nebraska Press.

———. 1994. "El Programa Nacional de Apoyo a Jefas de Hogar de Escasos Recursos." In María Elena Valenzuela (ed.), *De Mujer Sola a Jefa de Hogar: Género, Pobreza y Políticas Públicas,* pp. 187–214. Santiago: SERNAM.

———. 1998. "Women and the Democratization Process in Chile." In Jane S. Jaquette and Sharon L. Wolchik (eds.), *Women and Democracy: Latin America and Central and Eastern Europe,* pp. 47–74. Baltimore: Johns Hopkins University Press.

Verdugo, Patricia. 2001. *Chile, Pinochet, and the Caravan of Death.* Translated by Marcelo Montecino. Miami: North-South Center Press.

Vickers, Jill. 1997a. *Reinventing Political Science: A Feminist Approach.* Halifax: Fernwood.

———. 1997b. "Towards a Feminist Understanding of Representation." In Jane Arscott and Linda Trimble (eds.), *In the Presence of Women: Representation in Canadian Governments,* pp. 20–46. Toronto: Harcourt Brace.

Vogel, Isabel. 1995. "Gender and the Labour Market." In David E. Hojman (ed.), *Neoliberalism with a Human Face: The Politics and Economics of the Chilean Model,* pp. 82–91. Liverpool: Institute of Latin American Studies.

Walby, Sylvia. 1994. "Is Citizenship Gendered?" *Sociology* 28 (2): 379–395.

———. 1997. *Gender Transformations.* London: Routledge.

Waylen, Georgina. 1994. "Women and Democratization: Conceptualizing Gender Relations in Transition Politics." *World Politics* 46 (3): 327–354.

———. 1996. "Democratization, Feminism, and the State in Chile: The Establishment of SERNAM." In Shirin M. Rai and Geraldine Lievesley (eds.), *Women and the State: International Perspectives,* pp. 103–117. London: Taylor and Francis.

———. 1997. "Women's Movements, the State and Democratization in Chile: The Establishment of SERNAM." In Anne Marie Goetz (ed.), *Getting Institutions Right for Women in Development,* pp. 90–103. London: Zed Books.

———. 2000. "Gender and Democratic Politics: A Comparative Analysis of Consolidation in Argentina and Chile." *Journal of Latin American Studies* 32 (3): 765–793.

Weinstein, Marisa. 1996. "Estado, Mujeres de Sectores Populares y Ciudadanía." Santiago: FLACSO-Chile.

———. 1997. "Políticas de Equidad de Género y Participación de las Mujeres." Santiago: FLACSO-Chile.

West, Guida, and Rhoda Lois Blumberg (eds.). 1990. *Women and Social Protest.* New York: Oxford University Press.

Weyland, Kurt. 1997. "'Growth with Equity' in Chile's New Democracy?" *Latin American Research Review* 32 (1): 37–67.

Index

About the Book

Why have women remained marginalized in Chilean politics, even within a context of democratization? Addressing this question, Susan Franceschet traces women's political activism in the country—from the early-twentieth-century struggles for suffrage to current efforts to expand and deepen the practice of democracy.

Franceschet highlights the gendered nature of political participation in Chile, as well as changing perceptions of what is and is not political. Even as women enter electoral and bureaucratic politics in greater numbers, she argues, they are divided by ideology, competing interests, and unequal access to power. Clarifying the themes and challenges of the Chilean women's movement today, she finds an inextricable link between women's struggles for citizenship rights and the nation's broader struggles for democracy and social justice.

Susan Franceschet is assistant professor of political science at Acadia University, Wolfville, Nova Scotia.

Medieval and Renaissance Studies

Publication of this book has been made possible by a grant from the Hull Memorial Publication Fund of Cornell University

Theodor Mommsen's undergraduate seminar, Cornell University, November 10, 1954

THEODOR E. MOMMSEN

Medieval and Renaissance Studies

Edited by

EUGENE F. RICE, JR.

Cornell University Press

ITHACA, NEW YORK

CORNELL UNIVERSITY PRESS

First published 1959
Reissued 1966

PRINTED IN THE UNITED STATES OF AMERICA
BY VALLEY OFFSET, INC.
BOUND BY VAIL-BALLOU PRESS, INC.

Preface

THEODOR E. MOMMSEN published most of his work in the form of articles. He often said himself that he was an article man rather than a book man. Inevitably his writings are scattered, some of them in relatively inaccessible journals; and both the coherence and the variety of his scholarship have been correspondingly masked. So when several of his graduate students suggested after his death that his papers be collected in a single volume, the Cornell University Department of History welcomed the proposal as appropriate and useful. This book is the result. Its purpose is to serve the memory of an admirable scholar and to make the bulk of his work more conveniently available to a larger number of readers in this country and abroad.

Articles which appeared first in English are reprinted without change. Those which appeared in German or Italian have been translated. The essay on Augustine and Orosius is printed here for the first time. I have included, I believe, all of Mommsen's important articles. I have omitted notes and documents, reviews, articles on subjects too narrow, in my judgment, to warrant a second printing, and articles the inclusion of which would have confused the structure of the book. A comparison of the table of contents with the bibliography will indicate the papers I have chosen to omit and where they remain available.

Permission was kindly granted by the following editors and publishers to reprint the articles included in this book: the President of the *Monumenta Germaniae Historica,* the Accademia Lucchese di Scienze, Lettere ed Arti, the University of

Chicago Press, the editors of the *American Journal of Archaeology,* Pantheon Books, the Libreria Editrice Minerva of Bologna, the Mediaeval Academy of America and the editors of *Speculum,* the editors of *The Art Bulletin,* the editors of the *Journal of the Warburg and Courtauld Institutes,* the Cornell University Press, the Fordham University Press and the editors of *Traditio,* the editors of the *Journal of the History of Ideas,* and the Princeton University Press.

Mr. Craig Fisher, Stechert-Hafner, Inc., of New York, Mr. Richard Rouse, the College Art Association of America, Professor Kurt Weitzman, and Father Edwin Quain, S.J., generously gave up their offprints of Mommsen articles or copies of the journals in which they appeared. Professor Friedrich Baethgen very kindly secured for me a microfilm of the article "Karl der Grosse—Kaiser der Franzosen?"

Finally, I gratefully acknowledge my debt to friends, colleagues, and students who have helped and advised me: Felix Gilbert, Ernst Kantorowicz, Ludwig Edelstein, Roger Hahn, Karl Morrison, Walter Simon, Harry Caplan, Hajo Holborn, and Joseph Mazzeo. They have saved me time and mistakes.

EUGENE F. RICE, JR.

Ithaca, New York
May 18, 1959

Introduction

WHEN Theodor Ernst Mommsen came to Cornell University in 1954 as professor of medieval history, he was a mature teacher and scholar, a man in the prime of life. He had left Germany, his native land, in 1935 as an act of protest against the totalitarian government and anti-Semitic policy of Hitler, and on coming to the United States he had at once taken up again his academic career. Johns Hopkins University, Yale University, Groton School, and Princeton University gave him his first experience of the American academic scene; he adapted himself to it quickly and completely. Like every good teacher he had a strong desire to express himself; like every good scholar he was a versatile linguist. To the Greek and Latin, the French and Italian he had learned in school and university he soon added English, and, though his voice never lost the smooth vowels and throaty consonants of German speech, he spoke the new language fluently. By the time he left Princeton for Cornell his colleagues acclaimed him as an excellent teacher and scholar and gave him high place in the academic life of the United States. He had completed a new chapter in his career.

The first chapter, the German one, began with his birth in Berlin in 1905. He was member of a family famous in the scholarly world both for the achievements of his grandfather, Theodor Mommsen, the renowned historian of classical civilization, and of the sociologists, Max and Alfred Weber, who were his uncles. The young Theodor found himself committed to the life of a scholar almost before he left his mother's knee, and as he grew up he enjoyed the company of many scholars and professional men, some conservative, some liberal in their outlook upon the academic and political life of Germany. From them he derived intellectual tastes and standards which were to endure. He found among them men whom he regarded throughout his life with reverence and affection. Here his informal education began. Yet the actions of German scholars and professional men put before him his first dilemma. For while he admired much, he found much to condemn, particularly the tendency of the group as a whole to lack a sense of public duty and the readiness of many individuals to co-operate with the Hitler dictatorship.

His own formal studies took him to Heidelberg and Vienna during the years 1923 to 1925. In 1929 the University of Berlin gave him the degree of Doctor of Philosophy. He had already joined the staff of the great historical enterprise called *Monumenta Germaniae Historica* and continued as one of its resident associates until 1935, carrying on his scholarly pursuits at many research centers in Germany and Italy.

His departure for the United States in 1936 was the most striking event in his life. Not only did he leave the land of his birth, he left his family, his mother, sisters, and brothers, and he turned his back on a way of living which, despite its shortcomings, held many happy memories for him. He came to the United States because he hoped to find generosity and toleration in the relations of man and man and because he sought opportunity to associate freely with persons of all classes and creeds. He was not disappointed. And he himself, the newcomer, actively and joyfully took up the life of an American. He made friends in all branches of society. As if to wipe out the shame of Hitler, he reaffirmed his association with Jewish scholars, both native Americans whom he now met for the first time and those whom he had known in Europe and who in some instances had counseled him on his decision to live in the United States. During the Second World War he took part in the program of the United States Army for training American soldiers who were assigned to American universities, and he also helped to present his own interpretation of history to Germans who were held as prisoners of war in the United States. In the years immediately following the war he was a member of the faculty of

Princeton University, where the companionship of his colleagues and of members of the Institute for Advanced Study deepened his interest in scholarly work.

When he joined the history department of Cornell University, his colleagues welcomed him as a scholar and teacher and soon learned that he had other gifts, academic and personal, to give to the life of the community. He had many friends and acquaintances among scholars throughout the world, and he made available to his colleagues and graduate students the advantage of these associations. No one knew better than he where to turn for information about candidates for a university post or for judgment on an out-of-the-way piece of scholarship. He corresponded extensively and traveled often to keep fresh his knowledge and to renew his associations, for he enjoyed to the full the sense of intimacy with others which came from a leisurely meal, an informal conversation, or a long letter.

Such was the range of his interests and his capacity for friendship that he soon associated himself with the departments of classics and literature at Cornell and thus substantially strengthened the ties of the history department with all other scholars in the humanities. The great Petrarch collection in the Cornell University Library had attracted him before he became a member of the university faculty.

In the early pre-Cornell days his friendship with the local scholars who used the Petrarch collection and with others whose interest in medieval studies and the classics touched his own had given him a place, a visitor's place, in the Cornell community such as he enjoyed in a dozen American universities. Once he joined the Cornell faculty, he rapidly enlarged his circle of friends and acquaintances, young and old. He took a leading part in building up medieval and renaissance studies and promoted every cause which seemed likely to raise the quality of scholarship in the College of Arts and Sciences and the Graduate School. On one occasion, when offered an attractive post at another university, he agreed to stay at Cornell on condition that the university endow a fellowship in medieval studies, the George Lincoln Burr Fellowship.

The scholarly interests growing out of his own academic work were not his only sphere of activity. His love of music was another; a third was his love of the graphic arts, which caused him to assemble a small collection of modern paintings. He was a great concertgoer and led his friends on journeys, sometimes hazardous and snow-swept, to Rochester and Syracuse. He collected gramophone records and invited his friends—particularly graduate students—to musical evenings at his apartment. There, as the middle-aged bachelor who shared his pleasures with the young and told them stories of the Germany of his youth, he was, perhaps, at his happiest.

He was a noteworthy teacher throughout his career in the United States; indeed, at Princeton University the students nominated him as one of their best teachers. At Cornell he devoted himself to relatively small classes and to seminars. He also served as representative of the history department in its dealings with the Graduate School. His own graduate students were his special care; their training had first call upon his time. Although his interest in medieval history was wide, he kept to a narrow line in planning the work of his seminars, for his purpose was to give his students the tools of historical research rather than a detailed knowledge of history. His model was the training he himself had received in Germany, where the seminar was a co-operative workshop, the professor leading and directing but not dominating his students. He believed medieval history to be an ideal subject for the teaching of young historians because the relative scarcity of the records available for study made every fragment precious.

From term to term he chose a few documents—an early history, a biography, some letters—and led his students through a microscopic examination of them. They searched step by step, discussing here perhaps the phrases by which a pope described his authority or a king alluded to his powers, perhaps there a seemingly innocent word which suggested a new turn of thought in the relations of church and state. Together Mommsen and his students put before one another at these seminars the fruits of the studies each had made in preparation for the discussion, and in this exchange of knowledge and opinions they worked until, to use his phrase, they had "squeezed the sources dry."

While the labor continued there was no time for rest. So intense was the concentration that all felt the effects, not least Mommsen. He had prepared as assiduously as his students; he had guided and stimulated the conversation from idea to idea and called into play the whole range of his knowledge. The end of the week's seminar—the weekly crucifixion, as one of his students called it—left all exhausted. Mommsen repaired the ravages of the afternoon by leading the group, or most of it, away to dinner at the Faculty Club, where the rule was that no one should talk history. One of his musical evenings often continued the work of recreation.

His writings covered a wide range of subjects and displayed meticulous scholarship, as the following pages show. Regarded as a whole they resemble a thriving, wide-spreading tree whose roots were in the early middle ages and thus drew nourishment from the historical writings of his grandfather. His Petrarch studies, which he continued to the end, were the center of his scholarly interests; they were the trunk of the tree. The branches reached out in many directions to touch the history of Germany, Italy, France, and Britain; one of them, represented by his work with the *Monumenta Germaniae Historica,* followed the line of his apprentice days as a historian. He did not see his work in this way; to him it lacked unity, authority, and volume. But he was judging by the standards his grandfather had set; he had in mind the array of massive works usually associated with the name of Mommsen.

To criticize himself on this score was not reasonable. The younger Mommsen reached manhood in Germany during the desperate years following the First World War; he uprooted himself to come to the United States when his career as a historian was just beginning. Then, within four years, came the Second World War, and the whole academic system was out of joint again. What were his thoughts during these dark days? He had shown his own aversion to the Germany of the thirties, to the Germany of Hitler; yet in the eyes of the world Germany was Hitler. Even so he must have shuddered at the defeat of Germany, at her devastation and her dismemberment. When he visited Germany in 1948, he saw the home of his mother and the home of his father in ruins, only a few bricks standing; the Germany of his happier memories had vanished. The cataclysm was all the more difficult for him to bear because as a result of his visit he judged that Germany had learned nothing from her experience and because some within his own German circle had supported Hitler. In the light of these disasters what is remarkable is not the paucity of Mommsen's scholarly writings during the early and middle 1940's but the fact that he wrote anything at all.

In the late 1940's and the early 1950's he renewed his vigor as a scholar. As a teacher he had his success at Princeton University. During these years and when he came to Cornell he seemed to be beginning the most stable and promising period of his career. He was hard at work. One saw him in the early morning, a stocky figure striding across the campus. At lunch time he was never without two or three companions. Sometimes he dined alone in his apartment; often he spent his evenings with friends and students. They sought him eagerly for he was a gentle, genial man, lively in conversation and fond of describing the world he had known. His wit was a scholar's wit, precise in its focus on individual objects, yet ranging wide in the discussion of books and music, men and places, and always kindly in describing those with whom he had worked, particularly the young.

The zest with which he maintained a conversation and the energy of his physical movements made him appear to be a man of robust health, but this was not so. He moved energetically because his body was by nature sluggish and poorly co-ordinated. He conversed in a lively manner to drive away melancholy. The image of his grandfather cast a shadow on his own work, and the dark picture of a Germany that had destroyed itself was always with him. From these burdens death delivered him on July 18, 1958, and in so doing took away from family, friends, colleagues, and students an accomplished scholar and a generous companion.

FREDERICK GEORGE MARCHAM

Contents

PART I

Studies in the Diplomatic and Military History of Italy and the Empire, 1316-1687

1

The Habsburg-Angevin Marriage Alliance of 1316*

ON the 19th and 20th October, 1314, the dual election of Frederick the Fair and Louis of Bavaria as king of Rome had taken place in Frankfurt. In consequence of the resulting internal conflict in Germany, concern with conditions in Italy was relegated to the background; but it did not disappear altogether. In fact, significantly enough, the two pretenders to the throne adopted different policies in this respect. Louis remained loyal to the traditional practices of imperial law by appointing John of Beaumont, the brother of Count William of Holland, Vicar General of the empire in Italy on January 4, 1315,[1] and by announcing this action in Italy by means of a circular.[2] To be sure, no further significance attached to this appointment; we do not even know whether John took office in Italy in person. Subsequently, until the battle of Mühldorf in 1322 and apart from the politically insignificant granting of some privileges, Louis refrained from any further active intervention in Italy.[3]

* Reprinted from *Neues Archiv der Gesellschaft für ältere deutsche Geschichtskunde,* L (1935), 600–615. Translated by Walter M. Simon.

1 *Monumenta Germaniae Historica. Constitutiones,* ed. J. Schwalm, V, 178, nr. 195.

2 *Const.,* V, 179, nr. 196. See also *ibid.,* 291, nr. 347.

3 See *Const.,* V, 207, nr. 239; 282, nr. 333; 427, nr. 537; 428, nr. 538; 516, nr. 653.

By contrast, Frederick did not immediately appoint a Vicar General or imperial vicars for separate districts.[4] He attempted instead to prepare for his Italian policy by diplomacy. He was in a favorable position by virtue of the fact that as the husband of Elizabeth, the daughter of James II of Aragon,[5] he was the son-in-law of a monarch with exceptionally good diplomatic connections in all capitals, particularly in Avignon and Naples, the two centers of power most important for Italy; moreover, as a result of his campaigns for the conquest of Sardinia James was himself actively interested in Italian affairs. Indeed, on July 10, 1314, even before his election, Frederick had asked his father-in-law *quod, si fortuna nobis arriserit in hac parte* (i.e. in Germany), *in partibus Ytalie nostra promoveatis negocia.*[6] In his reply of October 17, 1314, James promised to further Frederick's policy *ubicumque poterimus.*[7] Frederick continued on several occasions to request James' support in Avignon and in Italy; [8] significantly, however, whereas James not only gave undertakings but actually took steps with respect to Avignon, he made no response whatever to Frederick's Italian plans.[9]

Early in 1315, Frederick also entered into negotiations with

[4] The first imperial vicar appointed by Frederick, without a precise demarcation of his jurisdiction, was Castruccio Antelminelli, on August 5, 1315 (*Const.*, V, 270, nrs. 314 and 315). Cf. my article on Castruccio in the *Atti della R. Accademia Lucchese,* N.S. III (1934), 35 ff. [See below, pp. 19–32.]

[5] See J. Schrader, *Isabella von Aragonien, Gemahlin Friedrichs des Schönen von Österreich,* 1915.

[6] Heinrich Finke, *Acta Aragonensia* (Berlin and Leipzig, 1922), III, 274, nr. 122.

[7] *Const.*, V, 78, nr. 82.

[8] Frederick's letter to James of Sept. 25, 1314, i.e. also before the election (*Const.*, V, 77, nr. 81); James' reply is lost. Further letters from Frederick to James on Jan. 13, 1315 (*Const.*, V, 187, nr. 210), and on May 23, 1315 (*Const.*, V, 241, nr. 281, incorrectly dated 13 May). See also the letter of Duke Rudolf of Saxony dated Jan. 1, 1315 (Finke, III, 275, nr. 123; Gross, *Regesta Habsburgica,* III, 249, nr. 56a), and the king of Aragon's answer of March 8, 1315 (*Const.*, V, 197, nr. 225). On Frederick's plan for an early Italian expedition in the summer of 1315 see also the letter of one of the queen's ladies-in-waiting of June 6, 1315 (*Const.*, V, 254, nr. 291, and Finke, I, 362, note 6).

[9] See *Const.*, V, 196, nr. 223; 198 ff., nrs. 226–228; 219 ff., nrs. 256–260; 238 ff., nrs. 276–280; 267 ff., nrs. 311–313; 283, nr. 335; 284, nr. 338; 285, nr. 339; 316, nr. 376; etc.

Sicily. His letter to King Frederick III, brother of James II, has been lost; but from the Sicilian's reply (May/June 1315) [10] we can deduce that it contained a notification of his election, a report on conditions in Germany, and a request for support. The king of Sicily promised his aid and reminded the Habsburg Frederick of the undeviating loyalty to emperor and empire that he had demonstrated in the time of Henry VII.

The arrival of this letter caused the king of Sicily's German friends to suggest that the formal exchange of assurances of friendship could be converted into a closer alliance by a marriage between Catherine, Frederick the Fair's sister, and Peter, the heir to the Sicilian throne.[11] Frederick responded by a letter (September 22, 1315) to his father-in-law leaving to him the decision and possible further steps in this matter,[12] which shows how dependent Frederick was on James in his Italian policy.[13]

10 On April 30, 1315, James sent Frederick's no longer extant letter to his brother in Sicily (*Const.*, V, 226, nr. 264), and on June 18 the latter sent James a copy of his reply to Frederick (see Finke, I, 353, note). Schwalm (*Const.*, V, 227, nr. 266) is therefore right in assigning the letter to the period between these two dates, as contrasted with Finke, I, 352, nr. 239: "1315 vor April 15." Gross' appendix to nr. 181, which follows Finke, should accordingly also be corrected.

11 The date is derived from the fact that there is no mention of the marriage project in Frederick of Sicily's letter of May/June 1315 referred to above, but that on the other hand Frederick the Fair on Sept. 22 informed his father-in-law of this plan, originated, as he said, *ad suggestionem sinceram quorundam ipsius Friderici* [of Sicily] *amicorum* (Finke, III, 293, nr. 132). This disposes of Davidsohn's conjecture (*Mitteilungen des österreichischen Instituts für Geschichtsforschung,* XXXVII, 200 f.) that consultations had already taken place between Frederick and his wife and sister, with a view to a Sicilian marriage for the latter, on the occasion of the wedding of Duke Henry of Carinthia (the beginning of February, see Gross, nr. 86). The assumption of E. Haberkern, *Der Kampf um Sizilien in den Jahren 1302–1337* (1921), p. 187, note 10, that Frederick was given the idea of the marriage project by the king of Sicily's letter of congratulation should be corrected to the extent that the initiative came from German friends of the latter from the period of his coalition with Henry VII.

12 Finke, III, 293, nr. 132; Gross, nr. 326a; cf. also the letter of Queen Elizabeth to her father of October 1, 1315 (Finke, III, 296, nr. 134; Gross, nr. 332a).

13 It is likewise characteristic that Frederick sent his reply to the Sicilian court via Barcelona (see *Const.*, V, 284, nr. 338); since he had left the final decision to his father-in-law, the letter must have been couched in very general terms.

Although Frederick had not concealed his eagerness to conclude such an alliance, James categorically advised against it on the ground that Peter of Sicily was bound by his earlier betrothal to Beatrix, the daughter of Henry VII, *iuxta sacrorum canonum instituta.*[14]

Nevertheless, the real reason for James' negative attitude is probably to be found in his disinclination to see his son-in-law involved in the conflict between the kingdoms of Naples and Sicily that resulted from the Sicilian Vespers. James, as the brother of the king of Sicily and the brother-in-law of the king of Naples, had consistently tried to mediate in this dispute, although in general he had tended to be on the side of his Angevin brother-in-law; and this policy of mediation was bound to be made more difficult if James' German son-in-law, the possible future emperor, committed himself to one of the two parties by a marriage alliance. Moreover, James' mediation appeared particularly necessary just at this time, for March 1, 1316, was the expiration date of the truce that on December 16, 1314, had put a temporary end to the war between the two countries which had broken out in connection with Henry VII's Italian expedition.[15]

An Aragonese diplomatic report of February 25, 1316, provides useful information concerning the prevailing mood in Naples and in Messina.[16] Both courts were at a complete loss as to the attitude of the future incumbents both of the vacant papal throne and of the imperial throne, disputed by two aspirants; both courts feared that the other might gain a decided advantage when these situations clarified, and they ob-

[14] *Const.*, V, 285, nr. 339 and note 1.

[15] On this Neapolitan-Sicilian conflict cf. Haberkern, *op. cit., passim.*, but especially pp. 68 f., and Caggese, *Roberto d'Angiò, passim.*, but especially vol. I (1915), 213 f. and vol. II (1931), 163 ff.

[16] The ambassador speaks of the favorable conditions for making peace that prevailed at the moment: in the first place because both parties had suffered considerable losses, in the second place "quia propter eventus incertos pape et imperatoris et aliqua alia negocium contingencia non potest sciri certitudinaliter, cuius conditio melior sit futura. Et talis papa posset creari, vel taliter imperator se posset habere, quo unus super alium videretur habere magnum avantagium, propter quod posset ad pacem difficilius inclinari" (Finke, II, 715, nr. 448. See also Caggese, II, 3 ff.).

served the activities of the other with appropriate care and anxiety, since every move in this involved game, with its international complications, might bring about tactical changes of great importance. There can therefore be little doubt that Robert of Naples was cognizant of the attempts to steer Frederick the Fair in the direction of a Sicilian alliance as well as of James of Aragon's negative attitude toward this project.

At exactly this same time, at the beginning of 1316, a mission from Frederick arrived in Naples, probably charged, like the similar mission to Sicily a year earlier, only with establishing diplomatic connections and not with making any concrete proposals, from which Frederick was prohibited so long as the Sicilian marriage negotiations were pending. It is highly probable that Robert seized the opportunity of this mission to take the initiative himself by proposing, in his turn, a marriage alliance between his house and the Habsburgs, that is to say, between Catherine and the heir to the Angevin throne, Duke Charles of Calabria. The German envoy to Naples returned home on February 3, 1316, in the company of a Neapolitan ambassador who, on this hypothesis, must have been the bearer of the marriage project.[17] If this was the case, the Neapolitan offer

[17] We have only one piece of evidence concerning the German embassy and the reply it received, an entry in the Angevin *exitus regestrum,* according to which on February 3, 1316 "Iohanni de Ypra clerico et familiari regis et Iohanni de Lusimburgo nuncio domini regis Romanorum . . . missis per dominum regem [i.e. Robert] ad certas partes," a payment to cover their expenses was made (Gross, nr. 387, regarded this entry as probably the first trace of the marriage negotiations). Frederick himself attested to the fact that the initiative in the negotiations came from Naples when on June 30, 1316, he informed his Italian adherents of the treaty and described the agreements as *per magnificum principem Robertum Ierusalem et Sicilie regem nuper a maiestate nostra petita* (*Const.,* V, 304, nr. 364). See also the corroborating passage in Queen Elizabeth's letter to her father of July 24, 1316 (Finke, III, 307, nr. 143). But even if this evidence is discarded as possibly tainted with subjectivity, it was objectively impossible for the German embassy which returned from Naples on February 3 to have been originally sent off with cognizance of James' letter dated January 8 from Barcelona. The distances (Barcelona–south Germany, south Germany–Naples) were too great and the time (a bare four weeks, from which must be subtracted the intervals necessary for consultations at the courts of Frederick and Robert) too short. But so long as the Sicilian project was pending Frederick could not conceivably launch discussions with another

would have been made about four weeks after James' rejection of the Sicilian offer, and would have arrived in Germany at a correspondingly later date.

Unfortunately we have no information as to how Frederick received these two missives, but we do know that he rapidly accomplished the change of front which they both suggested. No further mention was made of the Sicilian project. On the contrary a Habsburg-Angevin marriage agreement was concluded on June 23, 1316, only four months after the arrival of Robert's offer.[18] In the meantime the Neapolitan ambassador had received further instructions from his court.[19]

The actual treaty instruments probably prepared by both parties are not extant. Our knowledge of the matter is based on the following documents:

1) on Frederick's part: a circular to his Italian adherents, dated June 30, 1316,[20] and letters to James II from Frederick, dated July 18, [21] and from Queen Elizabeth, dated July 24; [22]

2) on Robert's part: a notification to the Iustitiarius of Montorio Superiore, dated August 1, obviously a specimen of a circular to a number of Neapolitan officials and towns,[23] a

---

party. Haberkern, *op. cit.*, p. 187, note 10, assumes without substantiation that the initiative for this marriage project also emanated from Frederick the Fair; Caggese, II, 10, declares that nothing is known on this question.

[18] Nothing is known about the place where the treaty was signed. We know only that on June 26, three days after the date of the treaty, the king was two days' journey distant from Schaffhausen (see Gross, nr. 480 and 479a; on the document allegedly issued by King Frederick in Vienna on June 26, 1316, see the remarks of Gross, nr. 462).

[19] According to the Angevin *exitus regestrum* in Naples, the couriers Annechinus and Franciscus de Flandria, *accessuris extra regnum* were paid over five ounces of gold on May 4, 1316 (Naples, State Archives, Reg. Ang. 209, fol. 333). On August 1 the same two persons, *redituris in Alamaniam,* received another payment (*ibid.,* fol. 333; see Gross, nr. 484). The word *redire* indicates that the couriers had just been in Germany; it was probably they who brought the news of the signing of the treaty to Naples on July 31 (this date is derived from Robert's circular printed below).

[20] *Const.,* V, 304, nr. 364 (copies for Treviso and Castruccio). See also *Const.,* V, 303, nr. 363, and 305, nr. 365.

[21] Finke, III, 306, nr. 142; Gross, nr. 477a.

[22] Finke, III, 307, nr. 143; Gross, nr. 479a.

[23] Hitherto unprinted, summary in Caggese, I, 654, note 3, printed below [pp. 17–18] from the original mandate in the State Archives in

letter to the Aragonese ambassador Petrus Ferrandi de Ixar, dated August 2,[24] and letters from the king and queen of the same date to James.[25]

From these conflicting sources we must try to deduce the probable contents of the agreements.

Frederick's accounts confine themselves largely to the fact of the marriage alliance. The king hoped that this agreement would lead to a pacification and settlement of the hostilities by which Italy was torn. At the same time, Frederick wished it "to attract [the Anjous] to the empire," *imperio atrahere, allicere et nuptiarum placare probabili blandimento,* terminology which, in view of the family pride of the house of Anjou, connected as it was with the French royal family, was not very diplomatic or wise when employed in an open circular. Queen Elizabeth made use of these same terms in her letter to her father on July 24, in which (like her husband in his letter to James a few days earlier) she also expressed the hope that the marriage would contribute to a settlement of the Neapolitan-Sicilian conflict too and would be welcome to James for this reason alone. The king of Aragon, who this time had not been asked for his agreement in advance, declared in his reply of September 19, 1316, that he shared these hopes, but otherwise expressed no opinion as to the concrete implications of the alliance.[26]

Frederick's letters are silent concerning the detailed provi-

---

Naples: Pergamene della R. Zecca, vol. 22, nr. 477. We cannot venture to explain the provenance of this document. That it is a specimen of a circular, accidentally preserved is clear in the first place from the fact that at the end of the document itself the king lists a number of places which he wishes to inform directly. But, in the second place, the condition of the document indicates that it took the form of a circular: the addressee was named originally only as *iustitiarius,* with a space left for a later indication of the district; the two dots before *iustitiario* took the place of the name of the individual in each particular case (see below, [p. 17], note a). I am much obliged for the friendly suggestions of Count Riccardo Filangieri de Candida, director of the State Archives in Naples, and of Professor Sthamer.

[24] Finke, III, 310, nr. 145; Gross, nr. 480a. In both Finke's and Gross' descriptive notices "imperial vicar in the Guelf districts of Italy" should be substituted for "imperial vicar in all of Italy."

[25] Finke, III, 310, nr. 145, note.

[26] *Const.,* V, 316, nr. 376. (Finke's note, III, 307: "Kein zeichen einer Antwort" should accordingly be corrected. See also *Const.,* V, 318, nr. 377.)

sions of the agreements,[27] for which we are therefore dependent on Robert's accounts. According to the latter the provisions were of two kinds. In the first place the two kings undertook not to attack each other, but to come to each other's aid with both advice and action. To be sure, Robert's words, taken literally, indicate a unilateral undertaking on Frederick's part; [28] and it is true that Robert would have been more interested in such a guarantee than Frederick, bearing in mind the possibility of a Roman expedition on Frederick's part and remembering the policy that Henry VII had adopted toward him for imperial considerations only a few years before. Nevertheless, in view of the prevalent practice known from numerous instances, it is to be assumed that Robert and Frederick in fact concluded a bilateral "non-aggression treaty," as we should say nowadays.[29]

But if in this respect King Robert had the greater interest and enjoyed the greater advantage, this was even more true of the second point, which provided nothing less than that King Frederick should appoint Robert's son, Duke Charles of Calabria, as imperial vicar for all Guelf areas in Italy. Robert's accounts of the meaning and implications of this appointment differ. According to his letter to the Aragonese ambassador the vicariate was to include all areas which had belonged to the Guelf party in the time of Henry VII, belonged to them now, or might belong to them in the future.[30] On the other hand, in his letter to the Iustitiarius, those districts only are defined as Guelf which had been ruled by Guelfs in the time of Henry VII.[31] In view of the importance of the appointment it would

[27] Communication of further details was probably left to the embassy which Frederick sent to Italy at the same time as the circular of June 30 (*Const.*, V, 303, nr. 363).

[28] See below, [p. 17].

[29] Robert himself, in his communication to the Aragonese ambassador, also speaks of *condicionibus et convencionibus, quibus ipse electus et nos invicem striccius obligamur* (Finke, III, 310, nr. 145).

[30] "Constituitque idem electus . . . ducem . . . eius vicarium in tota Ytalia in terris, que erant de parte Guelfa tempore domini Henrici quondam Romanorum regis, sunt ad presens vel erunt in futurum" (Finke, III, 310, nr. 145).

[31] ". . . dans et concedens (i.e. Frederick) eidem primogenito nostro per

be of great interest to know its precise terms, but owing to the loss of the agreements themselves this is very difficult. The problem is whether the imperial vicariate pertained to the area of Guelf power at the time of the Luxembourg emperors, or extended also to all areas since conquered by the Guelfs and even to those which might be conquered by them in the future. The probabilities are in favor of the former and against the latter supposition. In the first place a reference to the future, such as would be indicated by the latter supposition, would have introduced into a treaty too great a factor of uncertainty, which would have contained considerable potentialities of conflict and could scarcely have contributed to the goal of a settlement of Italian animosities. We should also consider the addressees of the various accounts. The more comprehensive version was addressed to the envoy of a foreign power; it was expressly designed for use in pending negotiations [32] with Sicily, Robert's most active opponent; [33] Robert was therefore likely to be tempted to exaggerate the concessions received from the German king beyond the actual provisions of the agreement in order to use them as a means of exercising pressure. In the account addressed to the officials and towns of Robert's own kingdom this factor was absent, and an unvarnished report of the facts was adequate.

According to these considerations the contents of the Habsburg-Angevin treaty of June 23, 1316, may be reconstructed as follows:

1) Catherine of Austria is betrothed by proxy to the heir to

---

totam Ytaliam in omnibus terris imperii vicariam Guelfis videlicet, que per Guelfos olim gubernate fuerunt tempore quondam domini Henrici de Lisimburg, regis Alamanie nominati" (see below, [p. 17]).

32 "Predictis (i.e. convencionibus) autem in tractato nobiscum negocio, pro quo itis, utamini, sicut prudencia vestra cognoverit promocioni ipsius negocii expedire" (Finke, III, 310, nr. 145).

33 It is clear from the identity of the addressee, Petrus Ferdinandi de Ixar, who in 1316 attempted to mediate between Robert and Frederick on behalf of James of Aragon, that these items of information were to be used in the course of the Neapolitan negotiations with Sicily (cf. Finke, II, 671, nr. 423; 718, nr. 450, especially the note about Petrus' mission on p. 725; 933, note; III, 279. For the general context of these negotiations see Haberkern, p. 75).

the Neapolitan throne, Duke Charles of Calabria, with the usual agreements concerning the dowry and its settlement [34] as well as concerning the embassy to be sent from the Neapolitan court to collect Catherine on Italian soil.[35]

2) Kings Frederick and Robert undertake not to attack each other.

3) King Frederick appoints Duke Charles of Calabria to be imperial vicar for all areas in Italy which were Guelf in the time of Emperor Henry VII.

According to Frederick the Fair's intentions the agreement was designed *imperio atrahere,* "to attract the king of Naples to the empire." For an understanding of this expression, as well as for a correct evaluation of the treaty as a whole, a brief examination of the situation in Italy, as well as of the recent Roman expedition of Henry VII, is necessary.

The Italian peninsula had for a long time been torn by the most violent animosities, partly between the communes and signories, partly within the several territories between the ruling families, social classes, or variously composed factions; the party names Guelf and Ghibelline actually served to designate the most widely divergent kinds of hostile relationships. Henry VII, however, had crossed the Alps with the intention of putting an end to these quarrels and of reconciling the several authorities by subordinating them to a new legal order, or rather to a revival of the old imperial legal order. But the result of his campaign was precisely the reverse of this original purpose. Even previously it had often been the case that, in view of the complicated involvements of the Italian state system, local conflicts had been fought out in larger arenas, but after the emperor's death Italy was manifestly divided into two camps: the *pars imperialis,* which had rallied under the imperial banner,[36] and the opposing party which styled itself the *devoti*

[34] This is evident from one of Robert's papers dated Dec. 31, 1316 (Gross, nrs. 545 and 629).

[35] In Robert's circular to his adherents it is said that Catherine "assignetur instanter gentibus nostris et ipsius primogeniti nostri in civitate Trivisii, deinde in regnum cum comitiva honorabili traducenda" (see below, [p. 18]). On the composition of this *comitiva* see Gross, nr. 484.

[36] It should be noted here that *pars imperialis* was the customary name

sanctae matris ecclesiae and which regarded the king of Naples as its patron. The party names Guelf and Ghibelline, therefore, acquired once more a significance similar to that which they had had in the days of the Hohenstaufen but which they had lost during the long period when the imperial power had left Italy virtually to its own devices and when any reference to the empire, positive or negative, had therefore become largely meaningless. Henry VII had attempted to superimpose the empire over these two "parties" and to absorb them in a higher unity. It is therefore no accident that the official sources (unusually plentiful for his reign) contain only one reference to the names Guelf and Ghibelline, and even this one with the meaning just suggested: in the summer of 1311 the king directed his ambassador to Pope Clement V to inform the latter of the state of affairs in Lombardy and Tuscany *et qualiter se habet* (i.e. Henry) *absque omni partialitate ad Guelfos et Guibellinos.*[37] These designations occur nowhere else in the extant letters or privileges issued by the emperor, whereas they appear frequently in all the contemporary Italian, Spanish, and papal documents.[38] The force of events and of circumstances gradually drove Henry increasingly in the direction of becoming the leader of the *pars imperialis,* i.e. of the Ghibellines; but he consistently refused to acknowledge this development formally by ignoring the party names.

After this backward glance at the period of Henry VII we can see clearly the radical change of policy that Frederick the Fair undertook by concluding the agreement of the summer of 1316. He abandoned all pretense of ignoring the existence of two rival parties, accepting it instead as an accomplished fact

---

for the Ghibelline party. For example, Frederick the Fair's appointment of Castruccio (April 4, 1320) as Vicar General of a number of specified places *cum aliis terris partis imperialis Pistorii subiectis* (*Const.,* V, 458, nr. 570) is to be translated as "together with other districts subject to the imperial (Ghibelline) party of Pistoia," that is to say, those districts belonging to the Pistoian exiles, constituted as an independent community. Gross' descriptive notice for nr. 928 should be corrected accordingly.

37 *Const.,* IV, 604, 21.

38 Cf., for example, the Index of *Const.,* vol. IV under "Gibellini" (p. 1477) and "Guelfi" (p. 1517) and Finke, *Acta Aragonensia,* vols. I–III.

and attempting merely to attract them to the empire (*imperio atrahere*) in one fashion or another and thus to make them, after all, a part of the empire. One of these parties, the Guelfs, with the Angevin royal house at its head, was in principle opposed and hostile to any claim to imperial suzerainty. Frederick sought to render this situation of fact as harmless as he could by legalizing it when he conferred the title of imperial vicar in the Guelf territories on Duke Charles. In so doing, to be sure, he acknowledged the existence of two spheres of interest in Italy, the control of which the empire was thenceforth to share with the Angevins.

The direct results of the agreement corresponded to Frederick's expectations (as expressed in his reports) in at least one area in which the conflict had raged with particular bitterness, Tuscany. The war-weariness prevalent there probably contributed to the conclusion of a truce (August 1316) between the Guelf and Ghibelline communes, as demanded by the heads of the two parties who were now in alliance; and this was followed in the next year by a definitive peace.[39] The wedding journey of Catherine, the daughter and the sister of German kings, through Italy, and her ceremonial welcome in such centers of Guelf sentiment as Bologna and particularly Florence might therefore have appeared as the symbol of the new harmony.[40]

At this same time, just before his son's wedding, Robert made an effort to buy a crown that had at one time belonged to Henry VII and had been left behind by him in Rome.[41] In the document dealing with this matter Robert referred to Henry as the "self-styled king of the Romans," (*se Romanorum regem dicentis*) that is to say, here as elsewhere, he disputed the legitimacy of the Luxembourg emperor's title. This phrase must be considered in conjunction with that of the circular of August 1 in which he informed his subjects of the conclusion of the marriage alliance and in which he referred to Frederick as duke

[39] The best treatment of these events is Davidsohn, *Geschichte von Florenz,* III, 604 ff.

[40] The available information on this wedding journey has been collected by Gross, nrs. 484, 499, 508–510, 519, 520a, 546; cf. Davidsohn, *op. cit.,* III, 607, and Caggese, I, 654 ff.

[41] See Robert's mandate of Sept. 20, 1316 (*Const.,* IV, 1307, note 1).

of Austria and king of Germany, but not as king of Rome.[42] Although Robert permitted his son to receive one of the highest imperial posts from the actual possessor of imperial power and thus formally to become a member of the official hierarchy of the empire, and although he used Frederick's correct title in diplomatic notes, he declined, in the last resort, to attribute its proper significance to the emperor's position. It appeared expedient to him, at a time when the international situation was obscure, to enter into an alliance with the emperor, especially since it did not affect the actual power position of the Guelfs, whereas it did imply some weakening of imperial authority. So far as Robert was concerned, the Habsburg marriage alliance represented above all a tactical move against Sicily and the danger of a Sicilian alignment with the empire. In fact, he continued his policy of attempting to enlist German forces for his own purposes when, after the expiration of the truce, the war with Sicily was resumed in the spring of 1317.[43] Robert must have been very reluctant to fulfil the *quid pro quo* demanded by Frederick, the use of his good offices with the Curia in order to obtain papal recognition of Frederick's kingdom;[44] not many years, after all, had passed since Robert himself had asked Pope Clement V to deny imperial claims to dominion in

[42] See below, [p. 17].

[43] See the report of Christian Spinula to James II, dated March 26, 1317, to the effect that it had been rumored for some time "quod dominus rex Robertus intendit de Theotonicis se munire et quod miserit ad ducem Austeriche pro mille Theotonicis habendis" (Finke, II, 574, nr. 374; Gross, nr. 581).

[44] We learn from a letter of Frederick the Fair to James II, dated April 14, 1317, that an embassy from Frederick to Robert had just returned from Naples; in his reply to Frederick's request for his good offices with the Curia, Robert "qui status et negocii nostri [i.e. Frederick's] apud summum pontificem . . . intendit et vult, ut fermiter asseruit et promisit, vigil et fervens esse promotor," had promised to exert himself "sicut facere disposuit" (Finke, III, 330, nr. 156). Cf. James' reply, dated June 6, 1317, saying that Robert "non potuit propter brevitatem termini ad hoc dare operam, sicut facere disposuit, efficacem, set quod brevi et congruo tempore in ipso negocio operacione sollicita laborabit" (*Const.*, V, 347, nr. 411). In the early summer of the same year another ambassador, Ersus, was apparently sent by Frederick to Naples. This is confirmed by a Neapolitan Exchequer note according to which Ersus had left for home on August 14, 1317 (Gross, nr. 626).

Italy by delaying his recognition of the German election after Henry VII's death and making it conditional, among other things, on a renunciation of Italy.[45]

Robert, therefore, who, so far as we know, never allowed his son to use the title of imperial vicar, was not likely to be much concerned when on March 31, 1317, the new pope, John XXII, forbade persons of all ranks, even royal, to accept or to use the title of vicar; [46] in so doing, in fact, John made himself the spokesman of Guelf principles and of Robert's personal views. Shortly thereafter, on July 16, 1317, Robert received from the pope the office of imperial vicar for the duration of the vacancy of the imperial throne which, in the papal view, existed in Germany.[47]

This event marked the failure of Frederick's first attempt at an Italian policy in alliance with the Guelfs.[48] Henry VII had striven to pacify Italy by imposing the higher idea of the empire and by deliberately ignoring the existing party alignments; Louis of Bavaria later embarked on his Italian expedition of 1327 at the behest of the Ghibellines; Frederick the Fair tried to find a middle way. While leaving the forces hostile to the empire intact he tried to associate them formally with the empire by means of an imperial title; but in so doing he disregarded the self-contradiction that such a policy implied for the Guelfs. The failure of all three of these entirely different policies demonstrates the impossibility of a recovery of Italy for the empire after the estrangement at the end of the Hohenstaufen era.

[45] *Const.*, IV, 1369, nr. 1253.

[46] *Const.*, V, 340, nr. 401.

[47] *Const.*, V, 367, nr. 443.

[48] We cannot here go any further into Frederick the Fair's subsequent Italian policy, which generally was concerned only with northern Italy, though in 1320 he concluded another alliance with the kingdom of Naples (Gross, nrs. 963 and 964). It may be noted, however, that in pursuit of this policy Frederick at times played the part of a leader and defender of Guelf interests and therefore departed even more markedly from the traditional imperial policy than he had done in 1316.

Appendix

King Robert the Wise informs the Iustitiarius of the Principato ulteriore of the marriage of his son, Duke Charles of Calabria and Catherine, the sister of King Frederick the Fair.

Naples August 1, 1316.

Robertus Dei gracia rex Ierosolem et Sicilie, ducatus Apulie et principatus Capue, Provincie et Forcalquerii ac Pedimontis comes . . iusticiario Principatus [a] ultra Serras Montorii [a1] fideli suo graciam suam et bonam voluntatem. Ad fidelium nostrorum noticiam libenter gaudiosa perferimus, qui eos frequenter de multis inculcatis oneribus inviti quodammodo fatigamus, set primum prompta voluntas delectabiliter efficit, secundum urgens articulus patule necessitatis indicit. Sane noverit [b] vestra sincera devocio nunciorum nostrorum, quos pridem ad ducem [b] Austrie, Alamanie regem illustrem, misimus, heri die ultima preteriti mensis Iulii certas nos litteras recepisse, quod ipsi ex precedente tractatu iam habito die vicesima tercia Iunii proximo nunc transacti in spectabilem iuvenem Catherinam sororem regis eiusdem sicut in sponsam Caroli primogeniti nostri ducis Calabrie ipsius nomine et eadem domicella in eos tanquam in ipsum primogenitum nostrum suum sponsum legitimum per verba de presenti legitime consenserunt dictaque sponsa sacerdotali benedictione premissa fuit in ecclesia publice desponsata dictusque rex in maioris amoris vinculum confederavit se nobis per amabilem unionem promittens nos ipsumque primogenitum et terras nostras nullo unquam tempore offendere vel molestare aut permittere pro suo posse offendi vel ab aliis molestari, quin pocius nobis patenter assistere auxilio, consilio et favore, dans et concedens eidem primogenito nostro per totam Ytaliam in omnibus terris imperii vicariam Guelfis videlicet, que per Guelfos olim gubernate fuerunt

[a] From *Principatus* to *Montorii* was added by another hand. Because the space left was so small, the writing is very cramped.
[b] From *noverit* to *ducem* is written over an erasure.

[1] Montorio Superiore east of Sarno; see E. Sthamer, *Die Verwaltung der Kastelle im Königreich Sizilien unter K. Friedrich II. und Karl I. von Anjou* (*Die Bauten der Hohenstaufen in Unteritalien,* Erg. Bd. I), 1914, p. 112.

tempore quondam domini Henrici de Lisimburg, regis Alamanie nominati, subiuncta ordinacione concordi inter eosdem regem et nuncios nostros, ut domicella prefata assignetur instanter gentibus nostris et ipsius primogeniti nostri in civitate Trivisii,[2] deinde in regnum cum comitiva honorabili traducenda. Per que faciente pacis auctore speramus et credimus, quod dicte unionis et confederacionis nexus amabilis nobis nostrisque fidelibus pausam placidam quietis et pacis affert et multa prepedia implicite contencionis elidct. Volumus et fidelitati tue districte iubemus, quatinus statim receptis presentibus in singulis terris et locis decrete tibi provincie, in quibus expedire videris, ad exultacionem nostrorum fidelium nova huiusmodi divulgare studeas vel facias divulgari, exceptis civitatibus infrascriptis, quibus ea notificamus per alias nostras litteras speciales, quarum nomina sunt hec: videlicet Avellinum,[c3] Arianum,[4] Aquaputida,[5] Guardia Lombardorum,[6] Frequentum,[7] Apicium [8] et Mons Fusculus.[9]

Dat. Neapoli per Bartholomeum de Capua militem logothetam et prothonotarium regni Sicilie, anno domini M°.CCCXVI°, die primo Augusti, XIIII[e] indictionis, regnorum nostrorum anno VIII.[c]

[c] The ending of the brief, from *Avellinus* on, was added later, apparently in several stages. The rather shakily written words *per Bartholomeum de Capua militem* might be in the hand of the Chancellor.

[2] Treviso.

[3] Avellino south of Benevento.

[4] Ariano di Puglia west of Benevento.

[5] The present Mirabella Eclano southeast of Benevento. See Sthamer, *op. cit.*, 104, note 5.

[6] Guardia Lombardi southwest of Melfi.

[7] Frigento southeast of Benevento. [8] Apice east of Benevento.

[9] Montefusco southeast of Benevento.

2

Castruccio Castracani and the Empire*

CASTRUCCIO Castracani degli Antelminelli, by birth a noble of Lucca, bore the following titles at his death: *Dei gratia dux Lucanorum, Lateranensis comes, sacri Romani imperii vexillifer et Pisarum vicarius generalis.*[1] These dignities, which placed him in one of the highest ranks of the imperial hierarchy, he owed to imperial authority. He himself explicitly acknowledged this when he wrote to the Pisans on January 17, 1322, the day on which Louis of Bavaria's coronation raised him to the height of his power, that the life and safety of him and his followers depended solely on the *imperialis celsitudo.*[2]

Castruccio himself was thus convinced that he owed his position to the empire. Was this in fact true? The present study seeks to answer this question, not by a chronological account of Castruccio's life, but rather by examining, with this particular question in mind, the successive stages of his rise to power.[3]

* Reprinted from *Castruccio Castracani degli Antelminelli. Miscellanea di studi storici e letterari edita della Reale Accademia Lucchese, Atti della R. Accademia Lucchese,* N.S. III (Florence, 1934), 33–45. Translated by Eugene and Charlotte Rice.

1 Castruccio used the title in a codicil to his will dated December 20, 1327.

2 *Monumenta Germaniae Historica. Constitutiones,* ed. J. Schwalm, VI, 285, nr. 383.

3 Two modern biographies of Castruccio are F. Winkler, *Castruccio Castracani, Herzog von Lucca* (Berlin, 1897), and C. Magnani, *Castruccio*

Castruccio, later to become leader of the Ghibellines, was descended from a family originally Guelf. In the factional strife which divided Lucca, as it did Pistoia, Florence, and other Guelf cities, strife caused by personal rivalries between the leading houses, the Antelminelli took the side of the Bianchi. They were defeated; in 1301 the family was banished and, like the Bianchi of other Tuscan cities, oppressed by the Neri. Thus Castruccio grew up as an exile, living for thirteen years in an anti-Guelf environment. The Italian expedition of Henry VII was the crucial turning point of his life. Until then Castruccio had been a *condottiere,* serving France, Verona, and Venice far from his native city. Now he joined the imperial army, first in Lombardy under its captain general Werner von Homburg, then under the emperor himself, whom he followed to Pisa in 1312. In a letter to the Florentines sixteen years later he called himself a *planta* of Henry VII.[4] He expressed the same feeling of devoted gratitude by naming his sons Arrigo, Giovanni, and Valerano, the names of the emperor, his son, and his brother. But since Castruccio had attained no real prominence during the lifetime of Henry VII,[5] it is impossible to determine if, and in what way, the emperor personally favored him. He was, in any case, to honor Henry VII as the man who had given a powerful impetus to his destiny and to that of the Ghibelline party.

The power of the Ghibellines continued to grow after the premature death of Henry VII, above all because they had found in Uguccione della Faggiuola, lord of Pisa, a valiant chief. Castruccio remained in the background. Only the peace concluded by Uguccione with Lucca on April 25, 1341, made it possible for him and the other Luccan exiles to return to their native city. His rise to power begins here; for a few months later when war broke out anew between Lucca and Pisa, he was able to give Uguccione effective support in the conquest of Lucca.

(Milan, 1926). R. Davidsohn, *Geschichte der Stadt Florenz* is indispensable for placing Castruccio in the historical context of his time. See also the bibliography which E. Lazzareschi has added to his article on Castruccio in the *Enciclopedia Italiana,* IX, 384.

4 *Const.,* VI, 382, nr. 464.

5 His name does not occur in the well-preserved diplomas of Henry VII. See *Const.,* IV.

But when Uguccione did not reward his services with a share in the government of the city, he sought to establish himself outside of Lucca. He persuaded bishop Bernardino Malespina to make him viscount of the bishopric of Luni-Saranza (July 4, 1314). Within the district were the communes of Saranza and Castro, subject only to the bishop for the spiritualities, but as *camera imperii* independent for the temporalities. But even if Castruccio was incontestably to exercise effective power over these imperial enclaves, that power could be legitimized only by imperial law.

He found a solution by having the communes elect him imperial vicar of the Lunigiana at the first news of the election of a new German king (December 5, 1314). From the wording of the act which records Castruccio's election, it might appear that he did not know that two kings had been elected at Frankfurt. This is possible, though hardly probable. The elections of Louis of Bavaria and Frederick the Fair had taken place on two consecutive days (October 19 and 20); and in the uproar which followed, the two names could not have been kept silent. Spreading contrary rumors was perhaps a premeditated means of hiding the fact of a double election and, therefore, of avoiding the need to opt for one of the two rivals.

But soon decision became inevitable, for already at the beginning of 1315 King Louis made clear his Italian pretentions by naming a Vicar General. No sooner had Uguccione received this news than he openly allied himself with the Bavarian and in return received a diploma of investiture (March 26, 1315).

What was Castruccio's attitude at this moment?

Had he really wished to further the interests of the empire against its enemies, he should have followed the example of Uguccione and recognized Louis of Bavaria in order to avoid a schism in the imperial party which could only benefit the Guelfs. His very different conduct is to be explained by his rivalry with Uguccione. Castruccio was seeking to found an independent power, and he was right in fearing that Uguccione would exercise his influence over Louis, if he had not already done so, to secure legal recognition of the same power for himself. So Castruccio sent an ambassador to Frederick the Fair and got a privilege (dated August 5, 1315) making him his councilor and familiar and, more important, naming him Vicar General of all the imperial fortresses, castles, cities, and villages then in his possession. This appointment as an imperial vicar was of great value to Castruccio because it gave him juridical sanction for his present possessions and his future conquests.

While these negotiations with Frederick were in progress in Germany, Castruccio maintained an apparent friendship for Uguccione, supporting him in his struggle against Florence and fighting on August 29 in the battle of Montecatini, Uguccione's splendid victory over the Guelfs, won under the banner of the Wittelsbachs. Only somewhat later, after Castruccio's ambassador returned with the privilege from the Habsburg king, did Uguccione become aware of his duplicity and open conflict break out between them. Castruccio had executed for high treason many citizens of Massa, a city subject to him. Uguccione called these death sentences assassinations, an implicit assertion that Castruccio's title of imperial vicar was invalid, for it alone granted the right to impose the death penalty. The Guelfs must have rejoiced to see Ghibellines, who boasted of representing the empire and its law, fighting for these titles, which thus appeared even more empty.

The Pisan revolt of April 11, 1316, rather than respect for Castruccio's distant royal lord saved him from the death penalty passed against him by Uguccione. The political situation in Tuscany changed significantly, and not through the intervention of the empire or its rival representatives. At one blow Uguccione, until then lord of Pisa and Lucca and the recognized head of the Tuscan Ghibellines, lost his power over the two cities, after Florence the most important in Tuscany. With his fall the conflict between Guelf and Ghibelline lost its sharpness, the more so because at the same moment King Robert of Naples and Frederick the Fair, the heads of the two factions, made an alliance which was supposed to extend to their adherents. Frederick addressed a request for such a truce to his Italian supporters on June 30, 1316. It is preserved in two copies, one of them addressed to Castruccio. On March 12, 1317, peace was concluded between Pisa and Lucca, on the one hand, and Florence and the other Guelf communes of Tuscany, on the other.

This period of peace, though brief, was precious to Castruccio, enabling him to build up and fortify the powerful position he had acquired in Lucca after the fall of Uguccione. It did not take him long to attain this objective, for already in 1318 he felt himself strong enough to take the offensive and get himself elected captain general of a group of irreconcilable Pistoian exiles who had not wished to recognize the peace. Given the relations between Florence and Pistoia, war between Castruccio and the Guelf communes was bound to follow. For the next ten years Pistoia became the center of the struggle in Tuscany.

Before openly declaring war, however, Castruccio sent an embassy to King Frederick in Germany. But this time he did not content himself, as he had at the beginning of his career in 1315, with a general and appropriately vague formulation of rights. The privilege he now asked for, and got (April 4, 1320), sanctioned his effective position by naming him imperial Vicar General of Lucca and the district for a six-mile radius around the city. More than this it took into consideration his wider ambitions. Since the imperial vicariate granted him extended over all territories subject to the *pars imperialis* of Pistoia, he was in fact made head of the Tuscan Ghibellines and Bianchi. This implied a particular threat to Florence, for he got from the German king authority over territories long controlled by Florence *de facto* and since the peace of 1317 held legally. No sooner had he obtained this privilege than Castruccio got himself declared captain general and lord of Lucca for life (April 26, 1320). The former exile had now completely legitimized his external and internal position as lord of Lucca and could very willingly give the German ambassador in exchange the oath of fealty and obedience Frederick of Hapsburg required (May 1, 1320).

Precisely at this moment a war broke out between Guelfs and Ghibellines, which soon spread as far as Liguria. In opposition to King Robert of Naples, who had seized the lordship of Genoa, Castruccio was elected Vicar General of the Genoese exiles (July 19, 1320). On May 27, 1321, he had himself acclaimed lord of Pontremoli, having already held the title of *dominus generalis* of the *pars imperialis* of the city.

In the meantime the struggle for the German throne had been decided by Louis of Bavaria's victory at Mühldorf on September 28, 1322. Castruccio did not hesitate to abandon Frederick's cause and give his support to the victor; and when a royal plenipotentiary arrived in Tuscany in the spring of 1323, he took the same oath of loyalty as the lords of Pisa and Arezzo. He proved his loyalty in the summer of the same year by contributing effectively toward the liberation of Milan during the struggle for the city between the Ghibelline army led by Louis of Bavaria's Italian lieutenant, the count of Neiffen, and a Guelf and papal army. And in the autumn he refused to allow the pope's sentences against Louis to be published in his territories.

But while he showed himself so loyal a defender of imperial interests and while he probably conducted negotiations in Germany to confirm his power as an imperial vicar, Castruccio also took steps in a quite different direction.[6] The war between Pisa and the kingdom of Aragon over Sicily was entering its final stage. The relations between Castruccio and the Ghibelline city had long been strained, and an alliance between Aragon and Castruccio was to be foreseen. This was in fact brought about at the end of 1323 by one of the most interesting political figures of the period, Cardinal Napoleone Orsini, who had relations with both Castruccio and King James of Aragon. At the beginning of 1324 Castruccio sent an embassy to Barcelona and initiated negotiations designed, according to the cardinal's proposals, to bring him into the service of the Aragonese king for the duration of the Pisan war and perhaps longer. Incalculable consequences would have flowed from the realization of such a project. A new political force—one openly hostile to the papacy—would have modified profoundly the character of the conflict between Guelfs and Ghibellines. The alliance did not come off. But it was not due to any lack of desire or deter-

[6] See the reports of the Aragonese ambassadors in H. Finke, *Acta Aragonensia* (Berlin and Leipzig, 1908), II, 606, nr. 389; 608, nr. 391; 621, nr. 395.

mination on Castruccio's part that the head of the Tuscan Ghibellines did not desert the imperial cause and enter the service of a new overlord. The project failed because it seemed too daring to the king of Aragon, who was anxious to limit, if possible, his war with Pisa to the conquest of Sardinia.

Once the Aragonese project had fallen through, Castruccio pressed his negotiations with the German king. These were concluded on May 29, 1324. He was confirmed in his post of imperial vicar of Lucca. His appointment as imperial vicar of Pontremoli made legitimate the lordship he had exercised over that city since 1321. He was also made imperial vicar of the city, county, and district of Pistoia, where before he had been vicar only of the *pars imperialis,* that is, of the Pistoian exiles. This was tantamount to an open declaration of war against the still independent commune and its Florentine protectors. Finally, to support Castruccio further, King Louis revoked, in the case of Lucca, the sentences of punishment which Henry VII had decreed against all the Guelf cities of Tuscany.

But if the head of the Ghilbellines had received imperial sanction for his struggle in Tuscany, his Guelf opponents replied in kind: the first papal ban was launched against Castruccio on April 30, 1324. Henceforth the adversaries called each other *rebelles sacri Romani imperii* and *rebelles sanctae matris ecclesiae.*

War now began. On March 5, 1325, Castruccio conquered Pistoia and on September 23 of the same year gained a splendid victory over the Florentines near Altopascio. Castruccio's victory caused a sensation, for it seemed to give the Ghibellines a decisive advantage in Tuscany. Florence felt defenseless before the threat of an immediate danger. She looked for help toward the most important Guelf power in Italy, and on December 23, 1325, elected Duke Charles of Calabria, the son of King Robert of Naples, lord of the city. Castruccio then disclosed his ultimate aim. On March 9, 1326, he accepted the captainship of the *pars imperialis,* that is of the Ghibelline party, of the city, county, and district of Florence.

These events explain Castruccio's attitude toward Louis of Bavaria's Italian expedition. His campaign in Tuscany had entered a decisive phase, aimed no longer at the single bastion of Pistoia but at the center of Guelfism itself, Florence. He needed a counterweight to the support Florence had found in the king of Naples. So toward the end of 1326 Castruccio and the Ghibellines of northern Italy dispatched an embassy to the German king, urging him to hasten his long-projected expedition to Italy. Louis decided to yield to the pressure of his Italian partisans and on January 4, 1327, wrote to Castruccio in this sense. Although Castruccio could not, like the Lombard *Signori,* participate in person in the conference which Louis called at Trent, he sent a plenipotentiary; and he remained in constant contact with the king until he could greet him personally in September at Pontremoli, the entrance to his dominions.

Louis found a very complicated situation in Tuscany, a complication for which Castruccio was largely responsible. His policy of annexation threatened not only Florence, which was Guelf, but also Pisa, which was Ghibelline. And so this most faithful city of the empire, once the principal support of Henry VII, although it offered Louis money and devotion, refused to allow him within its walls, obviously for fear that beside the king would ride the powerful Castruccio, a presence potentially fatal to its liberty. When Louis rejected so conditional a subservience, war began. The Pisans found support in the Florentines, traditionally their bitterest enemies. After a month's siege Pisa submitted to the king and on October 11, 1327, admitted him, but not Castruccio. But three days later, thanks to a popular insurrection, engineered perhaps by Castruccio himself, he too entered the city.

With the elimination of Pisa as an independent political force Castruccio took a long step forward on the road to predominance in Tuscany. He was disappointed in his ambition of being named lord of Pisa; but on conducting the king to Lucca, he was splendidly rewarded by being created hereditary duke of Lucca, Pistoia, and Volterra and *gonfaloniere* of the empire (November 11, 1327).

It is doubtful that this title made him a prince of the empire. But the real significance of Castruccio's new rank cannot, in any case, be understood in purely formal terms. There was, to be sure, no lay prince according to imperial law in Italy at this period, nor was it possible to adapt such an institution to the very different conditions of Italy. In fact, however, we have seen that Castruccio exercised rights of extreme importance: *mixtum et merum imperium,* the regalia, and feudal investiture. His exercise of these rights was now confirmed by a new title. The title *dux* itself was not of primary importance; the important fact was rather that the title made hereditary the rights it reconfirmed. An imperial vicar could be dismissed; Castruccio's new title raised him to the position of hereditary lord of a large territory including three cities. He therefore possessed, in fact, a princely authority which placed him above the other Italian dynasts.

It is perhaps no accident that the wording of the royal privilege was vague. The explicit recognition of Castruccio as a prince of the empire would have been an innovation in Italy; it would have created a precedent and aroused the jealousy of the other Ghibelline leaders. Instead it recognized Castruccio's authority as equal to that of the German princes; it granted him the ducal title, which after the royal dignity was the highest rank in the feudal hierarchy, while at the same time avoiding, formally, the title *princeps.* But Castruccio's contemporaries, careless of the niceties of imperial law, considered him and called him prince.[7]

A point of special interest in the *constitutio* of November 17 is the appointment of Castruccio as *Vexillifer imperii.* Such a title had never existed in imperial law. It must be seen as an imitation of the title *Vexillifer ecclesiae,* conferred by the popes since the end of the thirteenth century.[8] The king also granted Castruccio a new coat of arms, allowing him to quarter the Wittelsbach arms with his own. Here too he was perhaps following papal practice. Although we have no authentic document confirming this, Villani's testimony cannot be questioned.[9]

[7] For example, even after Castruccio's death a document from the court of the general vicariate of the Lunigiana dated January 21, 1329 refers to Castruccio as *illustris princeps* (*Const.,* VI, 452, nr. 544).

[8] See C. Erdmann in *Quellen und Forschungen aus italienischen Archiven und Bibliotheken,* XXIX, 239.

[9] See Fr. Bock in *Archivalische Zeitschrift,* 3. Folge, VIII, 52.

Both the grant of the coat of arms and the appointment as Gonfalnier of the empire are important for the history of German political institutions because such acts are here verified for the first time. In both cases the king imitated the pope in his effort to distinguish his most important partisans and so prepared the way for the acceptance in imperial law of uses and titles of papal origin.

Castruccio conducted the king from Lucca to Pistoia and showed him the sites of his battles against the Florentines. But for the time being he was unwillingly obliged to halt his campaign against Florence and, rendering an unwelcome service demanded by his royal privileges, accompany the king from Pisa to Rome early in December. The importance of Castruccio's political role is clear from Villani's detailed narrative of this memorable expedition. And even if it be admitted that Villani, with his contempt for Louis of Bavaria, profoundly admires Castruccio and overemphasizes his role, despite the hatred of the Guelf for the dangerous Ghibelline enemy of his city, even coloring certain things in his favor, it remains no less true that the facts of the Roman expedition confirm his narrative. The emperor heaped the most important posts and honors in his gift on the head of the duke of Lucca. According to custom the count of the Lateran figured in the coronation ceremonies at St. Peter's. This was a papal functionary; and the man then holding the office, Benedetto Gaetani, had left the city. In order to respect the ancient usages, Louis abolished the papal office, created an analogous imperial office, and conferred it on Castruccio and his heirs forever.[10] From this usurpation, dictated by a momentary need, derives the later imperial office of count Palatine.[11] After the coronation Louis knighted Castruccio and the same evening announced the engagement of his son Arrigo and the daughter of the chief of the Roman Ghibellines, Sciarra Colonna. Next day he was named Roman senator.

10 The document containing this appointment dates only from March 14, 1328 [*Const.*, VI, 316, nr. 415].

11 See Ficker, *Forschungen zur Reichs-und Rechtsgeschichte Italiens,* II, 112.

The singular importance the emperor attributed to Castruccio could not have been more strikingly shown than by these extraordinary favors showered on him.

Still Castruccio did not let himself be blinded by the splendor of the position he had attained in Rome, conscious that Tuscany was the basis of his power. Thus he did not hesitate to hasten home at the first news of Florence's reconquest of Pistoia. The emperor did not object; he could not keep Castruccio at his side by force, and he feared that other Guelf victories in Tuscany would imperil his return to Germany. Castruccio's haste probably saved King Robert and the kingdom of Naples from an attack by Louis, who now, without Castruccio's troops and the promised help of the Sicilians, felt himself too weak to undertake it.

The emperor spent several months in Rome in virtually complete military inactivity while his discussions with the papacy became increasingly sharp under the influence of his Franciscan advisors and Marsilius of Padua. In the meantime Castruccio vigorously pursued his energetic policy. He seized Pisa and on April 29, 1328, without the slightest consideration for the emperor and his imperial vicar, got himself acclaimed lord of the city for two years by a citizen body intimidated by his mercenaries. The emperor had no choice but to sanction this act of violence and on May 30, through a plenipotentiary, he made Castruccio imperial vicar of Pisa. And so Castruccio added a new imperial title to the many he held already.

His immediate aim was the reconquest of Pistoia. He arrived there on August 4, the very day the emperor was forced to leave Rome. The Florentines and the duke of Lucca were bound to assume that he was moving against Florence, which, according to Castruccio's past promises to him, could be conquered in two months. The alarmed Florentines asked King Robert for help. But then Louis suddenly changed his mind and turned south to join the Sicilian fleet, which had at last arrived for action against the kingdom of Naples.

The emperor's decision was a hard blow for Castruccio, who

had hoped he could count on his help in the conquest of Florence. He was of course aware by now of the emperor's relative weakness. He had profited from it only a few months earlier to usurp the lordship of Pisa. But even then, when the emperor's authority and power had seemed reasonably solid, Castruccio had acted only in his own interest and without any respect for imperial law, hoping at the same time to use Louis to further his Florentine plans. No wonder that he was less respectful than ever of imperial interests, now that his expectation was frustrated and Louis had deserted him. There is, therefore, no reason to doubt Villani's statement that Castruccio had decided to abandon the imperial cause and begin secret negotiations with Florence. These negotiations had barely begun when they were cut off by Castruccio's death.

When he heard that his most powerful Tuscan ally had died, the emperor went to Pisa. Here he learned of Castruccio's projected desertion. At last he must have realized clearly how weak the foundations were on which his rule in Italy rested, when the man whom he had raised above all others, whom he had sought to bind to the empire with its highest titles, honors, and privileges, so easily forgot his obligation of fealty to the emperor to whom he owed those privileges. Louis in his turn considered himself released from his promises and refused to recognize the right of Castruccio's sons to the ducal title and to the dominions which only a year before he had conferred on their father as an hereditary right.

To study a life like Castruccio's is to gain a clearer understanding of the political condition of Italy in the early fourteenth century. The fall of the Hohenstaufen had removed the peninsula's supreme source of law. A legal order binding on all men no longer existed. Italy, it can be said, was atomized. Only very slowly was a new unity being formed. Individuals, families, classes, communes, each took sides in accordance with its own interests. Yet ultimately every political authority had to be legitimized in law, however fictitious in origin. The Guelfs turned to the papacy; more specifically, the Guelf communes appealed to customary law, even though their customary law was in reality nothing more than a tissue of violations of the traditional imperial legal order.

The Guelfs, then, could consider themselves "conservatives." The case was very different for rulers like Castruccio, who had arisen out of nothing. Their rights rested on the *de facto* power they had themselves acquired rather than on a traditional dominion. In most cases they had used republican forms to rise to power in their own communes. But once on top they inevitably tried to secure their authority with other than democratic guarantees, in principle always revocable.

It is this search for legitimacy which explains why the majority of the *Signori*—the Visconti and the Scaligeri, for example, to mention only the most important—were Ghibellines, that is, based their authority on imperial law. Castruccio, to be sure, was anti-Guelf for family reasons. But this was not his only motive for being a Ghibelline; his very status as a *Signore* forced him to ally himself with the *pars imperialis.* And so we see him after each forward step in his career turn immediately to the German king in order to obtain legal sanction for what he had already acquired in fact. By studying the royal grants of 1315, 1320, 1324, and 1327 we can follow his rapid rise to power, but in estimating their real significance we must recognize that in none of them was Castruccio given anything he did not already possess.

The Ghibellines called themselves the *pars imperialis.* But Castruccio's career clearly reveals that they represented the empire in no significant sense at all: for example, his dubious game in 1315 at the time of the double imperial election; his desire in 1323–1324 to ally himself with the kingdom of Aragon; his secret negotiations with Florence at the end of his life. It was in fact precisely this last unforeseen change of sides by the head of the Ghibellines which was to convince the emperor of the impossibility of finding support in the "imperial party." Louis of Bavaria made the attempt and failed. In reality, of course, the Ghibellines wanted a fictitious empire, not a real authority. The emperors were to supply them with that theoretical legality which every ruler needs; but they had no intention of becoming his subordinates in any political hierarchy of significance. Dante reproached contemporary Ghibellines for having degraded the imperial idea to the level of a party label, crying out:

> Faccian li Ghibellin, faccian lor arte
> sott'altro segno; chè mal segue quello
> sempre chi la giustizia e lui diparte.[12]

His reproach remains valid for Castruccio and all the Ghibelline *Signori* of his time. The Guelfs called them tyrants, by this name emphasizing not only their despotism but also the illegitimacy of their rule.

That their rule was illegitimate is objectively true; for all these lordships were based on violence, not on the fictitious rights their rulers subsequently acquired. And yet it would be a mistake to question Castruccio's own subjective conviction of loyalty, his conviction that "he had acted justly for the empire and his commune." [13] Castruccio lived at a turning point of history, and he considered his own actions solely in terms of traditional imperial norms, however far they deviated from such norms. He bore the title of Gonfalonier of the empire, a title rightly his in the circumstances of the time. In reality, however, he was a new type of prince and *condottiere,* already corresponding in part to the type later exalted by Machiavelli.

[12] *Paradiso,* VI, 103–105.

[13] Giovanni Villani, *Cronica,* X, 86: *Biblioteca classica Italiana* (Trieste, 1857), s. XIV, nr. 21, I, 328.

3

The Accession of the Helvetian Federation to the Holy League: An Unpublished Bull of Pope Julius II of March 17, 1512*

THE Scheide collection of the Library of Princeton University contains, among many other documents from the eleventh century to the eighteenth, one piece which deserves special attention. It throws new light on one of the most interesting phases of the history of international relations during the Italian Renaissance—the war of the Holy League of 1511–1512 against King Louis XII of France and the methods used by Pope Julius II to bring about the entrance of the Swiss federation into this war. The document in question is a bull issued by the pope at St. Peter's in Rome on March 17, 1512, in which Julius excommunicates the French supporters of the rebels against the papal see and at the same time threatens the Swiss with excommunication in case they should conclude any kind of agreement with King Louis. For the right understanding of this hitherto unpublished papal bull it is necessary to sketch briefly the events leading up to its issuance.[1]

* Reprinted from *The Journal of Modern History,* XX (1948), 123–132.

[1] As to the general background see esp. M. Brosch, *Papst Julius II* (Gotha, 1878); Ch. Kohler, *Les Suisses dans les guerres d'Italie de 1506 à 1512* (Geneva and Paris, 1897); L. Pastor, *The History of the Popes,* Vol. VI (St. Louis, Mo., 1912); E. Gagliardi, *Geschichte der Schweiz,* Vol. I. (Zurich, 1920); W. Oechsli, *History of Switzerland, 1499–1914* (Cambridge, 1922); H. Nabholz, *Geschichte der Schweiz,* Vol. I (Zurich, 1932); F. Ercole, *Da*

On October 4, 1511, Pope Julius II, King Ferdinand of Aragon, and the Venetian Republic concluded "a league which the pope himself wanted and ordered to be called most holy because it was established and made entirely for the benefit of the church." [2] The stated purpose of this alliance was "the conservation of the holy church and the dignity of the holy papal see and the recovery of Bologna and the other territories of the holy Roman church which are now occupied by its enemies." [3] Actually, however, Julius II aimed at a much greater objective than the mere re-establishment of his authority over the papal states. His ultimate goal was the complete liberation of Italy from the French "barbarians." He was only too well aware of the fact that the "rebels" against the holy see, the Bentivoglio family of Bologna and Duke Alfonso of Ferrara, were continuously supported by the French king, who through his possession of the Duchy of Milan and through his alliance with the Florentine Republic had acquired a very strong position in Italy. Since the pope alone was too weak to break the predominant power of Louis XII, he resorted to an alliance with Spain and Venice and endeavored also to bring Henry VIII of England and Emperor Maximilian of Germany into this coalition. England did, in fact, join the Holy League shortly after its conclusion, on October 17, 1511, whereas Maximilian continued to adhere to a pro-French policy, motivated by the conflict of interests which for many years had existed between himself and Venice.

But if it is correct to say that the famous Holy League of 1511 was really a grand alliance of the great European powers against France and that its actual goal was the reduction of

---

Carlo VIII a Carlo V (Florence, 1932); and M. Darcy, *Louis XII* (Paris, 1935).

[2] See the letter of Bernardo da Bibbiena to Cardinal Giovanni Medici, Rome, Oct. 4, 1511: "Conclusa, stabilita, ferma e sancita si è stasera la lega, la quale Nostro Signore, per essere fondata e fatta tutta a beneficio della Chiesa, vuole e comanda che si chiami Santissima" (published in A. Desjardins, *Négociations diplomatiques de la France avec la Toscane* [Paris, 1861], II, 548).

[3] See the pope's letter to Medici, Oct. 5, 1511, *ibid.*, p. 551. For the full text of the treaty of the Holy League see T. Rymer, *Foedera,* VI, Part I (The Hague, 1741), 23–24.

French power in general and the expulsion of the French armies from Italy in particular, we have to keep in mind that this objective was not explicitly and formally stated in the text of the agreement between the allied states. Consequently, there developed a rather curious situation in the autumn of 1511. Although the armies of the Holy League had started some rather halfhearted campaigns in northern Italy against the lords of Bologna and Ferrara and their French associates who were commanded by the French governor of Milan,[4] this actual outbreak of hostilities was not accompanied by a formal rupture of the diplomatic relations among the various powers. On the contrary, at the papal and French courts, as well as in Venice and elsewhere, a great many open and secret negotiations took place in which attempts were made either to find a basis for the conclusion of a general peace or to reach some separate agreements between individual members of the two hostile camps.[5]

During the first months of 1512 things came more and more to a head. In contrast to the very slow start of hostilities in the preceding autumn, the fighting became increasingly serious in January and February of that year. The initial successes were with the French, and by the middle of March it seemed to be evident that their commander in Lombardy, Gaston de Foix, was intent on starting a large offensive in order to destroy the armies of the Holy League.[6] At the same time, there was a great deal of activity on the diplomatic front. In February and in the first part of March, Louis XII tried once more to make peace with the pope. The negotiations were carried on at the French court in Blois, where the Aragonese tried to serve as mediators,[7] and simultaneously at the papal court in Rome,

[4] Cf. Brosch, pp. 237–240; and Pastor, VI, 395.

[5] See esp. the collection of diplomatic dispatches, sent by various diplomats of the great powers between October and December 1511, in *Lettres du Roy Louis XII, avec plusieurs autres lettres, memoires et instructions écrites depuis 1504 jusques et compris 1514* (Brussels, 1712) (hereafter cited as *Lettres du Roy Louis XII*), III, 80–105.

[6] See the letter of Bernardo da Bibbiena to Medici, Rome, Mar. 19/22, 1512, Desjardins, II, 576; cf. the letter of Gaston de Foix, Mar. 8, 1512, *Lettres du Roy Louis XII*, III, 196–197; M. Sanuto, *I Diarii* (Venice, 1886), XIV, 49; and cf. Pastor, VI, 396–398.

[7] *Lettres du Roy Louis XII*, III, 175 and 193–196; and Sanuto, XIV, 49.

on the initiative of some pro-French cardinals.[8] A peaceful settlement could not be reached. Finally, a last attempt, it seems, was made in Rome on March 17, when the Roman nobleman, Domenico Massimo, saw Julius II in two successive audiences and urged him, in the name of the Roman people, to come to an understanding with Louis. The pope's answer was so evasive and guarded that it became clear that the conflicting interests and aims of the papal see and France were irreconcilable.[9]

While Julius and Louis were engaged in these peace negotiations, each tried simultaneously to lure his opponent's allies over to his own side. The pope endeavored to bring Maximilian into the fold of the League by reconciling him with the Venetians,[10] and Louis secretly made very favorable overtures to Venice in order to neutralize it.[11] By the end of March it was manifest that Louis was unable to draw Venice away from the League, whereas Julius was on the point of success in his mediation between the Venetians and the emperor. Thus in the spring of 1512 France found itself in a most dangerous situation; it was threatened by an imminent offensive of the pope, Venice, Spain, and England; and against this formidable coalition it could not even rely on further support from its only strong ally, the Habsburg emperor.[12]

In the Europe of that era there was, however, besides the six countries just mentioned a seventh state, the Helvetian federation, which, from the military point of view, at least, had to be counted among the great powers. The more the general tension over the Italian issues increased, the more important became the question whether and on whose side the Swiss would

[8] See Sanuto, XIV, 24; F. Guicciardini, *La storia d'Italia,* Book X, chap. 11 (ed. A. Gherardi [Florence, 1919], II, 418); O. Raynaldus, *Annales ecclesiastici* (Rome, 1663), XX (1512), Nos. 23 and 24; cf. Kohler, p. 302.

[9] See the dispatch of the Venetian ambassador in Rome, Mar. 17, 1512, quoted by Brosch, pp. 242–243 and 357, n. 8.

[10] See Pastor, VI, 383–384 and 412–413; and H. Kretschmayr, *Geschichte von Vendig* (Gotha, 1920), II, 439.

[11] Cf. Sanuto, XIV, 38–39 (Mar. 19), 47 (Mar. 22), 51 (Mar. 23), 61–62 (Mar. 30), and 78 (Apr. 2); and Kohler, pp. 312–313.

[12] As to contemporary documents illustrating this situation see, e.g., *Lettres du Roy Louis XII,* III, 119, 149–150, and 208; Desjardins, II, 573; Sanuto, XIV, 48 and 76; and see also Kohler, pp. 297–298.

participate in the coming hostilities. Ever since the French invasion of Italy in 1494, Swiss mercenaries had fought in the service of the French kings. But when in 1510 Louis XII failed to renew his old alliance with the federation, Julius II used this opportunity to secure for himself the support of the best soldiers of that time. In March 1510 he concluded an agreement which obliged the Swiss, in exchange for the papal promise of annual subsidies, to come to the defense of the holy see during the next five years, whenever the pope might request their help; the Swiss also engaged not to make an alliance with a third power without the pope's knowledge and consent.[13] As this treaty of 1510 was to last for five years, it would appear at first glance that at the time of the outbreak of the war of the Holy League the Swiss were still under obligation to fight on the papal side. But in spite of the fact that in December 1511 they had undertaken an expedition against the French in Lombardy,[14] the Swiss no longer considered themselves legally bound to the papal cause, for, according to their claims, Julius had not completely fulfilled the financial stipulations of the treaty of 1510.[15]

As things stood early in 1512, it was natural that both the Holy League and France should strive to win the military support of the Helvetian federation, and it was just as natural that the Swiss should try to use this favorable situation to their best advantage.[16] They were willing to listen to propositions made by representatives of both camps, but at the same time they made it very clear that their services could be obtained only for a heavy price. At the French court it was realized that "the whole victory of the king [Louis] against his enemies was based" on the support of the Swiss.[17] But after many conferences the French envoys to the Helvetian diet were finally, on March 24,

13 See Kohler, pp. 151–153; and Gagliardi, I, 250.

14 On this campaign see Kohler, pp. 229–280; Gagliardi, I, 252–253; and Nabholz, p. 303.

15 See Kohler, pp. 192, 203–205, and 288–292.

16 On these negotiations of the Swiss with France and with the Holy League see esp. Kohler, pp. 286–305.

17 Letter of Jean le Veau to Margaret of Austria, Blois, Jan. 29, 1511; ". . . sur laquelle resolution est fondée toute la victoire du Roy contre ses ennemys" (*Lettres du Roy Louis XII*, III, 133).

presented with "so great and unreasonable" financial demands [18] that they had to ask for an adjournment of the talks in order to get new instructions from Louis.[19] While carrying on these negotiations with the French, the Helvetian diet decided to send a large diplomatic mission to Venice to meet there a fellow-countryman, the cardinal and papal legate, Mathaeus Schiner,[20] and to discuss with him and the Venetians the possibilities of renewing or implementing the former alliance with Pope Julius.[21] Immediately after the arrival of Cardinal Schiner in Venice on March 26 the parleys between him and the Helvetian envoys started.[22]

The great question, then, in March 1512 was whether the Swiss would ultimately ally themselves with France or with the Holy League. As a matter of fact, Andreas of Burgos, one of the shrewdest observers of the rapidly shifting diplomatic scene of those days, who at that time was accredited to the French court, declared specifically that the future course of events depended largely on this Swiss decision. In a dispatch which he wrote from Blois to Margaret of Austria on March 15 he gave a detailed account of the intricate diplomatic game of the preceding weeks and reported the news from Italy concerning the probability of an imminent offensive of the French troops against the armies of the Holy League.[23] Then Andreas continued: "L'on attend de jours en jours nouvelles de ce que

[18] According to a dispatch of Andreas of Burgos of March 22, the Swiss "demandent choses si grandes et desraisonnables que jamais le Roy ne le fera si ce n'est par autre extreme necessité" (*Lettres du Roy Louis XII,* III, 206).

[19] Cf. Kohler, pp. 293–297.

[20] On Schiner cf. C. Wirtz, "Akten über die diplomatischen Beziehungen der römischen Curie zu der Schweiz, 1512–1522," *Quellen zur schweizerischen Geschichte,* XVI (Basel, 1895), esp. xiii–xix; A. Buechi, "Korrespondenzen und Akten zur Geschichte des Kardinals Schiner," *Quellen zur schweizerischen Geschichte,* Sec. III, Vol. V. (new ser., 1920); and A. Buechi, "Kardinal M. Schiner als Staatsmann und Kirchenfürst," in *Collectanea Friburgensia,* Vols. XXVII and XXXII (1923 and 1937).

[21] Cf. Kohler, pp. 292–293 and 311.

[22] On these negotiations see esp. Sanuto, XIV, 57–79 and *passim* (Mar. 26–Apr. 2); and Kohler, pp. 313–319.

[23] *Lettres du Roy Louis XII,* III, 197.

s'ensuyvra en Suysses, de quoy depend en grand partie ce qu'adviendra d'estre."

The picture painted by Andreas of Burgos of the European situation in mid-March 1512 provides us with an excellent key to the understanding of the content and the purpose of Pope Julius' bull of March 17, 1512, for there are two distinct issues with which Julius shows himself primarily concerned in this document—the war against the French army in Italy and the problem of the Swiss attitude toward the Holy League and France.

In regard to the first point, the pope complains bitterly about the continuous support given by Louis XII and his troops to the members of the Este and Bentivoglio families. According to Julius, this aid has frustrated so far all attempts made by himself and his ally, King Ferdinand of Aragon, to crush "the tyranny" of those lords of Ferrara and Bologna and to re-establish papal authority over the territories of the Roman church now "usurped" by them. To remedy the situation, the pope commands "the captains of King Louis and those fighting under them in the cities of Ferrara and Bologna and other lands belonging to the Roman church" to evacuate these territories within six days from the promulgation of this bull. In case the French should disobey this order of the pope, they will automatically fall under papal excommunication and other most severe punishments of the church.

In applying these ecclesiastical weapons against the French troops, the pope acted in accordance with an obligation which he had assumed at the time of the conclusion of the Holy League. One of the articles of this alliance stipulated that the pope was bound "to fulminate censures and ecclesiastical penalties against anyone of whatever authority or rank, ecclesiastical, secular or even royal, who opposed the League . . . both inside and outside Italy." [24] When the pope finally, after five

[24] "Item, quod Sanctissimus Dominus noster teneatur et debeat contra quoscumque, quavis auctoritate vel dignitate ecclesiastica vel mundana etiam regia fulgentes et praeditos, hujusmodi ligae et foederi se opponentes, eis auxilium consilium et favorem praestantes tam in Italia quam extra,

months of more or less open and direct hostilities between the armies of the Holy League and Louis XII, made good this threat of excommunication, he was certainly not under the illusion that the French generals would be so deeply impressed by his spiritual authority that they would automatically comply with his order. It is more plausible to assume that through the promulgation of this bull Julius wanted to put an end to the state of undeclared warfare and to brand publicly the French troops in Italy as enemies of the papal see.

If this interpretation of the bull as a kind of official declaration of war against the French in Italy is correct, the date of its issuance, March 17, is very interesting, for as we have seen before, it was on the very same day that Domenico Massimo made a last attempt to bring about a Franco-papal understanding. From our new document we are able to conclude not merely that on that day the pope gave an evasive answer to Massimo's entreaties but that he also decided to break openly with the French. In regard to this rupture it is, however, also worth noticing that Julius excommunicated only the French commanders and their troops in Italy and not the king himself. Throughout the bull, Julius speaks most respectfully of "our dearest son in Christ, the most Christian King of the French," in striking contrast to his denunciation of Alfonso of Ferrara and the members of the Bentivoglio families as "sons of iniquity." A past master of the diplomatic game of the Italian Renaissance and a great expert in the most subtle rules of this game, Julius knew how to hold the door still ajar for the possibility of a reconciliation with the French king.

What were, however, the specific reasons which, at that particular moment, motivated the pope to "formalize" his war against the French armies by excommunicating them? This question brings us to the second aspect of the document, its connection with the problem of the Swiss attitude and with the diplomatic negotiations then going on in Venice.

Whether or not the pope had any information concerning the secret overtures made by the French to the Venetians at that

censuras et poenas ecclesiasticas fulminare et publicare, prout et quotiens opus fuerit" (Rymer, VI, Part 1, 23).

time is impossible to decide. We know only that on March 19 and later some French proposals for the conclusion of a separate peace were submitted to the Venetian doge and council [25] and that on March 23 the same council was informed through a dispatch of the Venetian ambassador in Rome that the pope "has composed a bull in which he excommunicates all those who stay in the pay of France or give aid to it." [26] On the next day, the 24th, the papal nuncio in Venice presented certain proposals concerning the conclusion of an agreement between Venice and Emperor Maximilian and at the same time told the Venetian council of Julius' resolution of "chasing the French." [27] If the pope actually happened to know of the secret Franco-Venetian negotiations, the promulgation of his bull at that very moment could very well serve to keep the Venetians in the camp of the Holy League. But even if we discard the possibility of this specific objective, there is no doubt that through the excommunication of the French troops the pope intended to notify the Venetians that henceforth he wanted to wage the Italian war in a much more open and resolute fashion than had been the case hitherto. Thus, Cardinal Schiner, in his own words, "speaking as a good Italian, though born a barbarian" (i.e., a Swiss), certainly acted in accordance with Julius' ideas and instructions when, on March 28, he declared before the Venetian council that he would do everything in his power "to chase the barbarians out of Italy and to bring the Swiss into the [Holy] League." [28]

This last reference and other similar passages in Schiner's speech before the Venetian council on March 28 have to be connected with those parts of Julius' bull of March 17 which deal with the Swiss problem. In speaking of the hostile acts commit-

[25] Compare Sanuto, XIV, 38–39, 47, 51, 61–62 and 78; see also Kohler, pp. 312–313.

[26] "(Soa Santita) . . . ha fato una bolla che scomunicha tutti chi è a soldo di Franza e chi li dà aiuto, etiam sguizari si con lui saranno, et asolve tutti quelli che li va contra in servizio di la Chiexia e di colpa e di pena, benedicendoli etc" (Sanuto, XIV, 49; cf. also Kohler, p. 318).

[27] ". . . di la bona mente dil Papa in concluder questo acordo e cazar francesi" (Sanuto, XIV, 52).

[28] "[Schiner] parlando per tanto come bon italian, licet sia nasuto barbaro, vol far ogni suo poter che se caza barbari de Italia, et far li elvetii sia con la liga" (*ibid.*, p. 58).

ted by the French against himself, the pope says that he has been informed from several sources that Louis XII is trying to incite the Swiss to fight on the French side against Julius and his ally, King Ferdinand of Aragon. This complaint shows clearly that the pope had full knowledge of the French-Swiss negotiations which were taking place at that time before the Helvetian diet. In his bull the pope recalls the fact of the alliance which (since March 1510) had existed between himself and the Helvetian federation, and he reminds the Swiss of their promises and legal obligations which, in his opinion, are still valid. He forbids them, therefore, under the threat of excommunication to conclude an alliance with Louis or to give military assistance to him or any other enemy of the pope and his allies. He even requests the Swiss not to carry on negotiations or to have any direct or indirect dealings with the troops of the French king.

There is no doubt that these sections dealing with the Swiss problem were inserted into the bull of March 17 for a very definite and practical purpose. They were to be used by Cardinal Schiner in his negotiations with the envoys of the Helvetian federation in Venice. We know that rumors had been spread in Switzerland to the effect that the pope was on the point of reconciling himself with the French king.[29] From the papal point of view these rumors were very dangerous because they could easily give a pretext to the Swiss for the conclusion of an agreement of their own with the French. To deny the authenticity of these reports and to prove at the same time the pope's definite rupture with the French in Italy, Cardinal Schiner had only to produce the bull of March 17 and to point out to the Swiss envoys the fact of the papal excommunication of the French generals and troops. But even more, the threat of excommunication against the Swiss themselves enabled the papal negotiator to put strong pressure upon the envoys of the Helvetian federation, for if elsewhere the weapons of ecclesiastical penalties, because of their all too frequent use, had become rather blunt and ineffective, they could still be expected to make a deep impression upon the devout mountaineers.

To be sure, the most crucial point in the negotiations between

[29] Buechi, "Kardinal M. Schiner," *loc. cit.*, XXVII, 283.

Schiner and the Swiss envoys in Venice was the satisfaction of the financial demands of the federation, just as was the case in the simultaneous bargaining between the French envoys and the Helvetian diet in Zurich. Cardinal Schiner put this point very neatly before the council of Venice in his speech of March 28 when he said: "We know the malady of those Swiss. Through the medicine of money they will recover quickly." [30] But the cardinal was too good a diplomat not to use other, more intangible and immaterial inducements as well.

First, Schiner held out promises of some special and symbolic honors, like the gift of a sword. But eventually, after a whole week of negotiations, he told the Swiss delegation directly about the papal bull of March 17. According to the official report of the envoys, he informed them on April 2 that the "pope has heard about the presence of French ambassadors in Switzerland and about their proposal of a Franco-Swiss alliance. If such an agreement should be concluded, the pope is resolved to anathematize the Swiss in the same way as he has already anathematized the French." [31] This final threat seems to have turned the scale of the negotiations, for on the same day, April 2, a basic agreement for an alliance was reached between Cardinal Schiner and the Swiss envoys. Five days later the Helvetian delegation was ready to leave Venice to submit the treaty to the Helvetian diet for ratification.

After that events moved rapidly. While the Swiss envoys were still on their way home, on April 11, the French army under Gaston de Foix triumphed over the army of the Holy League in the great battle of Ravenna. For a moment Julius II believed his cause lost. But soon he recovered his courage and decided to

[30] ". . . cognoscemo la malatia di essi elvetii, quali con danari si risanano presto" (Sanuto, XIV, 58).

[31] See the dispatch of the Swiss envoys to the diet in Zurich: "Uff frytag vor dem palmtag [i.e., Apr. 2] hat unser gnaediger herr [i.e., Schiner] uns anzoigt, das Im brieff und Bullen kommen syen von baebstl[icher] H[eilig-kei]t, wie das baebstl. Ht. vernommen habe, das die franzoesische Botschaft in unserm land lige und da ein Vereynung mit uns machen welle; wo das bescheche, ist Sin Heiligkeit der Meynung, uns in bann zu thun mit allem fluch wie dann die Franzosen darinn sind" (*Amtliche Sammlung der älteren Eidgenössischen Abschiede,* III, Part 2 [Lucerne, 1869], 606; cf. V. Anshelm, *Berner Chronik,* III [Bern, 1888], 306).

fight on. Even more important for further developments was that on April 19 the Helvetian diet, still ignorant of the outcome of the battle of Ravenna, resolved to ratify the alliance with the pope and to start war against France early in May.[32] In a campaign of only a few weeks the Swiss, without much support from the other armies of the Holy League, conquered most of Lombardy and forced the French troops to withdraw completely from Italy.[33]

All these dramatic changes took place within three months after March 17, when the pope had issued his declaration of war against the French armies in Italy. On June 22 Julius received the news of the final collapse of the French power in Italy. He exclaimed exuberantly: "We have won. We have won. . . . May God give joy . . . to all the faithful souls whom he has at last deigned to deliver from the yoke of the barbarians." [34] But Julius II remembered also very well that above everything else it had been the power of the Swiss soldiers which allowed him to see the realization of his most cherished desire, the liberation of Italy from the French. Thus, on July 6, 1512, the same Swiss, who only a few months earlier had been threatened by the papal anathema, were granted by the pope the perpetual title of "Protectors of the Liberty of the Church."

TEXT OF THE BULL [35]

Julius episcopus servus servorum Dei. Ad futuram rei memoriam. Ad compescendos conatus nepharios perversorum, qui Dei timore postposito contra Romanam ecclesiam sponsam nostram, quam pro eorum honore et dignitate liberalem et gratiosam

[32] Compare Kohler, pp. 320–324; and Buechi, "Korrespondenzen," *loc. cit.*, pp. 139, No. 174, 140, No. 175.

[33] See Kohler, pp. 333–399.

[34] Account of the papal master of ceremonies, Paris de Grassis, as quoted by Pastor, VI, 416.

[35] The document which is preserved in the Scheide collection of the Library of Princeton University is not an original but a copy. This copy originated, however, in the papal chancery itself, for we find on the reverse side the following notes: "De curia[?] duplicata"; and beneath that line, in larger letters: "A[?] de Comitibus." Also on the reverse side we read: "Ita apud me Bal. Tuerdum." The name of Balthasar Tuerdus appears likewise

invenerunt, arma sumere non verentur, tanto magis nos decet oportuno remedio providere, quanto peramplius eorum detestanda iniquitas tendit in divine maiestatis offensam et ex illorum malefactis, qui ab aliis facile in exemplum trahuuntur [*sic*], possent ecclesie prefate maiora scandala provenire. Sane quod non sine magni animi displacentia referre cogimur, quod, cum anno proxime elapso potentissimum fortissimumque exercitum contra iniquitatis filium Alfonsum Esten(sem) civitatem nostram Ferrarie ad Romanam ecclesiam legitime devolutam occupatam indebite detinentem paravissemus, charissimus in Christo filius noster Ludovicus Francorum rex christianissimus non solum eiusdem Alfonsi protectionem recepit eique gentium armorum copiis auxilium prestitit, quominus civitatem ipsam recuperare valuerimus, verum etiam effecit, quod iniquitatis filii Bentivoli eiusdem regis exercitu suffulcti civitatem nostram Bononien(sem), que et eius cives ab eorum tiramnide opera nostra magno nostro incommodo liberata fuerat, occuparent et occupatam detinerent. Nuper ex pluribus locis ad nostrum pervenit auditum, quod idem rex Helvetiorum et Suetentium [*sic*] gentes manupromptas et in arte militari expertas, que nobis pro Romane ecclesie et nostrorum iurium conservatione fedus et ligam inierunt et nunquam contra nos et eandem ecclesiam, cuius semper devotissimi filii fuerunt, arma sumere promiserunt et ad id se astrinxerunt, contra nos et dictam ecclesiam provocare et in partis [*sic*] suas adducere et ad sua stipendia conducere satagit, ut valido et potenti exercitui, quem charissimus in Christo filius noster Ferdinandus Aragonum rex illustris et catholicus ex partibus Hispaniarum pro nostra et iurium dicte ecclesie defensione ac civitatum huiusmodi recuperatione misit, ac nostro aperte resistere seu illum profligare ac terras et

---

at the end of the bull itself; he was, as we know from other bulls of Julius II, a member of the papal chancery. From this provenance we may conclude that the Princeton document is a "transumptum auctenticum," i.e., one of the official copies which, according to the text of our bull itself, were to be used to propagate and publicize its content as widely as possible. The first line of the text, containing Julius' title and the invocation, is written in elongated capitals. Apart from a few small holes which have been caused by the folding of the parchment document, it is in an excellent state of preservation.

loca dicte ecclesie armata manu invadere possit, et ad hec se totis viribus preparat contra nos, qui summo desiderio cupimus non solum dictarum civitatum recuperationem ac pacem et tranquilitatem in ecclesia Dei conservare, sed etiam impedit sanctos cogitatus nostros de obviando infidelibus et quod per nos apparatum erat contra Christiani nominis hostes prosequi, ac verentes, ne ex hiis maiores tumultus, ut verisimiliter creditur, excitentur, quibus impediti premissa exequi ut optamus non possumus.

Conversi ad remedia, que pronunc offeruntur et in bulla que legitur "In cena Domini" continentur, videlicet quod omnes conspirantes aut coniurantes contra personam statum vel auctoritatem Romani pontificis, etiam regali dignitate fulgentes aut eis consilium auxilium vel favorem quomodolibet prestantes aut civitates terras et alia loca ecclesie Romane invadentes et illis adherentes excommunicantur et anathematizantur, prefati Ludovici regis capitaneos ac sub eis militantes in Ferrarien(si) et Bononien(si) civitatibus et aliis terris ad dictam Romanam ecclesiam pertinentibus existentes et alios tunc expressos, quos etiam per alias nostras litteras excommunicationis sententias ac alias penas in litteris nostris privationis dicti Alfonsi Esten(sis) olim ducis Ferrarie contentas incurrisse declaravimus in virtute sancte obedientie et sub penis infrascriptis et etiam in dicta bulla "Cene Domini" contentis, quas contrafacientes incurrere voluimus ipso facto, auctoritate apostolica tenore presentium requirimus et monemus eisque districte precipiendo mandamus, quatinus omni excusatione cessante appositionibusque exceptionibus et replicationibus quibuscunque infra sex dierum spatium, postquam presentes littere fuerunt publicate, quorum duos pro primo, duo [*sic*] pro secundo et reliquos duos dies pro tertio et ultimo ac peremptorio termino ac monitone canonica eis omnibus et eorum singulis assignamus, a Ferrarien(si) et Bononien(si) ac aliis civitatibus et terris ac locis dicte ecclesie recedant et a prestatione auxilii consilii vel favoris Alfonso et Bentivolis prefatis penitus desistant, alioquin lapsis sex diebus huiu(sm)odi [36] in dicti Ludovici regis capitaneos et sub eis militantes

[36] There is a hole in the parchment; the above conjecture seems to be most probable.

et quemlibet eorum maioris excommunicationis sententiam promulgamus in hiis scriptis et illos illam incurrere volumus eo ipso, a qua preter in mortis articulo constituti ab alio quam a Romano pontifice, et(iam pretex)tu [36] cuiuscunque facultatis cuicunque pro tempore desuper concesse, nequeant absolutionis beneficium obtinere. Et si moniti et excommunicati predicti dictam excommunicationis sententiam per alios tres dies dictos sex dies immediate sequentes animo, quod absit, sustinue(rint ob)durato,[36] sententiam ipsam aggravamus. Si vero moniti et excommuni(cati) [36] predicti per alios tres dies dictos ultimos tres dies immediate sequentes ad cor reverti et nostris motioni et mandato predictis obtemperare distulerint et in sua voluerint cordis duritia et perversa obstinatione permanere, eos et quemlibet eorum reaggravationis et anathematizationis ac maledictionis et damnationis iunctione percutimus ac omnium ecclesiasticarum censurarum laqueis ligatos et irretitos ac reos criminis lese maiestatis et ab omnibus dicte Romane ecclesie devotis cum eorum bonis perpetuo diffidatos ac honoribus et dignitatibus privatos auctoritate et potestatis plenitudine esse decernimus et civitates terras opida et loca, ad que aliquem eorundem excommunicatorum declinare contigerit, quamdiu ibidem permanserit et triduo post recessum eiusdem, ecclesiastico subiicimus interdicto.

Ac universis et singulis Christi fidelibus, presertim Helvetiis et Suetensibus prefatis sub eisdem penis, ne contra fedus nobiscum initum contra nos aut alios colligatos nostros arma sumere aut ad stipendia alicuius, qui contra nos et civitates et loca ad dictam Romanam ecclesiam et colligatos nostros legitime spectantia venirent, militare presumant, ac eis et quibusvis aliis sub eisdem penis iniungimus, ut excommunicatos anathematizatos et maledictos prefatos evitent et quantum in eis est evitari faciant ac cum eis comercium aliquamve conversationem non habeant nec eis prestent aliquod consilium auxilium vel favorem. Inhibemus quoque omnibus et singulis temporalia dominia obtinentibus, etiam regali ducali principatus marchionatus comitatus vel alia dignitate fulgentibus, universitatibus presertim eorun-

[36] There is a hole in the parchment; the above conjecture seems to be most probable.

dem Suetensium et Helvetiorum ac communitatibus quancunque potentiam et dominium obtinentibus, ne cum regis Gallorum gentibus huiusmodi directe vel indirecte maxime ad impediendum recuperationem civitatum terrarum et locorum ad dictam Romanam ecclesiam et colligatos nostros pertinentium vel ad defensionem seu auxilium eorundem se nobis vel pro eadem ecclesia agentibus aut ad motionem belli opponant in preiudicium Romane ecclesie tendentis ligam aut conferationem [*sic*] seu colligationem suscipiant vel intelligentiam ineant, quas, quatinus ille ad preiudicium dicte Romane ecclesie tendant, etiam si penarum adiectione iuramentoque sint vallate, non tenere et nemini, quominus eisdem monitis et excommunicatis favendo sub colore eorum censuras predictas incurrant, excusationem prestare posse declaramus, observent quoquo modo.

Et ut moniti ac alii, quos presentes littere contingunt quibusve aliquid mandatur vel prohibetur per easdem, nequeant de premissis ignorantiam allegare et pretextu ignorantie, si non paruerint, velamen excusationis assumant, et ut ad ipsorum notitiam deducantur, cum hee nostre littere eis tute publicari non possint, eas in valvis Basilice Principis Apostolorum de Urbe et apostolice Cancellarie affigi iubemus. Ac omnibus et singulis ordinariis locorum et civitatum tam in Italia quam extra eam consistentium ecclesiarum quarumlibet cathedralium et non cathedralium monasteriorum prioratuum et domorum ac locorum religiosorum ordinum quorumcunque etiam mendicantium exemptorum et non exemptorum episcopis capitulis canonicis abbatibus prioribus conventibus guardianis fratribus et personis aliis ecclesiasticis quibuscunque et ipsorum cuilibet, ita quod alter alterum in hiis exequendis non expectet, sub similibus excommunicationum censuris et penis etiam privationis beneficiorum ac dignitatum et privilegiorum eis et eorum ecclesiis et monasteriis a sede predicta vel alias quomodolibet concessorum dicta auctoritate mandamus, quatinus ipsi et quilibet eorum, cum desuper fuerint requisiti, has nostras litteras seu illarum transumptum auctenticum manu publici notarii subscriptum et sigillo alicuius prelati munitum in ipsarum ecclesiarum valvis affigant et alias etiam in eorum sermonibus ad populum publicent et sermocinent in locis, in quibus sit de verisimili coniectura, quod ad eorundem monitorum et aliorum, quos littere ipse contingunt quibusve aliquid mandatur vel prohibetur per easdem, possint notitiam verisimiliter pervenire, volentes quod ipse presentes littere et illarum transumpta ac huiusmodi publicatio extunc post affixionem et publicationem predictas factas in eisdem Basilice et Cancellarie valvis ipsos sic monitos et alios supradictos perinde arctent, ac si littere ipse eisdem monitis et aliis supradictis et eorum cuilibet intimate personaliter extitissent, non obstantibus constitutionibus et ordinationibus apostolicis contrariis quibuscunque. Aut si monitis prefatis vel quibusvis aliis communiter vel divisim ab eadem sit sede indultum, quod interdici suspendi vel excommunicari aut propterea privari et inhabiles reddi non possint per litteras apostolicas non facientes plenam et expressam ac de verbo ad verbum de indulto huiusmodi mentionem et quibuslibet aliis privilegiis indulgentiis et litteris apostolicis generalibus vel specialibus quorumcunque tenorum existunt, per que presentibus non expressa vel totaliter non inserta effectus earum impediri valeat quomodolibet vel differri, et de quibus quorumque totis tenoribus de verbo ad verbum sit in nostris litteris mentio specialis habenda, que quoad hoc cuiqua [*sic*] volumus suffragari.

Nulli ergo omnino hominum liceat hanc paginam nostre requisitionis monitionis mandati assignationis promulgationis aggravationis percussionis decreti suppositionis iniunctionis inhibitionis declarationis iussionis et voluntatis infringere vel ei ausu temerario contraire. Siquis autem hoc attemptare presumpserit, indignationem omnipotentis Dei ac beatorum Petri et Pauli apostolorum eius se noverit incursurum.

Datum Rome apud Sanctum Petrum, anno incarnationis dominice millesimo quingentesimo undecimo, sextodecimo kal. Aprilis, pontificatus nostri anno nono.

BAL.[AR] TUERDUS.

4

The Venetians in Athens and the Destruction of the Parthenon in 1687*

ON September 12, 1683, the Turkish army, which had laid siege to Vienna, was defeated by imperial and Polish troops under the command of Duke Charles of Lorraine and King John Sobiesky of Poland. This event marks a turning point in the relations between Orient and Occident. For after a period of more than three centuries of Turkish aggression and conquest it was now the turn of the western peoples to assume that offensive, which in the course of the next two centuries led to the almost complete exclusion of the Turks from southeastern Europe. The signal for this counter attack was given by an alliance concluded under the papal auspices by the Habsburg emperor, Poland, the Venetian Republic, and other powers. The Venetians had good reasons for their adhesion to the anti-Turkish coalition. Throughout the sixteenth and seventeenth centuries they had seen their position in the eastern Mediterranean more and more threatened by the Turkish advance. They were, therefore, only too eager to go to war against the Ottoman Empire by attacking it simultaneously on the Dalmatian coast and in Greece. In three campaigns, from 1685 to 1687, the Venetian commander-in-chief, Francesco Morosini, succeeded in conquering the

* Reprinted from *American Journal of Archaeology,* XLV (1941), 544–556.

whole Peloponnesus, which was to remain under Venetian rule until 1714.

However great this success was—and it was to be the last glorious chapter in Venetian history—Morosini's Greek campaign has always been remembered with rather bitter feelings for one particular episode: his landing in the Piraeus and the conquest of Athens in September 1687. From the standpoint of the political historian this event is quite insignificant, since the Venetians had to abandon Athens after an occupation of hardly more than half a year. But futile as the expedition was, it will always be recalled because of the irreparable damage which was inflicted on the Parthenon by a Venetian bomb during the siege of the Acropolis on September 26, 1687.

What were the detailed circumstances under which the Parthenon was destroyed? This question has been raised frequently during the last hundred years, but so far no uniformity of opinion has been reached. In his recent book on *The Venetians in Athens, 1687–1688,* Mr. James Morton Paton has presented new sources of information on the topic. In addition, there exist some other sources which have not been used in the earlier monographs on the destruction of the Parthenon. This new material makes it appear appropriate to approach the much discussed problem once more, with the hope of finding a solution. In undertaking this task, I wish to acknowledge my indebtedness to Mr. Paton's research, which has greatly facilitated my task.

In 1835 Leopold Ranke published an article entitled: "Die Venezianer in Morea."[1] Ranke concerned himself primarily with the Venetians' administration of the Peloponnesus during their brief rule over the peninsula from 1687 to 1714, but in a short retrospective chapter on the war of 1685–87 he spoke also of the conquest of Athens. In Ranke's opinion this conquest must be considered "a calamity rather than a stroke of fortune." For on this occasion "the most beautiful ruins of the world, the remains of perhaps the most perfect building that ever existed, were destroyed by an unfortunate accident." Ranke used as his source of information an account given by a con-

[1] *Historisch-politische Zeitschrift* ii, Berlin, 1835.

temporary Venetian officer, Muazzo by name, which he reprinted in a footnote.[2]

Whereas Ranke had expressed the view that the destruction of the Parthenon was due to "an unfortunate accident," the historian of Venice, S. Romanin, avoided committing himself to so definite an opinion. In his *Storia documentata di Venezia* he simply said that on the occasion of the shelling of the Acropolis a bomb fell in the Parthenon, which the Turks had transformed into a powder-magazine. He concluded his account with the statement that the Venetian commander-in-chief, Morosini, "gentilmente allevato al bello, al sentimento artistico in Venezia," could not help exclaiming: "O Atene, o delle arti cultrice, quale sei ora ridotta." [3] By telling this anecdote, which he found in an eighteenth-century biography of Morosini,[4] Romanin evidently implied that the Venetians themselves felt a profound regret for their work of destruction.

Ranke and Romanin had based their accounts on rather inadequate sources. Neither they nor anyone before them had made an attempt to collect all the sources relating to the siege and conquest of Athens and the Acropolis in 1687. The gathering of all the material available was the task which the Comte de Laborde set himself in his work: *Athènes aux XVe, XVIe et XVIIe siècles,* where he dealt in great detail with the events leading to the catastrophe of the Acropolis.[5] De Laborde's interest in the subject was not entirely that of an antiquarian, as is shown by the dedication of the second volume of his book: "Aux vandales, mutilateurs, spoliateurs, restaurateurs de tous les pays, hommage d'une profonde indignation." But despite his moral indignation over "cette détestable bombe" [6] and the incidents which led to the final disaster, de Laborde strove hard to be fair to the people responsible for it; especially to the com-

[2] *Historisch-politische Zeitschrift* ii, 1835, p. 425.

[3] S. Romanin, *Storia documentata di Venezia* vii (2nd, reprint. edit., Venice, 1914), p. 491.

[4] A. Arrighi, *De vita et rebus gestis F. Mauroceni,* Padova, 1749.

[5] (L.E.S.T.) Comte de Laborde, *Athènes aux XVe, XVIe et XVIIe siècles,* 2 vols., Paris, 1854; C. de Laborde, *Documents inédits ou peu connus sur l'histoire et les antiquités d'Athènes,* Paris, 1854, pp. 128–196, 214–239.

[6] De Laborde, *Athènes* ii, p. 149.

manding general, Count Koenigsmarck, upon whom he did not want to cast "un trop amer reproche." [7] The conclusion of the French scholar, however, was that the destruction of the Parthenon was not due to "an unfortunate accident," but that it was done intentionally. De Laborde's principal source of information was an account given in a diary of a German officer in the Venetian expeditionary army, Sobiewolsky by name.[8] According to this report, the Venetians were informed by a deserter that the besieged Turks used the Parthenon as a powder-magazine; consequently, the Venetians made the temple the target of their bombs and after a number of misses they eventually succeeding in hitting and blowing it up. At the end of his narrative de Laborde spoke of the admiration of the Venetian officers for the greatness of the ruined monument. But at that point, again, de Laborde expressed his moral condemnation by the remark that the feeling of remorse made Morosini decline "the responsibility for the misdeed." [9]

De Laborde's thesis met with quite different responses. In 1871, Adolf Michaelis published his book, *Der Parthenon,* where he gave a detailed account of the siege and conquest of Athens in 1687.[10] Michaelis, to be sure, did not take the standpoint of a moral judge, as de Laborde had done, but his presentation of the events followed that of the French scholar with only slight divergencies.[11] In Michaelis' opinion, too, "the fateful shot" was the result of the deserter's report concerning the powder-magazine in the temple, which gave "a definite target for the Venetians." [12]

Ranke certainly did not wish to make this his own opinion. When, a few years after the publication of Michaelis' book, he reprinted his essay on the Venetians in Morea, he did not change a single word in his text, in which he had attributed the destruction of the Parthenon to "an unfortunate accident." He

[7] *L.c.* ii, p. 139. [8] See de Laborde, *l.c.* ii, p. 151, n. 1.

[9] *L.c.* ii, p. 175.

[10] A. Michaelis, *Der Parthenon,* Leipzig, 1871, pp. 61–65.

[11] See Michaelis, *l.c.,* p. 61, n. 251. In appendix III of his book (pp. 345–347), Michaelis printed extracts from the most important sources concerning the siege of the Acropolis.

[12] *L.c.,* p. 62.

merely added a passage to his original footnote in which he rejected de Laborde's thesis.[13] He contrasted briefly his own authority (the account of the Venetian officer Muazzo), with that of de Laborde (the diary of the German officer Sobiewolsky), and came to the conclusion that, compared with Muazzo's narrative, that of Sobiewolsky was "ein kameradschaftliches Histörchen." He decided, therefore, that the story could be disregarded and that "Muazzo's account is here undoubtedly to be preferred." It is curious to note a certain sensitiveness on the part of Ranke against the imputation that, if Sobiewolsky were to be believed, an unnamed German artilleryman was responsible: "this honor," Ranke exclaimed ironically, "we Germans can refute with good conscience."

De Laborde had not raised this national issue; in his opinion "Christian Europe" as a whole, and not individual nations and their members, were responsible for the disaster of 1687.[14] But just as Ranke had sensed a certain attack against German honor in de Laborde's thesis, so had an Italian scholar seen in it a "slander" on the Venetian name. In 1881, A. Dall'Acqua Giusti published an essay: "I Veneziani in Atene nel 1687," [15] the purpose of which was to reply to de Laborde's book and its thesis, and to save Venice, "salvatrice della civiltà dell'Europa," from "la nuova invettiva," which charged her with the wilful destruction of Ictinus' masterpiece.[16] After a brief account of the beginnings of the siege and the bombardment of the Acropolis, Dall'Acqua Giusti came to the crucial question, how to account for the fateful bomb which blew up the Parthenon. "Was it by deliberate aim or by accident? By accident." [17] His authorities were primarily the accounts of three officers of the Venetian expeditionary force, among them Muazzo.[18] In Dall'Acqua Giusti's opinion, Sobiewolsky's testimony could be entirely discarded, since it was not only completely isolated, but taken by itself was hardly believable. For, according to Dall'Acqua Giusti, ballistics were not yet very far advanced, and therefore it was impossible to assume that a shot fired from a

[13] L. von Ranke, *Sämmtliche Werke* xxxxii, Leipzig, 1878, p. 297.

[14] See de Laborde, *Athènes* ii, pp. 149 ff.

[15] *Archivio Veneto* xxii, 1881, pp. 251–270.

[16] *L.c.*, p. 251.

[17] *L.c.*, p. 259.

[18] *L.c.*, pp. 259 ff.

great distance and to a much higher point could have been aimed so precisely as to hit the only vulnerable point in the middle of the temple. "So marvellous an artilleryman seems to me to be fabulous," Dall'Acqua Giusti concluded.[19] Thus he decided that de Laborde, to be sure, did excellent work in collecting all the sources available for the solution of the problem, but that he did not make the right use of them, since, because of his alleged prejudice against the Venetians, he relied exclusively on one source, the diary of Sobiewolsky, and neglected the other and more trustworthy testimony.[20]

Since the publication of Dall'Acqua Giusti's article, the problem of the causes responsible for the destruction of the Parthenon has never again been studied by itself. Those scholars who had to deal with the event in a larger connection, as, for instance, in histories of Venice or Athens, did not turn to the primary sources, but contented themselves with accepting the results of one of the earlier monographs. Thus we find one group of authors who, in accordance with Ranke and Dall'Acqua Giusti, attributes the destruction of the Parthenon to "an unfortunate accident." In this group we find F. Gregorovius,[21] W. C. Hazlitt,[22] and H. Kretschmayr.[23] A number of other scholars accepted de Laborde's and Michaelis' thesis and believed that the destruction had been intentional. This opinion we find in W. Miller,[24] M. L. D'Ooge,[25] and G. Fougères.[26] Finally, a third group of students avoids the whole issue and states simply the fact that the Parthenon was ruined during the siege of 1687. Among these are G. Finlay[27] and H. C. Brown.[28]

[19] *L.c.*, p. 266. [20] *L.c.*, pp. 267 ff.

[21] *Die Geschichte der Stadt Athen im Mittelalter* ii, Stuttgart, 1889, p. 420.

[22] *The Venetian Republic; its Rise, its Growth, and its Fall (410–1797)* ii, London, 1900, p. 279.

[23] *Geschichte von Venedig* iii, Stuttgart, 1934, p. 347; cf. pp. 626 f.

[24] "A History of the Acropolis of Athens," *AJA*. viii, 1893, pp. 548 f.

[25] *The Acropolis of Athens*, New York, 1908, pp. 321 ff.

[26] *Athènes*, Paris, 1923, p. 167. Also in all later editions of Baedeker's *Greece*.

[27] *A History of Greece from its Conquest by the Romans to the Present Time* v, Oxford, 1877, p. 185.

[28] *Venice, a Historical Sketch of the Republic*, New York and London, 1893, p. 378. Cf. H. C. Brown, *The Venetian Republic*, London, 1902, p. 177; H. S. Zwiedineck-Suedenhorst, *Venedig als Weltmacht und Weltstadt*,

This survey of the secondary literature on the destruction of the Parthenon shows clearly that in the opinion of the scholars who have dealt with the problem, there appeared to exist two completely contradictory accounts of the event, that of Muazzo and his Venetian fellow officers, and that of the German officer Sobiewolsky. Since these accounts seemed to be incompatible with one another, there was apparently no choice left but to accept one and to reject the other. In my opinion, however, there is a way out of this dilemma. For Muazzo's and Sobiewolsky's narratives are not the only accounts of the incident, and we are, therefore, enabled to compare their statements with those of other sources. By inspecting the entire material at our disposal we shall not only be able to establish certain facts on which all our sources agree, but we shall also be able to judge the total value of the individual sources and to appraise their trustworthiness in particular points where they disagree with one another.

Early in October, 1687, about a week after the final conquest of the Acropolis, Francesco Morosini, the Venetian commander-in-chief, dispatched a report to Venice with the news of the victory.[29] He related that on the twenty-first of September the Venetians had landed in the Piraeus and the Turks had withdrawn their troops to the Acropolis and refused a Venetian demand for capitulation. Morosini continued: "Fu perciò partito di necessità dar di mano ad invaderlo col furore dell'armi e disposto immediate l'attacco dalla versata sperienza dell'eminentissiomo signor generale Konismarch, si principò la mattina dei 23 con due batterie, l'una di sei pezzi di cannone, e l'altra di quattro mortari da bombe a tormentar gli assediati." [30] According to Morosini, this bombardment of the Acropolis met with great difficulties, because of the nature of the terrain. "Col getto poi delle bombe continuatosi a flagellar dal sopra intendente Costi di S. Felice (i.e., Antonio Mutoni, Count of San Felice, who was in command of the Venetian mortars) l'interno

---

Bielefeld and Leipzig, 1899, p. 180; C. Diehl, *Une république patricienne, Venise,* Paris, 1915, p. 280.

29 The report was printed by de Laborde, *Athènes* ii, p. 157, n. 1.

30 *L.c.,* p. 158, n. 1.

del barbaro luogo, s'ebbe il contento di vederne fra le altre cader una, la sera del 26, con fortunato colpo, mentre acceso un deposito di buona quantità di polvere, non potè più estinguersi la fiamma, che andò serpendo, e per due intieri giorni diroccando l'abitato coll'apportar loro notabili danni e crucciose mestizie." [31] But despite this calamity, Morosini reported, the besieged Turks held out bravely and surrendered the fortress only after their hope for relief from outside had proved to be vain.

In this report several points seem noteworthy. In the first place, Morosini did not claim any merit for himself, but attributed the direction of the attack and its success to the commander of the landing forces, Count Koenigsmarck. Should this fact lead us to assume that by disclaiming any personal responsibility, Morosini intended to put any possible blame for the work of destruction on another man? I do not think so. Morosini expressed very clearly his "satisfaction" over the "lucky shot" which played such an important part in the siege. Was this "fortunato colpo," then, according to Morosini, a merely fortunate accident? Certainly not. For it resulted from a systematic bombardment which had lasted for several days and the purpose of which could have been nothing else but such a direct hit. Finally, we should note that in this report Morosini simply spoke of the explosion of a powder-magazine and did not say anything about the destruction of the Parthenon.

About a week after this first account of the conquest of Athens, Morosini sent a second report to Venice.[32] He informed the Venetian Senate that he had appointed Count Pompei governor of the ruined fortress, "da cui s'applica di fronte a farlo sgombrar dalle rovine, e renderlo purificato dal fetore de' putrefatti cadaveri, sendone più di trecento periti di sesso diverso dalla sola prodigiosa bomba che causò la desolazione del maestoso tempio dedicato a Minerva, e che in empia moschea s'era convertito." [33]

[31] *L.c.*, p. 158, n. 1.
[32] Printed in de Laborde, *Athènes* ii, p. 162, n. 1.
[33] *L.c.*, p. 162, n. 1.

From this second letter we learn further details concerning the effects of this "prodigious bomb": it had caused the ruin of the Parthenon and had brought death to more than three hundred people of both sexes.

Count Koenigsmarck, the second in command of the Venetian army, did not report to Venice on the siege-works under him,[34] but we possess the testimony of a person who was in the general's entourage and who gives us precise information on his feelings at that critical moment. This evidence is contained in a long letter which, on the 18th of October, 1687, Anna Akerhjelm, lady-companion and friend of Countess Koenigsmarck, wrote from Athens to her brother in Sweden.[35] The relevant passage reads as follows: "The fortress (i.e., the Acropolis) lies on a mountain which was, as some say, most difficult to seize, since no mines could be used. How reluctantly His Excellency (i.e., Count Koenigsmarck) saw himself compelled to destroy this beautiful temple which has stood some three thousand years (sic) and is called the temple of Minerva. But it could not be helped. The bombs did their work, and this temple can never again be re-erected in this world." [36]

From the sources just quoted, we get a clear picture of both the actions and the feelings of the two highest commanders of the Venetian army. It was their task to complete the conquest of Athens with the seizure of the fortress, the Acropolis. Since the Turks refused to surrender, and since other means—such as sapping—were not applicable, they saw themselves forced to resort to a systematic bombardment of the citadel. The bomb-

[34] In this country there is unfortunately no copy of A. Schwencke's work, *Geschichte der hannoverschen Truppen in Griechenland, 1685–1689,* Hannover, 1854, "in welchem aus den Briefschaften Koenigsmarcks die wichtigsten Mittheilungen über die Belagerung vorkommen," Ranke, *Sämmtliche Werke* xxxxii, 297, n. 1; on Schwencke, see also de Laborde, *Athènes* ii, p. 139, n. 2. On Otto Wilhelm Graf von Koenigsmarck, see Krause's article in *Allgemeine Deutsche Biographie* xvi, Leipzig, 1882, pp. 532 ff.

[35] The Swedish text and a French translation are found in de Laborde, *Athènes* ii, pp. 276 ff.

[36] "Fästningen ligger på ett berg, som säges wara det slemmaste att bemäktiga sig ty ingen mine kunde göras: huru nödigt Hans Excellens wille förderfva det sköna tempel som uti 3000 är har stått och kallas Minerva Tempel, men det hjelpte inte, bomberna gjorde sin werkan och kan det tempel aldrig i denna werlden mer upprättas"; *l.c.*, p. 276.

ing had the desired effect: for one shot blew up a powder-magazine, which was in the Parthenon, and caused such damage that after two more days the besieged Turks capitulated. From the military point of view there was every reason for the satisfaction which Morosini expressed in his dispatches, although both he and Count Koenigsmarck felt great personal regret that this victory had to be bought at the price of the ruin of the Parthenon, the beauty of which both admired.

We must now turn to the second group of documents relating to the siege of Athens, the reports of Venetian officers. Here we have first the *Relazione dell'operato dell'armi venete dopo la sua partenza da Corinto e della presa d'Atene,* which was written by an unknown officer who took part in the siege.[37] In his account of the bombardment this writer discriminated sharply between the efficiency of the cannon and the mortars. The cannon-fire was well directed and soon silenced the batteries of the enemy. As to the mortars, however, the author of the report asserted: "Le bombe per il contrario non fecero alcuna danno alla fortezza, non so se per la troppa distanza de' mortari, ovvero per altra causa, non avendo il Moltoni (i.e., Mutoni, Count of San Felice), nemmeno quest'anno avuta fortuna di levare della mente di molti il concetto della sua poca abilità e la credenza ch'abbia più parole che fatti." According to the *Relazione,* Count Koenigsmarck summoned Mutoni and reprimanded him severely for the inefficiency of his work. When, despite this rebuke, Mutoni's efforts continued to be of no avail, Koenigsmarck was on the point of removing him from the post in which only Morosini's intervention had kept him. "Ma nel punto ch'era (i.e., Koenigsmarck) per farne la consegna, una bomba gettata a capriccio e senza regola andò a cadere sul tempio di Pallade dentro alla fortezza e diede il fuoco a molta polvere che per giornaliero deposito tenevano in quel loco." [38] A little farther on in the same *Relazione* we read: "In fortezza si vede il tempio dedicato a Pallade Protettrice, ma quello che restò illeso dall'ira e furore di Serse è rimasto rovinato dalle bombe gettatevi in questo assedio, non essendo restato in piedi che una

[37] Extracts in de Laborde, *Athènes* ii, p. 145, n. 1.

[38] De Laborde, *l.c.* ii, p. 145; supplemented by Paton, *l.c.*, p. 73, n. 17.

piccola parte della facciata." As to this last point, we may remark that the *Relazione* somewhat overstated the work of destruction by saying that only "a small part of the façade" remained. We may point out furthermore, that the author was inconsistent. At first he spoke of the explosion of only one bomb in the Parthenon; later, however, he used the plural, speaking of "the bombs thrown into it." But most noteworthy is the statement of the *Relazione* that the fateful bomb was thrown "capriciously and irregularly."

This assertion we find repeated in two more accounts. In a letter of June 8, 1688, written by a Venetian officer who had arrived in Athens about three months after the conquest, we read: "La conquista però della piazza si deve ad una bomba caduta a caso nel tempio di Minerva, ove i Turchi come asilo aveano riposte tutte le loro ricchezze ed il bassà tutta la munizione da guerra, la quale accesa, fè precipitosamente cadere quell'altissima mole, la quale, benchè caduta, non ha potuto non farmi restare estatico in contemplarla." [39]

Although this officer knew things only from hearsay, we possess testimony from a third Venetian officer, Francesco Muazzo, who had been an eye-witness of the conquest. In his *Storia della guerra tra li Veneti e Turchi dal 1684 a 1696,* Muazzo gave a detailed account of the siege of the Acropolis. Like the anonymous author of the *Relazione,* Muazzo asserted that the bombardment of the citadel was so badly managed that Count Koenigsmarck was forced to "corregger pubblicamente il Moltoni, direttor delle batterie, il quale per allora deposta le presunzione, lasciò la cura al governator Leandro assai provetto, benchè suppeditato dal fasto ambizioso dell'altro. Adoprate le macchine da mani più destre, fecer immediate l'effetto dentro la rocca, ed il 27 settembre casualmente penetrò una per l'unico foro della superficie del tempio di Minerva, decantato per architettura e scoltura impareggiabile, sostenuto negli archi massicci da raddoppiati corsi di smisurate colonne, alla divota sussistenza di cui (fatto meschita) la guarnigione tenea ricovrate le sostanze, le famiglie e le munizioni da guerra. Al cader della bomba s'accese la polvere. . . ." [40] This disaster greatly dis-

[39] De Laborde, *Athènes* ii, p. 188, n. 1.
[40] De Laborde, *l.c.* ii, p. 143, n. 1.

couraged the besieged Turks and eventually induced them to capitulate when their hope for outside relief proved vain.

It is on the basis of the three accounts quoted that the destruction of the Parthenon has been attributed by modern scholars to "an unfortunate accident." Before accepting or rejecting this thesis we must scrutinize these three sources more closely. In the case of the second we do not get very far, since the writer of the letter of 1688 simply stated that "one bomb fell by chance in the temple of Minerva." But in the *Relazione* and in Muazzo's account we obtain detailed information on the events preceding the fateful shot. According to both sources, the Venetians began a systematic bombardment of the besieged Acropolis. While the cannon did efficient work, the mortars did not achieve any success. Both Muazzo and the author of the *Relazione* ascribed this failure to the incompetency of Antonio Mutoni, Count of San Felice, who was in charge of the Venetian "bombisti." From sources collected by de Laborde and Paton we learn that Mutoni, because of his reputation as an expert in ballistics, had been put in charge of the Venetian mortars in 1685, but that his new theories and inventions did not work well during the campaigns of 1685 and 1686.[41] In this respect, therefore, the charges made by Muazzo and by the *Relazione* against Mutoni are borne out by independent witnesses, who establish the fact that within the Venetian army there were officers who considered Mutoni unfit for his job; he was able to keep it only through the protection of the commander-in-chief Morosini.[42]

On the other hand, we have to note an interesting divergence concerning an important point in the accounts of Muazzo and the *Relazione*. According to the *Relazione,* Mutoni was about to be replaced, when "a bomb, thrown capriciously and irregularly" fell into the powder-magazine in the Parthenon. According to this account, then, Mutoni was still in command when the decisive shot was fired; but, according to Muazzo, this was not the case. For he asserted that, after his rebuke by Count

[41] See de Laborde, *Athènes* ii, p. 141, n. 2; especially the following passage from a letter of a German officer: "Le comte Felice est un sot, il nous fait plus de mal avec ses bombes qu'à l'ennemi." Compare Paton, *l.c.,* p. 72, n. 17.

[42] See Paton, *l.c.,* p. 72, n. 17.

Koenigsmarck, Mutoni yielded the direction of the actual bombardment to his subordinate Leandro. Muazzo then stated that "under a more adroit direction, the machines (i.e., the mortars) achieved immediate effect within the fortress and on the 27th (sic) of September a bomb accidentally penetrated the only opening in the roof of the temple of Minerva." This last sentence of Muazzo is puzzling and at first glance seems to be rather illogical. For if the fire of the mortars under the direction of Leandro was now actually better aimed, how could the final success then be "accidental"? The only possible explanation appears to be that, in Muazzo's opinion, it was by chance that the bomb fell into "the only opening" of an otherwise hardly penetrable surface.[43]

When we accept this explanation, we cannot agree with Ranke and Dall'Acqua Giusti, who base their thesis of the "accidental" destruction of the Parthenon on the assertion that there exists concordant testimony of three Venetian officers on this point. For one of these officers, the writer of the letter of 1688, was not an eyewitness of the event, and his account is not very detailed; the two other accounts disagree as to whether or not Mutoni was still in charge of the bombing when the fateful shot was fired. According to the *Relazione,* moreover, it was by accident that the Parthenon was hit at all, whereas, according to Muazzo, it was by accident only that one particular and especially vulnerable spot in the building was hit. In addition we have to keep in mind that from the same sources we learn that within the Venetian army there existed two schools of opinion about the commander of the "bombisti," Mutoni, one group led by Count Koenigsmarck, the other by Morosini. We must take into consideration the possibility that the author of the *Relazione* and Muazzo were somewhat prejudiced and inclined to discredit the work, not only of Mutoni, but also of the mortars, by ascribing the final success of the bombs to a mere accident.

In addition to the accounts of the three Venetian officers, we

[43] For Muazzo's "unico foro della superficie del tempio," see a design of the Acropolis, drawn up in 1670 by an unknown artist, and reproduced by H. Omont, *Athènes au XVII siècle,* Paris, 1898, pl. XXIX.

possess narratives of the conquest of Athens written by two German officers in the expeditionary army. The first is found in a diary of a Hanoverian officer who fought in the Venetian service during the Greek campaign of 1686/87.[44] The anonymous diarist gave a detailed report of the landing of the Venetians in the Piraeus on the 21st of September, the beginning of the siege, and an attempt to mine the citadel. On the afternoon of the second day of the siege "schosze man zur probe die erste bombe hinein, welche sehr woll fiel; auch wurden 4 stücke aufgebracht." [45] The bombardment both with cannon and with mortars was continued throughout the next day: "auch wurden unterschiedliche Bomben hinein geworfen, welche guten Effect thaten, in dem unterschiedliche auf ihre Bolwerke gefallen und groszen Schaden gethan." [46] Under the date of the 26th of September, the diarist said: "Frühe morgendz wurd wieder angefangen mit Canonen und Bomben zu werfen, doch wurden viel derselben fehl geworfen; gegen abend fiel eine in den schönen Tempel der göttin Minerva, welche den ihre Pulver und munition, so sie daselbst gehabt, ergriffen, so dasz alles angegangen, dergestalt, dasz durch einen gewaltigen schlag das schöne gebäude gantz ruiniret worden. . . ." [47] The fire continued to rage for two days and destroyed the whole temple, "so dasz nichtz als die beiden mauren stehen blieben, welches den wohl zu bedauern war, in dem es noch von den eltesten und raresten gebäuden der welt gewesen. . . ." [48] On the 28th of September the Turkish garrison, five hundred men apart from women and children, surrendered the fortress.

From this account we get a description of the bombardment of the Acropolis which is quite different from that given by the three Venetian officers. According to the Hanoverian diarist, "the unfortunate bomb," which in one stroke blew up the Parthenon, was only the last and most successful in a series of hits within the Acropolis which had started two days earlier when the first bomb was fired with good effect into the fortress.

[44] Published by L. Dietrichson, "Zum zweihundertjährigen Gedächtnis der Zerstörung des Parthenon," in *Zeitschrift für bildende Kunst,* xxii, 1887, pp. 367–376.

[45] *L.c.,* p. 369.

[46] *L.c.,* pp. 369 ff.

[47] *L.c.,* p. 370.

[48] *L.c.,* p. 370.

The diarist's statement that quite a few of the bombs went astray strengthens his claim to reliability, since even in the course of a systematic bombardment it was inevitable that a number of shots should miss their mark.

The second account of a German officer is found in the *Marschroute des Hessischen Regimentes so nach Morea geschickt worden;* the author is Major Sobiewolsky, who served as lieutenant of the Venetian auxiliary troops in the campaign of 1687. Sobiewolsky reported that on the 22nd day of September his regiment began to build trenches and to bring batteries into position. At the same time his men began to sap mines in the hard rock of the Acropolis, an effort which, in Sobiewolsky's opinion, probably would have proved vain. At that moment, he continued, "there came a deserter from the castle with the news that the commander of the fortress had all the stores of powder and other precious things brought to the temple which is called the temple of Minerva, and that also the people of rank were there because they believed that the Christians would not do any harm to the temple. Upon this report, several mortars were directed against the temple, but none of the bombs was able to do damage, particularly because the upper roof of the temple was somewhat sloping and covered with marble, and thus well protected. A lieutenant from Lüneburg, however, offered to throw bombs into the temple, and this was done. For one of the bombs fell through (the roof of) the temple and right into the Turkish store of powder, whereupon the middle of the temple blew up and everything inside was covered with stone, to the great consternation of the Turks." [49]

[49] "In deme aber dieses geschahe (i.e., the mining), kame ein überläuffer aus dem Castell, welcher diese nachricht mitbrachte, das der Commendant der vestung allen vorraht von Pulver nebst anderen besten sachen in den Tempell, der Minervae Tempell genannt, hätte einbringen lassen, auch das die vornehmbste Personen sich darin befinden, in dem sie glaubeten, die christen würden dem Tempell keinen schaden zufügen. Hierauff sind unterschiedliche Mörsell auff den Tempell gerichtet, keine bombe hat aber schaden können, sonderlich weilen das oberdach am Tempell etwas abhängig mit Marmor bedecket, und woll verwahret war. Ein lüneburgischer lieutenant aber, derselbe erboste (sic) sich, in den Tempell Bomben einzuwerffen, welches auch geschehen, in dem eine davon durch den Tempell gefallen, und eben in der Türcken vorraht von Pulver; da dan die

This "description" of Major Sobiewolsky is the crucial account which de Laborde and Michaelis made the basis of their narratives of the destruction of the Parthenon, and which Ranke and Dall'Acqua Giusti rejected peremptorily. In weighing the value of this statement we may note first that Sobiewolsky did not claim any merit for himself or for any other specific person, not even for a member of his own regiment. He was not like Benvenuto Cellini who, at the occasion of the siege of Rome in 1527, ascribed to himself the glory of the death of the Constable of Bourbon. The complete lack of personal pretension on the part of Sobiewolsky makes it difficult to discard entirely his report, since there seems to be no reason for him to invent a story which he reported as a simple matter of fact and without any judgment of value.

But apart from this inner plausibility, there exist other and independent authorities which to a certain extent confirm the correctness of Sobiewolsky's account. According to him, it was an officer from Lüneburg who fired the decisive shot. Now we possess the text of the convention between the Duke Ernest of Brunswick and Lüneburg and the Venetian Republic concerning the sending of three regiments of eight hundred men each by the Duke to Venice in 1684. The 10th paragraph of this contract reads as follows: "L'artiglieria necessaria per queste Truppe con li bombardieri è la munition di guerra sarà fornita in ogni luogo dalla Republica à sue spese ed ella farà risarcir le armi rotte è perdute in fattion alli soldati." [50] This stipulation proves that the regiment, to which the officer from Lüneburg belonged, had mortars as part of its equipment.

Furthermore there exist several plans of the bombardment of the Acropolis which were drawn up by Verneda, an engineer in the Venetian expeditionary army, who took part in the siege of Athens.[51] In addition to bombs which are falling both inside

---

Mitte des Tempells auffgegangen, und alles was darinnen gewesen mit steinen bedecket ward, mit groszer Bestürzung der Türcken." Extract in Michaelis, *Der Parthenon,* p. 346, n. 18.

[50] Printed in de Laborde, *Athènes* ii, p. 75, n. 1.

[51] Reproduced by de Laborde, *Athènes* ii, *passim,* and by H. Omont, *Athènes au XVIIe siècle,* Paris, 1898, pls. XXXII–XXXVII. On Verneda, see de Laborde, ii, p. 180, n. 2.

and outside the Acropolis, we see the effect of the one fatal bomb which has just blown the Parthenon into the air. Since Verneda indicated the trajectories of the missiles, we can trace the bomb back to the point from which it was fired. The position of this particular battery was, according to one of Verneda's plans,[52] very close to the "Quartieri del Reg(imen)to del Principe di Bransuich," that is, of that regiment to which Sobiewolsky's officer from Lüneburg belonged.

Finally, Sobiewolsky's story seems to be somewhat confirmed by the account which was given by the contemporary Venetian chronicler Cristoforo Ivanovich in his *Istoria della Lega Ortodossa contro il Turco*.[53] For after having recounted the start of the bombardment of the fortress, Ivanovich continued: "Avvertito Sua Eccellenza (i.e., Morosini) trovarsi nel Tempio di Minerva le monizioni de'Turchi insieme con le loro principali donne e figli, stimandosi ivi sicuri per la grossezza delle mura e volti del detto tempio, ordinò al Conte Mutoni che dirizzasse il tiro delle sue bombe a quella parte. Nacque sino dal principio qualche disordine nel getto delle medesime, che cadeano fuori, e fu per l'inegualità del peso che si trovò in 130 libre di svario dall'una all'altra; ma pratticatosi il giusto peso non andò più fuori alcuna, si che una di quelle colpendo nel fianco del tempio finì di romperlo." [54] In the next sentence Ivanovich described the "terrible effect" of this shot. The following paragraph of the *Istoria* told how on the 28th of September the Venetians defeated Turkish troops who attempted to relieve the fortress; and how on the same day the *Proveditor di Campo*, Dolfin, by "accelerating the work of the cannon and mortars," strove "di necessitar i Turchi alla resa." Ivanovich continued: "Avertito il Mutoni da un Greco che in una casa erano ritirate alcune donne dell'Aga diresse i tiri alla medesima e una bomba fece si fiera stragge di quelle che atterrita tutta la Fortezza, desperata anco del soccorso fuggato, convenne esporre bandiera bianca per rendersi, e fu lo stesso giorno a ore 22." [55]

[52] This design has been reproduced by de Laborde, *l.c.* ii, after p. 182.

[53] See *The Venetians in Athens 1687–1688; from the Istoria of Cristoforo Ivanovich;* edited by J. M. Paton, Cambridge, Mass., 1940.

[54] Paton, *l.c.*, pp. 10 ff.

[55] *Ibid.*, *l.c.*, p. 11.

Ivanovich's narrative seems to agree with Sobiewolsky's assertion that the Venetians were apprised of the existence of the powder-magazine in the Parthenon, and that, therefore, they made this building the target of their bombs. Since it is not possible to assume that Ivanovich had seen and read the account of the German officer, he must have obtained his information from other sources, probably from accounts given by Venetian soldiers after their return home. Thus, Sobiewolsky's story seems to be borne out and confirmed by an independent source. Unfortunately, Ivanovich's account of the episode as a whole is of dubious value.[56] It is excusable that he attributed to Morosini a much greater personal share in the victory than any of the other sources, including Morosini's own reports; this may be explained, in the words of Mr. Paton, by Ivanovich's "wish to magnify the importance of the Captain General." [57] But our belief in Ivanovich's reliability is really shaken when we read in his account, first that the explosion of the powder-magazine in the Parthenon came about because Morosini had been informed of its location and had directed the fire of the Venetian mortars there; and next when we read in the following paragraph—in almost identical words—about the deliberate slaughter of a number of Turkish women, likewise, because of special information—an incident not reported by any other source. This duplication of destructive bombs in Ivanovich's narrative actually is due, as Mr. Paton points out, "to a failure to recognize that two accounts of the disaster caused by the 'prodigiosa bomba' . . . really referred to the same event." [58]

Although this confusion makes it impossible to accept at face value Ivanovich's narrative of the details of the siege of the Acropolis, we may safely draw one conclusion: there were rumors in Venice which attributed the destruction of the Parthenon to a deliberate bombardment.[59] The existence of these

[56] See Paton, *l.c.*, pp. 69 ff.

[57] *Ibid.*, p. 69, n. 9.

[58] Paton, *l.c.*, p. 70, n. 11.

[59] There was, however, at least one man in the Venetian army who even claimed personal credit for the final success of the bombardment. On November 8, 1687, Matteo del Teglia, Florentine *Maestro di Posta,* wrote a letter from Venice to Florence in which we find the following sentence: "La sorte di questo attaco toccò al Signore Rinaldo Buchett, o di vero La

rumors would speak in favor of Sobiewolsky's assertion. But despite the conformity of two different and independent sources on this point, I hesitate to say more than that there is a certain probability for the truthfulness of these reports, but no really conclusive proof.

But even if we discard completely these particular details, we are certain of the following facts as substantiated by concurring testimonies of the various eyewitnesses:

(1) In 1687 the Acropolis served as a fortress to which the Turks retreated after they had been forced to abandon the city of Athens to the Venetian expeditionary army.

(2) The commanding generals of the Venetian army, Francesco Morosini and Count Koenigsmarck, desiring to spare the fortress the horrors of a siege, summoned the Turkish garrison to surrender before they opened the battle; the Turks, however, refused to capitulate.

(3) By military necessity, therefore, though with personal reluctance, the Venetian generals ordered a systematic bombardment of the Acropolis, which began on the 24th of September. An earlier attempt to mine the citadel had failed, because of the hardness of the rock on which it was built.

(4) After the bombardment had started, the mortars, in contrast to the efficiency of the cannon, did not obtain immediate effect. Eventually, however, on the third day of the siege, that is, on the 26th of September, one of the bombs penetrated the roof of the Parthenon and blew up a large store of powder in the temple; the explosion resulted in the death of many people and in a fire which, two days later, forced the Turkish garrison to surrender.

(5) Although the Venetians regretted the ruin of the Parthenon, they were highly pleased by this quick success of their arms;

Rue, piantando esso la prima e la seconda batteria di commissione del suo Prefato (sic?) Conte di San Felice, che gli sortì felicemente, doppo alquanti tiri a vuoto; per lo che ne riportò la gloria meritata" (extract in Paton, *l.c.*, p. 70, n. 10). Whether the claim of del Teglia's friend La Rue, who served under Mutoni (see Paton, *l.c.*), was legitimate, is, of course, impossible to decide. The main value of this passage is that it confirms the accounts of the anonymous Hanoverian diarist and of Sobiewolsky concerning the systematic bombardment of the Acropolis.

they felt no need for apology when they announced the news of the conquest of Athens in the *Reporti di Venezia* and other official and semi-official publications which were sent all over Europe.[60]

In view of these various facts it seems impossible to call the destruction of the Parthenon "an unfortunate accident." For after the Turks had refused to capitulate, the Venetians were resolved to break their resistance by inflicting on them as much damage as possible. Thus all the buildings on the Acropolis became military objectives. By far the largest and the most outstanding building within the narrow enclosure of the Acropolis was the Parthenon, thus the central target of the Venetian fire.[61] The man who was in charge of the bombing,

60 See the accounts in the *Reporti di Venezia* of November 22 and December 6, 1687 (extracts in de Laborde, *Athènes* ii, p. 146, n. 1, and 176, n. 2).—In the fall of 1687, after the conquest of the Peloponnesus had been completed, an official account of the expedition was printed in Venice under the title: *Ragguaglio giornaliero delle trionfanti ed invittissime armate Venete maritime e terrestri con suoi acquisti distintamente descritti fatti contro la Potenza Ottomana . . . , seguiti l'anno 1687.* (In Venetia, 1687, per G. Albrizzi in Campo dalla guerra a S. Zulian.) While this report was in the process of publication, the news of the conquest of Athens arrived in Venice; and the editor decided immediately to insert at last a short account of this event in his book; see the edition of the text by H. Omont, "Une relation Vénitienne du siège d'Athènes," in *Revue des études Grecques* viii, 1895, p. 258. Immediately after its publication in Venice, the *Ragguaglio giornaliero* was translated into English under the title: *A Journal of the Venetian Campaign. A.D. 1687. Under the conduct of the capt. general Morosini, providitor gen. Cornaro, general Coningsmarch, general Venieri, etc.* (Translated from the Italian original, sent from Venice, and printed by the order of the most Serene Republick. Licensed, decemb. 16, 1687. R. L. Estrange, London; printed by H. C. and sold by R. Taylor, near Stationers-Hall, 1688); the description of the siege of the Acropolis has been inserted on pp. 38 ff.—The Venetian government of that time was greatly interested in publicizing the successes of the Venetian armies and lent active support to a number of publications, both in the form of books and pamphlets, which served this purpose; some of these publications were even illustrated with drawings of battle-scenes and sieges; on this practice, see de Laborde, *l.c.* ii, 98–109; H. Omont, *Athènes au XVIIe siècle,* pp. 10 ff. (descriptions of pls. XXXII–XXXVII).

61 The rocky plateau of the Acropolis is very small, its largest extension from east to west being less than 350 yards, that from north to south less than 150 yards. Within this narrow space, the Parthenon occupies a comparatively large room, since its platform, the *stylobate,* is 70 yards long and 33 yards broad.

Antonio Mutoni, Count of San Felice, failed at first in his task and was accused of incompetency by his adversaries in the Venetian army. This fact has been told by Muazzo and by the anonymous author of the *Relazione,* who have served as the main authorities for the "accidental" character of the explosion. But, in my opinion, the very fact that Mutoni was accused of incompetency, proves that it was considered perfectly feasible to effect direct hits on the Acropolis, and that such hits were demanded. That the Parthenon was finally hit, was not an accidental event, but an almost inevitable and, from the military point of view, desirable result of the systematic bombardment of the Acropolis. If there was "luck," then it was that kind of luck with which every artillery officer will reckon, the luck he is hoping for and is to a certain degree able to bring about. In this sense, then, but only in this sense, we may take the words in Morosini's official reports, which attributed his victory to the "fortunato colpo" of "una prodigiosa bomba."

PART II

Petrarchan Studies

5

An Introduction to Petrarch's Sonnets and Songs*[1]

PETRARCH presents in his life and work a most interesting example of a complete mutation in literary fame. For there exists in critical annals a very marked and curious contrast between his reputation among his contemporaries and in subsequent periods.

In the popular imagination of today his name is indissolubly linked with that of Laura,

> "La bella giovenetta ch'ora è donna."
>
> (*Rime* No. 127)

This tradition reaches back many centuries; in fact it had originated shortly after his death. To the majority of the generations of his admirers, Petrarch has been primarily the lover of Laura and the author of the *Rime,* the sonnets and songs which he began in his youth and in which he never tired of singing of his

* Reprinted from Petrarch's *Sonnets and Songs,* translated by Anna Maria Armi, Introduction by Theodor E. Mommsen (New York: Pantheon Books, 1946), pp. xv–xliii.

[1] I should like to thank my friend George W. Freiday, Jr., for his many valuable suggestions and for his constructive criticism.

The quotations from the "Letter to Posterity" and the letter describing Petrarch's ascension of Mont Ventoux are from the translations by Edward H. R. Tatham in *Francesco Petrarca. The First Modern Man of Letters; His Life and Correspondence (1304–1347).* 2 vols. 1925/26. The Sheldon Press, London.

love. Among Italians and non-Italians the image and fame of that Petrarch are just as much alive today as they were vivid towards the end of the fourteenth century when Geoffrey Chaucer glorified him in the *Canterbury Tales:*

> "Fraunceys Petrak, the lauriat poete,
> Highte this clerk, whose rethorike sweete
> Enlumyned at Ytaille of poetrie."

Through the mastery of language in his Italian poetry Petrarch not only made an everlasting contribution to world literature, but also rendered a very specific service to the development and moulding of the language of his own country. Since the Renaissance literary historians have referred to him as "the father of the Italian language," a title which he shares with the two other great Florentines of the fourteenth century, Dante and Boccaccio.

By later generations Petrarch was considered an initiator in still another respect. Through the influence of the *Rime* he became the originator of a whole school of poetry, that of the "Petrarchists," which appeared soon after his death both inside and outside Italy. He had brought his favourite form of expression, the sonnet, to such a classical perfection that for centuries to come he remained the admired and widely imitated model of many poets who endeavoured to write in the same pattern. For the Elizabethan period witness the statement made in 1593 by Gabriel Harvey in his *Pierces Supererogation:* "All the noblest Italian, French, and Spanish poets have in their several veins Petrarchized; and it is no dishonour for the daintiest or divinest muse to be his scholar, whom the amiablest invention and beautifullest elocution acknowledge their master." Among these Petrarchists of the Renaissance we find Sir Thomas Wyatt and the Earl of Surrey in England, the group of the *Pléiade* with their leader Ronsard in France.

In marked contrast to the judgment of posterity, Petrarch's own generation, however, found his principal merit in his Latin writings, not in his Italian poetry.

This contemporary estimate is most clearly shown by the fact that it was the authorship of the Latin epic *Africa* and not that of the *Rime* which brought Petrarch, in 1341, at the age of thirty-seven, the famous crown of the poet laureateship on the Roman Capitol. According to the tradition of the fourteenth century, in antiquity this ceremony had symbolized the greatest tribute which could be given to a living poet. To Petrarch's contemporaries no one was deemed more worthy of this ancient honour than he who seemed to re-embody the classical ideal. Through the conscious imitation of the *Aeneid* and the *Eclogues* in his own *Africa* and *Carmen Bucolicum* he appeared to have become a second Vergil. Moreover his numerous treatises dealing with problems of moral philosophy and especially the content and style of his hundreds of widely circulated letters placed him in juxtaposition with Cicero. And as King Robert the Wise of Naples asked Petrarch for the dedication of the *Africa* to himself, so the German Emperor Charles IV requested later on the same honour for Petrarch's main historical work, the collection of Roman biographies entitled *De viris illustribus,* in which Petrarch recounted the lives and deeds of the great political and military leaders of ancient Rome in order to inspire his readers to similar accomplishments.

Throughout all these various Latin writings Petrarch pursued the same purpose: he wished to teach his Italian contemporaries not to regard the great Roman statesmen and writers as figures of a dead past, but to look upon them as living models for the present and as harbingers of the future. The Italians alone, not "barbarians" like the French or Germans, Petrarch asserted, had a legitimate claim to the Latin inheritance. In the acceptance of this Roman legacy Petrarch saw an instrument of spiritual unity for his fellow-countrymen. With this motive he devoted many of his Latin poems, treatises, and letters to the task of awakening the consciousness of this legacy in the hearts and minds of the Italians of his day.

In this sense, then, Petrarch again stands at the beginning of a very important evolution in Italian culture, the great movement known as "the Revival of Antiquity" or "Humanism." He was destined to direct and stimulate these new ideas in many significant ways, as for instance through his zealous effort to write in a "pure," i.e., classical, Latin style, through his tireless and often extremely successful search for ancient manuscripts, and through his gift for textual emendation. In contrast to many of the later humanists, this "father of Humanism" did not, however, study Latin primarily from an antiquarian point of view, since for him this language was the medium through which the greatest aesthetic, intellectual, and political tradition ever created had found its timeless expression. It was as the voice of this tradition that Petrarch was most admired and revered in his lifetime. This reputation of Petrarch within his own generation has been well characterized in Jakob Burckhardt's *Civilization of the Renaissance in Italy:* "Petrarch, who lives in the memory of most people of today chiefly as a great Italian poet, owed his fame among his contemporaries far more to the fact that he was a kind of living representative of Antiquity."

In view of the fact that there exists such a divergence of opinion in the evaluation of the main aspects of Petrarch's lifework and such variety in the judgments rendered by his own generation and by posterity, it seems worth asking what conceptions Petrarch had concerning himself and his work. It is quite easy to find an answer to this question. For Petrarch was fully conscious of the fact that his life and work represented a unique and interesting phenomenon. Thus he says in the first sonnet of his *Rime:*

> ". . . I have seen enough that in this land
> To the whole people like a tale I seem."

When Petrarch wrote these lines in the proem to the collection of his *Rime,* he had reached the summit of his fame. He could rightly assume that to Italian and non-Italian eye-witnesses his accomplishments and his rise to glory would appear "like a tale." Naturally he wished this "tale" to be perpetuated accurately beyond the memory of his contemporaries, and consequently around the year 1351 he wrote a letter which he addressed explicitly "To Posterity." Later he included this epistle, in a revised form, in the first collection of his letters called the

Familiares, and thus made sure that the letter would actually come down to future generations.

The stated purpose of this letter is to tell posterity "what sort of man I was and what was the fate of my works." There is no better account of the main events during the first part of Petrarch's life than that given by himself in this "Letter to Posterity."

He introduces himself with a description of his outward appearance: "In my early days my bodily frame was of no great strength, but of great activity. I cannot boast of extreme comeliness, but only such as in my greener years would be pleasing. My complexion was lively, between fair and dark, my eyes sparkling, my sight very keen for a long time until it failed me unexpectedly after my sixtieth year, so that to my disgust I had to have recourse to glasses."

After this portrait of himself he begins the tale of his life: "I was but a mortal mannikin like yourself, with an origin neither very high nor very low. . . . I was of honourable parents, both natives of Florence but living in exile on a scanty fortune which was, to tell the truth, verging upon poverty. During this exile I was born at Arezzo, in the year of Christ 1304 of this present age, at dawn on Monday the 20th of July. . . . The first year of my life, or rather part of it, I spent at Arezzo where I first saw the light; the six following years, after my mother had been recalled from exile, at Incisa, an estate of my father's about fourteen miles from Florence. My eighth year I passed at Pisa, my ninth and following years in Transalpine Gaul on the left bank of the Rhone. The name of the city is Avignon, where the Roman Pontiff holds, and has long held, the Church of Christ in a shameful exile. . . . There then, on the banks of that most windy of rivers, I passed my boyhood under my parents' care, and, later, all my early manhood under my own vain fancies—not, however, without long intervals of absence. For during this time I spent four whole years at Carpentras, a small town not far east of Avignon; and in these two places I learnt a smattering of Grammar, Dialectic and Rhetoric suited to my age—as much, I mean, as is generally learnt in schools—and how little that is, dear reader, you know well enough. Then I went to Montpellier to study Law, where I spent four more years; and then three years at Bologna where I heard the whole Corpus of Civil Law, and was thought by many to be a youth of great promise if I would only persevere in what I had taken up. However, I abandoned that study altogether as soon as my parents abandoned the care of me; not because I did not respect the authority of Law, which is doubtless great and full of that Roman Antiquity in which I delight, but because it is degraded by the villainy of those who practise it. And so I revolted at learning thoroughly that what I would not turn to dishonourable, and could scarcely turn to honourable, uses; for such rectitude, if I had tried it, would have been laid to ignorance. Accordingly, in my twenty-second year (1326) I returned to Avignon—my exile home, where I had lived from the close of my childhood, for habit is second nature."

Petrarch continues to relate that there in Avignon he gained the friendship and patronage of many distinguished men. Among these patrons he mentions particularly some members of the great Roman family of Colonna who resided at that time at the papal court. He does not tell that after his renunciation of law he took minor orders which entitled him to receive ecclesiastical prebends without becoming a priest. He had now become "a worthy clerk," as Chaucer calls him in the prologue to *The Clerk's Tale*.

During that period, Petrarch's account goes on, "a youthful longing impelled me to travel through France and Germany; and though other causes were feigned to recommend my going to my superiors, yet the real reason was an eager enthusiasm to see the world. On that journey I first saw Paris; and I took delight in finding out the truth or falsehood of what I had heard about that city. Having returned thence, I went to Rome, which from my infancy I had ardently desired to see. And there I so venerated Stefano Colonna, the noble-minded father of that family, who was like one of the ancient heroes, and I was so kindly received by him in return, that you could scarcely have detected a difference between me and one of his own sons."

On his return from Rome, in 1337, Petrarch decided to establish himself in Vaucluse. According to the "Letter to Posterity" these were his reasons: "I could not overcome my natural ingrained repugnance to Avignon, that most wearisome of cities. Therefore I looked about for some bypath of retreat as a harbour of refuge. And I found a narrow valley, delightful and secluded, called Vaucluse (fifteen miles from Avignon), where the Sorgues, king of all fountains, takes its rise. Charmed with the sweetness of the spot, I betook myself thither with my books. It would be a long story if I were to go on to relate what I did there during many, many years. Suffice it to say that nearly every one of my works was either accomplished or begun or conceived there; and these works have been so numerous that they exercise and weary me to this day."

Now Petrarch's tale comes to the supreme moment of his life, his coronation as poet laureate: "While I was spinning out my leisure in Vaucluse, on one and the same day, strange to relate, letters reached me both from the Senate of the city of Rome and from the Chancellor of the University of Paris, bringing me rival invitations to accept the laurel crown of poetry—the former at Rome, the latter at Paris. In my youthful pride at such an honour, thinking I must be worthy of it as such eminent men so thought me, but weighing their verdict instead of my own merit, I yet hesitated for a while which invitation to accept. And on this point I asked by letter for the advice of Cardinal Giovanni Colonna. He was so near that although I had written late in the day, I received his answer the next morning before nine o'clock. In accordance with his advice I decided for the dignity of the city of Rome as superior to all others, and my two replies to him applauding that advice are still extant. I set out accordingly, and though, like all young men, I was a very partial judge of my own works, I still blushed to accept the verdict upon myself even of those who had invited me. Yet no doubt they would not have done so if they had not judged me worthy of the honour so offered. I determined, therefore, first to visit Naples, and appear before that distinguished king and philosopher, Robert—as illustrious in literature as in station, the only king of our time who was a friend of learning and of virtue alike—to see what judgment he would pass upon me. I still wonder at his flattering estimate of me and the kindly welcome that he gave me; and you, reader, if you knew of it, would wonder no less. On hearing of the reason of my coming, he was marvelously delighted, and considered that my youthful confidence in him—perhaps, too, the honour that I was seeking—might be a source of glory to himself, since I had chosen him of all men as the only competent judge in such case. Need I say more? After numberless conversations on various matters, I showed him that epic of mine, the *Africa,* with which he was so delighted that he begged me as a great favour to dedicate it to him—a request which I certainly could not refuse, nor did I wish to do so. At length he fixed a day for my visit and kept me from noon to evening. And since the time proved too short for the press of subjects, he did the same on the following two days. After having fully probed my ignorance for three days, he adjudged me worthy of the laurel crown. His wish was to bestow it upon me at Naples, and he earnestly begged me to consent. But my love of Rome prevailed over even the reverend importunity of so great a king. Therefore, when he saw that my resolution was inflexible, he gave me messengers and letters to the Roman Senate in which he declared his judgment of me in flattering terms. This royal estimate was then, indeed, in accord with that of many others, and especially with my own. Today, however, I cannot approve his verdict, though it agreed with that of myself and others. Affection for me and interest in my youth had more weight with him than consideration of the facts. So I arrived at Rome, and unworthy as I was, yet with confident reliance on such a verdict, I gained the poetic laurel while still a raw scholar with great applause from those of the Romans who could be present at the ceremony. On this subject, too, there are letters of mine, both in verse and in prose."

In the retrospective view of the "Letter to Posterity" Petrarch concludes the account of this event with a rather disillusioned comment: "This laurel gained for me no knowledge, but rather much envy, but that also is too long a story to be told here."

It may be true that in the full maturity of his age Petrarch sincerely regretted his early desire for "empty glory" and his "youthful audacity" in accepting the honour of the coronation. But there is no doubt that at the time of the event itself he drew a deep inspiration for his work from his public and official acclaim as "a great poet and historian." He himself tells in the "Letter to Posterity" why it was that after his departure from Rome he resolved to finish his Latin epic *Africa* which he always considered his greatest title to fame: "I was mindful of the honour I had just received and anxious that it should not seem to be conferred on one who was unworthy of it. And so one day when, during a visit to the mountains, I had chanced upon the wood called Selvapiana across the river Enza on the confines of Reggio, I was fired by the beauty of the place and turned my pen to my interrupted poem, the *Africa*. Finding my enthusiasm, which had seemed quite dead, rekindled, I wrote a little that very day and some on each successive day until I returned to Parma. There . . . in a short time I brought the work to a conclusion, toiling at it with a zeal that amazes me today." And in the last book of the *Africa* he did not hesitate to insert, in the form of a prophecy, an account of his coronation, "such as Rome has not seen for a thousand years."

While it is thus certain that Petrarch's greatest Latin poem owed its completion to the stimulus of the laurel crown, we might digress here for a moment from the account of the "Letter to Posterity," to point out that it seems at least probable that Petrarch's greatest Italian poem, the canzone "Italia mia," was conceived under the same inspiration.[2] This fervent appeal for Italian unity is addressed to the Italian princes.

> "In whose hands Fortune has put the rein
> Of the beautiful places. . . ."
>
> (*Rime* No. 128)

It is significant that Petrarch, a poet, not a man of politics, makes himself the mouthpiece of all his fellow countrymen when he reminds the rulers of Italy of their common inheri-

[2] [See Theodor E. Mommsen, "The Date of Petrarch's Canzone *Italia Mia*," *Speculum*, XIV (1939), 28–37. Mommsen argues that "Italia mia" was certainly composed "before the year 1347" and probably composed in the years 1341–1342, in the months following Petrarch's coronation as poet laureate on April 8, 1341.]

tance of "the gentle Latin blood" and implores them not to call in "barbaric" mercenaries from abroad and not "to ruin the loveliest country of the earth." He places his hopes for the unification and pacification of contemporary Italy in the revival of the ancient *virtus Romana:*

> "Virtue will fight and soon the debt be paid:
> For the old gallantry
> In the Italian hearts is not yet dead."

It is interesting to recall that Machiavelli concludes his *Prince* with "an exhortation to liberate Italy from the barbarians," and that he ends this final chapter with the quotation of those very verses of Petrarch.

There seems to be hardly any other moment in Petrarch's life in which he could feel better entitled to utter such an exhortation than that period following his coronation when he had been acknowledged symbolically not only as the greatest living poet of Italy, but also as the resuscitator of the spirit of ancient grandeur. It is by this spirit that "Italia mia" is inspired. In this canzone Petrarch created a poem which, because of its leitmotiv of national unity, might rightly be called the first Italian anthem. But beyond that he distinguished these verses by an intensity of feeling so powerful that all his readers, regardless of their national origin, then found it and have since found it a timeless expression of their sentiments towards their native country:

> "Is not this the dear soil for which I pined?
> Is not this my own nest
> Where I was nourished and was given life?
> Is not this the dear land in which we trust,
> Mother loving and kind
> Who shelters parents, brother, sister, wife?"

It is most significant that for the first time in the history of the western world patriotic feeling had found articulate expression in poetry and had come to consciousness in a man who had grown up and lived in exile and who, therefore, could more clearly perceive the idea of supreme unity which was hidden to the resident citizens through their very entanglement in local rivalry and disunity.

The "tale" of Petrarch's life had reached its climax on the Capitoline in the spring of 1341 and during the period of the greatest productivity of his poetical genius. From the artistic point of view it appears logical, then, that in his "Letter to Posterity" Petrarch deals only very briefly with the events during the ten years following his coronation and that he breaks off his account rather abruptly with the year 1351, never to take it up again. For everything he had to narrate concerning the second half of his life would have seemed anticlimactic in comparison with the story of his dramatic rise during the first half. Even more, the account would have necessarily become a record of Petrarch's increasing pessimism and feeling of personal frustration and disillusionment. The hopes which he continued to have for the pacification and unification of Italy were destined to remain unfulfilled, whether he was to place them on the Italian princes or on the Roman Tribune of the People, Cola di Rienzo, or on the German Emperor Charles IV. The fervent exhortations which he addressed to successive popes, admonishing them to return from Avignon to Rome, met with little or no response. To his passionate feelings against Avignon as the seat of the Frenchified papal court he gave frequent expression in both his Latin and Italian writings, as for instance in the *Rime* (No. 138), where he denounces the hated city as:

> "Fountain of sorrow, dwelling of revolts,
> The school of errors, place of heresy,
> Once Rome, now Babylon wicked and false,
> For which the world suffers in infamy."

The nearness of hateful Avignon poisoned even Petrarch's love for Vaucluse, where since 1337 he had so often sought refuge from the turmoil of the world and found inward peace and stimulation for his work. Thus in 1353 Petrarch decided to bring to an end his sojourn of more than forty years in southern France and to go back to Italy.

It was an outwardly restless life Petrarch spent during his remaining years in northern Italy. He did not choose to take up permanent residence in any one place, not even in his native Florence, where he had been offered, at the instigation of his friend and admirer Boccaccio, a professorship at the university. The Italian princes, among them the powerful Visconti family in Milan, as well as the patrician rulers of Venice, considered it a great honour when the poet accepted their hospitality. Petrarch's democratic and republican friends deplored the close relationship into which the herald of the grandeur of the Roman Republic seemed to have entered with the "tyrants" of his age. Petrarch defied these complaints, for he never considered himself the servant of any prince or the tool of any interest contrary to his own convictions. Free from all obligations of office, in complete independence, he lived solely for his literary work and for the cause of the revival of the eternal standards and universal values of classical antiquity.

If we can trust an old report, death overcame Petrarch in the midst of his studies late at night on July 18, 1374, while he was working in the library of his country house in Arquà near Padua.

An examination of Petrarch's literary opera shows that in the most complete edition, that of the year 1554, the various Latin works and letters occupy almost twenty times as much space as the Italian poetry, the *Rime* and the *Trionfi*. Thus Petrarch's Latin writings do not merely outweigh those in the vernacular in actual volume, but they seem also to have had definite preponderance in the mind and judgment of the author himself. For in the "Letter to Posterity" he speaks in some detail about most of the Latin works which he had written or begun by that time, but he does not mention specifically the collection of his Italian *Rime*. That this omission was not simply accidental becomes evident from the following passage in the same epistle: "My mind was rather well balanced than acute; and while adapted to all good and wholesome studies, its special bent was towards moral philosophy and poetry. But the latter I neglected, as time went on, because of the delight I took in sacred literature. In this I found a hidden sweetness, though at one time I had despised it, so that I came to use poetry only as an accomplishment. I devoted myself singly, amid a crowd of subjects, to a knowledge of Antiquity; for this age of ours

I have always found distasteful, so that, had it not been for the love of those dear to me, I should have preferred to have been born in any other."

This passage leaves no doubt as to which part of his work Petrarch himself considered most important. From his own point of view the judgment of his contemporaries certainly was right and that of later generations wrong. He himself desired to be renowned, above all else, for his "single devotion to the knowledge of Antiquity," and not for his Italian poetry.

The fact that Petrarch gave his personal preference to his humanistic endeavours and accomplishments ought not, however, to compel us to believe that he actually meant to disavow his Italian writings altogether. It is true that in a letter written two years before his death, he called his poems in the vernacular "little trifles" and "juvenile fooleries" and expressed the wish that "they might be unknown to the whole world and even to myself if that could be." But notwithstanding this wish for their obliteration, Petrarch, from the record of his work, actually took the greatest personal care in preserving and editing these very same poems. When in mid-life he decided to collect his "scattered rhymes" (*Rime* No. 1) in one volume, he never ceased working over them throughout the rest of his days, striving to bring them to what he considered the point of perfection.

The clearest evidence of the painstaking effort Petrarch made in this task of polishing his verse is manifestly shown by the great number of corrections and marginal notes in his working copy of the *Rime* which is preserved today in the Vatican Library. A few examples may suffice to illustrate this point. On the margin of the sonnet "Non fûr ma' Giove" (*Rime* No. 155) Petrarch remarks: "Note that I had once in mind to change the order of the four stanzas so that the first quatrain and the first terzina would have become second and vice versa. But I gave the idea up because of the sound of the beginning and the end. For (in the case of a change) the fuller sound would have been in the middle and the hollower sound at the beginning and at the end; this, however, is against the laws of rhetoric."

Another marginal note (to *Rime* No. 199) gives an interesting glimpse into Petrarch's working habits: "In 1368," he jots down, "on Friday, August the 19th, sleepless for a long time during the first watch of the night, I at last got up and came by chance upon this very old poem, composed twenty-five years ago." That Petrarch gave a great deal of thought to determining which of his earlier poems were worthy of inclusion in his final collection is well demonstrated by the following note at the end of the sonnet "Voglia mi sprona" (*Rime* No. 211): "Amazing. This poem was once crossed out by me and condemned. Now, by chance reading it again after a lapse of many years, I have acquitted it and copied it and put it in the right place. Shortly afterwards, however, on the 27th, in the evening, I made some changes in the final lines, and now I shall have finished with it."

Within the limited compass of this essay it is impossible to go into the intricate problems involving the chronology, the variant forms and arrangements of Petrarch's collection of sonnets and songs. It will be sufficient to state that despite his solemn declarations to the contrary Petrarch never, even during his old age, lost his interest in his "juvenile fooleries" but continued editing and re-editing them to the last. He worked on them until his sense of artistry was truly satisfied. There is tangible evidence of his own critical approval in the frequent recurrence of the word *placet* on the margins of his working copy. And if there is a legitimate suspicion that Petrarch was not quite candid in the denial of his personal interest in his Italian poems, the same doubt can assail our acceptance of the sincerity of his wish that "they might be unknown to the whole world." For he knew very well from the study of his beloved antiquity that glory depends solely on true distinction in whatever field of activity an individual might choose. In his own incessant striving after perfection he must, therefore, have been greatly inspired and impelled by the desire for approval of these poems by readers in his own era as well as in coming centuries.

In the final collection of his verse Petrarch included three hundred and sixty-six poems. Of this number, three hundred and seventeen were written as sonnets, twenty-nine as *canzoni,* nine as *sestine,* seven as *ballate,* and four as madrigals. The collection has no definite title but is known in Italian simply by the generic names of *Canzoniere* or *Rime,* or somewhat more specifically, *Rime Sparse.* For in contrast to Dante, who assembled his poems to Beatrice in a book named by himself *La Vita Nuova,* Petrarch never chose a precise name for his collected poems but was content to call them rather vaguely *Rerum vulgarium fragmenta,* "Fragments," or better "Pieces of matters written in the vernacular." This absence of a concrete title does not seem to be wholly fortuitous. For again in contrast to Dante's *Vita Nuova,* Petrarch's *Rime* do not form an organic unit but are in truth "scattered rhymes," as Petrarch calls them himself in the proem to the collection. The content of most of the longer poems is political, religious, or moral in nature whereas the theme of the overwhelming majority of the sonnets is Petrarch's love for Laura. The author did not arrange his poems according to their poetical form nor apparently did he attempt to divide the long series of the love sonnets to Laura into definite "sequences," although there are to be found certain groups of poems which are more closely interrelated than others.

Some of Petrarch's most beautiful verse is contained in his *canzoni,* as for instance in "Spirto gentil," "Italia mia," or "Vergine bella." But it was especially in the sonnet that his genius found the most adequate mode of expression. Petrarch did not invent the form of the sonnet. It had appeared long before his time and flourished greatly in the school of poets writing in the "dolce stil novo," which reached its climax with Dante. He surpassed, however, all his predecessors in the fashion in which he perfected the traditional form and filled it with a content at once richer and more variegated than ever before. The brevity of the fourteen lines actually permits no more than the expression of one idea or one mood or one emotion. These perceptions and feelings, however, are not allowed to remain vague and fleeting but are submitted to the discipline of rigid form. As no other poet before and only few after him, Petrarch, in many of his sonnets, succeeded in striking this delicate balance of form and content and in establishing a true harmony of feeling and thinking. As the unsurpassed master of the love sonnet of his day Petrarch became, as has been shown before, the model of innumerable sonneteers, in Italy as well as abroad, who were fully conscious of their discipleship and even proud of their denomination as "Petrarchists."

In creating the glory of the Italian sonnet Petrarch can lay claim to still another distinction, the tone colour which is one of the most outstanding characteristics of his Italian poetry. In this connection it is worth noting that the Italian terms *sonetto* and *canzone* are derived from the words for "sound" and "song." This derivation tells us very clearly that poems written in these particular two forms were meant to be intoned and that consequently their authors needed musical as well as literary talent. Petrarch in full measure possessed the gifts of the musician. His contemporary biographer, the Florentine Filippo Villani, states: "He played the lyre admirably. His voice was sonorous and overflowing with charm and sweetness." Among the few personal possessions which Petrarch deemed worthy of specific mention in his last will there appears "my good lyre."

In the working copy of his *Rime* we find the following note to one of his sonnets: "I must make these two verses over again, singing them (*cantando*), and I must transpose them. —3 o'clock in the morning, October the 19th." No better testimony than this intimate self-reminder can be found to illustrate both the importance which Petrarch attributed to the musical qualities of his verse and the method which he used to test these qualities. Whoever reads his sonnets and songs aloud in their rich Italian will immediately be impressed by their melodiousness and will readily agree with Filippo Villani who says: "His rhythms flow so sweetly that not even the gravest people can withstand their declamation and sound." Some of Petrarch's most beautiful verse, the poems in honour of the Virgin, were set to music by the greatest composer of the Italian Renaissance, Palestrina, in his *Madrigali Spirituali.*

The theme of the overwhelming majority of Petrarch's *Rime* is his love for Laura. This fact has led many editors since the sixteenth century to divide the collection up into two parts, the first containing the poems written "In vita di Madonna Laura," the second one consisting of those "In morte di Madonna Laura," beginning with the moving lamentation of the sonnet "Oimè il bel viso" (*Rime* No. 267). Although this division cannot be directly traced back to Petrarch himself there is no doubt that the main theme of the sonnets is Petrarch's love for Laura "in life and in death."

Who was Laura? With this question we come to that problem which more than almost any other has attracted the attention of scholars working on Petrarch and has, to an even greater degree, challenged and fascinated the popular imagination.

The crux of the problem is that Petrarch himself, both in his *Rime* and in his Latin writings, chose to give only very few details of a concrete nature concerning Laura and her personal circumstances. This discretion on the part of Petrarch in regard to the central figure in his life becomes particularly manifest in his "Letter to Posterity." For although in this epistle he speaks of a good many of his close friends in some detail, he condenses all he has to say about the person presumably nearest to his heart in one sentence: "In my youth I suffered from an attachment of the keenest kind, but constant to one, and honourable; and I should have suffered longer, had not death—bitter indeed, but useful—extinguished the flame as it was beginning to subside." The marked restraint and the curious detachment make it very evident that in this autobiographical record written for the perusal of later generations Petrarch was resolved to gloss over the crucial importance of Laura in his life, just as he attempted, in the same document, to belittle the significance and the value of those *Rime* whose principal theme was his love for Laura.

When not thinking of himself in the light of posterity but writing solely for his own record, Petrarch had a good deal more to say about Laura. It was his habit to make notes on the most intimate details of his personal life in the most cherished book of his library, on the fly-leaf of his manuscript of Vergil's works. There appears the following entry: "Laura, illustrious by her own virtues and long celebrated in my poems, first appeared to my eyes in the earliest period of my manhood, on the sixth day of April, anno Domini 1327, in the Church of St. Claire, at the morning hour. And in the same city at the same hour of the same day in the same month of April, but in the year 1348, that light was withdrawn from our day, while I was by chance at Verona, ignorant—alas!—of my fate. The unhappy tidings reached me at Parma in a letter from my friend Louis on the morning of May the 19th in the same year. Her chaste and lovely body was laid in the Church of the Franciscans on the very day of her death at evening. Her soul, however, I am persuaded—as Seneca says of Africanus—has returned to heaven whence it came. I have felt a kind of bitter sweetness in writing this, as a memorial of a painful matter—especially in this place which often comes under my eyes—so that I may reflect that no pleasures remain for me in this life, and that I may be warned by constantly looking at these words and by the thought of the rapid flight of years that it is high time to flee from the world. This, by God's preventing grace, will be easy to me when I keenly and manfully consider the empty, superfluous hopes of the past, and the unforeseen issue."

Neither in this most intimate record nor anywhere else does Petrarch say who Laura actually was. In truth, he kept this secret so well that apparently even among his closest friends the suspicion arose that "Laura" was merely a fictitious name for an imaginary love and that the word stood not so much for the name of a real person as for Petrarch's dearest goal in life, the "laurel," symbol of the poet's fame. Indeed Petrarch himself liked to play upon the similarity between the name of Laura and the Latin and Italian words for laurel. Against the charge of feigned love Petrarch defended himself in a letter written in 1336 to his intimate friend Giacomo Colonna, Bishop of Lombez, as follows: "You actually say that I have invented the name of 'Laura' in order to have some one to talk about, and in order to set people talking about me, but that, in reality, I have no 'Laura' in mind, except that poetical laurel to which I have aspired, as my long and unwearied toil bears witness; and as to this breathing 'laurel,' with whose beauty I seem to be charmed, all that is 'made up'—the songs feigned, the sighs pretended. On this point would that your jests were true! Would that it were a pretense, and not a madness! But, credit me, it takes much trouble to keep up a pretense for long; while to spend useless toil in order to appear mad would be the height of madness. Besides, though by acting we can feign sickness when we are well, we cannot feign actual pallor. You know well both my pallor and my weariness; and so I fear you are making sport of my disease by that Socratic diversion called 'irony,' in which even Socrates must yield the palm to you."

This letter is a convincing proof of the genuineness of Petrarch's love, but it is again noteworthy that even in this self-defense he did not deign to reveal the identity of the actual Laura. As the result of Petrarch's silence concerning the real circumstances of Laura's life there arose soon and grew and flourished throughout the centuries almost to the present a Laura-legend which was an interesting composite of romantic and fanciful imagination, pseudo-scholarly research, and half-truth. It would lead into too many bypaths to follow the story of this legend. May it suffice to say that according to modern scholarship it seems likely that the "historical" Laura was the daughter of a Provençal nobleman, Audibert de Noves, that she was married to Hugues de Sade, and that Petrarch probably met her for the first time about two years after her marriage.

That the object of Petrarch's love was a married woman and the mother of several children was a hypothesis that ran contrary to the popular and sentimental romanticization of the two lovers and their relationship, and for that reason this thesis was long and bitterly contested. But actually the "real" Laura does not matter at all. For whatever the facts of her life might have been, they do not provide us with any "background" for a better understanding of the collection of the *Rime* in the form in which Petrarch wanted them to endure. If he had not burnt many of his earlier poems, as he did according to his own statement, the picture would perhaps be quite different. But his final collection does not present a narrative pattern or sequence, and all attempts have completely failed to crystallize an account of a romance out of the *Rime*.

Everything the more curious need know for the understanding of the nature of Petrarch's relationship with Laura, he himself has told in the self-analysis of his book called the *Secretum,* which he composed in the form of a dialogue between himself and St. Augustine as his father confessor. He started writing this work in 1342 while Laura was still alive and finished it a few years after her death. Therein he states: "Whatever little I am, I have become through her. For if I possess any name and fame at all, I should never have obtained them unless she had cared with her most noble affection for the sparse seeds of virtues planted in my bosom by Nature." Laura's mind, Petrarch says, "does not know earthly cares but burns with heavenly desires. Her appearance truly radiates beams of divine beauty. Her morals are an example of perfect uprightness. Neither her voice nor the force of her eyes nor her gait are those of an ordinary human being." Petrarch asserts emphatically that he had "always loved her soul more than her body," though he has to admit that, under the compulsion of love and youth, "occasionally I wished something dishonourable."

But the purity of the relationship was saved by Laura, for "not moved by any entreaties nor conquered by any flatteries, she protected her womanly honour and remained impregnable and firm in spite of her youth and mine and in spite of many and various other things which ought to have bowed the spirit of even the most adamant. This strength of character of the woman recalled seemly conduct to the mind of the man. The model of her excellence stood before me so that in my own strife for chastity I lacked neither her example nor her reproach. And when finally she saw me break the bridle and fall (this is obviously a reference to a love affair with another woman), she left me rather than follow my course."

Eventually Petrarch succeeded in conquering himself, for in the dialogue he assures St. Augustine: "Now I know what I want and wish, and my unstable mind has become firm. She, on her part, has always been steadfast and has always stayed one and the same. The better I understand her womanly constancy, the more I admire it. If once I was grieved by her unyielding resolution, I am now full of joy over it and thankful." It was for spiritual reasons that Petrarch felt a sense of profound gratitude towards Laura, as he makes clear both in the *Secretum* and in the moving lines of thanksgiving in one of his later sonnets:

> "I thank her soul and her holy device
> That with her face and her sweet anger's bolts
> Bid me in burning think of my salvation."
> (*Rime* No. 289)

The autobiographical account in the *Secretum* provides the most valuable clue to the right understanding of Petrarch's conception of Laura's image and his relationship with her, as they are reflected in the *Rime*. For a clear comprehension of the passages quoted it should be remembered that they do not represent simply a personal record but are set forth in the solemn form of an imaginary dialogue with Petrarch's spiritual guide and conscience, St. Augustine. In this dialogue, which has an almost confessional character, Petrarch naturally felt bound to reveal himself fully and frankly, even if this meant his candid admission of aberrations from the right path of acting and feeling. It is purely incidental that he has satisfied our curiosity about certain external details of his relationship with Laura.

On the other hand, it is most significant that he depicted this relationship as one in which were linked together two beings who belonged to two entirely different spheres and therefore acted in an entirely different fashion. Whereas he himself was an ordinary human being with all of man's passions and desires, Laura was above earthly cares and burnt solely with heavenly desires. Whereas his own personality and sentiments underwent many radical changes, she remained always one and the same. The climax of this love was reached when Petrarch, inspired by the example of Laura's perfection, masters himself and his desires and begins, under her guidance, to strive for the salvation of his soul.

What Petrarch has recounted in the prose of his *Secretum* as his personal confession to St. Augustine, he has expressed in the lyrics of his *Rime* to all

". . . who hear in scattered rhymes the sound
Of that wailing with which I fed my heart."
(*Rime* No. 1)

For in the *Rime* he gives us the rapture of love in which there is only one subject, the man, who alone speaks and feels, acts and changes, while the woman is but the mute and passive object of this love, an ideal and therefore immutable being.

This ideal object of his love was, however, not imaginary or fictitious. As if to refute any doubt as to the existence of a "real" Laura, Petrarch makes repeatedly very specific chronological statements in the *Rime* themselves concerning the dates of his first meeting with Laura and of her death. Petrarch obviously had very good reasons for such an inclusion of dates into his verse, for his musical ear must have protested against these attempts at fitting bare figures into a rigid metre.

In other ways, too, Petrarch tries to assure his readers of Laura's reality. He describes her appearance, her golden hair and her fair eyes, or he pictures her in the beauty of nature, "walking on the green grass, pressing the flowers like a living girl." But all these descriptions are rather limited in range, for her beauty and charm are beyond the power of the poet's pen, as he himself confesses:

". . . I still seem to pass
Over your beauty in my rhyme . . .
But the burden I find crushes my frame
The work cannot be polished by my file.
And my talent which knows its strength and style
In this attempt becomes frozen and lame."
(*Rime* No. 20)

Petrarch is aware that he will be criticized for his endeavour to enshrine her above others in his song and that the temper of his praise will be considered false, but he cannot accept such criticism. For he knows that no matter what he says he will never be able to express his thoughts in verse as well as he feels them enclosed in his breast (*Rime* No. 95).

Eventually Laura assumes an ideal nature such as is disclosed in one of the sonnets in words which are almost identical with the quoted passage from the *Secretum:*

"In what part of the sky, in what idea
Was the example from which Nature wrought
That charming lovely face wherein she sought
To show her power in the upper sphere?"
(*Rime* No. 159)

This conception of Laura as the sublime ideal, expressed in terms strongly reminiscent of Platonic thought, shows most clearly the transformation which the picture of the "real" Laura had undergone in the poet's mind: she has become the image of the concept of the beautiful, and we might add from the reading of other poems in the *Rime,* the embodiment, too, of good and the right. The ultimate transfiguration of Laura is attained in one of the later sonnets where his

". . . inner eye
Sees her soar up and with the angels fly
At the feet of our own eternal Lord."
(*Rime* No. 345)

While Laura is thus elevated into "the upper sphere," Petrarch himself remains earthbound. The object of his love is an ideal, but his feelings for his beloved are human. From the time when, at the age of twenty-three, he met Laura first in the church in Avignon, to her death twenty-one years later, and from that time to his own death, this was the focusing passion of his life:

"I have never been weary of this love,
My lady, nor shall be while last my years."
(*Rime* No. 82)

Petrarch runs the whole gamut of emotions and passions of a lover, from the highest elation to the deepest despair. In this full scale only one note is missing which in ordinary love would naturally mark the supreme moment: the exaltation of physical consummation. That the love for Laura, by its very nature, was denied fulfillment in the common sense, has to be understood as the mode to which the whole tone of Petrarch's sonnets and songs is pitched. For above all the *Rime* sing of the sad and woeful beauty of love, of the longing for the unattainable, of the rebellion against denial, of the inward laceration of the lover and of his melancholic resignation. In the *Rime* all these moods of a lover have found their timeless representation. And the very fact that the figure of Laura is so idealized has made it possible for many readers of these sonnets and songs to see in the image of Laura the picture of their own beloved and to hear in the verse of the poet the expression of their own thoughts and the echoes of their own love.

While in the exalted conception of his beloved Petrarch was still bound by the tradition of the love poetry of the Provençal troubadours and the Italian poets of the "dolce stil novo," in the representation of himself and of his own humanity he was guided by a very different source of inspiration, the model of Latin poetry of classical times. There is hardly one poem in the *Rime* which does not show more or less definite traces of this influence as to form and content, figures of speech and comparisons, symbols and allegories. Petrarch went wholeheartedly (and with full consciousness of his debt) to school to the great Roman poets. And what he learned there he absorbed so completely that even in imitating he succeeded for the most part in creating something new. The splendour and richness of the *Rime* were to a large extent based on his lifelong devotion to the scholarly study of antiquity. Thus the accomplishments of Petrarch the sonneteer presuppose the research of Petrarch the humanist.

Petrarch once strikingly compares himself to the statue of Janus: like the double-faced Roman god he feels himself to be looking both backward and forward. This, his own comparison, characterizes well Petrarch's personal outlook on life. For often and with profound yearning he looked back to the glory of ancient Rome and drew from its grandeur the deepest inspiration for his work. He regarded the whole epoch of a thousand years, extending from the fall of the Roman Empire to his own days, as a period of "darkness." But throughout his life he hoped that the "revival" of the past would put an end to the process of decline and would usher in a new and better era. This ardent hope for the future Petrarch has voiced in the canzone "Italia mia" and in many other pieces, but nowhere more impressively than in that work which he himself considered as his greatest, the *Africa.* At the very end of this epic he addresses his own poem as follows: "My fate is to live amid varied and confusing storms. But for you perhaps, if, as I hope and wish, you will live long after me, there will follow a better age. This sleep of forgetfulness will not last forever. When the darkness has been dispersed, our descendants can come again in the former pure radiance."

Posterity may accept Petrarch's own judgment and may agree that the figure of Janus truly symbolizes his position in history. His outlook on the world indeed included views of two different ages. Yet to posterity his choice of the image of Janus might seem a simplification. He had, it would seem, more than the two aspects of the Roman god. Witness one of the most famous incidents in his life, the ascent of Mont Ventoux near Vaucluse, which he undertook in 1336, at the age of thirty-two. In a letter written under the immediate impression of this experience Petrarch relates how he decided to climb this mountain, "induced by the sole desire of seeing the remarkable height of the place." As a student of classical authors he knows of similar undertakings in antiquity and thus, in imitation of an ancient model, he does what no man during the Middle Ages had done, he scales a mountain with the sole motive of satisfying his curiosity. He describes in great detail the difficulties which he and his brother, his only companion, found on their way. Despite the warnings which the pair received from an old shepherd, they continue their strenuous ascent and finally reach the summit. What Petrarch sees and feels on that momentous occasion, he endeavours to express in the following sentences: "First of all, braced by the nip of the keen air and the extent of the view, I stood as dazed. I looked back; the clouds were beneath my feet. And now the stories of Athos and Olympus seem less incredible to me, as I behold on a mountain of lesser fame what I had heard and read of them. I turn my eye's glance in the direction of Italy, whither my heart most inclines. . . . I confess I sighed for the skies of Italy, which I looked upon with my mind rather than with my eyes, and an irrepressible longing seized me to behold my friend and my country."

But while he was thus gazing at the beauty of the panorama of the Alps, "a new thought" suddenly possessed him which drew him from the sight of the external world towards a consideration of himself and his past life. He thinks of Laura, saying: "What I used to love, I love no longer—nay, I lie, I do love, but with more restraint, more moderately, more regretfully." He continues: "While I marveled at these things in turn, now recognizing some earthly object, now lifting my soul upwards as my body had been, I thought of looking at the book of Augustine's *Confessions* . . . which I always have with me. I opened the little volume, of handy size but of infinite charm, in order to read whatever met my eye. . . . I call God to witness, and my listener too, that these were the words on which my eyes fell: 'Men go abroad to admire the heights of mountains, and the mighty billows, and the long-winding courses of rivers, the compass of the ocean, and the courses of the stars—and themselves they neglect.' I confess I was amazed; and begging my brother, who was eager to hear more, not to trouble me, I closed the book, indignant with myself that at that very moment I was admiring earthly things—I, who ought to have learnt long ago from even heathen philosophers that there is nothing admirable but the soul—in itself so great that nothing can be great beside it. Then, indeed, content with what I had seen from the mountain, I turned my eyes inward upon myself, and from that moment none heard me say a word till we reached the bottom."

By this narrative of the ascent of Mont Ventoux Petrarch revealed himself in the whole complexity of his personality and in the diversity of his thoughts, feelings, and interests. He was the man of a new age who set out to discover the beauty of the world and relive an experience forgotten for long centuries. He was the humanist who wanted not merely to devote himself to an antiquarian study of the arts and letters, the history and philosophy of Roman days, but who desired to revive the past in the present and for the future by re-enacting what the ancients had done. He was the Italian patriot whose inner eye beheld the unity and splendour of his native country. He was the lover of Laura who was still torn in his human feelings but was beginning to conquer himself. Yet at the end he found himself bound by the traditions of medieval Christianity in which he had been brought up and which he always revered in the person and work of his great guide, St. Augustine. Thus at the culminating point of his new experience Petrarch closed his eyes to the external world and turned to the spiritual problems of his soul.

All these manifold facets of Petrarch, which the account of his impressions on the peak of Mont Ventoux illumines in a most dramatic fashion, have found their expression in the *Rime*. The essential nature remains, but the colours are much more variegated and the pattern as a whole is infinitely richer. Only the most striking parallel may be pointed out. As the story of the mountain climbing ends with spiritual reflections stimulated by the reading of St. Augustine's *Confessions,* so the collection of love poetry concludes with a devout prayer to the Virgin Mary:

> "Recommend me to your Son, to the real
> Man and the real God,
> That Heaven's nod be my ghost's peaceful seal."

Petrarch lived in an era which in the history of western civilization marks the beginning of the turn from the medieval to the modern age. Petrarch's personal views and his literary work reflect fully the transitional character of his period. For if there are characteristic medieval features to be found in Petrarch, there are also just as many traits which point to a venture into a world of new ideas. Thus the English biographer of Petrarch, Edward H. R. Tatham, rightly names him "the first modern man of letters." It is Petrarch's interest in man and in the problems of human nature that makes him "modern" and differentiates him from medieval writers. All of Petrarch's works, whether they were written in verse or in prose, in Italian or in Latin, have as their main theme the spiritual and intellectual, the emotional and artistic aspects of man's life.

But Petrarch was not only concerned with "man" in general, but was also deeply engrossed in the phenomenon of man as an individual being, as he saw him in the history of the past or as a living actor on the contemporary stage. And above all Petrarch was interested in himself and in the phenomenon of his own individuality.

"In the Middle Ages," writes Jakob Burckhardt, "both sides of human consciousness—that which was turned within as that which was turned without—lay dreaming or half awake beneath a common veil. This veil was woven of faith, illusion, and childish prepossession through which the world and history were seen clad in a strange hue." Petrarch was among the first to tear this veil away by striving for a full understanding of his own individuality through continuous self-analysis and self-portrayal, as illustrated by the "Letter to Posterity" or the *Secretum* or, above all, the *Rime*. In this sense Petrarch may be called the founder of modern humanism.

6

An Early Representation of Petrarch as Poet Laureate*

THERE is an early fifteenth-century illustrated manuscript in the Rossi Collection of the Vatican Library which has a certain interest for Petrarch iconography.[1]

The body of the manuscript contains the texts of the twenty-three lives which make up Petrarch's most important historical work, the *De viris illustribus*. At the end of the last biography, that of Caesar (f. 178r), there is a note about Petrarch's death similar to those found in manuscripts of the same work copied in Padua after the poet's death.[2] The following pages contain Petrarch's Latin translation of Boccaccio's story about Griselda; and on the last page are two epigrams on Scipio Africanus the Elder and Scipio Africanus the Younger written by Francesco

* Reprinted from *Studi Petrarcheschi,* II (1949), 101–105. Translated by Eugene F. Rice, Jr.

1 Cod. Rossianus 526, formerly IX, 216. The manuscript has been described by H. Tietze, *Die illuminierten Handschriften der Rossiana in Wien-Lainz* (Leipzig, 1911), p. 105, nr. 194. In 1924 the Rossi Collection was transferred by its owners, the Jesuits, from Lainz to Rome and permanently located in the Vatican Library.

2 "His gestis Cesaris cum instaret, obiit ipse vates celeberrimus Franciscus Petrarca, millesimo trecentesimo septuagesimo quarto, decimo nono Iulii. Arquade, inter montes Euganeos, deno ab urbe Patavi miliario." See P. de Nolhac, "Le 'De viris illustribus' de Pétrarque," *Notices et extraits des manuscrits de la Bibliothèque Nationale,* XXXIV, 1 (Paris, 1891), 75, note.

da Fiano at the beginning of the fifteenth century as captions or *"tituli"* for a series of twenty heroes decorating the Sala dei Giganti of the Palazzo Trinci in Foligno.[3]

A short note by the copyist at the end of the text of the *De viris illustribus* tells us that this part of the codex Rossianus was commissioned in 1418 "from Naples." [4] Unfortunately the name of the first owner and the coat of arms at the bottom center of the first page have been defaced. Very probably the codex was later acquired by Cardinal Domenico Capranica (1400–1458), who left it in his will, together probably with another Petrarch manuscript, to the library of the Collegio Capranica.[5]

The manuscript contains many illuminated initial letters. According to Tietze their style would indicate Venetian and, more specifically perhaps, Paduan origin.[6] Three initial letters differ from the others because they contain human figures. Thus the miniature of the letter R, which begins the biography of Romulus (f. 2r), shows the bust of an armed warrior; the letter G, the first letter of the biography of Julius Caesar (f. 93r), represents an armed knight mounted on a white horse. Although both these figures look completely medieval, there can be absolutely no doubt that the intention was to portray the first king of Rome and the founder of the Roman Empire.

[3] The "Epigrama Scipionis Africani superioris" begins with the words *Columen infirmum.* It has been published by L. Bertalot, "Humanistisches in der Anthologia Latina," *Rheinisches Museum für Philologie,* LXVI (1911), 72 f. The "Scipionis Emiliani posterioris Africani epigrama" begins with the words *Altera lux patrie nitet.* It has not yet been published. Cf. Bertalot, *op. cit.,* pp. 64 and 75; M. Salmi, *Bollett. d'Arte,* XIII (1919), 165, n. 1, 176, and 180; and A. Messini, *Rivista d'Arte,* ser. II, XIV (1942), 85 ff.

[4] Cod. Rossianus 526, f. 178r: ". . . de Napoli fecit scribi hunc librum M°CCCC°XVIII."

[5] Cod. Rossianus 715 (formerly X, 95), which contains the *Familiari,* is stamped with the arms of Cardinal Domenico Capranica. Cod. Rossianus 526 is listed in the 1657 catalogue of the library of the Collegio Capranica under the following title: "Francisci Petrarcae illustrium virorum gesta manuscript. in fol. pergameno" (Tietze, *op. cit.,* p. XII).

[6] See Tietze, *op. cit.,* p. 105, nr. 194. G. Martellotti, who is working on the critical edition of the *De viris illustribus,* has kindly informed me that the codex Rossianus apparently derives directly from codex Ottobonianus 1833, which was in the possession of Salutati. In that case Florentine origin might seem more probable.

1. Rome, Vatican Library, Cod. Rossianus 526, fol. 1r: Petrarch as poet laureate

The third of these miniatures is much larger than the other two. It illustrates the first page of the codex where Petrarch's preface begins with the words: "Illustres quosdam viros." The letter I forms a gilded shaft, decorated with violet-colored leaves, which frames against a blue ground the figure of a bearded man, wrapped in a purple robe and wearing purple shoes. His brow is crowned with laurel.[7] The important position assigned this picture and the laurel crown are sure evidence that the aim here was to represent Petrarch himself.[8]

The question now arises to what extent this miniature is a real portrait of the poet. Any reference to Petrarch's actual appearance must be ruled out at once. This can be proved by confronting the miniature from the codex Rossianus with the most authentic Petrarch portraits, such as the miniatures in several of the earliest manuscripts of his works (for example, cod. Paris. Lat. 6069 F [9] and cod. Vatic. Lat. 3198) [10] or the portrait of Petrarch by Nardo di Cione in the fresco in the Strozzi Chapel in Santa Maria Novella in Florence.[11] These portraits of the poet, as indeed those whose real resemblance is less certain,[12] all have one element in common: Petrarch is

[7] [See Fig. 1.] Cf. the reproduction in Tietze, *op. cit.,* p. 106.

[8] Tietze, who discovered this figure and reproduced it for the first time, did not identify it with Petrarch, describing it simply as "ein bärtiger Mann." This omission probably explains why the miniature has not hitherto been considered in relation to Petrarch iconography.

[9] Cf. P. de Nolhac, *Pétrarque et l'humanisme,* 2nd ed. (Paris, 1907), II, 250 ff. The most recent reproductions of this portrait are in N. Festa's edition of the *Africa* (1926) and in U. Bosco, *Petrarca* (1946), plate I. Cf. also the tiny picture in the Biblioteca Ambrosiana, reproduced by A. Ratti (Pope Pius XI), *Un antico ritratto di Francesco Petrarca all'Ambrosiana* (Milan, 1907), p. 11.

[10] Reproduced by V. Rossi in the second volume of his edition of the *Familiari.*

[11] Reproduced in the fourth volume of the *Familiari* edited by Rossi and Bosco. On the specific worth of this portrait cf. H. Keller, "Die Entstehung des Bildnisses am Ende des Hochmittelalters," *Römisches Jahrbuch für Kunstgeschichte,* III (1939), 336–338 and fig. 301.

[12] For example, cod. Paris. Lat. 6069 T (in Rossi, ed., *Familiari,* III); Bibliot. Marciana, Cl. VI n. 86 (in de Nolhac, *op. cit.,* II); Bibliot. Trivulziana (Milan), cod. 905 (reproduced in *Petrarca e la Lombardia,* Milan, 1904; cf. *ibid.,* pp. 322 ff., and also Prince d'Essling and E. Müntz, *Pétrarque, ses études d'art, son influence sur les artistes, ses portraits et ceux de Laure, l'illustration de ses écrits,* Paris, 1902, p. 83); Darmstadt, cod. 101 (d'Essling-Müntz, *op. cit.,* p. 65); and, finally, the late-fourteenth-

pictured without a beard. Leaving aside other incongruities of the miniature from the codex Rossianus, the emphatic representation of a luxuriant beard is enough to prove conclusively that this picture does not portray the real appearance of the poet, but rather gives an idealized personification of the type executed later by painters like Castagno and Justus of Ghent.[13]

But although this miniature sheds no new light on how Petrarch really looked, it does have one element of importance for the study of Petrarch iconography: there can be no doubt that the painter wished to represent Petrarch as poet laureate. The laurel crown and purple robe are unequivocal. The miniaturist, or the unknown Neapolitan who commissioned the manuscript, by choosing the royal purple wished to celebrate Petrarch's coronation as poet laureate on the Capitol in 1341. On that occasion Petrarch in fact did wear a robe given him by King Robert of Naples, as he himself records with pride and gratitude in one of his Latin poems: "On that festive day I was clothed in royal robes." [14]

In 1418, moreover, the tradition was no doubt still alive in Padua that Petrarch had been buried in the purple gown of a

---

century frescoes in the Palazzo Vescovile and the Sala dei Giganti in Padua (reproduced respectively in G. Billanovich's edition of the *Rerum memorandarum libri,* 1943, and in Rossi, ed., *Familiari,* I). On Petrarch iconography, besides the older works of Prince d'Essling and de Nolhac and the list of portraits in M. Fowler, *Catalogue of the Petrarch Collection in the Cornell University Library* (Oxford University Press, 1916), pp. 497–503, see W. von der Schulenburg, *Ein neues Porträt Petrarcas* (Berne, 1918); F. Rougemont, "Ein neues Petrarca-Bildnis," *Imprimatur, ein Jahrbuch für Bücherfreunde,* VII (1936–1937), 22 ff.; and H. Keller, *op. cit.,* p. 336, nr. 392.

[13] The portraits followed by Justus and Castagno have been reproduced by Bosco, *op. cit.,* plates II and VI.

[14] *Ep. metr.* II, 1, ll. 60–64 (D. Rossetti, ed., *F. Petrarcae poëmata minora,* Milan, 1831, II, 100):

"Tum regia festo
Vestis honesta die me circumfusa tegebat,
Et dominum referens, et tanti testis amoris,
Quam, lateri exemptam proprio, regum ille supremus
Rex dederat gestare suo."

Cf. E. H. Wilkins, "The Coronation of Petrarch," *Speculum,* XVIII (1943), 182 ff.

"master of poetics and of history."[15] Perhaps the miniaturist, or the person who commissioned the work, knew, as Petrarch himself certainly knew, the ancient tradition which ruled the ceremonies and coronations on the Capitol. According to Suetonius, the emperor Domitian presided at such ceremonies "in half-boots, clad in a purple toga in the Greek fashion, and wearing upon his head a golden crown."[16]

Painters, and the innumerable engravers who imitated them, would later picture Petrarch robed in purple and crowned with laurel, as in Raphael's "Parnassus" or the portraits at the Musée Calvet in Avignon and the Uffizi in Florence.[17] One of the best-known, and hitherto one of the earliest-known, examples of this type illustrates a manuscript of the *Rime* and *Trionfi* in the Laurentian Library.[18] The 1418 miniature from the codex Rossianus, however, antedates this by more than fifty years, for the Laurentian manuscript was written in 1463.[19] But more interesting than the question of the priority of the Rossi miniature is the remarkable fact that a portrait of Petrarch as poet laureate has been used to illustrate the manuscript of one of his historical works. This is clear indication that the men of the early Quattrocento still remembered, according to the words of the *"Privilegium laureae"* of 1341, that the laurel crown bestowed on Petrarch consecrated in him "the great poet and the great historian."

[15] Cf. Billanovich, *Petrarca letterato,* I. *Lo scrittoio del Petrarca* (Rome, 1947), p. 340, n. 1.

[16] *Domitian,* IV, 4.

[17] Reproduced by d'Essling-Müntz, *op. cit.,* pp. 67, 69, and 73. For other portraits and engravings see the list in M. Fowler, *op. cit.,* pp. 499–503.

[18] Cod. Plut. XLI n. 1, f. 8v, reproduced by d'Essling-Müntz, *op. cit.,* p. 71.

[19] Cod. Plut. n. 1, f. 183r: "Finis sex triumphorum poete clarissimi Francisci Petrarche. Iacobus Macarius scripsit in civitate Senarum. 1463." Cf. A. M. Bandini, *Catalogus codicum manuscriptorum bibliothecae Mediceae Laurentianae* (Florence, 1778), V, 97.

7

Petrarch's Conception of the "Dark Ages"*

IN *The American Cyclopaedia* of 1883 we read: "The *Dark Ages* is a term applied in its widest sense to that period of intellectual depression in the history of Europe from the establishment of the barbarian supremacy in the fifth century to the revival of learning about the beginning of the fifteenth, thus nearly corresponding in extent with the Middle Ages." [1] This statement from a popular work is merely a reflection of opinions held at that time by quite a few students of the Middle Ages, a fact proved, for instance, by the very title of Samuel R. Maitland's book, *The Dark Ages.* In this work, which appeared for the first time in 1889, the author published a number of essays illustrating "the state of religion and literature in the ninth, tenth, eleventh and twelfth centuries," thus characterizing as "dark" centuries like the eleventh and the twelfth which, from the present point of view, represent the climax of the mediaeval period. In the scholarly world this usage of the term "Dark Ages" was either to be abandoned completely or at least to be restricted increasingly in its application. When in 1904 William Paton Ker published his work *The Dark Ages* in the collection *Periods of European Literature,* he stated: "The Dark Ages and the Middle Ages . . . used to be the same; two

* Reprinted from *Speculum,* XVII (1942), 226–242.

[1] *Op. cit.,* I, 186.

names for the same period. But they have come to be distinguished, and the Dark Ages are now no more than the first part of the Middle Age, while the term mediaeval is often resticted to the later centuries, about 1100 to 1500." [2] This restricted conception of the term found expression in a newer encyclopaedia, *The Americana,* in the 1909 edition of which the phrase "the Dark Ages" is defined as "a period supposed to extend from the fall of the Roman Empire, 475 A.D., to the revival of literature on the discovery of the Pandects at Amalfi in 1137." [3] In a similar manner the eleventh edition of the *Encyclopaedia Britannica* (1911) states that the period from the fifth to the tenth centuries is called "the dark Age," and affirms that "the dark Age was a reality." [4] It is important to note, however, that in the latest (the fourteenth) edition of the *Encyclopaedia Britannica* the term "Dark Ages" is no longer used. On the contrary, it is explicitly stated that "the contrast, once so fashionable, between the ages of darkness and the ages of light has no more truth in it than have the idealistic fancies which underlie attempts at mediaeval revivalism." [5]

Therefore, if we use the popular encyclopaedia as a means of ascertaining the nature of opinions commonly held, and the changes in such common opinions, it would seem that the notion of the mediaeval period as the "Dark Ages" is now destined to pass away for good. This idea, however, had a long and interesting history of its own, a history which has been described in a detailed monograph by Lucie Varga.[6] Miss Varga has shown very clearly that the expression "Dark Ages" was never primarily a scientific term, but rather a battle-cry, "a denunciation of the mediaeval conception of the world, of the mediaeval attitude toward life, and of the culture of the Middle Ages." [7] The slo-

[2] *Op. cit.,* p. 1; cf. *ibid.,* p. 1 ff., where Ker quotes a number of passages from English writers of the seventeenth and eighteenth centuries, illustrating their conceptions of the "dark ages." Other quotations are found in *A New Dictionary on Historical Principles,* III (Oxford, 1897), 34.

[3] *The Americana,* VI (New York, 1909/10), under "Dark Ages." This definition is repeated verbatim in the later editions of the same work.

[4] *Op. cit.,* XVIII, 411 and 412.

[5] *Op. cit.,* XV, 449.

[6] L. Varga, *Das Schlagwort vom "finsteren Mittelalter"* (Vienna-Leipzig, 1932).

[7] Varga, *op. cit.,* p. 2; cf. *ibid.,* p. 138.

gan attained its greatest currency in the age of the Enlightenment, and the very name of that period was a manifest declaration of war against the era of "darkness" and its scale of values.[8]

But the conception originated even earlier with the Italian humanists of the Renaissance.[9] In a recent essay on "La Coscienza della Rinascita negli Umanisti," [10] Franco Simone emphasizes the fact that "the idea of renovation brought with it, in a supplementary way, the idea of a period of absolute ignorance of the classical culture," and that "the humanists, in order to express this double conception of theirs, used another metaphor which was no less common than that of 'rebirth'; this other formula was that of light and darkness." [11] The metaphor as such was, of course, not at all new, for throughout the Middle Ages it had been used to contrast the light, which Christ had brought into this world, with the darkness in which the heathen had languished before His time.[12] It was in this sense that Petrarch used the old metaphor when he pitied Cicero who had had to die shortly before "the end of the darkness and the night of error" and before "the dawn of the true light." [13]

But the same Petrarch asserted that "amidst the errors there shone forth men of genius, and no less keen were their eyes, although they were surrounded by darkness and dense gloom; therefore they ought not so much to be hated for their erring but pitied for their ill fate." [14] These words are a good illustration of the attitude which Petrarch held throughout his life to-

8 *Ibid.*, pp. 113 ff. 9 *Ibid.*, pp. 36 ff.

10 Published in *La Rinascita,* II (1939), 838–871; III (1940), 163–186.

11 F. Simone, *op. cit.*, III, 169 f.

12 Cf. Varga, *op. cit.*, pp. 5 ff.; Simone, *op. cit.*, III, 177 ff.

13 Petrarca, *De sui ipsius et multorum ignorantia,* ed. M. Capelli (Paris, 1906), p. 45: ". . . paucis enim ante Cristi ortum obierat oculosque clauserat, heu! quibus e proximo noctis erratice ac tenebrarum finis et ueritatis initium, uereque lucis aurora et iustitie sol instabat." Compare Petrarch's remarks on Aristotle, *ibid.*, pp. 40 f.

14 "Nullo enim modo diuinarum illis uerum ueritas apparere illis poterat, quibus nondum uerus sol iustitiae illuxerat. Elucebant tamen inter errores ingenia, neque ideo minus uiuaces erant oculi quamuis tenebris et densa caligine circumsepti, ut eis non erranti odium, sed indignae sortis miseratio deberetur"; *Apologia contra cuiusdam anonymi Galli calumnias* (in *Opera omnia,* Basel, 1554, p. 1195); quoted by Simone, *op. cit.*, III, 182.

ward the classical poets and thinkers and of the way in which he justified the object of his life's work. But these sentences have an importance beyond this personal aspect. They mark, as Simone says, "the moment at which the metaphor of light and darkness lost its original religious value and came to have a literary connotation." [15] This concept was soon to be developed fully. Men like Boccaccio, Filippo Villani, Ghiberti and others contrasted the "rebirth" of the arts and letters which, they held, had been effected by Dante, Giotto, and Petrarch, with the preceding period of cultural darkness.[16] With this change of emphasis from things religious to things secular, the significance of the old metaphor became reversed: Antiquity, so long considered as the "Dark Age," now became the time of "light" which had to be "restored"; the era following Antiquity, on the other hand, was submerged in obscurity.

The use of the expression "the Dark Ages" was not, however, confined to the circles of artists and writers of the Renaissance. The term was also used, and in an even more comprehensive sense, by the humanist historians who, from a general point of view, attempted to assign to their own time its place in the course of history. This problem of periodization of history, as it appeared to the Renaissance scholars themselves, has recently been studied by Wallace K. Ferguson in an article on "Humanist Views of the Renaissance." [17] Ferguson concludes that "the Humanists . . . are in fairly general agreement that there was a decline of ancient civilization with the decline of Rome and that this decline led to a period of barbaric darkness." [18]

In this connection it is obviously important to find out which humanist first used the expression "the Dark Ages" as a term of periodization, since the figure of speech in itself implies a sharp chronological demarcation. Scholars have pointed to Petrarch as the man whose writings seemed to suggest such a conception.[19]

15 Simone, *op. cit.,* III, 182 f.

16 Cf. Varga, *op. cit.,* pp. 44 ff.; W. Goetz, "Mittelalter und Renaissance," *Historische Zeitschrift,* CII (1907), 31, 53 f.

17 Published in *The American Historical Review,* XLV (1939), pp. 1–28.

18 Ferguson, *op. cit.,* p. 28.

19 Cf. e.g., W. Rehm, *Der Untergang Roms im abendländischen Denken* (Leipzig, 1930), p. 45; Simone, *op. cit.,* II, 842 f.; Ferguson, *op. cit.,* p. 7.

But there is no definite agreement on this particular point.[20] I think, however, that sufficient material can be adduced to decide the disputed question. This problem must be approached with an investigation of the development of the conception which Petrarch held with regard to his main historical work, the *De viris illustribus*. This investigation will lead directly to a discussion of Petrarch's historical conceptions in general and and the part which the term "Dark Ages" played in them.

In a letter written from Parma in 1349, Petrarch recalls the years full of personal happiness and literary productivity which he once spent in the seclusion of his beloved Vaucluse.[21] In it he enumerates the various poems and works which he began there; then he continues: "No place gave more leisure or offered stronger stimulation. That solitude encouraged me to bring together the illustrious men of all countries and of all times." [22] This composition which Petrarch conceived in the solitude of Vaucluse was to become his work *De viris illustribus*.

It is possible to fix the approximate date of the conception of this plan. The earliest possible date is 1337, when Petrarch took up residence in Vaucluse. We learn moreover from another remark of Petrarch that the design of *De viris illustribus* formed itself in his mind before that of the *Africa*.[23] The date of this

[20] Cf. Varga, *op. cit.*, pp. 41 f.: "Petrarca und . . . Coluccio Salutati . . . bezeichnen im allgemeinen noch nicht das von ihnen abgelehnte Jahrtausend mit der Metapher der Finsternis; wohl aber sprechen sie, trotz aller Verehrung für die Antike, vom 'finsteren Heidentum.' . . . Bei Petrarca und Salutati ist somit die Verteilung von Licht und Schatten auf die Geschichte fast ausschliesslich vom christlichen Standpunkt aus bestimmt."

[21] *Fam.*, VIII, 3 (ed. V. Rossi, *Le Familiari*, II, 158–161).—As to the frequently controversial dates of Petrarch's letters, I refer once and for all to the valuable bibliography gathered by E. H. Wilkins, *Modern Discussions of the Dates of Petrarch's Prose Letters* (Chicago, 1929).

[22] *Fam.*, VIII, 3 (ed. Rossi, II, 160): "Nullus locus aut plus otii prebuit aut stimulos acriores: ex omnibus terris ac seculis illustres viros in unum contrahendi illa michi solitudo dedit animum."

[23] *De contemptu mundi*, Dial. III (in *Opera omnia*, Basel, 1554, p. 411). Cf. P. de Nolhac, "Le 'De viris illustribus' de Pétrarque," *Notices et extraits des Manuscrits de la Bibliothèque Nationale*, XXXIV, 1 (Paris, 1890), 61 f. —On Petrarch's historical conceptions in general cf. G. Koerting, *Petrarca's Leben und Werke* (Leipzig, 1878), pp. 592–617; H. W. Eppelsheimer, *Petrarca* (Bonn, 1926), pp. 77–96; L. Tonelli, *Petrarca* (Milan, 1930), pp. 253–266.

latter work is Good Friday 1338.[24] Thus we may conclude that the first plan of *De viris illustribus* dates from 1337/38.

According to his plan to write on "illustrious men of all countries and of all times," Petrarch went to work immediately and started writing "biographies" of Jewish and oriental, Greek and Roman figures, belonging to the realm of both myth and reality. This first version began with the life of Adam and ended with that of Caesar.[25]

A few years later, however, the original program was to undergo a decisive change. In Petrarch's *Secretum,* which was begun about 1342/43,[26] Saint Augustine addresses the poet in the following words: "You have been dreaming of becoming renowned to posterity and for this reason . . . you have ventured upon writing the history from King Romulus to Emperor Titus, an immense undertaking that requires much time and work." [27] This sentence shows that in 1342/43 Petrarch no longer intended, as he had done five years earlier, to write on the illustrious men of all ages.[28] By this time he had restricted his theme to the history of a very definite period, stretching from Romulus, the first king, down through the centuries of the Roman Republic to the first hundred years of the Empire.

[24] N. Festa, *Saggio sull'Africa del Petrarca* (Palermo-Rome, 1926), p. 4 ff.

[25] It was only at the end of the nineteenth century that this first text of *De viris illustribus* was discovered by P. de Nolhac, who published extracts from it, *op. cit.,* p. 110 ff.; cf. P. de Nolhac, *Pétrarque et l'Humanisme,* II (2nd edit., Paris, 1907), 1 ff.

[26] Cf. L. Tonelli, *op. cit.,* pp. 122 f.

[27] *Opera omnia* (Basel, 1554), p. 411: ". . . famam inter posteros concepisti, ideoque manum ad maiora iam porrigens, librum historiarum a rege Romulo in Titum Caesarem, opus immensum temporisque et laboris capacissimum aggressus es."

[28] R. Tatham, *Francesco Petrarca, the First Modern Man of Letters; His Life and Letters,* II (London, 1926), p. 66, believes that Petrarch started out with writing "a series of lives of Roman warriors and statesmen from Romulus to Titus," and that "afterwards—at what date is not clear—he extended his design so as to include famous men of all ages and countries." Tatham argues as follows (II, 66, n. 3): "(Petrarch) alludes to the longer design in *Fam.,* VIII, 3, which was written in 1349; and since the *Secret* was written in 1342–1343, the change must have been between these dates." This argument is wrong: Tatham did not notice that in *Fam.,* VIII, 3, Petrarch does not speak of books he was working on in 1349, but of plans which he had conceived in a happy past when he was living in Vaucluse.

How are we to account for this alteration of the original design? Must we believe that Petrarch abandoned the initial project because he had come to realize that the task was "too vast and beyond his power"? [29] Surely no mere external difficulties could offer an impulse strong enough to make Petrarch discontinue his original plan and even discard all the lives of biblical and Greek personages which he had already written. It seems more logical to assume that it was a new concept of history which necessitated these alterations. A search for possible causes of this decisive change, which took place in Petrarch's mind between the years 1337 and 1342/43, reveals that one of the most important events in the poet's life fell in this period: his coronation as poet laureate on the Capitol on April 8, 1341. The question, then, arises whether Petrarch's new concept of history as Roman history is to be connected with his Roman coronation?

To answer this question we have to consider Petrarch's relation to Rome.[30] Ever since his childhood his thoughts had centered around "the city to which there is none like, nor ever will be." [31] But when in 1337 he came to Rome for the first time and actually saw the remains of her ancient grandeur, he was so overwhelmed by the impressions he received that he was unable to express his feelings in words.[32] The fact that Petrarch saw

[29] Cf. P. de Nolhac, in *Notices et extraits . . .* , XXXIV, 1, p. 109, who says that Petrarch "a fini par abandonner un sujet trop vaste et trop au dessus de ses forces, pour se consacrer de préférence à l'histoire romaine. Sur ce terrain, pour lui, les sources abondaient, et il était soutenu dans son œuvre par le sentiment d'un hommage rendu à des aïeux directs, aux ancêtres et aux modèles de la patrie italienne qu'il rêvait." Cf. P. de Nolhac, *Pétrarque et l'Humanisme,* II, 2; E. C.(arrara), "Petrarca," in *Enciclopedia Italiana,* XXVII (Rome, 1935), p. 13: "Poi l'audace disegno giovanile gli si venne restringendo ai personaggi romani da Romolo a Tito."

[30] On this point compare Tatham, *op. cit.,* I, 328–348; in his text Tatham gives large extracts from a number of Petrarch's letters dealing with Rome, viz. *Fam.,* II, 9, 12, 13, 14; VI, 2; VIII, 1.

[31] *Fam.,* II, 9 (ed. Rossi, I, 96): ". . . de civitate . . . illa, cui nulla similis fuit, nulla futura est"; translat. by Tatham, I, 331.

[32] Thus Petrarch wrote in a letter of 1337, dated "Rome, idibus Martii, in Capitolio," to his great patron, the Cardinal Giovanni Colonna: "Ab urbe Roma quid expectet, qui tam multa de montibus acceperit? Putabas me grande aliquid scripturum, cum Romam pervenissem. Ingens michi forsan in posterum scribendi materia oblata est; in presens nichil est quod

himself reduced to an almost complete silence in viewing the city and wonders for which he had longed throughout his life, seems the more remarkable when we remind ourselves that under normal circumstances he was very well able to describe his travelling experiences; we have only to think, for instance, of the two journal-letters, which he wrote during his journey in Germany in 1333, and the brilliant picture which he drew in them of the city of Cologne.[33] The entirely different reactions of Petrarch toward his impressions in Cologne and in Rome is, of course, easily explained. Whereas in Germany he could and did take the attitude of a "tourist" interested in new sights and in the observation of foreign people and strange customs, he went to Rome as to "that queenly city, of which I have read, aye, and written so much, and shall perhaps write more, unless death break off my efforts prematurely." [34] This first visit to Rome, therefore, evoked emotions in Petrarch so deep that he was unable immediately to express them in concise words but had first to ponder over them for a long time.[35]

Quite different was the case when in 1341 Petrarch paid his second visit to Rome. On the actual ceremony of his coronation as poet laureate, it is true, he left only one—and that rather general—description to posterity in one of his *Epistles*.[36] But this time he was able to render a real account of the impression which Rome had made upon him. Witness the letter which at the end of the same year he addressed to his friend,

---

inchoare ausim, miraculo rerum tantarum et stuporis mole obrutus"; *Fam.*, II, 14 (ed. Rossi, I, 103); translat. by Tatham I, 338. Cf. *Senil.*, X, 2 (in *Opera omnia*, Basel, 1554, p. 963).

[33] *Fam.*, I, 4 and 5 (ed. Rossi, I, 24–31); compare the notes in P. Piur's edition of these letters in K. Burdach, *Vom Mittelalter zur Reformation*, VII (Berlin, 1933), 161–174.

[34] *Fam.*, II, 9 (ed. Rossi, I, 96): ". . . hec cursim attigi, ut intelligeres non parvipendere me regine urbis aspectum, da qua infinita perlegi et ipse multa iam scripsi, plura forte scripturus, nisi primordia mea precipitata dies mortis abrumpat"; translat. by Tatham, I, 331.

[35] Cf. Tatham, *op. cit.*, I, 338 ff.

[36] *Epist. metr.*, II, 1, ed. D. Rossetti, *F. Petrarchae poëmata minora*, III (Milan, 1834), 1 ff.; see also *Fam.*, IV, 7, 8, 9, 13; *Africa*, IX, 237 ff. Cf. Tatham, *op. cit.*, II, 104–156; A. Marpicati, "L'incoronazione del Petrarca in Campidoglio," *Annali della Cattedra Petrarchesca*, VII (Arezzo, 1937), 1–25.

the mendicant friar Giovanni Colonna.[37] Petrarch had first met Giovanni in Avignon and had carried on a correspondence with him, after this scion of the great Colonna family had gone to Rome to conclude his life as a monk. When Petrarch came to Rome in 1341, Giovanni often accompanied him on his promenades around the city. These common wanderings of theirs Petrarch recalls in that letter to Giovanni which begins: "Deambulabamus Rome soli." After a digresson on the relative values of the various ancient schools of philosophy Petrarch continues: "We were wandering together in that mighty city, which, though from its extent it seems empty, has an immense population; we were wandering not merely in it but all around it; and at every step we encountered food for musing and for conversation." [38] There follows a long list of the localities which the two friends visited on their walks through Rome. It is to be noted that for the most part Petrarch recalls spots which were connected with the great figures and events of the history of pagan Rome, especially of the time of the Roman Republic, whereas only a very small part of the enumeration is devoted to scenes of Christian Rome: the proportion shows where Petrarch's main interest lay.[39] This is the more noteworthy, since in the beginning of the same letter Petrarch affirms: "We are to read philosophy, poetry, or history in such fashion that the echo of Christ's gospel, by which alone we are wise and happy, may ever be sounding in our hearts,—that gospel, without which the more we have learnt, the more ignorant and

[37] *Fam.*, VI, 2 (ed. Rossi, II, 55–60); partly translated by Tatham, *op. cit.*, I, 343–346. The date of the letter was controversial and it was doubtful whether it referred to Petrarch's first or second visit to Rome. However, L. Foresti, *Aneddoti della vita del Petrarca* (Brescia, 1928), pp. 81–84, has proved beyond any doubt that "la lettera fu invero scritta in cammino per la campagna di Parma il 30 Novembre 1341" (*op. cit.*, p. 82); F. E. H. Wilkins, *A Tentative Chronology of Petrarch's Prose Letters* (Chicago, 1929), p. 6 (under November 30).

[38] "Vagabamur pariter in illa urbe tam magna, que cum propter spatium vacua videatur, populum habet immensum; nec in urbe tantum sed circa urbem vagabamur, aderatque per singulos passus quod linguam atque animum excitaret" (ed. Rossi, II, 56; translat. by Tatham, *op. cit.*, I, 344).

[39] In Rossi's edition of the letter in *Le Familiari,* the ratio is about ten to one: lines 47 to 105 are devoted to the description of pagan Rome, lines 106 to 111 to that of Christian Rome.

wretched shall we be; to which, as the highest citadel of truth, all things must be referred; on which alone, as the firm foundation of sound learning, all human toil is built." [40] Here a strong inconsistency appears: on the one hand Petrarch denies the intrinsic value of secular knowledge and declares that everything must be referred to eternal religious truth; on the other he puts an almost exclusive emphasis on the history of pagan Rome and neglects the Christian aspects of the eternal city.[41]

After enumerating the historical spots, Petrarch complains bitterly that the contemporary Romans know nothing about Rome and things Roman. In his opinion this ignorance is disastrous. For he asks: "Who can doubt that Rome would rise up again if she but began to know herself?" [42] After this emotional outburst, Petrarch continues the reminiscences of his wanderings with Giovanni Colonna: "After the fatigue of walking over the immense circuit of the city, we used often to stop at the Baths of Diocletian; sometimes we even climbed upon the vaulted roof of that once magnificent building, for nowhere is there a healthier air, a wider prospect, or more silence and desirable solitude. There we did not talk of business nor of private or public affairs on which we had shed tears enough. As we walked over the walls of the shattered city or sat there, the fragments of the ruins were under our very eyes. Our conversation often turned on history, which we appeared to have divided up between us in such a fashion that in modern history

[40] "Sic philosophica, sic poetica, sic historias legamus, ut semper ad aurem cordis Evangelium Cristi sonet: quo uno satis docti ac felices; sine quo quanto plura didicerimus, tanto indoctiores atque miseriores futuri sumus; ad quod velut ad summam veri arcem referenda sunt omnia; cui, tanquam uni literarum verarum immobili fundamento, tuto superedificat humanus labor." (ed. Rossi, II, 56); translat. by Tatham, *op. cit.*, I, 344.

[41] In this connection it is interesting to contrast this letter of 1341 with a passage in a letter which Petrarch wrote to Barbato da Sulmona in 1352 (*Fam.*, XII, 7; ed. Rossi, III, 28). "Id quidem quod non in ultimis adversitatum numeras, ut me Rome non inveneris, divinitus factum reor, ne si congredi licuisset, non templa Dei devotione catholica sed Urbis ambitum lustraremus curiositate poetica, non anime curam agentes sed negotium literarum, quod licet sit iocundissimum pabulum intellectus, nisi tamen ad unum verum finem redigatur, infinitum quiddam et inane est."

[42] *Fam.*, VI, 2 (ed. Rossi, II, 58): "Quis enim dubitare potest quin illico surrectura sit, si ceperit se Roma cognoscere?"

you, in ancient history I, seemed to be more expert; and ancient were called those events which took place before the name of Christ was celebrated in Rome and adored by the Roman emperors, modern, however, the events from that time to the present." [43]

What strikes the modern reader of this letter is the fact that the poet looked at Rome and the Roman scene primarily from a historical and not from an aesthetic point of view. And even this historical point of view is quite unique. This becomes evident in the climax of the letter where Petrarch recalls the conversations which he had with his old friend on the roof of the Baths of Diocletian, the ruins of the city spread beneath them. The reader of these sentences is immediately reminded of the words with which in his *Memoirs* Gibbon records the conception of his great history: "It was on the fifteenth of October (1764), in the gloom of evening, as I sat musing on the Capitol, while the barefooted fryars were chanting their litanies in the temple of Jupiter, that I conceived the first thought of my history. My original plan was confined to the decay of the City; my reading and reflection pointed to that aim; but several years elapsed, and several avocations intervened, before I grappled with the decline and fall of the Roman Empire." [44] To Gibbon, true son of the age of *Ruinen-Romantik*,[45] those Roman ruins bore witness to "the greatest, perhaps, and most aw-

[43] "Solebamus ergo, post fatigationem quam nobis immensa urbs ambita pepererat, sepius ad Termas Dioclitianas subsistere, nonnunquam vero supra testudinem illius magnificentissime olim domus ascendere, quod et aer salutaris et prospectus liber et silentium ac votiva solitudo nusquam magis. Ibi de negotiis nichil omnino, nichil de re familiari nichilque de publica, quam semel flevisse satis est. Et euntibus per menia fracte urbis et illic sedentibus, ruinarum fragmenta sub oculis erant. Quid ergo? Multus de historiis sermo erat, quas ita partiti videbamur, ut in novis tu, in antiquis ego viderer expertior, et dicantur antique quecunque ante celebratum Rome et veneratum romanis principibus Cristi nomen, nove autem ex illo usque ad hanc etatem." (ed. Rossi, II, 58); compare Tatham's translation, *op. cit.*, I, 345.—The rest of the letter deals with the problem of the beginnings of the liberal and mechanical arts.

[44] Quoted by D. M. Low, *E. Gibbon* (London, 1937), p. 184; cf. the similar words at the very end of *The Decline and Fall of the Roman Empire.*

[45] Cf. W. Rehm, *Der Untergang Roms im abendländischen Denken* (Leipzig, 1930), pp. 120 ff.

ful scene in the history of mankind";[46] and thus was he inspired to inquire and to describe the decadence of Rome. Petrarch's reaction as shown by his letter was entirely different. To him those ruins evidently bore witness to the time when Rome and the Romans had been great: "Of minute things," he exclaims, "there are no great ruins; . . . he never will fall from a height who already lies in the abyss";[47] thus Petrarch shows his main interest, the rise and greatness of the *Respublica Romana.* In Gibbon's opinion Rome had fallen once and for all; in Petrarch's opinion there was a hope of resurrection, "if Rome but began to know herself."

This interpretation of the letter of 1341 reveals that by this time a new concept of history existed in Petrarch's mind. It would be highly gratifying to our sense of the logical if we were able to prove conclusively that this gravitation toward ancient Rome originated in and resulted directly from Petrarch's coronation which made him a *civis Romanus* both legally and ideally.[48] The material at our disposal, however, is too scanty to show this with absolute certainty.[49] But one conclusion we may safely draw from Petrarch's letter to Giovanni Colonna in 1341: here for the first time he ventured to state explicitly that his primary interest was in the history of pagan rather than of Christian Rome, thus drawing a sharp boundary-line between "ancient" and "modern" history. As in this letter he spoke almost exclusively of the remains of the classical time in Rome, also shortly afterwards he stated in his *Secretum* that he

[46] E. Gibbon, *The Decline and Fall of the Roman Empire,* last page.

[47] "Minutarum rerum ruina magna esse non potest; procul absunt ab hoc metu; nunquam cadet ex alto, qui in imo iacet; Roma igitur ex alto cecidit, non cadet Auinio"; *Apologia contra cuiusdam anonymi Galli calumnias* (in *Opera omnia,* Basel, 1554, p. 1180).

[48] In the *Apologia contra cuiusdam anonymi Galli calumnias* (in *Opera omnia,* Basel, 1554, p. 1185) Petrarch proudly proclaims: "Sum uero Italus natione et Romanus ciuis esse glorior." In a letter of January 5, 1342, i.e. shortly after his coronation, Petrarch speaks of Rome as the city, "in qua civis (sum)"; *Fam.,* IV, 12 (ed. Rossi, I, 185). Cola di Rienzo calls Petrarch his "concivis" in a letter of July 28, 1347 (ed. K. Burdach, *Vom Mittelalter zur Reformation,* II, 3 [Berlin, 1912], 85).

[49] There exists the possibility that Petrarch had conceived of this idea before he went to Rome, and that his laurel crown merely fortified his belief in the focal importance of Roman history.

had confined his work *De viris illustribus* to the time "from Romulus to Titus."

The same demarcation of two clearly separated epochs of history is found in a letter of 1359, which Petrarch addresses to another member of the Colonna family, Agapito Colonna.[50] Petrarch's main purpose in writing this letter is to defend himself against Agapito's reproach of ingratitude and haughtiness and against the accusation that he intended to use Agapito as an example of vanity. Petrarch repudiates these charges and assures Agapito that he never had introduced his name in any of his works, "not because I lacked affection but because I lacked occasion." [51] Petrarch continues: "And yet had I touched upon illustrious men of our time, I will not say that I should have introduced your name (lest in my present anger I should seem to flatter you, a thing which is not my habit even when well disposed), but most assuredly I should not have passed over in silence either your uncle or your father. I did not wish for the sake of so few famous names, however, to guide my pen so far and through such darkness. Therefore sparing myself the excess both of subject-matter and of effort, I have determined to fix a limit to my history long before this century." [52]

In accordance with the passages quoted above from the letter of 1341 and from the *Secretum,* Petrarch states in this letter of 1359 that he had resolved to set a precise date limit to his historical studies. At the same time, however, he qualifies his judgement of the epoch following the period to which he was devoting his attention: this epoch was to him an era of *"tenebrae,"* of "darkness."

What did Petrarch mean to say by using this word *"tenebrae"?* In his opinion was this period dark simply because the lack of sources prevented the historian from shedding light on

[50] *Fam.,* XX, 8 (ed. J. Fracassetti, *Epistolae de rebus familiaribus,* III, 28–34).

[51] "Caeterum nusquam ibi, nusquam alibi hactenus tuum nomen inserui, destituente quidem materia, non affectu" (ed. Fracassetti, III, 30).

[52] "Quamquam si illustres aevi nostri viros attigissem, non dicam te, ne tibi, quod placatus non soleo, iratus adulari videar, at certe nec patruum nec patrem tuum silentio oppressurus fuerim. Nolui autem pro tam paucis nominibus claris, tam procul tantasque per tenebras stilum ferre: ideoque vel materiae vel labori parcens, longe ante hoc saeculum historiae limitem statui ac defixi." (ed. Fracassetti, III, 30 f.).

it? Or was it dark because "the lamps had gone out all over Europe" for a time of more than a thousand years? With this alternative we come to the crucial point in the interpretation of Petrarch's conception of history. For the acceptance of the second assumption would mean that by the use of the word "darkness" Petrarch passed a very definite judgement of value upon the long era in question.

To solve this problem we turn to statements made by Petrarch elsewhere in his writings. In a famous passage in the second book of the *Africa* he makes the father of the elder Scipio Africanus predict the future of Rome to his son. Lucius Scipio breaks off his prophecy with the reigns of the Emperors Vespasian and Titus. "I cannot bear," he exclaims, "to proceed; for strangers of Spanish and African extraction will steal the sceptre and the glory of the Empire founded by us with great effort. Who can endure the thought of the seizure of supreme control by these dregs of the people, these contemptible remnants, passed over by our sword"? [53]

Similar ideas Petrarch expresses in a letter which he directed to the German King Charles IV in 1351.[54] The second half of this letter is a speech which Roma herself addresses to Charles. She describes in detail the rise of the Roman Republic up to the Augustan era: hundreds of years of effort and struggle, she says, resulted in the foundation of the Empire and in the establishment of eternal peace. At this point Roma suddenly breaks off her narration. She declares emphatically that she does not wish to begin "the lamentable story" of the decline: "where things have retrograded," Charles will see for himself.[55]

In the history of the later Roman emperors of "foreign" ex-

[53] Ulterius transire piget; nam sceptra decusque
Imperii tanto nobis fundata labore
Externi rapient Hispane stirpis et Afre.
Quis ferat has hominum sordes nostrique pudendas
Relliquias gladii fastigia prendere rerum; *Africa,* II, 274–278 (ed. N. Festa, p. 40); cf. *Africa* II, 255 ff.

[54] *Fam.,* X, 1 (ed. Rossi, II, 277–284); cf. P. Piur's edition of this letter in K. Burdach, *Vom Mittelalter zur Reformation,* VII (Berlin, 1933), 1–11.

[55] ". . . voti compos, omnia sub pedibus meis vidi. Inde sensim nescio quonammodo, nisi quia mortalium opera decet esse mortalia, in labores meos irrepsit aliena segnities, ac ne lacrimabilem ordiar historiam, quorsum res redierint, vides" (ed. Rossi, II, 282).

traction Petrarch is no more interested than he is in the history of all those rulers of non-Roman nations, "whose names," as he says in the preface to the second version of *De viris illustribus,* "were always obscure and are now entirely obliterated because of the long lapse of time." [56] In this connection it is noteworthy that in an early letter (written in 1333) Petrarch calls Charlemagne simply "King Charles whom, by the cognomen of 'the Great,' barbarous peoples dare to raise to the level of Pompey and Alexander." [57] If in this letter and elsewhere Petrarch denies to Charles both his official and his popular titles,[58] he denies more than the personal greatness of a single individual: he expresses his disregard of the whole institution—the first and greatest representative of which Charlemagne had been—the mediaeval Empire, the self-proclaimed heir and successor of the *Imperium Romanum.* That Petrarch does not contest the imperial idea, according to which the Empire had been transferred from the Romans to the Byzantines, the Franks and eventually the Germans, is shown by the prediction which in the *Africa* he puts in the mouth of Lucius Scipio.[59] But in contradiction to the political theorists and historians of the Middle Ages, Petrarch looks with scorn at this continuity. For in his

[56] "Quis enim, queso, Parthorum aut Macedonum, quis Gothorum et Unnorum et Vuandalorum atque aliarum gentium reges ab ultimis repetitos in ordinem digerat, quorum et obscura semper et iam senio deleta sunt nomina?" (ed. P. de Nolhac, in *Notices et extraits de la Bibliothèque Nationale,* XXXIV, 1 [Paris, 1890], 112).

[57] ". . . Carolum regem quem magni cognomine equare Pompeio et Alexandro audent"; *Fam.,* I, 4 (ed. Rossi, I, 25).

[58] See the canzone "Il successor di Carlo" (in *Le Rime sparse e i trionfi,* ed. E. Chiòrboli, Bari, 1930, n. 27, p. 22), and the first version of the "Trionfo della Fama" (ed. Chiòrboli, *op. cit.,* p. 376, v. 163).—On Charlemagne's cognomen compare P. Lehmann, "Das literarische Bild Karls des Grossen vornehmlich im lateinischen Schrifttum des Mittelalters," *Sitzungsberichte der Bayerischen Akademie der Wissenschaften, philosoph.-histor. Klasse* (Munich, 1934).

[59] Vivet honos Latius, semperque vocabitur uno
Nomine Romanum imperium; sed rector habenas
Non semper Romanus aget; quin Siria mollis
Porriget ipsa manum, mox Gallia dura, loquaxque
Grecia, et Illiricum: tandem cadet ista potestas
In Boream: sic res humanas fata rotabunt; *Africa,* II, 288–293 (ed. Festa, p. 40).

opinion the Roman Empire "had been impaired, debilitated, and almost consumed at the hands of the barbarians." [60]

From these passages it is clear that Petrarch discarded the whole history of the Roman Empire during late Antiquity and the Middle Ages because within that age, everywhere in the western world, had come into power "barbarous" nations which brought even Rome and the Romans under their domination. Because Petrarch could think of this whole development only with a feeling of scornful grief, he consciously and consistently consigned it to oblivion in all his writings. In his letters time and again he conjures up the great shades of Antiquity, but scarcely ever does he refer to a mediaeval name. In his *Rerum memorandarum libri quatuor,* more than half of the examples are drawn from Roman history, about two-fifths from ancient Greek history, and only the rest from "more recent" times, which in this case meant almost exclusively from the fourteenth century; the Middle Ages proper are passed over in complete silence.[61] Exactly the same is true of his *Trionfi,* where nearly all of the handful of mediaeval figures mentioned belong to the realm of legend or poetry or to the period close to Petrarch's own time.[62] To realize the peculiarity of Petrarch's standpoint, we have only to think of the entirely different picture of the past in the *Divine Comedy,* where Dante usually

[60] In the *Apologia contra cuiusdam anonymi Galli calumnias* Petrarch says of the Empire: "quod licet inter manus barbaricas imminutum atque debilitatum et pene consumptum sit, Romanas inter manus tale fuit, ut omnia mundi illi admota pueriles ludi fuisse videantur et inania nomina" (in *Opera omnia,* Basel, 1554, p. 1187).

[61] Compare *Rerum memorandarum libri IV* (in *Opera omnia,* Basel, 1554, pp. 442–550). The work contains 20 chapters, each of which is arranged in the three sections of the history of the Romans, the "externi," and the "recentiores." There are about 350 entries in the work; of these, 30 entries are grouped under the heading of "recentiores," more than 130 under that of "externi"; the remaining more than 180 stories are from Roman history.—On the general character of this work cf. L. Tonelli, *Petrarca* (Milan, 1930), pp. 261 ff.

[62] Out of more than 400 names mentioned in the *Trionfi,* I count only 14 mediaeval names: King Arthur, Charlemagne, Godfrey of Bouillon, Saladin, Admiral Ruggero di Lauria, Duke Henry of Lancaster, King Robert of Sicily, Stefano Colonna, Tristan and Iseult, Lancelot and Guenevere, Paolo and Francesca Malatesta da Rimini; compare the index of names in C. Calcaterra's edition of the *Trionfi* (Turin, 1923).

couples ancient and mediaeval figures in his representation of the various vices and virtues of man.[63]

Petrarch's conception of history, I think, cannot be better expressed than by the words which he wrote in the *Apologia contra cuiusdam anonymi Galli calumnias:* "What else, then, is all history, if not the praise of Rome?" [64] This peculiar notion of history, very impressive in its Latin succinctness, was formulated by Petrarch only at the end of his life. But evidently he conceived of it much earlier, in the beginning of the 1340's, when he started work on the second version of *De viris illustribus.* When in his historical work Petrarch emphasized everything that was Roman and excluded everything that was outside Rome, he was entirely in accord with all his other writings; both in his letters and in his poetical works he confined himself to the same topic as in *De viris illustribus.*

This consistent restriction to subjects taken from Roman history makes it clear that Petrarch did not narrow down the scope of his historical studies for mere external reasons, but that he rather limited himself on principle. This limitation was based on a very definite judgement of value: the praise of Rome corresponded to the condemnation of the "barbarous" countries and peoples outside Rome. This point of view Petrarch expressed when in 1341 he drew a line of demarcation between "ancient" and "modern" history, and when later on he called the period stretching from the fall of the Roman Empire down to his own age a time of "darkness." In Petrarch's opinion that era was "dark" because it was worthless, not because it was little known. The sooner the period dropped from man's memory, the better. Therefore Petrarch, personally at least, was resolved to bury it in oblivion.

This notion, however, has an importance beyond its relation

[63] Cf. J. Burckhardt, *The Civilization of the Renaissance in Italy,* b. III, ch. 4: "In the *Divine Comedy* (Dante) treats the ancient and the Christian worlds, not indeed as of equal authority, but as parallel to one another. Just as, at an earlier period of the Middle Ages types and antitypes were sought in the history of the Old and New Testaments, so does Dante constantly bring together a Christian and a pagan illustration of the same fact."

[64] "Quid est enim aliud omnis historia quam Romana laus?" (in *Opera omnia,* Basel, 1554, p. 1187); cf. H. W. Eppelsheimer, *Petrarca* (Bonn, 1926), p. 77.

to the life and works of Petrarch. It offers not only a key to the understanding of Petrarch's personal standards of value, but it deserves attention as well in connection with the problem with which our discussion started, the problem of the humanist periodization of history.

As we have seen, Petrarch divided the course of history into two sharply separated periods and set as a dividing point between them either the time when Christianity became the state religion in the Roman Empire or the time when the Roman Empire began to "decline" under the rule of "barbarian," that is, non-Roman emperors. Mediaeval historiography was based on essentially different principles.[65] Whereas after the modification of his original plan Petrarch concerned himself exclusively with the first period and concentrated upon the secular history of Rome "from Romulus to Titus," the mediaeval historians almost without exception wrote universal history, that is, in the words of Benedetto Croce, "a history of the universal, of the universal by excellence, which is history in labor with God and toward God."[66] Even the most meager monastic chroniclers and annalists dealt usually with their particular monasteries within the framework of a history of the world from its creation to the present. In doing so they followed very definite schemes according to which universal history was divided up into the succession either of the four world-monarchies or of the six ages.[67] These two patterns were first drawn up by Jerome in his *Commentaries* on Daniel's famous prophecy on the statue composed of different metals and on the four

[65] Compare M. Ritter, *Die Entwicklung der Geschichtswissenschaft an den führenden Werken betrachtet* (Munich-Berlin, 1919); B. Croce, *Theory and History of Historiography,* translat. by D. Ainslie (London, 1921), pp. 200–223; H. von Eicken, *Geschichte und System der mittelalterlichen Weltanschauung* (4th edition, Stuttgart-Berlin, 1923), pp. 641–671; H. E. Barnes, *A History of Historical Writing* (Norman, 1937), pp. 41–98.

[66] B. Croce, *op. cit.,* p. 206.

[67] On these two schemes cf. H. F. Massmann, *Der keiser und der kunige buoch oder die sogenannte Kaiserchronik* (Quedlinburg-Berlin, 1854), III, 353–364; M. Ritter, *op. cit.,* pp. 84 f.; B. Croce, *op. cit.,* pp. 206, 213 f.; H. Spangenberg, "Die Perioden der Weltgeschichte," *Historische Zeitschrift,* CXXVII (1923), 7 f.; G. Falco, *La polemica sul medio evo* (Turin, 1933), pp. 1–6; W. K. Ferguson, "Humanist Views of the Renaissance," *The American Historical Review,* XLV (1939), 5 f.

beasts (*Daniel,* 2, 31 ff. and 7, 1 ff.); and by Augustine in the *City of God* (XXII). Both schemes had in common the conception of the world and its various countries and peoples as a unity, which implied the notion both of universality and of continuity in history. This idea originated in Hellenistic times,[68] and later on was taken over by the greatest of the early Christian historians, Eusebius of Caesarea. Because of the authority of Jerome and Augustine the patterns of the four world-monarchies and the six ages became the models of almost all the mediaeval universal histories, those of Isidore of Seville, Bede, Otto of Freising, Vincent of Beauvais, to mention only the greatest names. As late as in the seventeenth century we find histories of the world organized in accordance with the interpretation of Daniel's prophecy.[69] In these two schemes the beginnings of the last period coincided, since in the one it began with the foundation of the Roman Empire by Caesar or Augustus, in the other with the birth of Christ. "And thus," as Comparetti says, "history was divided into two distinct periods—a long period of error and darkness, and then a period of purification and truth, while midway between the two stood the Cross of Calvary." [70]

Against this background we may now place Petrarch's division of history: he certainly drew an entirely different line of demarcation. Since he concerned himself exclusively with one particular state, Rome, he was not interested in the four world-monarchies. He started out from the very beginnings of Rome and showed her growth under the leadership of the great men of the republican period, whereas the mediaeval historians paid very little attention to the epoch preceding the foundation of the Empire.[71] "The lamentable story of how things retrograded," Petrarch did not want to recount (*Fam.,* X, 1), and therefore he

[68] Cf. C. Trieber, "Die Idee der vier Weltreiche," *Hermes,* XXVII (1892), 311–342.

[69] Cf. E. Fueter, *Geschichte der neueren Historiographie* (3rd edition, Munich-Berlin, 1936), pp. 187 f., 288, 618.

[70] D. Comparetti, *Vergil in the Middle Ages,* translat. by E. F. M. Benecke (London, 1908), p. 174.

[71] Cf. A. Graf, *Roma nella memoria e nelle immaginazioni del Medio Evo,* I (Turin, 1882), 230 f.: "Il periodo della storia romana che più sta a cuore al medio evo è il periodo imperiale. . . . L'interesse per Roma repubblicana è, generalmente parlando, un frutto del Rinascimento avanzato." Cf. Comparetti, *op. cit.,* pp. 177 f.

stopped precisely at the point where in his opinion the "decline" of the Empire began. The mediaeval historians, on the other hand, continued the history of the Empire straight through to their own time: in their opinion the *Imperium Romanum* still existed although the rule over it had been "transferred" from the Romans to other peoples.

By setting up the "decline of the Empire" as a dividing point and by passing over the traditional marks either of the foundation of the Empire or of the birth of Christ, Petrarch introduced a new chronological demarcation in history. This scheme has been distinguished from the older mediaeval or "Hellenistic" ones by the name "humanistic," [72] for it formed the underlying principle of most of the historical works written by Italian humanists.[73] Its most manifest expression is found in the title of Flavio Biondo's work *Decades historiarum ab inclinatione imperii,* a history of the period stretching from 410 to 1440. The origin of this new chronological demarcation, therefore, has usually been dated hitherto from the middle of the fifteenth century.[74] But, since Petrarch consciously confined his historical studies to the period *"usque ad declinationem imperii,"* if we may say so, we are justified in stating that thereby he implicitly anticipated ideas of the fifteenth-century Italian humanists.

This statement with regard to Petrarch's demarcation of "Antiquity" raises another question. The humanists were to replace the older patterns with a division of history into three periods which, under the names of "ancient," "mediaeval," and "modern" times, live to the present day.[75] Is it possible to con-

[72] Cf. A. Dove, "Der Streit um das Mittelalter," *Historische Zeitschrift,* CXVI (1916), 210.

[73] On humanist historiography see P. Joachimsen, *Geschichtsauffassung und Geschichtschreibung in Deutschland unter dem Einfluss des Humanismus* (Leipzig-Berlin, 1910), pp. 15–36; M. Ritter, *Die Entwicklung der Geschgichtswissenschaft* (Munich-Berlin, 1919), pp. 125–204; B. Croce, *op. cit.,* pp. 224–242; H. Baron, "Das Erwachen des historischen Denkens im Humanismus des Quattrocento," *Historische Zeitschrift,* CXXXVII (1933), 5–20; E. Fueter, *op. cit.,* pp. 1–36 (cf. the bibliography, pp. 607 ff.); H. E. Barnes, *op. cit.,* pp. 99–111; W. K. Ferguson, "Humanist Views of the Renaissance," *The American Historical Review,* XLV (1939), pp. 1–28.

[74] Cf. P. Joachimsen, *op. cit.,* pp. 22 ff.

[75] On the question of division of history compare K. Heussi, *Altertum, Mittelalter und Neuzeit; ein Beitrag zum Problem der historischen Periodi-*

nect Petrarch also with the origin of this division? I think that the question can be answered in the affirmative. To be sure, this threefold division we shall nowhere find expressed directly by Petrarch. As we have seen, he speaks only of "ancient" and "modern" history.[76] The use of the word "modern" in this connection cannot be interpreted otherwise than that Petrarch thought of his own time as still a part of the period which had begun with the "decline" of the Empire. His was an age of decadence: this idea Petrarch has expressed time and again in his letters. The feeling of profound pessimism finds perhaps its most impressive wording in an early letter where Petrarch says: "As conditions are, I foresee worse things from day to day; but, although I can fear worse things, I can scarcely imagine them." [77] But like so many men of all ages, Petrarch was a pessimist because he was an idealist at heart. In measuring the actual conditions of his time with the standards of his lofty ideals he could not escape despair, a despair, however, which did not always mean hopelessness. His "Golden Age," it is true, lay in the past but, on occasion at least, he was able to visualize the possibility of its return in the future. Thus, in a letter to Pope Urban V, he expresses his belief that Christ desires the re-establishment of the papal court in Rome *"pro aurei saeculi principio."* [78] In similar, though less religious language Petrarch phrases his passionate appeals to the Roman Tribune of the People, Cola di Rienzo, and to the German Emperor Charles IV, urging them to take over the legacy of Antiquity and to follow the models of the great men of ancient Rome: by so doing they were to revive the grandeur of times past. It was this same con-

---

sierung (Tübingen, 1921); H. Spangenberg, "Die Perioden der Weltgeschichte," *Historische Zeitschrift,* CXXVII (1923), 1–49.

[76] *Fam.,* VI, 2 (ed. Rossi, II, 58).

[77] *Fam.,* II, 10 (ed. Rossi, I, 98): "Sed, ut res eunt, in dies peiora conicio; quamvis iam peiora vix possim nedum timere, sed fingere"; cf. Tatham, *Petrarca,* II, 72.

[78] *Senil.,* VII (in *Opera omnia,* Basel, 1554, p. 903): "Incipit, credo, Christus Deus noster suorum fidelium misereri, uult ut arbitror, finem malis imponere, quae multa per hos annos uidimus, uult pro aurei saeculi principio Ecclesiam suam, quam uagari propter culpas hominum diu sinit, ad antiquas et proprias sedes suas et priscae fidei statum reuocare."

viction which impelled Petrarch to pursue historical studies.[79] Since he believed that "Rome would rise up again if she but began to know herself," he strove throughout his life and his work to make his contemporaries conscious of the great traditions of the eternal city. In spite of his often expressed pessimism Petrarch evidently was convinced that there existed the chance of a spiritual rebirth which would put an end to the process of decline, and bring about the beginning of a "new time." This ardent hope of his for the future Petrarch voices nowhere more impressively than in the work which he himself considered as his greatest: at the very end of the *Africa* he addresses his own poem as follows: "My fate is to live amid varied and confusing storms. But for you perhaps, if as I hope and wish you will live long after me, there will follow a better age. This sleep of forgetfulness will not last for ever. When the darkness has been dispersed, our descendants can come again in the former pure radiance." [80]

These verses of the *Africa* show clearly Petrarch's views on the periodization of history. He holds that there was an era of "pure radiance" in the past, Antiquity, and that there is an era of "darkness" succeeding this former period and lasting to the poet's own days. Thus, in Petrarch's opinion, there exists, for the time being, only a twofold division of history. But, since he hopes for the coming of "a better time," the conception of a third era is expressed, or at least implied, in his thoughts. This is illustrated most distinctly in one of his *Epistles,* in which he complains against Fate for having decreed his birth in such sad times, and in which he wishes that he had been born either earlier or much later; for he says, "there was a more fortunate age and probably there will be one again; in the middle, in our

[79] I shall give this question detailed treatment in a monograph on *Petrarch's Historical and Political Ideas.* [This monograph was never written.]

[80] *Africa,* IX, 451–457 (ed. Festa, p. 278): . . . Michi degere vitam.

Impositum varia rerum turbante procella.
At tibi fortassis, si—quod mens sperat et optat—
Es post me victura diu, meliora supersunt
Secula: non omnes veniet Letheus in annos
Iste sopor! Poterunt discussis forte tenebris
Ad purum priscumque inbar remeare nepotes.

time, you see the confluence of wretches and ignominy." [81] In these lines Petrarch plainly distinguishes between three eras: the fortunate ages of the past and, possibly, of the future; between them there is a "middle" time which has not yet come to an end. For the humanists of the fifteenth century periodization of history was to be much simpler. In their opinion the "new" era had actually come to light, because of the work of the great artists and poets of the fourteenth century, among them Petrarch himself. Thus, in their minds, there was no doubt about the reality of three periods: a "middle" period separated the Golden Age of Antiquity from a "modern" time of "renascence." [82] It would be asking too much to expect Petrarch to proclaim himself explicitly the inaugurator of a new era, although occasionally he comes close to making such a claim.[83] But implicitly he certainly paved the way to the idea which was to be set forth by the humanists of following generations. In this sense, then, our modern threefold division of history can be traced back to Petrarch.

The strength of Petrarch's hope for a revival of the Golden Age varied throughout his life, in accordance with general circumstances and his personal moods. But he never vacillated in his firm conviction that the era following the decline of the

[81] *Epist. metr.*, III, 33 (ed. D. Rossetti, *F. Petrarchae poëmata minora,* II [Milan, 1831], 262) begins as follows:

Vivo, sed indignans, quae nos in tristia fatum
Saecula dilatos peioribus intulit annis.
Aut prius, aut multo decuit post tempore nasci;
Nam fuit, et fortassis erit, felicius aevum.
In medium sordes, in nostrum turpia tempus
Confluxisse vides; gravium sentina malorum
Nos habet; ingenium, virtus et gloria mundo
Cesserunt; regnumque tenent fortuna, voluptas;
Dedecus ingenti visu! nisi surgimus actum est.

[82] The first written proofs of the expression "Middle Ages" used in the technical sense, date from the middle of the fifteenth century; cf. P. Lehmann, "Mittelalter und Küchenlatein," *Historische Zeitschrift,* CXXXVII (1928), 200–206.

[83] Cf. *Rerum memorandarum,* I, 2 (in *Opera omnia,* Basel, 1554, p. 448); "Ego . . . uelut in confinio duorum populorum constitutus, ac simul ante retroque prospiciens . . ."— Cf. N. Sapegno, "Petrarca e l'Umanesimo," *Annali della Cattedra Petrarchesca,* VIII (Arezzo, 1938), 77–119; F. Simone, *op. cit.,* II, 843 f.

Roman Empire was a period of "darkness." The fact that we are able to associate this conception with Petrarch, means more than merely the fixation of a date. For the whole idea of the Italian "rinascita," is inseparably connected with the notion of the preceding era as an age of obscurity. The people living in that "renascence" thought of it as a time of revolution. They wanted to break away from the mediaeval past and all its traditions and they were convinced that they had effected such a break. They believed that in their time, to use the words of Petrarch, "the darkness had been dispersed," and that they had "come again in the former pure radiance." Their model was Antiquity, "and the Middle Ages did seem to be a ditch or a declivity." [84]

From our modern point of view we may find it impossible to draw such a sharp line of demarcation between the Renaissance and the preceding period. We have, however, to keep in mind one very essential fact which has been expressed by Joachimsen as follows: "If there is one thing that unites the men of the Renaissance, it is the notion of belonging to a new time." [85] It is precisely this notion of a "new time" which distinguishes the Italian Renaissance from all the so-called earlier "Renaissances" in the Carolingian and Ottonian times or in the twelfth century. These times may have experienced a certain revival of classical studies, but the people living in them did not conceive of or wish for a complete break with the traditions of the times immediately preceding.[86] This idea was peculiar to the Italian Renaissance and it found its expression in the condemnation of the mediaeval epoch as an era of "darkness." Petrarch stands at the very fountainhead of Renaissance thought. It is logical that the "Father of Humanism" is also the father of the concept or attitude which regards the Middle Ages as the "Dark Ages."

[84] B. Croce, *op. cit.*, p. 201; cf. *ibid.*, p. 241.

[85] P. Joachimsen, *op. cit.*, p. 24.

[86] On the problem of the earlier "Renaissances" compare E. Patzelt, *Die karolingische Renaissance; Beiträge zur Geschichte der Kultur des frühen Mittelalters* (Vienna, 1924); H. Naumann, *Karolingische und Ottonische Renaissance* (Frankfurt, 1926); C. H. Haskins, *The Renaissance of the Twelfth Century* (Cambridge, 1927). Cf. the remarks of F. Simone, *op. cit.*, II, 867.

8

Petrarch and the Decoration of the Sala Virorum Illustrium in Padua*

PETRARCH and the Arts is a topic which has often claimed the attention of scholars interested in the history of ideas current during the early Italian Renaissance.[1] For throughout his life Petrarch took a great personal interest in the art of his own time, as well as in that of the classical era; he owned works of Giotto and Simone Martini and he concerned himself on many occasions with the archaeological and other remains of Roman antiquity. That the greatest poet then living in Italy distinguished himself also as a connoisseur and collector must have helped the "new" art considerably and increased the critical regard for it of the people of his generation. It is noteworthy that Petrarch remained faithful to his original love although, after the middle of the fourteenth century, there developed among his younger contemporaries "a certain kind of adverse criticism

* Reprinted from *The Art Bulletin,* XXXIV (1952), 95–116.

[1] The nature of the problems treated in this article forced the author to move into areas of research which are somewhat outside his own field. He therefore feels most grateful for the helpful advice and the valuable suggestions which he received from his friends B. Degenhart, E. Mandowsky, E. Panofsky, and W. L. Woodfill, as well as from the members of the University Seminar on the Renaissance at Columbia University, to whom the paper was presented in Spring 1950. Acknowledgment for the use of photographs is made to Danesin, Padua, for Figs. 2, 3, and 4.

of the work of Giotto and his followers." [2] Of Petrarch's "fervent, yet systematic and scientific labors devoted to antiquity," it has justly been said that they "mark a phase of the greatest moment in this development." [3]

But perhaps even more important than this personal interest in contemporary art and in ancient archaeology is the fact that through his literary work Petrarch gave many ideas to the artists of later generations. In the standard work on this topic, Prince d'Essling and Eugène Müntz came to the conclusion that "a historian who neglects [this influence] passes over one of the most operative factors of the Renaissance." [4] Above all it was, of course, the *Trionfi* which inspired artistic imagination, and so we find throughout the Renaissance a large number of representations of Petrarch's triumphs, some of the whole series and some of only a single triumph.[5] But other works of Petrarch were also to exert a definite influence upon artistic creation, as Prince d'Essling and E. Müntz have shown.[6]

The case of Petrarch's main historical work, *De viris illustribus,* a collection of biographies of great Roman statesmen and generals, is of particular interest. In most of the other instances Petrarch's influence was posthumous. But here we know that his book was adapted by painters during his lifetime and under his very eyes. Moreover, we even know the motive which inspired his patron, Francesco il Vecchio da Carrara, to commission the frescoes representing Petrarch's historical work in the palace at Padua. This information we obtain from Petrarch's faithful disciple, Lombardo della Seta, whom he appointed his

[2] M. Meiss, *Painting in Florence and Siena after the Black Death,* Princeton, 1951, p. 6; see *ibid.,* pp. 70–71; for Petrarch's remarks concerning Giotto, see R. Salvini, *Giotto, bibliografia,* Rome, 1938, p. 5 notes 9–11.

[3] F. Antal, *Florentine Painting and Its Social Background,* London, 1947, p. 103.

[4] [V. Masséna] Prince d'Essling and E. Müntz, *Pétrarque: ses études d'art, son influence sur les artistes, ses portraits et ceux de Laure, l'illustration de ses écrits,* Paris, 1902, p. 60; see also L. Venturi, "La critica d'arte e F. Petrarca," *L'Arte,* XXV, 1922, pp. 238–244; L. Chiovenda, "Die Zeichnungen Petrarcas," *Archivum Romanicum,* XVII, 1933, pp. 1–61 (with bibliography).

[5] See W. Weisbach, *Trionfi,* Berlin, 1919, *passim.*

[6] D'Essling and Müntz, *op. cit.,* ch. III (pp. 83–100).

literary executor.[7] In 1379, five years after Petrarch's death, Lombardo completed his continuation of the work *De viris illustribus,* which Petrarch had left unfinished. In his dedicatory preface Lombardo addresses Francesco il Vecchio as follows: "As an ardent lover of the virtues, you have extended hospitality to these *viri illustres,* not only in your heart and mind, but also very magnificently in the most beautiful part of your palace. According to the custom of the ancients you have honored them with gold and purple, and with images and inscriptions you have set them up for admiration. . . . To the inward conception of your keen mind you have given outward expression in the form of most excellent pictures, so that you may always keep in sight these men whom you are eager to love because of the greatness of their deeds." [8]

If the decoration of the Sala Virorum Illustrium in Padua had been preserved in the original form inspired by Petrarch and commissioned by Francesco da Carrara, we would have a singular opportunity to study and understand how the essence of an important literary work was expressed in painting. The almost complete destruction of the frescoes seems, at first glance, to have deprived us of that opportunity. However, sufficient evidence remains so that we can attempt to reconstruct, to a certain extent at least, the original decoration.[9]

The first problem which arises is the question as to when the

[7] On Lombardo, see G. Ferrante, "Lombardo della Seta umanista padovano," *Atti d. R. Istituto Veneto d. Scienze, Lettere ed Arti,* XCIII, part II, 1933–34, pp. 445–487; G. Billanovich, *Petrarca letterato,* Rome, 1947, I, part III, *passim.*

[8] Paris, Bibliothèque Nationale, Cod. Lat. 6069 F, fol. 144r: "Hos non modo mente et animo ut uirtutum amantissimus hospes digne suscepisti, sed et aule tue pulcerrima parte magnifice collocasti et more maiorum hospitaliter honoratos auro et purpura cultos ymaginibus et titulis admirandos ornatissime tua prestitit magni animi gloriosa conceptio, que cum similes sui ut supra dictum est reddat effectus, nec tui nec innate uirtutis oblitus in forma excellentissime picture extrinsecus expressisti, quod intus ab arduo erat conceptum ingenio, ut assidue in conspectu haberes, quos diligere ob magnitudinem rerum studueras." Compare the somewhat faulty edition of Lombardo's preface by D. Rossetti, *Petrarca, Giulio Celso e Boccaccio,* Trieste, 1828, pp. 226–232.

[9] The first and most basic treatment of the problem was by J. von Schlosser, "Ein Veronesisches Bilderbuch und die höfische Kunst des XIV. Jahrhunderts," *Jahrbuch der Kunsthistorischen Sammlungen des Allerhöchsten Kaiserhauses,* XVI, 1895, pp. 183–193.

frescoes of the hall were painted. The dates which have been assigned so far vary from the late 1340's [10] to a date before 1370.[11] It is, however, possible to fix the date somewhat more precisely by taking into consideration the fact that Francesco da Carrara comissioned the frescoes only after Petrarch had dedicated his work *De viris illustribus* to him.[12] The final preface, containing this dedication, is undated. But a study of the relationship which existed between Petrarch and Francesco il Vecchio permits us to establish quite definitely the date *post quem* of the dedication of the book and, consequently, also that of the beginning of the decoration.

Francesco was the son of Giacomo da Carrara with whom Petrarch, in his younger years, had been on very close terms.[13] The news of Giacomo's assassination by members of his own family, in 1350, came as a terrible shock to Petrarch, and for more than seven years he avoided Padua. It was only in 1358 that he revisited the city, of which Francesco il Vecchio had by then assumed the government. From that year on, Petrarch again frequented Padua for longer or shorter periods and ultimately, from 1367 to his death in 1374, he resided there and in nearby Arquà more often than anywhere else. During his stays in Padua, Petrarch of course got to know the lord of the city but, to judge from a letter written in 1361, his relationship with Francesco remained at first quite formal.[14] Evidently, it was only after Petrarch had become a more or less permanent

10 A. Fitzgerald, "Guariento di Arpo," *Memoirs of the American Academy in Rome,* IX, 1931, pp. 170 and 176.—H. Keller, "Die Entstehung des Bildnisses am Ende des Hochmittelalters," *Römisches Jahrbuch für Kunstgeschichte,* III, 1939, p. 355, dates the frescoes "between 1347 and 1365."

11 P. de Nolhac, "Le 'De viris illustribus' de Pétrarque," *Notices et Extraits des Manuscrits de la Bibliothèque Nationale et autres Bibliothèques,* XXXIV, 1891, p. 64, n. 3, and, following him, d'Essling and Müntz, *op. cit.,* p. 46.

12 On this dedication, see de Nolhac, *op. cit.,* pp. 63–65; G. Martellotti, "Epitome e Compendio," *Orientamenti Culturali,* II, 1946, pp. 209–211.

13 On Petrarch's relationship with the Carrara family, see A. Zardo, *Il Petrarca e i Carraresi,* Milan, 1887; A. Gloria, *Documenti inediti intorno al Petrarca,* Padua, 1878; A. Medin, "Il Petrarca a Padua e ad Arquà," *Padova a F. Petrarca,* Padua, 1904, pp. 3 ff.; A. Limentani, "L'amicizia fra il Petrarca e i principi di Carrara," *Padova: Rassegna Mensile del Comune di Padova,* X, 1937; G. Billanovich, *op. cit.,* I, pp. 297 ff.

14 See *Fam.* (ed. V. Rossi) XXIII, 20, §§ 5–6.

resident of the principality of the Carrara that a true friendship developed between the two men, as a large number of letters indicates, which Petrarch either addressed directly to Francesco or in which he spoke of him. These letters were all written between the years 1367 and 1374.[15] We learn from them that the prince endeavored in every possible way to show the respect and the admiration which he felt for the poet. Thus, for instance, he appeared in person to greet Petrarch on his return from a journey, had his own physician attend him, and called on him to deliver personally unhappy news of one of Petrarch's closest friends, news which later fortunately proved to be false.[16] Theirs was not a relationship between lord and subject but between man and man, and consequently their conversations were characterized by complete frankness and cordiality.[17] Petrarch, on his side, had high regard for Francesco's statesmanship and took a great interest in the political affairs of Padua.[18] He even went so far, not long before his death, as to write for the prince a treatise in which he undertook to outline and discuss in quite meticulous fashion the administrative problems and tasks of the government of the city.[19] Petrarch's gratitude toward Francesco found its ultimate expression in one of the stipulations of his last will in which he left to him his picture of the Virgin by Giotto.[20] This gift was a token of his appreciation of the fact that his closing years in Padua and Arquà had been so pleasant because "the lord of these places, a very wise man, loves and honors me, not as a master but as a son does, both on account of his own affection for me and in memory of his magnanimous father who loved me like a brother." [21]

The intimate friendship between the two men bore rich fruit

[15] *Sen.* x, 2; xi, 2, 3, and 17; xiii, 8; xiv, 1 and 2; xv, 5; *Epistola Posteritati,* ed. E. Carrara, *Annali d. Istituto Superiore d. Magist. di Torino,* iii, 1929, p. 308, § 40.—As to the dates of these letters, compare the extremely helpful chronological list and the bibliographical references given by E. H. Wilkins, *The Prose Letters of Petrarch: A Manual,* New York, 1951.

[16] *Sen.* xi, 2; xiii, 8; xi, 3.

[17] Cf. *Sen.* xiii, 9; xiv, 1 and 2.

[18] *Sen.* x, 2; xiv, 2.

[19] *Sen.* xiv, 1 (ed. V. Ussani, Padua, 1922).

[20] G. Fracassetti, *F. Petrarcae epistolae de rebus familiaribus,* Florence, 1863, iii, p. 541; the document dates of 1370, not of 1361, as R. Salvini, *Giotto,* p. 5, n. 11, assumes.

[21] *Sen.* xv, 5.

because it resulted, on the part of Petrarch, in the resumption of his work *De viris illustribus* [22] and, on the part of Francesco da Carrara, in the commissioning of the painting of the Sala Virorum Illustrium.

Petrarch's interest in history dated back to his early youth, and, after his first visit to Rome in 1336, he resolved to write a great historical work in the form of a collection of biographies of "the illustrious men of all countries and ages." [23] Soon after starting this ambitious undertaking Petrarch apparently realized that the only history which truly interested him was that of Rome, and thus he decided to limit himself to writing the biographies of all the famous statesmen of Rome "from the time of Romulus to that of Titus." [24] In consequence, during the late 1330's and early 1340's, he wrote a number of lives of great figures in Roman history. After this brief period of intensive historical work, other interests monopolized his attention so that he never completed even this more restricted project. But although Petrarch actually did very little work on *De viris illustribus,* he kept it in his mind and mentioned it rather frequently in other works and in his letters and conversations.[25] In spite of this continuous interest it seems likely,

[22] Cf. Zardo, *op. cit.,* pp. 180 ff.; de Nolhac, *op. cit.,* pp. 63 ff.; Martellotti, *op. cit.,* pp. 209 f.

[23] *Fam.* VIII, 3, § 12.

[24] On the complex question of the chronology of the various versions of *De viris illustribus,* see especially de Nolhac, *op. cit.,* pp. 61–109; E. Carrara, *Petrarca,* Rome, 1937, pp. 37–40; T. E. Mommsen, "Petrarch's Conception of the Dark Ages," *Speculum,* XVII, 1942, pp. 228–234 [see above, pp. 106–129]; G. Martellotti, "Sulla composizione del De viris e dell'Africa del Petrarca," *Annali d. Scuola Normale Superiore di Pisa,* ser. II, X, 1941, pp. 247–262; "Petrarca e Cesare," *ibid.,* XVI, 1947, pp. 149–158; "Epitome e Compendio," *Orientamenti Culturali,* II, 1946, pp. 205–216.—In a recent article, "Linee di sviluppo dell'umanesimo Petrarchesco," *Studi Petrarcheschi,* II, 1949, pp. 51–80, Prof. Martellotti attempts to show that "il più vasto 'De viris' [i.e., that version which contains the Biblical lives] sarebbe posteriore a quello da Romolo a Tito" (*op. cit.,* p. 53). Prof. Martellotti's arguments for this thesis (which is also maintained, though for different reasons, by C. Calcaterra, *Nella selva del Petrarca,* Bologna, 1942, pp. 415 ff.), are very interesting, but in my forthcoming study of Petrarch's historical works I hope to be able, on the basis of additional evidence, to reaffirm the validity of P. de Nolhac's chronology. [See above, p. 127, n. 79.]

[25] See, e.g., *Rerum Memorandarum libri,* I, 2 (ed. G. Billanovich, Florence, 1943, p. 273); *De vita solitaria,* I, 10 (in Petrarch's *Opera,* ed. Basel, 1581,

however, that Petrarch would never have attempted any final "editing" of that work, had it not been for Francesco da Carrara. For we learn from Petrarch himself that it was Francesco who requested him "to collect his scattered biographies in one book." [26] After Petrarch's death, Lombardo della Seta likewise stated that the collection of biographies of a number of illustrious men was "ordered" by Francesco il Vecchio.[27] It is evident that we owe the final redaction of Petrarch's main historical work in the form in which it has come down to posterity to the initiative of Francesco da Carrara.

When one considers Francesco's decisive role, it seems only just that Petrarch should have inscribed the work to him. But from Petrarch's point of view this final dedication actually signified a much higher and more unusual honor than appears at first glance. For when he started the work in 1337 and 1338, far from dedicating it to a prince, he declared explicitly that "the princes of our days furnish material merely for satire, not for history." [28] Fifteen years later, in 1354, when the German king and later emperor Charles IV asked that the book *De viris illustribus* be inscribed to himself, Petrarch replied frankly and to Charles' face: "Know, Caesar, that you will be worthy, at long last, of this gift and of the dignity of the title of this

---

p. 240); *Invectiva contra medicum quendam*, I. II (*ibid.*, p. 1095); *Fam.* VIII, 7, § 5; IX, 15, § 1; XIX, 3, §§ 12–13; XX, 8, § 11.

[26] See Petrarch's final preface to *De viris illustribus* (ed. Razzolini, Bologna, 1874, I, p. 2), in the following, quoted from Cod. Paris. Lat. 6069 F, fol. 1r: "Illustres quosdam uiros, quos excellenti gloria floruisse doctissimorum hominum ingenia memorie tradiderunt, in diuersis uoluminibus tanquam sparsos ac disseminatos rogatu tuo, plaustrifer insignis, qui modestissimo nutu inclite urbis Patauine sceptra unice geris, locum in unum colligere et quasi quodammodo stipare arbitratus sum." G. Martellotti (*Orientamenti Culturali*, II, 1946, p. 207) was the first to point out the importance of the fact that it is only in this preface that the qualifying term "quidam viri illustres" is used; before that Petrarch always spoke of *the* illustrious men; cf. Martellotti, *ibid.*, p. 210.

[27] See Lombardo's preface to his continuation of the *Compendium* (in Petrarch's *Opera*, ed. 1581, p. 502), in the following, quoted from Cod. Paris. Lat. 6069 G, fol. 9v: "Iussisti enim multa et maxima quorundam uirorum facta prius quodam epithomate neque prolixo neque artato, sed mediocri stilo declarari."

[28] See Petrarch's first preface to *De viris illustribus*, ed. de Nolhac, *op. cit.*, p. 111, ll. 22–24.

book, not simply because of a resplendent name or a meaningless diadem, but only when, because of your deeds and the *virtus* of your mind, you have finally joined the company of illustrious men and when you have lived so that posterity will read of you what you read about the ancients." [29] The bitter disappointment which Petrarch was soon to feel about Charles' Italian policy ended any thought he may have had of ever inscribing the book to him. Nor did Petrarch deem any of the other powerful men with whom he was connected throughout his life worthy of the honor. It was saved for the last of his princely patrons, Francesco il Vecchio, whom, in a letter of 1373, he indeed calls "vir illustris." [30]

In view of the fact that Petrarch attributed such great significance to the dedication of this particular work, it seems safe to assume that he inscribed it to Francesco da Carrara only after he had established a really close relationship with him. As we have seen from Petrarch's correspondence, this was not before the year 1367, which therefore appears to be the earliest possible date of the final preface to *De viris illustribus.* Since the resumption of Petrarch's historical work was directly connected with the prince's desire for its pictorial representation in his palace,[31] it follows that the same year 1367 has to be regarded also as the *terminus post quem* for the beginning of the decoration of the hall. Because the painters had to know which men and how many of them were to be depicted in the hall, Petrarch must have made, at the same time, his final selection of the Roman heroes. We can therefore assume that not only the twenty-four biographies of *De viris illustribus* which were written by Petrarch himself, but also the twelve others which, after Petrarch's death, were added by Lombardo della Seta, formed part of the plan agreed upon with Francesco il Vecchio in or shortly after the year 1367.[32]

[29] *Fam.* XIX, 3, § 13: "Quod autem ad te, Cesar, ita demum hoc te munere et eius libri titulo dignum scito, si non fulgore nominis tantum aut inani dyademate, sed rebus gestis et virtute animi illustribus tete viris ascripseris et sic vixeris, ut, cum veteres legeris, tu legaris a posteris."

[30] See the last sentence of *Sen.* XIV, 1 (ed. V. Ussani, p. 47).

[31] See Lombardo's statement, quoted supra, note 8.

[32] See de Nolhac, *op. cit.,* pp. 64 f.; Martellotti, *op. cit.,* pp. 209 f.

By 1370 the decoration of the hall was so far advanced that the project was known even outside Padua. For we learn from a notice in Piero Buoninsegni's *Florentine History* concerning the death of the Florentine condottiere Manno Donati and his burial in Padua that "the lord [i.e., Francesco il Vecchio] had Manno's portrait painted in a hall among the other men famous for their feats of arms." [33] A letter from Lombardo asks Petrarch "to insert Manno in the work *De viris illustribus* . . . and thus to make him deservedly eternal among the mortals." [34] Petrarch could not assent to this request because long ago he had decided to exclude men of his own era from the work, but it is likely that he composed at least an inscription for Manno's tomb.[35] Francesco da Carrara, on the other hand, evidently deemed his Florentine contemporary worthy of the same honor which he was rendering to the great war lords of ancient Rome and had Manno portrayed in one of the halls of his palace, though not in the Sala Virorum Illustrium itself, which remained reserved for the heroes of antiquity.[36]

As to when the decoration of the hall was completed, long discussion is unnecessary: the *terminus ante quem* is January 25, 1379, the day on which Lombardo della Seta, according to his own statement, finished his continuation of *De viris illustribus*.[37] Shortly before he set down that date, at the beginning of his last biography, that of Trajan, Lombardo addresses himself

[33] P. Buoninsegni, *Historia Fiorentina,* Florence, 1580, p. 548 (ad. a. 1370): ". . . hauuta la vittoria ne venne a Padoua e dopo pochi gironi passò di questa vita e fu sepellito in Padoua con grandissimi honori, e fecelo il signore dipignere in una sala fra gli altri huomini famosi in fatti d'arme." Buoninsegni's account was repeated by Sozomeno da Pistoia in his *Chronicon Universale* (ed. Muratori, *Rerum Italicarum Scriptores,* Milan, 1730, XVI, p. 1090); see also Scipione Ammirato, *Istorie Fiorentine,* Florence, 1848, III, p. 213.—The date of Manno Donati's death is controversial; A. Zardo, *Il Petrarca e i Carraresi,* pp. 119–124, believes that Manno did not die until 1374, but his arguments are not convincing.

[34] The letter was edited by de Nolhac, *op. cit.,* p. 103, n. 3: "Hunc [i.e., Manno] scilicet te intra opus Illustrium inserere rogo. . . . Arripe, quaeso, illum tuum disertissimum calamum, quo soles strenuos illustrare viros, et hunc merito fac inter mortales eternum."

[35] See de Nolhac, *op. cit.,* p. 64, n. 3.

[36] See von Schlosser, *op. cit.,* p. 185.

[37] See de Nolhac, *op. cit.,* p. 73 (from Cod. Paris. Lat. 6069 F, fol. 195).

to Francesco il Vecchio as follows: "I know that you, gracious lord of Padua, are eagerly waiting for the conclusion of this work so that you can learn briefly and in the right order about the deeds of your famous heroes. For this reason, just as you have placed Trajan among the others in the extreme corner of your beautiful hall, so I, in this work, set out to treat him as the last one." [38]

The frescoes in the Sala Virorum Illustrium of the Carrara palace in Padua which illustrated the lives of the great Romans in Petrarch's *De viris illustribus* must, therefore, have been painted between the years 1367 and 1379.

In regard to the dates of the portraits of Petrarch and Lombardo della Seta which were painted on one of the small sides of the same hall, we are somewhat less certain. If the portrait of Petrarch which is still to be seen in the hall, although greatly retouched (Fig. 4), was actually the work of Guariento, as some scholars believe,[39] it must have been painted before 1370, the year of Guariento's death. This attribution can be supported by the fact that Guariento worked in Padua from early in 1368 until he died, that is, during the years when the decoration of the hall had already been started. Furthermore, such a likeness from life would not have been unusual, because other portraits, executed while Petrarch was alive, were in various Italian palaces.[40] However, in view of the complete silence of all our sources, including the naturally well-informed eye-witness Lombardo della Seta, it seems more likely that the portrait was made only after Petrarch's death in 1374 or even after Lombardo had

[38] Cod. Paris. Lat. 6069 F, fol. 194r, ed. de Nolhac, *op. cit.*, p. 81, n. 1: "Scio enim te, urbis Patavi inclite rector, tuorum clarissimorum heroum gradatim ut breviter acta cognoscas, huiusce opusculi avide finem exposcere. Ideoque ut in ultimo angulo tue venustissime aule Trayanum inter ceteros collocasti, ita et in hoc opere novissimum tradere perquiro. . . ."

[39] E.g., A. Moschetti, "Per un antico ritratto del Petrarca," *Padova a F. Petrarca,* Padua, 1904, pp. 8 f.; A. Fitzgerald, "Guariento," *Memoirs of the American Academy in Rome,* IX, 1931, pp. 176 f.; the portrait was reproduced by V. Rossi in the first volume of his edition of Petrarch's *Familiari,* Rome, 1933, with the caption: "forse dipinto dal Guariento."

[40] See d'Essling and Müntz, *op. cit.*, pp. 62 ff.; A. Ratti (Pope Pius XI), *Un antico ritratto di F. Petrarca all'Ambrosiana,* Milan, 1907; R. Weiss, *Il primo secolo dell'umanesimo,* Rome, 1949, pp. 75–77, 81.

written, in 1379 and 1380, the two prefaces to his continuations of Petrarch's historical works. Consequently, the portrait has been attributed to a number of other masters active in Padua during the last decades of the fourteenth century, including Altichiero of Verona, Jacopo Avanzo of Padua and Giusto de' Menabuoi.[41] It has even been held to have been painted in the early fifteenth century because "the forms of the furniture, which are still Gothic, and the acquaintance with, though still awkward employment of, linear perspective, point to the time of Pisanello." [42] Most scholars have rejected this later dating,[43] and their arguments seem to be supported by a fresco in the church of the Abbey of Viboldone near Milan representing the Doctors of the Church and showing in one part a monk studying in his cell (Fig. 5). The whole setting of this monastic study is very much like that of the portrait of Petrarch in the Sala Virorum Illustrium, in respect both to the particular kind of perspective used and to the Gothic milieu. The fresco in Viboldone was painted between 1363 and 1365 and has been assigned either to a painter who was strongly influenced by the Tuscan school of Giotto's followers [44] or, more specifically, to Giusto de' Menabuoi.[45] The question of whether or not the two frescoes were painted by the same master can be answered only on the basis of additional comparative material. But the noticeable similarity of the perspective certainly allows the assumption that the Paduan portrait of Petrarch was painted about the same time as the picture in Viboldone, that is, in the last third of the fourteenth century. In view of the political developments which took place in Padua

[41] E.g., G. Cittadella, "Petrarca a Padova e ad Arquà," *Padova a F. Petrarca,* Padua, 1874, p. 67, n. 3, and R. Van Marle, *The Development of the Italian Schools of Painting,* The Hague, 1924, IV, p. 152, attributed it to Altichiero; L. Coletti, "Studi sulla pittura del Trecento a Padova," *Rivista d'Arte,* XII, 1930, p. 360, to Giusto; S. Bettini, *Giusto de' Menabuoi e l'arte del Trecento,* Padua, 1944, pp. 71 and 123, n. 22, to Avanzo.

[42] Schlosser, *op. cit.,* p. 189; see d'Essling and Müntz, *op. cit.,* p. 64.

[43] See especially Moschetti, *op. cit.,* pp. 8 f.; Fitzgerald, *op. cit.,* p. 176.

[44] F. Wittgens, *Gli affreschi della Badia degli Umiliati a Viboldone,* Milan, 1933, pp. 29 ff.

[45] Bettini, *op. cit.,* pp. 45–50; see *ibid.,* pl. 21, the reproduction of the whole fresco in question.

at that time, it appears possible to determine the date *ante quem* even more closely. For in 1388 Francesco il Vecchio was vanquished by a coalition of Milan and Venice and condemned to end his life as a prisoner of Gian Galeazzo Visconti. His son Francesco Novello reconquered Padua in 1390 but his position remained precarious, politically as well as financially, until the final collapse of the power of the Carrara family in 1405. These external difficulties, and the fact that Francesco Novello showed himself quite uninterested in Petrarch's literary legacy,[46] seem to justify the conclusion that the portrait of Petrarch was painted when the older Francesco was still in power, that is, before the year 1388.[47]

The portrait of Lombardo della Seta, the counterpart of the Petrarch portrait in the hall, was so completely painted over in the sixteenth and seventeenth centuries that its original style and appearance cannot be determined. It has been rightly assumed, however, that it was painted during the reign of Francesco il Vecchio, probably in recognition of Lombardo's completion of Petrarch's *De viris illustribus,* that is, between the years 1380 and 1388.[48] In the case of this portrait, it is absolutely certain that it was not done under the rule of Francesco Novello. For, during the Milanese occupation of Padua, Lombardo entered the service of the victors and on Francesco Novello's return to power, in 1390, had to flee to Venice where he died a few weeks later. In accordance with his last wishes, he was to be buried near Petrarch in Arquà. But Francesco Novello resented so deeply his collaboration with the Viscontis that he ordered the body to be sent back to Venice.[49]

46 See Billanovich, *Petrarca letterato,* I, pp. 336–341.

47 The popularity of the Paduan fresco portrait is shown by the fact that in the early fifteenth century it was copied by the illuminator of a manuscript of Petrarch's *Rime* (Florence, Biblioteca Nazionale, Cod. Palat. 184 fol. Ov; see Fig. 7); a copy of this illumination is to be found in another manuscript of the *Rime,* which was written in the later fifteenth century (Florence, Biblioteca Laurenziana, Cod. Strozz. 172 fol. Or).

48 See G. Ferrante, "Lombardo della Seta umanista padovano," *Atti d. R. Istituto Veneto d. Scienze, Lettere ed Arti,* XCIII, part II, 1933–34, p. 457; Billanovich, *op. cit.,* I, p. 320.

49 The documentary evidence of this interesting incident was recently discovered by G. Billanovich, *op. cit.,* I, pp. 334 f.

Use in this article of the designation "Sala Virorum Illustrium" is appropriate, for it is found in two Paduan documents of the years 1382 and 1390.[50] The very name of the hall as it appears in these official records demonstrates most clearly the close connection which in the eyes of contemporaries existed between the decoration and Petrarch's homonymous work.

The earliest descriptive information about the hall as a whole is obtained through the treatise *De laudibus Patavii,* which was composed by Michele Savonarola in 1446 or 1447.[51] In his description of the "Capitanei curia," that is, the former palace of the Carrara family, which by that time had become the residence of the Venetian governor of Padua, Michele Savonarola says: "There are two very large rooms which are elaborately decorated with pictures. The first of these rooms is called the 'Sala Thebarum,'[52] the other one, which is larger and more glorious than the first, is named the 'Sala Imperatorum.' In this room are depicted the Roman generals [*Romani imperatores*], in wonderful figures and with their triumphs, painted in gold and with the best colors. The representation of these men was the work of the famous painters Ottaviano and Altichiero. This is indeed an imperial palace and worthy of an emperor."[53]

[50] See A. Gloria, *Documenti inediti intorno al Petrarca,* Padua, 1878, p. 36 (ad a. 1382): "in sala virorum illustrium"; *ibid.* (ad a. 1390): "super podiolos iuxta salam novam illustrium virorum." Gloria's documentary material gives a very illuminating insight into the variety and the wealth of decorations in the many rooms of the Carrara palace of the fourteenth century.—In Galeazzo and Bartolomeo Gatari's *Cronaca Carrarese,* which was composed at the end of the fourteenth century, the hall is called "[la] grande salla de l'inperadori" (ed. A. Medin and G. Tolomei, in Muratori, *Rerum Italicarum Scriptores,* Città di Castello, 1914, XVII, part I, p. 408, ad a. 1390).

[51] Ed. A. Segarizzi, in Muratori, *Rerum Italicarum Scriptores,* Città di Castello, 1902, XXIV, part 15; as to the date of the treatise, see *ibid.,* p. viii; on the reliability of Savonarola's statements concerning the various works of art in Padua, see Segarizzi's remarks, *ibid.,* p. 44, n. 2.

[52] On this hall, see Schlosser, *op. cit.,* p. 184.

[53] Ed. Segarizzi, *op. cit.,* p. 49: "Cumque honoratas scalas ascendis, podiola lodiam parte in superiori circuentia, columpnis marmoreis ac magnificis fenestris, que ad utranque curiam aspectum habent, etiam ornata invenis. Stantque due amplissime et picturis ornatissime sale ad latera horum situate, quarum prima *Thebarum* nuncupatur, altera *Imperatorum*

The details of this statement will be discussed later. At this point, only one particular item requires immediate clarification. In speaking of the figures of the *Romani imperatores* in the Sala Virorum Illustrium, Savonarola certainly did not mean to imply that the hall contained pictures of "emperors" exclusively.[54] He rather made use purposely of the double meaning of the word, because this allowed him to say that "the hall of the Roman generals" was truly "imperial" or majestic. This interpretation of the phrase in question is confirmed by the observation that a hall in the Palazzo Trinci in Foligno, which contains a similar series of frescoes depicting a number of great men of the Roman Republic and Empire, was in the fifteenth century likewise called "la sala de l'imperatori." [55]

The next information about the hall is found in the *Notizia d'opere del disegno* by the so-called Anonimo Morelliano, that is, by Marcanton Michiel, who wrote about a hundred years later than Michele Savonarola. Michiel says: "In the Sala dei Giganti, according to Campagnola, Jacopo Avanzo painted on the left side the captivity of Jugurtha and the triumph of Marius; on the right side, Guariento of Padua painted the twelve Caesars and their deeds. According to Andrea Riccio, the painters working there were Altichiero and Ottaviano of Brescia. There are portrayed Petrarch and Lombardo who, I believe, supplied the subject-matter of these pictures." [56]

---

nominatur prima maior atque gloriosior, in qua Romani imperatores miris cum figuris cumque triumphis, auro optimoque cum colore depicti sunt. Quos gloriose manus illustrium pictorum Octaviani et Alticherii configurarunt. Hec vero domus imperatoria est et imperatore digna: cui camere, amena viridaria, ecclesia, officialium loca et advenarum hospitia quam magnifica minime desunt."

[54] As to the name "la salla de l'inperadori," as used in Gatari's *Cronaca Carrarese,* see supra, note 50.

[55] See M. Salmi, "Gli affreschi del Palazzo Trinci a Foligno," *Bollettino d'Arte,* XIII, 1919, p. 160, n. 1.

[56] Anonimo Morelliano (Marcanton Michiel), *Notizia d'opere del disegno,* ed. T. Frimmel, Vienna, 1888, p. 34: "Nella sala di Giganti, segondo el Campagnola, Jacomo Dauanzo dipinse a man mancha la captiuita di Giugurta, et triompho di Mario. Guariento Padoano li XII Cesari a man dextra e li lor fatti. Segondo Andrea Rizzo ui dipinsero Altichierio et Octauiano Bressano. Iui sono ritratti el Petrarcha et Lombardo, i quali credo dessero l'argomento di quella pittura."

In the evaluation of this statement, it is important to notice that Marcanton Michiel merely expresses an opinion of his own in the last sentence quoted, concerning the portraits of Petrarch and Lombardo and their presumable participation in the choice of the pictorial topics. In regard to the other frescoes, however, Michiel declares explicitly that his account is based on the information of two earlier Paduan authorities, Gerolamo Campagnola (who flourished in the second part of the fifteenth century), and Andrea Riccio (who lived from 1470 to 1532).[57] Of these two, Riccio's information confirms, or simply repeats, Michele Savonarola's statement that the Sala Virorum Illustrium was decorated by Altichiero of Verona (died ca. 1385),[58] and by Ottaviano Prandino of Brescia (flourished 1370–1420).[59] Gerolamo Campagnola on the other hand, attributes the frescoes to two entirely different painters, Guariento (died 1370) and Jacopo Avanzo of Padua (flourished in the second part of the fourteenth century).[60]

As we have seen before, Guariento was active in Padua between 1368 and 1370, so that his participation in the decoration of the Sala Virorum Illustrium, which is also asserted by Vasari,[61] could well be fitted into the chronology of the work. The fact that he died so shortly after the start of the enterprise could be taken as an explanation of why it had to be completed by other artists. But in view of the scarcity of the documentary material at our disposal, the thesis of Guariento's share in the decoration of the hall cannot claim more than a hypothetical

57 On Gerolamo Campagnola, see Milanesi's remarks in his edition of Vasari's *Vite,* III, p. 385, notes 1 and 2, p. 634, n. 1, p. 636, n. 4; W. Kallab, *Vasaristudien,* Vienna, 1908, pp. 347–354; Thieme-Becker, *Künstler-Lexikon,* V, p. 451; on Andrea Riccio, see Thieme-Becker, *op. cit.,* XXVIII, p. 259.

58 Thieme-Becker, *op. cit.,* I, p. 351; E. Sandberg Vavalà, *La Pittura Veronese,* Verona, 1926, pp. 156–189; L. Coletti, *Rivista d'Arte,* XII, 1930, pp. 323–380.

59 See Thieme-Becker, *op. cit.,* XXVII, p. 346.

60 See Thieme-Becker, *op. cit.,* II, p. 270; L. Coletti, *Rivista d'Arte,* XIII, 1931, pp. 303–363.

61 Vasari, *Vite,* ed. Milanesi, III, pp. 636 f.: "Guariero pittor padovano . . . dipinse . . . la sala degl'Imperadori romani, dove nel tempo di carnovale vanno gli scolari a danzare." Vasari, in this connection, does not mention any of the other painters named in Michiel's statement.

value. Nor does it seem possible to decide with any real certainty whether Campagnola and Riccio supplement or contradict one another in their statements quoted by Marcanton Michiel concerning the participation of Avanzo, Altichiero, and Ottaviano Prandino in the work.[62] It seems significant that Michiel himself did not choose to make any decision between these conflicting authorities.

Another puzzling question is raised by the statement attributed to Campagnola that the hall contained the portraits of "the twelve Caesars." For the book *De viris illustribus* included the biographies of only four of the Roman emperors, and certainly neither Petrarch nor Francesco da Carrara ever intended to glorify in their Hall of Fame the memory of all of the first twelve Roman emperors portrayed in Suetonius' work. Thus it seems more likely to assume that Campagnola, like Michele Savonarola before him and Vasari after him, knew that the room was called "the Hall of the *Romani Imperatores*," but did not realize that in this case the word *imperatores* had the meaning of "general"; consequently, he saw in the name of the hall a reference to the popular title of Suetonius' book on "the twelve Caesars." The assumption of such a linguistic misunderstanding would appear to offer a very simple explanation, were it not for the fact that Campagnola was a native of Padua and ought therefore to have known that there were no portraits of "the twelve Caesars" in the palace. Two alternatives remain: either Marcanton Michiel did not quote verbatim from Campagnola's letter and is therefore himself responsible for the misinterpretation of the word *imperatores;* [63] or Campagnola

[62] The authorship of Guariento has been assumed, e.g., by A. Venturi, *Storia dell'Arte Italiana,* Milan, 1907, v, p. 929: A. Moschetti, *Atti e memorie d. R. Accad. d. Scienze, Lettere e Arti in Padova,* XL, 1924, p. 25; Fitzgerald, *op. cit.,* pp. 176 f. On the other hand, Schlosser, *op. cit.,* p. 185, and Van Marle, *op. cit.,* IV, p. 126, have attributed the frescoes to Altichiero and Avanzo.

[63] In accordance with Campagnola's, or Marcanton Michiel's, misstatement, modern scholars, including Venturi, *op. cit.,* v, p. 929, L. Chiovenda, in *Archivum Romanicum,* XVII, 1933, p. 10, and H. Keller, *Römisches Jahrbuch für Kunstgeschichte,* III, 1939, p. 355, have spoken of the portraits of "the twelve Caesars" in the Carrara palace; P. Schubring, in Thieme-Becker, *op. cit.,* I, p. 351, speaks of the "Kaisersaal"; Van Marle,

did not know the actual subjects of the portraits because the decoration of the Sala Virorum Illustrium had been destroyed before his time.

It was indeed during that very same period, around the turn of the fifteenth century, that the interior of the former Carrara palace suffered damage to such an extent that practically all the earlier decorations disappeared. Unfortunately, no written sources exist which give an account of that destruction, its causes and its exact date. But the restoration of the hall which was undertaken by the University of Padua in the year 1928 led to discoveries which permitted the following conclusion: "It seems that between the end of the fifteenth and the beginning of the sixteenth century a fire destroyed the ceiling of the hall and also did irremediable damage to the pictorial decorations on the walls. Abundant traces of fire were noticed on the remains of the walls of the Trecento." [64] Of all the original frescoes of the late fourteenth century, apparently only one, the portrait of Petrarch, survived that fire and even that picture had evidently been somewhat damaged, for it was partly repainted in the sixteenth and seventeenth centuries.

The present decoration of the hall was initiated in 1539 or 1540 [65] when, according to an inscription above the main door, it was resolved "to restore, in its full splendor, the hall which was near to collapse because of old age." [66] Two prominent citizens of Padua were in charge of the selection of the subject-matter and decided which heroes were to be portrayed and what scenes of their lives were to be depicted by the two painters chosen for the work, Domenico Campagnola and Stefano dall'Arzere. Giovanni Cavazza composed the *eulogia* which one of the best calligraphers of the time, Francesco de Puciviglianis,

---

op. cit., IV, p. 43, wrongly asserts that "Charlemagne . . . no doubt also figured in the hall of the giants that . . . Altichiero [frescoed] in Padua."

64 Translated from a pamphlet entitled *Appunti sulla storia della Sala dei Giganti,* which was published (ca. 1930) by the R. Università degli Studi in Padova; Professor Carlo Anti of the University of Padua was kind enough to refer me to this pamphlet and to give me a copy of it.

65 On the history of the rebuilding of the Sala dei Giganti, see A. Moschetti, in *Padova a F. Petrarca,* Padua, 1904, pp. 9 f.; the *Appunti* quoted in note 64; and O. Ronchi, *Guida di Padova,* 1932.

66 Quoted by Moschetti, *op. cit.*, p. 9: ". . . aulam vetustate pene colapsam in hunc egregium nitorem restituit."

2. Sala dei Giganti: *Eulogia* of L. Quinctius Cincinnatus and C. Fabricius Luscinus

3. Sala dei Giganti: Figures and scenes from the lives of Caesar, Q. Fabius Maximus Rullianus and Cunctator, and Augustus

4. Sala dei Giganti: Petrarch

5. Fresco in the church of the abbey of Viboldone (detail)

6. State Library of Darmstadt, Cod. 101, fol. 1v: Petrarch

7. Florence, Bibl. Nazionale, Cod. Palat. 184 (E. 5.7), fol. 0v: Petrarch

8. State Library of Darmstadt, Cod. 101, fol. 2v: King Amulius; Rhea Silvia; soldier carrying Romulus and Remus

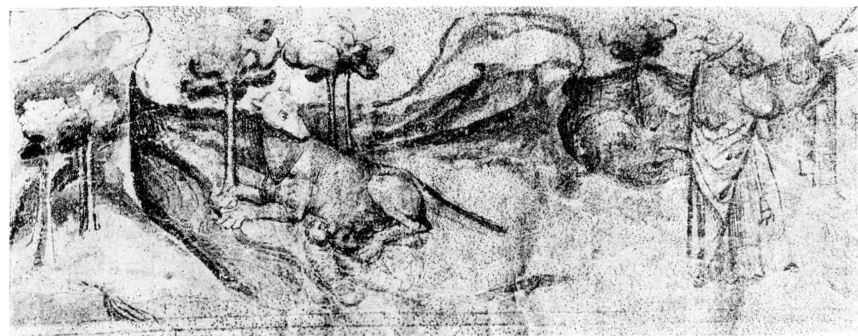

9. Cod. 101, fol. 3r: The she-wolf and the twins; Ara Larentia and the twins

10. Cod. 101, fol. 3v: Romulus (with a crown) and a group of farmers

11. Cod. 101, fol. 4r: Romulus attacking Alba; the killing of Amulius

12. Cod. 101, fol. 4v: The building of the walls of Rome; the quarrel between Romulus and Remus

13. Cod. 101, fol. 6v: The Horatii and Curiatii between the armies of Rome and Alba

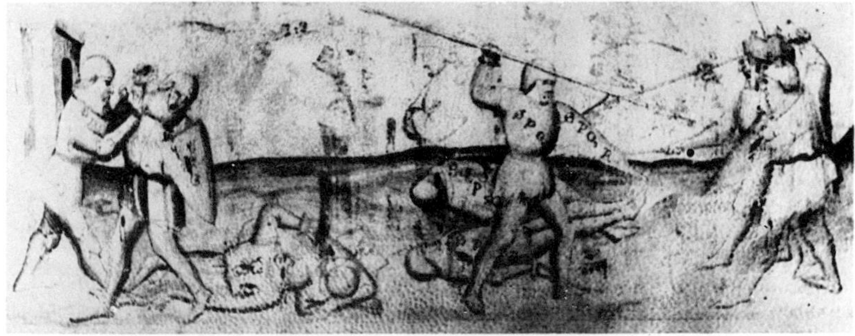

14. Cod. 101, fol. 7r: The fight between the Horatii and Curiatii (traces of buildings similar to those in Fig. 12 are visible in the background)

15. Cod. 101, fol. 7v: Ancus Martius and some nobles; the worshiping of a god (Jupiter Feretrius)

16. Cod. 101, fol. 8r: Lucretia and nobles; expulsion of Tarquinius by Brutus

17. Cod. 101, fol. 8v: Cocles beneath the Tiber bridge; the recalling of Cincinnatus

18. Cod. 101, fol. 9r: The triumph of Camillus

19. Cod. 101, fol. 11r: Camillus expelling the Gauls from Rome

20. Cod. 101, fol. 14r: T. Manlius Torquatus threatening the tribune Pomponius

21. Cod. 101, fol. 15r: Valerius Corvinus receiving the banners and shields of conquered Samnites

22. Cod. 101, fol. 18r: Fabricius and Pyrrhus' slave; extradition of the slave to Pyrrhus

23. Cod. 101, fol. 19r: The siege of a city by Alexander's army

24. Cod. 101, fol. 19v: The battle between the armies of Alexander and Darius

25. Cod. 101, fol. 20r: The finding of Darius' body

26. Cod. 101, fol. 21r: Alexander and a prisoner

27. Cod. 101, fol. 22r: Alexander worshiping a goddess

28. Cod. 101, fol. 24v: The oath of Hannibal; Hamilcar

29. Cod. 101, fol. 51v: The triumph of Claudius Nero and Livius Salinator

30. Cod. 101, fol. 53v: The triumph of P. Cornelius Scipio Africanus

31. Cod. 101, fol. 54r: Scipio Africanus, King Massinissa, Hannibal

32. State Library of Darmstadt, Cod. 101, fol. 2r: The Triumph of Fame

33. Harvard, Houghton Library, Ms. *The City of God* (ca. 1380), fol. 66v: Cain and Abel; Romulus and Remus

34. Cod. 101, fol. 5r, initial: Numa Pompilius

35. Cod. 101, fol. 7v, initial: Ancus Martius

36. Cod. 101, fol. 8r, initial: Tarquinius Superbus and Junius Brutus

37. Cod. 101, fol. 9r, initial: Camillus

38. Cod. 101, fol. 8v, initial: Horatius Cocles

39. Cod. 101, fol. 8v, initial: Cincinnatus

inscribed underneath the paintings. Because of the over life-size of the figures, the hall was immediately called the "Sala dei Giganti" and has kept the name to the present day.[67] After many vicissitudes the room was once more completely restored in 1928 and serves now as the assembly hall of the University of Padua.

The brief survey of the history of the hall has shown that the Sala dei Giganti of today represents almost entirely work of the Cinquecento and not of the late Trecento. Nevertheless, the question arises whether it is not possible to draw at least indirect inferences from the present room as to the aspect of the original Sala Virorum Illustrium.

For this purpose it seems best to list the heroes of Petrarch's book *De viris illustribus* who had been portrayed in the old hall, and to compare this series with that of the men who in the sixteenth century were represented in the Sala dei Giganti. If we assume that the images of the original *viri illustres,* like those of the latter *giganti,* were arranged on the two long walls only and not on the short ones, we obtain the following arrangement of the portraits in the old Sala Virorum Illustrium:[68]

M. Claudius Marcellus
C. Claudius Nero
M. Livius Salinator
P. Cornelius Scipio Africanus
M. Porcius Cato (Censor)
P. Cornelius Scipio Nasica
T. Quinctius Flaminius
L. Cornelius Scipio Asiaticus
L. Aemilius Paullus Macedonicus
Q. Caecilius Metellus Macedonicus
P. Cornelius Scipio Aemilianus Africanus
C. Marius
Cn. Pompeius
C. Julius Caesar
Augustus
Vespasianus
Titus
Trajanus

Romulus
Numa Pompilius
Tullus Hostilius
Ancus Martius
L. Junius Brutus
Horatius Cocles
L. Quinctius Cincinnatus
M. Furius Camillus
M. Valerius Corvinus
T. Manlius Torquatus
P. Decius Mus
L. Papirius Cursor
M. Curius Dentatus
C. Fabricius Luscinus
Alexander
Pyrrhus
Hannibal
Q. Fabius Maximus Cunctator

[67] For the first time, we find this name in Marcanton Michiel's *Notizia* (see supra, note 56), which was written between 1515 and 1541.

[68] In the following arrangement, it has been assumed that the series of the portraits of the Trecento, like that of the sixteenth century, started in the northwest corner, i.e., on the right side, of the hall.

Before giving the scheme of the portraits in the Sala dei Giganti, it is necessary to describe briefly the present aspect of the hall as a whole.[69] The main door is in the center of the north wall, and another door is on the opposite wall near the southeast corner. On each of the two short sides of the room are three large windows which leave space for four portraits on the west wall and for only two on the east wall. The decorations on the two long sides are divided by pilasters into fifteen panels on each side. The upper part of each of the panels contains from one to three standing figures, the *giganti*.[70] Underneath these figures each panel contains frescoes of historical scenes and, beneath these, inscriptions of the *eulogia* of varying length.[71] The number of scenes and inscriptions (or *tituli*) in each panel always agrees with the number of figures portrayed above in the same panel.[72]

The arrangement of the portraits in the Sala dei Giganti presents the following scheme: [73]

West Wall

Petrarch (*window*) Asinius Stella (*window*) C. Valerius Flaccus (*window*) Lombardo della Seta

South Wall	North Wall
Charlemagne	Romulus
M. Tullius Cicero M. Attilius Regulus M. Junius Brutus	A. Cornelius Cossus M. Claudius Marcellus
Theodosius	Numa Pompilius

[69] See Fig. 1; the picture has been taken from the east wall; in the upper left-hand corner is the portrait of Petrarch (see Fig. 4). [Fig. 1 of this article has been omitted for technical reasons.]

[70] See Fig. 3, which shows, in one panel, the figures of Q. Fabius Maximus Rullianus and Q. Fabius Maximus Cunctator, flanked by single figures of Julius Caesar and Augustus; underneath are scenes from the lives of these men.

[71] See Fig. 2, which shows the *eulogia* or *tituli* of L. Quinctius Cincinnatus and C. Fabricius Luscinus.—According to G. A. Moschini, *Guida di Padova,* Venice, 1817, p. 197, these inscriptions were published by J. Zabarella, *Aula heroum,* Padua, 1671.

[72] See Fig. 3.

[73] The grouping of names in the scheme, whether one, two, or three, indicates that there are one, two, or three portraits in a panel.

T. Licinius Lucullus L. Cornelius Sulla Cn. Pompeius	L. Junius Brutus D. Valerius Publicola
Constantine	Tullus Hostilius
P. Cornelius Scipio Africanus P. Cornelius Scipio Aemilianus Africanus	M. Valerius Corvinus T. Manlius Torquatus
M. Aurelius Antoninus	Ancus Martius
M. Porcius Cato (Censor) M. Porcius Cato (Uticensis)	*(door)*
Antoninus Pius	Tarquinius Priscus
T. Quinctius Flaminius C. Claudius Nero	L. Quinctius Cincinnatus C. Fabricius Luscinus
Trajanus	Servius Tullius
M. Furius Camillus M. Curius Dentatus	L. Papirius Cursor L. Aemilius Paullus Macedonicus
Titus	C. Julius Caesar
Q. Sertorius (*underneath: door*) C. Marius	Q. Fabius Maximus Rullianus Q. Fabius Maximus Cunctator
Vespasianus	Augustus

East Wall

(*window*) Francesco Zabarella (*window*) Q. Asconius Paedianus (*window*)

When we compare the two lists, we find that only twenty-seven of the thirty-six *viri illustres* of Petrarch's and Lombardo's book are represented in the series of forty-four portraits in the Sali dei Giganti. In regard to the omissions, the exclusion of the three non-Roman heroes (Alexander the Great, Pyrrhus, and Hannibal) might be explained by the assumption that the sixteenth century planners wanted to give their hall an entirely Roman character. It seems impossible, however, to find any good reasons why the other six men (Horatius Cocles, P. Decius Mus, M. Livius Salinator, L. Cornelius Scipio Asiaticus, P. Cornelius Scipio Nasica, and Q. Caecilius Metellus Macedonicus) were omitted. On the other hand, among the men who were added in the sixteenth century we find quite a number whom Petrarch himself, for various reasons, definitely did not consider *viri illustres* in the true sense and whom he therefore purposely excluded—for instance, men like the two kings Tarquinius Priscus and Servius Tullius, Sulla, M. Porcius Cato Uticensis, and the younger Brutus.[74] According to his definition of the term, which comprised only great men of action—that is, generals and statesmen [75]—Petrarch did not regard Cicero as a *vir illustris,* although he admired him tremendously, of course, as the outstanding Roman writer and thinker. Furthermore, whereas Petrarch and Lombardo ended their series, as we have seen, with the emperor Trajan, the planners of the sixteenth century added five more emperors, Antoninus Pius, Marcus Aurelius, Constantine, Theodosius, and Charlemagne. The inclusion of the last of these rulers would have caused particular displeasure to Petrarch if he had seen it, because throughout his writings he denied consistently the cognomen of "the Great" to the founder of the mediaeval Roman empire.[76] In conclusion, then, we can state that the Sala dei Giganti of the sixteenth century was very definitely not a Sala Virorum Illustrium according to Petrarch's conception of the term.

In looking over the series of portraits in the Sala dei Giganti, we see that each of the Roman monarchs, whether king or emperor, occupies a panel by himself, while the figures belonging to the republican era of Rome are always represented in groups of two or even three men within one panel. Again one wonders whether Petrarch would have approved of an arrangement in which the representatives of the monarchical form of government were given such strikingly prominent positions. The whole tenor of his writings makes it more likely that he would have preferred a uniform and equal treatment in the pictorial representation of his great Romans.

In the Sala dei Giganti the six kings and the ten emperors (including Julius Caesar) are portrayed in chronological order,

[74] Petrarch's inclusions and omissions of biographies in his book *De viris illustribus* express a very definite judgment of value on his part, as I shall attempt to show in my forthcoming study of Petrarch's historical works.

[75] *Invectiva contra medicum quendam,* I. II (in Petrarch's *Opera,* ed. Basel, 1581, p. 1095): "Nihil ibi de medicis nec de poetis quidem aut philosophis agitur, sed de his tantum, qui bellicis virtutibus aut magno rei publicae studio floruerunt et praeclaram rerum gestarum gloriam consecuti sunt."

[76] See, e.g., *Fam.* I, 4, § 7: "Carolum regem, quem Magni cognomine equare Pompeio et Alexandro audent."

beginning with Romulus in the northeast corner and going clockwise around the room. The sequence of the other figures is not at all chronological and appears on the whole quite arbitrary. In this respect, too, it is most likely that the arrangement differs from that in the original Sala Virorum Illustrium, which seems to have followed the chronological order. Witness the remark which Lombardo makes concerning the identical location of Trajan's image in the Sala Virorum Illustrium and his literary portrait in the book of the same name, which is, of course, chronologically arranged.[77]

Comparison, then, of the number, the subject-matter, and the arrangement of the portraits in the hall shows that on all three counts the Sala dei Giganti differs greatly from the original decoration of the Sala Virorum Illustrium, an observation borne out by the discoveries made on the occasion of the recent restoration of the hall. Then it was found that the fifteenth century fire was so devastating that it left hardly any traces of the former decoration, with the exception of the portrait of Petrarch. Thus the work of the sixteenth century was one of complete refinishing rather than of restoration.

But after all these negative remarks have been made, it has to be stated that in one respect at least we can obtain very important information from the present Sala dei Giganti about the former Sala Virorum Illustrium. For, irrespective of all the changes in detail, the general scheme and aspect of the decoration of the original hall can be assumed to have been identical with that of the room of today. The most characteristic feature of the sixteenth century decoration is the division into panels and the tripartite division of each panel into figures of the heroes, scenes from their lives, and inscriptions or *tituli.* That the same scheme was already employed by the artists of the late Trecento is clearly shown by the statements concerning the old hall which were quoted earlier. In the dedication of his continuation of *De viris illustribus,* Lombardo della Seta praises Francesco il Vecchio because he honored those men in his palace "with images and inscriptions." [78] Michele Savonarola states explicitly that in the Sala Imperatorum "the Roman generals

[77] See supra, note 38.

[78] See supra, note 8.

are depicted in wonderful figures and with their triumphs," that is, with glorious scenes from their lives.[79] The existence of historical scenes in the frescoes is also confirmed by Gerolamo Campagnola, who is obviously describing one of them when he says that "Avanzo painted on the left side of the room the captivity of Jugurtha and the triumph of Marius." [80]

In regard to the inscriptions or *tituli* mentioned by Lombardo, the question arises as to whether they were composed by Petrarch himself. We learn from Lombardo that Francesco da Carrara asked Petrarch "to compress in an abridged form" his larger work *De viris illustribus.*[81] Petrarch started to comply with this wish of his princely friend, but at the time of his death he had composed only fourteen biographies in this series, so that this *Compendium,* like the more extensive *Epitome,* had to be completed by Lombardo della Seta.[82] In his dedication of the *Compendium* to Francesco da Carrara, Lombardo describes the character of this collection of abridged biographies, *De viris illustribus,* very strikingly by saying: "I shall draw and not paint the image of the subject so that the quality of the linear contours can be seen without an adumbration of the inward character." [83]

It has been claimed that with this statement Lombardo seems to establish an analogy between the literary portraits in the *Compendium* and the pictorial images in the Sala Virorum Illustrium, which were probably simple grisailles.[84] And on the basis of this parallel it has been furthermore asserted by some scholars that Petrarch and Lombardo wrote these abbreviated

[79] See supra, note 53. [80] See supra, note 56.

[81] In the preface to his continuation of the *Compendium,* Lombardo writes (Cod. Paris. Lat. 6069 G, fol. 9v): "Nunc quodammodo, ut ita dixerim, eadem stipare compendiosius imperas, ut cognitioni tradantur. . . . Hoc enim idem et celeberrimo Petrarce commiseras, inuictissime eloquentie uiro, qui cum desiderio tui satisfacere lucubraret, terris elatus euanuit rediturus ad astra in eternum et lacrimabile funus." Compare the somewhat faulty text in the Basel edition of 1581 of Petrarch's *Opera,* p. 502.

[82] On the history of the *Compendium,* see de Nolhac, *op. cit.,* pp. 65 and 76 f., and especially G. Martellotti, "Epitome e Compendio," *Orientamenti Culturali,* II, 1946, pp. 205–216.

[83] Cod. Paris. Lat. 6069 G, fol. 9v: "Itaque rei designabo ymaginem, non pingam, ut liniamentorum qualitas sine indolis specie considerari possit."

[84] See Schlosser, *op. cit.,* pp. 185 and 189, n. 4.

biographies specifically to serve as *tituli* underneath the portraits and scenes in the Carrara hall.[85]

Although this hypothesis is rather tempting, it must be rejected for two reasons. In the first place, neither Petrarch nor Lombardo ever made any direct statement to that effect. Their silence is more significant in this case than it would be ordinarily, because it must be remembered that Lombardo pointed out in most explicit terms the close connection which in other respects existed between Petrarch's historical portraits and their pictorial representation by Francesco da Carrara.[86] Apart from this *argumentum e silentio,* the very length of the biographies contained in the *Compendium* seems to bar the thesis, or at least makes it rather improbable that these accounts were meant to be used as *tituli.* When we look over the edition of 1581 of the *Compendium,* we find that only five of these biographies are fairly short (from twelve to eighteen lines); two thirds of them vary in length from about thirty to more than forty lines, and one, that of Julius Caesar, is fifty lines long. In view of the size of the panels of the hall into which the inscriptions had to be inserted, it can be assumed that the number of words in each line there must have roughly corresponded to the number of words in each line of the printed edition, that is, from ten to twelve words. Such *tituli* of thirty to forty lines, however, would certainly have made very clumsy reading and would have looked unsightly. It is more likely, therefore, that Petrarch and Lombardo composed the *Compendium* so that Francesco il Vecchio and others could use it as a convenient little manual for the Sala Virorum Illustrium. The actual inscriptions beneath the scenes were probably rather brief, perhaps similar to those which are still to be found in the Libreria of the Cathedral of Siena under Pinturicchio's frescoes representing the main events of the life of Pope Pius II.[87]

If it is impossible, then, to reconstruct the original *tituli* in the hall, we are more fortunate in regard to the historical scenes

[85] That is the assumption of Schlosser, *op. cit.,* p. 185, and of d'Essling and Müntz, *op. cit.,* p. 46.

[86] See supra, notes 8 and 38.

[87] See the reproductions in P. Misciattelli, *The Piccolomini Library in the Cathedral of Siena,* Siena, 1924.

from the lives of the great Romans, with which the room was once decorated. For we can gain a certain impression of the outward appearance and the subject-matter of the lost frescoes from a number of illuminations in a manuscript of Donato degli Albanzani's translation of Petrarch's *De viris illustribus.* The manuscript was written around the year 1400 in northern Italy, probably in Padua, for the Paduan family Papafava, and is now preserved in the State Library of Darmstadt. It is a codex on vellum of forty-five leaves and measures about 9 x 14 inches.[88] Each page is divided into two columns and at the bottom of every page space has been left by the copyist for the illuminations. However, there are only twenty-four illuminations altogether, which measure on the average about 2½ x 7 inches; and, whereas most of the biographies begin with ordinary decorated letters, seven of them contain an image of their hero in their initials.[89] The reverse side of the fly-leaf of the manuscript shows a large portrait of Petrarch in his study (Fig. 6), and the upper part of the first page of the text has a representation of the *Triumph of Fame* (Fig. 32).

Julius von Schlosser, who first discovered and described the Darmstadt Codex, noticed immediately that the portrait of Petrarch on the fly-leaf is undoubtedly a copy, and a very accurate copy, of the Trecento portrait of the poet still preserved, though in badly retouched form, in the present Sala dei Giganti in Padua.[90] He observed moreover that the manuscript was written for a Paduan family closely related with the Carrara dynasty,[91] and concluded that it was most likely that the other illuminations also were derived from the paintings in the original Sala Virorum Illustrium. In short, Schlosser decided that the illuminations in the Darmstadt manuscript "give us an approximate idea as to what the [lost] frescoes . . . looked like." [92]

[88] See the description of the manuscript by Schlosser, *op. cit.,* pp. 185 ff.

[89] See Figs. 8–31, 34–39; ten of the illuminations were reproduced by Schlosser. . . . [Cod. 101, fol. 6v, initial: The Horatii is omitted here.]

[90] Compare Figs. 4 and 6.

[91] According to P. P. Vergerio's *Vitae principum Carrariensium* (ed. Muratori, *Rerum Italicarum Scriptores,* Milan, 1730, XVI, p. 117), the Papafava family was a younger branch of the Carrara family.

[92] Compare Schlosser, *op. cit.,* p. 190; see also d'Essling and Müntz, *op. cit.,* pp. 47 f.; W. Weisbach, *Trionfi,* Berlin, 1919, pp. 20 f.

Furthermore, Schlosser pointed out that among the original frescoes in the hall there was probably also one showing the *Triumph of Fame*.[93] For the representation of this subject which is found in the Darmstadt manuscript (Fig. 32) resembles strongly the headpieces in two other manuscripts of *De viris illustribus,* both of which were written in Padua about the same time, one in 1379, the other at the end of the century.[94] The similarity of these three illuminations and their common Paduan origin make it probable that they were all derived from a fresco in the Carrara palace. Considering the general arrangement of the Sala Virorum Illustrium, it seems likely that this representation of the *Triumph of Fame* was placed on the east wall, opposite the other short side of the room, which still contains the portraits of Petrarch and Lombardo. On the two long walls in between were the pictures of the men whom the goddess and the poet-historian deemed worthy of eternal fame.

One additional observation in this connection: Schlosser and other scholars have pointed out that the three Paduan illuminations and later representations of the *Triumph of Fame* follow the concept of the Triumph of Fame which Boccaccio presents in his poem *Amorosa Visione,* and that the artists had to depend on Boccaccio because Petrarch, in his *Trionfi,* fails to give a precise description of the setting of that particular triumph.[95] It must be added that in one respect at least the three Paduan illuminations, and presumably therefore also their lost model in

[93] Schlosser, *op. cit.,* pp. 190 f.

[94] The most recent reproductions of these two illuminations were given by D. Shorr, "Some Notes on the Iconography of Petrarch's *Triumph of Fame,*" *Art Bulletin,* xx, 1938, p. 101, figs. 1 and 2. However, Mrs. Schorr states wrongly that they appear as headpieces of manuscripts of the Italian translation of *De viris illustribus:* they are actually found in Cod. Paris. Lat. (and not Ital.) 6069 F and I. On these manuscripts and the illuminations, see also de Nolhac, *op. cit.,* pp. 70 f., 99 f.; E. Müntz, *Histoire de l'Art pendant la Renaissance,* Paris, 1889, I, 228; P. de Nolhac, *Pétrarque et l'Humanisme,* Paris, 1907, II, pp. 250 ff.—The two illuminations have been attributed by P. Toesca, (*Monumenti e Studi per la Storia della Miniatura Italiana,* Milan, 1930, p. 36) to the school of Altichiero; by Longhi (in *Critica d'Arte,* v, 1940, p. 180, n. 4) to Giusto; S. Bettini, *Giusto de' Menabuoi,* Padua, 1944, p. 142, does not declare himself on the question of their authors.

[95] Schlosser, *op. cit.,* pp. 191 f.; Shorr, *op. cit.,* p. 103; Antal, *Florentine Painting and Its Social Background,* London, 1947, p. 368.

the Sala Virorum Illustrium, differ from all other Triumphs of Fame. Whereas in the later pictures Fame is always shown surrounded by both men and women, only men appear in the headpieces of the three Paduan manuscripts (See Fig. 32). And with good reason, for it is obvious that neither in these manuscripts nor in the Hall of the Illustrious Men was there properly a place for women. It was only when the artists began to represent the *Triumph of Fame* in general, not just as an illustration of Petrarch's historical work, that they began also to show women in their pictures, in accordance with Petrarch's own *Trionfi* and with Boccaccio's *Amorosa Visione*. The first example of this later kind seems to be offered by the picture of the *Triumph of Fame* on a Florentine *cassone* of ca. 1400; although it is "closely connected with the Darmstadt illustration," [96] it shows, in contrast to it, Fame attended by women as well as by men.

When we now turn to an analysis of the historical scenes as they were depicted in the Sala Virorum Illustrium and are preserved to a certain extent in the "copies" of the Darmstadt manuscript, we must remember that they were meant to illustrate the main scenes of Petrarch's *De viris illustribus*. A comparison of the pictorial representations with the historical text shows indeed that the artist, or the artists, almost always depicted incidents to which Petrarch himself had assigned a central, or at least a very prominent, position within the framework of his biographies.[97]

Thus, for instance, more than half of the biography of King Tullus Hostilius is devoted to the account of the combat between the three Horatii and the three Curiatii,[98] illustrated twice in the Darmstadt manuscript (Figs. 13 and 14). In Figure 15 we see King Ancus Martius worshiping the statue of a god who

[96] Shorr, *op. cit.*, p. 104; see the reproduction of the *cassone, ibid.*, p. 102, fig. 4.

[97] It should be noted, however, that the illuminator apparently added some scenes on his own initiative. For, considering the size of the panels in the hall, it is hard to see how, e.g., the two sets of five scenes, each illustrating the lives of Romulus (Figs. 8–12) and of Alexander (Figs. 23–27), could have been fitted into the scheme of the decoration.

[98] Ed. L. Razzolini, *F. Petrarchae De viris illustribus vitae*, Bologna, 1874, I, pp. 40–44.

from Petrarch's text can be identified as Jupiter Feretrius; in other passages of the same biography Petrarch emphasized strongly the attention which Ancus Martius gave to things religious.[99] Another illumination (Fig. 17) shows Horatius Cocles swimming under the Tiber bridge, in accordance with Petrarch's statement at the very beginning of the biography: "About this man nothing comes to mind but that famous and hardly believable battle and defense of the *Pons Sublicius.*"[100] The illumination in the biography of Cincinnatus (Fig. 17) illustrates accurately the literary account of how he was found by the emissaries of the Senate while "he was alone on his land, busy with farm work."[101] The miniaturist likewise depicted very well the climax in the life of Marcus Valerius Corvinus (Fig. 21) when, after the battle of Suessula, he was presented by his soldiers "with forty thousand shields and one hundred and seventy ensigns of the enemy."[102] Finally, the picture of young Hannibal taking the oath to fight the Romans (Fig. 28) represents an excellent choice, because the incident foreshadowed his whole career, as Petrarch himself declares at the beginning of his biography of Hannibal.[103]

In a number of instances, the pictures contain details which to a surprising degree correspond to the particular items indicated in the text. In his biography of Brutus, for example, Petrarch tells how Lucretia related her sad story to her friends and then committed suicide. After that Petrarch continues: "Whereas the others burst out in tears and lamentations . . . Brutus showed himself the leader of the public revenge."[104] The illuminator succeeded very well in bringing out the contrast between mere compassion on the part of the people watching Lucretia's suicide and the dramatic action taken by Brutus (Fig.

[99] Ed. Razzolini, p. 50: ". . . auctumque Feretrii Jovis templum"; compare *ibid.*, p. 48; see also the account of the king's life in the *Compendium* (in Petrarch's *Opera*, ed. Basel, 1581, p. 496).

[100] Ed. Razzolini, p. 54; *Compendium*, p. 497.

[101] Ed. Razzolini, p. 58; compare *ibid.*, p. 56, and *Compendium*, p. 497.

[102] Ed. Razzolini, p. 108; *Compendium*, p. 498.

[103] Ed. Razzolini, p. 422: ". . . a patre . . . aris applicitus et sacramento obstrictus esse iam tunc animo inimicum Romanorum et futurum rebus, ubi primum facultas affuisset."

[104] Ed. Razzolini, pp. 50 f.; *Compendium*, p. 496.

16). In the same picture Brutus' breastplate bears the inscription *Libertas,* a reflection of the statement made by Petrarch in the first sentence of his biography that Brutus was "the founder of Liberty." In his various representations of the triumphs of Roman war lords, the illuminator depicts in only one case, that of Camillus, a chariot drawn by four, instead of two, horses (Fig. 18). This is in exact agreement with Petrarch who asserts (apparently without the support of any ancient source) that on the occasion of his first triumph Camillus entered Rome seated "in a golden chariot drawn by four white horses." [105] In his life of T. Manlius Torquatus, Petrarch relates how Manlius went to the house of the tribune Pomponius in order to prevent him from prosecuting his father; he continues: "After the bystanders had been removed, Manlius was admitted alone, whereupon he suddenly brandished his sword over the head of the tribune." [106] The illumination (Fig. 20), showing Manlius threatening the tribune with his sword while three soldiers stand guard outside the house, illustrates the scene very accurately. In his account of the triumph of the older Scipio Africanus, Petrarch says that "according to Polybius King Syphax was among the prisoners of war made to march in front of the triumphal chariot." [107] The illumination depicting this scene (Fig. 30) does indeed show the African king, distinguished by the crown on his head.

It can be argued that the close similarity between the pictorial representations and the literary accounts simply resulted from a thorough study of Petrarch's historical text by the illuminator and that, therefore, it is not necessary to assume that Petrarch himself supervised the illustration of his work. In the case of at least one of the illuminations, however, the first explanation does not seem to suffice. In the biography of Romulus we find a picture which represents the building of Rome by Romulus and Remus and the quarrel between the two brothers who are

[105] Ed. Razzolini, p. 64: "[Camillus] urbem est ingressus . . . currum aureum equis quatuor niveo candore trahentibus"; see the similar statement in the *Compendium,* p. 497.

[106] Ed. Razzolini, p. 102; see *Compendium,* p. 499.

[107] Ed. Razzolini, p. 610: "Inter captivos vero hostium ante currum actos fuisse Syphacem regem Polybius scribit"; Petrarch's reference to Polybius is based on Livy, XXX, 45.

shown facing one another across the walls under construction (Fig. 12). It seems curious that the illuminator did not choose to depict the actual killing of Remus by Romulus, although this dramatic climax of the quarrel has always been one of the best known facts of Roman history and although, from the point of view of a painter, it would also seem to offer an interesting and thankful subject. Note, for example, the illuminations in two French manuscripts of St. Augustine's *City of God* also made in the late fourteenth century, which illustrate the parallel between the killing of Abel by Cain and that of Remus by Romulus (Fig. 33).[108] A look at the two versions of Petrarch's work *De viris illustribus* appears to provide the explanation for the singular representation of the famous incident by the Paduan artists. For in the longer text of the biography of Romulus, Petrarch states that "Remus was killed" but does not mention the tradition that Romulus had any responsibility for the murder.[109] In the condensed version of the *Compendium* he goes even further and omits the whole incident.[110] From his reading of *The City of God* Petrarch knew, of course, the famous parallel which St. Augustine had drawn between the two fratricides standing at the beginnings of "the earthly city" and of "the second Babylon." [111] The fact that he had this knowledge makes it the more noteworthy that, on this particular point, he deviated so markedly both from his ancient Roman sources and from the authority of St. Augustine.[112] Since Petrarch took such great care to de-emphasize this famous event and the significance commonly attributed to it and for that reason in his *Compendium* even

[108] Both illuminations were reproduced by Comte A. de Laborde, *Les manuscrits à peintures de la Cité de Dieu de Saint Augustin,* Paris, 1909, III, pl. VII; the manuscript, which formerly belonged to the collection of H. Yates Thompson, is now in the collection of Mr. Philip Hofer at the Houghton Library of Harvard University (see Fig. 33); compare A. de Laborde's description of the manuscript, *op. cit.,* I, pp. 241–244.

[109] Ed. Razzolini, p. 16: "Ceterum seu hinc orto certamine seu contempto fratris edicto Remus nova moenia transcendens interficitur; sive imperii cupiditas sive ille iustitiae rigor fuit, variat enim in multis vetustissimae rei fides."

[110] See *Compendium,* p. 495.

[111] See Augustine, *De civitate Dei,* XV, 5.

[112] A fuller discussion of this problem will be found in my forthcoming study of Petrarch's historical works.

went so far as to ignore it completely, the assumption seems warranted that, at the same time, he suggested to the artists of the Paduan hall that they omit the fratricide and depict simply the quarrel between the brothers. This instance, then, would seem to support the statement made by Marcanton Michiel that "Petrarch supplied the subject-matter of these pictures." [113]

Very little need be said about the small illuminations (Figs. 34–39) which are contained in the initial letters of seven of the biographies. Some of their features reveal the same close dependency on the text of Petrarch's work which can be observed in the pictures of the historical scenes. For instance, King Numa Pompilius "the law-giver," as he is called in his biography,[114] is shown holding a book in his hand (Fig. 34); Ancus Martius, "who built a wall around the Gianicolo," [115] is represented carrying the model of a walled city (Fig. 35); and Cincinnatus the farmer appears in a typical peasant dress (Fig. 39). At first glance one might be inclined to believe that these illuminations were meant to reproduce, on a minute scale, the series of large portraits which, as we have seen, must have been painted above the historical scenes in the hall. But this assumption cannot be maintained in view of the fact that some of those initial letters do not contain individual "portraits" but rather depict historical scenes (see Figs. 36–38).

A particularly interesting feature of the illuminations in the Darmstadt manuscript, and presumably therefore also of the lost frescoes in the Carrara palace, is the architectural background which appears in some of the historical scenes. In his discussion of Paduan painting during the late fourteenth century, R. Van Marle has pointed out that one of its characteristics is the attention given by the leading masters of that school to the representation of architecture.[116] But whereas most of the buildings shown in the other Paduan paintings of that pe-

[113] See supra, note 56.

[114] Ed. Razzolini, p. 34: ". . . primus apud Romanos legifer"; see *ibid.*, p. 38, on the later finding of the fourteen Latin and Greek books of the king, ". . . de iure pontificio, . . . de sapientia conscripti."

[115] Ed. Razzolini, p. 50: "murusque Ianiculo circumductus."

[116] Van Marle, *op. cit.*, VII, p. 40 (with specific reference to Guariento, Semitecolo, Altichiero, and Avanzo); see *ibid.*, IV, p. 175.

riod seem to be either local or imaginary edifices, the decorators of the Sala Virorum Illustrium apparently attempted to place their scenes from Roman history against the background of the city of Rome and of some of its main buildings as they actually existed around the year 1400.

Thus we find the following Roman buildings depicted in the illuminations of the Darmstadt manuscript.[117] Fig. 11: the Janus Quadrifons (or Arco di Giano) which is identified by the three arched gates visible. Fig. 12: the Castel Sant'Angelo, the Colosseum, the Vatican Obelisk, and again the Janus Quadrifons. Fig. 16: the Vatican Obelisk, the Pantheon, and once more the Janus Quardifons. Fig. 19: the Pantheon, the Vatican Obelisk, and one of the Columns, either that of Trajan or of Marcus Aurelius. Fig. 23: the Church of S. Nicola in Carcere.[118] The

[117] L. Schlosser, in his discussion of the Darmstadt manuscript, did not comment on the Roman background of the scenes; but on the basis of Schlosser's reproductions, E. Müntz, in *Bulletin de la Société Nationale des Antiquaires de France,* 1899, pp. 350 f., identified some of the buildings; see also d'Essling and Müntz, *op. cit.,* p. 48.—It is interesting to compare the group of ancient monuments depicted by the Paduan artists of the late Trecento with the representation of the city of Rome on the golden bull of Louis IV (the Bavarian), which was made at the time of the imperial coronation at Rome in 1328; see the reproductions by O. Posse, *Die Siegel der deutschen Kaiser und Könige,* Dresden, 1909, I, pl. 50, nr. 8, and by W. Erben, *Rombilder auf kaiserlichen und königlichen Siegeln des Mittelalters,* Graz, 1931, pl. III (with bibliography). According to W. Erben, *op. cit.,* pp. 61–68, the following ancient monuments can be identified on that imperial seal: the Colosseum, the Pantheon, the Castel Sant' Angelo, the Vatican Obelisk, the Arch of Titus, the Pyramid of Cestius, the Column of Marcus Aurelius, the Mausoleum of Augustus.

[118] On this particular identification, see T. E. Mommsen, "Un problema riguardante la topografia medioevale di Roma: S. Nicola in Carcere nell'anno 1400," *Atti d. Pontif. Accad. Romana d. Archeologia, Rendiconti,* XXIV, 1949, pp. 309–315. [Mommsen remarks that S. Nicola in Carcere was probably reproduced because it is an example of a Christian church built around an antique temple. The article concludes as follows: "Sembrerà un caso fuori del comune quello di trovare una miniatura primitiva che rappresenti una fra le chiese secondarie e minori di Roma, perchè queste si trovavano troppo adombrate da numerosi edifici d'interesse superiore, o religioso o artistico o storico. Quando il disegnatore padovano del 1400 si decise ad illustrare proprio questa chiesa, a preferenza di tante altre, avrà dovuto fare tale scelta perchè essa interessava per i suoi elementi antichi. Anche nelle altre sue miniature egli ha mostrato la stessa tendenza; perchè si ricorderà che la maggior parte degli edifici da lui indicati erano di origine classica. In tale senso, dunque, il modesto schizzo di San Nicola

churches which appear in Figs. 11, 12, 16, 18, and 19 are drawn in such a highly stylized fashion that identification with particular buildings seems to be impossible.[119] Likewise, the Gothic palace which is shown in Figs. 12, 16, 19, and 23 cannot be identified; for a survey of the pictorial representations and the literary descriptions of Rome during the fourteenth and fifteenth centuries definitely excludes the identification of this building with the Senatorial Palace; [120] nor does the same material seem to show any other building of an aspect similar to that indicated in these figures.[121]

It will be noted that all the buildings which can be identified are either of classical origin or at least contain ancient elements, like the Church of S. Nicola in Carcere which incorporates the remnants of two pagan temples.[122] As a matter of fact, the list of the edifices shown in the Darmstadt manuscript includes some of the most representative monuments of ancient Rome still extant at the end of the Middle Ages and, above all, of course, the Pantheon, the Colosseum, and the Castel Sant' Angelo. That the Vatican Obelisk was depicted in no less than three of the illuminations is explained not merely by the fact that it was the only one of the Roman obelisks which remained standing throughout the Middle Ages, but even more by the popular legend connected with it.[123] According to the *Mirabilia urbis Romae,* the

---

in Carcere costituisce una notevole espressione del rinascente spirito umanistico di quell'età."]

119 It has to be noted that Fig. 16 shows two quite similar churches, both of which have their campanile on the left side, whereas in Figs. 12, 18, and 19 the campanile appears on the right side.

120 E. Müntz, in *Bullet. d. l. Soc. Nat. des Antiquaires de France,* 1899, p. 351, says of the palace shown in Fig. 16: "un chateau crénelé, probablement le Capitole." Against this identification see, however, the representation of the Senatorial palace on the golden bull of Louis IV of 1328, mentioned above, note 117. On the aspect of the Palazzo Senatorio during the later Middle Ages, see also E. Lavagnino, "Il Campidoglio al tempo del Petrarca," *Capitolium,* XVI, 1941, pp. 103–114.

121 Compare the bibliography given by C. Scaccia Scarafoni, *Le Piante di Roma possedute dalla Biblioteca dell'Istituto e dalle altre Biblioteche Governative della Città,* Rome, 1939.

122 The drawing (Fig. 23) shows clearly six Ionic columns along one side of the church.

123 On the cycle of legends concerning the Vatican Obelisk, see R. Lanciani, *The Ruins and Excavations of Ancient Rome,* Boston and New York, 1897, pp. 549 f.

Agulia, as it was called in the Middle Ages, was a memorial to Julius Caesar: "There his ashes nobly rest in his sarcophagus, to the intent that as in his lifetime the whole world lay subdued before him, even so in his death the same may still lie beneath him forever." [124] Petrarch was familiar with that tradition, for in one of his letters he speaks of "that stone, amazing in size, sitting upon bronze lions and sacred to the divine emperors, upon the top of which, according to the legend, the bones of Julius Caesar are resting." [125]

Whereas the inclusion of the Vatican Obelisk probably resuted from the legendary association of the monument with the memory of Caesar, the illustrator of Petrarch's *De viris illustribus* very definitely deviated from the same mediaeval tradition in his representation of the Colosseum. The *Mirabilia urbis Romae* had asserted that the Colosseum was "all covered with an heaven of gilded brass." [126] and this statement was often repeated—for instance, by Petrarch's Florentine contemporary Fazio degli Uberti in his cosmographical poem *Il Dittamondo.*[127] Accordingly, on two maps of Rome which were drawn in the third decade of the fourteenth century,[128] and in an illuminated manuscript of *Il Dittamondo* of the mid-fifteenth century,[129] the Colosseum is shown covered by a dome. The Paduan illuminator of 1400, on the contrary, depicts the Colosseum in its real appearance to the best of his ability (see Fig. 12).[130]

124 From the translation of the *Mirabilia* by F. M. Nichols, London, 1889, pp. 71 f.; the best edition of the Latin text is to be found in H. Jordan, *Topographie der Stadt Rom im Alterthum,* Berlin, 1871, II, p. 625.

125 *Fam.* VI, 2, § 11: "Hoc est saxum mire magnitudinis eneisque leonibus innixum, divis imperatoribus sacrum, cuius in vertice Iulii Cesaris ossa quiescere fama est." See M. Mercati, *Gli Obelischi di Roma,* 1589, pp. 239–244, who, in his discussion of the Vatican Obelisk, refers explicitly to this statement by Petrarch.

126 Nichols, *op. cit.,* p. 63; Jordan, *op. cit.,* II, 638.

127 Ed. Jordan, *op. cit.,* II, 391: ". . . come un castel ch'è quasi tondo, coperto fu di rame. . . ."

128 The maps are contained in the manuscripts of two versions of Paulus Minorita's *Chronicle;* see the reproductions by W. Holtzmann, *Jahrb. d. Deutsch. Archaeolog. Instituts,* XLI, 1926, pls. I and II; compare G. B. de Rossi, *Piante iconografiche e prospettiche di Roma,* Rome, 1879, pp. 81–86, 139 ff.; Holtzmann, *op. cit.,* pp. 56–66.

129 See de Rossi, *op. cit.,* p. 88.

130 In this respect, the Paduan illuminator somewhat resembles his contemporary, the Milanese Leonardo da Besozzo who, in the early fifteenth

Throughout his life Petrarch was greatly interested in the monuments of the cities which he visited and especially, of course, those of Rome, as various passages in his letters and other literary works show.[131] In his epic *Africa* (VIII, 862–951), he describes in great detail the sights of Rome as they presented themselves to the Carthaginian ambassadors who, at the end of the second Punic War, were taken on a tour around the city. Of this description it has been rightly said that "it testifies to a direct knowledge of the monuments, nay, even to an affectionate familiarity with them." [132] In view of Petrarch's interest and knowledge, one is led to believe that the choice of an actually Roman background, and perhaps even the selection of the particular monuments shown in the Sala Virorum Illustrium, were due to the advice of Petrarch, who in this respect, too, would have "supplied the subject-matter of these paintings." Further support for such an assumption can be found in the fact that, during his last years in Arquà and Padua, Petrarch used to employ in his household, in addition to his copyists, some illuminators as well, as we learn from a letter written in 1371.[133] We may conclude that he was quite accustomed to giving precise instructions to

---

century, drew a panoramic view of Rome in which he attempted "di raffigurare Roma nella sua attualità intera"; see F. Gregorovius, "Una pianta di Roma delineata da Leonardo da Besozzo milanese," *Atti d. R. Accad. d. Lincei,* 1882/83, ser. III, *Memorie d. Class. d. Scienze Morali,* XI, p. 210.—See also the representation of the Colosseum on the golden bull of Emperor Louis IV of 1328 (reproduced by Posse, *op. cit.,* I, pl. 50, nr. 8, and by Erben, *op. cit.,* pl. III), and the images of the Colosseum which appear on the seals of the earlier German rulers Frederick I, Henry VI, and Henry VII (see Erben, *op. cit.,* pp. 49 ff., 53 f., 71 ff., also pl. II).

[131] See, e.g., *Fam.* VI, 2, §§ 5–15, where Petrarch mentions, among others, four of the buildings illustrated in the Darmstadt codex, i.e., the Vatican Obelisk, the Castel Sant' Angelo, the Pantheon, and the Columns; see furthermore: *Africa* (ed. N. Festa, Florence, 1926), Book VIII, vv. 862–951; *Ep. Metr.* II, 5 (ed. D. Rossetti, *F. Petrarchae poëmata minora,* Milan, 1834, III, pp. 4–30); *De remediis utriusque fortunae,* Book I, dial. 118 (in Petrarch's *Opera,* ed. 1581, pp. 99 f.).

[132] P. P. Trompeo and G. Martellotti, "Cartaginesi a Roma," in P. P. Trompeo, *La scala del Sole,* Rome, 1945, p. 58.

[133] *Var.* 15 (ed. G. Fracassetti, *F. Petrarcae Epistolae de rebus familiaribus,* III, pp. 332 f.): "Soleo habere scriptores quinque vel sex; habeo tres ad praesens, et ne plures habeam, causa est, quia non inveniuntur scriptores; sed pictores utinam non inepti."

illustrators of his own works, as well as of books of other authors collected by him. Petrarch was also gifted with the eyes of a painter and proved himself able, in another passage in *Africa* (III, 140–262), to offer a remarkably graphic picture of the appearances and characteristic attributes of the ancient gods.[134]

Prince d'Essling and Eugène Müntz have pointed out that "one of the most striking features of the illuminations" of the Darmstadt manuscript is the fact that "the costumes, as well as the architecture, are decidedly those of the fourteenth century, not those of ancient Rome." [135] This observation is correct, and one could go even further and point to the naïve anachronism to be found in the consistent representation of Christian churches in scenes of pagan history. In this respect, the Paduan illustrators of Petrarch's *De viris illustribus* were still encumbered by the artistic tradition of their era. For, although "during the fourteenth century the representation of antiquity became one of the favorite themes of Western book-illustrators," [136] these men, like most of the painters of that day, tended to depict ancient buildings in the style of their own period.[137] Thus we see the graphic artists of the Trecento still unable to present antiquity in its own aspects and terms, whereas Petrarch succeeded in doing it remarkably well in his poetical and historical works.

But if it is true that the accomplishments of the decorators of the Sala Virorum Illustrium fell short of the later achievements of men like Mantegna, they must at least be credited with a definite endeavor to create a specifically Roman background, by showing some of the most characteristic antique buildings of

[134] See E. Panofsky, *Hercules am Scheidewege,* Leipzig and Berlin, 1930, pp. 11–18, esp. p. 14: "Die Bildbeschreibungen der *Africa* stehen zwischen ihren Vorläufern und ihren Nachfolgern als ein Stück echter Renaissance-Kunst zwischen zwei Denkmälern des Mittelalters." On the above passage in *Africa,* see also the comment made by J. Seznec, *La Survivance des dieux antiques,* London, 1940, p. 150.

[135] D'Essling and Müntz, *op. cit.,* pp. 47 f.; the same opinion was expressed by Schlosser, *op. cit.,* p. 190, and by Weisbach, *Trionfi,* p. 20.

[136] F. Saxl, "Rinascimento dell'Antichità," *Repertorium für Kunstwissenschaft,* XLIII, 1922, p. 242.

[137] See C. Hülsen, *La Roma antica di Ciriaco d'Ancona,* Rome, 1907, pp. 37 f.

the city. Another instance of this endeavor is to be found in the two pictures of ancient temples (Figs. 15 and 27): the nude statues of the deities being worshiped, which we see placed on the altars in these temples, are employed, without any apparent disapproval by the artist, as a typical feature of a "classical" environment, and not as a frightening example of pagan idolatry, as was the case in so many mediaeval representations of hagiological or other sacred subjects.[138] And although the Roman statesmen and warriors in the Darmstadt manuscript, their battles and triumphs, do not look exactly antique to the modern critic, they certainly appear to be less feudal or chivalrous than the armor-clad knights shown in practically all of the contemporary manuscripts which include illuminations of Roman history.[139] We have to remember that what Erwin Panofsky and Fritz Saxl have stated of the mediaeval mind in general was still true of the artist around the year 1400: "Being incapable of realizing, as the modern mind automatically does, the unity of classical form and classical subject-matter, [the mediaeval mind] actually avoided bringing the two together—for we must remember that any combination of what were regarded as two separate things would have been meaningless to both the average artist and the average beholder." [140]

[138] When Schlosser, *op. cit.*, p. 190 (and, following him, d'Essling and Müntz, *op. cit.*, p. 86), said that "das archäologische Beiwerk gipfelt etwa in jenem S.P.Q.R." (on the shields, breast plates, and banners of the soldiers, and on the gates of Rome; see Figs. 13, 14, 16, 17, 19 and 21), it must be noted that this example was badly chosen; for the knowledge and use of that abbreviation was not at all "archaeological" but has rather to be traced back to a medieval tradition, as we learn, e.g., from Giovanni Villani's *Chronicle;* see L. Magnani, *La Cronaca figurata di G. Villani,* Vatican City, 1936, p. 23, and *ibid.*, pls. VII, X, and XI.

[139] See, e.g., the illuminations in a manuscript of Livy's first ten decades, which was written in Venice in 1373 (cf. G. Fogolari, "La prima deca di Livio illustrata nel trecento a Venezia," *L'Arte,* X, 1907, pp. 330–345), or the "antique" scenes in a late fourteenth century manuscript of Villani's *Chronicle* (see Magnani, *op. cit.*). Compare also P. d'Ancona, *La Miniature italienne du Xe au XVIe siècle,* Paris, 1925 (see esp. pp. 20–48 on the various schools of the fourteenth century); E. Panofsky and F. Saxl, "Classical Mythology in Mediaeval Art," *Metropolitan Museum Studies,* IV, 1932/33, pp. 262 f.; Antal, *op. cit.*, p. 273, n. 33.

[140] Panofsky and Saxl, *op. cit.*, pp. 268 f.; cf. E. Panofsky, "Renaissance and Renascences," *Kenyon Review,* VI, 1944, esp. pp. 219–222.

Petrarch's whole creative work was marked by a conscious effort to unite classical content and its form and expression. The poet was more advanced in this regard than the contemporary artists. But a reflection, at least, of this new approach can be found in the illustrations to Petrarch's historical work, imperfect as these attempts are.

One more question remains. During the Middle Ages it had become common practice for princes and nobles all over Europe, and even for rich burghers, to have the walls of their residences decorated with frescoes depicting people and events belonging to the realms of both history and legend. Among the great variety of topics chosen, we find representations of the popular romances, like those of Alexander the Great, of Troy and of Thebes, of the cycles of King Artus and the Holy Grail, or of the famous series of the *Neuf Preux,* which included three examples each of Hebrew, pagan, and Christian heroes (Joshua, David, Judas the Maccabaean; Hector, Alexander the Great, Caesar; Artus, Charlemagne, and Godfrey of Bouillon); sometimes these men were accompanied by the *Neuf Preuses.*[141] How does the Paduan series of the *viri illustres* fit into that tradition? The large mass of material bearing on this question makes it advisable to confine ourselves to a survey of the most important schemes of decoration executed in Italy during the fourteenth and early fifteenth centuries.

The first example to be mentioned seems to be by the hand of Giotto. In about 1332 he executed for King Robert of Naples a number of paintings which included the decoration of "la sala dei uomini famosi" in Castelnuovo, a work which unfortunately was destroyed in the fifteenth century.[142] These frescoes portrayed nine heroes who, however, were not identical with the traditional Nine Worthies, there being among them no Christians, only two Hebrews (Solomon and Samson), and seven

[141] On this "höfische Kunst," compare, e.g., Schlosser, *op. cit.,* pp. 156–194; P. d'Ancona, "Gli affreschi del Castello di Manta nel Saluzzese," *L'Arte,* VIII, 1905, pp. 94–106, 183–198; Antal, *op. cit.,* p. 273, n. 33.

[142] See L. Ghiberti, *I Commentari,* II, 3, ed. O. Morisani, Naples, 1947, p. 33; G. Vasari, *Vita di Giotto,* ed. Milanesi, I, pp. 390 f. As to the date of the commission, see R. Caggese, *Roberto d'Angiò,* Florence, 1922, I, p. 679.

pagans (Alexander, Hector, Aeneas, Achilles, Paris, Hercules, and Caesar); their wives were probably also represented.[143]

A few years later, in about 1340, Azzo Visconti commissioned in his newly built palace in Milan "a large hall . . . in which Vainglory was depicted and also illustrious pagan princes of the world, such as Aeneas, Attila, Hector, Hercules, and several others; but among them is only one Christian, Charlemagne, and then Azzo Visconti." [144]

About the time of the frescoing of the hall of Francesco il Vecchio da Carrara, Altichiero painted, according to Vasari, in neighboring Verona, "the great hall of their palace [i.e., of the della Scala]. . . , depicting therein the war of Jerusalem, according as it is described by [Flavius] Josephus. In this work, Aldigieri showed great spirit and judgment, distributing one scene over the walls of that hall on every side, with a single ornament encircling it right round; on the upper part of which ornament, as it were to set it off, he placed a row of medallions, in which it is believed that there are the portraits from life of many distinguished men of those times, particularly of many of those Signori della Scala. . . . And among many portraits of men of distinction and learning, there is seen that of Messer Francesco Petrarca." [145] According to the same passage in Vasari's *Lives*, "Jacopo Avanzo shared the work of this hall with Aldigieri, and below the aforesaid pictures he painted two most beautiful Triumphs, likewise in fresco, with so much art and so good a manner, that Gerolamo Campagnola declares that Mantegna used to praise them as pictures of the rarest merit." [146]

If we can trust another notice in Vasari's *Lives*, at about the same time (ca. 1370) Giottino painted a "Hall of Famous Men" in the palace of the Orsini family in Rome.[147]

[143] Cf. G. de Blasiis, in *Napoli Nobilissima*, IX, 1900, pp. 65 ff.; P. Schubring, *Repertorium für Kunstwissenschaft*, XXIII, 1900, pp. 424 f.; Venturi, *Storia dell'Arte Italiana*, V, p. 448, n. 1.

[144] See Galvano Fiamma, *Opusculum de rebus gestis ab Azone, Luchino et Johanne Vicecomitibus*, ed. C. Castiglioni, in Muratori, *Rer. Ital. Scriptores*, XII, part 4, Bologna, 1938, p. 17; see Schlosser, *op. cit.*, p. 178.

[145] Vasari, *Vita de Vittore Scarpaccia*, ed. Milanesi, III, p. 633; English translation by G. du C. de Vere, IV, pp. 54 f.

[146] Schlosser, op. cit., pp. 180 f., assumes that these decorations were executed for Cansignorio della Scala, who died in 1375.

[147] Vasari, *Vita di Tommaso detto Giottino*, ed. Milanesi, I, p. 626;

Around the turn of the century several cycles of "famous men" seem to have been executed in Florence. We hear that portraits of four Florentine poets of the Trecento (Dante, Petrarch, Zenobio da Strada, and Boccaccio) were commissioned by the guild of the judges and notaries,[148] and that another series was in the "aula minor palatii Florentini," in which the Florentine poets, including Claudianus, were represented among ancient heroes such as Ninus, Alexander, Brutus, Camillus, Scipio, and Cicero; Coluccio Salutati was supposed to have written the *tituli* for these portraits.[149] According to Vasari, Cosimo Medici's father Giovanni commissioned Lorenzo di Bicci "to paint in the hall of the old house of the Medici . . . all those famous men that are still seen there to-day, very well preserved." [150] Of all these Florentine frescoes, unfortunately nothing seems to remain.

Between 1407 and 1414, Taddeo di Bartolo decorated the chapel of the Palazzo Pubblico in Siena. Only the vestibule of this chapel concerns us. Here Taddeo painted, besides a panoramic view of contemporary Rome and the images of Jupiter, Mars, Apollo, and Pallas, nine famous figures of antiquity (Aristotle, Caesar, Pompey, Cicero, Cato, Curius Dentatus, Scipio Nasica, Camillus, and Scipio Africanus), whose characters and deeds are described underneath in Latin verses. We also see, besides the images of Brutus and Laelius, the symbolizations of the virtues of Justice, Magnanimity, Prudence, Fortitude, and Religion, and representations of St. Christopher, Judas the Maccabaean, and the blessed Ambrogio Sansedoni. At first glance this combination of pagan and Christian elements seems to be strange and incongruous, but its meaning is made clear by an inscription of fifteen lines in the vernacular, which begins with the words: "You who are the regents, look upon these [images]

---

cf. P. Schubring, in *Jahrb. d. Preuss. Kunstsammlungen,* XXI, 1900, p. 174.

148 See L. Mehus, *Vita Ambrosii Traversarii,* 1759, pp. cclxvi, cccxxix f.; A. M. Bandini, *Catalogus codicum Latinorum Bibliothecae Mediceae Laurentianae,* Florence, 1776, III, col. 714.

149 See Mehus, *op. cit.,* pp. cclxvi, cccxiv; L. Bertalot, "Humanistisches in der Anthologia Latina," *Rheinisches Museum für Philologie,* LXVI, 1911, p. 73, n. 2; Antal, *op. cit.,* p. 273, n. 33.

150 Vasari, *Vita di Lorenzo di Bicci,* ed. Milanesi, II, p. 50; English trans. by de Vere, II, p. 67.

if you want to govern for thousands and thousands of years." [151] On their daily walks to the chapel, the ruling authorities of Siena were to be reminded of their moral obligations by the images of the virtues and of some of the great pagan and Christian figures of the past.

About the same time, between the years 1413 and 1424, the Trinci family of Foligno in Umbria built in their palace "la sala de l'imperatori," in which twenty great Roman statesmen and generals, from Romulus to Trajan, were commemorated both with paintings and with Latin epigrams composed by Francesco da Fiano.[152]

And, finally, we obtain an example of the representation of the *Neuf Preux* and *Neuf Preuses,* dating from the third decade of the fifteenth century and located in one of the halls of the Castle of Manta near Saluzzo.[153] It appears to be the only representation of this typically mediaeval and chivalrous subject to have been preserved on Italian soil and, appropriately, it was painted by a French painter and is found in Piedmont where the influence of French culture was always strong. For throughout the later Middle Ages this particular topic of the *Neuf Preux* was even more popular in France than anywhere else.[154]

Painting of the series of "famous men" continued, of course, throughout the fifteenth century all over Italy,[155] and the great-

[151] See the first two and the last four lines of the poem, which was published by L. Schorn in the footnotes to his German translation of Vasari's *Vite* (Stuttgart and Tübingen, 1832, I, p. 405, n. 1); Van Marle, *op. cit.,* II, pp. 547 and 567.

[152] See M. Salmi, "Gli affreschi del Palazzo Trinci a Foligno," *Bollettino d'Arte,* XIII, 1919, pp. 139–180; Van Marle, *op. cit.,* VIII, pp. 320–326; A. Messini, "Documenti per la storia del Palazzo Trinci di Foligno," *Rivista d'Arte,* XXIV, 1942, pp. 74–98.

[153] See P. d'Ancona, "Gli affreschi del Castello di Manta nel Saluzzese," *L'Arte,* VIII, 1905, pp. 94–106, 183–198; Van Marle, *op. cit.,* VII, pp. 190 f.; G. Ring, *A Century of French Painting: 1400–1500,* New York, 1949, p. 202, n. 84 (with attribution to Jacques Iverny, about 1420–30).

[154] J. J. Rorimer and M. B. Freeman, "The Nine Heroes Tapestries at the Cloisters," *Metropolitan Museum of Art Bulletin,* N.S. VII, 1949, pp. 244 f.—On the series of frescoes of famous heroes and sages in the Piedmontese Castle of Fénis, see d'Ancona, *op. cit.,* pp. 94 f.; Van Marle, *op. cit.,* VII, p. 192; Ring, *op. cit.,* p. 202, n. 85.

[155] See, e.g., the "Baedecker-Liste" compiled by L. Bertalot, *Rheinisches Museum,* LXVI, 1911, p. 73, n. 2, which lists for the later fifteenth century

est and best known collection of this kind was ultimately brought together by Paolo Giovio, who called the museum which contained his collection of portraits the "Templum Virtutis." [156]

From this survey we learn that there are certain similarities between the Paduan Sala Virorum Illustrium and other "Halls of Famous Men" belonging to the same period. For instance, just as *tituli* were inscribed underneath the images in Padua, so were *tituli* also under the lost frescoes in Florence, in the vestibule of the chapel of the Palazzo Pubblico in Siena, in the Castle at Manta, and in the Palazzo Trinci in Foligno.[157] And if the Paduan hall included a picture of the *Triumph of Fame,* as it almost certainly did, it was in that respect like the halls which were decorated by the two great princely families of northern Italy, the Visconti in Milan and the della Scala in Verona.

But more noteworthy than these resemblances is the fact that the exclusively Roman subject-matter of the Paduan hall seems to have been unique,[158] and it deserves special attention, there-

---

the decorations in the palace of Braccio Baglioni in Perugia, in the audience hall of the "Riformatori dello Stato della Libertà" in Bologna, and in the Ferrarese castle of Belriguardo. One might also add Paolo Uccello's "Giganti" in the palace of the Vitaliani in Padua, and the portraits of famous men and women which Andrea del Castagno painted in a country-house outside Florence.—Compare also M. Wackernagel, *Der Lebensraum des Künstlers in der florentinischen Renaissance,* Leipzig, 1938, pp. 154 f.

156 See Giovio's description of his collection in *Elogia doctorum virorum,* Basel, 1571, pp. 5–14; especially p. 12: "Publicatis ac in Musaeo tanquam augusto Virtutis templo dedicatis clarorum virorum tabulis, illae ipsae veluti spirantes imagines aequissimo iure deposcunt, ut Musaeum quoque, sua sacrata sedes, eodem conditoris stylo describatur."

157 The poems celebrating the *Neuf preux* in Naples did not form a part of the decoration but were composed shortly afterwards; see G. de Blasiis, *Napoli Nobilissima,* IX, 1900, pp. 65 f.; Schubring, *Repertorium für Kunstwissenschaft,* XXIII, 1900, p. 424.

158 If we can trust a somewhat inconclusive Sienese tradition of the early fifteenth century, there existed in the fourteenth century another decoration depicting stories from Roman history. For the *Cronaca Senese attribuita ad Agnolo di Tura del Grasso detta la Cronaca Maggiore* (ed. A. Lisini, in Muratori, *Rerum Italicarum Scriptores,* Bologna, 1931–35, XV, part VI, p. 518) contains the following statement (under the year 1337): "Sanesi avendo fatto el palazo co' la prigione nuova, e sopra la sala del conseglio fecero le camere de' Signori e d'altri famegli nella sala del

fore, in the history of Italian art of the early Renaissance. This uniqueness resulted from an idea which was conceived, it seems to me, by none but Petrarch himself. As has been mentioned before, he intended originally to write about "the illustrious men of all countries and ages." Such a plan was entirely in accordance with the customary mediaeval conception of universal history. In his *Trionfi,* especially in the Triumph of Fame, Petrarch remained faithful to the mediaeval tradition, listing among his famous men and women great figures of the Old Testament, of Greco-Roman antiquity, and of the mediaeval romances and legends. But as far as his historical work was concerned, Petrarch decided very early to confine himself exclusively to one people and one period, the era of Roman greatness from Romulus to Titus or Trajan. This new conception of history was formulated most succinctly by him when he asked in one of his latest writings: "What else, then, is all history, if not the praise of Rome?" [159] And even within this limited compass Petrarch did not propose to write about all the men who had been outstand-

Palazo del mezo, e fecelle dipegnare di fuore a storie romane di mano di maestro Ambruogio Lorenzetti da Siena." E. von Meyenburg, *Ambrogio Lorenzetti,* Heidelberg, dissertation, 1903, p. 16, quotes the above passage and refers in this connection also to the following passage in Vasari's *Vita di Ambruogio Lorenzetti* (ed. Milanesi, I, p. 523): ". . . e nel medesimo palazzo [i.e., the Palazzo Pubblico of Siena] fece otto storie di verdeterra, molto pulitamente"; according to Milanesi, *ibid.,* p. 523, n. 4, those Roman scenes "furono dipinte nel 1345, ma da gran tempo sono perdute."—If the attribution to Ambrogio Lorenzetti can be accepted as reliable and correct, that lost representation of an exclusively Roman subject-matter could be interpreted as another instance of Ambrogio's "interesse per il passato, nella duplice qualità di artista e di archeologo," which was noted by G. Rowley, "Ambrogio Lorenzetti il pensatore," *La Balzana,* XX, 1927, p. 214; on Ambrogio's interest in classical antiquity, see also von Meyenburg, *op. cit.,* p. 13; G. Sinibaldi, *I Lorenzetti,* Siena, 1933, pp. 82 ff.; Meiss, *op. cit.,* p. 157. However, it ought to be noted in this connection that Lorenzo Ghiberti in his *Commentarii* does not mention those alleged "storie romane," despite his recognition of Ambrogio's special interest in the antique. Since the representation of an entirely classical subject appears to be foreign to the whole spirit of the early Trecento, the assumption of such a work by Ambrogio Lorenzetti seems rather doubtful, a doubt which my friend George Rowley shares with me.

[159] *Apologia contra cuiusdam anonymi Galli calumnias* (in Petrarch's *Opera,* ed. 1581, p. 1076): "Quid est enim aliud omnis historia quam Romana laus?'

ing in Roman history, but only about those whose personalities and characters, as he saw them, were shaped and dominated by their innate *virtus* in such a manner that they were able to perform deeds worthy of being remembered and imitated by posterity.

The galaxy of the great men of Rome that we find in the final version of his work *De viris illustribus* derived from and expressed a very definite judgment of value on the part of Petrarch. It is evident that the images of the same men in the Sala Virorum Illustrium and the representations of their main deeds, which were given underneath the portraits in the pictorial scenes and the inscribed *tituli,* were meant to imply the same normative character.

If we now look over the schemes of the other "Halls of Famous Men" decorated during Petrarch's lifetime, we see immediately that none of them was in accordance with this fundamental conception of Petrarch. There was nothing Roman and not even the slightest homogeneity in the hall at Verona in which illustrations of Flavius Josephus' *Jewish War* were combined with portraits of political and literary figures of the fourteenth century. Men like Attila or Charlemagne, who were portrayed among others in the Castle at Milan, certainly did not qualify, in Petrarch's opinion, as *viri illustres,* but they were men whose power was the gift of *fortuna* and not of *virtus.*[160] In regard to the pictures of the strange "Nine Worthies" and their wives in Castelnuovo at Naples, it has been considered curious that in his *Iter Syriacum* Petrarch does not refer to this work of Giotto although he commends Giotto's activity in Naples.[161] If any conclusion at all can be drawn from this omission, it may be that Petrarch considered that selection of heroes to be completely arbitrary and therefore hardly worth noticing; in other instances as well, in order to show his rejection of matters alien to him, Petrarch simply passed them over in silence.

[160] On this distinction between men who are merely "homines fortunati" and those who are truly "viri illustres," compare Petrarch's final preface to *De viris illustribus* (ed. de Nolhac, *op. cit.,* p. 112, ll. 69–72).

[161] *Iter Syriacum,* ed. G. Lumbroso, *Atti d. R. Accad. d. Lincei,* 1888, ser. IV, Rendiconti, IV, 398, ll. 232–234; see G. de Blasiis, *Napoli Nobilissima,* IX, 1900, p. 65.

Of the later "Halls of Famous Men," only that in the Palazzo Trinci at Foligno seems to come close to Petrarch's ideas. For it contains only Roman statesmen and generals from the time of Romulus to Trajan, and we even find that sixteen of the twenty men portrayed in Foligno belong also to Petrarch's series of *viri illustres*. But among the four others are three whom Petrarch explicitly considered disqualified, Cato Uticensis on account of his suicide, Tiberius and Caligula because of their vices.

Thus it seems that the Sala Virorum Illustrium in Padua stands by itself in the series of decorated halls of the early Italian Renaissance. From this point of view it appears logical that the room also reveals, together with the *Triumph of Fame* and the representations of the images and the deeds of the great men of Rome, the portrait of the man who inspired this remarkably unified work of program-painting.

Throughout all his writings Petrarch endeavored to recall to the memory of his Italian contemporaries the great personifications of the antique *virtus Romana*. In the preface to his work *De viris illustribus* he declares: "Indeed, if I am not mistaken, it is the fruitful task of the historian to make known that which the reader should imitate or which he should avoid, so that of these two a number of illustrious examples are available." [162]

In the Sala Virorum Illustrium of Francesco il Vecchio da Carrara in Padua, Petrarch's conception of the exemplary value of the history of Rome personified by her great men found its visual expression. And the words written by Lombardo della Seta to the prince who commissioned this unique decoration might also have been addressed as an admonition and a challenge to every beholder of these pictures: "Keep always in sight these men whom you ought to be eager to love because of the greatness of their deeds."

[162] Ed. de Nolhac, *op. cit.*, p. 113: "Hic enim, nisi fallor, fructuosus historici finis est illa prosequi, que vel sectanda legentibus vel fugienda sunt, ut in utramque partem copia suppetat illustrium exemplorum."

9

Petrarch and the Story of the Choice of Hercules*

IN his book *Hercules am Scheidewege,* Erwin Panofsky has shown how the ancient tale of the choice of Hercules became during the Renaissance a favourite theme of humanist writers and playwrights, and of artists, especially in Italy and Germany.[1] The great popularity of the theme in antiquity as well as in the Renaissance and afterwards is striking in contrast to its complete absence from the work of mediaeval writers and artists. According to Panofsky, "the topic was revived in literature only around the year 1400," making its first appearance in Coluccio Salutati's treatise *De laboribus Herculis.*[2] Panofsky supported this point by remarking that "neither do Petrarch and Boccaccio mention the decision of Hercules nor do the mediaeval mythographers, Berchorius, Villena and the *Livre du fort Hercules.*" [3]

* Reprinted from the *Journal of the Warburg and Courtauld Institutes,* XVI (1953), 178–192.

[1] E. Panofsky, *Hercules am Scheidewege und andere antike Bildstoffe in der neueren Kunst: Studien der Bibliothek Warburg,* XVIII, Leipzig and Berlin, 1930; see also E. Tietze-Conrat, "Notes on Hercules at the Crossroads," this *Journal,* XIV, 1951, pp. 305–309.

[2] Panofsky, *op. cit.,* p. 155. Salutati's treatise has just been edited by B. L. Ullman, *De laboribus Herculis,* 2 vols., Zürich, 1951; on this treatise, see the remarks made by E. Garin in the preface to his edition of Salutati's *De nobilitate legum et medicinae,* Florence, 1947, pp. xxviii f., and by Ullman, *op. cit.,* pp. vii–xiv.

[3] Panofsky, *op. cit.,* p. 155, n. 2.

This statement requires a modification as far as Petrarch is concerned, for he actually did know the story.

Petrarch, to be sure, does not mention the choice of Hercules where one would expect to find it, in the "Life of Hercules," which formed a part of the first version of his biographical collection *De viris illustribus* and which was probably written in the year 1337 or shortly afterwards.[4] It is true that he never finished that biography, but if he had intended to tell of the decision made by the young Hercules, he would have done so at the beginning. The name of Hercules appears a number of times in Petrarch's *Rerum Memorandarum Libri*,[5] and in his correspondence,[6] but always without any reference to the choice. However, in his *De vita solitaria,* which he began in 1346, Petrarch referred in two different places (1, 4, 2; 2, 9, 4) very explicitly to the choice of Hercules.

Before starting the discussion of these passages it is necessary to ask why the ancient tale was so completely neglected throughout the Middle Ages. At first this phenomenon seems rather strange, because mediaeval scholars certainly must have come upon the story in Cicero's *De officiis* (1, 32, 118; 3, 5, 25), and, one might think, must have found its moral lesson highly commendable. Actually, however, as Panofsky proved very convincingly, the story implied a moral conception which from the Christian point of view was much too pagan and secular and therefore had to be passed over in silence.[7] In the first place, the two ways of life were represented in the tale by the personifications of what was considered praiseworthy and bad *(virtus* and *voluptas)* in a strictly earthly sense and not at all in accord-

[4] Edited by P. de Nolhac, "Le *De viris illustribus* de Pétrarque," *Notices et extraits des manuscrits de la Bibliothèque Nationale,* XXXIV, Paris, 1891, pp. 134–136; on the complex question of the chronology of the various versions of Petrarch's historical works, see the bibliography in my article, "Petrarch and the Decoration of the *Sala virorum illustrium* in Padua," *The Art Bulletin,* XXXIV, 1952, p. 97, n. 24. [See above, p. 135, n. 24.]

[5] See the index in G. Billanovich's edition of *Rerum Memorandarum Libri,* Florence, 1943, p. 294.

[6] See the index in V. Rossi's and U. Bosco's edition of *Le Familiari,* IV, Florence, 1942, p. 326.

[7] Panofsky, *op. cit.,* p. 156.

ance with the Christian interpretation of the eternal meaning of good and evil. And secondly, no Christian was given the right, which in the story was claimed for Hercules, to make an entirely free and wholly individual choice concerning the basic direction of his life; it was granted only to Christ that "he may know to refuse the evil and choose the good" (Isaiah vii. 15).

Panofsky discussed this tacit rejection of the tale of the choice of Hercules in connexion with his observation that throughout the Middle Ages artists created many pictorial and sculptural images of the various *virtutes* and *vitia,* either in whole cycles or individually, but no representations of *virtus* or *vitium* in general.[8] The ancients had held, of course, the concept of a supreme Virtue, the *dea virtus,* which could be depicted in an anthropomorphic figure, but such deification of *virtus* was not acceptable to any Christian theologian. Thus it was denounced in the most explicit terms by St. Augustine who wrote in *The City of God:* "[The pagans] made also *virtus* a goddess; if she really were a goddess, she would indeed have to be preferred to many others; but since actually she is not a goddess but a gift of God, she is to be obtained by Him by whom alone she can be given." [9] The *virtus Dei* as the power of God in the fullest sense was personified by Christ alone, as St. Paul taught.[10] It was therefore in complete accordance with the Christian refutation of the pagan concept of the *dea virtus,* Panofsky said, that "mediaeval thinking could no longer seek for the supreme Virtue in the anthropomorphic but only in the metaphysical sphere." [11] On the other hand, since the individual *virtutes* were to be achieved by man in this world, they could be represented by earthly personifications, such as the life-like figures of women.[12]

8 Panofsky, *op. cit.,* pp. 151 f.

9 *De civitate Dei,* ed. J. E. C. Welldon, IV, 20 A: "Virtutem quoque deam fecerunt; quae quidem si dea esset, multis fuerat praeferenda. Et nunc quia dea non est, sed donum Dei est, ipsa ab illo inpetretur, a quo solo dari potest, et omnis falsorum deorum turba vanescet"; quoted by Panofsky, *op. cit.,* pp. 152 f.; see also *De civitate Dei,* IV, 21 A, and V, 12 K.

10 I Cor. i. 24: ". . . Christum Dei virtutem et Dei sapientiam."

11 Panofsky, *op. cit.,* p. 153.

12 Panofsky, *op. cit.,* pp. 151 ff.; see also E. Mandowsky, *Untersuchungen zur Iconologie des Cesare Ripa,* Dissertation, Hamburg, 1934, pp. 18 f.;

The Augustinian distinction between the supranatural character of the supreme *virtus Dei* on one side, and the variety of the cardinal, theological and other *virtutes* entering into the realm of human life on the other side, apparently dominated artistic tradition to the very end of the Middle Ages. Whosoever wanted to deviate from that tradition and create an image of the supreme Virtue could do so only in full awareness of the novelty of his attempt. This becomes evident to the reader of the remarks which the Tuscan writer and designer Francesco da Barberino (1264–1348) made in the Latin commentaries to his work *Documenti d'Amore* (published in 1314).[13] In connexion with his discussion of "the three kinds of *virtus* (i.e., *naturalis, spiritualis, and animalis*)," Francesco da Barberino said that he intended "to represent the *virtus moralis in genere*." As he knew, "some people declared that although it is possible to represent in images the *virtutes in specie,* it is impossible to depict the *virtus in genere*." But in spite of those objections Francesco decided "to proceed *ad istam generalitatem figurandam*," and actually drew a sketch of the *virtus in genere* or *virtus generalis*. He did so "not without some great hesitation," as he admitted himself, because he was conscious of "the novelty of the image" to be introduced by him.[14]

A. Katzenellenbogen, *Allegories of the Virtues and Vices in Mediaeval Art from Early Christian Times to the Present Century,* London, 1939.

[13] The work was edited by F. Egidi, 4 vols., Rome, 1905–27; as to the date of its composition, see *ibid.,* IV, pp. XXXIII–XLI; on Francesco da Barberino's life and works, compare Egidi's article in *Enciclopedia Italiana,* VI, 1930, p. 141 (with bibliography). I owe the reference to the subsequently discussed passage in the *Documenti d'Amore* to Professor Panofsky who discovered it only after he had published his *Hercules am Scheidewege.*

[14] Ed. Egidi, *op. cit.,* I, 66: "Sed primo quidem nobis videndum est et sciendum, quod tres species sunt virtutis: naturalis, spiritualis et animalis. Forma tamen virtutis, quam representare intendo, est moralis in genere, ut ad omnem se moralem hoc genus extendat, et ita idem dico de vitiis, que consistunt in omnia. Nec obmicto, quamvis aliqui dixerint, quod licet possibile sit representare in figuris virtutes in specie, tamen in genere figurare virtutem impossibile videbatur, quin ad istam generalitatem figurandam procedam non in contentum illorum sed ad quandam qualem novitatis effigiem inducendam in amoris honorem servorumque suorum gaudium aliquale. Et quia facto rei cuilibet fundamento, ut dicitur supra circa principium prohemii ibi ubi de amoris forma tractatur [see *op. cit.,*

Francesco da Barberino's allegorical image of the *virtus generalis* remained, it seems, unique of its kind for a long while, and the artists of the Trecento and Quattrocento continued to depict, in accordance with the mediaeval tradition, merely the "special" virtues and vices.[15] It was only a century and a half after the composition of the *Documenti d'Amore* that another Italian, Antonio Averlino, who chose to call himself Filarete, "the friend of Virtue," attempted again to design an allegorical image of the supreme *virtù*, as distinguished from the allegories representing the "special" virtues. In his *Trattato d'Architettura*, which was written between the years 1460 and 1464,[16] Filarete described an imaginary "House of Virtue and Vice" to be erected in the future city of *Sforzinda*, and said that this temple was to be crowned by a statue personifying *virtù*. In this connexion he declared that he tried to find out "through reading and through inquiry whether *virtù* and *vitio* had ever been represented in such a way that either one of them could be perceived in a single figure." But, he said, "I have not found as yet that they were represented in one figure," whereas there existed,

I, 8 f.], igitur reservatis rationibus formarum et locorum hic designatorum infra loco suo antequam ad aliorum expositionem divertatur, et reservato etiam ipsius moralis virtutis tractatu similiter loco suo hic figuras ipsius generalis virtutis et vitiorum, secundum quod capere potuit mei modicitas intellectus, non sine quadam magna dubitatione represento." With the remark: "Vide illas: hic sunt," Francesco refers to a sketch on the same page which shows the *virtus in genere* being attacked by ten figures which represent the vices, under the heading: "hec sunt opposita"; see *ibid.*, I, 66, Egidi's drawing of Francesco's sketch; a photographic reproduction of the original sketch (from Cod. Barber. 4076, f. 6^{v}) was published by Egidi in his earlier article "Le miniature dei codici barberiniani dei *Documenti d'Amore*," *L'Arte*, V, 1902, p. 89. See also Francesco's discussion of the *virtus moralis* and the question of its representation, as well as that of the *vitia*, somewhat later in the same chapter of the *Documenti d'Amore*, ed. Egidi, I, 72–76.

[15] See, e.g., the illuminated German manuscript of the early 15th century, which was described and analysed by F. Saxl, "Aller Tugenden und Laster Abbildung," *Festschrift für J. Schlosser*, 1926, pp. 104–121; see esp. the picture of the assault made by the vices upon the castle of the virtues (*ibid.*, fig. 52); see also Panofsky, *op. cit.*, p. 79.

[16] The text of Filarete's *Trattato d' Architettura* was edited, partly in the Italian original and partly in German translation, by W. v. Oettingen, *Quellenschriften für Kunstgeschichte und Kunsttechnik des Mittelalters und der Neuzeit*, N. F. III, Vienna, 1890.

of course, many representations of the four cardinal and the three theological virtues or of the seven principal vices.[17] According to Filarete, the only personifications of *virtù* and *vitio* were to be found in the story of the choice of Hercules, as told by Xenophon.[18] Since Filarete considered these latter allegories "unsatisfactory," he decided to use his own mind and imagination and proceeded "to represent *virtù* and *vitio,* each alone and by itself in one figure." [19] These remarks indicate that in the second part of the fifteenth century the conception of an allegorical representation of *virtus generalis* was still as much of "a novelty" as had been the case around the year 1300 when Francesco da Barberino wrote his *Documenti d'Amore.* In fact, Filarete himself made it very manifest how proud he was of his innovation, which he called "a worthy and memorable enterprise, not yet undertaken in any other place." [20]

It is worth noticing that while Francesco da Barberino, in his

[17] The Italian text of this passage in bk. XVIII of Filarete's treatise was published by Panofsky, *op. cit.,* pp. 188 f: "Si che immaginando io più volte, a che cose si potesse asomigliare questa virtù et questo vitio si possa asomigliare che più propria paresse, et leggendo et domandando, se mai alcuno di questi avessi figurati immodo che in una figura comprendere si potesse l'uno essere il vitio et l'altra la virtù, io non o ancora trovato che in una figura figurate fussono come impiù, come a dire le quattro virtù cardinali et le tre theologiche, et così i septe vitii principali, che chi a uno animale et chi a un altro et così ancora la virtù a varie figure asimigliate." Compare the abridged German translation of this passage by v. Oettingen, *op. cit.,* p. 500.

[18] Ed. Panofsky, *op. cit.,* p. 189: "Vero è che Seneca [according to Panofsky, *op. cit.,* pp. 194 f., a misreading in the text for Senofonte] le discrive in forma di donna vestita di biancho e 'l vitio pure in forma di donna molto adornata di begli vestimenti et figure, che in sonno venissono dinanzi a Ercole et a dimostrargli, che ciascheduno dovesse seguitare le sue vestigie, così il vitio come la virtù, ogniuno gli profferiva de' suoi fructi et chi dolci et chi bruschi, et lui, come savio, prese più presto le bruschi che dolci."

[19] Ed. Panofsky, *op. cit.,* p. 189: "Si che, vedute tutte queste similitudini et intese, non nella mente mi sodisfaceva, immodo che collo 'ngegnio mi missi a fantasticare et pensare tanto, che pure mi venne nella mente di figurare il vitio et la virtù in una figura sola ciascuna di per se, le quali stanno in questa forma, che qui narrerò et anche per disegnio potrete la sua forma vedere." Compare the rest of the passage, ed. Panofsky, *op. cit.,* pp. 189–192, and the reproductions of three of Filarete's drawings, *ibid.,* figs. 117–119.

[20] *Trattato d'Architettura,* bk. IX, ed. v. Oettingen, *op. cit.,* p. 306: "Per la loggia dinanzi dalla porta, sotto il portico, io ò pensato quello a me

discussion of the problem of *virtus generalis,* had abided by the mediaeval tradition in so far as he avoided any reference in his *Documenti d'Amore* to the choice of Hercules, Filarete, in his search for previous representations of the single or supreme *virtù* and *vitio,* did recall it. In five or six generations humanistic studies had made so much progress that Filarete could not only tell the story but could allude to its Greek version in Xenophon's *Memorabilia.*[21] This observation brings us back to Petrarch who, one generation later than Francesco da Barberino, first revived that tale, in two places in his *De vita solitaria.*

The first of these passages (1, 4, 2) reads as follows: "It were an excellent thing, if want of counsel, the unavoidable concomitant of youth, did not stand in the way, that each one of us at the very beginning of his maturity should give careful and earnest thought to the selection of some particular kind of life, nor ever turn aside from the path he had once chosen, except for important reasons or for some grave necessity; Hercules did so on entering manhood as is testified by Xenophon, the pupil of Socrates, and by Cicero." [22]

Petrarch did not know Greek, and Xenophon had not yet

---

pare ci stia bene; e sarà cosa degnia e memorabile, e non è ancora fatta in altri luoghi. Quello che a me pare, che ui stia bene, si è la Virtù e 'l Vitio, e nel modo ch'io l'ò figurato nel libro del bronzo" (a reference to a passage in book IV of the *Trattato,* ed. v. Oettingen, p. 132). See also Panofsky, *op. cit.,* pp. 192–194. On the "esoteric character" of some late 14th-century French manuscripts of Aristotle's works, which contain representations of the general Virtue, see Panofsky, *op. cit.,* pp. 150 ff., 160, 193.

21 That Filarete derived his account from Xenophon's text and not from the Latin version of the story in Cicero's *De officiis,* is clearly shown by a comparison of the text in the *Trattato d'Architettura* with that in the *Memorabilia* (2, 1, 21–34).

22 Quoted from the excellent translation of Petrarch's *Life of Solitude,* which was made by J. Zeitlin, Urbana, Ill., 1924, p. 133; the Latin text, in Petrarch's *Opera,* Basle, 1581, p. 234, reads as follows: "Optimum quidem esset, nisi consilii inopia iugis adolescentiae comes obstaret, ut ab ineunte aetate circa unum aliquod vitae genus apprehendendum unusquisque nostrum accuratissime cogitaret nec ab illo calle, quem semel elegisset, nisi magnis ex causis aut gravi necessitate diverteret. Quod initio pubertatis fecisse Herculem auctor Xenophon ille Socraticus testis est et Cicero"; see also A. Altamura's edition of *De vita solitaria,* Naples, 1943, pp. 36 f. On the history of the work, see B. L. Ullman, "The composition of Petrarch's *De vita solitaria* and the history of the Vatican manuscript," *Miscellanea Giovanni Mercati,* 1946, IV, 107–142.

been translated into Latin. Therefore Petrarch's source of information was exclusively Cicero's *De officiis* (1, 32, 118; 3, 5, 25). When he very learnedly cited Xenophon as his first authority, he derived that knowledge also from Cicero and not from any personal acquaintance with the *Memorabilia;* there are many similar examples of this method of indirect quotation to be found in Petrarch's writings.

It will be noted that in this first passage Petrarch referred to the decision made by Hercules only in a rather general fashion, without any indication of the specific choice between the two ways of life, personified as they were in Cicero's account by *virtus* and *voluptas.* And it is interesting to observe that somewhat later in the same chapter Petrarch expressed the problem of finding the right way in an entirely Christian fashion and not at all in the terms of pagan antiquity: "If a man has been illumined by the celestial light at his very entrance into life, when, as I have already said, not a spark of judgment is active, and if he has been able to find a safe road or one whose dangers are slight and easily avoided, he has reason for everlasting gratitude to God." [23]

In the second passage of *De vita solitaria* (2, 9, 4), Petrarch spoke about people of the past who loved solitude. After a brief discussion of Romulus and Achilles he said: "Hercules too attained in solitude that wholesome plan of life which I have mentioned in the preceding book [1, 4, 2], when, hesitating long and much as though at a parting of the ways, he ultimately spurned the way of pleasure and took possession of the path of virtue, and marching indefatigably along its course, he was raised not only to the apex of human glory but even to a reputation of divinity. Although the fame of this man extends its branches high and wide, if you look for its roots, your mind must turn back to solitude." [24]

[23] Translat. by Zeitlin, *op. cit.,* p. 133; ed. *Opera,* 1581, p. 234: "Cui autem in ingressu viae huius, quando ut dixi, scintilla nostri consilii nulla erat, coeleste aliquod lumen affulsit, ut vel securum vel periculi minoris et facile remediabile iter arriperet, habet unde semper Deo gratias agat."

[24] Translat. by Zeitlin, *op. cit.,* pp. 286 f.; ed. *Opera,* 1581, p. 283: "Ipse Hercules in solitudine sanum illud consilium vitae coepit, cuius libro priore mentionem feci, quando velut in bivio diu multumque haesitans ad

It is evident that in this passage Petrarch followed the text of Cicero much more closely than in the earlier one although this time he did not cite his authority. But it was obviously Cicero's text which led him to say that Hercules went into solitude and pondered there for a long while over the question of the right choice, and it was also in accordance with Cicero when Petrarch spoke of the two roads as the ways of *virtus* and *voluptas*. Petrarch's remark that Hercules was raised to "the reputation of divinity" likewise agreed with Cicero's statement that "popular belief has given him a place in the council of the Gods." [25]

But in this second passage in *De vita solitaria* Petrarch used one very interesting phrase which did not occur in Cicero's text, although one might say that it was implied in it. For whereas

---

postremum spreta voluptatis via semitam virtutis arripuit, quam indefesse gradiens non ad humanae modo gloriae verticem, sed ad opinionem divinitatis evectus est, quamlibet alte lateque ramos porrigat viri fama, si radicem quaeras, ad solitudinem erit animo recurrendum"; compare the text edited by Altamura, *op. cit.*, p. 137.

[25] In the following two passages from Cicero's work, I have italicized those words which Petrarch transcribed in his treatise. *De officiis*, 1, 32, 118: "Nam quod *Herculem* Prodicus dicit, ut est apud *Xenophontem, cum primum pubesceret, quod tempus a natura ad deligendum, quam quisque viam vivendi sit ingressurus, datum est, exisse in solitudinem* atque ibi sedentem *diu secum multumque dubitasse, cum duas cerneret vias, unam Voluptatis, alteram Virtutis, utram ingredi melius esset,* hoc Herculi 'Iovis satu edito' potuit fortasse contingere, nobis non item, qui imitamur, quos cuique visum est, atque ad eorum studia institutaque impellimur." *De officiis*, 3, 5, 25: "Itemque magis est secundum naturam pro omnibus gentibus, si fieri possit, conservandis aut iuvandis maximos labores molestiasque suscipere imitantem *Herculem* illum, quem *hominum fama* beneficiorum memor *in concilio caelestium collocavit,* quam vivere in solitudine non modo sine ullis molestiis, sed etiam in maximis voluptatibus abundantem omnibus copiis, ut excellas etiam pulchritudine et viribus." It may be noted that Petrarch, though following the text of Cicero in other respects, deviated on one rather personal point very markedly from his authority. For, whereas Cicero declared it to be "more in accord with nature to emulate Hercules and undergo the greatest toil and trouble for the sake of aiding or saving the world, if possible, than to live in solitude, not only free from all care but revelling in pleasures . . . ," Petrarch, in accord with his high praise of the solitary life in his treatise of this title, asserted explicitly that, "if you look for the roots of Hercules' fame, your mind must turn back to solitude"; cf. also *De vita solitaria*, 1, 3, 2 (translat. by Zeitlin, p. 125). The English translation of the two passages in *De officiis*, is that given by W. Miller in *The Loeb Classical Library*, 1903, pp. 121, 291 f.

Cicero said (*De officiis,* 1, 32, 118) that Hercules "saw two ways," Petrarch stated more explicitly that the hero found himself "as it were *in bivio*," at a parting of the ways. The assumption seems warranted that Petrarch inserted this particular term *in bivio* because he remembered that it appeared quite regularly in another traditional allegory symbolizing the two ways of life, the concept of "the Pythagorean letter," the Y, which was developed in antiquity and remained alive throughout the Middle Ages.[26] For instance, in the second part of the fourth century, Servius wrote in his *Commentarii in Vergilii Aeneidos:* "As we know, Pythagoras of Samos divided human life according to the form of the letter Y; in the uncertainty of early age men have not yet given themselves to virtues and vices; but the parting of the ways *(bivium),* [symbolized by the two upper shafts] of the letter Y, begins with adolescence at the time when men follow either the vices, that is the left side, or the virtues, that is the right side." [27] The allegorical meaning of the *bivium* as illustrated by the Y was interpreted in a very similar fashion by Ausonius, St. Jerome and Martianus Capella.[28]

[26] On this concept see especially C. Pascal, "Il bivio della vita e la littera Pythagorae," *Miscellanea Ceriani,* Milan, 1910, pp. 57–67; furthermore: C. Taylor, "The Two Ways in Hermas and Xenophon," *The Journal of Philology,* XXI, 1893, pp. 247 ff.; W. Schultz, "Herakles am Scheidewege," *Philologus,* LXVIII, 1909, pp. 488–499; A. Brinkmann, "Ein Denkmal des Neupythagoreismus," *Rheinisches Museum für Philologie,* N. F. LXVI, 1911, pp. 616–625; J. Alpers, *Hercules in bivio,* Dissertation, Göttingen, 1912, passim; F. Dornseiff, *Das Alphabet in Mystik und Magie* (*Stoicheia,* VII), 1925, pp. 24, 172; E. Panofsky, *op. cit.,* pp. 44, 64–68; A. Friberg, *Den Svenske Herkules; Studier I: Stiernhielms Diktning,* Stockholm, 1945, pp. 122–161 (see the French summary, *ibid.,* pp. 264–266); see also *Thesaurus Linguae Latinae,* II, col. 2024 f., s.v. "bivium."

[27] Servius, *In Aeneid.,* VI, 136 (ed. G. Thilo, II, 30 f.): "Novimus Pythagoram Samium vitam humanam divisisse in modum Y litterae, scilicet quod prima aetas incerta sit, quippe quae adhuc se nec vitiis nec virtutibus dedit; bivium autem Y litterae a iuventute incipere, quo tempore homines aut vitia, id est partem sinistram, aut virtutes, id est dexteram partem sequuntur.' Compare also the much earlier lines in Persius, *Satirae,* 3, 56–57, where, however, the word *bivium* does not appear: "Et tibi, quae Samios diduxit littera ramos, / Surgentem dextro monstravit limite callem."

[28] Martianus Capella, *De nuptiis philologiae et Mercurii,* 2, 102; Ausonius, *De litteris monosyllabis* (348), 9; St. Jerome, *Epistolae,* 107, 6, 3 (ed. I. Hilberg, in *Corpus scriptorum ecclesiasticorum Latinorum,* LV, 1912, p. 297).

The allegory met, however, also with pronounced opposition among some early Christian theologians, as Lactantius' *Divine Institutes* shows. Lactantius knew that the pagan philosophers had spoken of the two ways and "represented the one as belonging to the virtues, the other to the vices," but he objected that "these men because they were ignorant or in doubt in regard to the fact that the souls of men are immortal, evaluated both virtues and vices in terms of earthly honours or punishments." [29] He also remembered that "they say that the course of human life resembles the letter Y," but again he rejected the purely secular interpretation of that symbol by which "they referred the end of those ways to the body, and to this life which we lead on earth." [30] Lactantius granted that the poets had perhaps more correctly dealt with that *bivium* than the philosophers had done,[31] but nevertheless he felt obliged to ask "what need is there of the letter Y" in a matter, the choice of the right life, concerning which pagans and Christians held so completely divergent views.[32] Thus he stated most emphatically: "We bring forward these ways in a very different manner from that in which the philosophers are accustomed to present them: first of all, because we say that a guide is proposed to each, and in each case an immortal one: but that the one is honoured who presides over virtues and over the good, the other is condemned who presides over vices and the bad." [33]

[29] Lactantius, *Div. Instit.*, 6, 3, 1–2 (ed. S. Brandt, *Corp. script. eccl. Lat.*, XIX, 1890, p. 485): "Duae sunt uiae, per quas humanam uitam progredi necesse est, una quae in caelum ferat, altera quae ad inferos deprimat; quas et poetae in carminibus et philosophi in disputationibus suis induxerunt. Et quidem philosophi alteram uirtutum esse uolerunt, alteram uitiorum"; *ibid.*, 6, 3, 5: "Hi uero quia ignorabant aut dubitabant animas hominum inmortales esse, et uirtutes et uitia terrenis honoribus aut poenis aestimauerunt"; translat. by W. Fletcher, *The Ante-Nicene Fathers,* VII, 1905, p. 164.

[30] *Div. Instit.*, 6, 3, 6: "Dicunt enim humanae uitae cursum Y litterae similem"; *ibid.*, 6, 3, 9: "Ad corpus ergo et ad hanc uitam, quam in terra ducimus, fines earum uiarum rettulerunt."

[31] *Div. Instit.*, 6, 3, 9.

[32] *Div. Instit.*, 6, 3, 17: "Quid enim opus est Y littera in rebus contrariis atque diuersis?"

[33] *Div. Instit.*, 6, 3, 14: "Has igitur uias longe aliter inducimus, quam induci a philosophis solent, primum quod utrique praepositum esse dicimus

In spite of the serious objections expressed by Lactantius, the Pythagorean letter was often recalled by Christian writers. For instance, Isidore of Seville declared in his *Etymologiae:* "Pythagoras of Samos was the first to form the letter Y as an example of human life. For its lower shaft signifies early age in its uncertainty, which has not yet given itself either to the vices or the virtues. The *bivium,* however, which is above, starts with adolescence; its right side is steep but reaches to the blessed life; the left side is easier but leads down to fall and ruin." [34] This inclusion of the traditional concept of the Y in Isidore's encyclopaedia probably accounts for the great popularity which the symbol enjoyed from the Carolingian era to the end of the Middle Ages. As Manitius has stated, it became quite a common practice to use the phrase *ad Pythagoricae litterae bivium pervenire.*[35] For example, the Friar Salimbene of Parma said in his *Cronica* that he entered the Franciscan Order at the age of fifteen years, "when I arrived at the parting of the ways of the Pythagorean letter." [36] In the fourteenth century, Richard de

---

ducem utrumque inmortalem, sed alterum honoratum, qui uirtutibus ac bonis praesit, alterum damnatum, qui uitiis ac malis." Compare on this passage, C. Taylor, *op. cit.,* p. 247; see *ibid.,* p. 256, Taylor's remarks about the general background of the idea that "the Christian two ways may have had good and evil angels placed upon them"; see also C. Pascal, *op. cit.,* pp. 59–61; J. Alpers, *op. cit.,* pp. 60–72, and W. Jaeger's remarks in *Göttingische Gelehrte Anzeigen,* CLXXV, 1913, pp. 590 ff.

[34] Isidorus, *Etymolog.,* 1, 3, 7 (ed. W. M. Lindsay, Oxford, 1911): "Y litteram Pythagoras Samius ad exemplum vitae humanae primus formavit; cuius virgula subterior primam aetatem significat, incertam quippe et quae adhuc se nec vitiis nec virtutibus dedit. Bivium autem, quod superest, ab adolescentia incipit: cuius dextra pars ardua est, sed ad beatam vitam tendens: sinistra facilior, sed ad labem interitumque deducens"; Isidore concluded with the lines quoted above [n. 27] from Persius, *Sat.,* 3, 56.

[35] M. Manitius, "Beiträge zur Geschichte römischer Dichter im Mittelalter," *Philologus,* XLVII, 1889, p. 713, n. 3; see also C. Pascal, *op. cit.,* pp. 65–67; F. Dornseiff, *op. cit.,* p. 24; *Die Cambridger Lieder,* ed. K. Strecker, 1926, pp. 22 nr. 3a, 37 nr. 3b; H. Walter, in *Degering-Festschrift,* 1926, pp. 299 nr. 8, 302 f.

[36] Salimbene, *Cronica,* ed. O. Holder-Egger, *Mon. Germ. Script.,* XXXII, 1905–13, p. 38, lines 16–18: ". . . ego frater Salimbene, qui, quando perveni ad bivium Pythagorice littere, id est finitis tribus lustris, . . . ordinem fratrum Minorum intravi . . ."; Salimbene used the same phrase in four other passages in the *Cronica* (pp. 166, l. 25 f., 187 l. 13 f., 265 l. 33 f., 277 l. 25).

Bury, writing in his *Philobiblon,* accused the corrupt clergy of his era in the following words: "At last, yielding your lives to wickedness and reaching the parting of the ways of the Pythagorean figure, you choose the left branch and, turning backward, forsake the lot of the Lord, which you had first chosen, and become partakers with thieves." [37]

Petrarch was well acquainted with the traditional interpretation of the symbol Y. Thus he advised a friend who had started on a political career not to despair of his final salvation for that reason, "as if you had chosen the devious and, as the Pythagoreans call it, the left road." [38] In a letter in which he recommended his young son Giovanni to the care of the grammarian Giberto Baiardi of Parma, Petrarch wrote that the boy "has come in his life to the Pythagorean *bivium:* never is there less prudence, never more peril." [39] After this allusion Petrarch discussed in the rest of the letter the problem of the two ways very much in Christian terms, beginning with the quotation of the famous passage in St. Matthew (vii. 13–14): "Enter ye in at the strait gate: for wide is the gate, and broad is the way, that leadeth to destruction, and many there be which go in thereat; because strait is the gate, and narrow is the way, which leadeth unto life, and few there be that find it." But it is very characteristic of Petrarch that within the subsequent string of quotations from the Old Testament concerning the right way of life he inserted also two passages from "our poet," that is, from Vergil's *Aeneid.*[40] In one of his *Epistles,* Petrarch likewise talked about

[37] *The Philobiblon of Richard de Bury,* translat. by A. F. West, New York, 1889, II, 35; the Latin text, *ibid.,* I, 33: "Tandem aetate succumbente malitiae, figurae Pythagoricae bivium attingentes, ramum laevum eligitis, et retrorsum abeuntes, sortem Domini praeassumptam dimittitis, socii facti furum"; see also West's explanatory note, *ibid.,* III, 109.

[38] *Famil.,* 3, 12, 5: "Tu igitur ne desperes, quasi devium et, ut Pithagorici vocant, levum iter ingressus sis, aut quasi tuorum cura civium, quam geris, divine quam petis gratie sit adversa."

[39] *Famil.,* 7, 17, 1: "Adolescentulum nostrum, consilii inopem et etatis agitatum stimulis, paterne solicitudinis ope complectere. Iam, ut vides, ad bivium pithagoricum vivendo pervenit; nusquam prudentie minus, nusquam periculi magis est."

[40] *Famil.,* 7, 17, 11–13 (with quotations from Proverbs ii. 13; iii. 17; iv. 19 and 27; xv. 19; Psalm xxxv. 6; Liber Ecclesiastici, 21, 11; Jerem. 21, 8; Vergil, *Aen.,* 9, 641 and 6, 542–543).

the two ways of life, "one lofty and hard" which leads to the life eternal but is chosen only by the very few, the other extending in "a deep valley" and leading to Tartarus or, as he said in a later line, to eternal death. "What is it," Petrarch asked, "that compels men, at the *bivium* of the old man of Samos, to deviate to the left side and to hold the right path in such contempt?" [41]

The most interesting discussion of the meaning of the letter Y is to be found in a letter which Petrarch addressed to Zanobi da Strada. He described "that grave matter placed before those who are entering the way of life," the choice of "the path which is more to the right, steep and narrow, thorny and stony." This path, Petrarch explained in Christian terms, is the narrow way to "the true life," whereas the left road, and here Petrarch again quoted Vergil, "wreaks punishment of the wicked and sends them on to pitiless Tartarus." Petrarch continued: "Neither our Maro was ignorant of this nor was Pythagoras when he, following the steps of Cadmus, hammered out on the anvil of his mind that letter which, though superfluous as far as writing goes, is useful for life." [42]

[41] *Epistolae metricae,* 3, 32, ed. D. Rossetti, *Petrarchae poëmata minora,* II, Milan, 1831, p. 150, lines 1–15:

"Artibus ut variis agitur brevis orbita vitae
Et per mille vias metam properamus ad unam.
Ast iter optatum pariter non prendimus omnes,
Altum iter et durum; in primis nec mole gravatis
Corporea ascensus facilis scopulosaque saxis
Undique praeruptis anceps via turbat euntes;
Undique terribiles lapsus atque undique mors est;
Per medium securus eas; hoc tramite pauci
Incedunt. Plures videas in valle profunda
Errantes passim coecos ad Tartara gressus
Ferre. Quid heu tantum fessis mortalibus obstat?
Quid Samii senis in bivio deflectere cogit
Ad laevam atque iter usque adeo contemnere dextrum?
Excelso stat vita loco, nos ima sequentes
Vergimus ad mortem."

As Panofsky, *op. cit.,* p. 67, n. 1, has shown, Petrarch used "in freier Weise" the poem of Maximinus (or Pseudo-Vergil), ed. A. Riese, *Anthologia Latina,* I, 2, 1906, p. 98 nr. 632; on Maximinus, see also C. Pascal, *op. cit.,* pp. 64 f.

[42] *Famil.,* 12, 3, 5–6: "Sentis . . . illud grande discrimen, illud grave negotium, quod intrantibus viam vite huius obicitur: longum iter asperumque, breve tempus et adversum; dexterior trames arduus angustus

It is clear that in this passage, as in the previous one, Petrarch supported the allegorical significance of the Pythagorean letter with references to both the Christian and the classical traditions. But this time he commented on the meaning of the symbol in still another and, it seems, entirely personal and original fashion. "The two-horned form of the letter" he found to be "of exemplary value." For, "with its right horn, though it is narrower, the letter reaches to the stars, whereas on the left side the letter is broader but, through the curve of the horn on that side, is bent toward the earth." [43] The editor of Petrarch's *Familiari,* Vittorio Rossi, has most ingeniously pointed out that for the correct understanding of this passage one has to realize that Petrarch wrote his Y in exactly the same manner in which he described it in this letter: one shaft was drawn in a rather thin stroke, turned somewhat to the right but pointed upward; the left shaft was much broader but on its top the curve was pointed downward.[44] This particular interpretation of the Y, then, was just as much in accordance with Petrarch's handwriting as the explanation of the symbolism of that letter, given by Persius and other Latin writers of antiquity, agreed with their practice of writing it. In their case, "the right way" was represented by the straight main shaft from which the left shaft forked off, at first in a slight angle but after that also going straight up.[45] Thus they could say that the right path rises very steeply and that the ascent on the wrong road seems at first easy and offers

---

vepricosus scrupeus; ea nobis ad veram vitam semita est; 'at leva malorum / Exercet penas et ad impia Tartara mittit' [*Aen.,* 6, 542–543]; quod nec Maro noster ignorat nec Pythagoras ignorabat, dum Cadmi vestigiis insistens scripture supervacuam, sed vite utilem literam in incude ingenii mallearet." On Cadmus and Pythagoras as inventors of the letters of the alphabet, see F. Dornseiff, *op. cit.,* pp. 5 f., 8, 13 f., 24, 114, 170.

[43] *Famil.,* 12, 3, 7: "Bicornis et exemplaris litera dextro cornu arctior tendit ad sidera, levo latior in terram curvata reflectitur; ea, ut aiunt, ad inferos est via, et illa quidem incessu letior ac dulcior, exitu mestissima atque amarissima est, et cuius omnino nil possit miserie superaddi; dextrum vero iter ingressis ut labor ingens sic finis optimus."

[44] See V. Rossi's note in Vol. III, p. 18, of his edition of Petrarch's *Le Familiari* (with a facsimile showing the form in which Petrarch wrote the letter Y).

[45] This observation was made by J. Conington, in a note to his translation of Persius' *Satirae,* Oxford, 1893, p. 61.

its real difficulties only along its later course. But these ancients could not say that the left way ultimately pointed toward a downfall, as Petrarch was to abstract from his own calligraphical usage.

Original though Petrarch was in this specific interpretation of the allegorical significance of the form of the letter Y, in other respects he adhered to the conception of the *bivium,* which had been customary throughout the Middle Ages. For the above three passages in the *Familiari* and the lines in the *Epistola metrica* indicate clearly that the idea of the parting of the ways was to him symbolized primarily by the Pythagorean letter and was in no way connected with the choice of Hercules, which he did not mention at all in those four places. On the other hand, when he resolved, for the only time, it seems, in his own writings, and for the first time in western literature since antiquity, to include in his treatise *De vita solitaria* the story of that choice, he put into his account the phrase *in bivio,* which did not occur in his source, Cicero's *De officiis,* but was well known to him through the mediaeval saying *ad Pythagoricae litterae bivium pervenire.* By combining two literary traditions which in ancient times had been related though never completely tied together, Petrarch was the first, it appears, to coin the phrase *Hercules in bivio,* which for his own era was a real novelty but finally became quite proverbial in Italian as well as in German.[46]

When Coluccio Salutati wrote his long letter to Giovanni of Siena commenting on Seneca's tragedy *Hercules furens,* which he later elaborated into the treatise *De laboribus Herculis,*[47] he included the story of the decision made by the hero in his

[46] See, e.g., the title of an opera by J. A. Hasse, *Alcide al bivio,* which was performed in 1760 with a libretto written by Metastasio (*Opere,* VIII, 1781, pp. 207–248); cf. Panofsky, *op. cit.,* pp. 134 ff.; see *ibid.,* pp. 42 and 48. As to the popularity of the German expression "Herkules am Scheidewege," see G. Büchmann, *Geflügelte Worte,* 1929, p. 194; F. Riedl, "Der Sophist Prodikus und die Wanderung seines 'Herakles am Scheidewege' durch die römische und deutsche Literatur," *Jahresbericht des Staatsgymnasiums zu Laibach,* 1907/8, pp. 34–46.

[47] *De laboribus Herculis,* 3, 7, 1–4, ed. B. L. Ullman, I, 181–183; (see also 3, 15, 17, *ibid.,* p. 249); Salutati's letter to Giovanni da Siena was published by Ullman, *ibid.,* II, 585–635, as "prima editio" of the *De laboribus;* the relevant passages are: 2, 26 and 59 (*ibid.,* pp. 622 and 635).

youth, without taking cognizance, however, of the fact that the tale had made a previous reappearance in Petrarch's *De vita solitaria.*[48] Salutati took his account from the passage in the first book of *De officiis* and did not refer to the other passage in the third book of the same work. He felt obviously somewhat uncertain about the truthfulness of the story, for he concluded his quotation from Cicero with the words: "Whether this is true, I cannot otherwise ascertain." But after this cautious remark he added that "a man of the greatest authority, Basilius, testifies" to the moral lesson of the story as it had been taught by Prodicus and related by Xenophon and Cicero.[49] In this allusion Salutati referred to a passage in St. Basil's treatise *De legendis gentilium libris,* a work known to him through the Latin translation which Leonardo Bruni Aretino had just made and dedicated to him.[50] For the rest of his treatment of the incident it is interesting to note that Salutati, like Petrarch, combined Cicero's account of the choice of Hercules with the traditional allegory of the Pythagorean letter and also employed once, in the letter addressed to Giovanni of Siena, the phrase *in bivio,* which Petrarch had used in the same connexion.[51]

[48] Petrarch's *De vita solitaria* was known, of course, to Salutati; see, e.g., the references to it in two of his letters, one of 1374, the other of 1405 (*Epistolario,* 3, 15, and 14, 19, ed. F. Novati, I, 180, and IV, 135). In his writings on Hercules, according to the index in Ullman's edition, Salutati referred only to one work of Petrarch, the *De remediis utriusque fortunae;* his ignorance of Petrarch's "Life of Hercules" is explained by the fact that Salutati's manuscript of *De viris illustribus* did not contain the non-Roman biographies of the earlier version; cf. G. Martellotti, "Il codice Ottoboniano 1883 e l'opera di Lombardo della Seta nella tradizione manoscritta del *De viris illustribus,*" *Convivium,* 1947, pp. 739–752; G. Billanovich, *Petrarca letterato,* Rome, 1947, I, 322.

[49] Salutati, *De laboribus Herculis,* 3, 7, 1, quoted the passage in Cicero's *De officiis,* 3, 32, 118, from the words "Herculem Prodicus dicit" to "utram ingredi melius esset" (see Cicero's text, [n. 25 above]) and then continued: "Hec ille. Quod an verum fuerit, aliter compertum non habeo"; after that Salutati said (3, 7, 2): "Miror tamen, licet hoc idem testetur maxime autoritatis Basilius . . ." (ed. Ullman, p. 182).

[50] See Basilius, *Ad adolescentes de legendis libris gentilium,* 5, 12, ed. F. Boulenger, 1935, pp. 48–49 (Greek text and French translation); the text of Bruni's Latin translation of the relevant passage was given by Panofsky, *op. cit.,* p. 53; on Bruni's translation and its dedication to Salutati, see the remarks made by F. Novati in his edition of Salutati's *Epistolario,* IV, 184, n. 1; cf. *ibid.,* IV, 516.

[51] The sources used by Salutati (3, 7, 3) in his discussion of the Py-

It ought to be noted that Petrarch, thus reviving a story dormant for almost a millennium, used it only once. This uniqueness stands in marked contrast to Petrarch's customary habit of alluding time and again in his writings and, above all, in his correspondence, to those historical or legendary figures and events, stories and anecdotes, which allowed him to draw moral lessons from them. In order to account for the apparent reserve which he maintained in regard to that particular tale, it may be permissible to assume that he was conscious of the fact that, from the strictly Christian point of view, the story was somewhat problematic. When Petarach wrote his *De vita solitaria,* he knew Lactantius's works and he must have remembered the passage in *The Divine Institutes* (6, 3, 9), in which Lactantius protested sharply against the pagans who "referred the end of those two ways to the body, and to the life which we lead on earth." [52] To be sure, Lactantius had also said that the one path was the *via virtutis* and that on the other way "cupidity and pleasure (*voluptas*) dragged men headlong;" [53] but at the same time Lactantius had made it very clear what in the eyes of a true Christian ought to be the nature of "the two ways which God has assigned to human life: . . . in the one case God has pointed out that there will be first temporal evils which will be followed by eternal goods. . . ; in the other, first temporal goods which will be

---

thagorean letter were identical with those quoted by Petrarch in the same connexion: Persius, *Sat.,* 3, 56 f.; Servius, *Ad Aeneid.,* 6, 136; Vergil, *Aen.,* 6, 541–543; see also *De laboribus Herculis,* 4, part 2, ch. 9, 3 (ed. Ullman, p. 572). The passage in the letter to Giovanni da Siena (2, 59, ed. Ullman, *op. cit.,* p. 635) reads as follows: "Cum itaque in illo bivio tum carnis sarcina ab illa virtutis ardua et arcta via deterreretur, et voluntate apud terrena detenta ad declivem sinistram viam voluptatis invitaretur, Hercules noster rate, hoc est voluntate, relicta virtutem eligendo suggestionibus carnis superatis emersit."

[52] See above, [n. 30]. On Petrarch's knowledge of Lactantius, compare P. de Nolhac, *Pétrarque et l'humanisme,* Paris, 1907, I, 183 f., 259 n. 3; II, 111, 184, 190 n. 4, 211 f.; see also, s.v. "Lattanzio," in the indices of Billanovich's edition of *Rerum Memorandarum Libri,* and of Rossi's and Bosco's edition of *Le Familiari,* the many references to passages in which Petrarch quoted from the *Divinae Institutiones.*

[53] *Divin. Instit.,* 6, 4, 1: "Una est itaque uirtutis ac bonorum uia . . ."; *ibid.,* 6, 4, 10: "Omnes . . . quos cupiditas aut uoluptas praecipites trahit . . ."

followed by eternal evils."[54] The goal reached by Petrarch's *Hercules in bivio* was very different indeed; for after "Hercules had spurned the way of *voluptas* and taken possession of the path of *virtus,* . . . he was raised to the apex of human glory."[55] Petrarch must have realized that to Lactantius, as well as to any other Christian thinker, "human glory" represented merely a temporal good and certainly not that "*gloria* that cometh from God alone."[56] Therefore it seems very likely that he refrained quite consciously from emphasizing the story of *Hercules in bivio* too strongly and too frequently in his writings.

In spite of the personal reserve which Petrarch may have felt, his revival of the story appears to be hardly accidental but quite logical, both within the whole context of his own writings and within the general frame-work of the history of the ideas marking the period of transition from mediaeval to Renaissance thought. For the tale implied a basic maxim which is characteristic of one of the aspects of Petrarch's thinking as well as of that of the generations following him: the demand that every man, on reaching in his life the fateful point of the parting of the ways, ought to choose, as Hercules had done, the right path, that of *virtus,* through which he will obtain fame.

As Panofsky showed, the concept of a supreme Virtue had no proper place within the mediaeval moral system, and it was only in the fifteenth century that "the ancient concept of *virtus* as a state of perfection in this world was re-established to its full extent and at the same time reconciled with the Christian dogma: no longer was it considered to be a diminution of the divine omnipotence but on the contrary its most profound confirmation that in the centre of the universe stood the free man—free,

[54] *Divin. Instit.,* 6, 4, 12: "Hae sunt uiae, quas Deus humanae uitae adsignauit: in quibus singulis et bona ostendit et mala, sed ordine praepostero atque conuerso. In sua enim monstrauit temporaria prius mala cum aeternis bonis, qui est ordo melior, in altera temporaria prius bona cum aeternis malis, qui est ordo deterior . . ."

[55] See the text above, [n. 24].

[56] See the text of St. John v. 44, in the *Vulgata:* "Quomodo vos potestis credere, qui gloriam ab invicem accipitis, et gloriam, quae a solo Deo est, non quaeritis?"; compare St. Paul's Epistle to the Hebrews ii. 6–9.

not any longer because of the aid of heavenly grace but because of his innate *virtus*." [57] To a certain degree Petrarch anticipated that idea of the later humanists although he still conceived of it in a somewhat unsystematical fashion since classical and Christian notions often appeared in his work side by side and had not yet become really integrated.[58] This is especially true of his concept of *virtus*. On one side it would be easy to quote many passages in his writings in which he defined *virtus* or *virtutes* in complete accordance with the traditional views of the Middle Ages. On the other side, almost as frequently it seems, he set forth a concept of *virtus,* which definitely foreshadowed the later concept of *virtù*.[59] For instance, Petrarch, like many humanists after him, recalled Cicero's statement that the word *virtus* is derived from *vir,* that is to say that *virtus* is that quality which makes a human being into a man in the fullest sense.[60] "Through the might of *virtus*," Petrarch wrote in his *Apologia contra cuiusdam Galli calumnias,* "do outstanding men conquer everything." [61] The same fervent belief in the power of *virtù* manifests itself in the famous lines of the canzone *Italia mia:* "vertú contra furore prenderà l'arme . . . ," with which Machiavelli was to conclude *Il Principe. Virtus* was the basic theme of Petrarch's main historical work, the *De viris illustribus.* As he made it clear in the preface to that book, the great men of history were to him the embodiments of *virtus;* they were "illustrious" because their fame is "the gift of *virtus* and *gloria,* not that of *fortuna*." [62]

[57] Panofsky, *op. cit.,* p. 164.

[58] This peculiar feature of Petrarch's thought has been very well characterized by Panofsky, *op. cit.,* p. 165, n. 4, with the remark that Petrarch "hier wie überall die Renaissance-Anschauung in einer eigentümlich zartverschleierten, man möchte sagen: noch nicht dogmatisierten Gestalt an den Tag treten läst."

[59] On the history of that idea, compare, e.g., E. W. Mayer, *Machiavellis Geschichtsauffassung und sein Begriff virtù,* 1912; I. Wyss, *Virtù und Fortuna bei Boiardo und Ariosto,* 1931.

[60] *Famil.,* 23, 2, 28: "At profecto sive 'a viro virtus,' ut vult Cicero [*Tusc.,* 2, 18, 43], sive a virtute vir dicitur, nil hac vere viro carius, nil amabilius esse potest."

[61] Ed. E. Cocchia, in *Atti della R. Accademia di Archeologia, Lettere e Belle Arti,* N.S., VII, Naples, 1920, p. 148: "Viri enim egregii virtutis ope vincunt omnia."

[62] See the preface to the first version of *De viris illustribus,* ed. P. de

It ought to be pointed out that nowhere in his historical work did Petrarch indicate what the source was of that *virtus* which "chooses men as perpetual leaders necessary for the commonwealth and forces them to spend their lives under arms," as he declared in one of his letters.[63] He knew, of course, that passage in *The City of God,* in which St. Augustine had protested against the pagans who "made *virtus* a goddess," [64] and he certainly did not have any personal intention to deify *virtus.* But the fact is that in his work *De viris illustribus* he never, either explicitly or implicitly, derived *virtus from* God, as St. Augustine and every other Christian theologian had done very specifically. Thus he provided no answer to the fundamental question as to who was ultimately responsible for the power which he considered the most important driving force in history. Through this omission he leaves his readers with the impression that he believed that a truly "illustrious" man, who by his own choice is possessed of *virtus,* is able to shape his own destiny, as well as being the maker of history. Such a conception was indeed highly secular and did not at all conform with the mediaeval tradition according to which all history is ruled over by God. Only one generation before Petrarch, Dante had still called the great men of Rome "instruments through which Divine Providence proceeded in the Roman Empire where many times the arm of God was seen to be present." [65]

In the story of *Hercules in bivio,* as told in *De vita solitaria,* the hero who chose the path of *virtus* was ultimately "raised to

---

Nolhac, *Notices et extraits des manuscrits de la Bibliothèque Nationale,* XXXIV, 1891, pp. 110–114, esp. lines 69–72: "Neque enim quisquis opulentus et potens confestim simul illustris est; alter enim fortune, alter virtutis et glorie munus est, neque ego fortunatos, sed illustres sum pollicitus viros describere."

[63] In *Famil.,* 13, 4, 12, Petrarch enumerated a number of great Roman war leaders who could not have achieved their deeds, "nisi eos spectata virtus . . . duces perpetuos reipublice debitos ac necessarios elegisset coegissetque sub armis evum agere"; see also, *ibid.,* the phrase: "quisquis es, qui virtutis specie illectus eius contubernium concupiscis, scito rem te maximam optare neque parvo parabilem, sed que totum te poscat in precium."

[64] See above, [n. 9].

[65] Dante, *Convivio,* 4, 5, 17: "e manifesto esser dee, questi eccellentissimi essere stati strumenti, con li quali procedette la divina provedenza ne lo romano imperio, dove più volte parve esse braccia di Dio essere presenti."

the apex of human glory." This close relationship and interdependence existing between *virtus* and *gloria* is again one of Petrarch's favourite ideas, which found expression in many of his writings and, above all, in his historical work. By his very definition of the topic of *De viris illustribus* he called only those men "illustrious" whose *virtus* enabled them to achieve true fame through great deeds.[66] Glory represented to Petrarch "the companion and herald of *virtus*." [67] In one of his canzoni, *gloria* is pictured as "una donna più bella assai che 'l sole," who reveals to the poet the personification of *virtù*, "che farà gli occhi tuoi via più felici." [68]

It seems worth noticing that in the *Documenti d'Amore* Francesco da Barberino set forth a very similar idea by declaring in regard to the *virtus moralis in genere:* "It is that *virtus* which increases the fame of every man." [69] Just as Francesco da Barberino had been the first artist since the days of antiquity to attempt to create an image of the supreme or "general" Virtue, so a generation later Petrarch revived the memory of the ancient story in which *Hercules in bivio* figured as the representative of the truly "illustrious" man, that highest type of man who by his own free decision chooses the path of *virtus* on which he will ascend to the peak of earthly glory. These were novel ideas which form, in Panofsky's words, "a part in that great process which we still may define as *Rinascimento dell' Antichità*." [70] The full development of these concepts was left to the later writers and artists of the Renaissance.

[66] See above, [n. 62].

[67] *Famil.*, 9, 11, 3: "Hoc nimirum interest, quod ut nos ipsos quos non vidimus amemus, natura est; ut alios, virtus facit et fama, virtutis comes ac nuntia"; see also *Famil.*, 1, 2, 25: ". . . virtutem fama, ceu solidum corpus umbra, consequitur" (cf. Cicero, *Tuscul.*, 1, 45, 109); likewise, *Famil.*, 15, 1, 8; 14, 27; 23, 11, 1; compare *De remediis utriusque fortunae,* I, dial. 92 (in Petrarch's *Opera*, ed. 1581, pp. 76 f.).

[68] *Le Rime,* CXIX, lines 1 and 60; cf. Panofsky, *op. cit.*, p. 165, n. 4.

[69] Ed. F. Egidi, *op. cit.*, II, 240: "Est igitur virtus illa, que cuiuslibet famam auget"; in his commentary on this passage Francesco da Barberino referred back to his earlier discussion of the *virtus generalis* (see above, [n. 14]); compare Francesco's remark in a later section of the *Documenti d'Amore* (ed. Egidi, III, 254): "Dicit Seneca in VIII[a] epistula [*Ad. Lucil.*, 79, 11]: 'Gloria ut umbra virtutis etiam invitos commitabitur.' "

[70] Panofsky, *op. cit.*, p. 166.

10

The Last Will: A Personal Document of Petrarch's Old Age*

"I HAVE often reflected on a matter concerning which no one can reflect too much and only a few reflect enough, namely, the last things and death." With these words starts the Testament which Petrarch drew up in Padua on April 4, 1370. That the thought of "the last things and death" had indeed been with Petrarch throughout his life is shown by innumerable passages in his writings and letters.[1] It is the more noteworthy, therefore, that apparently he did not decide to compose a formal will be-

* Reprinted from *Petrarch's Testament,* edited and translated, with an Introduction, by Theodore E. Mommsen (Ithaca, N.Y.: Cornell University Press, 1957), pp. 3–50.

[1] For the older literature on Petrarch, see M. Fowler, *Catalogue of the Petrarch Collection Bequeathed by Willard Fiske to Cornell University Library* (London, 1916). Of the more recent publications only the following can be mentioned: E. Carrara, *Petrarca* (Rome, 1937; first published in *Enciclopedia Italiana,* XVII [1935], 8–23); U. Bosco, *Petrarca* (Turin, 1946); G. Billanovich, *Petrarca letterato,* vol. I (Rome, 1947); E. H. Wilkins, *The Making of the "Canzoniere" and Other Petrarchan Studies* (Rome, 1951); N. Sapegno, *Il Trecento,* 6th ed. (Milan, 1952), pp. 165–276; P. G. Ricci, "Petrarca," *Enciclopedia Cattolica,* IX (1952), coll. 1288–1299; E. H. Wilkins, *Studies in the Life and Works of Petrarch* (Cambridge, Mass., 1955); see also the bibliography in the most recent anthology: *Francesco Petrarca, Prose* (vol. VII of *La letteratura italiana, storia e testi*), ed. by G. Martellotti, P. G. Ricci, E. Carrara, and E. Bianchi (Milan and Naples, 1955), pp. XXII–XXV; henceforth quoted as *Petrarca, Prose.*

fore he reached the age of almost sixty-six years.[2] Only a few years earlier he had been seriously wondering whether or not he would safely survive his sixty-third year, as we learn from a letter which he addressed to Boccaccio on the very day on which he entered that year of his life, on July 20, 1366.[3] In this letter he recalled "the very old belief" in the unpropitious character of the numbers seven and nine and their even more ominous combination in the number sixty-three, relating in detail the views held by such ancient writers as Aulus Gellius, Censorinus, and, above all, Julius Firmicus Maternus, whose opinions he summed up as follows: "During the sixty-third year of his life man runs extreme danger, either of great misfortune or of sickness, be it of the mind or of the body or, finally, of death." [4] It cannot be denied that on this occasion Petrarch "displayed," in Lynn Thorndike's words, "considerable anxiety concerning his own safe passage of the grand climacteric . . . year." [5] But it also ought to be noted that in this same letter to Boccaccio he expressed quite definite reservations in regard to the value

[2] In a letter of 1352 (*Fam.* XIV, 4) Petrarch defended himself against the charge of avarice and declared that the smallness of his estate would become manifest on the day of his death; the very vagueness by which Petrarch referred in this connection to "heredi meo," seems to exclude the assumption that by that time he had already composed a formal will; see esp. *Fam.* XIV, 4, 17–19 (here and elsewhere *Le familiari* has always been quoted from V. Rossi's publication in the Edizione Nazionale, 4 vols., Florence, 1933–1942).

[3] *Sen.* VIII, 1 (ed. *Opera,* 1581, pp. 827–830); in my quotations from the *Seniles* I have always used, if not indicated otherwise, the texts which are found in the (unnumbered) Venetian edition of 1501 of *Librorum Francisci Petrarche impressorum annotatio,* and have added (in parenthesis) page references to the more commonly available Basel edition of 1581 of *Francisci Petrarchae . . . opera quae extant omnia;* see also the Italian translations by G. Fracassetti, *Lettere senili di F. Petrarca volgarizzate e dichiarate,* 2 vols. (Florence, 1869–1870). As to the dates of Petrarch's letters, see the most helpful bibliographical references which were compiled for each letter by E. H. Wilkins, *The Prose Letters of Petrarch: A Manual* (New York, 1951).

[4] *Sen.* VIII, 1 (ed. *Opera,* 1581, p. 829); the passages quoted by Petrarch in this letter are: Aulus Gellius, *Noctes Atticae,* XV, 7 (see also III, 10, 9); Censorinus, *De die natali,* XIV, 13–15; Julius Firmicus Maternus, *Matheseos,* IV, 20. Compare also *Fam.* I, 7, 8.

[5] L. Thorndike, *A History of Magic and Experimental Science* (New York, 1934), III, 220.

of such astrological speculations.[6] In any case, these fears did not prove strong enough to induce him at that time to take legal cognizance of the possible imminence of his death by drafting a last will.

As a matter of fact, "during that terrible year [of a man's life] whatever it has been like or is going to be like for others," Petrarch wrote to Boccaccio on his next birthday, on July 20, 1367, "no adversity befell me in my private life, and in public life two most fortunate events occurred in those days." [7] One of these events, the conquest of Alexandria by the King of Cyprus, proved to be merely a temporary success, but the other event, the return of Pope Urban V to Rome in the year 1367, meant a great deal to Petrarch. Throughout his life he had addressed the most fervent appeals to the successive popes and implored them to re-establish the papal see in the traditional center of the Christian world. It was natural, then, that he greeted the ultimate fulfillment of that ardently cherished hope with the greatest enthusiasm and declared himself eager to accept the invitations which Urban V repeatedly extended to him.[8] More than two and a half years, however, were to pass before Petrarch finally felt able, in April 1370, to pay his often-promised visit to Rome.

It was at that particular moment, on April 4, that Petrarch resolved to compose his Testament. During the previous autumn he had been very sick, as he told the pope in a letter of December 24, 1369,[9] and he must have been fully aware of the risks which the long and strenuous journey from northern Italy to Rome was bound to involve for a man of his advanced age. If Petrarch actually had had such fears, they proved indeed to be only too well justified. For shortly after he had started for Rome in late April, he was taken gravely ill in Ferrara and

[6] *Sen.* VIII, 1 (ed. *Opera,* 1581, p. 829): "Est autem hec ratio, quam prefatus sum mihi mirabilem uideri; que quanti sit ponderis, librent, qui hiis animum curis applicuere. Ego enim, ex equo fateor, et rem ipsam et rei causam despicio." See also the beginning of *Sen.* VIII, 8 (ed. *Opera,* 1581, p. 843).

[7] *Sen.* VIII, 8 (ed. *Opera,* 1581, p. 843).

[8] See *Sen.* IX, 1; XI, 1, 15 and 16.

[9] *Sen.* XI, 16; see also *Sen.* XIII, 11.

was forced by the advice of the doctors to return to Padua, and from there, on May 8, 1370, he notified Urban V of the reason for the frustration of his visit.[10] Petrarch was never to regain his full health. In a letter which he wrote a few months later to his friend Giovanni Dondi he described his condition as follows: "During this year [1370] I have been reduced to such a state that for many days now I have been unable to move without the help of my servants; I have become a sad burden, noxious to others and odious to myself." [11] His physical weakness did not prevent him, however, from pursuing his literary activities just as resolutely as ever throughout the remaining four years of his life. "I read, I write, I think; this is the life, this the pleasure, which since my youth have always been mine," he wrote in a letter of 1371.[12]

Of all the writings and letters belonging to this period of Petrarch's old age his Testament of 1370 may rightly be called one of the most personal documents. There are many indications which bear out the truth of the statement he made toward its end (§ 30): [13] "I have written this with my own hand." On all technical points and on the legal terminology he must have taken counsel, of course, with the two notaries who subscribed the document (§ 31), and thus we find that the style of the Will deviates in some respects from his customary mode of expression. But the assertion of a literary critic of the sixteenth century, Girolamo Ruscelli, that "it is undeniable that in this Testament Petrarch shunned elegance on purpose in order to keep within the notarial style" can be accepted only in a very limited sense.[14] For a mere glance at the wording of an-

[10] *Sen.* XI, 17.

[11] *Sen.* XII, 1, in Seminario di Padova, ed., *Nel VI centenario dalla nascita di F. Petrarca la Rappresentanza Provinciale di Padova* (Padua, 1904), p. 48 (ed. *Opera,* 1581, p. 899).

[12] *Sen.* XIII, 8 (XIII, 7, ed. *Opera,* 1581, p. 921).

[13] The references are to the text and the translation of the Testament . . . [in Mommsen, *Petrarch's Testament,* pp. 68–93].

[14] In the prefatory remarks to the edition of the Testament which G. Ruscelli included in his publication of the *Canzoniere* (*Il Petrarca nuovamente con la perfetta ortografia della lingua volgare, corretto* [Venice, 1554]), he declared that at first he intended to give an Italian translation but then decided to present the original text so as to enable the reader to see "che

other deed actually composed by one of the notaries who a few weeks earlier had assisted in the drafting of the Will shows clearly how basically different in language and syntax the purely notarial style employed by the legists of the time was from the Latin used by Petrarch on this formal occasion.[15] And it may be noted that even in such a strictly legal document the humanist Petrarch could not refrain from alluding in at least two places (§§ 1 and 5) to passages in Cicero's *De senectute.*

Just as the style of the Testament is to a considerable extent that of Petrarch, so is its arrangement his also. To be sure, the organization as a whole follows the customary pattern, and therefore we find that in the main sections of the Will Petrarch dealt first with the question of his burial and made provisions for the Church and the poor (§§ 4–10), then listed the special legacies to his friends and servants (§§ 11–24), and finally ended with stipulations regulating the bequest of the residuary estate to his principal legatee (§ 25). If a notary had written the final form of the Will, he would certainly have seen to it that every provision appeared at the right place and within the proper context, but Petrarch himself apparently worried not at all at making no less than three addenda (§§ 26–28, 32), the last of which, moreover, followed the reference to the attesta-

lingua s'usasse in quei tempi, et quanto men felicemente il Petrarca scriuesse nella latina lingua che nella sua"; according to Ruscelli this relative inferiority of Petrarch's Latin style manifested itself in the Will, as well as in all his other writings, whether poetry or prose, and in his letters: "benche non sia da negare che in questo testamento egli à studio fuggisse l'eleganza, sì per tenersi nello stile notaresco, de' quali è come proprio tal'ufficio; come ancora perche in pensieri et ragionamenti che ci tengano come presente la morte, non si conuien mostrar ricordo non che affettatione d'ornamenti, et di politezze, per non dir lussuria di fauella." See also G. Fracassetti's remark in *F. Petrarca, Lettere delle cose familiari* [Florence, 1864], II, 353, n. 1) that Petrarch wrote the Will "in quel latino semibarbaro ch'era proprio de' contratti e degli altri atti pubblici notarieschi."

[15] See the contract for the purchase of some landed property in Arquà which, in the name of Petrarch, was negotiated by Lombardo della Seta and drafted by the notary Niccolo, son of the late Ser Bartolomeo, in Padua on June 22, 1370 (ed. by C. Leoni in A. Malmigiati, *Petrarca a Padova, a Venezia e ad Arquà* [Padua, 1874], pp. 92–95). See *ibid.,* p. 91, C. Leoni's comment: "Un pubblico notaio, che dettava con lingua e stile si barbaro (come questo Atto) digiuno persino delle più elementari regole ortografiche e grammaticali, è cosa strana e degna di studio."

tion by the two notaries.[16] Neither did he hesitate to insert in such a strictly legal document remarks of a very intimate or, occasionally, even humorous nature.

The same personal character manifested itself also in the introductory part of the Testament in which Petrarch stated in the traditional fashion the reasons for making his last will; death, he said, may come at any moment, and intestacy might provoke litigation among his heirs. In this connection he declared (§ 1): "To confess the truth, my possessions are so slight and so few that I am somewhat ashamed to bequeath them." Although this remark, taken by itself, would not seem at all unusual, it must be noted that Petrarch also stressed the littleness of his worldly estate in some other passages of the Will. Thus he concluded the list of the bequests to his friends by saying (§ 21): "As to the smallness of these legacies, let my aforesaid friends accuse not me but Fortune—if there be any such thing as Fortune." In order to understand the full meaning of this interesting, though rather casually expressed, doubt concerning the existence of Fortune, one has to turn to a letter which he had addressed a few years earlier to the physician Tommaso del Garbo, because there he had discussed in great detail the whole problem of Fortune and, in agreement with the views of Lactantius and Augustine, had come to the conclusion that "Fortune by herself does not exist." [17] By telling his friends, then, in the Testament that they should charge Fortune and not himself for the insignificance of his bequests, he told them in fact that they could not bring charges against anything or anybody. But the most startling remark concerning the small size of the estate is to be found at the very end of the Will, where he concludes as follows: "I . . . would have drawn up

[16] It is also possible, of course, to assume with H. Cochin (*Le frère de Pétrarque et le livre "Du repos des religieux"* [Paris, 1903], p. 148, n. 1) that Petrarch added this last bequest as a codicil to the Will at a somewhat later date.

[17] *Sen.* VIII, 3 (ed. *Opera,* 1581, p. 838): "Hiis atque aliis inductus fortunam per seipsam nihil esse dicentibus assentiri cogor, de quo, ne aliena mihi tribuam, a multis, inter quos ab hiis, quorum supra memini, Augustino et Lactantio Firmiano Institutionum libro, et argute satis ut arbitror et fideliter disputatum est"; see, e.g., *De civitate Dei,* IV, 18; V, 9; VII, 3; *Divin. Institut.,* III, 29.

a different Testament if I were rich, as the mad rabble believes me to be."

This rather jarring note with which the Testament ends indicates that Petrarch felt self-conscious about his economic status, and there are to be found indeed quite a few passages in his correspondence which reveal his awareness of the fact that his alleged wealth had incited envy against him among many of his contemporaries.[18] How large his fortune actually was, we do not know, and the Testament is of no help in this respect since it does not specify the value of the residuary estate. The various monetary legacies add up to a sum of about six hundred gold ducats, which at that time represented a fair though by no means an unusually large amount. In this connection it may also be noted that in the Will (§ 16) he acknowledged himself to be indebted to his friend Lombardo della Seta to the amount of one hundred and thirty-four gold ducats, and he declared in another provision of the Testament (§ 8) that "because of other expenses" he had been unable to buy some land for a bequest to the Paduan Cathedral. These statements seem to be hardly indicative of a rich man. As is well known, Petrarch drew his income exclusively from Church benefices.[19] On the basis of a detailed study of his ecclesiastical appointments, Ernest H. Wilkins has reached the following conclusion: "In his earlier years, while his financial status was still precarious, he was, I think, definitely acquisitive"; in later years, Wilkins declares, "he seems to have been, in point of fact, rather well satisfied—though he was willing enough to receive such supplementary appointments as might not interfere with his freedom. . . . He had no desire for great possessions." [20]

It was in regard to the possibility of such a supplementary appointment that Petrarch described his economic situation in a most objective fashion to Francesco Bruni, then a papal

[18] See, e.g., *Sen.* X, 2 (ed. by Martellotti in *Petrarca, Prose,* p. 1104), in which Petrarch spoke of the honest wealth "que me, mirum dictu, solitarium contemptorem, profugum in medias silvas, usque ad invidiam insecute sunt"; see also *Fam.* XIX, 16 and 17; XX, 8, §§ 12–18.

[19] See chapter, "Petrarch's Ecclesiastical Career," in Wilkins, *Studies,* pp. 3–32.

[20] *Ibid.,* p. 31.

secretary in Avignon.[21] This letter, written on May 24, 1371, helps us greatly to understand the personal conditions under which, one year earlier, Petrarch had composed his Will, and this letter also clarifies some of the details of the Testament, as we shall see. "If I were to say," Petrarch told Francesco Bruni, "that I lacked anything necessary for the life of a single canon, I should lie; but perhaps I should not be lying when I say that I have more acquaintances and consequently more burdens than almost the whole of the cathedral chapter to which I belong; I do not know whether or not I could avoid these obligations by some device." [22] Not only did he have to entertain the many people who constantly came to visit him, but even more, Petrarch wrote, he needed in his household a large staff of servants—"though I wish I knew how to live without them"—and usually employed five or six copyists; [23] ordinarily he also kept at least two horses.[24]

In regard to Petrarch's income we learn from a papal bull of the year 1390 that the annual revenue from one of his ecclesiastical appointments, the canonry in Padua, was estimated to be two hundred and sixty ducats.[25] It may be permissible, therefore, to assume that Petrarch's total income amounted to more than four hundred ducats. In order to evaluate the meaning of this figure it may be useful to observe that in the first part of the fifteenth century a member of the patrician merchant class of neighboring Venice, Andrea Barbarigo, was able to live with his family comfortably on an annual budget of about the same amount.[26] Petrarch himself, as his letter to Francesco Bruni shows, was quite willing to admit that he had a fair income, but he was certainly also justified in asserting that both his fame and his literary activities were forcing upon

[21] *Var.* 15, in G. Fracassetti, ed., *F. Petrarcae epistolae de rebus familiaribus et variae* (Florence, 1863), III, 331–337. In my quotations from the *Variae* I have always used Fracassetti's edition of the *Epistolae.*

[22] *Ibid.,* p. 332.

[23] *Ibid.,* pp. 332 f.

[24] See also the mention of his horses in a letter of Dec. 24, 1369, in *Sen.* XI, 16 (ed. *Opera,* 1581, p. 894) and in the Testament (§ 15).

[25] Compare A. Medin, "Il successore di F. Petrarca nel canonicato di Padova," in *Padova in onore di F. Petrarca* (Padua, 1904), II, 50; Wilkins, *Studies,* p. 22.

[26] See F. C. Lane, *Andrea Barbarigo, Merchant of Venice, 1418–1449* (Baltimore, 1944), p. 33.

him a style of living and the maintenance of a staff of servants and copyists for which his means were barely adequate. He stated his personal situation in a similar way in the treatise *On His Own Ignorance and That of Many Others,* which he completed in the year 1370; people know, he said, that "what I have is moderate, not my own property but to be shared with others; it is not magnificent but very modest without haughtiness and pomp; they know that it really does not deserve any envy." [27] His remark, then, that "to confess the truth, my possessions are so slight and so few that I am somewhat ashamed to bequeath them," has to be understood as a rhetorical exaggeration; it is contradicted by the very contents of the Will, which show that he was able to afford legacies of rather considerable value. On the other hand, he was right, though perhaps somewhat too vehement in his form of expression, when he declared at the end of the Will that he was not "rich, as the mad rabble believes me to be."

In the main section of the Testament, Petrarch took up first the matter of his burial. It was in accordance with religious conventions when he voiced the desire (§ 4) to be buried "without any pomp but with utmost humility and all possible lowliness," and it was just as natural that after his death his family and friends paid no attention to this demand but gave him a very ceremonial funeral.[28] When he further asked (§ 5) that "no one is to shed tears for me, but to address prayers for me to Christ," we find in this request a combination of conventional Christian ideas and of the thoughts expressed in the epitaph of the ancient poet Ennius which he read in Cicero.[29]

"As to the burial place," Petrarch declared (§ 6), "I do not

[27] Trans. by H. Nachod in *The Renaissance Philosophy of Man,* ed. by E. Cassirer, P. O. Kristeller, and J. H. Randall (Chicago, 1948), p. 52; for the Latin text, see the edition of *De sui ipsius et multorum ignorantia* by L. M. Capelli (Paris, 1906), p. 20.

[28] Galeazzo and Bartolomeo Gatari, *Cronaca Carrarese,* in L. A. Muratori, ed., *Rerum Italicarum Scriptores* (Città di Castello, 1909), vol. XVII, pt. 1, 138; compare Carrara, *op. cit.,* p. 37; U. Mariani, *Petrarca e gli Agostiniani* (Rome, 1946), p. 102; Billanovich, *op. cit.,* p. 340, n. 1.

[29] Cicero, *De senectute,* 20, 73; see also *Tuscul. disput.,* 1, 15, 34; for the remark in the preamble to the Will (§ 1) that "et mors omnibus certa sit et hora mortis incerta" and that death "semper nobis impendet," compare *De senectute,* 20, 74.

care greatly. I am content to be laid to rest wherever it shall please God and those who shall deign to assume this task." But after having made this statement, Petrarch proceeded to enumerate seven different places in which he might possibly die and stipulated specifically in which of the churches situated in these localities he desired to be buried.

That whole list is most characteristic of Petrarch. For it shows that he, who had led a migratory existence throughout his life, still expected to continue his travels into his old age. He said (§ 6 g) of the first six towns that those are the "places which I had been wont to frequent in Italy," and we find indeed, by looking over his itinerary during the decade previous to the date of the Will, that he had resided for longer or shorter periods in five of them, that is, in the two Visconti cities of Milan and Pavia, in Venice, and in the Carrara towns of Padua and Arquà.[30] The inclusion of Rome as the sixth normally frequented place is, of course, accounted for by Petrarch's intention in April 1370 to visit the pope; actually he had not been in Rome since the year 1350. That he no longer ordinarily visited the seventh city mentioned, Parma, Petrarch made clear by the disarmingly frank admission (§ 6 h) that "I have been a useless and almost always absent archdeacon for many years" of the Cathedral there. The silence regarding foreign countries and especially France indicates that Petrarch no longer intended to travel abroad; in fact his embassy to Paris in the year 1360 proved to be his last absence from Italy.

In regard to the various churches which Petrarch selected as possible burial places, he demonstrated a certain preference for those belonging to the mendicant orders (§ 6 a, c, and e), and he showed the same predilection for these four orders, above all the Franciscans, in two other passages of the Testament (§§ 6 i, 9).

In the event that his death were to take place in Padua, Petrarch wished to be buried in the Dominican church of S. Agostino and not in the Cathedral, although he was a canon of the latter church.

[30] On Petrarch's itinerary, see the chapter "Peregrinus ubique" in Wilkins, *Making of the "Canzoniere,"* pp. 1–8.

He explained this particular wish in one of the most touching passages of the Will (§ 6 a): "For not only is this place [S. Agostino]," he said, "dear to my soul but it is also there that that man lies who loved me very much and who, through his devoted entreaties, brought me to these parts, Jacopo da Carrara of most illustrious memory, sometime Lord of Padua." His contemporaries, as well as later scholars, have often expressed their regret that Petrarch strove consistently for the favors of the great of his time, and they have charged that he was rather inclined to ingratiate himself with the powerful and the rich through undue compliments and insincere flatteries. There is no doubt that Petrarch knew well on occasion, perhaps even on too many occasions, how to speak the language of the courtier. But he also knew very well how to keep faith with those princes whom he genuinely respected, during and after their lifetimes. His attitude toward King Robert of Naples would be one case in point. But nowhere in his writings did he voice in a more moving fashion the gratitude and the loyalty which he felt for a great patron than he did with these simple words dedicated to the memory of the long-deceased Jacopo da Carrara, in a document which was not, like most of his letters, to be broadcast to the world, but was to be opened only after his own death.[31]

In discussing the possibility of his dying in Arquà "where my country-place is," Petrarch declared (§ 6 b) that he desired to be buried in the small chapel which he intended to build there in honor of the Virgin Mary. One year later he referred to the same project in the letter to Francesco Bruni which has been mentioned before; according to this letter of 1371 he had already started the construction and was resolved to carry it through "even if I should have to mortgage or sell my books." [32] Actually that "little oratory," as he called it in his letter to Bruni, was never finished,[33] and Petrarch was finally buried

[31] Petrarch spoke of Jacopo da Carrara with equal warmth in his *Letter to Posterity*, ed. by Ricci in *Petrarca, Prose*, pp. 16 f.; see also *Fam.* VIII, 5, 13; XI, 2, 4–5; XI, 3; XIII, 11, 6; compare Billanovich, *op. cit.*, p. 103.

[32] *Var.* 15, in *Epistolae*, III, 333.

[33] Two of the sixteenth-century biographers of Petrarch, Fausto da Longiano (1532) and G. A. Gesualdo (1533), asserted erroneously that

outside the parish church of Arquà, in a sepulchral monument which was completed six years after his death by his son-in-law, Francescuolo da Brossano. Although this plan never did materialize, it deserves attention, for it shows that Petrarch in his old age was particularly devoted to the cult of the Virgin Mary, a devotion which manifested itself also in other parts of the Testament (§§ 3, 8, 18). In this connection it is worth remembering that it was just about the time of the composition of the Will that Petrarch himself transcribed his great *canzone* "Vergine bella" in his own manuscript of the *Canzoniere* (now Codex Vaticanus Latinus 3195) in such a way as to indicate clearly that this was to be and remain the terminal poem in the collection.[34] In the *canzone* Petrarch used a rather unusual phrase which he most probably adopted from one of the apocryphal sections of the Latin Vulgate, the Oratio Manassae regis Iuda; "I pray," he said in the *canzone*,[35] "to the Virgin with the genuflexion of the mind." In the Testament (§ 3), on the other hand, he prayed to Christ "with the genuflexion of this very soul." No precise date can be assigned to the composition of "Vergine bella," but the similarity between the two passages just quoted may permit us to assume a fairly close connection between the *canzone* and the Testament. And it is certainly safe to assert that the Virgin Mary occupied a most important place in the thoughts of Petrarch during his last years: just as the beautiful *canzone* written in her praise was to terminate the collection of his lyrical poetry, so he himself wished to be laid to rest in a chapel erected by him in her honor.

Petrarch's desire (§ 6 d and e) to be buried in the church of S. Ambrogio if he were to die in Milan, or in the church of S. Pietro in Ciel d'Oro if in Pavia, resulted from a long and

---

Petrarch had actually erected a chapel in Arquà; see the edition of these biographies by A. Solerti, *Le vite di Dante, Petrarca e Boccaccio scritte fino al secolo decimosesto* (Milan, 1904), pp. 379 and 408.

[34] See Wilkins, *Making of the "Canzoniere,"* pp. 175–180, 358.

[35] Petrarca, *Le rime*, CCCLXVI, vv. 63–65:

> "Con le ginocchia de la mente inchine
> prego che sia mia scorta
> e la mia torta via drizzi a buon fine."

The Vulgate text of the passage in Oratio Manassae regis Iuda, 15, reads as follows: "Et nunc flecto genu cordis mei, precans a te bonitatem."

strongly felt attachment to those churches. For more than six years, from 1353 to 1359, he had lived in Milan in a house situated beside the basilica of S. Ambrogio and for that reason had spoken of himself as "the guest of Ambrose." [36] The church of S. Pietro in Ciel d'Oro contained the tomb of St. Augustine and, joined with it in "pious and devoted fellowship," also the remnants of Boethius: "One might wish," Petrarch wrote to Boccaccio from Pavia in the year 1365, "to lie very close to so holy and so learned men." [37]

Turning now to the disposal of those things which, in Petrarch's words (§ 7), "men call goods, although frequently they are rather impediments to the soul," we find first a number of conventional bequests made to the Church and the poor. The most important of these provisions (§ 8) dealt with the establishment of "a perpetual anniversary mass for my soul," which was to be celebrated in the Cathedral of Padua, "from which I have received both advantages and honors." In accordance with the custom of the time, Petrarch wanted to secure the endowment of that mass by deeding some land and the revenues from it to the Cathedral. In this connection there existed certain problems. In the first place, Petrarch had to admit that, "because of other expenses," he had been unable so far to buy such a piece of land. Moreover, although by 1370 he had been for a number of years a more or less permanent resident of Padua and of the territory ruled by the lord of that city, Francesco da Carrara the Elder, Petrarch had remained, in legal terms, an "alien" in Padua, as he himself stated explicitly in the treatise on good government which he addressed to Francesco da Carrara in 1373.[38] Being an alien, he needed formal

[36] *Fam.* XIX, 16, 16; XX, 8, 23; see also *Fam.* XVI, 11, 11; XVII, 10, 14; XXI, 14, 2.

[37] *Sen.* V, 1 (ed. *Opera,* 1581, p. 791).

[38] In *Sen.* XIV, 1 (in V. Ussani, ed., *F. Petrarchae . . . rerum senilium liber XIV ad . . . Franciscum de Carraria . . . epistola I* [Padua, 1922], p. 21), Petrarch told the prince that the swamps around Padua should be drained; he added in this connection: "Utque te in risum cogam, ne nil aliud quam uerba ponere dicar in hanc rem, arculam ipse meam alienigena in particulam impense huius offero. Quid ciuibus debitum? quid domino? Ac si forsitan nominatim auxiliaris quantitas collationis exigitur, scies in tempore."

authorization by the prince for the acquisition of any kind of real estate in and around Padua.[39] When he drew up the article under discussion in the Will, he had obtained, as he said (§ 8), merely "the oral permission" of Francesco, but ten days later, on April 14, 1370, he received, "by decree of the magnificent and mighty Lord Francesco da Carrara, Lord of Padua etc., imperial Vicar General, the favor of buying and acquiring immovable goods and possessions in Padua and the Paduan district." [40] In spite of this official authorization, Petrarch actually never bought a piece of land for the endowment of his future anniversary mass, and for that reason the alternative provision of the Will became valid, by which he bequeathed the sum of two hundred gold ducats to the cathedral chapter of Padua for that purpose. But as we learn from a recently discovered document, it was only after a protracted litigation with Petrarch's son-in-law and heir, Francescuolo da Brossano, that the chapter finally secured that endowment in the year 1391.[41] From that time on, an annual mass for the dead was celebrated in the Cathedral of Padua on the anniversary of Petrarch's death, as is proved by a number of documents belonging to the first part of the fifteenth century.[42]

[39] Compare, e.g., A. Zardo, *Il Petrarca e i Carraresi* (Milan, 1887), p. 71: "Difatti, per gli Statuti allora vigenti in quella città, nessun forestiere poteva acquistare immobili in Padova e nel territorio padovano, se non con la permissione del Principe."

[40] See the contract for the purchase of land which was negotiated by Lombardo della Seta in the name of Petrarch on June 22, 1370 (quoted above, note 15); according to the document (Malmigiati, *op. cit.*, p. 92), the price for the land was paid with the money "venerabilis et sapientis viri domini Francisci Petrarce canonici Paduani . . . ad presens Padue habitantis . . . , habentis decretum et gratiam a magnifico et potente domino Francisco da Carraria Padue et cetera imperiali vicario generali, emendi et acquirendi bona immobilia et possessiones in Padua et Paduano districtu, prout de dictis decreto et gratia evidenter constat in quodam publico et autentico instrumento dicti decreti scripto sub anno millesimo et indictione suprascriptis, die dominico, quarto decimo mensis Aprilis." Compare A. Gloria, *Documenti inediti intorno al Petrarca* (Padua, 1878), pp. 22 f.; Zardo, *op. cit.*, pp. 97–101; Billanovich, *op. cit.*, pp. 427 f.

[41] P. Sambin, "Nuove notizie su eredi e discendenti del Petrarca," *Atti dell'Istituto Veneto di Scienze, Lettere ed Arti,* CX (Classe di Scienze Morali e Lettere, 1952), 255 ff., 261–263.

[42] See the documentary material compiled by Billanovich, *op. cit.*, p. 362, n. 1. According to a note in the edition of the Will, which is

After this bequest to the Cathedral of Padua and after further gifts to other churches and to "the poor of Christ" (§§ 9, 10), Petrarch listed his individual legacies. He placed first (§ 12) "my aforesaid magnificent Lord of Padua," then (§§ 13–22) "my friends who are of lesser condition, though they are very dear to me," and finally (§ 23) his servants, of whom he mentioned two by name. It is interesting to compare this list of men who, at the end of his life, were close enough to Petrarch to be remembered by him in his Will with a letter which he wrote in 1350.[43] Of the ten men whom Petrarch had enumerated in 1350 as having been closest to him during the first part of his life, we find that in 1370 only two were still alive, his brother Gerardo and Giovanni Boccaccio. With the exception of these two, then, all the other legatees were men with whom Petrarch had become intimate only during the later years of his life. On the other hand, it is evident that these were the people whom Petrarch now considered to be closest to himself, and the nearness of his relations with them can indeed be proved in almost every case by additional material.

Among the intimates of Petrarch's old age there seems to be only one name missing in the Testament, that of Philippe de Cabassole.[44] Their friendly relationship had begun in 1337, when Petrarch took up residence in Vaucluse, over which Philippe, then Bishop of Cavaillon, held both spiritual and temporal jurisdiction. The two men remained in close contact up to the death of Philippe in 1372, as is shown by the warm tone of Petrarch's numerous letters to Philippe, as well as by the fact that he dedicated to him his treatise *On the Solitary Life.* In his *Letter to Posterity,* Petrarch stated explicitly that "he is now the only one alive of all my old friends." [45] The fact that

contained in the Paduan (Comino) publication of 1722 of *Le rime,* p. LI, the anniversary mass "fedelmente anche oggidì si pratica in questa Cattedrale adì 9. Luglio, o in altro giorno da' maggiori ufficij non impedito."

[43] *Fam.* IX, 2.

[44] On Philippe de Cabassole see, e.g., Martellotti's introductory remarks to his edition and Italian translation of "De vita solitaria" in *Petrarca, Prose,* p. 286.

[45] Ed. by Ricci in *Petrarca, Prose,* p. 12: ". . . michi iam solus omnium veterum superstes, non me epyscopaliter, ut Ambrosius Augustinum, sed fraterne dilexit ac diligit."

in spite of this undoubtedly very intimate friendship Petrarch did not remember Philippe in his Will is perhaps best explained by the assumption that he could not think of any bequest suitable to a man who through his elevation to the cardinalate in 1368 had become one of the highest dignitaries of the Church.

A similar problem faced Petrarch in regard to the great princely patron of the last period of his life, Francesco da Carrara,[46] "since he neither, by the grace of God, is in need of anything," we read in the Testament (§ 12), "nor have I anything else worthy of him." In this case, however, Petrarch was in fact capable of making a bequest truly worthy of a prince. For he left to Francesco da Carrara "my panel or icon of the blessed Virgin Mary, a work of the eminent painter Giotto." Besides Simone Martini there was no painter of the Trecento whom Petrarch esteemed more highly than Giotto.[47] Thus he spoke of Giotto's "enormous fame among the moderns"[48] and said that "this fellow-countryman of mine, the prince of painters of our era, left great monuments of his hand and genius" in the royal chapel at Naples.[49] But whereas Petrarch had acquired quite early in his life a work of Simone Martini by commissioning the famous miniature of his codex of Virgil's writings, which is now in the Ambrosian Library in Milan,[50] he came

[46] On Petrarch's relationship with Francesco da Carrara, see Zardo, *op. cit.;* A. Medin, "Il Petrarca a Padova e ad Arquà," *Padova a F. Petrarca* (Padua, 1904), pp. 3 ff.; A. Limentani, "L'amicizia fra il Petrarca e i principi di Carrara," *Padova: Rassegna mensile del comune di Padova,* X (1937); Billanovich, *op. cit.,* pp. 297 ff.; T. E. Mommsen, "Petrarch and the Decoration of the Sala Virorum Illustrium in Padua," *Art Bulletin,* XXXIV (1952), 96 ff. [See above, pp. 133 ff.]

[47] Compare Prince d'Essling and E. Müntz, *Pétrarque: ses études d'art, son influence sur les artistes* (Paris, 1902), pp. 1, 4, 8–16, 44, 54 f., 58, 106 f.

[48] *Fam.* V, 17, 6: "Atque ut a veteribus ad nova, ab externis ad nostra transgrediar, duos ego novi pictores egregios, nec formosos: Iottum, florentinum civem, cuius inter modernos fama ingens est, et Simonem senensem."

[49] *Itinerarium Syriacum,* ed. by G. Lumbroso, in his *Memorie Italiane del buon tempo antico* (Turin, 1889), p. 37 (ed. *Opera,* 1581, p. 560): Petrarch advised his friend Giovanni di Mandello to visit in Naples "capellam regis . . . in qua conterraneus olim meus, pictorum nostri aevi princeps, magna reliquit manus et ingenii monimenta."

[50] A colored reproduction of Simone Martini's illumination is to be found in G. Galbiati's facsimile edition of *F. Petrarcae Vergilianus codex* (Milan, 1930), fol. 1v.

into the personal possession of a work by Giotto only in his old age. According to the Testament it was sent to him "by my friend Michele di Vanni of Florence." Recent investigations of Giuseppe Billanovich [51] have identified this friend as a member of the great Albizzi family of Florence, whom Petrarch got to know in Venice in 1365 and to whom he took such an instant liking that he recommended him in very cordial words to Boccaccio: "At the moment I have here," Petrarch wrote from Venice, "a friend who is new but has proved himself to be very good, Michele di Vanni; if I am dear to you, I wish him also to be dear to you." [52] We can assume, therefore, that Petrarch received the Giotto painting from that new friend between the years 1365 and 1370.[53]

In bequeathing the Giotto picture to Francesco da Carrara, Petrarch added the following comment: "The ignorant do not understand the beauty of this panel but the masters of art are stunned by it." Long before Petrarch wrote this sentence, his friend Boccaccio had expressed the same idea in almost identical terms by declaring in *The Decameron* that Giotto "brought to light again that art which for many centuries had lain buried through the mistaken notions of those who painted more to flatter the eye of the ignorant than to satisfy the intel-

[51] Billanovich, *op. cit.*, p. 275, n. 1.

[52] This passage is contained in the text of the original version of *Sen.* III, 6, which Professor Billanovich found in Cod. 146 B of the Library of Balliol College in Oxford; it reads as follows (*op. cit.*, p. 275, n. 1): "Habeo in presentia amicum novum sed probatum optimum, Michaelem Vannis, quem, si tibi carus sum, carum habeas velim." In addition to the material concerning Michele di Vanni degli Albizzi, which was collected by Billanovich, my friend Professor Gene Brucker of the University of California very kindly furnished me the following information: "Michele was declared eligible for the *Signoria* in the *scrutinio* of February 1364, but as a result of the prohibition of members of the Albizzi and Ricci families holding office in the commune (*Provvisioni* of April 1372), his name was removed from the *borsa* when it was drawn out in November 1373."

[53] The picture apparently does no longer exist; see A. Moschetti, "La Madonno trecentesca del duomo di Padova e la creduta sua originale appartenenza al Petrarca," *Padova in onore di F. Petrarca* (Padua, 1904), II, 139–156; S. Bettino, "Una Madonna di Giusto de' Menabuoi nella Biblioteca Capitolare di Padova," *Bollettino d'Arte,* XXIV (1930/31), 70–75; R. Salvini, *Giotto: Bibliografia* (Rome, 1938), pp. 25, nr. 48; 59, nr. 130; 64, nr. 143; 68, nr. 149; 317, nr. 683. Salvini (p. 5, n. 11), assumed wrongly that Petrarch's Testament dated of the year 1361.

lect of the wise." [54] When Petrarch thus, in 1370, expressed the belief which Boccaccio had expressed even earlier, that Giotto's art appealed primarily to the "intelligent" and not to the "ignorant," this view differed greatly from the one which a few years later, around 1375, was to be set forth by Benvenuto da Imola, who wrote in his *Commentary on Dante's Divine Comedy:* "Giotto still holds the field because no one subtler than he has yet appeared, even though at times he made great errors in his paintings, as I have heard from men of outstanding talent in such matters." [55] In his discussion of the significance of this passage Millard Meiss has rightly pointed out that "Benvenuto's comment . . . reflected current criticism of Giotto's pictorial style," which was in accordance with, and resulted from, "an important change in style and in taste around the middle of the fourteenth century." [56] But while it is true that most of the Florentine masters of the latter half of the fourteenth century were, to use Millard Meiss's term, "in a sense anti-Giottesque," [57] the situation in Padua was quite different because there the Giottesque tradition was still very much alive. Precisely around the year 1370 a group of those northern fol-

[54] G. Boccaccio, *Il Decameròn,* VI, 5 (ed. by E. Bianchi; Milan and Naples, 1952, p. 440): "E per ciò, avendo egli quella arte ritornata in luce, che molti secoli sotto gli error d'alcuni, che più a dilettar gli occhi degl'ignoranti che a compiacere allo 'ntelletto de' savi dipigneano, era stata sepulta, meritamente una delle luci della fiorentina gloria dir si puote; e tanto più, quanto con maggiore umiltà, maestro degli altri in ciò vivendo, quella acquistò, sempre rifiutando d'esser chiamato maestro"; the above translation, with slight changes, is that of F. Winwar in the Modern Library edition of *The Decameron* (1955), p. 366. See also Boccaccio's remarks on Giotto in *L'amorosa visione,* IV, 13–18 (ed. by V. Branca; Bari, 1939, p. 131).

[55] Benvenuto da Imola (*Comentum super Dantis Aldigherii Comoediam,* ed. by J. P. Lacaita [Florence, 1887], III, 312 f.) remarked in the context of his commentary on the Giotto passage in Dante's *Purgatorio,* XI, 91–96, that both Petrarch and Boccaccio had mentioned and praised Giotto and that Boccaccio had stressed above all the naturalness of Giotto's art; after that Benvenuto continued as follows (p. 313): "Et sic nota, quod Giottus adhuc tenet campum, quia nondum venit alius eo subtilior, cum tamen fecerit aliquando magnos errores in picturis suis, ut audivi a magnis ingeniis." The above translation is that given by M. Meiss, *Painting in Florence and Siena after the Black Death* (Princeton, 1951), pp. 4 f.

[56] Meiss, *op. cit.,* p. 6. [57] *Ibid.,* p. 7.

lowers of Giotto—including Altichiero of Verona, Jacopo Avanzo of Padua, and Giusto de' Menabuoi—adapted Petrarch's main historical work, the *De viris illustribus,* in the decoration of the great hall of the Carrara palace, which had been commissioned by Francesco il Vecchio da Carrara.[58] These painters and other men of their school working in Padua at that time were certainly known to Petrarch, and it is among them that "the masters of art" must be found, who according to Petrarch were "stunned" by the beauty of his Giotto painting. The strength of the Giottesque tradition in the Padua of the late Trecento is further illustrated by a statement made by the humanist Pietro Paolo Vergerio more than twenty years after Petrarch's death. In a letter, written in Padua in 1396, Vergerio found it logical that "the painters of our era, although they look carefully at the pictures of others, follow nevertheless the example of only one man, Giotto." [59]

None of Petrarch's other bequests was quite so outstanding in its kind and value as the unique gift which he left to his "magnificent Lord" Francesco da Carrara. But at the same time it should be noted that every one of the legacies to "the friends of lesser condition" reveals the most thoughtful endeavor on Petrarch's part to make a present which he considered to be fitting, as well as pleasing, to each individual. Thus it was very appropriate that he bequeathed to two of his socially prominent Paduan friends two of his horses, asking them (§ 15) "to draw lots to decide who shall have the first choice and who the second." The name of one of these Paduans, Bonzanello da Vigonza, seems to appear nowhere else in Petrarch's works or letters. But we learn from contemporary chronicles [60] that the

58 Mommsen, [*Art Bulletin,* XXXIV], 97–102. [See above, pp. 134–145.]

59 In L. Smith, ed., *Epistolario di Pier Paolo Vergerio* (Rome, 1934), ep. 75, p. 177: "Faciendum est igitur, quod etatis nostre pictores, qui, cum ceterorum claras imagines sedulo spectent, solius tamen Ioti exemplaria sequuntur."

60 See Guglielmo and Albrigetto Cortusi, *Chronica de novitatibus Padue et Lombardie,* in Muratori, ed., *Rerum Italicarum Scriptores* (Milan, 1728), XII, coll. 759–988; only the beginning of this chronicle has so far been republished in the new edition of Muratori's *Rerum Italicarum Scriptores* (Bologna, 1941), vol. XII, pt. v; Galeazzo and Bartolomeo Gatari, *op. cit.;* see the index, *ibid.,* p. 847, s.v. "Vigonza."

"casa da Vigonza" played quite an active role in Paduan affairs during the fourteenth century,[61] and the memory of at least one member of the family, Corrado da Vigonza, must have been very much alive in the Arquà of Petrarch's time, for in 1322 he had led a band of Paduan exiles to Arquà and burned down its castle. Three years later Corrado was captured by Niccolo and Marsiglio da Carrara and beheaded in Padua.[62] Of Petrarch's friend Bonzanello da Vigonza, we learn from the same narrative sources that he participated in Francesco da Carrara's unsuccessful war of 1372 against Venice and was made a prisoner by the Venetians. He and other Paduan noblemen obtained their freedom only as a result of the peace mission of Francesco the Younger of Carrara and Petrarch, which the older Francesco was forced to send to Venice in 1373.[63]

The second of those two Paduans to whom Petrarch bequeathed his horses was Lombardo della Seta. Whereas Petrarch's relationship with Bonzanello da Vigonza must be presumed to have been of a purely social nature, there existed the closest possible ties between him and Lombardo, who has rightly been called "Petrarch's favorite pupil in the last period of his life." [64] Lombardo was a humanist in his own right, though of rather limited talent and achievement, and he became best known by the fact that he completed the two historical works which had been left unfinished by his master, the *De viris illustribus* and its abridgment, the so-called *Compendium.* During Petrarch's lifetime Lombardo helped him in the management of his financial affairs and acted occasionally as his business agent, as we learn both from the Testament and from other documentary evidence. After Petrarch's death he served as his literary executor and played a very important, though not altogether fortunate, role in editing and publishing the works of his master. It was he who took charge of most of

[61] See Gatari, *op. cit.*, pp. 10 and 51.

[62] See Cortusi, *op. cit.*, (1941 ed.), pp. 40 f., 44, 45.

[63] See Gatari, *op. cit.*, pp. 115, 116, 127; compare *ibid.*, p. 115, n. 1.

[64] Martellotti in *Petrarca, Prose*, p. 1127, note; see also G. Ferrante, "Lombardo della Seta umanista padovano," *Atti d. R. Istituto Veneto di Scienze, Lettere ed Arti*, XCIII, pt. II (1933/34), 445–487; Billanovich, *op. cit.*, pp. 299 ff., 333 ff.

the task of having Petrarch's works copied and distributing them among all the friends and other persons interested in them; indeed, he copied some with his own hand.[65] Petrarch was fully and gratefully conscious of Lombardo's loyalty toward him, which, he said in a letter of 1373, had manifested itself "not through meaningless words and flattery, a fragile link of transitory friendship, but through the infallible proof of acts by which minds become linked together in a strong and lasting fashion." [66] In the Testament, Petrarch expressed the love and gratitude which he felt for this faithful friend, not merely by leaving him one of his horses, but by adding a highly personal present, "my little round cup made of silver and gilded"; [67] and he added to this bequest the charming remark (§ 17): "Let him drink water from it, which he drinks with pleasure—indeed with much greater pleasure than he drinks wine." Of Lombardo's predilection for water Petrarch spoke approvingly in the same letter of 1373 which has just been mentioned.[68]

Petrarch also made a like personal gift to Tommaso Bombasi, a native of Ferrara.[69] Very little seems to be known about this friend, and that information is derived mostly from a letter of

[65] On this whole matter see Billanovich, *op. cit.,* pt. III ("Da Padova all'Europa"), esp. pp. 318–323.

[66] *Sen.* XV, 3 (XIV, 4, ed. *Opera,* 1581, p. 933).

[67] J. F. P. A. de Sade, *Mémoires pour la vie de F. Pétrarque* (Amsterdam, 1757), III, 743, note b, said in regard to this drinking cup: "C'est sans doute le gobelet que l'Empereur Charles lui envoya l'an 1362 [actually in 1361]"; see also *ibid.,* pp. 559 f. But this identification is contradicted by the fact that according to Petrarch's letter of thanks (*Fam.* XXIII, 8, 1–2) the "crater" given by Charles IV was "auro solidus," whereas in the Testament he described his little round "scyphus" as "argenteus et auratus."

[68] According to *Sen.* XV, 3 (ed. *Opera,* 1581, p. 934), Lombardo had been asked by someone what he liked to drink and, in reply, had simply pointed to his well; on this answer Petrarch commented: "Preclare; nam quid aliud siquis illam roget?" In a letter to the physician Giovanni Dondi, who warned him constantly against the drinking of water, Petrarch defined his own attitude toward wine as follows: "Nunc uero bibo et edo ut ceteri, nec tamen laudo, sed consuetudine rapior ad id etiam quod non probo"; *Sen.* XII, 2 (ed. *Opera,* 1581, p. 913).

[69] On Bombasi, see C. Culcasi, *Il Petrarca e la musica* (Florence, 1911), pp. 19 ff.; N. Leonelli, *Attori tragici, attori comici* (Milan, 1940), I, 82.

1364, in which Petrarch described the festivities with which the Venetians celebrated their successful suppression of a dangerous revolt in Crete.[70] For the direction of one of the equestrian games, which was performed on that occasion by twenty-four young Venetian patricians, Tommaso Bombasi had been called from Ferrara to Venice. Petrarch wished "with a few words to make this man known to posterity," for, he said in his letter, "he is today as renowned in the whole of Venice as Roscius was once renowned in Rome"; and he added: "He is just as dear and close to me as Roscius was to Cicero." In 1364 the friendship between the two men must already have been at least five years old. For, although Petrarch did not choose to include in his epistolary collections any of the letters which he may have written to Tommaso, we know from several marginal notes in the autograph manuscript of the *Canzoniere* that on October 8, 1359, as well as on another occasion, he sent some copies of his sonnets to Tommaso in Ferrara.[71] To this friend who, if we may judge from the account of his activities in Venice and from the comparison with the famous Roman actor Roscius,[72] must have been a combination of stage director, actor, and musician, Petrarch bequeathed "my good lute," and he added the characteristic admonition (§ 20) "that he may play it, not for the vainglory of this fleeting world, but in praise of God everlasting."

In the Testament, Petrarch mentioned specifically only one other of his personal possessions, "my great breviary which I bought in Venice for the price of one hundred pounds." He bequeathed it (§ 18) to "the priest Giovanni a Bocheta, custodian of our cathedral." Giovanni a Bocheta appeared under the same title of "custos ecclesiae maioris Paduanae" in a Paduan document of 1358.[73] Petrarch called him in two of his letters

70 *Sen.* IV, 3, ed. by Martellotti in *Petrarca, Prose,* pp. 1082 f.

71 See the facsimile edition of *Il Codice Vaticano Latino 3196,* ed. by M. Porena (Rome, 1941), foll. 3^{v}, 4^{r}, 5^{v}; compare K. Appel, *Zur Entwicklung italienischer Dichtungen Petrarcas* (Halle, 1891), pp. 42, 46, 52; Wilkins, *Making of the "Canzoniere,"* pp. 158, 159, 289.

72 On Q. Roscius Gallus see Pauly-Wissowa, *Real-Encyklopaedie der classischen Altertumswissenschaft* (Stuttgart, 1920), ser. II, vol. I, col. 1123 ff.

73 Gloria, *op. cit.,* p. 27, nr. 1. On Giovanni a Bocheta see also G. Cittadella, "Petrarca a Padova e ad Arquà," *Padova a Petrarca* (Padua, 1874),

"my priest," [74] and in the letter of 1371, in which he described to Francesco Bruni his household, he spoke of Giovanni as follows: "I have a priest, a venerable man, who attends to me whenever I am in church." [75] As we may conclude from these passages, it was evidently Giovanni's function to assist Petrarch, or to substitute for him, in the performance of the clerical and administrative duties which were connected with his position of a canon of the cathedral chapter in Padua. Petrarch was in most definite need of such a priestly attendant since he was frequently absent from Padua and, moreover, had himself never taken any priestly orders. In view of this relationship it was fitting that Petrarch left his breviary to Giovanni a Bocheta. After the latter's death the breviary was "to remain in the sacristy of Padua for the perpetual use of the priests," whom Petrarch asked to pray to Christ and the blessed Virgin on his behalf.[76]

While Petrarch was residing in Venice between the years 1362 and 1367, one of the men closest to him there was the grammarian Donato degli Albanzani, a native of Pratovecchio in the Apennines, "teacher of literature, now living in Venice," as we read in the Testament (§ 14).[77] In 1366 Donato became the godfather of Petrarch's oldest grandson, Franceschino da

---

pp. 36 f.; Zardo, *op. cit.*, pp. 74 f.; Fracassetti in his translation of *Lettere delle cose familiari*, V, 356.

[74] *Var.* 11, in *Epistolae*, III, 326, and *Sen.* VI, 4 (ed. *Opera*, 1581, p. 809). See also *Var.* 39, and Fracassetti's note to his translation of that letter (*Lettere*, V, 356).

[75] *Var.* 15, in *Epistolae*, III, 333.

[76] P. de Nolhac, *Pétrarque et l'humanisme*, 2d ed. (Paris, 1907), I, 93, n.2, stated in regard to this breviary that he searched in vain for it in Padua; according to an old tradition the Paduan chapter had presented it in the early seventeenth century to Pope Paul V, and some scholars identified it, therefore, with a specific breviary now extant in the Vatican Library; De Nolhac, however, questioned this identification by stating: "J'ai examiné attentivement le manuscrit sans trouver, sur un volume qui aurait été un des plus familiers au poète, le moindre signe extérieur venant à l'appui de la tradition." See also A. Foresti, *Aneddoti della vita di F. Petrarca* (Brescia, 1928), pp. 243 f.

[77] On Donato see F. Novati, "Donato degli Albanzani alla corte estense," *Archivio storico italiano*, ser. V, vol. VI (1890), 365–385; V. Rossi, "Nell'intimità spirituale del Petrarca," *Nuova antologia*, CCCLVI (July 1931), 5–7; Billanovich, *op. cit.*, pp. 129, n. 2; 293, 310, 373, 390; Martellotti in *Petrarca, Prose*, p. 1126, note.

Brossano, and two years later the two friends shared their grief over the simultaneous deaths of Franceschino and of one of Donato's sons.[78] When Petrarch departed from Venice in 1367 or early in 1368, he left his library in charge of Donato,[79] and it was to Donato that he dedicated in 1370 the treatise *On His Own Ignorance and That of Many Others* in which he polemized sharply against some of his Venetian critics. Donato served later in the chancery of the Este princes, and at the end of the century, while in Ferrara, he translated Petrarch's work *De viris illustribus* into Italian. From Petrarch's correspondence we learn that Donato showed himself quite concerned about the fact that he was under certain financial obligations to Petrarch and thus seemed to have gained material advantages from their friendship. Petrarch called Donato's worries "laughable," and declared that he was not certain whether "you have said this jokingly or whether you have made a mistake in regard to the state of our accounts." [80] In another letter he told Donato: "Between friends the principle holds that in the event of an exigency there is nothing which belongs only to one of them." [81] It was in accordance with this notion of friendship that in the Will he remitted to Donato "whatever he owes me on loan" and at the same time depreciated very tactfully that gift by adding: "How much it is I do not know, but in any case it is little."

In the case of Giovanni Boccaccio, Petrarch even offered an explicit apology in the Testament for the bequest of fifty gold florins which he made to this very old and intimate friend, by saying (§ 19) that he was "ashamed" to leave "such a trifling legacy to so great a man." In fact, this sum of money was not

[78] See *Sen.* X, 4 (ed. *Opera,* 1581, p. 874).

[79] See Petrarch's remark in *De sui ipsius et multorum ignorantia* (ed. by Ricci in *Petrarca, Prose,* p. 756): "bibliotheca nostra tuis in manibus relicta . . ."

[80] *Sen.* VIII, 6 (ed. *Opera,* 1581, pp. 840 f.).

[81] In *Sen.* X, 5 (ed. *Opera,* 1581, p. 881) Petrarch complained about the frequent gifts which Donato had sent him and objected to them as follows: "Non est operosa res amicitia mea, quippe que nec magni eciam precii res est, ut sit autem maximi, nihilo erit operosior. Et amare et amari gratis didici. Si necessitas amicorum ingruat, nil cuiquam proprium uolo. Ubi id cessat, quid sibi uult, precor, ista largitio?"

a mere trifle but represented "a rather ample share of goods," as Boccaccio himself acknowledged in the letter of November 3, 1374, in which he expressed to Francescuolo da Brossano his sincere gratitude for "the munificence" of the bequest forwarded to him by Da Brossano.[82] Boccaccio's friends knew him to be poor, "a fact which I have never denied," as he stated in a letter in which he told Petrarch how, on his departure from Venice in the summer of 1367, Francescuolo da Brossano "gripped my poor small arms with his giant hands and pressed on me, despite my reluctance and blushes, a liberal sum of money." [83] In full knowledge of the straightened circumstances under which Boccaccio lived, Petrarch with great tact avoided embarrassing him with an outright monetary present, but gave to his bequest a nicely intimate and personal note by asking his learned friend (§ 19) to purchase with the money "a winter garment to be worn by him while he is studying and working during the night hours."

To his Paduan friend Giovanni Dondi dall'Orologio, the famous scientist and physician,[84] Petrarch bequeathed fifty gold ducats, the same amount which he left to Boccaccio. There is, however, a marked difference between these two bequests. In

[82] *Ep.* 24, in A. F. Massèra, ed., *G. Boccaccio, Opere latine minori* (Bari, 1928), pp. 225 f. On this "lascito notevolmente generoso" see also Billanovich, *op. cit.*, p. 284.

[83] *Ep.* 14, in Massèra, ed., *op. cit.*, p. 181; the above translation is that of F. MacManus, *Boccaccio* (New York, 1947), pp. 268 f. The fact that Boccaccio's material means were much more limited than those of Petrarch becomes evident also from a comparison of his Testament of 1374 (in Corazzini, ed., *Le lettere edite e inedite di G. Boccaccio* [Florence, 1877], pp. 425–433) with Petrarch's Will; but Michel de Montaigne exaggerated greatly when, after a perusal of Boccaccio's Will, he commented on it in his *Journal de voyage en Italie* (ed. by A. Armaingaud; Paris, 1929, II, 166) as follows: "Questo testamento mostra una mirabile povertà e bassezza di fortuna di questo grand'uomo."

[84] On Giovanni Dondi see A. Gloria, "I due orologi meravigliosi inventati da Jacopo e Giovanni Dondi," *Atti d. R. Istituto Veneto di Scienze, Lettere ed Arti,* LIV (1895/96), 675–736; see also *ibid.*, LV (1896/97), 1000–1017; V. Lazzarini, "I libri, gli argenti, le vesti di Giovanni Dondi dall'Orologio," *Bollettino del Museo Civico di Padova,* n.s., I (1925), 11–36; Thorndike, *op. cit.*, III, 386–397; IV, 190–201; Billanovich, *op. cit.*, pp. 343–346; see also the "annotazioni" to the edition of *Sen.* XII, 1, published by the Seminario di Padova, *op. cit.*, pp. 75–80.

contrast to Boccaccio, Giovanni Dondi was a wealthy man, and in his case, therefore, Petrarch stipulated (§ 22) not the purchase of a utilitarian object such as a warm cloak, but rather asked Dondi to buy for that amount "a small finger-ring to be worn by him in my memory." Petrarch held Dondi in high esteem, as he stated clearly in the Testament: "I have postponed to the last him who deserved to be the first." But throughout their relationship Petrarch left never any doubt in Dondi's mind that he respected him, not because of, but rather in spite of the fact that he was "the prince of doctors of this era," and time and again he professed very frankly to this friend the deep-rooted aversion which he felt against most of the physicians of his day.[85] Thus he wrote to Dondi on November 17, 1370: "Looking at you I see a double personality, that of the friend and that of the physician; with the friend I find myself in such a complete accord that nothing which seems right and pleasing to you does not also seem right and pleasing to me, and I cannot conceive of any other kind of friendship than that by which two minds are becoming one; on the other hand, with the physicians I have a long and unresolved quarrel over many and important matters." [86]

One of Giovanni Dondi's special claims to distinction was the famous clock on which he had worked in Pavia between the years 1348 and 1364 and which was placed in the tower of the Visconti palace there. According to Lynn Thorndike, Giovanni's work was not an ordinary clock but an even more elaborate astronomical clock than the one which had been built earlier by his father Jacopo Dondi for the Carrara palace in Padua; [87] both instruments were devised, in Thorndike's words,

[85] *Sen.* XII, 1, in Seminario di Padova, ed., *op. cit.*, p. 45: "Et non quidem artem ipsam, sed artifices parvipendi, preter aliquot raros, quos dilexi, quoniam veri michi medici viderentur; quomodo inquam talis ego cum principe medicorum huius temporis, aut unico aut uno ex paucis, disputarem de rebus ad medicum spectantibus?"

[86] *Sen.* XII, 2 (ed. *Opera,* 1581, p. 904). Dondi himself testified to the intimacy of his relationship with Petrarch by stating in a letter addressed to Guglielmo da Verona (quoted by De Nolhac, *op. cit.*, I, 139): "ego familiaris fui multumque domesticus, presertim in posteris eius annis."

[87] On these two clocks see Thorndike, *op. cit.*, III, 386–388; compare the letter written by Petrarch in Milan in 1353 (Foresti, *op. cit.*, pp. 279–285,

"to mark the courses of the planets instead of merely the hours." [88] The two Dondi clocks from which the family derived the name dall'Orologio are unfortunately no longer in existence, but we still possess a treatise entitled *Planetarium* or *Opus Planetarii* in which Giovanni Dondi dealt with the problem of mechanical clocks.[89] If the text of the stipulation concerning Giovanni Dondi which appears in the *editio princeps* of the Testament were authentic, it would indicate that Petrarch used this particular opportunity to give specific recognition to the scientific achievements of his friend; for according to this version he spoke of him as follows: "Giovanni dei Dondi, physician, easily prince of astronomers, who is called dall'Orologio because of the admirable astronomical clock (*planetarium*) made by him, which the ignorant rabble believe to be an ordinary clock (*orologium*)." [90] But although both the style and the didactic tone of these remarks seem quite characteristic of Petrarch, the authenticity of this version of the text appears highly dubious in view of the fact that it is not to be found in any of the various other traditions of the Testament, whether manuscript or printed.

In the legacies to his servants (§ 23) Petrarch followed the conventional pattern by leaving them small sums in cash, varying in amount according to their positions in his household. In passing we may note the surprisingly direct and personal admonition which he added to his bequest of twenty ducats to Bartolomeo da Siena called Pancaldo (§ 23 a): "May he not use them for gambling." Petrarch evidently had certain reservations about this particular servant, for we find that in a letter of 1373 he called Pancaldo "a great simpleton." [91]

292), in which he mentioned "publicum horologium, quo ultimo invento per omnes fere iam Cisalpinae Galliae civitates metimur tempus" (*Var.* 44, in *Epistolae,* III, 419).

88 Thorndike, *op. cit.,* III, 389. 89 *Ibid.,* pp. 389–392, 740 f.

90 See [Mommsen, *Petrarch's Testament*], p. 84, n. 51, in the edition of the text of the Will, the variant readings provided by the *b*- and *m*-traditions. The Paduan editors of 1904 of *Sen.* XII, 1 (see above, note 84) accepted (*op. cit.,* p. 78) the authenticity of this insertion on the basis of the Comino-edition of 1722 of the Will which, however, was simply derived from the *m*- and *b*-traditions; see *op. cit.,* p. 61.

91 *Var.* 9, in *Epistolae,* III, 322: "Et nunc tandem per Pancaldum sim-

As has been mentioned before, Petrarch added to his list of individual legacies some further provisions at the end of the Will. One of them, he said (§ 27), "concerns that little piece of land which I own beyond the Alps . . . in the village or castle district of Vaucluse. . . . Since undoubtedly it would cost somewhat more than the property is worth to go there or send someone, I stipulate that this piece of land become the property of the hospital of the said place and be used for the poor of Christ." In the case of legal obstacles to this bequest, Petrarch provided that the land in Vaucluse was to become "the property of the brothers Jean and Pierre, sons of the late Raymond of Clermont, commonly called Monet, who was most obedient and faithful to me"; in the event that one or both of the two brothers mentioned had died, "the land should fall to their sons or grandsons in memory of the said Monet."

With this alternative bequest to the descendants of Raymond Monet, Petrarch remembered the services of the man who for fifteen years had tended "the few acres of arid land," which he owned in Vaucluse.[92] Ever since Petrarch had begun to live in Vaucluse in 1337, Monet had been his caretaker in the fullest sense of the word, a man whom he could trust, not only with the management of his small estate there, but above all with the custody of his most treasured possession, his library.[93] We learn all these and other details regarding the truly intimate

plicissimum hominum mittebam, nisi tuus hic nuntius advenisset." In the revised edition of this letter (*Sen.* XIII, 11) Petrarch omitted that reference to Pancaldo, as Wilkins, *Making of the "Canzoniere,"* p. 177, has observed. It may be noted that the name of the other servant mentioned in Petrarch's Will (§ 23 b) appears in a letter addressed by Giovanni Dondi to Petrarch (ed. by Zardo, *op. cit.*, p. 279): "Zilius noster, qui literam istam defert, retulit michi hodie de te grata, optime pater, quoniam iuxta modum non firme, sed labentis tue ac recidentis persone satis bene ad presens te valere testificatus est."

92 See the letter of Jan. 5, 1353 (*Fam.* XVI, 1, 1), in which Petrarch told the cardinals Elie de Talleyrand and Guy de Montfort that "villicus . . . meus vobis non ignotus, qui michi pauca itidem sicci ruris iugera colebat, hesterno die obiit." See also the reference to Vaucluse in *Sen.* VI, 3 (ed. *Opera*, 1581, p. 808): "tellus ipsa licet aridula et angusta."

93 On Raymond Monet see Fracassetti's notes to his translations of *Fam.* XVI, 1 (*op. cit.*, III, 412 f.) and of *Sen.* IX, 2 (*op. cit.*, II, 62 f.). In *Fam.* XVI, 1, 5, Petrarch said that "totum me illi [i.e., Monet] et res meas librosque omnes, quos in Galliis habeo, commiseram"; Monet had always taken such diligent and loving care of the books that now, after his death,

relationship between master and servant from a letter which Petrarch addressed to two cardinals on the day after Monet's death on January 4, 1353: "The earth has never borne, I believe, a more faithful being,"[94] Petrarch declared, and added that during the fifteen years of their relationship Monet's house had become to him "a temple of loyalty."[95] In almost identical terms he stated in a letter written to Francesco Bruni many years after Monet's death that "he was loyalty personified."[96] Through the legacy made in memory of the humble bailiff "who was most obedient and faithful to me," Petrarch revealed the same feeling of gratitude and devotion to a man long departed but still vividly remembered which we found in the words of the earlier passage of the Testament, in which he conjured up the friendship and love once shown to him by one of his great princely patrons, Jacopo da Carrara.

In the last of the addenda to the Testament (§ 32) Petrarch made provisions for his brother Gerardo, who lived as a Carthusian monk in the monastery of Montrieux near Marseilles.[97] Although the two brothers always remained very close to one another, we find in the whole collection of Petrarch's correspondence during the later period of his life, the *Seniles,* only one letter addressed to Gerardo.[98] From this letter, which was probably written around 1373, we learn that four years earlier he had been asked by Gerardo "to leave him in his Will a certain sum of money to be transmitted in small payments appropriate to his occurring needs."[99] It was apparently in accordance with that request that Petrarch stipulated in the Testament (§ 32) that "immediately after my death my heir is to give

---

Petrarch declared (*Fam.* XVI, 1, 3): "bibliothece mee, quam michi in filiam adoptavi, sentio deesse custodem." See also *Fam.* XII, 6, 6, and XVII, 5, 9. In *Sen.* X, 2 (ed. *Opera,* 1581, p. 870) is a reference to the good care which one of Monet's sons ("uillici mei filius") had taken so as to prevent Petrarch's books from being robbed on Christmas Day of the year 1353.

[94] *Fam.* XVI, 1, 4. [95] *Fam.* XVI, 1, 7.

[96] *Sen.* IX, 2 (ed. *Opera,* 1581, p. 854): "Nam fidelem dicere detrahere est, ipsa siquidem fides erat."

[97] See Cochin, *op. cit.*

[98] *Sen.* XV, 5; see the analysis of this letter by Cochin, *op. cit.,* pp. 142–155.

[99] *Sen.* XV, 5 (XIV, 6, ed. *Opera,* 1581, p. 939): "Scripsisti interdum, ut si ante te morerer . . . certam pecunie summam tibi testamento legarem ad te minutis pro occurrenti necessitate solutionibus peruenturam."

written notice of this event to my brother Gerardo Petracco . . . and let him choose whether he wishes one hundred florins [at once] or five or ten florins annually, as he may please." Naturally enough Petrarch did not notify his brother of this testamentary provision of 1370. It was evidently only in reply to a renewed request by Gerardo for financial help that around 1373 Petrarch finally decided to write to his brother and discuss the entire matter with him. In this letter he declared that he would have gladly anticipated Gerardo's requests for help, "if I had not known that the small sum of money which I once sent you never reached you because the severe rule of your monastic order, I assume, prevented it." [100] In regard to the small legacy for which Gerardo had asked previously, Petrarch assured him that he had already acted upon it and left him in his Will "a sum three times as large as the one requested by you." [101] Moreover, he asked his brother to let him know whether he would like to have some part of this legacy transmitted immediately to him, "for," he explained, "both to you and to myself will be more welcome what I shall have done personally than what my heir will do." [102] In the absence of any further letters we do not know whether Gerardo actually expressed some preference concerning the disbursement of the amount of money promised to him. But it has been ascertained through the archival investigations of Henry Cochin that three years after Petrarch's death, in 1377, at least one part of that bequest to Gerardo, the sum of twenty florins, was used in the monastery of Montrieux for the endowment of a mass "for the soul of the venerable lord Francesco, son of Petracco, the most eloquent poet of late"; [103] many centuries later it was still re-

[100] *Ibid.:* "Scribe modo, quid fieri uelis; non frustrabor tuum desiderium nec differam neque uero ut peteres expectarem sed uolens occurrerem, nisi didicissem, quod pecuniola illa, quam alioquotiens tibi misi, non peruenit ad manus tuas, rigore ut credo tue religionis obstante."

[101] *Ibid.:* "Enimuero id iampridem factum noris et legato quantitas triplo maior quam petebatur inserta est."

[102] *Ibid.:* "Nec tamen expectari mortem testamenti confirmatricem expedit; iube, parebitur; et tibi gratius erit et mihi, quod ipse fecero quam quod heres meus."

[103] See the excerpts from a contract of Dec. 31, 1377, which were published by Cochin, *op. cit.*, pp. 232–236; see also *ibid.*, pp. 145 f., 223, 236–238.

membered in the charterhouse of Montrieux that this anniversary mass for Petrarch was to be celebrated annually on St. Michel's day (September 29).[104]

Petrarch bequeathed his whole residuary estate, consisting, as he said (§ 25), "of all my movable and immovable goods which I have now or may have in the future, wherever they are or may be," to Francesco da Brossano. Francesco, or, as he was commonly called, Francescuolo, was a native of Milan, who held administrative positions first in the service of the Visconti, later in the service of the Carrara.[105] In or about the year 1361 he married Petrarch's daughter Francesca, by whom he had a number of children. Since Petrarch's only other child, his son Giovanni, had already died in 1361, it may be assumed that Petrarch resolved long before the formal composition of his Testament to bequeath his estate to his son-in-law and his family, and thus it seems most likely that it was Francescuolo da Brossano whom he had in mind when he wrote in a letter of the year 1363: "My heir himself—if indeed it will be he whom I desire and upon whom I have decided—hopes for more from me being alive than having died." [106] Petrarch always showed a deep affection for Francescuolo and for "the little family" of the Da Brossano who shared his life and household during his old age.[107] But in view of the fact that both Francesca and Giovanni were of illegitimate birth, it is worth noticing that

[104] Cochin, *op. cit.*, pp. 150, 155, 237 f.

[105] On Francescuolo's name, see a document of Dec. 11, 1375, in Gloria, ed., *op. cit.*, p. 34: ". . . providus vir Franciscus dictus Franciscolus q. d. Amizoli de Broxano de Mediolano." On Francescuolo's career and his marriage with Petrarch's daughter Francesca, see A. Serena, *Francesca figlia del Petrarca* (Milan, 1904), and the various articles published by Serena in *Atti d. R. Istituto Veneto di Scienze, Lettere ed Arti,* LXXXIV, pt. II (1924/25), 379–396; XCI, pt. II (1931/32), 241–256; XCV, pt II (1935/36), 13–24; G. Liberali, *La dominazione carrarese in Treviso* (Padua, 1935), pp. 66–82; Billanovich, *op. cit.*, pp. 277, 298 f., 318 ff., 325 f., 352 ff.

[106] *Sen.* III, 7 (III, 6, ed. *Opera,* 1581, p. 777): "Certe, nisi fallor, nullus est hominum, cui aut damnosa uita aut mors utilis mea sit. Ipse heres meus, si tamen is erit, quem cupio quemue disposui, plusculum ex uita mea sperat, ut arbitror, quam ex morte."

[107] *Sen.* V, 6 (V, 7, ed. *Opera,* 1581, p. 805): "Franciscus meus quo nemo . . . adolescens melior, . . . charitatis et constantiae plenus . . ."; see the references in *Sen.* XIII, 17 (XIII, 16, ed. *Opera,* 1581, p. 930) and in *Var.* 9 (in *Epistolae,* III, 321) to "familiola mea."

throughout his correspondence Petrarch carefully avoided making any direct statement as to the exact nature of the existing relationship. As long as Giovanni was alive he spoke of him simply as "our boy" or "our youth" or used even vaguer terms,[108] and only after his death he called him "my Giovanni."[109] In the same way he always referred to his son-in-law as "my Francescuolo"[110] or, more familiarly, "our Checcus."[111] His daughter he never mentioned by name, not even in the letter of 1368 in which he expressed to Donato degli Albanzani his deep sorrow over the death of his little grandson Franceschino da Brossano: "He was the son of the two people who for a long time have been closest to me," he wrote to his friend; and he added, "He was called by the same name as myself and as both his parents and thus he became the fourth Francesco, a great solace in our life and the hope and delight of the whole house."[112] It will be noted that even in these highly personal words the actual relationship between Petrarch and Francesca's son Franceschino is merely implied.[113] It was in accordance with his customary practice, then, that in the Will Petrarch did not call Francescuolo outright his son-in-law and that he chose to couch his bequest to Francesca in com-

[108] See, e.g., *Fam.* VII, 17, 1 and 3; XIII, 2, 1 and 3; XIX, 5, 1; XIX, 17, 9; XXIII, 12, 15; *Var.* 35; see also the two letters addressed to Giovanni (*Fam.* XVII, 2, and XXII, 7).

[109] *Sen.* I, 2 (I, 1, ed. *Opera,* 1581, p. 736). See also the note in which Petrarch recorded the death of "Iohannes noster" in his Vergil manuscript, in De Nolhac, ed., *op. cit.,* II, 284. At the beginning of *Sen.* I, 3 (2), Petrarch spoke of the death "adolescentis mei."

[110] *Var.* 4 and 12; *Sen.* V, 6 (7).

[111] See Petrarch's autograph note in one of his manuscripts (now Cod. Vatic. 2193, fol. 156v; published by De Nolhac, *op. cit.,* II, 267), in which he referred to some trees "quas donauit nobis Checcus noster."

[112] *Sen.* X, 4 (ed. *Opera,* 1581, p. 875): "noster utriusque parentis meumque simul nomen nactus erat, ita et solatium uite ingens et spes domus ac iucunditas, et nobis tribus quartus iam Franciscus accesserat"; Fracassetti, *Lettere senili,* II, 113, translated this passage very freely as follows: "Era figliuolo di Francesca e Francesco . . ."

[113] See Serena's observation (in *Atti d. R. Istituto Veneto di Scienze, Lettere ed Arti,* LXXXIV, pt. II [1924/25], 382), that Francesca was "cinta di geloso silenzio" by Petrarch throughout his life; compare also Fracassetti's remarks in the preface to his translation of *Lettere delle cose familiari,* I, 50 f.

pletely veiled terms by instructing Francescuolo as follows: (§ 25) "I ask him—not only as an heir but also as a very dear son—to divide into two parts whatever money he may find in my possession. . . . Let him keep one part for himself and count out the other part to the person to whom he knows I wish it to go; and in regard to the latter sum he is to follow my wishes, which are also known to him."

In the event that Francescuolo da Brossano were to die before his own death, Petrarch stipulated (§ 29) that "my heir is to be the aforementioned Lombardo della Seta." In view of everything we know about Petrarch's love for his daughter, coupled with the discreet language used by him in referring to her, and also in view of his close ties with Lombardo, the assumption seems justified that through this provision Petrarch did not really mean to bequeath to Lombardo the full possession of his residuary estate for his own benefit but wanted him merely to act as a fiduciary in the interests of Francesca and her children. This interpretation appears to be implied in the words with which Petrarch referred in this connection to Lombardo (§ 29): "He knows my mind fully, and I hope that he whom I have found to be most faithful during my lifetime will be no less faithful after my death." No problem ever arose on this particular point, since Francescuolo da Brossano survived both Petrarch and Francesca.

At the end of this survey of Petrarch's testamentary provisions, attention must be turned to one most notable omission. Of all his possessions there was none which he personally treasured more highly than his library, "which," he once said, "I have adopted as my daughter"; [114] the large collection of books which he had brought together with so much zeal and so systematically throughout his life certainly represented also in material terms a very considerable investment.[115] But besides the bequest of "my great breviary" to the priest Giovanni a Bocheta (§ 18), there is not a single reference to the library in

[114] Petrarch said of Monet that he was the custodian "bibliothece mee, quam michi in filiam adoptavi" (*Fam.* XVI, 1, 3).

[115] See the list of books owned by Petrarch which De Nolhac, *op. cit.*, II, 239–242, compiled.

the Will. Petrarch's silence on this matter appears the more remarkable as we know that eight years earlier, in 1362, he had shown great concern about the question as to what was to become of his books after his death.[116] At the beginning of that year Boccaccio advised him of his decision to give up once and for ever all his literary and scholarly work and to sell his books. In a long letter, dated on May 28, 1362, Petrarch endeavored to dissuade his friend from such a radical renunciation of his previous studies. In the event, however, that Boccaccio were to insist on his intention Petrarch declared himself willing to make use of the option on the library, which had been offered to him by Boccaccio. He explained this, not merely by admitting that he was indeed "covetous for books," [117] as Boccaccio had said, but by giving an even better reason: "I do not wish that the books of so great a man as you are be scattered here and there and be handled, as it may happen, by profane hands; as the two of us, though separated in body, are one in spirit, so I desire if God will aid my wish, that after our deaths these scholarly instruments of ours may go together and undivided to some pious and devout place in perpetual memory of us." Petrarch had conceived that plan, he told Boccaccio, "since he died who, I had hoped, would succeed me in my studies"—an evident allusion to the death of his son Giovanni in the previous year 1361.[118]

The project of combining those two libraries was not materialized because Boccaccio mastered his emotional crisis and decided to keep his books. When in his Will of 1374 Boccaccio bequeathed his entire library to Father Martino da Signa and, after Martino's death, to the monastery of S. Spirito in Florence,[119] he may have remembered Petrarch's words that a collection of scholarly books ought not to be dispersed but preserved as a whole in "some pious and devout place." It was in accordance with the same principle that Petrarch himself acted almost

[116] See the letter (*Sen.* I, 5, or, in ed. *Opera,* 1581, I, 4), which he addressed to Boccaccio on May 28, 1362.

[117] *Sen.* I, 5 (ed. *Opera,* 1581, p. 744): ". . . gratum, hercle, habeo me librorum auidum, ut tu ais."

[118] *Ibid.*, pp. 744 f.

[119] See the text of the Testament, edited by Corazzini, *op. cit.*, pp. 428 f.; see also Billanovich, *op. cit.*, pp. 262, n. 1, 263 ff., 268, n. 1, 283.

immediately after he had propounded it to Boccaccio. For in August 1362 he entered into negotiations regarding his library with the government of Venice, where he had just decided to take up residence.[120] In a proposal which he submitted to the Venetian authorities he declared his wish "to have Saint Mark the Evangelist as [my] heir of those books, unknown in number, which [I have] now or will have in the future." He stipulated that "these books were not to be sold nor dispersed in any way but perpetually preserved . . . in some fire- and rain-proof location to be assigned for this purpose." He made this donation "in honor of the said saint and in [my] own memory and also for the encouragement and the benefit of those noble and superior minds of this city, to whom it will be given to take delight in such things." He wished to do this not because he thought that "the books are very numerous or very valuable" but because he hoped "that later from time to time this glorious city will add other books at public expense and that also private individuals—noble and patriotic-minded citizens, as well as perhaps even foreign-born persons—will follow the example and leave in their last wills a part of their books to the church of San Marco; in this fashion it might easily be possible to establish a large and famous library, equal to those of antiquity." At the end of his proposal Petrarch declared that "he desired to obtain for himself and his books a house, not large but respectable," in which he promised to reside as extensively as would be feasible for him.[121] On September 4, 1362, the Grand Council met to discuss the proposal made by Petrarch, "whose fame," the official records of that meeting stated,[122] "is so great today in the whole world that in men's memory there never was nor is now a moral philosopher and a poet comparable to him." The offer was gratefully accepted, and authorization was given for

[120] On this whole matter see Fracassetti's note to his translation of *Var.* 43 (*Epistolae,* V, 375–383) and De Nolhac, ed., *op. cit.,* I, 93–98.

[121] Petrarch's proposal was inserted in the records of the deliberations of the Venetian Senate on Sept. 4, 1362 (see De Nolhac, ed., *op. cit.,* I, 94, n. 1); a facsimile reproduction of these particular records is to be found in the publication *La Biblioteca Marciana nella sua nuova sede* (Venice, 1906), after p. 6.

[122] *Ibid.*

the expenses necessary for the house which was to be used by Petrarch during his lifetime and in which his books were to be installed. For more than five years Petrarch lived in fact on the Riva degli Schiavoni in "a vast palace—flanked by two square towers—which this free and munificent city has dedicated to my use." [123]

This is not the place to discuss the general implications of Petrarch's highly original and novel plan to bequeath to the Republic of Venice his collection of books as the nucleus of a future "public library," as he called it in a letter to his friend Benintendi dei Ravignani, the head of the Venetian chancery, who helped him in his negotiations with the state authorities.[124] Here it suffices to state that the silence concerning his books, which Petrarch observed in his Will, must be accounted for by the agreement which he had concluded eight years earlier with Venice. To be sure, he had departed from Venice at the end of the year 1367 and in fact never returned to Venice except on the occasion of a brief diplomatic mission in the service of Francesco da Carrara in 1373. But even in the treatise *On His Own Ignorance and That of Many Others,* in which, after his departure, he dealt sharply with a group of Venetian critics of his works and ideas, he still called Venice "that most noble and good city" against which he raised merely one objection: "Much freedom reigns there in every respect, and what I should call the only evil prevailing—but also the worst—far too much freedom of speech." [125] There seems to be no indication whatsoever that at the time of the composition of the Will Petrarch was already definitely resolved never again to live in his house on the Riva degli Schiavoni. In this connection it must be remembered that in the Testament (§ 6 c) he placed Venice third in the list of places normally frequented by him; it is listed as a possible burial place right after Padua and Arquà. Even more

[123] See *Sen.* II, 3 (ed. *Opera,* 1581, p. 760). This house was the Palazzo Molin which became later the Convento del Sepolcro and finally the Caserma Aristide Cornoldi; it was located near the Ponte del Sepolcro; see *Guida d'Italia; Venezia* (Milan, 1951), p. 177; compare M. Oliphant, *The Makers of Venice* (London, 1889), pp. 347 ff.

[124] *Var.* 43, in *Epistolae,* III, 414: "bibliothecae decus publicae."

[125] Trans. by Nachod, *op. cit.,* p. 121; Capelli, ed., *op. cit.,* pp. 84 f.

important, it seems quite certain that in the beginning of the year 1370 the bulk of Petrarch's books was still in Venice. For in the treatise *On His Own Ignorance,* which he started late in 1367 and completed in Arquà on June 25, 1370,[126] he not only stated that he "had left his library behind" in Venice and in charge of Donato but he also made a very specific reference to it. Petrarch's Venetian critics had asserted that "Plato, whom they hate, whom they do not know, and whom they dislike, did not write anything except one or two small little books." To this assertion Petrarch replied as follows: "I am not versed in letters and am no Greek; nevertheless, I have sixteen or more of Plato's books at home, of which I do not know whether they have ever heard the names." Therefore he asked Donato "to let them come and see" for themselves about Plato's work.[127] We may conclude, then, that Petrarch did not need to, or even could, say anything about his library in the Testament of 1370. Since the majority of the books was certainly still in Venice and since also his house there was most probably still at his disposal, he was definitely bound by the contract of 1362 through which he had bequeathed his library to the Republic of Venice.

A short time after he had drafted the Testament, however, Petrarch must have changed his mind and must have decided to gather all his books together in Arquà, where he was to reside more or less permanently for the remaining four years of his life. It seems impossible to ascertain the exact date on which the removal of the books he had left behind in Venice took place.[128]

126 On the history of the composition of this work see Nachod, *op. cit.,* p. 133, note; Ricci in *Petrarca, Prose,* pp. 1173 f. On the background of this work see P. O. Kristeller, "Il Petrarca, l'umanesimo e la scolastica a Venezia," in *La Civiltà Veneziana del Trecento* (Florence, 1956), pp. 149–178.

127 Trans. by Nachod, *op. cit.,* p. 112; ed. by Capelli, *op. cit.,* p. 76; by Ricci, *Petrarca, Prose,* p. 756.

128 By the year 1372 the library must have been in Arquà, for we learn from a letter of Nov. 17, 1372 (*Sen.* XVII, 17 = XIII, 16, ed. *Opera,* 1581, p. 930) that because of the war which at that time was raging between Padua and Venice, Petrarch had taken refuge in Padua and brought with him "libellos quos ibi [i.e., in Arquà] habui." It may also be noted that the Augustinian friar Bonaventura Badoer da Peraga who lived in Padua between 1368 and 1377 (see Mariani, *op. cit.,* pp. 100–102) mentioned in his funeral oration on Petrarch that he had seen him "aliquando in sua

But we can state definitely that by spring 1371 he felt free to make dispositions concerning his library if need arose. For in the letter of May 24 of that year, in which he told Francesco Bruni, as has been mentioned before, about his plan of building a little chapel in Arquà, he declared to be determined to carry that project through, "even if I should have to mortgage or sell my books." [129] Petrarch would have hardly inserted that phrase in his rather businesslike letter to Bruni if he had still felt to be under obligation to his contract with Venice.

Petrarch never added to his Will a codicil concerning the library.[130] He may have expressed his wishes as to the eventual fate of his books in a less formal fashion, for instance by giving instructions to his son-in-law Francescuolo da Brossano, or to his friend Lombardo della Seta. If he did so, we seem now to be just as ignorant of his ultimate intentions in regard to this question as the circle of his Florentine intimates was at the time of his death. For we read in the letter of condolence which Boccaccio addressed to Francescuolo da Brossano on November 3, 1374: "I should like to hear what has been decided about the most precious library of the illustrious man; for among us some believe this, others report that." [131] From a strictly legal point of view the answer to that question was simple. Petrarch himself obviously considered his former agreement with the Republic of Venice to be void, and we have no evidence to show that after his death the Venetian authorities ever attempted to lay claim to the library on the basis of the contract of 1362. In the absence of any other explicit testamentary provision it was clear, then, that the library formed a part of the residuary estate and was covered by the following article of the Will (§ 25): "Of all my movable and immovable goods which I have now or may have in the future, wherever they are or may be, I institute as

---

bibliotheca." See the text of Bonaventura's oration, edited by Solerti, *op. cit.*, p. 270.

[129] *Var.* 15, in *Epistolae*, III, 333.

[130] The only book which we definitely know Petrarch to have given away after the composition of the Will was the copy of St. Augustine's *Confessions* which he had once received from Dionigi di Borgo San Sepolcro and which he sent as a present to Luigi Marsili in January 1374 (*Sen.* XV, 7).

[131] *Ep.* 24, in Massèra, ed., *op. cit.*, p. 226.

the heir general Francescuolo da Brossano." Since Francescuolo was not a scholar himself, he could hardly be expected to be interested in keeping the collection as a whole in the possession of the family; on the contrary, it was natural that he would attempt to dispose of this highly valuable property to the best interest, as he saw it, of his own family, of his employer, Francesco da Carrara the Elder, of Petrarch's friends, and of the cause of scholarship in general; he was probably advised in this entire matter by Lombardo della Seta.[132]

"Habent sua fata libelli"—the truth of this saying is certainly borne out by the history of Petrarch's library, which has been investigated and is still being investigated in great detail and with most revealing results by some of the most outstanding scholars in the field of Petrarch studies, including Pierre de Nolhac and Giuseppe Billanovich, who found Petrarch's former books dispersed over all of western Europe, from London and Paris to Florence, Rome, and Naples. Thus the very thing happened against which Petrarch had endeavored to warn his friend Boccaccio in the year 1362: "I do not wish that the books of so great a man . . . be scattered here and there and be handled . . . by profane hands." And the establishment of a "public library" in Venice had to wait another hundred years until the year 1469, when the great Greek humanist, Cardinal Bessarion, bequeathed his vast collection of books to the Republic of Venice[133] and through this donation laid the foundation of the Biblioteca Marciana, which has fulfilled the hopes voiced by Petrarch in 1362 and has become "a large and famous library, equal to those of antiquity."

[132] According to Billanovich, *op. cit.*, p. 298, "la parte più ampia e migliore della sua libreria venne scelta dagli agenti di Francesco il Vecchio per la reggia carrarese."

[133] See, e.g., H. Kretschmayr, *Geschichte von Venedig* (Gotha, 1920), II, 490 f., 658.

11

Rudolph Agricola's Life of Petrarch[*][1]

AMONG the many personal faults with which Petrarch, in his dialogue entitled *The Secret* or *The Soul's Conflict with Passion,* let himself be charged by St. Augustine, there was one which he found harder to renounce than any other. In reply to Augustine's reproach: "You are seeking fame among men and the immortality of your name more than is right," Petrarch could only say: "This I admit freely and cannot find any remedy to restrain that desire." [2] In fact, throughout his life Petrarch was well aware that "to the whole people I have been a *favola,*" as he declared in the introductory sonnet of his *Rime Sparse,* and he showed himself constantly determined to perpetuate his fame beyond death, as his *Epistle to Posterity* and numerous other autobiographical documents demonstrate. His effort bore fruit, for the life of no other literary figure of the fourteenth century, not even that of Dante, was told more frequently and fully by the writers of the Renaissance than that of Petrarch.[3] Among his biographers we find some of the greatest Italian humanists, including Giovanni Boccaccio, Filippo Villani,

* Reprinted from *Traditio,* VIII (1952), 367–386.

1 This paper was first read in the University Seminar on the Renaissance at Columbia University.

2 Petrarca, *Opera Omnia* (ed. Basel 1581) 364; compare the translation by W. H. Draper, *Petrarch's Secret* (London 1911) 166.

3 See the collection of biographies published by A. Solerti, *Le vite di Dante, Petrarca e Boccaccio scritte fino al secolo decimosesto* (Milan 1904) 237–359.

Leonardo Bruni Aretino, Pietro Paolo Vergerio and Gianozzo Manetti. But, interestingly enough, for the period of the first century after Petrarch's death in 1374, there exists not a single biography which was composed by a non-Italian writer. This fact is the more notable when we remember the tremendous reputation which Petrarch enjoyed, during his own era and afterwards, in France and Germany, and even in remote England, where Chaucer, in *The Clerk's Prologue,* sang the praise of "this clerk whose rethoryke so sweete enlumed al Itaille of poetrye." The anonymous Bohemian scholar who, at the beginning of the fifteenth century, brought together an anthology of Petrarch's works, did not himself write a biography but simply used the one written by Vergerio.[4] Interest in the personalities and achievements of the great poets and artists arose first in Italy, and it was there that the traditional literary form of "the lives of the illustrious men" was filled with a new spirit and content. From this point of view it appears characteristic that the first biography of Petrarch by a non-Italian was composed only after the passage of a hundred years following his death and that it was written by a man like Rudolph Agricola who was more than any of his northern fellow humanists influenced by Italian traditions and who, at the same time, was to become "the founder of the new intellectual life in Germany." [5]

Agricola's *Life of Petrarch* was not included in the edition of his works published by Alardus in Amsterdam in 1539, neither was it mentioned in some of the early biographies of Agricola.[6]

[4] See K. Burdach, *Vom Mittelalter zur Reformation,* IV: *Aus Petrarcas ältestem deutschen Schülerkreis* (Berlin 1929) 4–26.

[5] L. Geiger, *Renaissance und Humanismus in Italien und Deutschland* (Berlin 1882) 334. On Agricola see esp. F. von Bezold, *Rudolf Agricola: Ein deutscher Vertreter der italienischen Renaissance* (Munich 1884); G. Ihm, *Der Humanist Agricola: Sein Leben und seine Schriften* (Paderborn 1893); W. H. Woodward, *Studies in Education during the Age of the Renaissance, 1400–1600* (London 1906) 79–103; H. E. J. M. van der Velden, *Rodulphus Agricola* (Dissertation Leyden 1911); G. Ritter, *Die Heidelberger Universtität* I (Heidelberg 1936) 467–474.

[6] Cf. Gerard Geldenhauer, "Vita Rodolphi Agricolae," in J. Fichard, *Virorum qui . . . illustres fuerunt vitae* (Halle 1536) fol. 83–87; Melanchthon's letter of 1539 to Alardus of Amsterdam, in *Corpus Reformatorum* 3 (1836) 673–676; "Oratio de vita R. Agricolae habita a Ioanne Saxone Holsatiensi," in *Corpus Reformatorum* 11 (1843) 438–446.

This omission seems to explain why it remained relatively little noticed although Trithemius and some scholars of the seventeenth and eighteenth centuries referred to it.[7] It was only in 1873 that the biography became more widely known through a brief notice by Ludwig Geiger.[8] Professor Geiger and, following him, a number of German and Dutch scholars writing on Agricola, gave short accounts of Agricola's *Life of Petrarch,*[9] but did not edit the full text. These notices did not come to the attention of the Italian scholars working on Petrarch. For instance Angelo Solerti knew of the existence of the *Life* but not of the extant manuscripts and therefore did not include it in his collection of *Le Vite di Dante, Petrarca e Boccaccio* (1904). Thus, it was only fairly recently that the *Life of Petrarch* was finally edited in the original Latin—by the Dutchman J. Lindeboom and by the German Ludwig Bertalot, who published their texts independently of each other.[10]

Since the autograph of Agricola's work seems to be lost, both editions were based on two copies, one of which was written around the year 1500 (now preserved in the State Library at Stuttgart, Cod. Poet. et Philol. nr. 36, 4°, fol. 284^{r}–297^{r}) and the other in the first part of the sixteenth century (now in the State Library at Munich, Cod. Lat. 479, fol. 1^{r}–19^{v}). Of these

[7] Trithemius, at the end of a short biography published as preface to the edition of Agricola's *De inventione dialectica* (Cologne 1548), began his list with "Vita F. Petrarchae, liber unus." See also G. F. Tomasini, *F. Petrarcha redivivus* (2nd ed. Padua 1650) 36; J. de Sade, *Mémoires pour la vie de F. Pétrarque* I (Amsterdam 1764) p. xlviii.

[8] L. Geiger, "Die erste Biographie Petrarca's in Deutschland," *Magazin für die Literatur des Auslandes* 42 (1873) 613–614; see also Geiger's summary of Agricola's works in "Petrarca und Deutschland," *Zeitschrift für deutsche Kulturgeschichte,* N. F. 3 (1874) 224–228.

[9] Cf. (titles at n. 5 *supra*) Bezold, *op. cit.* 6, 10, 12–14, 17; Ihm, *op. cit.* 7 f.; van der Velden, *op. cit.* 108–111.

[10] J. Lindeboom, "Petrarca's Leven, beschreven door Rudolf Agricola," *Nederlandsch Archief voor Kerkgeschiedenis,* N. S. 17 (1923) 81–107; L. Bertalot, "Rudolf Agricolas Lobrede auf Petrarca," *La Bibliofilia* 30 (1928) 382–404. The Dutch edition is preceded by a detailed summary of the content of the biography. Bertalot supplied his text with a valuable apparatus in which he identified Petrarch's direct quotations from the classical authors; furthermore, he accompanied his edition with a brief critical appraisal of Agricola's work.

two manuscripts the earlier is of some special interest.[11] It owed its existence to the initiative of two of Agricola's pupils and closest friends, the brothers Dietrich and Johann von Plieningen.[12] They planned an edition of the principal works of their late teacher.[13] Johann von Plieningen, at the request of his older brother, Dietrich, had a large number of Agricola's writings and letters copied by a certain Johannes Pfeutzer. According to his own statement, Johann von Plieningen supervised and corrected the work of the copyist.[14] On the basis of his personal recollections he also wrote a short *Life of Agricola* which he meant to use as the preface to the prospective edition.[15] However, neither Johann von Plieningen's *Life of Agricola* nor his collection of Agricola's works and letters was published in the sixteenth century, for Johann himself died in 1506 and his brother Dietrich was apparently too much involved in public affairs [16] to take care of the edition.

11 On this Stuttgart manuscript, see F. Pfeifer, "Rudolf Agricola," *Serapeum* 10 (1849) 97–107, 113–119; H. Hagen, in *Vierteljahrsschrift für Kultur und Literatur der Renaissance* 2 (1886) 265 f.; P. S. Allen, "The Letters of Rudolph Agricola," *English Historical Review* 21 (1906) 302 f., 307; van der Velden, *op. cit.* 2 f.; Bertalot, *op. cit.* 383 n. 1.

12 On the two brothers, see T. Schott, in *Allgemeine Deutsche Biographie* 26 (1888) 299 f.

13 See the letter (ed. Pfeifer, *op. cit.* 99) in which Dietrich von Plieningen asked his brother that "locos insuper dialecticos et reliqua sua opuscula excribi unumque in volumen redigi facias." Dietrich concluded his letter as follows: "Debes preterea hoc universe reipublice litterarie, quod cui satisfacies, si curaveris omnia monumenta sua unum in volumen scribantur, quo tandem, quemadmodum cupio, imprimi in vulgusque edi emittique possint."

14 See the letter in which Johann von Plieningen told Dietrich about the completion of his collection (ed. Pfeifer, *loc. cit.*): "Satisfecit desiderio tuo . . . Johannes meus Pfeutzer, adolescens optimus; locos namque dialecticos Rhodolphi Agricole, preceptoris nostri, viri doctissimi, et reliqua sua opuscula, que aut nova fecit aut e Greco in Latinum convertit, excripsit unumque in volumen, quemadmodum voluisti, perdiligenter emendateque redegit. Omnia namque cum exemplaribus ipse contuli."

15 Johann von Plieningen's *Life of Agricola* was published by Pfeifer, *op. cit.* 101–107, 113–115.

16 According to the letter to his brother (ed. Pfeifer, *op. cit.* 99) Dietrich did not take upon himself the preparation of the edition, but rather entrusted Johann with it, "dum assidua negotia reipublice me impediant."

The text of Agricola's *Life of Petrarch* in the Stuttgart manuscript is unfortunately not as good as one would be led to expect from the fact that it was copied under the supervision of one of Agricola's intimate friends, who even stated that "I myself have collated everything with the originals." [17] For that reason the other manuscript, which is now in the State Library at Munich, demands some attention although it has a few omissions and other shortcomings of its own.[18]

Agricola dedicated his *Life of Petrarch* to Antonio Scrovigni of Pavia. This is the same friend to whom he addressed, during the time of his stay at Pavia, another little work, a Latin translation of a letter written by Arnold de Lalaing, provost of St. Mary's at Bruges.[19] Antonio Scrovigni became later a professor of medicine at the University of Pavia.[20]

The exact date of the composition of *The Life of Petrarch* presents a certain problem. According to the Stuttgart manuscript (fol. 284^{r}) Agricola wrote it "in the year 1477 in Pavia"; the Munich manuscript (fol. 1^{r}) gives the same year but omits the place. From some of Agricola's other works and his letters we learn that he studied in Pavia for several years until 1475 and left the city at that time in order to study Greek at the University of Ferrara, where he was still in 1477. Agricola's latest biographer, as well as some other scholars, attempted to save the date indicated by the two manuscripts and therefore set forth the hypothesis that the work was written during a brief second sojourn in Pavia, of which we have no other information.[21] This assumption is, however, contradicted by two passages in the *Life of Petrarch* itself which clearly date the

[17] See the passage quoted above (n. 14). On the shortcomings of the Stuttgart manuscript in general, compare Hagen, *loc. cit.* (n. 11 *supra*); K. Hartfelder, *Unedierte Briefe von Rudolf Agricola: Ein Beitrag zur Geschichte des Humanismus* (Karlsruhe 1886, also in *Festschift der Badischen Gymnasien, gewidmet der Universität Heidelberg*, pp. 1–36).

[18] On the Munich manuscript, see Bertalot, *op. cit.* 383.

[19] See Allen, *op. cit.* (n. 11 *supra*) 310 f.; Bertalot, *op. cit.* 399.

[20] Antonio Scrovigni is first mentioned as professor of medicine in Pavia in the year 1493: see *Memorie e documenti per la storia dell' Università di Pavia e degli uomini più illustri che v'insegnarono* (Pavia 1878) 121.

[21] Allen, *op. cit.* 312: Woodward, *op. cit.* (n. 5 *supra*) 89; van der Velden, *op. cit.* (n. 5 *supra*) 78 f.; Lindeboom, *op. cit.* (n. 10 *supra*) 83.

work. For there (pp. 394 and 395)[22] Agricola spoke of the death of Duke Amedeo IX of Savoy as having taken place "superiore anno"; Amedeo actually died on March 3, 1472, and therefore the biography must have been written in 1473 or perhaps 1474.[23] This earlier date is confirmed by a statement made by Johann von Plieningen, who stayed with Agricola both in Pavia and in Ferrara. In his *Life of Agricola* he mentioned the legal studies which Agricola pursued in Pavia before he turned to the study of Greek in Ferrara, and declared in this connection: "At that time he wrote *The Life of Petrarch,* at the request of, and persuaded by, Antonio Scrovigni."[24] Agricola explained why he wrote his *Life of Petrarch* as follows (p. 384):

> . . . in view of the large number of men distinguished through their eloquence, who have been flourishing in our era, it seems to me to be inappropriate that nobody has elucidated the achievements and the life of that man [i.e., Petrarch] in an oration; although I, because of the smallness of my mind, do not dare to hope to do justice to his glory, nevertheless I shall try, to the best of my abilities, to treat this subject in the form of a survey, limning it in rough strokes after the fashion of the less accomplished painters.[25]

This statement is somewhat puzzling. To be sure, Agricola might have been right in saying that nobody before him had celebrated Petrarch in an "oration," and if he actually delivered his work as a speech at the University of Pavia, he could indeed claim that this was a novel honor he rendered

[22] The pages, here as elsewhere in the paper, refer to the edition of the *Life of Petrarch* by Bertalot, *op. cit.* 383–398.

[23] According to Bertalot, *op. cit.* 399, it was begun in 1473 and finished in 1474.

[24] Ed. Pfeifer, p. 102: "Id quoque temporis, precibus ac suasu Anthonii Scrophini, viri haud illiterati, permotus vitam Petrarchae, viri prestantissimi et quem cunctis ingeniis seculi sui haud cunctanter pretulit cuique sua sententia omnis eruditio seculi nostri plurimum honoris debet, doctissime descripsit."

[25] From Johann von Plieningen's biography we learn that in fact Agricola "pictura . . . mirum in modum delectabatur" (ed. Pfeifer, pp. 113 f.); on Agricola's interest in drawing and in the other arts, cf. Woodward, *op. cit.* 81, 92, 103.

to his hero.[26] But this oration in its finished form was, in fact, a biography and as such it had, of course, quite a few precursors. When Agricola did not mention the existence of any previous biography, he differed in that respect quite markedly from his contemporary Girolamo Squarzafico, who said, at the beginning of his *Life of Petrarch,* that "many have described it," and who stated even more definitely in his epilogue: "I have followed Vergerio, Sicco Polenton, Leonardo Bruni and Filelfo." [27]

Agricola's silence on this point raises the question as to whether or not he was actually ignorant of all the earlier biographies of Petrarch. A comparison of his work with the other extant lives of Petrarch shows definitely that it was not based on independent investigation but, on the contrary, that its factual details were derived almost exclusively from one source, and moreover one which at that time was much more easily accessible than any other, because it had appeared in print precisely at the time of Agricola's coming to Italy.[28]

That source was a *Life of Petrarch* written in Italian and first published in the second edition of the *Rime Sparse,* which came out in Rome in the year 1471. Neither this edition nor two others of the *Rime Sparse,* which appeared in Rome and in Venice in the year 1473,[29] indicated the name of the author of the biography, and this fact may, perhaps, explain Agricola's failure to acknowledge his indebtedness. Only in the year 1477, that is, a short time after the composition of Agricola's oration, another editor of the *Rime Sparse,* Domenico Siliprandi, assigned an author's name to the previously anonymous *Life,* asserting that it was written by "il doctissimo

[26] In this case we must assume that the beginning of the *Life,* in which Agricola dealt in a rather personal fashion with Antonio Scrovigni and his grandfather Enrico, was added later, when he edited the speech for publication. On several other orations composed by Agricola in Pavia, see Allen, *op. cit.* 310 f.

[27] Squarzafico's *Vita F. Petrarchae* was first published in the two editions of Petrarch's *Opera* which appeared at Venice in 1501 and 1503; on Squarzafico's life, cf. N. Quarta, "I commentatori quattrocentisti del Petrarca," *Atti d. R. Accad. d. Archeol., Lett. e Belle Arti di Napoli* 23 (1905) 280–287.

[28] See Bertalot, *op. cit.* 401.

[29] On these editions, see M. Fowler, *Catalogue of the Petrarch Collection of the Cornell University Library* (London and New York 1916) 71–73.

Iurista Misser Antonio da Tempo." [30] It has been proved that this attribution to Antonio da Tempo, a mediocre poet of the early fourteenth century, is entirely impossible, and that the printed version of that biography was actually a condensation of a *Life of Petrarch* composed, also in Italian, in the middle of the fifteenth century by either Francesco Filelfo or Pier Candido Decembrio.[31] Whoever wrote the original version based his account primarily on Petrarch's own *Epistle to Posterity*. The unknown editor of the *Rime Sparse* of 1471 abridged the text considerably but at the same time inserted a number of facts concerning Petrarch's later years, which he took from Leonardo Bruni's biography.[32]

A careful analysis of Agricola's *Life of Petrarch* shows that for most of his factual data he depended on his printed source, which he simply translated into Latin. Unlike most of the other biographers, Agricola did not make any direct use of Petrarch's *Epistle to Posterity*.[33] If he had done so, it would have been easy for him to correct, for instance, the erroneous statement of his source that Petrarch's birth had taken place on the Calends of August instead of the thirteenth day before the Calends.[34] Or, to give another example, when Agricola found in his source the somewhat ambiguous phrase that Petrarch's "eyesight was singularly good to the time of his old age," [35] he translated this by saying (p. 395) that "the sharpness of his eyes was very great and singular to the very end and never dulled." If he had read the *Epistle to Posterity*, he would have found that Petrarch himself declared that his eyesight

[30] See Fowler, *op. cit.* 75 f.

[31] See Quarta, *op. cit.* 274 f., 288–292, 317. The longer version was first published by Solerti, *op. cit.* (n. 3 *supra*) 329–335; the shorter one, which appeared in the early editions of the *Rime Sparse*, was republished by Solerti, pp. 335–338, and, more correctly, by Quarta, pp. 320–322. In the following I shall always quote Agricola's source, the short Italian *Life* of 1471, from Quarta's reprint.

[32] See Quarta, *op. cit.* 290.

[33] L. Geiger, in *Zeitschrift für deutsche Kulturgeschichte*, N. F. 3 (1874) 225 n. 3, and Lindeboom, *op. cit.* (n. 10 *supra*), *passim*, assumed that Agricola used the *Epistle to Posterity*. Bertalot, *op. cit.* 400 n. 4, believed that Agricola undoubtedly knew the *Epistle* but made no direct use of it.

[34] Ed. Quarta, p. 320; compare Agricola's *Life* (pp. 384 f.).

[35] Ed. Quarta, p. 322: "di singular vista insino nella sua vechieza."

was excellent through most of his life but that after his sixtieth year he was forced, to his great dismay, to resort to glasses.[36] In his account of Petrarch's relationship with Laura, Agricola did not make any use of the personal note which Petrarch had inserted in his copy of Vergil's works. The omission is interesting in view of the fact that this famous document and also Petrarch's letter about Laura addressed to Bishop Giacomo Colonna (*Famil.* 2.9) were reprinted in the same editions of the *Rime Sparse* which contained the source of Agricola's biography.[37] In another case Agricola's exclusive reliance on his source led him to repeat a serious error made there. For the author of the Italian *Life* of 1471 misunderstood the title of Petrarch's treatise *De secreto conflictu curarum suarum*[38] and made two works out of it, calling them *De secreto combattimento* and *De le sue sollecitudine*.[39] These titles Agricola in his turn translated (p. 394) as *De secreta pugna* and *De sua sollicitudine*.

In connection with Agricola's shortcomings it must also be stated that he proved himself to be quite ignorant of historical chronology. In his enumeration of Petrarch's works (p. 394) he listed the *Invectiva contra medicum quendam*. The "certain doctor" in question was the personal physician of Pope Clement VI (1342–1352), but Agricola believed that in this *Invectiva* Petrarch advised "Pope Innocent III to stay away from the mass of doctors";[40] the most charitable explanation might be that Agricola confused the earlier Innocent who died in 1216 with another pope of that name, Innocent VI (1352–1362), who actually was a contemporary of Petrarch. Agricola accepted without hesitation (p. 387 f.) the statement of his source that it was Pope Urban V who suggested a marriage between Petrarch and Laura.[41] This curious story will be discussed later in more

[36] Ed. E. Carrara, "L'Epistola Posteritati e la leggenda Petrarchesca," *Annali dell' Istituto Superiore di Magistero di Torino* 3 (1929) p. 298 § 4.

[37] See Fowler, *op. cit.*, 72 ff.

[38] Under this title the work was listed by Villani, Vergerio, and Manetti; see Solerti, *op. cit.* 279, 299, 317.

[39] Ed. Quarta, p. 322.

[40] In the list of Petrarch's works in the Italian *Life* of 1471, the pamphlet was merely called "Invectiva contra medico bestiale."

[41] Ed. Quarta, p. 321.

detail; at this point we have only to say that Agricola evidently did not know that Urban V reigned at the end of Petrarch's life, from 1362 to 1370. Even worse was Agricola's assertion (p. 385) that it was the same Pope Urban V who transferred the Papal See to Avignon, because this confusion of Urban V with Clement V (1305–1314) cannot be attributed to Agricola's source but was entirely his own responsibility.[42] Agricola's contemporary Squarzafico was obviously a better historian. In his *Life of Petrarch* he spoke correctly of Clement V as the first of the Avignonese popes, and when he assigned the proposal of marriage to Benedict XII (1334–1342), this would have been, chronologically speaking, more easily possible than the attribution to Urban V.[43]

After this enumeration of a number of rather gross errors in Agricola's *Life of Petrarch* we have to state in all fairness that on two points at least it contains factual information that is not to be found in any of the biographies previous to its own era or even, to be more precise, previous to the late nineteenth century. Both these informative statements were made in connection with the list of Petrarch's works drawn up by Agricola.[44]

In regard to the *Africa,* Agricola mentioned the tradition (p. 394) that in his later years Petrarch always sighed when this work came up in conversation.[45] This attitude, Agricola apparently thought, had its most likely explanation in the fact that the poet, "driven by a youthful desire for fame," had pub-

[42] The Italian *Life* of 1471 said simply (ed. Quarta, p. 320): "[Petracho] senando Avignone, dove la corte Romana nuovamente era transferita."

[43] See Squarzafico's *Life of Petrarch,* ed. Solerti, pp. 348, 353.

[44] A comparison of Agricola's enumeration of Petrarch's works with that given in the Italian *Life* of 1471 shows that his list can be called quite complete. For, although he did not mention the *Septem psalmi poenitentiales* and the little *Itinerarium Syriacum,* which were listed there (ed. Quarta, p. 322), he added, on the other hand, as a separate item, Petrarch's Latin rendering of Boccaccio's *Novella di Griselda,* which was contained in the collection of Petrarch's *Seniles* (8.3); the title given to the work by Agricola, *De constantia Griseldis,* is very similar to the one used in the *editio princeps,* published in Cologne around the year 1472 (cf. Fowler, *op. cit.* 47).

[45] Agricola referred here to a tradition which is to be found in both Vergerio's and Manetti's biographies of Petrarch; see Solerti, *op. cit.* 300, 317.

lished his epic much too early and later found it impossible to call it back and revise it although his mature judgment made him want to do so. Another explanation, Agricola declared, might have been that Petrarch had come to realize that "the palm of victory had been snatched away from him, because, in the times of Nero, Silius Italicus had already written on the second Punic War." But Agricola considered this second alternative to be less probable, for he added: "I do not believe, however, that those books [i.e., Silius' *Punica*] were known to Petrarch, since it is certain that they were found only within our memory." With this remark he referred obviously to the fact that around the year 1417 a manuscript of Silius' epic had been discovered by Poggio Bracciolini in a monastery near Constance and its text had become accessible to the Italian humanists.[46] That scholars of the later fifteenth century were familiar with the history of that recent discovery of the *Punica* is proved, to name only one witness, by several letters written by Filelfo in 1460 and 1464.[47] It was therefore easy for Agricola to obtain this information from one of his humanist friends in Pavia. If this observation had not remained unpublished and therefore unknown, it would have prevented the later charge that Petrarch had plagiarized his *Africa* from Silius' poem. This accusation was first made in 1781 by a French editor of the *Punica,* Lefebvre de Villebrune, and was repeated by several other scholars during the first part of the nineteenth century.[48]

In the same enumeration of Petrarch's works (p. 394), Agricola listed the *Invectiva contra Gallum* with the following comment: "This [Frenchman] was Ioannes Hesdiniensis; when the pope had left Avignon and returned to Italy, he grieved over that change and disgorged many insults against Italy." The

[46] Cf. H. Blass, "Die Textesquellen des Silius Italicus," *Jahrbücher für classische Philologie,* Supplementband 8 (1875/6) 162–172; see also J. Duff's preface to his edition of the *Punica* (London 1934) I p. xvi.

[47] See Blass, *op. cit.* 168 ff.

[48] On this curious question, see the long note which G. Fracassetti added to his translation of Petrarch's *Variae* 22 (in *Lettere delle cose familiari* V 290–292); see also P. de Nolhac, *Pétrarque et l'humanisme* (2nd ed. Paris 1907) I 193.

explanatory remark is of some interest.[49] For Petrarch himself, in accordance with his consistent practice of not honoring a literary adversary by mentioning his name,[50] never indicated who "the Frenchman" was whom he attacked so vehemently in the treatise he addressed to Uguccione da Thiene in 1373; he even asserted that "he was unknown to me by face and name." [51] The occasion of the controversy was the return of Pope Urban V to Rome in the year 1367. That papal decision was, of course, highly welcome to Petrarch, who throughout his life had implored the popes to transfer the Papal See back to Italy and had always spoken of Avignon as another "Babylon." But the departure of the pope from Avignon, as well as Petrarch's fulminant censures of France, naturally aroused strong resentment among the French. As the spokesman of the French interests and sentiments, Jean de Hesdin, a Cistercian monk in the entourage of Cardinal Guido of Boulogne, composed between the years 1367 and 1370 a pamphlet directed against Petrarch. The quality of Jean de Hesdin's treatise was of such a nature that Petrarch felt compelled to take it very seriously and to reply to it. Both pamphlets were frequently copied and later often printed. But Petrarch succeeded so well with his customary tactic of condemning his opponents to oblivion that Jean de Hesdin's authorship was soon totally forgotten. For example, in the two editions of Petrarch's *Opera omnia* published at Basel in 1554 and 1581, Jean de Hesdin's treatise appeared under the title of *Galli cuiusdam anonymi in Franciscum Petrarcham invectiva,* and that of Petrarch under the title *Francisci Petrarchae contra cuiusdam anonymi Galli calumnias ad Ugutionem de Thienis apologia.*[52] Nor did any of the early or later biographers of Petrarch give the name of the French-

[49] In the *Life* of 1471, the work is simply listed as "Invectiva contra i Franciosi" (ed. Quarta, p. 322).

[50] See the discussion of Petrarch's polemical writings by E. Carrara, *Petrarca* (Rome 1937) 77–84; Jean de Hesdin's treatise and Petrarch's reply to it were edited by E. Cocchia, in *Atti d. R. Accad. d. Archeol., Lett. e Belle Arti di Napoli,* N. S. 7 (1920) 91–202.

[51] Ed. Cocchia, p. 140: "mihi nec vultu nec nomine notus est."

[52] See P. de Nolhac, "Le Gallus calumniator de Pétrarque," *Romania* 21 (1892) 598–606.

man. It was only at the end of the nineteenth century that two scholars, a Frenchman and a German, simultaneously but independently of each other, determined the identity of Petrarch's hitherto unknown adversary by finding some early manuscripts of Jean de Hesdin's treatise in which his name was given.[53] The explanation for the fact that, of all the biographers of Petrarch, Agricola alone established the identity of the anonymous must be that he had seen, either in Pavia or elsewhere in Italy, a manuscript containing the two treatises and giving the name of Jean de Hesdin.[54]

Agricola's observations concerning Petrarch's ignorance of Silius Italicus' *Punica* and his identification of Jean de Hesdin are noteworthy achievements, but his biography as a whole does not add much to our knowledge of the details of Petrarch's life. If, nevertheless, it can claim a definite value, this value is to be found in the information we obtain from it about its author and in the insight it gives us about his conceptions regarding the development and the nature of the humanist movement. The most interesting chapters in the *Life of Petrarch* are, therefore, those in which Agricola elaborates on, or disgresses from, his source. That such passages are very numerous, is indicated by the fact that Agricola's work is more than twice as long as the Italian *Life* of 1471.

Agricola's *Life of Petrarch* has a deeply personal, in parts almost autobiographical character which is accounted for by the fact that the author identified himself to a large extent with his subject and closely associated his own outlook on life, his basic interests and his sincerest aspirations with those of the kindred hero.[55] For instance, when he told the story (p. 385)

[53] See B. Hauréau, "Jean de Hesdin," *Romania* 22 (1893) 276–281; M. Lehnerdt, "Der Verfasser der Galli cuiusdam anonymi in F. Petrarcham invectiva," *Zeitschrift für vergleichende Literaturgeschichte,* N. F. 6 (1893) 243–245; see also Cocchia, *op. cit.* 110 f.

[54] It seems quite possible that Agricola saw such a manuscript in Pavia, for it is well known that a number of Petrarch's books and of his own writings were preserved there at that time; see P. de Nolhac, *Pétrarque et l'humanisme* (2nd ed. 1907) I 100 ff.; G. Billanovich, *Petrarca letterato* I (Rome 1947) 372 ff.

[55] Compare the remarks made by Bertalot, *op. cit.* 403, concerning "die Seelenverwandtschaft des Friesen und des Toskaners."

of how Petrarch was compelled by his father to study law, Agricola expanded the account given in his source by adding: "His mind was too noble to be wasted on things of slight and small importance like those of which the civil law consists for the most part, and he did not take lightly his being tied down to them." Agricola spoke here from his own experience. For he, too, had seen himself forced to comply with the wishes of his family and to start his studies at the University of Pavia as a student of the law. Therefore he was only too well able to appreciate Petrarch's relief when he could finally devote himself fully and without subterfuge to the "humanitatis artes." It is interesting to note that in his *Life of Agricola,* Johann von Plieningen quoted explicitly the passage just cited when he related how Agricola renounced his legal studies and turned to humanist scholarship.[56] Both Petrarch and Agricola professed their profound respect for "the great authority and the dignity of the civil law," but both men also shared the conviction that law and justice had become deeply degraded through the invidious, or even openly corrupt, practices of the lawyers of their times. Thus Petrarch quoted, in his *Rerum Memorandarum Libri* (3.93.2),[57] "the old proverb" cited by Cicero (*De officiis* 1.10.33): "Summum ius summa iniuria," and Agricola quoted (p. 385) the similar saying from Terence's *Heautontimorumenos* (796): "Ius summum saepe summast malitia." [58]

In the same connection (p. 385 f.), Agricola made some very bitter remarks about the customary disparagement of the "politores litterae": they were considered "sterile," he declared, "by the opinion of perhaps all the people in Petrarch's days

[56] Ed. Pfeifer (see nn. 15, 11 *supra*) pp. 101 f.: "Ac primis annis iuris civilis auditor fuit magisque id agebat, ut suorum obsequeretur voluntati quam quod eo delectaretur studio. Fuit namque in homine animus excelsior atque generosior quam ut ad levia illa exiguaque rerum momenta, quibus magna ex parte, ut ipsius verbis utar, ius civile constat, abjici posset neque passus est se ad ipsum alligari, precipue cum putaret vix constanti fide ac integritate a quoquam posse tractari. Relicto itaque iuris studio ad maiora eluctans, litteris pollicioribus et artibus, quas humanitatis vocant . . . animum applicuit."

[57] Ed. G. Billanovich (Florence 1943), p. 180.

[58] See also Petrarch's remarks concerning law and justice in his *Epistola Posteritati,* ed. Carrara (see n. 36 *supra*), p. 302 § 17.

and by the opinion of certainly the great majority in our time."[59] In that earlier period, Agricola said, even more than now, the vulgar crowd was interested only in mercenary activities directed at the gain of empty splendor and the accumulation of material goods: "they have no knowledge of the better things because they have never desired the better." In another chapter (p. 386) Agricola exclaimed: "By Hercules, great praise deserve those men who despised the price of 'the more salable arts,' to use Cicero's words,[60] and devoted themselves to the 'litterae,' contented with the sole pleasure of knowledge." To Agricola, Petrarch had proved to be a man of such a real and true dedication because in his studies of the ancients "he did not merely touch upon them but offered himself wholly to them."[61] To the very same studies Agricola finally resolved to devote his own life, as he stated in a letter to a friend, which he wrote in Ferrara, shortly after he had discussed this whole problem of the "studia humanitatis" in his *Life of Petrarch*.[62]

Another personal aspect becomes apparent in the great interest which Agricola took in Petrarch's travels. From his source he learned that Petrarch, in his early thirties, "felt a youthful desire to get to know new lands and thus undertook a journey through France and Germany."[63] Agricola evidently considered "a youthful desire" to be a rather weak and in-

[59] In a letter written in Ferrara (ed. Hartfelder, *op. cit.* [n. 17 *supra*] 17 nº 8), Agricola spoke about his own studies as follows: "studia nostra eadem sunt que semper, hoc est steriles et contumaces melioris consilii litterulae nostrae, quibus omnem dedicavimus vitam."

[60] See Cicero, *De fin.* 1.4.12. Agricola used the same phrase in his treatise *De formando studio* (ed. J. Rivius [Augsburg 1539] p. 77), where he talked about the study of law and medicine and then continued: "Et quas certe uendibiliores, ut Ciceronis uerbo utar, sciam et plane fatear, aliis nonnullis, quas steriles et ieiunas uocant, ut quae magis possunt animum explere quam arcam." See also Cicero, *De off.* 1.42.150–151.

[61] Johann von Plieningen again used exactly the same words in his *Life* to characterize Agricola's devotion to these studies (ed. Pfeifer, p. 102): ". . . studiosissime non solum attigit, sed totum eis se ingessit."

[62] See n. 59 *supra*.

[63] Italian *Life* of 1471 (ed. Quarta, p. 321): "Inquesto tempo mosso pergiovinile desiderio divedere nuove regioni lafrancia et lamagna accerchar simisse"; this is a literal translation of the statement made by Petrarch himself in his *Epistola Posteritati* (ed. Carrara, p. 303 § 21): "Quo tempore iuvenilis me impulit appetitus, ut et Gallias et Germaniam peragrarem."

appropriate motive in this case. Therefore he omitted this phrase entirely and said instead (p. 389): "At that time it came to Petrarch's mind how much 'auctoritas' and useful aid it would convey to him if he had viewed the sites, customs and civilizations of foreign people." Agricola was himself a great lover of travelling and consequently he took occasion, in this place as well as in others, to stress its educational value. Thus, in his dedicatory chapter (p. 383) he emphasized the many journeys which Enrico Scrovigni,[64] the grandfather of his friend Antonio, had made all over the world. Agricola was convinced that Enrico had acquired through his travels more than mere knowledge, for "he had proved through experience those things which the great majority of people have to accept on belief by simply reading about them" (p. 383). His own experiences encouraged Agricola to add to the account of his source a few remarks (pp. 389 and 392) glorifying the University of Paris, the number and the erudition of her professors of philosophy and theology, and the multitude of her students "coming from the ultimate ends of the world, from Scythia, Norway and Denmark." In view of Petrarch's rather critical attitude towards everything French, one wonders whether he himself would have been pleased by such an unreserved recognition of the greatness of the city and the University of Paris as his biographer imputed to him.

The discussion of Petrarch's numerous journeys led Agricola to a long digression in another direction. He was aware of the fact (p. 390 f.) that some people, "if they do not make it a cause of accusation, then at least they wonder why it could have been pleasing to a man, who in all other respects was steadfast in purpose, to change his residence so frequently and to live continuously in different places." Agricola admitted that this kind of unsettled existence might be considered harmful to any consistent pursuit of scholarly studies, and he quoted a statement made by Aristotle (*Physics* 8.3) to the effect that "knowledge is acquired by sitting quietly." [65] But in spite of these plausible

[64] On Enrico Scrovigni, see Bertalot, *op. cit.* 404 n. 3.

[65] On this quotation, see the interesting remarks made by Bertalot, *op. cit.* 390 n. 7.

objections to a migratory life, Agricola believed that still better arguments could be brought forth in its defense. In the first place he declared that steady and ever new exercises are just as necessary for the mind as they are for the body "if people want to avoid becoming lax and burdened down by their own weight." Thus, Agricola asserted, some of the most studious men of antiquity lived now in the country, now in the city, while others delighted in hunting, in sports, in games or in drinking. Agricola followed up this first argument with another that he obviously deemed even more striking. He stated: "We are a composite of opposite elements and therefore we are made over by the alternation of things diverse; hence what is pleasant and agreeable to one part of our nature, necessarily will weigh heavily upon another part if we do it too long." By referring to the authority of Plato, who had defined the soul as "that which is agitating in perpetual motion," [66] he considered his thesis to be valid that the most learned man must find his "re-creation"—this word must obviously here be understood in its basic meaning—in a variety of things and actions and not in exclusive attention to any one single matter. The rather personal tone of this long digression makes it quite evident that Agricola wrote this apology for Petrarch's "peregrinations" in self-defense, to justify his own innate aversion against the settled life.

The same personal character manifested itself in the way in which Agricola elaborated on the account which his source gave of the central event in Petrarch's life, his love for Laura. He showed himself deeply concerned both with the problem of love as a general phenomenon and with the question whether or not Petrarch's particular love was praiseworthy. In regard to the first problem he pointed out (p. 387) that the Stoics counted among the vices every state of mind which was not in accord with reason, whereas Aristotle and his followers took a much more tolerant view.[67] Agricola did not try to decide between

[66] According to Bertalot, *op. cit.* 391 n. 8, this is a reference to *Timaeus* 36 and 43; one may also think of *Phaedrus* 245 C–E.

[67] Agricola probably derived this information concerning the views of the Stoics and the Peripatetics from Cicero, *De fin.* 3.10.35; 3.12.41 ff.; *Tusc. Disput.* 4.9.22 f., 17.38 f., 19.43, 21.47.

those contradictory views since he did not consider his *Life of Petrarch* the right place for a discussion of the whole problem in all its aspects. Although one might perhaps sense a certain inclination on his part to condemn every over-ardent passion, he made sure to state at the same time that a compensation for the faults common to mankind may be found in the possession of great virtues, and in his opinion Petrarch certainly possessed such great virtues. Thus Agricola declared (p. 387): "The steadfastness and the moderation of his mind, with which he restrained himself, burning as he was with such a fire, will assuage even a stern censurer."

In this connection Agricola chose to insert into his *Life of Petrarch* one of the longest and most curious elaborations of his source. As has been mentioned before, he found there the apocryphal story that Pope Urban V had encouraged Petrarch to marry Laura and had promised to provide him with a living in the case he did.[68] Agricola not only accepted the story at face value but even decided to expand it greatly. Whereas his source related the whole incident in a few short sentences, Agricola let Petrarch reply to the papal proposition in a long and rather rhetorical speech (p. 387 f.). It was still in agreement with the original source when Petrarch, in this speech, rejected the marriage with Laura because he did not wish to make himself ridiculous by becoming "a domestic panegyrist," and because he also feared that "in those things which are most desired, abundance yet has often brought about weariness." But Agricola went far beyond his source when he made Petrarch offer himself and his conduct as a model of exemplary value for mankind in general. Thus we read in this speech to the pope: "Above everything else I must endeavor to make people understand that I could be afflicted and agitated by the fervor of my heart but that I could not be conquered by it; through the authority of Petrarch all men ought to learn that they can abstain from those things which they have desired

[68] Italian *Life* of 1471 (ed. Quarta, p. 321): "Et quantunque livolse essere data perdonna adinstantia di papa Urbano quinto ilquale lui singularmente amava concedendoli ditener colla donna i benefitii insieme; nol volse mai consentire; dicendo che i fructo che prendea dellamore ascrivere dipoi; che lacosa amata conseguito avessie tutto siperderia."

vehemently." Agricola let this speech conclude with a sentence which, like the ones just quoted, seems to reflect remarkably well the spirit and the mode of thought of the biographer, as well as of his hero: "How powerful the *virtus* of anything is, you will never know if you do not test it through an adverse experience."

This whole imaginary speech illustrates clearly the way Agricola felt about Petrarch's love for Laura. He admired greatly the sonnets and *canzoni* which testified to that love, and he declared (p. 388) that "in that art Petrarch surpassed everybody who wrote before or after him." Nevertheless Petrarch was to him primarily the great scholar and humanist and not the poet of the *Rime Sparse*. Therefore Agricola had to regret, to a certain degree at least, the fact that Petrarch fell victim to such an ardent and long-lasting passion, and he could even find some justification (p. 393) for the criticism of "those malevolent critics of another man's distress, who said that he took Laura's death in a weaker manner than befitted his years and his erudition." Agricola seems to have become reconciled with that passion for Laura only because Petrarch had always succeeded in restraining and sublimating it. For the right understanding of Agricola's attitude toward the problem of love and enduring attachment to one woman, one might remember that he himself stayed a bachelor throughout his life.

The numerous additions which Agricola made to his source reveal not only his personality but also demonstrate that he possessed a considerable knowledge of the classical authors, both Latin and Greek. Ludwig Bertalot, in his edition of the *Life of Petrarch,* has ascertained that in this work Agricola quoted from Vergil's *Aeneid,* the odes of Horace, Terence's *Heautontimorumenos,* Cicero's *De finibus,* Seneca's *De tranquillitate animi,* Suetonius' *Julius Caesar,* Plato's *Timaeus* (or *Phaedrus*) [69] and Aristotle's *Physics.* To this list can be added quotations from the following works: Cicero, *De senectute* [70] and *Pro L. Murena,*[71] Seneca's letters *Ad Lucilium,*[72]

[69] See n. 66 *supra.* [70] See n. 80 *infra.*

[71] When Agricola (p. 387) called Stoicism "asperioris frontis philosophiam," it seems likely that he thought of *Pro L. Murena* 29.60, where Cicero spoke of Stoicism as "doctrina paulo asperior et durior."

[72] See n. 74 *infra.*

and Juvenal's satires.[73] Because of his interest in the symbolism of numbers, Agricola found it significant (p. 391) that Laura died precisely twenty-one years after she and Petrarch had met; the figure twenty-one represents a combination of the numbers three and seven, "both of which," according to Agricola, "are celebrated among those who scrutinize the more occult mysteries of things." In the same connection Agricola declared, evidently on the basis of information he found in one of Seneca's letters (*Ep.* 58.31), that Plato had died at the age of eighty-one, that is nine times nine, and that he was therefore considered semi-divine by the magi.[74] It appears also worth noticing that in his brief discussion of the literary form and the metre of the sonnet and the *canzone* Agricola pointed out (p. 388) that the word "rhythmus" had assumed a meaning in modern times which it did not have in antiquity, that of "rhyme."

The short statement of his source that Petrarch had died of epilepsy[75] caused Agricola to write a brief but quite learned commentary on that disease, in which he said (p. 394 f.): "The general public calls it the falling sickness ('morbus caducus') but the ancients called it the 'morbus comitialis' because it was considered to be an unfavorable omen when somebody was afflicted by it during an assembly of the people."[76] Like some of the other humanists of the Renaissance, Agricola believed (p. 395) that epilepsy found its victims particularly among great men,[77] and as examples he pointed out that Julius Caesar

[73] When Agricola (p. 383) said: "ora ut dicitur praebere capistro bene monentis," he referred probably to Juvenal, *Sat.* 6.42 f.: ". . . si moechorum notissimus olim / stulta maritali iam porrigit ora capistro."

[74] On this belief, see G. Boas, "Fact and Legend in the Biography of Plato," *The Philosophical Review* 57 (1948) 450 n. 21. Bertalot, *op. cit.* 393 n. 3, did not identify the passage in Seneca's letter but quoted a remark very similar to that of Agricola made by Ficino in a letter written in 1477, that is, shortly after the composition of Agricola's *Life of Petrarch.*

[75] Italian *Life* of 1471 (ed. Quarta, p. 322): ". . . del male della epilensia diche per la eta sua era stato molto molestato lo extremo di della sua vita virtuosamente concluse."

[76] The same explanation of the name "morbus comitialis" is to be found in the writings of some of the later humanists, e.g., Erasmus and Johann Agricola; on this whole problem, see the detailed study of O. Temkin, *The Falling Sickness: A History of Epilepsy from the Greeks to the Beginnings of Modern Neurology* (Baltimore 1947) esp. pp. 7, 83, 131, 152 ff.

[77] On this belief, see Temkin, pp. 152 ff.

had suffered from it [78] and that "in the preceding year Duke Amedeo [IX] of Savoy had died of it." [79]

Agricola liked to quote old proverbs and sayings. These are sometimes easily identified, like the proverb taken (p. 397) from Cicero's *De senectute* (3.7),[80] which Robert Burton in his *Anatomy of Melancholy* turned into the saying: "Birds of a feather will gather together." In other cases it seems to be impossible to discover Agricola's sources. When he asserted (p. 395), for instance, that "according to an old proverb one ought to beware of those whom nature has marked," he might have referred to a medieval and not a classical saying; [81] a century and a half later this idea found again its literary expression in George Herbert's warning in the *Iacula Prudentum:* "Take heed of a person marked." Although Agricola's Latin style was often quite involved and even faulty, he succeeded occasionally in coining a very fortunate phrase. Perhaps the most striking example of that sort is offered by the maxim he pronounced in the course of his discussion of the value of traveling: "Nothing can appear to be more proper to man than the knowledge of man." [82] With this epigram, written at the end of the fifteenth century, Agricola expressed an idea which was to be formulated in almost identical terms by Pierre Charron at the beginning of the seventeenth century,[83] and by Alexander Pope in 1733.

In Agricola's opinion Petrarch certainly had been a true student of man. Indeed he considered him (p. 383) the initiator of that kind of studies in modern times, "to whom all the erudi-

[78] Suetonius, *Divus Julius* 45.1.

[79] This fact is correct; see *Enciclopedia Italiana* 2 (1929) 829 f.

[80] Bertalot, *op. cit.* 397 n. 2, referred this quotation to Jesus Sirach (= *Liber Ecclesiastici*) 13.20; but Agricola's phrasing ("in veteri proverbio est pares paribus facillime convenire") makes it more likely that he quoted from Cicero's *De senect.* 3.7: "Pares autem vetere proverbio cum paribus facillime congregantur." See also A. Otto, *Die Sprichwörter der Römer* (Leipzig 1890) 264.

[81] The proverb is, however, not listed in J. Werner's collection, *Lateinische Sprichwörter des Mittelalters* (Heidelberg 1912).

[82] *Life of Petrarch* (p. 389): "hominis magis proprium nihil videri potest quam hominem nosse."

[83] P. Charron, *De la sagesse* (Bordeaux 1601) I 1: "La vraye science et le vraye estude de l'homme, c'est l'homme."

tion of our century is owed."[84] He called (p. 383 f.) Petrarch "another father and restorer of the 'bonae artes,' who single-handedly recalled from the dead the 'litterae' which were almost extinct and nearly buried; he filled them with life through the infusion of a new spirit as it were."

This conception of Petrarch as the restorer of the "studia humanitatis" did not, of course, originate with Agricola, for he found that idea expressed in a very similar figure of speech in his source,[85] which, in its turn, had taken it over from Leonardo Bruni's *Life of Petrarch*.[86] There is, however, in spite of this similarity, a marked difference between Agricola and the other biographers of Petrarch. Explanation of this difference might be found in the fact that the northern scholar, being an outsider, was more detached from the development of Italian humanism and consequently could view the whole movement, and Petrarch's position within it, with better historical perspective than Italians themselves could. To be sure, Leonardo Bruni and his contemporaries were willing to acknowledge that Petrarch stood at the fountain-head of the new scholarly and literary current and "had opened the road to the perfection of their own days."[87] But they also began to voice rather severe criticism of the style of his works, as we learn, for example, from the *Dialogi ad Petrum Histrum*, which Bruni composed around the year 1406.[88] This critical attitude became gradually

[84] This statement was repeated by Johann von Plieningen in his *Life of Agricola* (ed. Pfeifer, p. 102): "[Petrarchae] sua sententia [i.e., that of Agricola] omnis eruditio seculi nostri plurimum honoris debet."

[85] Italian *Life* of 1471 (ed. Quarta, p. 320): "Et ebbe tanta gratia dingegno che fu il primo che questi sublimi studii lungo tempo caduti in oblivione rivoco alluce."

[86] Ed. Solerti (see n. 3 *supra*), p. 289: "[Petrarca] ebbe tanta grazia d'intelletto che fu il primo che questi sublimi studi lungo tempo caduti ed ignorati rivocò a luce di cognizione."—The same phrase is to be found in Gianozzo Manetti's *Life of Petrarch* (ed. Solerti, pp. 306 f.).

[87] See, e.g., Bruni's *Life of Petrarch* (ed. Solerti, p. 290): "Petrarca fu il primo . . . che riconobbe e rivocò in luce l'antica leggiadria dello stile perduto e spento, e posto che in lui perfetto non fusse, pur da se vide ed aperse la via a questa perfezione . . . ; e per certo fece assai, solo a dimostrare la via a quelli che dopo lui avevano a seguire."

[88] See the edition of the *Dialogi* by G. Kirner (Livorno 1889); compare D. Vittorino, "I dialogi ad Petrum Histrum di Leonardo Bruni Aretino," *Publications of the Modern Language Association* 55 (1940) 714–720.

more and more outspoken and vociferous until in the middle of the fifteenth century, in the words of Georg Voigt, "people usually passed their judgment on Petrarch with a sense of superiority and condescension," which allowed them to find the only excuse for his stylistic and other shortcomings in the "barbarousness" of his era.[89]

Agricola was, of course, familiar with that kind of criticism but he made a conscious effort to get beyond its merely negative aspects and to reach a more positive evaluation. He not only knew the general charges which were made against the deficiencies of Petrarch's Latin style but he showed himself also acquainted (p. 398) with a very specific accusation according to which "Petrarch, since his childhood, had been misled by too great an admiration for Seneca and had expressed himself, therefore, in a fashion which was too abrupt and too disorderly." Agricola did not state the source of his information but it seems likely that this sort of criticism was widespread among the scholars and students at the Italian universities of that period. It is interesting to note that Girolamo Squarzafico, who was in northern Italy at the same time that Agricola was there,[90] wrote in his *Life of Petrarch:* "Because Petrarch imitated more the 'densitas' of Seneca than the 'amplitudo' of Cicero, I have frequently called him the modern Seneca."[91]

Agricola made a very astute observation in regard to this criticism of Petrarch's style (p. 397 f.). He admitted that Petrarch did not, perhaps, follow the best model. At the same time, however, he suggested that the critics ought not to excuse this shortcoming simply with "the barbarousness of that era" but that they rather ought to give recognition to the much more important fact that Petrarch, working as he was under such unfavorable conditions, did, after all, turn to "stricter precepts" than were customary at that time. Agricola, who had grown up north of the Alps under circumstances which somewhat re-

[89] L. G. Voigt, *Die Wiederbelebung des classischen Altertums* I (3rd ed. Berlin 1893) 381; see also E. Carrara, in *Annali dell' Istituto Superiore di Magistero di Torino* 3 (1929) 338 ff.

[90] On Squarzafico's stay in northern Italy during the 1470's, see Quarta, *op. cit.* 283.

[91] Ed. Solerti, p. 357.

sembled those under which Petrarch had lived, understood much better than the Italian scholars of the third and fourth generations of humanism what it meant to work in "an era of barbarousness," that is among people whose outlook on life and expression of thought were still primarily bound by medieval and not by classical traditions.[92] Throughout his *Life of Petrarch,* Agricola emphasized a fact never particularly stressed by the other biographers—that "he became his own teacher since there was no other from whom he might learn" (p. 384).

In Agricola's opinion, then, Petrarch's greatest claim to fame was that he was a self-made man. This chief theme of the *Life of Petrarch* is clearly indicated at its very beginning, where Agricola quoted a saying of Enrico Scrovigni with wholehearted approval and with specific application to Petrarch's case (p. 383):

> It is glorious to have deserved praise on account of some achievement, and the glory of whatever has been excellently done remains; but it is most glorious to create for oneself those things for which one is praised. . . . To such a glory, it seems to me, nobody is more entitled than Francesco Petrarca, to whom all the erudition of our era is owed.

Petrarch's fame would have been great, Agricola asserted (p. 393), "even in an age of learning but in that scarcity of erudite people it shone with still greater splendor." If in one respect, then, the dearth of erudition and the absence of competition naturally enhanced Petrarch's reputation in his own century, in another respect the uniqueness of that position put him at a very definite disadvantage. For, as Agricola said (p. 398), "whereas even the most learned people of earlier times [i.e., of antiquity] received the counsel of other men in regard to their writings, it is a fact that Petrarch lacked a critic and emendator." That the creative mind needs for its own develop-

[92] Compare, e.g., the letter Agricola wrote to his friend Friedrich Mormann in 1480 (ed. Allen, *op. cit.* [n. 11 *supra*] 316); in this letter he congratulated Mormann particularly for the reason that "tantum eruditionis, hunc literarum cultum, hanc gratiam Musarum assecutus es, et assecutus quod difficillimum est in medio stridore rudis huius horridaeque barbariae, quantum in mediis penetralibus ac, ut ita dicam, officina illa omnis politioris eruditionis Italia hique Itali frustra sperarunt, pauci rettulerunt."

ment and productivity the stimulation provided by the constructive criticism of others, could also be realized much more readily by Agricola than by his Italian contemporaries. Agricola, like Petrarch, had been forced to make his intellectual start in comparative isolation and after his return from Italy to Germany he found himself again very much alone and thrown on his own resources. He stated the problem of intellectual isolation most clearly in a letter he addressed to Alexander Hegius in 1480; he told his friend that he had done little writing, and very poorly at that, ever since he had left Italy, and he attributed that unproductiveness to the lack of exchange of ideas and the absence of friends who could help his work through their approval or disapproval.[93]

Considering all the difficulties under which Petrarch labored, Agricola came to the conclusion that his literary and stylistic achievements deserve very high praise. But in Agricola's opinion, Petrarch deserved even greater acclaim because he had revived the "studia humanitatis" in his own era and had continued to spur on those studies long beyond his death. The other biographers of the fifteenth century were willing to give recognition to Petrarch as the initiator of the humanist movement. But to them, as well as to the later humanists, Petrarch's importance was a thing of the past. Probably only a few of them would have subscribed to the condemnation expressed by the representative of extreme Ciceronianism in Erasmus' *Dialogus Ciceronianus,* who declared that Petrarch's "whole style smacks of the horrible character of an earlier age." Most of the humanists of the fifteenth century, however, would have accepted the more moderate statement made by the other interlocutor in Erasmus' dialogue to the effect that Petrarch was "the first leader of eloquence flowering anew among the Italians, a man celebrated and great in his own times, but whose works are now scarcely in anyone's hands." [94]

[93] See Allen, *op. cit.* 321, nº 21; Ihm, *op. cit.* (n. 5 *supra*) 67.

[94] The whole passage in the *Ciceronianus* concerning Petrarch reads as follows (Erasmus, *Opera omnia* [Leyden 1703] col. 1008): "(Bulephorus:) Age redibimus ad aliud scriptorum genus nostro seculo vicinius. Nam aliquot aetatibus videtur fuisse sepulta prorsus eloquentia, quae non ita pridem reviviscere coepit apud Italos, apud nos multo etiam serius. Itaque

Rudolph Agricola certainly did not share such views, for he was firmly convinced that his own generation, though it had made great progress in erudition, still was under deep obligation to Petrarch as an ever-living example of the pursuit of true scholarship. And so he concluded his *Life of Petrarch* as follows:

Petrarch was in truth the liberator and the restorer of the "litterae." When they lay prostrate and altogether oppressed, he suffused them with new light and lustre. Through his great and memorable example he taught us that that end which is desirable is also realizable by the best of men, since nature has ordained that nothing that is honorable is impossible.

---

reflorescentis eloquentiae princeps apud Italos videtur fuisse Franciscus Petrarcha, sua aetate celebris ac magnus, nunc vix est in manibus: ingenium ardens, magna rerum cognitio, nec mediocris eloquendi vis. (Nosoponus:) Fateor. Atqui est ubi desideres in eo linguae Latinae peritiam, et tota dictio resipit seculi prioris horrorem. Quis autem illum dicat Ciceronianum, qui ne affectarit quidem?" Cf. the English translation of the *Ciceronianus* by I. Scott (New York 1908) 94.

PART III

Studies in Early Christian Historiography

12

St. Augustine and the Christian Idea of Progress: The Background of The City of God*[1]

IN the summer of the year 410 Rome fell to a Visigothic army under King Alaric. Since the city suffered relatively little external damage, modern historians have sometimes been inclined to regard that conquest or sack of Rome as a rather insignificant incident. We should be wary, however, of any tendency to belittle the event, remembering that it impelled Augustine to write *The City of God*. In view of the impact this work has

* Reprinted from the *Journal of the History of Ideas,* XII (1951), 346–374.

[1] This article was already in the hands of the printer when I got a copy of the essay by J. Straub, "Christliche Geschichtsapologetik in der Krisis des römischen Reiches," *Historia* (1950), 52–81. Prof. Straub's article does not discuss the idea of progress and the other Christian and pagan conceptions of history which were current before and throughout the fourth century. His main objective is rather, for the period from 378 to the aftermath of the fall of Rome in 410, to deal "mit der Rolle, welche die christlichen Apologeten in jenem epochalen Umwandlungsprozess gespielt haben, in dem der römische Staat zugrundeging, aber die mit dem Staat aufs engste verbundene Kirche ihre eigene Existenz zu behaupten und sich für die Teilnahme an der neu zu bildenden Völkergemeinschaft der Welt des Mittelalters freizumachen suchte" (p. 54). Of particular value is Prof. Straub's clarification of the views which Augustine and Orosius had concerning the Christian attitude toward the Roman empire.—Unfortunately I was unable to consult the articles by H. v. Campenhausen, O. Herding, and W. Loewenich, all of which, according to Straub, *l.c.,* p. 52, n. 1, deal with Augustine's historical conceptions.

had upon the development of Christian thought, it can certainly be said that the fall of Rome in the year 410, which motivated its composition, marks a momentous date in the intellectual history of the western world.

Moreover, Augustine was not the only contemporary to be profoundly impressed by that event, as several other writings show. It may suffice here to quote a few sentences from St. Jerome, who was at that time living in Bethlehem. When he received the news of "the havoc wrought in the West and, above all, in the city of Rome" (*Epist.* 126, 2), he expressed his feelings in the preface to the first book of the *Commentaries on Ezekiel,* which he was then writing: "When the brightest light on the whole earth was extinguished, when the Roman empire was deprived of its head and when, to speak more correctly, the whole world perished in one city, then 'I was dumb with silence, I held my peace, even from good, and my sorrow was stirred' (*Psalm* 39, 2)." And in the preface to the third book of the same work Jerome asked: "Who would believe that Rome, built up by the conquest of the whole world, has collapsed, that the mother of nations has also become their tomb?" [2]

To understand the profound consternation of Jerome and his contemporaries we must realize that the fate of Rome meant infinitely more to the people of late antiquity than the fate of any city, even the most renowned, would mean to the western world today. For many deeply rooted ideas and beliefs, and numerous superstitions, were connected with the very name and existence of that city. One need recall only the famous lines of Vergil's *Aeneid* (1, 278 f.), in which Jupiter says: "To the Romans I assign limits neither to the extent nor to the duration of their empire; dominion have I given them without end." This notion of "the eternal city," the capital of a universal empire, "the golden Rome," we find reflected in the works

[2] Throughout this article I have based the text of my quotations from the Church Fathers on the translations in the three series of *The Select Library of the Ante-Nicene Fathers,* and of the *Nicene and Post-Nicene Fathers* (1885–1900); very frequently, however, I have found it necessary to make changes in the translations, for which I have to take the responsibility.

of almost all the pagan writers and poets of the first centuries of our era, whether they were of Latin, Greek or Oriental origin.[3] Thus, at the end of the fourth century, the pagan general and historian Ammianus Marcellinus declared (*Histor.*, 14, 6, 3) that "as long as there are men, Rome will be victorious so that it will increase with lofty growth." And around the year 400 the Christian poet Claudianus wrote (*On the Consulate of Stilicho,* 3, 159 f.): "There will never be an end to the power of Rome, for luxury and pride resulting in vices and enmities have destroyed all other kingdoms."

During the same period the attitude of the Christians toward the Roman empire was divided. On the one hand there ran within early Christianity an undercurrent of strong hatred of the Roman state and of everything that state stood for. This hostility, nourished by Jewish traditions and strengthened by the persecutions, manifested itself in the apparently widespread expectation that some day the prediction of the angel in the *Book of Revelation* (14, 8) would be fulfilled: "Babylon [i.e., Rome] is fallen, is fallen, that great city, because she made all nations drink of the wine of the wrath of her fornication." On the other hand, the official spokesmen of the early Church always remembered that Jesus himself had ordered his disciples to "render therefore unto Caesar the things which are Caesar's" (*Matthew,* 22, 21), and that St. Paul had demanded obedience to the empire when he wrote in his *Epistle to the Romans* (13, 1): "Let every soul be subject unto the higher powers. For there is no power but of God: the powers that be are ordained of God." In accordance, then, with these explicit orders of Christ and St. Paul, every adherent of the faith had to pay his outward respect, at least, to the established authorities of the state.

But many Christians showed themselves willing to go even farther and actually hoped and prayed for the continuance of the Roman empire. This affirmative attitude grew out of certain historical and eschatological ideas which went back to both pagan and Jewish traditions.[4] In the Hellenistic era there had

3 See E. K. Rand, *The Building of Eternal Rome* (1943).

4 The most recent treatments of this question have been given by J. W.

developed in the East a theory which saw history take its course in a sequence of great or, rather, universal monarchies. Four of these empires were to follow one another, and the series was to conclude with a fifth monarchy which, it was believed, would last to the end of the world. This idea of the four or five monarchies was adopted by some of the Roman and Greek historians, and it appeared likewise in Jewish literature. For the great image seen in a dream by Nebuchadnezzar (*Daniel*, 2, 31 ff.) and the four beasts seen by Daniel himself (7, 1 ff.), were explained by the pre-Christian tradition in terms of an interpretation of world history: these visions were believed to signify symbolically that history takes its course through the succession of four universal monarchies; the disintegration of the last of the four empires was assumed to usher in the end of the world.

In the latter part of the second century and in the first part of the third century Christian theologians like Irenaeus of Lyons, Tertullian and Hippolytus adopted these pagan and Jewish traditions and expressed their opinion that the Roman empire "which now rules" (Irenaeus, *Against Heresies*, 5, 26, 1), should be considered to be the fourth monarchy.[5] All these Christian authors shared the belief that the fall of the last empire would be a most ominous event. Thus, Tertullian said in his treatise *On the Resurrection of the Flesh* (ch. 24), in which he interpreted a passage in St. Paul's *Second Epistle to the Thessalonians* (2, 7), that the Antichrist will appear after the Roman state has been scattered into ten kingdoms. On the basis of this eschatological belief Tertullian declared very emphatically in his *Apology* (ch. 32, 1): "There is also another and greater necessity for our praying in behalf of the emperors and the whole status of the empire and Roman affairs. For we know that only the continued existence of the Roman Empire retards the mighty power which threatens the whole earth, and post-

Swain, "The Theory of the Four Monarchies: Opposition History under the Roman Empire," *Classical Philology* (1940), 1–21; H. L. Ginsberg, *Studies in Daniel* (1948), 5–23.

[5] See the list of authors who identified the fourth monarchy with the Roman empire, which has been compiled by H. H. Rowley, *Darius the Mede and the Four World Empires in the Book of Daniel* (1935), 73 ff.

pones the very end of this world with its menace of horrible afflictions." In the early fourth century Lactantius stated even more explicitly in his *Divine Institutions* (7, 25, 6–8): "The fall and the ruin of the world will shortly take place, although it seems that nothing of that kind is to be feared as long as the city of Rome stands intact. But when the capital of the world has fallen . . . who can doubt that the end will have arrived for the affairs of men and the whole world? It is that city which still sustains all things. And the God of heaven is to be entreated by us and implored—if indeed His laws and decrees can be delayed—lest sooner than we think that detestable tyrant should come who will undertake so great a deed and tear out that eye by the destruction of which the world itself is about to fall."

During the fourth century a number of commentators on the *Book of Daniel,* including Eusebius and John Chrysostom in the East, Jerome and Sulpicius Severus (*Sacred Histories,* 2, 3) in the West, continued to identify the fourth monarchy with the Roman empire. Cyril of Jerusalem (*Catechetical Lectures,* 15, 12) followed even more closely the line of Irenaeus, Tertullian and Lactantius, by declaring: "The Antichrist is to come when the time of the Roman empire has been fulfilled and the end of the world is drawing near."

In view of the persistence of this concern for the continuance of Rome it seems safe to assume that in the year 410 many contemporaries regarded Alaric's conquest of Rome as the realization of the long-dreaded "fall of Rome" and considered the end of the world to be imminent. A reflection of this superstitious fear we find, I think, even in the words of Jerome, that "the whole world has perished in one city."

Augustine was, of course, well aware of both the pagan belief in "eternal Rome" and the eschatological speculations of his fellow-Christians. He rejected emphatically the one idea as well as the other. As to the pagan notion, he pointed out (*Sermon* 105, 9) that "the earthly kingdoms have their changes" and that only of the Kingdom of Christ it can be said: "There shall be no end" (*Luke,* 1, 33). He continued (*ibid.,* § 10): "They who have promised this to earthly kingdoms have not been guided by truth but have lied by flattery." He quoted the famous line from Vergil—whom he calls rather slightingly "a certain poet of theirs"—and remarked: "This kingdom which you [Jupiter] have given 'without limits to its duration,' is it on earth or in heaven? Certainly it is on earth. And even if it were in heaven, yet 'heaven and earth shall pass away' (*Matthew,* 24, 35). Those things shall pass away, which God Himself has made. How much more rapidly shall that pass away which Romulus founded?" As to the meaning of the passage in St. Paul's *Second Epistle to the Thessalonians* (2, 7): "Only he who now holdeth, let him hold until he be taken out of the way,"[6] Augustine was much less certain than Tertullian, who had concluded from these words that the duration of this world is bound up with the duration of the Roman empire. Augustine knew (*City of God,* 20, 19 E–F)[7] that "some think that this refers to the Roman empire," and he granted that such an interpretation, in contrast to some others, "is not absurd." But at the same time he felt obliged to state: "I frankly confess that I do not know what St. Paul meant."

In reply to those Christian thinkers who attempted to figure out the exact date of the end of the world and connected the coming of that event with concrete developments and with definite historical incidents like "the fall of Rome," Augustine declared (*City of God,* 18, 53 A–B) that such a question "is entirely improper." For he pointed out that Christ himself told his disciples: "It is not for you to know the times and the seasons which the Father hath put in His own power" (*Acts,* 1, 7). "In vain, then," Augustine stated, "do we attempt to compute and determine the years which remain to this world." Whoever undertakes that kind of calculation, Augustine concluded, "uses human conjecture and brings forward nothing certain from the authority of the canonical Scriptures."

[6] The above translation is based on the text of the *Itala* quoted by Augustine; the version in the *King James Bible* reads: "Only he who now letteth will let, until he be taken out of the way."

[7] My quotations from *De civitate Dei* are based on the Latin text edited by J. E. Welldon, 2 vols. (1924), and on the translation by M. Dods, *The City of God,* 2 vols. (1872); frequently, however, I have replaced Dods' translation with my own.

Another argument which in several of his sermons Augustine employed, though in a more incidental fashion, is the observation that, after all, Rome was still standing, in spite of the disaster of the year 410. For instance, in the *Sermon on the Ruin of the City* he said that Rome, unlike Sodom, was not completely destroyed, and in another discourse (*Sermon* 105, 9) he declared: "The city which has given us birth, according to the flesh, still abides, God be thanked." He added (§ 11): "An end there will be to all earthly kingdoms. If that end be now, God alone knows. Perhaps the end is not yet, and we, because of a certain weakness or mercifulness or anguish, wish that it may not yet be." Augustine confessed (§ 12) that he himself was "entreating the Lord for Rome," not because he believed the duration of that one city would guarantee the duration of the whole world, but simply because there were many fellow-Christians in Rome, dear to him as all other Christians were.[8]

Since Rome did, in fact, survive, the old belief in its eternity also survived for many centuries to come, and with it persisted the popular superstition, in spite of its rejection by Augustine, that the final "fall" of the city would signify the coming end of the world. Only one of many testimonials to that belief may be quoted. In a British text of the early eighth century, which was wrongly ascribed to the Venerable Bede, we find the following lines:

> As long as the Colosseum stands, Rome also stands.
> When the Colosseum falls, Rome also will fall.
> When Rome falls, the world also will fall.[9]

The denial of the pagan belief in the eternity of Rome and the rejection of any connection between Christian eschatology and specific historical events occupy, however, only a rather

[8] Cf. also *Sermon* 81, 9; all three sermons mentioned were preached in the years 410 and 411: see A. Kunzelmann in *Miscellanea Agostiniana* (1931), II, 449 f., 500. On these sermons see also M. Pontet, *L'exégèse de S. Augustin prédicateur* (1944), 454, 471–476.

[9] Pseudo-Bede, *Flores ex diversis, quaestiones et parabola,* ed. Migne, *Patrologia Latina,* 94, col. 543; cf. F. Schneider, *Rom und Romgedanke im Mittelalter* (1926), 66 f., 251.

minor place in the whole context of *The City of God.* Augustine felt justified in making short shrift of these ideas because he regarded them as either mere superstitions or futile conjectures.

The real purpose of his great book he stated in a number of places but nowhere more concisely than in the work entitled *Retractations* (2, 68, 1), which he wrote after the completion of *The City of God* in the year 426. He defined his primary objective as follows: "In the meantime Rome had been overthrown by the invasion of the Goths under king Alaric and by the vehemence of a great defeat. The worshippers of the many and false gods, whom we commonly call pagans, attempted to attribute that overthrow to the Christian religion, and they began to blaspheme the true God with even more than their customary acrimony and bitterness. It was for that reason that I, kindled by zeal for the house of God, undertook to write the books on *The City of God* against their blasphemies and errors."

The accusation was very old that Christianity was responsible for the miseries of the world. The pagans claimed that the Christians, through their refusal to honor the traditional deities, were provoking the wrath of the very gods whose favor had raised Rome to her universal power. The Christian apologists found it easy to refute the charge. One of the most precise expressions of their customary reply is contained in Tertullian's *Apology* (40, 3, 5). Tertullian addressed the pagans as follows: "Pray, tell me, how many calamities befell the world as a whole, as well as individual cities, before Tiberius reigned, before the coming, that is, of Christ?" He asked: "Where were your gods in those days when a deluge effaced the whole earth or, as Plato believed, merely its plains?" And he concluded: "The truth is that the human race has always deserved ill at God's hand. . . . Therefore one ought to know that the very same God is angry now, as he always was, long before Christians were so much as spoken of."

Augustine used exactly the same kind of argument throughout the first five books of *The City of God,* only in a much more elaborate and detailed fashion than Tertullian, Arnobius,

Lactantius and other apologists of the third century had done before him. He went still further and commissioned his younger friend Orosius to write an entire history of the world from a point of view which is best described by Orosius himself in the dedication to Augustine of his *Seven Books of Histories against the Pagans:* "You bade me to discover from all the available data of histories and annals, whatever instances past ages have afforded of the burdens of war, the ravages of diseases, the horrors of famine, terrible earthquakes, extraordinary floods, dreadful eruptions of fire, thunderbolts and hailstorms, and also instances of the cruel miseries caused by murders and crimes against man's better self." [10] Orosius proved himself indeed "the true compiler of the evils of the world," as Petrarch (*Familiares,* 15, 9, 10) was to characterize him scornfully many centuries later. But in spite, or perhaps because, of their admitted prejudices and their preconceived ideas, Augustine's and Orosius' systematic expositions of the old apologist conceptions of world history in general and of Roman history in particular were to determine the historical outlook of most western writers to the time of the Italian Renaissance.

However, that traditional apology fills only one section in the first part of *The City of God.*[11] In the second half of the work (books XI to XXII) Augustine wanted to offer much more than a mere defense, as he stated himself in his *Retractations* (2, 68, 2): "In order that no one might raise the charge against me that I have merely refuted the opinions of other men but not stated my own, I devoted to this objective the second part of the work."

Of the vast number of ideas which Augustine set forth as his "own opinions," only one problem will be discussed here, that of "History": how does history take its course and is there any

[10] Quoted from J. W. Woodworth's translation of Orosius's *Seven Books* (1936), 1.

[11] The second section of the first part of the work, which consists of books VI to X, can be passed over in this article because Augustine did not deal in it with historical problems but set out to disprove the assertions of those philosophers who "maintain that polytheistic worship is advantageous for the life to come" (*Retractations,* 2, 68, 1).

meaning to be found in the sequence of events from the beginning of this world to the present age and to the day of the Last Judgment?[12]

How deeply Augustine was concerned with the question of the philosophical or rather, from his point of view, the theological interpretation of the meaning and course of history, is shown by those chapters of *The City of God* in which he discussed the problems of the origin of the world and the uniqueness of its creation. He rejected the view that this world is eternal and without beginnings, and he stated that it was definitely created in time and will come to an end in another definite moment in time, a moment known to God alone. In connection with his discussion of "this controversy about the beginnings of things temporal" (12, 13 E) Augustine wrote (12, 14 A): "The philosophers of this world believed that they could or should not solve that controversy in any other way than by introducing cycles of time, in which they asserted that the revolving of coming and passing ages would always be renewed and repeated in the nature of things and would thus go on without cessation." In this sentence Augustine was obviously referring to the cyclical theory of history held by Platonists, Stoics and other Greek schools of philosophy.[13] But although he mentioned no name, it becomes evident from the context of

[12] See the comprehensive analysis of the main body of ideas of Augustine's main work, which has been recently presented by W. J. Oates in his introduction to *Basic Writings of St. Augustine* (1948), I, ix–xl; and by E. Gilson in his introduction to D. B. Zema's and G. G. Walsh's translation of *The City of God* (1950), I, pp. xi–xcviii.—Of the vast literature dealing with Augustine's historical ideas, I can list only some of the most recent treatments: R. J. Defferari and M. Keeler, "St. Augustine's City of God: Its Plan and Development," *American Journal of Philology* (1929), L, 109–137; U. A. Padovano, "La Città di Dio: teologia e non filosofia della storia," *Rivista di Filosofia Neo-scolastica* (1931), supplem. vol. to vol. XXIII, 220–263; H. I. Marrou, *S. Augustin et la fin de la culture antique* (1938; see esp. 131–135, 417–419, 461–467); H. Fuchs, *Der geistige Widerstand gegen Rom in der antiken Welt* (1938); C. N. Cochrane, *Christianity and Classical Culture; A Study of Thought and Action from Augustus to Augustine* (1944; esp. 397–516); W. M. Green, "Augustine on the Teaching of History," *University of California Publications in Classical Philology* (1944), XII, 315–332; K. Löwith, *Meaning in History* (1949), 160–173.

[13] Cf. K. Löwith, *l.c.*, 162–165, 248 n. 15; J. Baillie, *The Belief in Progress* (1951), 42–57.

the passage just quoted that he knew that this cyclical view was also maintained by Origen, who attempted to support it in a somewhat qualified fashion through quotations from the Scriptures, for instance the famous sentence in *Ecclesiastes* (1, 9): "There is no new thing under the sun." In his Latin translation of Origen's text Rufinus considerably modified these views, but this did not prevent Jerome from attacking them sharply. Augustine was even more emphatic in his refutation when he exclaimed in *The City of God* (12, 14 E): "Far be it from the right faith to believe that by these words of Solomon [*i.e., Ecclesiastes*] those cycles are meant in which [according to these philosophers] the revolving of the same periods and things is repeated." He found it logical that those thinkers "erroneously wandering around in cycles, find neither entrance nor exit," for he was convinced that "they do not know how the human race and this mortal condition of ours took its origin nor how it will be brought to an end" (12, 15 A). Those "false cycles which were discovered by false and deceitful sages," he believed, "can be avoided in the sound doctrine, through the path of the straight road (*tramite recti itineris*)." [14]

To Augustine, then, history takes its course, not in cycles, but along a line. That line has a most definite beginning, the Creation, and a most definite end, the Last Judgment. Within this definite period of time the greatest single event was, of course, the appearance of Christ. "For," Augustine said (12, 14 F), "Christ died once for our sins and 'raised from the dead dieth no more' (*Romans,* 6, 9); . . . and we ourselves, after

[14] *City of God,* 12, 14 B.—C. N. Cochrane, *l.c.,* 245, stated that "we find Origen, for instance, protesting vigorously against the Platonic theory of cycles." But Cochrane and, following him, R. Niebuhr, *Faith and History* (1949), 65, based their assertion exclusively on one passage in Origen's writings (*Against Celsus,* 4, 68) and neglected the much more detailed treatment of this problem in Origen's book *On First Principles,* 2, 3, 1–5; 3, 5, 3; 4, 13. P. Koetschau, in his edition of Rufinus' translation and of the Greek fragments of *On First Principles* (*Origenes Werke* [1913], V, 113 f., 120), commented on Rufinus' modifications of the original text and printed the relevant remarks made by Jerome on Origen's belief in a series of many worlds: see the English translation of Koetschau's edition by G. W. Butterworth, *Origen, On First Principles* (1935), 83–89, 238 f.; J. Baillie, *l.c.,* 74 ff., seems to overlook, too, the fact that Origen shared the cyclical theory, although in a modified form.

the resurrection, 'shall ever be with the Lord' (*I Thessalonians*, 4, 17)." It seems that here Augustine was arguing again indirectly against Origen who, according to Jerome, "allowed himself to assert that Christ has often suffered and will often suffer, on the ground that what was beneficial once, will always be beneficial," and who also, "in his desire to confirm the most impious dogma of the Stoics through the authority of the Divine Scriptures, dared to write that man dies over and over again.[15]

From Augustine's conception of the course of history it follows that every particular event that takes place in time, every human life and human action, is a unique phenomenon which happens under the auspices of Divine Providence and must therefore have a definite meaning. The roots of this linear conception of history, as distinguished from the cyclical theories of the Greeks, went back to Hebrew ideas which had been further developed by the early Christian theologians.[16] But it was Augustine who elaborated those ideas most fully and consistently and thus determined the theology of history which prevailed throughout the Middle Ages and was to influence the philosophies of history of modern times.

When Augustine decided to combat the cyclical theories, he was probably motivated, as we have seen, by his knowledge that this pagan view was shared, to a certain extent at least, by a prominent, though suspect and even heretical, Christian thinker, Origen. But it appears that there existed still another philosophy of history at that time, which from Augustine's point of view was even more dangerous than the cyclical theory because it was very widespread among the Christians of his own as well as previous generations. To Augustine the truly problematic and the most objectionable theory of history must

[15] See Butterworth, *l.c.*, 88 n. 4 (Jerome, *Apology*, 1, 20) and 83 n. 1 (Jerome, *Epist.*, 96, 9).

[16] On the Hebrew conceptions, see H. Butterfield, *Christianity and History* (1950), esp. 1–4, 57–62, 68–88; on the Christian views, see O. Cullmann, *Christus und die Zeit; die urchristliche Zeit- und Geschichtsauffassung* (1946); R. G. Collingwood, *The Idea of History* (1946), 46–52; J. Baillie, *l.c.*, 57–87; Th. Preiss, "The Vision of History in the New Testament," *Papers of the Ecumenical Institute* (1950), V, 48–66; J. Daniélou, "The Conception of History in the Christian Tradition," *ibid.*, 67–79.

have been a conception which may be called "the Christian idea of progress."

When in 1920 J. B. Bury published his book *The Idea of Progress,* he wrote (20 f.) that "the idea of the universe which prevailed throughout the Middle Ages and the general orientation of men's thoughts were incompatible with some of the fundamental assumptions which are required by the idea of progress." But more recently, a number of scholars have pointed out that, to a certain degree, such an idea can actually be found among some of the early Christian thinkers.[17] A systematic treatment of this complex topic does not yet exist and it connot be given in a brief essay. But in the following an attempt will be made at least to set forth some examples from early Christian writings, which may serve to illustrate the nature of that idea.

One might be inclined to find the first instance of the conception of progress in that part of Christian literature which dealt with the question of the Millennium. For some of the early theologians, including Justin, Irenaeus and Lactantius, interpreted the apocalyptic prediction of Christ's future reign of one thousand years in terms of a very material bliss. But this peculiar notion cannot be truly said to express a belief in "progress," because the Messianic kingdom of the future was not to come into existence through a gradual or evolutionary process but rather through the dramatically sudden second coming of Christ. Moreover, even before Augustine's time thinkers like Origen and Tychonius had successfully discredited that very materialistic notion of the Millennium and had interpreted the conception in a primarily spiritual sense.[18] This became Augustine's own opinion also, because in the writings

[17] See, e.g., E. K. Rand, *Founders of the Middle Ages* (1929), 13–22, 291; Rand, *The Building of Eternal Rome* (1943), 72, 189 ff.; C. N. Cochrane, *l.c.,* 242–247, 483 f.; K. Löwith, *l.c.,* 60 f., 84, 112 f., 182 ff.; J. Baillie, *l.c.,* 19–22, 94–96.

[18] On the ideas concerning the Millennium, see, e.g., E. Bernheim, *Mittelalterliche Zeitanschauungen in ihrem Einfluss auf Politik und Geschichtschreibung* (1918), esp. 63–109; A. Wikenhauser, "Das Problem des tausendjährigen Reiches in der Johannes-Apokalypse," *Römische Quartalschrift* (1932), XL, 13–36; Wikenhauser, "Die Herkunft der Idee des tausendjährigen Reiches in der Johannes-Apokalypse," *ibid.* (1937), XLV, 1–24; J. Baillie, *l.c.,* 60–64, 79–83.

of the later period of his life, which dealt with eschatological speculations, he made it very clear that the question of the Millennium has nothing to do with any kind of earthly prosperity but has reference only to the necessarily imperfect realization of the divine in this world.

But apart from these speculations concerning the Millennium we find that some of the most prominent Christian apologists voiced views which implied the belief that under the auspices of Christianity the world had made concrete progress in historical time and that further progress could be expected. Those writers asserted that the new creed was bringing blessings to the whole of mankind, not merely to its own adherents. They pointed to the historically undeniable fact that the birth of Christ had taken place at the time of the foundation of the Roman empire by Augustus and the establishment of the *Pax Romana* on earth. As the appearance of Christ coincided with a marked improvement of all things secular, so, the early apologists argued, the growth of the new faith will be accompanied by further progress.[19]

The first testimony to this conception is to be found in the *Apology* which Bishop Melito of Sardis addressed to Emperor Antoninus Pius in the middle of the second century. According to Eusebius' *Ecclesiastical History* (4, 26, 7–8), Melito wrote: "Our philosophy [*i.e.*, Christianity] flourished first among the barbarians; then, during the great reign of your ancestor Augustus, it spread among your people and, above all, it has become to your own reign an auspicious blessing. For from that time the power of Rome has grown in greatness and splendor. To this power you have succeeded as the desired heir and you will continue it with your sons if you safeguard that philosophy which grew up with the empire and took its start under Augustus. . . . The best evidence that our doctrine has been flourishing for the good of an empire happily started is this: since the reign of Augustus no misfortune has befallen it; on the contrary, all things have been splendid and glorious, in accordance with the wishes of all."

[19] On the discussion of these arguments, see also E. Peterson, *Der Monotheismus als politisches Problem* (1935), 66–88; J. Geffcken, *Zwei griechische Apologeten* (1907), esp. 63, 92.

Around the year 200, Tertullian expressed the same idea, though somewhat more cautiously. He wrote in his *Apology* (ch. 40, 13): "And for all that is said, if we compare the calamities of former times [with those of our own era], we find that they fall on us more lightly now, since the earth has received from God the believers of the Christian faith. For since that time innocence has put restraint on the wickedness of this world and men have begun to plead with God for the averting of His wrath."

These two apologists, then, did not merely content themselves with rejecting the pagan accusation that Christianity was responsible for the misfortunes of the era; on the contrary, they dared to take the offensive and claimed that their faith was making a positive contribution to the well-being of the Roman empire.

From this assertion there was but a single step to the expression of the belief that the universal acceptance of the Christian religion by the Roman world would lead to a still greater degree of security and prosperity. The pagan Celsus, in the middle of the third century, raised the question as to the consequences of such an event. Origen replied to Celsus' question with utmost confidence (*Against Celsus,* 4, 69): "If all the Romans were to pray together in full harmony, then they would be able to put to flight many more enemies than those who were discomfitted by the prayers of Moses when he cried to the Lord." Fifty years after Origen, around the year 300, Arnobius expressed the same belief in his treatise *Against the Pagans* (1, 6): "If all without exception, who consider themselves men, not in form of body, but in power of reason, were willing to lend, for a little while, an ear to [Christ's] salutary and peaceful prescriptions and were not, swollen with pride and arrogance, to trust to their own senses rather than to His admonitions, then the whole world, having turned the use of iron into more peaceful occupations, would live in the most placid tranquillity and would unite in blessed harmony, maintaining inviolate the sanctity of treaties."

This conviction that the appearance of Christ has led to a general improvement of the material conditions of the world and that its universal acceptance will lead to a still greater progress, was set forth by Melito and Tertullian, by Origen and Arnobius, during a period when their faith was suppressed by the official authorities of the Roman state. When, in the reign of Constantine, the great turning-point arrived and Christianity was not only tolerated but became the religion most favored by the emperor, it was natural that hope for progress rose still higher. Thus even Lactantius, once the champion of eschatological ideas in their most extreme and pessimistic form, dared to express rather optimistic expectations at the very end of his book *On the Death of the Persecutors* (ch. 52): "The Lord has destroyed and erased from the earth those proud names [of the anti-Christian rulers]. Let us therefore celebrate the triumph of God with joy. Let us frequently praise the victory of the Lord. Day and night let us offer our prayers to the Lord that He may establish for all time the peace which has been given to His people after [a warfare of] ten years."

Constantine showed himself most eager to adopt the idea that the worship of the true and omnipotent God was bound to benefit his empire in a material sense. In a letter written shortly after his decisive victory at the Milvian Bridge in the year 312, he declared (Eusebius, *Eccles. Hist.*, 10, 7, 1): "From many facts it appears . . . that the lawful recognition and observance [of the Christian faith] has bestowed the greatest success on the Roman name and singular prosperity on all affairs of mankind, blessings which were provided by the divine beneficence." Constantine's highly materialistic conception of his relationship with the Christian God was very much in accordance with the religious notions of the ancient Romans.[20] It was the old principle of *do ut des:* "I give that you may give." The emperor argued: I, Constantine, do something for you, God, so that you may do something for me; likewise, of course, God himself was assumed to expect gifts in return from those to whom he had extended favors. This idea of a commutative contract between God and man found reflection in the politico-ecclesiastical writings of quite a few of the Christian authors of the fourth cen-

[20] On this point, see H. Berkhof, *Kirche und Kaiser; eine Untersuchung der Entstehung der byzantinischen und theokratischen Staatsauffassung im 4. Jahrhundert* (1947), esp. 14–18, 31–34, 55–59, 66, 70.

tury, beginning with Constantine's court-bishop, Eusebius of Caesarea. It was a complete ideological reversal: once the pagans had charged that the worship of the Christian God was the source of all the calamities of the empire; now, Constantine had the symbol of the cross displayed in the principal room of his new imperial palace in Constantinople; according to Eusebius' *Life of Constantine* (3, 49), "this symbol seemed to the beloved of God [Constantine] to have been made as a safeguard of the empire itself."

The principle of *do ut des* was most emphatically rejected by Augustine, for it was wholly contrary to his conception of the relationship between God and man, even the great of this world.[21] Thus he stated in *The City of God* (4, 33) that in God's eyes earthly power and all similar things temporal are not important gifts and that therefore God "bestows them on both the good and the bad." In discussing the question of the *imperator felix,* Augustine admitted (*City of God,* 5, 25 A) that God "gave to the emperor Constantine, who was not a worshipper of demons but of the true God Himself, such fulness of earthly gifts as no one would even dare to wish for." But Augustine continued: "Lest, however, any emperor shall become a Christian in order to merit the blessed felicity of Constantine—when everyone ought to be a Christian for the sake of the eternal life —God took away [the Christian prince] Jovian far sooner than [his pagan brother, the emperor] Julian, and He allowed [the Christian emperor] Gratian to be slain by the sword of a tyrant."

These sentences in *The City of God* sound as if they were written expressly against Eusebius, who had declared in his *Life of Constantine* (1, 3, 3), with specific reference to the emperor: "God, that God who is the common Saviour of all, has treasured up with Himself, for those who love religion, far greater blessings than man can conceive, and He gives even here and now the first-fruits as a pledge of future rewards, thus assuring in some sort immortal hopes to mortal eyes."

Eusebius based his belief in the effectiveness of the principle of *do ut des* on a very definite interpretation and philosophy

[21] Cf. Berkhof, *l.c.,* 205–209.

of history.[22] He emphasized (*Demonstratio Evangelica,* 3, 7, 139) even more strongly than Melito and other Christian thinkers during the previous centuries, that "it was not through human merit that at no other time but only since the time of Christ most of the nations were under the single rule of the Romans; for the period of His wonderful sojourn among men coincided with the period when the Romans reached their summit under Augustus, who was then the first monarch to rule over most of the nations." [23] This concurrence of the appearance of Christ on earth and the founding of the universal empire by Augustus "was not by mere human accident" but it was "of God's arrangement." Whereas the earlier interpreters of that concurrence had stated it simply as a historical fact, Eusebius believed himself capable of adducing proof from the Scriptures that those events were long before predicted by God. Thus he quoted in all the works in which he discussed the "synchronising" of the birth of Christ with the reign of Augustus, the following passages from the Old Testament: "In His days the righteous shall flourish and abundance of peace" (*Psalm* 72, 7); "He shall have dominion also from sea to sea, and from the river unto the ends of the earth" (*Psalm* 72, 8); "And they shall beat their swords into plowshares, and their spears into pruninghooks: nation shall not lift up sword against nation, neither shall they learn war any more" (*Isaiah,* 2, 4).

These quotations are highly remarkable. For according to tradition those prophecies were to be understood as predictions of the future Messianic Kingdom, as we can learn from their interpretation by men like Irenaeus (*Against Heresies,* 4, 56, 3), Tertullian (*Against Marcion,* 3, 21) and Lactantius (*Divine Institutions,* 4, 16, 14). It seems that previous to Eusebius only Origen (*Against Celsus,* 2, 30) had ventured to refer the passage in *Psalm* 72, 7 to the *Pax Romana.*[24] But the full elabora-

[22] Cf. H. Berkhof, *Die Theologie des Eusebius von Caesarea* (1939), 45–50, 55 f., 58 f.; E. Peterson, *l.c.,* 66 ff.

[23] See the similar passages in Eusebius' *Theophania,* 3, 2; *Praeparatio Evangelica,* 5, 1.

[24] It may be noted that Origen interpreted the passage in *Isaiah,* 2, 4 in an entirely spiritual sense; see *Against Celsus,* 5, 33; *Against Heresies,* 6, 16.

tion of Origen's suggestion was left to Eusebius, who gave the most bluntly secular interpretations to these scriptural texts. Witness the passage in Eusebius' *Praeparatio Evangelica* (1, 4): "In accordance with these predictions [*i.e.*, of *Psalm* 72 and of *Isaiah*, 2, 4], the actual events followed. Immediately after Augustus had established his sole rule, at the time of our Saviour's appearance, the rule by the many became abolished among the Romans. And from that time to the present you cannot see, as before, cities at war with cities, nor nation fighting with nation, nor life being worn away in the confusion of everything." Eusebius saw a close parallel between the victory of Christian monotheism and the growth of the Roman monarchy. Thus he stated in his *Theophania* (3, 2): [25] "Two great powers sprang up fully as out of one stream and they gave peace to all and brought all together to a state of friendship: the Roman empire, which from that time appeared as one kingdom, and the power of the Saviour of all, whose aid was at once extended to and established with everyone. For the divine superiority of our Saviour swept away the authority of the many demons and gods, so that the one Kingdom of God was preached to all men, Greeks and barbarians, and to those who resided in the extremities of the earth. The Roman empire, too—since those had been previously uprooted who had been the cause of the rule by many—soon subjugated all others and quickly brought together the whole race of man into one state of accordance and agreement."

To Eusebius the greatest gains made by mankind since the days of Christ and Augustus were the abolition of wars, foreign and civil, and the establishment of peace and security, the time-hallowed ideals of the *Pax Romana*. But he saw also other improvements. For instance, he declared in his *Praeparatio Evangelica* (1, 4): "Of the benefits resulting from God's doctrines which have become manifest on earth, you may see a clear proof if you consider that at no other time from the beginning until now, and not through the merits of any of the illustrious men

[25] Translated from the Syriac by S. Lee, *Eusebius on the Theophania* (1853), 156 f.; cf. the very similar passage in Eusebius' *Praise of Constantine*, 16, 4–5.

of old but only through Christ's utterances and teachings, diffused throughout the whole world, the customs of all nations have been set aright, even those customs which before were savage and barbarous." Because of the strict discipline of the new faith men have learned to lead a moral life, to refrain from hostility toward others and to master their own emotions and passions. Eusebius concluded his enumeration of all the improvements made in the political, legal and moral spheres by asking: "How, then, can anyone . . . refuse to admit that our doctrine has brought to all men good tidings of very great and true blessings, and has supplied to human life that which is of immediate advantage toward happiness?"

There was no doubt in Eusebius' mind that mankind, under divine guidance, had made progress from the pre-Christian era through the three centuries of the gradual ascent of the new Church to the reign of Constantine in which he himself lived. He declared in his *Praise of Constantine* (16, 8): "As those predictions concerning our Saviour [*i.e., Psalm* 72, 7–8, and *Isaiah,* 2, 4] were foretold and delivered in the Hebrew tongue many ages before, so in our own times they have become really fulfilled and the ancient testimonies of the prophets clearly confirmed." Great as the advances made by mankind were, still further progress was expected by Eusebius. For he asserted (*ibid.,* 6): "Although the object of the Roman empire to unite all nations in one harmonious whole has already been secured to a large degree, it is destined to be still more perfectly attained, even to the final conquest of the ends of the habitable world, by means of the salutary doctrine and through the aid of that Divine Providence which facilitates and smooths the way [of the Empire]."

In his recent essay on *The Idea of Progress,* G. H. Hildebrand stated [26] that this idea includes three principles: "First, the belief that history follows a continuous, necessary, and orderly course; second, the belief that this course is the effect of a regularly operating causal law; and third, the belief that the course of change has brought and will continue to bring

[26] *The Idea of Progress; a Collection of Readings;* selected by F. J. Teggart; revised edition with an introduction by G. H. Hildebrand, 4.

improvement in the condition of mankind." The first two of these principles were always implied in the Christian belief that every single event and consequently also the course of historical events as a whole take place under God's will and in accordance with the plan of Divine Providence. But it remained for Eusebius to add the third principle, the optimistic belief in continuous improvement, and thus to develop a full-fledged Christian idea of progress.

Eusebius' idea was taken up by some of the most prominent theologians of the fourth and early fifth centuries, both in the eastern and the western parts of the Church.[27] This is shown by the interpretations which John Chrysostom, Ambrose, Jerome, Cyril of Alexandria and Theodoret of Cyrus gave in their various commentaries on *Psalm* 72 and *Isaiah* (2, 4), and we may add, on the passage in *Psalm* 46 (v. 9), which reads: "He maketh wars to cease unto the end of the earth." Like Eusebius all the writers just mentioned explained these passages in terms of the *Pax Romana* and its earthly achievements, and it seems that of the great theologians of the fourth century only Athanasius and Basil expounded them in a strictly spiritual sense.

When Augustine wrote his *Enarrations on the Psalms,* he replaced the explanations of the above passages with interpretations wholly different and entirely his own. For instance, Origen, Eusebius, John Chrysostom and Ambrose had declared that the words of *Psalm* 46: "He maketh wars to end," had been realized in the reign of Augustus; Basil alone had explained that passage in exclusively religious terms. But whereas Basil had contented himself with simply setting forth his personal exposition, Augustine accompanied the commentary which he wrote in 412, two years after the fall of Rome, with a polemic directed against the interpretation given by so many of his famous predecessors.[28] For although he did not mention any name, there seems to be no doubt that he was taking issue with

27 Cf. E. Peterson, *l.c.,* 71–88.

28 Cf. E. Peterson, *l.c.,* 97 f.; as to the date of *Enarration on Psalm 45,* cf. S. M. Zarb, "Chronologia enarrationum S. Augustini in Psalmos," in *Angelicum* (1947), XXIV, 275–283.

the current view when he denied categorically that the prediction of a reign of peace had been fulfilled in any material or historical sense: "There are still wars, wars among nations for supremacy, wars among sects, wars among Jews, pagans, Christians, heretics, and these wars are becoming more frequent" (*Enarration on Psalm 45, 13* = 46, 9). In Augustine's opinion, external peace was not yet achieved and, in fact, it would not even matter if it actually had. Only that peace matters which, through divine grace, man finds in himself, by his complete submission to the will of God. "When man learns that in himself he is nothing and that he has no help from himself," Augustine said, "then arms in himself are broken in pieces, then wars in himself are ended. Such wars, then, destroyed that voice of the Most High out of His holy clouds whereby the earth was shaken and the kingdoms were bowed; these wars He has taken away unto the ends of the earth."

In his *Enarration on Psalm 71, 10* (= 72, 7), Augustine commented on the passage: "In His days righteousness (*iustitia*) shall arise and abundance of peace until the moon be exalted." [29] These words, Augustine declared, "ought to be understood as if it were said: there shall arise in His days righteousness to conquer the contradiction and the rebellion of the flesh, and there shall be made a peace so abundant and increasing 'until the moon be exalted,' that is until the Church be lifted up, through the glory of the resurrection to reign with Him." Righteousness and peace in the words of the psalmist ought not to be confused, then, with the notions of *iustitia* and *pax* of the earthly state. Those highest Christian ideals have not yet been nor will they ever be embodied in the secular organization of the Roman empire, but they will be realized in the spiritual community of the eternal Church. The theologically untenable identification of the Messianic ideal with the historical reality of the *Imperium Romanum* could not have been rejected more radically than was done by Augustine in his commentary.

[29] The above translation of *Psalm* 72 is based on the text of the *Itala* used by Augustine.— This *Enarration* was written between 415 and 416; see S. M. Zarb, *op. cit., Angelicum* (1935), XII, 77–81.

Augustine was fully aware of the fact that in his exegetical works he was frequently deviating from his predecessors on essential points. No less a man than Jerome had told him so very bluntly in two letters written in the year 404 (*Epist.* 105 and 112), that is, long before Augustine wrote his *Enarrations on Psalms 45 and 71*. It is interesting to note that Jerome specifically referred to Augustine's "little commentaries on some of the Psalms, which, if I were disposed to criticise them," Jerome said (*Epist.* 105, 2), "I could prove to be at variance, I shall not say with my own opinion, for 'I am nothing' (*I Corinth.*, 13, 2), but with the interpretations of the older Greek commentators." [30] In his reply Augustine stated in unmistakable terms (*Epist.* 82, 3) that he felt justified in deviating from views held by previous commentators in any instance in which he considered himself to be in full accordance with the Scriptures; for he declared that "of only those books of the Scriptures, which are now called canonical, do I most firmly believe that their authors have made no error in their writing." He continued: "But the others I read in such a way that, however outstanding the authors are in sanctity and learning, I do not accept their teaching as true on the mere ground of the opinion held by them, but only because they have succeeded in convincing my judgment of its truth either by means of those canonical writings themselves or by arguments addressed to my reason." The definite nature of this statement entitles us to ascribe great significance to the fact that Augustine interpreted the Messianic predictions of the Old Testament in a fashion so fundamentally different from that of some of the most renowned earlier theologians, both Greek and Latin, who had found in those passages the promise of material well-being and progress to be achieved by man on earth and in the course of history.

Augustine's rejection of these conceptions appears even more noteworthy when we remember that it was during his own lifetime that the Christian idea of progress as developed by Eusebius became the crucial issue in a basic controversy. This

[30] We do not know to which of Augustine's "little commentaries" Jerome referred; Augustine started writing his *Enarrations* in the last decade of the fourth century; cf. Zarb, *op. cit.*

was the famous affair of the Altar of Victory in Rome, the great conflict, the last one in history, between pagan traditionalism and Christian progressivism.[31] That incident, with its later repercussions, forms the immediate background of the composition of *The City of God.*

Ever since the days of the Republic the statue of Victory had stood in the building of the Roman Senate, and the meetings of the Senate used to be opened with the burning of incense at the altar of the goddess. In the mid-fourth century emperor Constantius ordered the removal of the statue, but Julian the Apostate had it restored to its old place. It was taken away once again in the year 382. The pagan members of the Roman Senate were naturally very much disturbed, and in the year 384 the most highly respected member of that group, Symmachus, submitted an impressive plea to the reigning emperors for the restoration of the Altar of Victory. Symmachus argued on the basis of the principle of *do ut des,* but he used the principle, of course, according to the pagan mode of thought. The ancient deities, he declared, have raised Rome to her great position, and for that reason Rome owes them gratitude (Symmachus' *Relatio,* §§ 3 and 8). Symmachus let the personification of Rome address herself to the emperors (§ 9): "Excellent princes, fathers of the country, respect my years to which pious rites have brought me. Let me use the ancestral ceremonies, for I do not repent of them. Let me live after my fashion, for I am free. This worship has subdued the world to my laws, these sacred rites repelled Hannibal from my walls and the Gauls from the Capitol." In the same spirit Symmachus sounded an emphatic warning (§ 4): "We are cautious as to what may happen in the future, and we shun portentous actions."

The leading Christian figure of that time, Bishop Ambrose of Milan took it upon himself to reply to the plea made by the great pagan statesman. In his refutation of Symmachus' assertion that Rome rose to power through the favor of the pagan

[31] On this affair, see esp. J. R. Palanque, *S. Ambroise et l'empire Romain* (1933), 131–136, 221 f., 278 f., 307, 358–364, 510, 536; J. Wytzes, *Der Streit um den Altar der Viktoria* (1936); L. Malunowicz, *De ara victoriae in curia Romana quomodo certatum sit* (1937); M. Lavarenne in his edition of the works of *Prudence* (1948), III, 85–90.

gods, Ambrose employed, of course, the old arguments of the Christian apologists. But he went farther. He, too, let Rome speak for herself (*Epist.* 18, 7). But whereas Symmachus' *Roma* had pleaded for the preservation of the time-honored traditions of the past, Ambrose's *Roma* appealed to the idea of progress. "It is no disgrace," she declared, "to pass on to better things." And in answer to Symmachus' traditionalist argument that "the rites of our ancestors ought to be retained," Ambrose asked (§ 23): "Why should we do so? Has not everything made advances in the course of time toward what is better?" In both the memoranda which he addressed to the then reigning emperors, Ambrose made it clear that he shared the current belief that Christianity was a progressive factor in history. It may be remarked in passing that Ambrose, like Eusebius and Symmachus, believed that the relationship between God and man is largely determined by the principle of merit and reward. For instance, in his treatise *On Faith* (2, 16), Ambrose did not hesitate to find the explanation for the defeat of the emperor Valens in the battle of Adrianople in 378 in the fact that Valens was an Arian heretic: on the other hand he predicted with full confidence the victory of the emperor Gratian over the Visigoths because the new ruler confessed the orthodox faith.[32]

In the year 384, the question of the Altar of Victory was settled in accordance with Ambrose's wishes, but during the next two decades the pagan faction of the Roman Senate continued to work, with varying success, for the restoration of the statue. Thus around the year 403, the poet Prudentius decided to present once more the Christian point of view in regard to that problem.[33] His poem entitled *Against Symmachus* was the greatest poetical expression the Christian idea of progress ever found in early western Christendom. According to Prudentius, God had assigned to the Romans the task of conquering the world and establishing a universal empire so as to pave the way for the spread of the universal religion. The mission of the Roman empire was to become finally the

[32] Cf. H. Berkhof, *Kirche und Kaiser,* 90–94, 173–182.

[33] On the date of Prudentius' *Contra Symmachum,* cf. L. Malunowicz, *l.c.,* 99 f.; M. Lavarenne, *l.c.,* III, 89 f.

Christian empire. That great turn took place under Constantine who, in Prudentius' words (1, 539 f.), "accustomed Romulus' state to be powerful for ever in a dominion derived from above." In his description of the universal and eternal Christian empire as it was established by Constantine, Prudentius used phrases (1, 541–43) which are almost identical with those which Vergil once had made Jupiter say: "[Constantine] did not set any boundaries nor did he fix limits of time; he taught an imperial power without end so that the Roman valor should no longer be senile nor the glory which Rome had won should ever know old age." This Christian Rome, Prudentius said (1, 587–90), "has dedicated herself to Thee, O Christ, and has passed under Thy laws, and is willing now, with all her people and her greatest citizens, to extend her earthly rule beyond the lofty stars of the great heavens." Prudentius recalled Symmachus' assertion that it was only because of the help of the ancient gods that neither the Gauls nor Hannibal had succeeded in completely overwhelming Rome. He let his personification of the Christian *Roma* reply as follows (2, 690–95): "Whosoever tries to impress me again with the memories of past defeats and ancient calamities, he ought to see that in this age of yours [*i.e.*, that of the Christian emperors] I no longer suffer anything of that sort. No barbaric enemy shatters my walls with a javelin and no man with strange weapons, attire and hairdress wanders around the city he has conquered and carries off my young men into transalpine prisons."

These lines were written around the year 403. In 410 Rome fell to Alaric and Visigothic "strangers wandered around the city they had conquered." Under these circumstances many contemporaries, pagan as well as Christian, must have remembered the sombre warnings of Symmachus, which had been so recently discussed again and so optimistically rejected by Prudentius. In the year 410 Alaric had achieved that complete conquest of Rome which hundreds of years before Hannibal had failed to accomplish, and the long-dreaded "fall of Rome" had taken place almost immediately after a Christian poet had assured his listeners that it could not happen now and never would.

The reactions of the pagan and Christian contemporaries were profound and radical, as we learn from the *Sermon on the Fall of the City,* which Augustine preached shortly after the event.[34] The pagans said to the Christians (§ 9): "As long as we brought sacrifices to our Gods, Rome stood; now when the sacrifice to your God is triumphant and abounds and the sacrifices to our gods are prevented and forbidden, see what Rome is suffering." And the Christians, according to Augustine's sermon (§ 6), were shocked and bewildered by the fact that in spite of the many holy places in the city, in spite of the tombs of St. Peter and St. Paul and many other martyrs, "Rome is miserable and devastated, Rome is afflicted, laid waste and burnt." Augustine was naturally much more concerned about the reactions of the Christians than about those of the pagans. For in the aftermath of the year 410 it had become evident that Christianity included within its ranks many people who had been won over to the new faith simply because of its external triumph. To them Christianity meant primarily the belief in the effectiveness of the principle of *do ut des,* which had been taught by Eusebius and his followers. Such a faith, based as it was on essentially materialistic foundations, and such a shallow optimism were of necessity badly shaken by the turn of events. How deeply conscious Augustine was of the problem presented by those worldly-minded Christians is revealed by another sermon which he preached after the fall of Rome. In bitter words he condemned (*Sermon* 105, 13) "those blasphemers who chase and long after things earthly and place their hopes in things earthly. When they have lost them, whether they will or not, what shall they hold and where shall they abide? Nothing within, nothing without; an empty coffer, an emptier conscience."

This was the situation, from the ideological point of view a very critical situation, which motivated Augustine to write *The City of God.* He realized that one single event, the "fall of Rome," had an impact upon the thinking and the feeling of his contemporaries which went far beyond its material im-

[34] The Latin text of Sermon 296 has recently been re-edited by G. Morin, in *Miscellanea Agostiniana* (1930), I, 401–419.

portance. The significance attributed to the event resulted from the central position which the destiny and fate of "eternal" Rome occupied in the existing conceptions of history, whether they were pagan or Christian. If Augustine, then, wanted to combat in a truly fundamental fashion the interpretations of that "fall of Rome," he could do so only by setting forth his own ideas concerning the course and the meaning of history. Therefore he was willing to devote thirteen years of his life to the most comprehensive study of the problem of history, a problem which up to the year 410 had been of merely incidental interest to him.

In attempting to solve that problem, Augustine found, as we have seen, that he had to reject practically all the current conceptions of history. He did not share the sentiments of those among the early Christian writers to whom any concern about history was superfluous in view of the presumably imminent end of this world, and he had no interest in eschatological speculations and calculations regarding the future Millennium. Neither could he, of course, accept the cyclical theory as it was held by some of the pagan schools of philosophy and, in a modified form, by Origen. And he saw most clearly how perilous it was for the Christian faith to proclaim, as Eusebius and others had done during the fourth century, a belief in "progress," if that notion was understood in any kind of materialistic sense. For under the existing circumstances it was inevitable that "most of the pagans," as Augustine said in his *Enarration on Psalm 136, 9,* asked the question: "Is it not true that since the coming of Christ the state of human affairs has been worse than it was before and that human affairs were once much more fortunate than they are now?" [35] Every emphasis on the idea of secular progress was bound to lay the Christian cause wide open to attacks by the pagans and to the disillusionment of the half-hearted Christians. Both groups could rightly find that all promises of worldly success were totally disproved by the catastrophe of the year 410—and there might be more and worse disasters to come.

[35] This *Enarration* was written between 410 and 413; see Zarb, *l.c.* (1939), XVI, 289 f.

In contradistinction to all these conceptions Augustine's own views concerning history represent a basic reiteration and systematic elaboration of Hebrew and early Christian ideas.[36] To him history was the *operatio Dei* in time, it was "a one-directional, teleological process, directed towards one goal—salvation," the salvation of individual men, not of any collective groups or organizations.[37] Ever since the creation of the world there have existed two cities, the city of God or the community of those who "wish to live after the spirit," and the earthly city or the community of those who "wish to live after the flesh" (*City of God,* 14, 1 C). Of the twelve books of the second part of *The City of God,* eight books deal with the origin (*exortus*) and the end (*finis*) of those two cities, that is with the Creation and the Last Judgment. Only the middle section (books XV to XVIII) deals with that period of time which is commonly considered to be the historical era, and even within that section Augustine gave his main attention to those men and events which belonged to "the heavenly city which is a pilgrim on earth" (18, 54 K). The fact that only one book of *The City of God* (b. XVIII) treats historical developments proper, shows clearly that Augustine regarded the purely secular aspects of the drama of mankind as relatively insignificant.

The content of that middle section of *The City of God* comprising books XV to XVIII has been defined by Augustine as follows (15, 1 C): "It now seems right to me to approach the account of the course [of the two cities] from the time when those two [*i.e.,* Adam and Eve] began to propagate the race to the time when men shall cease to propagate. For this whole time or world-age, in which the dying give place and those who are born succeed, is the course of the two cities which are under discussion." Twice in the passage just quoted, and in two other passages (11, 1 C and 18, 54 K), Augustine used the word *excursus* to define the historical process which is taking place between the Creation and the Last Judgment.[38] In other

36 See above, note 16.

37 See K. Löwith, *l.c.,* 170 f.; E. Frank, "The Role of History in Christian Thought," *The Duke Divinity School Bulletin* (1949), XIV, 74.

38 Cf. *City of God,* 15, 9 D: *praeterit saeculi excursus.*

passages of *The City of God,* and more frequently, he employed the words *procursus* and *procurrere* for the development within the same span of time.[39] What is the meaning of these words? When we look in the translations of *The City of God* by John Healey and by Marcus Dods, we find that they translated the noun *procursus* most frequently with "progress," but also with "history," "proceedings" and "advance," the verb *procurrere* with "run its course," "run on," "proceed" and "progress," and the word *excursus* with "progress," "progression," "career" or "course." In their recent translation of *The City of God,* Fathers Demetrius B. Zema and Gerald G. Walsh translated the word *procursus* with "progress" and *excursus* with "development." Do we have to assume, then, that Augustine believed that the course of the two cities on earth takes place in some form of evolutionary progress? Such an assumption appears highly improbable. For not only were the two words *procursus* and *excursus* used interchangeably throughout *The City of God* and in the description of this work in Augustine's *Retractations* (2, 69, 2),[40] but in a letter which was written shortly after the completion of *The City of God,* Augustine said explicitly that the section under discussion "sets forth the *procursus* or, as we have preferred to say, the *excursus* [of the heavenly city]." [41] In retrospect, then, Augustine himself considered the term *excursus* more adequate. To equate that word with "progress" seems very questionable, both from the linguistic point of view and in consideration of the modern connotation of this term.

The best key to the right understanding of this particular terminology seems to be provided by a passage in *The City of*

[39] E.g., *City of God,* 1, 35 B; 10, 32 U; 15, 1 D; 16, 12 A, 35 A and 43 I; 17, 1 A, 4 A and 14 A; 18, 1 A, B, C and 2 G.

[40] M. Dods, *The City of God* (1872), I, p. viii, and, following him, G. H. Hildebrand, *The Idea of Progress* (1949), 110, translated the words *excursum earum siue procursum* in *Retractat.* 69, 2, with "their history or progress."

[41] The text of this newly found letter to Firmus has been published by C. Lambot in *Revue Bénédictine* (1939), LI, 212; the passage reads: *procursum siue dicere maluimus excursum;* it has been translated by Zema and Walsh, *l.c.,* I, 400, with "its progress, or, as we might choose to say, its development."

God (15, 21 E), in which Augustine said: "The reckoning of the times [in the Scripture] begins after the two cities have been set forth, the one founded in the business of this world, the other in the hope for God, but both coming out from the common gate of mortality, which is opened in Adam, so that they might run on and run out (*procurrant et excurrant*) to their separate proper and merited ends." The history of the two cities, according to this passage, has the same starting-point, the fall of Adam; from that point they follow each its own course to the terminal point in time, the Last Judgment. Thus Augustine conceived of the historical process in the form of two tracks the courses of which have been laid out by God and are to be followed by the successive generations of the citizens of the two communities. In the terms of that figure of speech it was possible for Augustine to use the words "run on" and "run out" as synonyms and to say that the city of God on earth "proceeded in running out its course." [42]

With regard to the course of the heavenly city it may be said that there is a "progress," not of any materialistic nature, but in the sense that there is a gradual revelation of the divine truth communicated by God to man, especially through the prophecies predicting the future Messiah (see, e.g., 18, 27).[43] Augustine declared (10, 14 A): "Like the correct knowledge of an individual man, the correct knowledge of that part of mankind which belongs to the people of God, has advanced by approaches through certain epochs of time or, as it were, ages, so that it might be lifted from the temporal to the perception of the eternal and from the visible to that of the invisible." In the spiritual realm, therefore, according to Augustine, mankind has grown up from the time of its infancy through the phases of childhood, adolescence, young manhood and mature manhood to its old age (*senectus*) which has begun with

[42] *City of God,* XIX, 5 A: . . . *ista Dei civitas . . . progrederetur excursu. . . .*

[43] Cf. K. Löwith, *l.c.,* p. 172: ". . . there is only one progress: the advance toward an ever sharper distinction between faith and unbelief, Christ and Antichrist . . ." ; according to J. Daniélou, *l.c.,* 70, it was Irenaeus of Lyons who first saw that "the reason for this progression is of a pedagogical nature."

the birth of Christ. That growth of the spiritual enlightenment of the human race found its clearest expression in the scheme of "the six ages," to which Augustine alluded in the passage just quoted and into which he divided the course of the heavenly city on earth.[44] The summit has been reached with the appearance and the gospel of Christ, and no further fundamental change will take place in the spiritual realm to the end of time.

In regard to the developments in the sphere of the earthly city, Augustine emphasized repeatedly in his historical survey the mutability and the instability of human affairs. Cities, kingdoms and empires have risen and fallen throughout the course of history, and this will always be the case. For, Augustine declared (17, 13 C) "because of the mutability of things human no security will ever be given to any nation to such a degree that it should not have to fear invasions inimical to its very existence." Augustine admitted that the Roman empire had achieved more than any other state, and he granted that the pagan Romans had possessed certain qualities which might be called virtues, though not in the full and true sense of the word. At the same time Augustine, like his pupil Orosius, maintained that for many centuries the Roman empire was involved in a process of moral disintegration, in a decline which had started long before the times of Christ and Augustus.[45]

Eusebius and the other Christian progressivists of the fourth century had strongly stressed the coincidence of the birth of Christ and the reign of Augustus, for they saw the counterpart of the religious summit in the erection of the "eternal" Roman empire and in the establishment of the "universal" *Pax Romana.* Whereas that observation occupied a central position in their conceptions of history, Augustine passed over it in a single sentence, by simply stating (18, 46 A): "While Herod reigned in Judaea and, after the change of the republican government, Caesar Augustus was emperor in Rome and paci-

[44] See *City of God,* 15 C A; 16, 24 F and 43 G; 22, 30 O–P; the most detailed exposition of that scheme is to be found in Augustine's treatise *De Genesi contra Manichaeos,* I, 23–24, in Migne, *Patrologia Latina,* XXXIV, 190–194; cf. W. M. Green, *l.c.,* 320–327.

[45] Besides many passages in *The City of God,* see a letter written by Augustine in the year 412 (*Epist.* 138).

fied the world, Christ, man manifest out of a human virgin, God hidden out of God the Father, was born of Judah in Bethlehem." Whereas according to Eusebius and his followers the history of man had taken a fresh start at that time and had "progressed" toward a new culminating-point under Constantine, when the Roman empire reached the fulfillment of its mission by becoming Christian, Augustine stopped his historical account precisely with the appearance of Christ. To him the period following that event and extending to his own days and to the end to come, was not a modern era but it was "the *senectus* of the old man, the last age in which the new man is born who now lives according to the spirit." [46] God has revealed all the truth that is to be communicated to man in this world, and henceforth the history of both the heavenly and the earthly cities has no fundamentally new lessons to teach. Augustine did not share the optimism of Eusebius and others; on the contrary, he spoke of his own era as "this malignant world, these evil days" (18, 49 A), and he reckoned even with the possibility of future persecutions of the Church and the faith (18, 52). He reminded his readers (16, 24 H) that, according to Christ's own words, the terminal period of history will not be an era of secular peace and earthly prosperity but just the opposite: "About the end of this world the faithful shall be in great perturbation and tribulation, of which the Lord has said in the Gospel: 'For then shall be great tribulation, such as was not since the beginning of the world to this time, no, nor ever shall be' (*Matthew*, 24, 21)."

In Augustine's opinion, then, there is no true "progress" to be found in the course of human history. He was, of course, well aware of the fact that "the human genius has invented and put to practical use many and great arts . . . and that human industry has made wonderful and stupefying advances" (22, 24 K–L). But at the same time he pointed out a fact which has been overlooked all too often by believers in the blessings of material progress, the fact that the ingenuity and the inventiveness of man have also their destructive aspects: "And for the

[46] Augustine, *De Genesi contra Manichaeos,* I, 23, 40, in Migne, *l.c.,* XXXIV, 192.

injury of men, how many kinds of poison, how many weapons and machines of destruction have been invented." This dual aspect of the development of human history results from the very nature of the forces determining its course. "In this river or torrent of the human race," Augustine said toward the end of *The City of God* (22, 24 A), "two things run the course together, the evil which is derived from the parent [Adam], and the good which is bestowed by the Creator."

13

Aponius and Orosius on the Significance of the Epiphany*

IN the history of the feasts of Christmas and Epiphany, the early fifth century marks an important period.[1] By that time, the Roman practice of celebrating the birth of Christ on

* Reprinted from *Late Classical and Mediaeval Studies in Honor of Albert Mathias Friend, Jr.*, Kurt Weitzmann, ed. (Princeton, N.J.: Princeton University Press, 1955), pp. 96–111.

1 The interest in the topic and the idea for this article grew out of a number of highly stimulating conversations concerning questions of the Western and Eastern liturgy, which I had during the last few years with Albert M. Friend and Ernst Kantorowicz. On the general history of the development of these two festivals, see esp. H. Usener, *Das Weihnachtsfest,* Bonn 1889 (reprinted in *Religionsgeschichtliche Untersuchungen,* 2nd ed., I, Bonn 1911); K. Holl, "Der Ursprung des Epiphanienfestes," *Gesammelte Aufsätze zur Kirchengeschichte,* Tübingen 1928, II, 123–154; B. Botte, *Les origines de la Noël et de l'Epiphanie,* Louvain 1938; K. Prüm, "Zur Entstehung der Geburtsfeier des Herrn in Ost und West," *Stimmen der Zeit,* 135 (1939), pp. 207–225; H. Lietzmann, *Geschichte der alten Kirche,* Berlin 1938, III, 321–329 (English translation by B. L. Woolf, London 1950, III, 314–322); A. Strittmatter, "Christmas and the Epiphany, Origins and Antecedents," *Thought,* XVII (1942), 600–626; O. Cullmann, *Weihnachten in der alten Kirche,* Basel 1947; H. Frank, "Frühgeschichte und Ursprung des römischen Weihnachtsfestes im Lichte neuerer Forschung," *Archiv für Liturgiewissenschaft,* II (1952), 1–24 (with an excellent critical bibliography); H. Engberding, "Der 25. Dezember als Tag der Feier der Geburt des Herrn," *Archiv für Liturgiewissenschaft,* II, 25–43; C. Mohrmann, *Epiphania,* Nijmegen 1953.

December 25 [2] had found an almost general acceptance both in the Western and the Eastern churches, above all in Antioch and Constantinople.[3] In only a few of the oriental provinces, for instance in Egypt [4] and Palestine,[5] the faithful still adhered, and continued to do so for some time to come, to their old custom of commemorating the birth of Christ on January 6, a practice observed even today in Armenia.[6]

As for the significance of the feast of the Epiphany, however, two entirely different traditions had started to devèlop in the Christian world by the beginning of the fifth century. On the one hand, the Church of Rome had made the decision that the day of January 6 should be dedicated almost exclusively to the commemoration of the adoration of Christ by the Magi; [7] this view was shared by St. Augustine, who, in all of his six sermons on the feast of the Epiphany, preached that this was the day on which Christ had been worshiped by the three Magi from the East and was thus "manifested to the firstlings of the gentiles." [8] On the other hand, in most of the remaining parts of

[2] See esp. Lietzmann, *op. cit.*, p. 317; Strittmatter, *op. cit.*, pp. 609–617; Cullmann, *op. cit.*, pp. 19–24; F. Dölger, "Natalis solis invicti und das christliche Weihnachtsfest," *Antike und Christentum*, VI (Münster 1950), 23–30; Frank, *op. cit.*, pp. 4–15.

[3] See Usener, *op. cit.*, pp. 215–227, 240–266; Strittmatter, *op. cit.*, pp. 600–604; Botte, *op. cit.*, pp. 22–24, 27–31; Cullmann, *op. cit.*, pp. 24–26.

[4] See Botte, *op. cit.*, pp. 11 f.; Strittmatter, *op. cit.*, pp. 604 f.

[5] O. Heiming, "Die Entwicklung der Feier des 6. Januar zu Jerusalem im 5. und 6. Jahrhundert," *Jahrbuch für Liturgiewissenschaft*, IX (1929), 144–148; cf. Holl, *op. cit.*, pp. 126 f., 156 f.; Botte, *op. cit.*, pp. 13–21; Strittmatter, *op. cit.*, pp. 604–608.

[6] See K. Holl, *op. cit.*, p. 126, n. 1; Botte, *op. cit.*, pp. 30 f.

[7] On the reasons for that decision, see Strittmatter, *op. cit.*, pp. 624–626; Cullmann, *op. cit.*, pp. 19–24; cf. also the eight Epiphany sermons preached by Pope Leo the Great (*Sermones* 31–38), which were thoroughly analyzed by E. Flicoteaux, "L'Epiphanie du Seigneur," *Ephemerides Liturgicae*, XLIX (1935), 401–412.

[8] Augustine, *Sermones* (ed. Migne, *Pat. Lat.*, XXXVIII, cols. 1026–1039; translated by T. C. Lawler, *St. Augustine's Sermons for Christmas and Epiphany*, London 1952, pp. 154–182); cf. Holl, *op. cit.*, p. 135; Botte, *op. cit.*, pp. 39 f.; Frank, *op. cit.*, p. 15.—See esp. *Serm.* 204, 12 (ed. Migne, col. 1038; translat. by Lawler, p. 180): *Oportebat itaque nos, hoc est ecclesiam, quae congregatur ex gentibus, huius diei celebrationem, quo est Christus primitiis gentium manifestatus, illius diei celebrationi, quo Christus ex Iudaeis natus, adiungere et tanti sacramenti memoriam geminata solemnitate servare;* cf. J. Leclercq, "Aux origines du cycle de Noël," *Ephemerides Liturgicae*, LX 1946, 7–26.

Christendom, the feast of the Epiphany was given a much more far-reaching and deeper meaning than the Church of Rome and St. Augustine were willing to grant to it. As Dom Anselm Strittmatter has said, the day of January 6 "became in the East, once the Western feast of December 25 had been introduced, the commemoration of Christ's Baptism and in addition to Easter a day set aside for the public baptism of the catechumens." [9] To the present day, the Eastern Christian churches celebrate on the day of the Epiphany primarily the memory of Christ's baptism on the Jordan River and the establishment of the sacrament of baptism.[10] In the West, however, the Church of Rome, supported by the great authority of St. Augustine, was gradually, in the course of the following centuries, to succeed in enforcing the almost complete exclusion of the liturgical commemoration both of Christ's baptism and of the foundation of the sacrament itself, and in reducing the significance of the feast of the Epiphany to the celebration of the adoration of the Magi.[11]

But around the year 400 this Roman conception of the feast, though clearly stated, was as yet by no means universally accepted by the Christians of the occidental world. Most of the important churches—including Milan under the leadership of St. Ambrose, Spain, Gaul, and Ireland—still continued the practice of solemnizing on January 6 the baptism of Christ, as well as the adoration of the Magi and the miracle of Cana.[12] This state of affairs is best illustrated by a remark which John Cassian made in his *Conferences,* written between the years 420 and 428. He observed that in Egypt "the priests regard

[9] Strittmatter, *op. cit.,* p. 623; see also Holl, *op. cit.,* p. 124; Botte, *op. cit.,* pp. 82 f.

[10] On this development in the Eastern churches, see esp. Holl. *op. cit.,* pp. 124–133; Botte, *op. cit.,* pp. 24 f., 27–31; Strittmatter, *op. cit.,* p. 623 and notes 86 and 87.

[11] See Holl, *op. cit.,* pp. 133–136.

[12] See Holl, *op. cit.,* pp. 133, n. 4, 135–142; H. Frank, "Zur Geschichte von Weihnachten und Epiphanie," *Jahrbuch für Liturgiewissenschaft,* XIII (1933), 10–23, 36–38; Frank, "Das mailändische Kirchenjahr in den Werken des hl. Ambrosius," *Pastor Bonus,* LI (1940), 42 f.; Frank, "Hodie caelesti sponso iuncta est ecclesia," *Odo Casel-Gedenkschrift,* Düsseldorf (1951), pp. 192–226; Lietzmann, *op. cit.,* pp. 316–318; Strittmatter, *op. cit.,* pp. 609, 624, n. 89; Botte, *op. cit.,* pp. 40 ff.

the Epiphany as the time both of our Lord's baptism and of His birth in the flesh, and consequently they celebrate the commemoration of either mystery on the single festival of this day, and not separately as in the western provinces." [13] From the last part of this statement, it becomes evident that John Cassian believed that in the Western churches of that time the celebration of Christ's baptism was just as generally observed on the day of the Epiphany as the celebration of Christ's birth was universally observed in them on Christmas Day.

In view of the basic divergence of opinion concerning the significance of the Epiphany, which existed within the church as a whole at the beginning of the fifth century, it may be warranted to introduce into the discussion of the problem two passages which, it seems, have not hitherto gained sufficient attention in this connection. Both of the authors of these passages, Aponius and Orosius, wrote in the early fifth century, both held views which differed widely from those held by the Church of Rome and by St. Augustine, and finally both of them attempted in a most curious fashion to relate the Epiphany of Christ to events in the realm of secular history, which took place in the reign of the Emperor Augustus.

Aponius is a rather obscure figure among the early theologians of the church.[14] His name, it seems, is not mentioned by

[13] Johannes Cassianus, *Conlatio,* x, 2 (ed. M. Petschenig, *Corpus Scriptorum Ecclesiasticorum Latinorum,* xiii, 2, Vienna 1886, 286): . . . peracto Epiphaniorum die, quem illius prouinciae [i.e. Egypt] sacerdotes uel dominici baptismatis uel secundum carnem natiuitatis esse definiunt et idcirco utriusque sacramenti sollemnitatem, non bifarie ut in occiduis prouinciis, sed sub una diei huius festiuitate concelebrant . . . ; English translation by E. C. S. Gibson, in *The Nicene and Post-Nicene Fathers,* 2nd series, xi (1894), 401; see Strittmatter, *op. cit.,* pp. 604 f.

[14] See esp. J. Witte, *Der Kommentar des Aponius zum Hohenliede,* Dissertation Erlangen 1903; cf. A. Hauck, "Aponius," *Realencyclopädie für protestantische Theologie und Kirche,* 3d ed. (1896), i, 757 f. (*ibid.,* 1913, xxiii, 106); A. Harnack, "Vicarii Christi vel Dei bei Aponius," *Delbrück-Festschrift,* Berlin 1908, pp. 37–46; O. Bardenhever, *Geschichte der altkirchlichen Literatur,* Freiburg 1924, iv, 601–603; A. Miller, "Aponius," *Lexikon für Theologie und Kirche,* i (1930), 574; A. Harnack, *Lehrbuch der Dogmengeschichte,* 5th ed., Tübingen 1932, ii, 248, n. 1, 304, n. 1, 309, 310, n. 1, 316, n. 2, 361; iii, 31, n. 1; P. Courcelle, *Les lettres Grecques en Occident de Macrobe à Cassiodore,* 2nd ed., Paris 1948, pp. 128 f.; M. L. W. Laistner, "Some Early Medieval Commentaries on the Old

any contemporary source, nor can any reference to his only extant work, *In Canticum Canticorum explanationis libri XII*,[15] be found before the eighth and ninth centuries when the Venerable Bede [16] and Angelomus of Luxeuil [17] made use of it in their own commentaries on *The Song of Songs.* Internal evidence offered by the *Explanatio* appears, however, to allow the conclusion that Aponius was a Syrian of Jewish origin, who went into the western part of the Empire and composed his work there, probably in Rome, between the years 405 and 415.

In the last book (XII) of the *Explanatio,* Aponius commented at great length on the passage in *The Song of Songs* (8: 10) which reads: "I am a wall and my breasts like towers; then I was in his eyes as one that found peace." [18] In Aponius' opinion this passage represents a prefiguration of Christ because here, he said, "is introduced the voice of that speaking soul through which that peace was spread over the lands, which would put to flight the wrath of wars and wretched struggles." [19] Aponius

---

Testament," *Harvard Theological Review,* XLVI (1953), 39–45. E. Dekkers, *Clavis patrum Latinorum* (1951), p. 32, n. 194, says of Aponius: "natione Syrus, floruit in Italia circa 405–415 secundum communiorem sententiam; potius vero cum J. H. Baxter and P. Grosjean, Hibernus saec. VII aestimandus est"; it remains to be seen how these two scholars will prove that this later date and the Irish origin of Aponius should displace the hitherto accepted view.

15 The first complete edition of this work was published under the above title by H. Bottino and J. Martini, Rome 1843.

16 Beda Venerabilis, *In Cantica Canticorum allegorica expositio,* referred twice to Aponius' commentary (Migne, *Pat. Lat.,* 91, col. 1112A and col. 1162C); see Witte, *op. cit.,* p. 3.

17 On Angelomus' use of Aponius' commentary, see Laistner, *op. cit.,* pp. 40 ff.

18 *Canticus Canticorum,* 8: 10: Ego murus, et ubera mea sicut turris, ex quo facta sum coram eo, quasi pacem reperiens. In the King James version, the last words are translated "as one that found favour"; but the context of Aponius' interpretation makes it necessary to translate the word *pax* with "peace."

19 Aponius, *op. cit.,* p. 233: Quidquid igitur in mysterio praefiguratum est, in omnium gentium, in sanctorum persona, a capite huius cantici usque ad praesentem versiculum, intelligitur esse completum; nunc vero quae sequuntur, proprie singularis electae per quam diabolus victus est et humanum genus de eius manibus liberatum est, animae vox loquentis inducitur per quam pax terris infusa est, quae iram bellorum et nequissima iurgia effugaret.

centered his whole exposition of this passage on the theme of peace: "Just as at the time of the birth of Christ the angels proclaim peace to men of good will (Luke 2:14), and just as Christ, according to the power of divinity, is all things to men, being God of gods, Lord of lords, King of kings, Prince of princes, Prophet of prophets, Anointed of the anointed, Judge of judges, Emperor of emperors, Saint of saints, Martyr of martyrs, so now according to the nature of the flesh, He asserted with proof and reason that He himself is 'the Wall of walls.' "[20] Aponius declared that the peace taught by Christ "is not the peace and perpetual tranquillity which the saints will enjoy after the end of this secular world, of which the prophet said (Psalm 37:11): 'The meek shall inherit the earth and shall delight themselves in the abundance of peace' . . . , but it ought to be understood as the peace of re-atonement found again between God and man."[21] Aponius' interpretation of the passage in *The Song of Songs* concluded by attributing to the peace, given to man through the birth of Christ, still another meaning—one which lay outside the strictly spiritual sphere. By the very fact that Christ assumed a human body and "*in humanitate* died most voluntarily for those who hate peace," Aponius said, "it was shown to the world that not only a peace of souls illuminates the world." He proved this point by con-

[20] *Ibid.*, p. 233: Sicut in eius nativitate Angeli nuntiant pacem in terris hominibus bonae voluntatis et sicut secundum divinitatis potentiam omnia hominibus Christus est ut Deus deorum, et Dominus dominorum, et Rex regum, Princeps principum, et Propheta prophetarum, et Christus christorum, et Judex judicum, et Imperator imperatorum, et Sanctus sanctorum, et Martyr martyrum, ita nunc secundum carnis naturam, pro loco vel causa, asseruit se Murum esse murorum.

[21] *Ibid.*, p. 236: Docuit utique non illam pacem perpetuamque tranquillitatem, quam fruituri sunt sancti post huius saeculi finem, de qua dixit propheta: "Mansueti possidebant terram et delectabuntur in multitudine pacis"; sed tantam, quam possit capere mundus, se reperisse nascendo pronuntiat, non illam quam iudicando daturus est dignis, sed illam quam iudicatus ab indignis reperit mundo. Non enim inconcussa pax est nec pacis est multitudo, ubi innumerabilia et antiqua bella grassantur quotidie; ubi dicitur: Vae mundo a scandalis; ubi in colluctatione positi sunt fideles; ubi non coronantur, nisi qui legitime certaverint; ubi adiutorii auxilia a bellatoribus quotidie implorantur; sed illa intelligitur repropitiationis pax, inter Deum et hominem reperta, per quod docuit a protoplasto Adam usque ad partum Virginis, bellum fuisse inter Creatorem et creaturam.

tinuing: "When the Roman Empire was exalted, foreign as well as civil wars were laid to rest and all peoples, civilized and barbarian, rejoice in the peace which has been found; since that time, the race of men wherever on earth it is located, is bound together by one bond of peace." [22] Aponius supported this argument as follows: "On the day of His *apparitio,* which is called the Epiphany, Caesar Augustus, after his return from Britain, announced to the Roman people during the spectacles, as Livy says, that the whole world was subjugated in the abundance of peace to the Roman Empire, by means of war as well as through alliances." [23] As an example of that pacification of the world, Aponius pointed to the fact that "when at that time, at the instigation of the Devil, wars broke out in Syria, it is proved that they were settled as quickly as possible through the intervention of peace, that is, through the presence of Christ." [24] Aponius concluded in this way: "In His indescribable *fabrica* was fulfilled the prophecy predicted by David (Psalm 72, 3 and 7): 'The mountains shall bring peace and the hills righteousness,' and 'In his days shall righteousness flourish and abundance of peace.' " [25] If any of his readers still doubted that the peace established on earth through the birth of Christ had also to be interpreted in a secular sense, Aponius stated explicitly that "the gift of peace, which the Creator has given us through the re-atonement," manifested itself in the sphere of earthly kings

[22] *Ibid.,* p. 237: Reperit pacem, inter Deum et homines mediatrix existens, cum ex altero latere Deo Verbo Patris, ex altero immaculatae carni coniungitur, cum vere vivit in deitate in patibulo Crucis et vere pro odientibus pacem libentissime moritur in humanitate. Nam ex quo facta est et mundo ostensa, non solum animarum pax illuminat mundum, sed publica etiam civilia, Romano imperio exaltato, bella sopita pacem omnium gentium barbarorum repertam exultant: et omnium hominum genus, quocumque terrarum loco obtinet sedem, ex eo tempore uno illigatur vinculo pacis.

[23] *Ibid.:* In cuius apparitionis die, quod Epiphania appellatur, Caesar Augustus in spectaculis, sicut Livius narrat, Romano populo nuntiat regressus a Britannia insula, totum orbem terrarum tam bello quam amicitiis Romano imperio pacis abundantia subditum.

[24] *Ibid.:* Ex quo tempore etiam et Syrorum, instigante diabolo, bella oriuntur; tamen interveniente pace, hoc est Christi praesentia, quantocius sedari probantur.

[25] *Ibid.:* In cuius fabrica inenarrabili completum illud propheticum, quod praedixit David: "Suscipiant montes pacem, et colles iustitiam"; et "orietur in diebus eius iustitia et abundantia pacis."

and judges. To be sure, Aponius granted that "there are still some kings who, in their desire for money, break the peace, and there are still judges who dispense justice blinded by bribes." Nevertheless, he asserted, "they do not rage as insanely and revel as much in evil as kings and judges of diverse peoples used to do before the coming of Christ, as we learn from the histories of ancient times; for how much so ever the aforesaid judges vent their fury against their subjects, or the most cruel kings wage wars among one another, still they are prevented, even against their own will, from their evil intentions by Christ, the author of peace, on account of the misery of the helpless and the lamentations of the poor and innocent who invoke Him." [26] This invocation led Aponius to the discussion of the next verse in *The Song of Songs* (8:11), telling of Solomon's vineyard, which does not concern us here.

It has seemed necessary to quote rather extensively from the text of Aponius' discussion of the nature of the peace established by Christ on earth because his remarks raise several interesting questions. In the first place, which event in Christ's life did Aponius have in mind when he spoke of "the day of his *apparitio*, which is called Epiphany"? From the context it is evident that he meant the day of Christ's birth. For twice, once at the beginning of his comment on that verse in *The Song of Songs* and also a few lines before he discussed the earthly peace, he quoted the annunciation of the angels to the shepherds, which he explicitly declared to have taken place *in eius nativitate* (or *in eius ortu*).[27] Furthermore, in the whole context there

[26] *Ibid.:* Quod utique in regibus et iudicibus terrae accipiendum est. Qui, ex quo facta est saepedicta gloriosa anima, quae nobis Creatorem repropitiando pacis munus donavit, et reges inter se pacis dulcedinem et iudices iustitiae obtinent suavitatem. Quamvis enim, ut diximus, fame pecuniae perurgente, nonnulli reges pacem irrumpant vel iudices excaecati muneribus solvant iustitiam, tamen non usque adeo ita insaniunt vel debacchantur in malis, sicut ante eius adventum fecisse reges et iudices diversarum gentium antiquitatum historiis edocemur. Quantumvis igitur saeviant contra subiectos praedicti iudices vel contra se crudelissimi reges bella indicant, prohibentur licet inviti a malis intentionibus a pacis auctore Christo propter miseriam inopum gemitumque pauperum vel innocentum invocantium eum.

[27] See above, note 20, and Aponius, *op. cit.*, p. 236: Quae magnitudine humilitatis suae sola inter Creatorem Deum et hominem, quem utrumque

is to be found not the slightest reference either to the adoration of the Magi or to Christ's baptism by John. It is certain, therefore, that to Aponius the word Epiphany, or its Latin equivalent *apparitio,* signified the birth of Christ in the flesh. The same meaning, then, must hold true for another passage of the *Explanatio,* namely the one in which Aponius dealt with the verse in *The Song of Songs* (7:1) which reads: "How beautiful are thy feet with shoes, O prince's daughter." After associating this verse with the words of Isaiah (52:7): "How beautiful upon the mountains are the feet of him that announces peace and preaches salvation," he commented upon the two passages as follows: "Undoubtedly these are the beautiful steps of the Church, which, by her instructive speech, were the first to announce to the Roman people the salvation of the soul and the peace of the body: for the histories of wars teach that the cruel conflicts between nations ceased *in Christi apparitione.*" [28]

It is thus apparent that this theologian of the early fifth century, presumably a Syrian living in Rome, employed the word Epiphany in a sense which was in accord neither with the usage of the Church of Rome nor with that of the Church of Antioch. In the Church of Rome Epiphany meant the commemoration of the adoration of the Magi; in the Church of Antioch, ever since St. John Chrysostom's famous sermon on the Baptism, "not that day on which Christ was born but rather the one on which he was baptized was called Epiphany." [29] In

---

gestabat, pacem reperit et inventam Angelorum ore tradidit mundo nascendo . . . clamantibus Angelis in eius ortu: "Gloria in excelsis Deo, et in terra pax hominibus bonae voluntatis." See also *ibid.,* p. 99: Et quis alius potest intelligi pacificus nisi Christus Redemptor noster? Qui secundum apostolum Paulum pacificavit "quae in coelo sunt, et quae in terra" (Ephes. 1:10), et reconciliavit Deo Patri humanum genus per sanguinem assumpti hominis sui. Cuius in adventu pacem terris nuntiavit Angelorum exercitus; qui reversurus ad coelum pacem viaticum suis Apostolis dereliquit dicendo: "Pacem meam do vobis, pacem meam relinquo vobis." (John 14:27)

[28] *Ibid.,* p. 192: Hi sunt procul dubio pulchri gressus ecclesiae, qui primi suo sermone doctrinae plebi Romanae salutem animae et pacem corporis annuntiaverunt; quoniam proeliorum historiae docent in Christi apparitione cessasse crudelia gentium bella.

[29] Migne, *Pat. Gr.,* XLIX, 365; on this sermon see Usener, *op. cit.,* pp. 238 f., Strittmatter, *op. cit.,* pp. 601 ff., and esp. H. Frank, *Jahrbuch für Liturgiewissenschaft,* XIII (1933), 5, n. 22, who argues that whoever followed the trend

maintaining a view of the Epiphany at variance with the usages of the Churches of Rome and Antioch, Aponius may have felt justified by knowledge of the fact that in the preceding fourth century such authorities as Ephraim the Syrian and Epiphanius of Cyprus had regarded the Epiphany as the feast of Christ's birth, and that in his own day the same view was still held in the Church of Jerusalem.[30]

In Aponius' opinion, the day of the Epiphany marked the most important date in the history of mankind, in the spiritual realm as well as in the secular. The peace which the angels announced to men at the birth of Christ has to be understood not only as "the peace of re-atonement found again between God and man" [31] or as "the peace of the soul," [32] but also as "the peace of the body." [33] To prove this latter point, Aponius referred explicitly to "the histories of ancient times," [34] which, he declared, "teach that the cruel wars of the nations ceased at the appearance of Christ." [35] For a specific example of that pacifying effect of Christ's "presence" on earth, he chose the quick settlement of the Syrian wars.[36]

But Aponius went still further and saw an even closer and more direct connection between the establishment of the spiritual and earthly peace brought about by Christ's appearance. On the very day of the Epiphany, on which Christ was born,[37]

---

of thought set forth by John Chrysostom after the introduction of the Christian festival on the 25th of December "durfte den Namen *apparitio* = ἐπιφάνεια nicht mehr der Geburt Christi zukommen lassen, weil bei dieser Christus verborgen gewesen und nicht erschienen sei."

[30] See Epiphanius of Salamis, *Haereses*, 51, 22, 3 (quoted in translation by Strittmatter, *op. cit.*, pp. 617 f.); cf. Holl, *op. cit.*, p. 146, n. 6; p. 147, n. 1; Botte, *op. cit.*, pp. 21 ff.

[31] See above note 21.

[32] See above note 22: *animarum pax*.

[33] See the passage (above note 28) in which Aponius juxtaposed the terms *salutem animae* and *pacem corporis*.

[34] See the phrase (above note 26): *antiquitatum historiis edocemur*.

[35] See above note 28; cf. note 19: . . . *pax terris infusa est, quae iram bellorum et nequissima iurgia effugaret*.

[36] See above note 24.

[37] Schneidewin, *op. cit.*, p. 46, denied that Aponius asserted this actual coincidence of the two events on the same day; but Witte, *op. cit.*, p. 36, noted rightly that "Aponius nicht meint, diese Friedensverkündigung des Augustus habe an irgendeiner Jahrestagswiederkehr der Erscheinung Christi stattgefunden, sondern an dem Tage, an welchem die Epiphanie

he declared, the Emperor Augustus "announced to the Roman people . . . that the whole world was subjugated to the Roman empire in the abundance of peace, by means of war as well as through alliances." [38] Whether or not there actually existed in Livy's *Ab Urbe Condita* a statement to that effect, as Aponius claimed, need not concern us in this connection; likewise, it does not matter that the passage in Livy, even if it is authentic as it seems likely, must be referred to a much earlier date, the year 24 B.C.[39] What is important, however, is that Aponius believed it to be an undeniable historical fact that the birth of Christ in Bethlehem and the proclamation of universal peace made by Augustus in Rome were events which took place on the same day.

With this expression of the belief in the providential coincidence between the appearance of Christ and the establishment of the Pax Romana on earth, Aponius placed himself within an old and very common tradition of Christian thought.[40] Ever since Bishop Melito of Sardis and Tertullian, the early Christian thinkers had strongly emphasized the fact that the birth of Christ occurred at the time of the foundation of the Roman empire by Augustus, and after the triumph of Christianity under Constantine, the champions of the faith, led by Eusebius and other theologians of the fourth century, had stressed the providential character of that coincidence with even greater conviction than ever before. As we have seen, Aponius did not hesitate, in the passage just quoted and in another place,[41] to use the Biblical phrase "abundance of peace" in reference to the peace established by Augustus. According to the original tradition, as represented by Irenaeus, Tertullian, and Lactantius, these words of the Psalm 72:7: "In his days shall righteousness flourish and abundance of peace," were to be

---

wirklich geschah, denn er redet von den Veränderungen, welche die Menschwerdung Christi hervorgerufen habe."

[38] See above note 23.

[39] I have dealt with this problem in an article "Augustus and Britain: A Fragment from Livy?," *American Journal of Philology,* LXXV, 1954, 175–183.

[40] See my article on "St. Augustine and the Christian Idea of Progress," *Journal of the History of Ideas,* XII (1951), 346–374. [See above, pp. 265–298.]

[41] See above note 25.

understood as predictions of the future Messianic Kingdom. But in delineating his own bluntly secular interpretation, Aponius could feel supported by the fact that some of the greatest ecclesiastical authorities of the third and fourth centuries, including Origen, Eusebius of Caesarea, John Chrysostom, Ambrose, and Jerome, had explained that prophecy of the psalmist in terms of the Pax Romana and its earthly achievements.[42]

Aponius found still another Biblical reference which, he believed, illustrated the role assigned to the Roman Empire in the plan of divine providence. In commenting on the passage in *The Song of Songs* (4:16): "Awake, O north wind; and come, thou south; blow upon my garden, that the spices thereof may flow out," he maintained that "just as the rigor of the north wind and the warmth of the south wind, through the tempering of the air, effect the growth of fruit in paradise," [43] so there existed also in the secular sphere the need for "a tempered air," to be brought about by the coexistence of, or rather the conflict between, two opposite elements. "While the almighty God," declared Aponius, "exalts above all kingdoms of the world the kingdom of the north wind, which is the kingdom of the Romans, He commands the prophets to arise, lifting them up from the south and bringing forth through the Virgin His Christ of whom the prophets sang that He would come from the South, as the prophet Habakkuk says: 'God will come from the South.' " [44] Aponius considered the persecutions of the Christians to be the work of the Devil who operated through the Roman Empire. Nevertheless, in his opinion, "the evil

[42] See [above, pp. 282–285].

[43] Aponius, *op. cit.*, p. 136: "Surge Aquilo et veni Auster, perfla hortum meum, et fluent aromata illius"; ut rigor Aquilonis et calor Austri temperato aere efficiant poma paradiso provenire, quo possint commixto rigore tribulationis, non inane nimio securitatis calore baccae animarum paradisi defluere ad terrenos actus delapsae.

[44] *Ibid.*: Exaltando igitur regnum Aquilonis super omnia regna orbis terrarum omnipotens Deus, quod est regnum Romanum, surgere iubet suscitando ab austro prophetas, ostendendo Christum suum per Virginem, quem prophetae ab austro cecinerunt venturum, ut ait Abacuc propheta: "Deus ab austro veniet," idest sermo Patris: "Et sanctus de monte umbroso" (Habakkuk, 3:3), qui assumptus intelligitur homo, et condenso intactoque corpore processisse.

spirit of the north wind," with all the harm wrought by it, worked, "though unknowingly," for the ultimate good of mankind. "In the struggles," Aponius asserted, "which the north wind and the south wind, that is, infidelity and faith, impiety and piety, the spirit of sorrow and that of consolation, fought against each other, while the bride [i.e., the Church] looked on, it is proved that the precious fragrant liquid, the blood of the martyrs, was shed." From this point of view, Aponius found it meaningful that the Roman Empire or, as he said, "the kingdom of the north wind, is permitted to arise, like a very harsh wind, above all other kingdoms." [45]

In this way Aponius assigned to the Roman power a role which differed considerably from the peace-giving mission he ascribed to it in his comment on the later verse in *The Song of Songs* (8:10). Both passages, however, reveal with equal clarity how deeply Aponius was convinced that the universal dominion of Rome occupied a central position in the divine plan of his-

[45] *Ibid.*, pp. 137–138: Sed quia gloriosus fructus occultus erat populo nascituro et suavitatis odor, quem per amicitias diaboli amiserat imparentis, aliter non poterat nisi per eius inimicitias reparari, permittitur regnum aquilonis veluti durissimus ventus surgere super omnia regna. In quo diabolus glutinatus durissimi praecepti flamine contritioneque poenarum ad subtilitatem spiritalis sensus redactas credentium Christo animas, ut tempestas decussis corporibus interficiendo, pretiosa aromata paradiso fudit. Lex enim vel Evangeliorum doctrina, ab Austro spiritalem virtutem suo calore inspirans, humanis mentibus ut arbusculis indidit dulcissimi succi medullam; quam Aquilonis immundus spiritus super regnum Romanorum manibus truculentium sanctorum corpora laniando ad odorem suavitatis nesciens coelorum virtutibus ut aromata perfruendam produxit. . . . Pugnantibus igitur Aquilone et Austro, id est infidelitate et fide, impietate et pietate, moeroris spiritu et consolationis, inter se, spectante sponsa, pretiosus aromaticus liquor martyrum sanguis fluxisse probatur. Agit namque horticuli vice nesciens satanas, qui vere ut damnaticius obcoecatus malitia et suo crudeli labore hortum Domini aromaticis sanctorum floribus picturavit. Laboravit in malo eius famulos persequendo, qui in bonis suo Creatori servire contempsit. Ex quo enim per regnum Romanorum quasi perturbatum ab Aquilone, coepit persequutionis lolium serere et rastris ungularum diversisque poenarum ferramentis sanctorum effodere carnes, immanem copiam pomorum iustitiae diverso meritorum sapore paradisus exuberat. Ibi namque martyrum confessorum, virginum, continentium, gratissimi iustitiae fructus; ibi virentia gramina castissimae copulae lege concessa, diversi sexus vel aetatis credentium Christo, dulcissima poma meritorum de animae voluntate prolata.

tory. In stating this conviction he remained in accordance with the views held by many of the most prominent Greek and Latin theologians of both his own and earlier times.[46] Only in one respect did he go further than those thinkers had gone. They stressed merely the providential character of the fact that the birth of Christ had taken place sometime during the reign of the founder of the Augustan peace. Aponius believed himself capable, mistakenly to be sure, of proving from a passage in Livy's *Ab Urbe Condita* that the earthly peace had actually been proclaimed on the day of the Epiphany, the very day of the birth of the founder of "the peace of re-atonement found again between God and men."

When we turn to Orosius' *Seven Books of Histories against the Pagans,* we find there at the end of the sixth book (VI, 20, 1-2), in the account of the deeds of Augustus, the following passage: "In the seven hundred and twenty-fifth year after the founding of the City, when Caesar Augustus was consul for the fifth time and the other consul was L. Apuleius, Caesar returned as conqueror from the East and entered the city in triple triumph on the sixth of January. It was at that time when all the civil wars had been laid to rest and brought to an end, that he first ordered the closing of the gates of Janus. It was at that time, too, that he was first saluted as Augustus. This title . . . signifies that such seizure of the supreme rule over the world was legitimate; and from that time on the sum of all things and powers began to rest in the hands of one man and remained there, [a form of government] which the Greeks call

[46] The fact that Aponius' views on this particular point conformed so closely to the opinions of many of the prominent theologians of the fourth century speaks in favor of the assumption that he composed his work in the early fifth century and not as late as the seventh century (see above, note 14). It is worth noticing in this connection that neither Bede nor Angelomus seems to have made any reference in their commentaries on *The Song of Songs* to Aponius' interpretation of the Augustan peace and the role of the Roman Empire within the plan of divine providence, although Bede knew Aponius' whole work and Angelomus the first six books, of which he made ample use (see Laistner, *op. cit.,* pp. 40 ff.); compare Bede's commentary on *Canticus Canticorum,* 4:16 and 8:10 (Migne, *Pat. Lat.,* 91, coll. 1150 ff. and 1217) and Angelomus' commentary on *Canticus Canticorum* 4:16 (Migne, *Pat. Lat.,* 115, col. 611).

monarchy." [47] Orosius continued as follows (VI, 20, 3): "Nobody of those who believe or even of those who are opposed to the faith, is ignorant of the fact that that day, i.e. January 6, is the same day on which we observe the Epiphany, that is, the *apparitio* or *manifestatio* of the Lord's Sacrament." [48]

This passage shows clearly that the feast of the Epiphany signified to Orosius the celebration of the establishment of the sacrament of Baptism: [49] it commemorated the day on which Christ, through his baptism by John, was manifested to mankind by the voice from heaven, saying: "This is my beloved Son, in whom I am well pleased" (Matt. 3:17). For the evaluation of his view we have to remember that Orosius was a member of the Spanish church, in which he was ordained priest. It has been asserted that the celebration of Christ's baptism on the day of the Epiphany did not start in Spain before the sixth or seventh centuries.[50] The validity of these late

[47] *Orosii historiarum aduersum paganos libri vii,* ed. K. Zangemeister, *Corpus scriptorum ecclesiasticorum Latinorum,* v, Vienna 1882, 418: "Anno ab Urbe condita DCCXXV ipso imperatore Caesare Augusto quinquies et L. Apuleio consulibus Caesar uictor ab Oriente rediens, VIII idus Ianuarias Urbem triplici triumpho ingressus est ac tunc primum ipse Iani portas sopitis finitisque omnibus bellis ciuilibus clausit. Hoc die primum Augustus consalutatus est; quod nomen, cunctis antea [inuiolatum] et usque ad nunc ceteris inausum dominis, tantum Orbis licite usurpatum apicem declarat imperii, atque ex eodem die summa rerum ac potestatum penes unum esse coepit et mansit, quod Graeci monarchiam uocant." The above and later translations are, with slight modifications, those given by I. W. Raymond in his English rendering of Orosius' *Seven Books of History against the Pagans,* New York 1936, p. 310.

[48] Ed. Zangemeister, *op. cit.,* p. 418: "Porro autem hunc esse eundem diem, hoc est VIII idus Ianuarias, quo nos Epiphania, hoc est apparitionem siue manfestationem Dominici sacramenti, obseruamus, nemo credentium siue etiam fidei contradicentium nescit." Translated by Raymond, *op. cit.,* p. 310. Cf. E. v. Frauenholz, "Imperator Octavianus Augustus in der Geschichte und Sage des Mittelalters," *Historisches Jahrbuch,* XLVI (1926), 86–122; see esp. 90 ff.

[49] A parallel for Orosius' use of the phrase *Dominicum sacramentum* in the sense of "the sacrament of baptism" is offered in a later passage of *Historiarum aduersum paganos,* VII, 33, 7 (ed. Zangemeister, p. 517) in which Orosius related that Count Theodosius, the father of the emperor, before his execution *baptizari in remissionem peccatorum praeoptauit ac postquam sacramentum Christi quod quaesierat adsecutus est,* willingly died.

[50] Flicoteaux, *op. cit.,* p. 410, n. 33 (and also Botte, *op. cit.,* pp. 67 ff.) considered it likely that the celebration of Christ's baptism and of the

dates has already been questioned by some scholars on the basis of evidence from the late fourth century, especially that of a letter which Pope Siricius wrote after his election in 385 to Bishop Himerius of Tarragona.[51] As Dom Anselm Strittmatter has pointed out,[52] this letter indicates that in Spain, as well as in many other regions in the West, "January 6 was one of the days on which catechumens were publicly baptized." The passage in *The Seven Books of Histories* provides us now with the definite proof that this practice resulted from the fact that on that day the Spanish church, as Orosius said, "observed the Epiphany, that is, the *apparitio* or *manifestatio* of the Lord's sacrament." It may be noted in passing that in some of the manuscripts of Isidore of Seville's *Etymologiae* the word "Epiphany" is defined in terms which are almost identical with those used by Orosius.[53]

When Orosius made his statement concerning the Epiphany, apparently he knew quite well that St. Augustine, at whose suggestion he had undertaken, and to whom he was to dedicate his book, held a view according to which this festival commemorated merely the adoration of the Magi and not the baptism of Christ. Orosius' awareness of this divergence of opinion between himself and his master found expression in the rather

---

miracle of Cana "prirent également place dans la fête occidentale du 6 janvier, de bonne heure certainement et Italie et en Gaule (début du Ve siècle), plus tard en Espagne et en Afrique (VIe et VIIe s.)."

[51] Migne, *Pat. Lat.*, XIII, cols. 1134–1136 (ch. 2); cf. Strittmatter, *op. cit.*, p. 609.

[52] Strittmatter, *op. cit.*, p. 624.

[53] Isidore of Seville, *Etymologiae*, VI, 18, 6–7 (ed. W. M. Lindsay, I, Oxford 1911): "Epiphania Graece, Latine apparitio [sive manifestatio] (the last two words appear in three manuscripts and are omitted in three others) vocatur. Eo enim die Christus sideris indicio Magis apparuit adorandus. Quod fuit figura primitiae credentium gentium. Quo die [et] Dominici baptismatis sacramentum et permutatae in vinum aquae, factorum per Dominum signorum principia extiterunt." In his discussion of the Ephiphany in *De ecclesiasticis officiis*, I, 27, 1–3 (Migne, *Pat. Lat.*, 83, cols. 762 f.) Isidore stated likewise that the feast commemorated the adoration of the Magi, the baptism of Christ and the miracle of Cana, and declared that "it is called in Latin *apparitio vel ostensio*"; cf. P. Séjourné, "Saint Isidore de Séville et la liturgie wisigothique," *Miscellanea Isidoriana*, Rome 1936, pp. 237 f. See also Botte, *op. cit.*, pp. 50 f.: "Le terme d'*apparitio*, pour désigner l'Epiphanie, est caractéristique de la liturgie espagnole."

curious words with which he accompanied his remarks on the meaning of the feast (VI, 20, 4): "In order that we might seem to have laid it open for inquirers and not to have inflicted it upon those who disregard it, there is no reason now nor does the occasion call for a fuller discussion of this sacrament which we most faithfully observe." [54] It seems permissible to assume that Orosius, when he asserted that "we most faithfully observe this sacrament," referred to himself and the Spanish Christians, and when he said "that we might seem . . . not to have inflicted it upon those who disregard it," he alluded to St. Augustine and to everybody else who had accepted the Roman interpretation of the meaning of the feast.

When Orosius dared in such a polite and respectful but yet very determined fashion to disagree with the view held on this question by St. Augustine, he may have felt encouraged by the knowledge that his opinion was shared by the other great Latin theologian of the time, St. Jerome, whom he had just visited in Bethlehem. For St. Jerome, too, the day of the Epiphany solemnized the baptism of Christ, as he stated most explicitly in a sermon preached on the feast of the Epiphany: [55] "The day of the Epiphany is thus called by a Greek word: for what we call *apparitio* or *ostensio,* the Greeks call ἐπιφάνεια. The reason is that [on that day] our Lord and Saviour appeared on earth. Although he was born of Mary and had already reached the age of thirty, he was nevertheless not yet known to the world. He became known at that time when he came to John the Baptist in order to be baptized in the Jordan River and when

[54] Ed. Zangemeister, *op. cit.,* pp. 418 f.: "De quo nostrae istius fidelissimae obseruationis sacramento uberius nunc dicere nec ratio nec locus flagitat, ut et quaerentibus reseruasse et neglegentibus non ingessisse uideamur." Trans. by Raymond, *op. cit.,* p. 310.

[55] This sermon was published by Dom B. Capelle, *Revue Bénédictine,* XXXVI (1924), 169: "Dies epiphaniorum Graeco nomine sic uocatur: quod enim nos adparitionem seu ostensionem dicimus, hoc Graeci ἐπιφάνειαν uocant. Hoc autem ideo quia dominus noster et saluator adparuit in terris. Licet enim olim natus esset ex Maria et xxx iam annorum explesset aetatem, tamen ignoratur a mundo. Eo tempore cognitus est, quo ad Iohannem Baptistam, ut in Iordane baptizaretur, aduenit et uox de caelo patris intonantis audita est: 'Hic est filius meus dilectus, in quo mihi complacui.' " This passage is also quoted by Strittmatter, *op. cit.,* p. 607, n. 25.

the voice of the Father was heard sounding from heaven: 'This is my beloved Son, in whom I am well pleased.' " St. Jerome, it must be noted, occupied a rather interesting position in the history of the interpretations of the festivals of Christmas and the Epiphany. On the one hand, in regard to Christmas, it has rightly been said that in all likelihood he "urged the Roman feast upon his eastern friends.' " [56] On the other hand, in regard to the Epiphany, he believed that this feast commemorated primarily the baptism of Christ, signifying the spiritual rebirth as distinguished from his birth in the flesh, and thus he maintained a view which was very different from that held by the Church of Rome and by St. Augustine,[57] but conformed closely with the opinions of all of the great contemporary theologians of the Eastern church. To give just one example, St. John

[56] Strittmatter, *op. cit.*, p. 600, n. 1.

[57] The fact that St. Jerome represented the Roman point of view only in regard to the celebration of Christmas day on December 25, but not in regard to the meaning of the feast of the Epiphany, does not seem to have found sufficient attention. For instance, H. Frank, *Archiv für Liturgiewissenschaft* (1952), II, 7, noted that "der dem Papste Damasus so nahestehende heilige Hieronymous von seinem römischen Standpunkt aus (auch wenn er in Bethlehem lebte und predigte) Epiphanie als Geburtstag des Herrn kategorisch ablehnte," and in this connection Frank and also Strittmatter, *op. cit.*, p. 607, n. 24, rightly quoted the passage from the sermon preached by St. Jerome on Christmas day 410 in Bethlehem, which begins with the words (ed. Dom G. Morin, *Anecdota Maredsolana,* III, 2, Oxford 1897, 396): "Alii putant quod in Epiphaniis nascitur; non damnamus aliorum opinionem, nostram sequimur doctrinam." But neither Strittmatter nor Frank quoted the continuation of this passage, in which St. Jerome told the members of the Church of Jerusalem what his own interpretation, as opposed to theirs, was concerning the meaning of the Epiphany (ed. G. Morin, *op. cit.*, p. 397): "Nos ergo dicimus, quia hodie (i.e. on Christmas day) Christus natus est, post in Epiphaniis renatus est. Vos adstruite nobis generationem et regenerationem, vos qui dicitis in Epiphaniis natum: quando ergo accepit baptismum, nisi verum eventum dicitis, ut in eadem die natus sit et renatus?" From this passage, as well as from those quoted in notes 55 and 59, it must be concluded that St. Jerome believed, contrary to the view of the Church of Jerusalem, that the birth of Christ should be celebrated on December 25, and not on January 6; but it must also be concluded that he believed, contrary to the view of the Church of Rome, that the day of the Epiphany on January 6 was to be dedicated to the commemoration of Christ's "rebirth," that is, his baptism by John.

Chrysostom [58] used exactly the same argument which St. Jerome set forth both in the Epiphany sermon just quoted and in his *Commentaries on Ezekiel* (1:3),[59] namely, that Christ was virtually unknown to the world during the first thirty years of his life and "appeared" in the true sense of the word only on the day of his baptism, which for that reason is called the "Epiphany" in Greek, or the *apparitio* or *manifestatio* in Latin. St. Jerome, who resided at that time in the East, apparently did not feel any need for an explicit defense of his own opinion on this point against the quite different attitude taken by the Roman church. Orosius, on the other hand, who wrote in the very presence of the greatest champion of the Roman point of view, granted implicitly the existence of two different interpretations of the meaning of the Epiphany, but evidently felt himself sufficiently supported by the tradition of his own Spanish church and by St. Jerome's opinion to maintain his personal standpoint even against the authority of St. Augustine. Since we know very little about Orosius' personality, this observation may have a certain value because it enables us to see that in spite of his intimate relationship with, and tremendous respect for, St. Augustine, he endeavored to maintain his independence on issues which were important to him.

After he had given his account of the events which took place on Augustus' return to Rome on January 6 of the year 29 B.C.—the closing of the gates of Janus and the proclamation of the universal monarchy—and after he had commented upon the

[58] In his *Sermon on the Baptism* (Migne, *Pat. Gr.*, 49, col. 366), St. John Chrysostom asked: "Why is this day called the Epiphany?", and he answered this question thus: "For the reason that Christ did not become manifest to all when he was born but only then when he was baptized; for until that day he was unknown to the many." To prove the assertion that Christ was virtually unknown, St. Chrysostom quoted St. John 1:26: "There standeth one among you, whom ye know not." On this sermon of Chrysostom's, cf. Botte, *op. cit.*, pp. 22 ff.

[59] Migne, *Pat. Lat.*, xxv, col. 18 f.: "Quintam autem diem mensis (on this date see Holl, *op. cit.*, p. 124, n. 3) adjungit, ut significet baptisma, in quo aperti sunt Christo coeli, et Epiphaniorum dies huiusque venerabilis est, non, ut quidam putant, Natalis in carne; tunc enim absconditus est et non apparuit; quod huic tempori congruit, quando dictum est: 'Hic est filius meus dilectus, in quo mihi complacui.' "

meaning of the feast of the Epiphany, Orosius concluded thus: "It was right to have recorded faithfully all this, so that the empire of Caesar might be proven in every respect to have been prepared for the sake of the future coming of Christ." [60] The sentence just quoted served as the leitmotiv for a summary account of three miraculous events in the reign of Augustus, in which, according to Orosius, the hand of God manifested itself. That they are events which took place in Rome and on occasions when Augustus made his entry into the capital is common to all three of these miracles. The first of them occurred on Augustus' return to Rome after Julius Caesar's assassination, when "a circle resembling a rainbow suddenly formed around the sun's disk." [61] The second miracle happened after Augustus' victory over Lepidus when "an abundant spring of oil . . . flowed through the course of a whole day from an inn" in Trastevere.[62] The third marvelous event was the closing of the gates of Janus and Octavian's acclamation as Augustus on Epiphany day, which has been discussed before. At the end of this summary, Orosius pointed ahead to the account which he was to give in some of the later chapters of his history concerning the events which occurred "on the occasion of a fourth return" of Augustus to Rome during the year of Christ's birth.[63] In this later narration, Orosius emphasized once more the close correspondence between "the firmest and truest peace which Caesar (Augustus) established through God's *ordinatio,*" and that peace which had been announced to mankind by the angels.[64] He also called to the attention of his readers the fact

[60] VI, 20, 4 (ed. Zangemeister, *op. cit.,* p. 419): "Hoc autem fideliter commemorasse ideo par fuit, ut per omnia uenturi Christi gratia praeparatum Caesaris imperium conprobetur."

[61] VI, 20, 5 (*ibid.,* p. 419); cf. Frauenholz, *op. cit.,* pp. 93 f., 104 f.

[62] VI, 20, 6–7 (*ibid.,* pp. 419 f.); see also VI, 18, 34 (*ibid.,* p. 413); *cf.* E. v. Frauenholz, *op. cit.,* pp. 101 ff.

[63] VI, 20, 9 (*ibid.,* p. 421): "Quid autem in quarto reditu, cum finito Cantabrico bello pacatisque omnibus gentibus Caesar Urbem repetiit, ad contestationem fidei, quam expromimus, actum sit, ipso melius ordine proferetur."

[64] VI, 22, 5 (*ibid.,* p. 428): "Igitur eo tempore, id est eo anno quo firmissimam uerissimamque pacem ordinatione Dei Caesar composuit, natus est Christus, cuius aduentui pax ista famulata est, in cuius ortu audientibus

that it was at that time that Augustus declined the appellation of "lord (*dominus*) on the ground that he was only a man."[65] And finally, Orosius found it noteworthy that in the very year Augustus had ordered the taking of a universal census and that consequently "Christ's name was entered in the Roman census list immediately after his birth."[66]

In drawing these parallels between the establishment of the universal monarchy by Augustus and the founding of the universal religion by Christ, Orosius stood at the end of a long tradition which had started early in the history of Christianity, had been greatly developed by Eusebius of Caesarea, and had remained quite generally accepted throughout the fourth century. But nobody before Orosius had ever attempted to set forth such an elaborate religio-political ideology, a veritable "Augustus-Theologie," as Erik Peterson rightly called it.[67]

The peculiarity of Orosius' thought becomes particularly evident in the way he treated the above-mentioned closing of the gates of Janus and Octavian's acclamation as Augustus. For, when he interpreted these two facts as signifying the proclamation of universal peace and the establishment of the world monarchy, he was in complete accordance with his source, St. Jerome's translation of Eusebius' *Chronica*. But when he declared that these two events had taken place on January 6, he made a statement which is supported neither by St. Jerome nor, as far as we can see, by any other extant source.[68] The insertion of the reference to that specific day, however, enabled Orosius to draw the closest possible analogy between the figures of Augustus and Christ: "Since the establishment of peace, the bestowal of the name [Augustus] and the day [Epiphany] oc-

---

hominibus exultantes angeli cecinerunt 'Gloria in excelsis Deo, et in terra pax hominibus bonae uoluntatis.' "

[65] VI, 22, 4 (*ibid.*, p. 427): "[Augustus] domini appellationem ut homo declinauit." See E. v. Frauenholz, *op. cit.*, pp. 92 f., 109 f.

[66] VI, 22, 6–8 (*ibid.*, pp. 428 f.).

[67] E. Peterson, "Der Monotheismus als politisches Problem," in *Theologische Traktate,* Munich 1951, p. 97.

[68] See Zangemeister's notes (*op. cit.*, p. 418) on the passage in Orosius (VI, 20, 1–2); the actual date was January 11 (see Pauly-Wissowa, *Real-Encyclopädie,* XI, 1 [1917], col. 338).

curred together for the purpose of such a *manifestatio*," he asks, "what can be believed and recognized more faithfully and truly than that, by the hidden order of events, Augustus was predestined to accommodate the preparation for Christ? For Augustus carried forward the banner of peace and assumed the name of supreme power on the same day on which a little later Christ was to be manifested to the world." [69] We have to remember that a few paragraphs earlier Orosius had spoken of the *manifestatio Dominici sacramenti* in connection with the occasion of Christ's baptism on Epiphany day. When we now find that in the passage just quoted he used the same word *manifestatio,* not only in regard to Christ, but also in regard to the secular peace and power established by Augustus, we may be justified in concluding that the Christian Orosius credited the pagan world monarch and bringer of earthly peace with a sort of mundane Epiphany.[70]

Orosius was destined to be one of the most widely read and most frequently quoted historians during the Middle Ages. In view of his authority, it is interesting to note that none of the medieval historians who used *The Seven Books against the Pagans* seems to have adopted his ideas concerning the Epiphany and the significance of that day in the life of Augustus. For instance, Paulus Diaconus mentioned the miracles of the rainbow around the sun and of the spring of oil, but in connection with Octavian's third entry into Rome he related only that he was saluted as Augustus and thus recognized as the supreme and universal monarch, and omitted any reference to the specific

[69] VI, 20, 8 (*ibid.,* pp. 420 f.): ". . . quid fidelius ac uerius credi aut cognosci potest, concurrentibus ad tantam manifestationem pace nomine die, quam hunc occulto quidem gestorum ordine ad obsequium praeparationis eius praedestinatum fuisse, qui eo die, quo ille manifestandus mundo post paululum erat, et pacis signum praetulit et potestatis nomen adsumpsit?"

[70] On the background of this idea in late antiquity, see A. Deissmann, *Licht vom Osten,* 4th ed., Tübingen 1923, pp. 314–320 (on παρουσία, ἐπιφάνεια and *adventus*); E. Peterson, "Die Einholung des Kyrios," *Zeitschrift für systematische Theologie,* VII (1930), 682–702; A. Alföldi, "Die Ausgestaltung des monarchischen Zeremoniells am römischen Kaiserhof," *Mitteilungen des Deutschen Archäologischen Instituts,* 49 (1934), pp. 88 ff. (with further bibliography); cf. also E. Stauffer, *Christus und die Caesaren,* Hamburg 1952, esp. pp. 34–39; C. Mohrmann, *Epiphania,* 1953, *passim.*

day, January 6.[71] Landolfus Sagax, whose *Additamenta ad Pauli Historiam Romanam* dates from the early tenth century,[72] mentioned the day, *octavum idus Ianuarias,* but made no reference whatsoever to the Epiphany, and Frutolf, in his *Chronicon Universale,* proceeded in the same way.[73] It was left to the most philosophically minded and erudite of the medieval historians, Bishop Otto of Freising, in his work on *The Two Cities,* really to take issue with Orosius' concept of the Epiphany and to interpret the whole problem in an entirely different fashion.[74] As far as all the factual details of the various miraculous events were concerned, he followed Orosius very closely and he believed, too, that "the reign of Augustus was in many ways a prophecy of the reign of Christ who was born in his times." [75] Thus in agreement with Orosius, he asserted: "Augustus, returning from the East on the sixth of January, after he had made kings subject to himself and put down civil strife, was received in the city with a threefold triumph and was called Augustus." [76] After this statement, however, Otto departed in the most decided fashion from Orosius' text, for he continued: "And Christ, being born and veiling Himself humbly in the flesh, was in a similar manner on that same day, that is, the 6th of January, which we call the Epiphany, worshipped with three kinds of gifts, a star serving as a guide [for the three kings] from the East, and He who before had been hidden was declared Augustus and King of Kings. At that time indeed this was only foreshadowed, but it is seen more clearly than light itself that

[71] Paulus Diaconus, *Historia Romana,* VII, 8 (ed. H. Droysen, *Mon. Germ. Hist., Scriptores Antiquissimi,* II, 119).

[72] VII, 116 ff. (ed. Droysen, *op. cit.,* II, 295 ff.).

[73] Ed. G. Waitz and P. Kilon, *Mon. Germ. Hist., Scriptores,* VI, 91–92.

[74] Otto of Freising, *Chronica sive historia de duabus civitatibus,* III, 6 (ed. A. Hofmeister, *Mon. Germ. Hist., Scriptores rerum Germanicarum,* LVIII [1912], 141 f.); the following translations are, with slight modifications, those given by C. C. Mierow, *The Two Cities,* New York 1928, pp. 229 f.; cf. E. v. Frauenholz. *op. cit.,* pp. 97 ff.

[75] III, 6 (ed. Hofmeister, *op. cit.,* p. 142): "Notandum preterea, quod Augusti regnum regni Christi, qui eius temporibus est natus, in pluribus fuit prenuntium."

[76] *Ibid.:* "Ille enim VIII. Idus Ian. ab oriente rediens regibusque sibi subiugatis ac civilibus sedatis motibus cum triplici triumpho in Urbe suscipitur Augustusque vocatur."

by this time it has been brought to accomplishment, namely that Christ not only reigns in heaven but also governs all kings on the earth." [77]

Like Orosius, then, Otto of Freising stated that one of the most important events in Augustus' life had taken place on the day of the Epiphany, but from this coincidence he drew an analogy between the figures of Christ and Augustus, which was totally unlike the one drawn by Orosius. To Otto, in agreement with the tradition and the practice of the Roman church which by that time prevailed all over the Western world, the feast of the Epiphany commemorated no longer the "manifestation" of Christ through the baptism by John, as Orosius had believed, but rather the adoration of the Magi. Otto illustrated his interpretation of the meaning of the Epiphany by specifically referring to the liturgy of that feast.[78] "Whence the Church," he said, [79] "with beautiful fitness sings to His praise on that day on which, as we have said, this was foreshadowed: 'Behold the Lord, the Conqueror, comes, and in His hand are the kingdom and the power and the empire,' [80] and in the offertory: 'And all the kings of the earth shall worship Him, and all nations shall serve Him.' " [81] Otto's explanation concluded: "In that

[77] *Ibid.*: "Iste natus humiliterque in carne latens similiter eadem die, id est VIII. Ian., quam nos epiphaniam dicimus, stella duce ab oriente trinis adoratur muneribus apparensque, qui ante latuerat, augustus ac rex regum declaratur. Quod quidem tunc prefigurabatur, sed iam completum esse, Christum scilicet non solum in caelis regnare, sed et in terris regibus omnibus imperare, luce clarius cernitur."

[78] Cf. L. Arbusow, *Liturgie und Geschichtsschreibung im Mittelalter*, Bonn 1951, p. 20.

[79] III, 6 (ed. Hofmeister, *op. cit.*, p. 142): "Unde pulchre ea, qua hoc prefiguratum esse diximus, die in laudem eius canit ecclesia: 'Ecce advenit dominator dominus, et regnum in manu eius et potestas et imperium.' Et in offerterio: 'Et adorabunt eum omnes reges terrae, omnes gentes servient ei.' "

[80] *Missale Romanum* (Milan 1474), ed. R. Lippe (H. Bradshaw Society, XVII), London 1899, 31, *in Epiphania Domini; introitus;* see also the so-called *Liber Antiphonarius* of Pope Gregory the Great (ed. Migne, *Pat. Lat.* 78, col. 649).

[81] *Missale Romanum, op. cit.*, p. 32, *offertorium; Liber Antiphonarius* of Gregory I, *op. cit.*, col. 649. It may be added that in the *Liber Responsalis* of Gregory, ed. Migne, *op. cit.*, col. 742 (*responsio in tertio nocturno*) and col. 743 (*Antiph. in matutinis laudibus*), we find the *tria*

He is called 'the Lord, the Conqueror,' the name Augustus is ascribed to Him; and in that 'the kingdom' and 'the empire' are said to be 'in His hand,' imperial dignity is ascribed to Him; and in that it is said that 'kings worship Him and all nations serve Him,' the supreme power of monarchy, that is, the singular principate over the whole world, is declared to be His." [82]

Through Orosius' exposition of the significance of the Epiphany, as Erik Peterson has rightly said,[83] "Augustus became christianized and Christ who had been made a *civis Romanus* became romanized." This ideology represented the culminating point of a trend of thought which had started among some of the earliest theologians of the church and which had been fully developed by Eusebius of Caesarea and other thinkers of the fourth century. Aponius belonged in the same tradition, although he and Orosius certainly set forth their theories in complete independence from each other and even interpreted the meaning of the feast of the Epiphany in entirely different ways. The fact that the universal world monarch had proclaimed his Augustan peace in Rome on the very same day on which the universal saviour of mankind was born in Bethlehem, was very strongly emphasized by Aponius. With this interpretation, he made exactly the same point which Orosius endeavored to make with his observation that the public recognition or "manifestation" of the supreme monarch and peace-giver occurred on the day on which Christ was later to be made "manifest" to the world through His baptism. On this particular question, Aponius undoubtedly could have subscribed to Orosius' statement that "by the hidden order of

---

munera mentioned to which Otto referred (see above, note 77). The phrase *stella duce* (see note 77) appears in the *Missale Romanum* (*op. cit.*, p. 31) in the *oratio:* "Deus, qui hodierna die unigenitum tuum gentibus stella duce revelasti."

[82] III, 6, ed. Hofmeister, p. 142: "Per hoc enim, quod 'dominator dominus' vocatur, augusti ei nomen adtribuitur, per hoc vero, quod 'regnum et imperium in manu eius' dicitur, imperatoria ei dignitas asscribitur, per hoc autem, quod 'reges eum adorare omnesque gentes servire' asseruntur, monarchiae apex, id est singularis super totum mundum principatus, eius esse declaratur."

[83] Peterson, *op. cit.*, p. 100.

events, Augustus had been predestined to accommodate the preparation for Christ."[84] With Otto of Freising we are in a different world. He was much more interested in "imperializing Christ" than in "christianizing" Augustus. Octavius, he admitted, had returned from the East as conqueror, he had made kings subject to him and he entered Rome in triple triumph. But the fact that this supreme moment in Augustus' life fell on the day on which later the three kings from the East were to worship Christ with their three kinds of gifts, indicated to Otto of Freising that Divine Providence had now prepared the world for the coming of the true "Augustus and King of Kings" whom "all the kings of the earth shall worship and all nations shall serve."

[84] See above, note 69.

14

Orosius and Augustine*

ABOUT a year ago a rather curious controversy took place in the correspondence columns of the *New Statesman and Nation.* In an article dealing with Jacob Burckhardt and the problem of "the universal historians," H. R. Trevor-Roper declared that Karl Marx, "as a historian . . . is dead as mutton, or at least as dead as Orosius, Baronius and Bossuet." To this statement the Marxian author E. J. Hobsbawn replied: "Orosius, Baronius and Bossuet are dead as historians because no historian today cares a rap what they wrote, thinks their views worth a minute's consideration, or modifies his work because of theirs." In his rebuttal, Mr. Trevor-Roper asserted: "Orosius may be dead as a historian, but he supplied the essential material for St. Augustine's *City of God,* which has had greater influence in history even than *Das Kapital.*" [1]

This English debate shows that the memory of Orosius as one of the outstanding "universal historians" is still quite alive

* Mommsen left three drafts of this paper. The first was read at a meeting of the Medieval Club in New York, the second to the Cornell University Research Club on November 14, 1956. The text printed here is, with minor revisions, the third draft, as it was read to the Yale Classical Club on April 15, 1957. The references have been added by the editor. Without exception, however, notes which do more than identify quotations are based on indications by the author in the margins of his typescript.

[1] August 6, 20, and 27, 1955, pp. 164, 217, and 243.

(regardless of the fact that no modern writer, whether Marxian or not, "modifies his work" because of his). Therefore Orosius' ideas may deserve, *pace* Mr. Hobsbawn's categorical rejection, a minute's (or even an hour's) consideration.

When Mr. Trevor-Roper defended the importance of Orosius' work in the history of ideas by saying that "he supplied the essential material for St. Augustine's *City of God*," he was echoing a common medieval view. In the *Paradiso*, for example, Dante calls Orosius "that defender of Christian times of whose treatise Augustine availed himself." [2] For some medieval thinkers, moreover, the relationship between the two men was not only close but reciprocal as well. As Augustine had availed himself of Orosius' *Seven Books of Histories against the Pagans*, so, it was generally assumed, Orosius was even more indebted to Augustine, under whom he had studied and whose fundamental ideas he reflected in his historical work. John of Salisbury concluded a long paraphrase of a passage from *The Seven Books* as follows: "Thus in substance Orosius, whose text and thought I use the more readily since I know that he, as a Christian and as a disciple of the great Augustine, . . . searched diligently for the truth." [3]

The medieval opinion that *The Seven Books* offers an interpretation of history from the Augustinian point of view is still maintained by most modern scholars who have written on Orosius. For instance, in 1936 I. W. Raymond stated in the Introduction to his translation of *The Seven Books* that the "basic principles upon which he [Orosius] founded his philosophy of history were those which he held in common with his guide and friend St. Augustine." [4]

The belief that there exsited a definite personal relationship

[2] X, 118–120:

> "Nell'altra piccioletta luce ride
> quello avvocato de tempi cristiani
> del cui latino Augustin si provide."

[3] *Policraticus,* VIII, 18, 788 C (ed. C. C. I. Webb, Oxford, 1909, II, 363): "Haec Orosius fere; cuius uerbis et sensu eo libentius utor quod sciò Christianum et magni discipulum Augustini propter religionem fidei nostrae ueritati diligentius institisse."

[4] *Seven Books of History against the Pagans,* tr. Irving Woodworth Raymond (New York, 1936), p. 10.

between the two men and a close connection between their historical works and ideas is well supported by the few established facts of Orosius' life. We know that around the year 414 Orosius went from his native Spain to Hippo in Africa, "prompted by the report," as Augustine said in one of his letters, "that he could learn from me whatever he wished on the subjects on which he desired information." Augustine gained a favorable opinion of Orosius, for he called him "a man of quick understanding, of ready speech and burning zeal who desires to be in the Lord's house a vessel rendering useful service." After Orosius had been in Hippo for about a year, studying under Augustine, the master felt in his own words that "I have taught him all that I could," and therefore urged him to go to Palestine and visit St. Jerome, "from whom," Augustine said, "he may learn those things which I could not teach him." [5] When in the following year, 416, Orosius returned from that journey, Augustine honored him with the greatest mark of confidence which the master could show his former pupil. He asked him, as Orosius himself put it, "to reply to the empty chatter of those who, as aliens to the city of God, are called pagans": [6] he commissioned him to write his *Seven Books of Histories against the Pagans.*

That derogatory reference to "the empty chatter" of the pagans illuminates clearly the background against which the composition of Orosius' work has to be placed. A few years earlier, in 410, the city of Rome had fallen to the onslaught of the Visigoths under King Alaric. In a purely material sense, this event was of slight importance. The city suffered relatively little damage. But this was not the way in which contemporaries viewed the event. All of them, whether Christian or pagan,

[5] *Ep.* 166, 1, 2 (to Jerome). For Jerome's answer see *Ep.* 172. Cf. *Ep.* 169, 4, 13 (ed. A. Goldbacher, *Corpus Scriptorum Ecclesiasticorum Latinorum,* Vienna, 1904, XLIV, 621): "occasionem quippe cuiusdam sanctissimi et studiosissimi iuuenis, presbyteri Orosii, qui ad nos ab ultima Hispania, id est ab Oceani litore solo sanctarum scripturarum ardore inflammatus aduenit, amittere nolui."

[6] *Pavli Orosii Historiarvm adversvm paganos libri VII,* I, Prol., 9 (ed. K. Zangemeister, *CSEL,* Vienna, 1882, V). All references to Orosius' *Seven Books* are to this edition. Translations are based on those of I. W. Raymond.

were profoundly disturbed by the fall of "eternal" Rome; and all of them asked why it had fallen, thus posing, more urgently than ever before, the old problem of the causes of the splendors and miseries of human history. To the pagans the answer was obvious: they attempted, said Augustine, "to attribute that overthrow of Rome to the Christian religion, and began to blaspheme the true God with even more than their customary acrimony and bitterness" [*Retractationes,* II, xliii, 1]. It was in these circumstances that Augustine began to write *The City of God.* He went far beyond his immediate purpose, that of an apology, and propounded the most comprehensive philosophy of history ever written from the Christian point of view. At the same time he evidently realized the need for another kind of apology, one which would present, in a strictly historical way, the calamitous aspects of the human record throughout the ages. Orosius obeyed Augustine's "instructions" and finished his work in little more than a year. When he dedicated it to Augustine, he expressed once more his deeply felt obligation to the master: "I humbly owe all that I have accomplished to your fatherly advice, and my entire work is yours, because it proceeds from you and returns to you, so that my only contribution must be that I did it gladly." [7]

In view of Orosius' undoubted closeness to St. Augustine and especially in view of his own conception of the task assigned to and carried out by him, it seems hardly possible to question the view held throughout the Middle Ages and also by most modern scholars that *The Seven Books* represents basically the Augustinian interpretation of history. Nevertheless certain doubts have been expressed recently, above all by German theologians such as Erik Peterson and Wilhelm Kamlah, doubts which suggest that the problem can be usefully re-examined.[8]

[7] I, Prol., 8. In the *Liber apologeticus* Orosius called Augustine and Jerome the "columnae et firmamenta Ecclesiae catholicae" (1, 4) and referred again to Augustine as "beatus pater meus" (31, 3).

[8] Wilhelm Kamlah, *Christentum und Geschichlichkeit,* 2nd. ed. (Stuttgart, 1951), pp. 176 ff. and Erik Peterson, "Der Monotheismus als politisches Problem," in *Theologische Traktate* (Munich, 1951), p. 97. Very full Orosius bibliographies will be found in G. Fink, "Recherches bibliographiques sur Paul Orose," *Revista de Archivos, Bibliotecas y Museos,*

In my own approach to the problem of the relationship between *The Seven Books* and *The City of God* I wish to deal primarily with two questions. First, if indeed Orosius wrote under the influence of Augustine's ideas, then in what sense did he interpret those ideas and how did he apply them in his own account? In other words, to what extent do Orosius' historical ideas actually reflect those of Augustine? The second question will be: what did Augustine himself think of the work and ideas of his pupil and to what degree, if any, did he "avail himself" of Orosius' treatise, as Dante asserted he did?

The dating of the composition of *The City of God* puts us in the fortunate position of being able to look for answers to both of these questions. For we learn from Orosius' Preface that at the time when he had finished his book and dedicated it to his master, Augustine was "intent on completing the eleventh book" of *The City of God* [I, Prol., 11]. Since we know that Augustine "published" each individual book or section of his work immediately after its completion, this means that Orosius had been able to use, while writing his own history, the whole first part of *The City of God,* which consists of Books I to X. Therefore a comparison of *The Seven Books of Histories* with the first part of *The City of God* will permit us to determine to what degree Orosius' ideas agree with, or differ from, those of Augustine. On the other hand, since Augustine worked on the second part of *The City of God* (Books XI to XXII) only after he had received Orosius' text, we can learn from an analysis of that section to what extent he utilized the factual material and the historical interpretation of his pupil.

If we start our investigation by comparing the basic themes of the two works, each taken as a whole, one essential difference becomes immediately evident, a difference which has not been sufficiently stressed by most modern scholars but which was clearly noticed by one of the greatest historians of the high

---

LVIII (1952), 271–322 and Berthold Altaner, *Patrologie,* 5th ed. (Freiburg, 1958), pp. 218–219. See also Guy Fink-Errera, "San Augustín y Orosio. Esquema para un estudio de las fuentes de 'De Civitate Dei,' " *La Ciudad de Dios. Revista Agustiniana,* CLXVII, vol. II (1954), 455–549.

Middle Ages, the German Bishop Otto of Freising. Bishop Otto observed that Augustine "has discoursed most keenly and learnedly on the origin, the course and the ordained end of the glorious city of God, setting forth how it had ever spread among the citizens of the world and who of its citizens or princes stood forth preëminent in the various epochs among the princes and citizens of the world." Orosius, on the other hand, "has composed a very valuable history of the fluctuations and wretched issues of human actions, of wars and the hazards of wars, and of the shifting of thrones, from the foundation of the world down to his own time." In other words, Otto put Orosius among the numerous historians, both pagan and Christian, who related "the tale of human miseries" or dealt "with the temporal and earthly city of the Devil." He considered Augustine unique because of his primary concern with the eternal and heavenly city of Christ.[9]

Bishop Otto's observation is correct. Throughout his *Seven Books of Histories* Orosius used the words "heavenly city" and "earthly city" only once, in the Preface addressed to St. Augustine [I, Prol., 9]. Nowhere else in his account did he attempt to interpret actual events or people in accordance with these two terms which are of such crucial importance in Augustinian thought. Yet the consistent avoidance of these terms need not be explained by the assumption that Orosius meant to slight, or even deviate from, Augustinian principles. The omission indicates rather that he simply conceived of his task more narrowly than Augustine had done. In fact, this limitation was imposed upon him by Augustine himself; for in his dedication Orosius said to Augustine: "You bade me discover from all the available data of histories and annals whatever instances past ages have afforded of the burdens of war, the ravages of disease, the horrors of famine, of terrible earthquakes, extraordinary floods, dreadful volcanic eruptions, thunderbolts and hailstorms, and also of the cruel miseries caused by parricides and by crimes against man's better self; I was to set forth these

[9] *Ottonis Episcopi Frisingensis Chronica sive Historia de duabus civitatibus,* ed. A. Hofmeister (Hanover and Leipzig, 1912), p. 6, ll. 22–26; 7, ll. 5–10; 9, ll. 8–20.

matters systematically and briefly in one volume" [I, Prol., 10]. It is obvious that the man who assigned this kind of historical account to his disciple had a rather narrow and, from a non-theological point of view, perhaps questionable concept of the task of the historian. But this was evidently Augustine's view, as is shown by a remark he made in the first part of *The City of God* (which Orosius almost certainly knew). In this passage Augustine began to enumerate the various disasters resulting from the second Punic War, but suddenly decided to break off his narrative by saying: "Were we to attempt to enumerate [all those calamities], we should become nothing but mere writers of history." [10] Augustine's own purpose, then, was to discuss fully "the origin, the course, and the end of the two cities" [XVIII, i, 1–4], especially of the heavenly city, whereas the task assigned by him to Orosius was to tell the tale of human misery in history.

Limited though this theme was in one sense, it was very comprehensive in another. For, as we have seen, Orosius' declared intention was to collect his material "from all the available data of histories and annals." Thus he began his history with the first man, Adam. In doing so, he rejected explicitly a tradition shared both by pagan and Christian writers according to which history began only with Ninus, King of the Assyrians and alleged contemporary of Abraham [I, i, 1–4]. In his own choice of Adam as the true starting point of the history of mankind, Orosius felt himself supported by the authority of Augustine. This marks an important change in the development of Christian historiography. For Augustine's and Orosius' contemporary St. Jerome and, before him, Eusebius, Bishop of Caesarea, had still begun their famous chronological tables with King Ninus and Abraham, following in that respect the models of earlier pagan authors of universal histories.[11] On the

[10] *De Civitate Dei,* III, xviii, 11–12 (ed. B. Dombard and A. Kalb, *Corpus Christianorum,* 1955, XLVII and XLVIII). All references to *The City of God* are to this edition. Translations are based on that of M. Dods, *The City of God,* 2 vols., 1872.

[11] *Eusebii Pamphilii Chronici Canones latine vertit, adauxit, ad sua tempora produxit S. Eusebius Hieronymus,* ed. J. K. Fotheringham (London, 1923), p. 11: "Verum in curiositate ne cesses, et cum diuinam scrip-

other hand, most of the world chronicles and annals which were written by western Christians after the publication of Orosius' *Seven Books* were to begin, as he did, with Adam.

Starting, then, with Adam and continuing his account to his own time, the early fifth century, Orosius related whatever instances he could find in his sources of the miseries which mankind as a whole, individuals as well as nations, had been suffering throughout history—a *catalogue raisonné,* as it were, more or less chronologically arranged in accordance with one of his main sources, St. Jerome's translation of Eusebius' chronological tables. There is no need here to go into details of the historical picture drawn by Orosius. It suffices to state that he performed his task in a painstakingly thorough and, one must admit, inevitably rather tiresome way. There is justification for the sarcasm of Petrarch who called Orosius "that collector of the evils of the world." But in fairness to Orosius we have to realize that this was precisely what Augustine wished him to be, "a collector" of all earthly miseries. A comparison of Orosius'

turam diligenter euolueris, a natiuitate Abraham usque ad totius orbis diluuium inuenies retrorsum annos DCCCCXLII, item a diluuio usque ad Adam annos $\overline{\text{II}}$CCXLII, in quibus nulla penitus nec Graeca nec barbara et ut loquar in commune gentilis inuenitur historia: quam ob rem praesens opusculum ab Abraham et Nino usque ad nostram aetatem inferiora tempora persequetur." Cf. Tertullian, *De Pallio,* ii, 5 (ed. A. Gerlo, Wetteren, 1940, pp. 66–67): "Bellis quoque plurimum licuit. Sed piget tristia non minus quam et regnorum vices recensere, quotiens et ista mutaverint iam inde a Nino, Beli progenie, si tamen Ninus regnare primus, ut autumat superiorum profanitas. Ferme apud vos ultra stilus non solet: ab Assyriis, si forte, aevi historiae patescunt. Qui vero divinas lectitamus, ab ipsius mundi natalibus compotes sumus"; and Justin, I, i, 1–7 (ed. O. Seel, 1935): "Principio rerum gentium nationumque imperium penes reges erat, quos ad fastigium huius maiestatis non ambitio popularis, sed spectata inter bonos moderatio provehebat. Populus nullis legibus tenebatur; arbitria principum pro legibus erant. Fines imperii tueri magis quam proferre mos erat; intra suam cuique patriam regna finiebantur. Primus omnium Ninus, rex Assyriorum, veterem et quasi nativum gentibus morem nova imperii cupiditate mutavit. Hic primus intulit bella finitimis et rudes adhuc ad resistendum populos terminos usque Libyae perdomuit. Fuere quidem temporibus antiquiores Vezosis Aegyptius et Scythiae rex Tanaus, quorum alter in Pontum, alter usque Aegyptum excessit. Sed longinqua, non finitima bella gerebant nec imperium sibi, sed populis suis gloriam quaerebant contentique victoria imperio abstinebant. Ninus magnitudinem quaesitae dominationis continua possessione firmavit."

Seven Books with the first part of *The City of God* shows indeed a close similarity between the ways in which the theme of material calamity was handled by the two authors. On occasion Orosius cut his own account short by referring explicitly to Augustine's treatment of the same topic. "Where your reverence," he said in one passage, "has exercised your zeal for wisdom and truth, it is not right for me to venture beyond it" [III, 4, 6]. In general, however, Orosius had ample opportunity to elaborate and prove, with innumerable historical details, the point that "the local miseries of the individual peoples have existed from the beginning" [I, 2, 106]. Augustine, after all, had dealt with that particular problem only incidentally; Orosius, in his own words, was to treat it "systematically."

Moreover, in the first part of *The City of God* Augustine confined his historical discussion almost entirely to events which had taken place in ancient Rome. In Orosius' opinion, too, "the deeds of the Romans have to be evaluated most of all," but he added in the same sentence that "the deeds of the Greeks must not be omitted" [I, 12, 3]. He even included in his narrative accounts of the principal misfortunes which had occurred in the great oriental monarchies: Assyria and Egypt, Babylonia and Persia. (When in his treatment of the pre-Christian era Orosius dealt primarily with pagan, and only very seldom with Jewish calamities, we have to remember that he wrote his work, as its title indicates, in the traditional form of an apology directed "against the pagans.")

Orosius concentrated so exclusively on the somber aspects of human history that hardly a bright spot appears in his picture, or at least not in that of pre-Christian times. He showed no interest in the development of the basic institutions of state and society or in the cultural achievements of the ancient world. Nor was he willing to concede that there had been great personalities during that era, who through their deeds had truly benefited mankind. To him, for example, Alexander the Great was nothing but "a veritable whirlpool of evils" [III, 7, 5]. But although Orosius' representation of ancient history is definitely one-sided and frequently unfair, it offers in one respect a notable, and perhaps necessary, corrective of views which were quite commonly held in his own time. Many of the ancient historians had emphasized and praised above all the glory of individual personalities and particular states and had devoted most of their attention to the victorious achievements of the leading men and nations. To Orosius it appeared that those historians had looked at things merely through the eyes of the victors, men who had gained great fame for themselves but had brought nothing but untold misery upon their vanquished enemies. "Times and events," Orosius declared, "must be considered not from the standpoint of one place only, but by taking the whole world into account; then it will become clear that just as much as Rome was made happy by having been the conqueror, so the non-Roman lands were made unhappy by having been conquered" [V, 1, 3]. When Orosius emphasized in such strong terms the reverse side of imperialism, he was partly influenced by St. Augustine, who expressed himself in a very similar vein in several passages of *The City of God.*[12] But his profound and often deeply moving comprehension of the problems of greatness and glory in history also manifestly resulted from his personal background. As a Spaniard he belonged to a people which had once been conquered by the Romans and was now, in his own lifetime, overrun by Germanic invaders. At one point he exclaimed: "Did I not make the terrible experiences of my ancestors my own, seeing in them the common lot of man?" [III, 20, 5]. And at the end of the account in which he recalled some of the harrowing incidents of his flight from Spain, he made a remark which might be addressed just as well to his own contemporaries as to all those historians who have found only grandeur and triumph in history: "Only men who themselves have never undergone suffering are insensible to the suffering of others" [III, 20, 7].[13]

[12] For example, III, x, or III, xiv, 55–65.

[13] Compare Orosius on the conquests of Philip of Macedon (III, 14) and of Alexander (III, 20). He reminds his pagan opponents that the "destruction wrought by an enemy is one thing, the reputation of a conqueror is another," and warns them that should the Goths master the Roman world, posterity "will call mighty kings those whom we now regard as our most savage enemies" (III, 20, 12).

In giving the fullest possible attention to the occurrence of material calamity as a constant in history, Orosius certainly believed himself to be in complete accord with Augustine. Augustine had made this topic the main theme of the third Book of *The City of God,* beginning it as follows: "I see that now I must speak of those evils which are the only things the pagans do not wish to suffer—famine, disease, war, pillage, captivity, massacre and similar horrors" [III, i, 4–7]. But it should be noted that Augustine attributed to physical disasters merely secondary importance. As he saw it, "the things which are to be avoided above all others are the evils afflicting men's morals and souls [III, i, 1–2]; for that reason he discussed these matters at length in Book II of *The City of God*—before he took up the question of material calamities. For his part, Orosius certainly paid some attention to the moral and spiritual evils which had beset the pagan world of antiquity, but within the general framework of his narrative and interpretation of events this theme was definitely stressed much less than in Augustine's system of thought. The fact that Orosius put his primary emphasis on the material aspects of man's misery throughout history again was the result of the very commission he had received from his master. It was Augustine's view that physical evils were "the only things really dreaded by the pagans," and he knew that ever since the beginnings of Christianity pagans were wont to blame all natural and other catastrophes on the adherents of the new faith. Two hundred years earlier, as we learn from Tertullian, whenever there were earthquakes or epidemics the cry had been: "Throw the Christians to the lions" [*Adversus Gentes,* xl]. In Augustine's and Orosius' own era there still existed "a common proverb: when the rain fails to fall, it is because of the Christians" [*De Civitate Dei,* II, iii, 3–4]. It was inevitable that the "Fall of Rome" in 410 should confirm the pagans in their conviction that "the present times are to an extraordinary degree infested with evils for the sole reason that Christ is venerated . . . and the pagan idols are worshipped less" [Orosius, I, Prol., 9]. Augustine had already taken it upon himself in *The City of God* to provide the theological refutation of that belief. But at the same time he thought it necessary to fight the pagans on their own ground and with material and arguments adapted to their own mode of thought. Thus he commissioned Orosius to prove, through a purposely nontheological account of secular history, the absurdity of the charges which the pagans had for many centuries made against the Christians. Orosius' very title, *The Seven Books of Histories against the Pagans,* makes clear his audience and his purpose. His book is an "Apology" in the conventional sense.

The preoccupation with the material evils of this world and the relative lack of emphasis on the spiritual and moral evils of mankind represent, then, the basic approach of Orosius to his task. This was the approach to universal history Augustine considered necessary in the particular circumstances created by the "Fall of Rome" in 410. The question now arises whether in the actual execution of his plan Orosius always adhered, at least on significant issues, to those views of his master with which he could have acquainted himself through his reading of the first part of *The City of God.* In the search for an answer only a few points can be taken up within the compass of this lecture.

One topic which both Augustine and Orosius considered of crucial importance was the evaluation of the role played by the Roman state and the people of Rome in the course of history. If we examine the first part of *The City of God* from this point of view, we find that Augustine showed rather mixed feelings in his attitude toward the Roman people. On the one hand as a Christian theologian, he had time and again to stress the fundamental fact that "by the hidden judgment of Divine Providence the true religion was not offered to their choice" [II, xxix, 9–10]. For that reason all the achievements of the Romans during the pre-Christian era belonged exclusively to the sphere of the earthly city. In fact Rome represented to him the outstanding embodiment of that earthly city: Rome was "the second Babylon" [XVIII, ii, 65–66]. But although he made it unmistakably clear that there could be no true virtues except those inspired by, and directed toward, things spiritual and supramundane, Augustine was ready to concede that the Romans possessed at least what we may call relative virtues; and among these laudable *mores* [I, xxxvi, 9] he singled out specifically "liberty and the desire for fame, which impelled the Romans to admirable deeds" [V, xviii, 20–21]. To clarify his meaning he devoted the whole fifth Book of *The City of God* to the question "Why God . . . has seen fit to grant such vast and long-lasting dominion to the Roman Empire?" [V, Praef., 5–8]. His answer was as follows: the establishment of Roman supremacy "was God's way of overcoming the many evils which existed among the nations; He put this task in the hands of men who sought their own fame in striving for the honor, praise and glory of their fatherland, and who were willing to sacrifice their private interests to the common good." Thus the ancient Romans, in Augustine's words, "conquered greed for wealth, and many other vices, for the sake of their one vice, the love of glory" [V, xiii, 1–9].[14] It was in accordance with this idea that throughout the first five Books of *The City of God* Augustine praised highly a number of great Romans and even went so far as to hold up some of their acts of self-sacrifice as commendable models for imitation by his fellow Christians [V, xviii].[15] It may be noted that nine hundred years later Dante was to adopt Augustine's view, and even his specific choices of the illustrious men of Rome; but Dante went still further than Augustine and called the great Romans "instruments through which Divine Providence proceeded in the Roman Empire; for there the hand of God was many times manifest." [16]

Orosius' attitude toward Rome was completely different. While Augustine could speak of *indoles Romana laudabilis* [II, xxix, 1], Orosius wrote: "Like an insatiable stomach that consumes everything and yet remains always hungry, that city, more wretched than other cities which she has made wretched,

[14] Cf. V, xii, 46–48: "Amore itaque primitus libertatis, post etiam dominationis et cupiditate laudis et gloriae multa magna fecerunt."

[15] Augustine especially praised Regulus (I, xv, for example). Orosius mentions Regulus several times (IV, 8–10, *passim*), but without any specific praise.

[16] *Convivio,* IV, v, 17 (ed. G. Busnelli and G. Vandelli, Florence, 1954, II, 56): ". . . e manifesto esser dee, questi eccellentissimi essere stati strumenti con li quali procedette la divina provedenza ne lo romano imperio, dove più volte parve esse braccia di Dio essere presenti."

left nothing untouched, and yet she herself had nothing; and she was forced by the pinch of hunger at home to continue in that state of unrest which war engenders" [V, 18, 29]. While Augustine spoke with open, though necessarily qualified, admiration of some of the great Romans, Orosius showed no respect for any figure of the pre-Christian era and made no attempt to explain the rise of Roman dominion in terms of the human qualities or personal virtues of the Romans, relative in value though such virtues might have been, or in fact were, from the Augustinian point of view. His explicit purpose was to "teach that all historical events have been arranged by the ineffable mysteries and the most profound judgments of God, and have not taken place either on the strength of human forces or as the results of fickle chance" [II, 2, 4]. His conception of the workings of Divine Providence prevented him, quite in contrast to Augustine, from assigning any importance to the role played by individuals, and even from taking any interest in their personal qualities. Consequently his answer to the question why God had granted so vast an empire to the Romans differed entirely from Augustine's. Orosius started from the Pauline statement that "the powers that be are ordained of God" [Rom., 13:1]; if this was true, then "all the more are the kingdoms, from which all powers proceed, ordained of God"; and he concluded: "If the kingdoms, however, compete with one another then it is better that some one kingdom be supreme, and to it all the other kingdoms be subject" [II, 1, 3–4].

In other words, Orosius believed it to be God's will that there exist in the political sphere the *ordinatio ad unum* [VI, 1, 6], the subjugation of all the separate states in the world to one universal monarchy. He saw the course of history as a succession of "four main kingdoms, pre-eminent in successive stages at the four cardinal points of the earth, to wit the Babylonian kingdom in the East, the Carthaginian in the South, the Macedonian in the North, and the Roman in the West" [II, 1, 4–5]. Apart from the inclusion of Carthage in the series, and apart, too, from the curious geographical distribution of these powers, Orosius reproduced the ancient idea of the four great monarchies, an idea accepted by the early Christians and given a prominent place in the universal chronicles of Eusebius and St. Jerome. (It ought to be noted, however, that in this connection Orosius never alluded to the famous passages in the *Book of Daniel* [Chapters 2 and 7] on which all earlier Christian writers had based their adaptations of the originally pagan concept of a succession of predominant monarchies.) Orosius' treatment of the scheme differs from those of his predecessors only in its more elaborate detail; while his attempt to draw the closest possible parallels between the two most important monarchies, those of Babylon and Rome, led him to construe some historical dates and chronological coincidences in ways which were not only peculiar but on occasion not even in accordance with his own sources, among them Jerome's *Chronici Canones*. It is relevant to our question about Orosius' dependence on, or independence from, Augustine that nowhere in the first part of *The City of God* did Augustine even mention in any explicit way the scheme of the four monarchies.

Since Orosius thought that none of the great monarchies, not even the Roman Empire, owed its dominion to the personal merits of its leaders and people, we must ask: according to Orosius, how did God work during the pre-Christian era for the attainment of His object, the elimination of the rivalry of the many by the hegemony of one state? Orosius evidently believed that for the most part God used the various pagan nations, regardless of their actual unworthiness, as mere puppets or tools for the furtherance of His divine purposes. But he was apparently convinced that on certain very important occasions God also influenced the turn of events by means of natural phenomena. Let me give one striking example. From Livy's account of Hannibal's siege of Rome Orosius learned that on two successive days heavy rainstorms had prevented the two armies from joining battle and for that reason "the Carthaginians, overcome by religious awe" finally decided to withdraw from the city [Livy, XXVI, xi, 4]. To Orosius it was "evident . . . that this rain, coming as it did at the necessary and opportune moment, was sent by Christ alone who is the true God." Thus in Orosius' opinion not Roman bravery preserved

Rome but it was "beyond dispute . . . the *ordinatio* of Jesus Christ . . . which in those days saved the city of Rome so that she might accept the faith in the future" [IV, 17, 8–11].[17]

Orosius climaxed his analysis of the workings of Divine Providence in history when he came to discuss the fact that the birth of the Universal Saviour of mankind coincided with the establishment of the universal monarchy by Augustus. In this case he was willing to admit that Augustus was "most brave and most clement," epithets he hardly ever used in reference to pagan figures. But at the same time Orosius made it very clear that Augustus owed his outstanding position to God alone, who "through his *ordinatio* conferred all things upon one emperor" [VI, 1, 6]. The fourth world monarchy was established by God; and world peace was secured not through Augustus' personal greatness but "through the power of Christ who made his appearance in the days of Augustus." The divine purpose was that "the glory of the new Christian name and the report of the promised salvation might spread abroad quickly and without hindrance in the midst of the state of great tranquility and universal peace that prevailed" [VI, 1, 8]. Many earlier Christian writers and, above all, Eusebius, had also stressed the providential character of the coincidence of the birth of Christ and the reign of Augustus and had explained the *raison d'être* of the Roman Empire in very similar terms. But it was left to Orosius to elaborate those ideas in the most systematic fashion. There were especially three miraculous events—a circle which formed around the sun, a fountain of oil which burst forth in Trastevere, and the closing of the gates

[17] His other source, Florus, I, xxii, 44–45 (ed. E. S. Forster, 1929, p. 108), explained the storms even more pointedly as meaning "that the gods . . . resisted Hannibal's progress." ("Quid ergo miramur moventi castra a tertio lapide Annibali iterum ipsos deos—deos inquam, nec fateri pudebit—restitisse? Tanta enim ad singulos illius motus vis imbrium effusa est, tanta ventorum violentia coorta est, ut divinitus hostem summoveri non a caelo, sed ab urbis ipsius moenibus et Capitolio videretur.") Again we may note that Orosius developed this special kind of reasoning in complete independence of Augustine, who made no attempt to explain the rainstorms as signifying an intervention of the Christian God (III, xx, 28 ff.).

of Janus—[18] which, Orosius believed, ought to be recorded with greatest faithfulness so as to "prove in every respect that the empire of Augustus had been prepared for the advent of Christ" [VI, 20, 4]. All these events occured at certain crucial moments in the career of Augustus, but they had at the same time to be understood as "prodigies and signs" revealing the coming of Christ and His Church. Orosius emphasized the providential and miraculous aspects of the reign of the first Roman world monarch to such an extent that Erik Peterson, a modern Catholic scholar has called the sum total of these ideas a "veritable Augustus-theology" and thus found it highly questionable from the strictly religious point of view.

In developing these concepts Orosius certainly felt himself supported by a tradition of thought which had started early in the history of Christianity and had, through the impact of Eusebius' writings, become quite generally accepted in the fourth century. But there was nothing he could learn from his master Augustine in this respect. For when we turn to the first part of *The City of God* we find that Augustine attributed no particular significance whatsoever to the reign of Augustus. On the subject of the coincidence of the birth of Christ and the beginnings of Roman hegemony over the world Augustine was content to note the bare fact that "Christ was born in the reign of Augustus" [III, xxx, 15–16]. From the same context in the third Book of *The City of God* it becomes clear that, in contrast to what Eusebius had said before and Orosius was to say later, Augustine did not put much faith in the universal peace allegedly secured by Augustus, for he stated explicitly that "Augustus waged numerous wars, in which many of the foremost men perished . . . among them Cicero" [III, xxx, 17–19]. That "Augustus-theology" which occupied such an important place in Orosius' work and thought, therefore, was derived from a tradition which Augustine had silently rejected.

There is at least one other and even more basic divergence concerning the interpretation of the general course of history between Orosius' *Seven Books* and the first part of *The City of*

[18] See above, p. 318.

God. The original intentions of both men were identical: they wanted to prove that the calamities of their own era were not unique and that they could not be blamed upon the prevalence of the Christian religion; for history taught that there had been many disasters in the past when the various pagan gods had allegedly protected their peoples. But while Augustine contented himself with that thesis and accepted the constant misery of this world as the divinely ordained fate of mankind, Orosius came to turn the argument in quite different directions. As a result of his researches he "discovered that the days of the past were not only as oppressive as those of the present but that they were the more terribly wretched the further they were removed from the consolation of true religion" [I, Prol., 14]. As Orosius saw it, there had been not only more grievous disasters in the period before the rise of Christianity than afterwards, but there existed now, in his own times, positive "blessings which our ancestors never had in their entirety: the tranquility of the present, the hope for the future and the possession of a common refuge" [V, 2, 8].[19] When we compare the last of *The Seven Books against the Pagans,* which deals exclusively with the Christian era, with the previous books, we find indeed that there emerges in Orosius' account a definite pattern of progress made by mankind with the help of the Christian God. Thus the emperor Claudius easily succeeded in conquering Britain in the year 43 A.D., Orosius declared, while Divine Providence had not favored Julius Caesar's earlier attempts.[20] Or, to give even more curious examples of Orosius'

[19] Cf. I, 21, 17–19: "What we at present find difficult to bear is any interference whatsoever in our pleasures or any restraint placed upon our passions, even for a moment. There is this difference, however, between men of that age and of this: the men of that age endured with patience those unbearable burdens because they were born and raised amid them and knew no better times, whereas men of our age, accustomed to perpetual peace in a life of tranquility and pleasure, are disturbed by every little cloud of anxiety that envelops them. If only they would pray to Him who can end this period of unrest, trifling though it be, and to whom they owe this continued peace which was unknown to other ages!"

[20] VII, 6, 9–11. Orosius goes on to point his moral sharply: "Any person of the present day who pleases may make comparisons in regard to this one island, period with period, war with war, Caesar with Caesar. I say nothing of the outcome, since in this case it was the most fortunate

notions concerning the material blessings bestowed upon mankind by the appearance of the Christian faith, there were now much less terrible plagues of locusts [V, 11, 6], and the volcano Aetna, "which in former days used to boil over from frequent eruptions that brought ruin upon fields and cities, at present only smokes harmlessly, as if to prove that it had been active in the past" [II, 14, 3].

With these and similar remarks Orosius clearly placed himself in that tradition of thought which may be described as the school of "Christian progressivists," a school whose most outstanding representative had been Eusebius of Caesarea. According to this view the universal faith and the universal empire had been established simultaneously by God and were destined by the same divine providence to grow together for all future times; it was the conviction of Eusebius, and in even greater degree of Orosius, that the larger the number of people to accept the spiritual truth, the more material benefits would befall mankind as a whole.

Both Eusebius and Orosius derived this conviction from their belief that the relationship between God and man was based on a kind of commutative contract which resembled strongly the old pagan principle of *do ut des.* If one does something that pleases God, the argument ran, God will do something for him in return; on the other hand, if one does something that displeases God, one must just as surely expect God's wrath. For example, the pagan and, later, the heretical emperors persecuted faithful Christians; consequently, Orosius asserted, God punished those imperial "tyrants" by allowing the outbreak of civil wars and by causing natural catastrophes [VII, 22 and 27].[21]

---

of victories, previously the bitterest of disasters. Thus Rome may finally come to see that the God through Whose Providence she formerly enjoyed partial success in her undertakings is the God through Whose recognition she now enjoys success in all its fullness to the extent that she does not become corrupted through the stumbling block of her blasphemies."

[21] Cf. VI, 22, 11: ". . . ut, quoniam ab initio et peccare homines et puniri propter peccata non tacui, nunc quoque, quae persecutiones Christianorum actae sint et quae ultiones secutae sint, absque eo quod omnes ad peccandum generaliter proni sunt atque ideo singillatim corripiuntur, expediam."

In Orosius good and evil men are almost always punished or rewarded on earth and not only at the Last Judgment, a notion echoed across the centuries in the final chorus of *Don Giovanni:* "This is the end of evildoers; and the doom of the wicked always corresponds to the life they lead." Orosius expressed this idea most succinctly in his summary of the career of the Theodosian general Mascezel: "By his own fate Mascezel showed that the judgment of God ever watches with a double purpose; for when he trusted in it, he received help, and when he despised it, he was put to death" [VII, 36, 13].

For this confident belief in the possibility of "a partial exposition of God's ineffable judgments" in history [II, 3, 5], Orosius certainly could draw no support from anything he had read in the first part of *The City of God.* Augustine was very far indeed from asserting, as Orosius did, that virtue and good deeds will usually receive their earthly rewards. On the contrary, he declared that in God's eyes neither the good nor the bad things of this world are of any real significance and value, and consequently that God "bestows them on both good and bad men . . . according to an order of things and times which is hidden from us but thoroughly known to Himself" [IV, xxxiii, 1–4].[22] Augustine demonstrated the mysterious workings of that divine providence in a specific reference to a number of fourth century emperors, Christian and pagan as well as orthodox and heretical [V, xxv, 1–19]. When Orosius discussed the same rulers—Constantine, Julian, Jovian, and Gratian—in the seventh Book of his history [chs. 28, 30, 31, 34] and drew his own lessons from their lives, he gave no evidence whatever of having understood the meaning of the profound warning which his master had directed against Eusebius' overoptimistic belief in the idea of progress and against the Christian acceptance of the pagan principle of *do ut des.* Any assumption of a direct, causal connection between things spiritual and material, any

[22] Cf. *De Civitate Dei,* I, viii, 13–19: "Placuit quippe diuinae prouidentiae praeparare in posterum bona iustis, quibus non fruentur iniusti, et mala impiis, quibus non excruciabuntur boni; ista uero temporalia bona et mala utrisque uoluit esse communia, ut nec bona cupidius adpetantur, quae mali quoque habere cernuntur; nec mala turpiter euitentur, quibus et boni plerumque adficiuntur."

assumption of a commutative contract between the Creator and his creatures, had to be most emphatically rejected by Augustine as wholly contrary to his conception of the relationship between God and men, even the great and best of this world.

This divergence of opinion concerns points of central importance in the systems of thought of Orosius and Augustine. Other differences between the views of the two men resulted, as we have seen, from the very nature of the task assigned to Orosius, or they can be explained by the fact that Orosius took the right of developing his own ideas in regard to problems to which his master appeared not to have given definite answers. But when Orosius came to the most crucial questions, the interpretation of the course of history as a whole and the elucidation of the workings of God and divine providence in time and on earth, then, it must be said, he set forth views which ran directly counter to much of what Augustine had said or left unsaid in the first part of *The City of God.* Perhaps Orosius himself was completely unaware of these fundamental deviations and believed himself in full accord with Augustine. But in spite of this subjective conviction, it is objectively impossible to maintain that "the basic principles upon which Orosius founded his philosophy of history were those he held in common with his guide and friend St. Augustine." On the contrary, we must say that the basic principles of Orosius' philosophy of history were those of Eusebius and his Greek and Latin followers in the fourth century, principles most explicitly rejected by Augustine in the first part of *The City of God.*

There still remains the second group of questions asked at the beginning of this lecture: how much use of Orosius' work did Augustine make in the second part of *The City of God,* and what did he think of the ideas of his pupil? In answer to these questions we must notice first that in the entire latter part of *The City of God* Augustine did not mention once either the name or the work of Orosius. When he referred to "our [i.e., Christian] historians who have written chronicles," he always meant Eusebius and St. Jerome, not Orosius [XVIII,

viii, 49–50]. This omission is the more remarkable since for some of the events he discussed Augustine could have found more information in *The Seven Books* than he himself presented. For example, in regard to the question of the role played by the four universal monarchies in world history, Augustine completely disregarded Orosius' elaborate treatment and instead referred the reader to Jerome's *Book on Daniel*, "which is written with sufficient care and erudition" [XX, xxiii, 42–46]. Another point which, it will be remembered, was strongly stressed by Orosius, was the providential coincidence of the birth of Christ and the foundation of the Roman Empire by Augustus. In the first part of *The City of God* Augustine had paid no particular attention to this fact. Evidently he remained unwilling to attribute to it any true significance, for in the second part of his work he still stated simply that Christ was born "when Herod was king in Judea and . . . Augustus was emperor in Rome" [XVIII, xlvi, 1–3]. The brevity of this one sentence contrasts most sharply with the long discussion of the same fact in no less than seven chapters of Orosius' work. It seems permissible to conclude from this difference of treatment that Augustine not only was uninterested in, but even disapproved, that whole "Augustus-theology" which occupied such a central position in Orosius' philosophy of history.

There is at least one important passage in the second part of *The City of God* which represents an outright rejection of an argument set forth in *The Seven Books against the Pagans*. In one of the last chapters of his work Orosius drew a curious and rather absurd parallel between the ten plagues of Egypt and the ten persecutions of the Christians by the pagan emperors; and from that parallel he drew the comforting conclusion that there would be no further persecutions of the Christians before the coming of Antichrist [VII, 27]. Such optimism was in full accord with Orosius' acceptance of the Eusebian idea of progress, but it was just as definitely contrary to everything Augustine believed. Indeed Augustine refuted the validity of the whole comparison by pointing out that there had actually been more than ten persecutions before the reign of Constantine and that there had also been persecutions since that time, by both pagan and heretical emperors. For that reason it seemed to him "an audacious presumption . . . to attempt foretelling what further persecutions may come from rulers." The whole context of Augustine's remarks makes it certain that it was Orosius with whom he took issue here, although he avoided any direct disavowal of his former student, who, after all, had dedicated his work to him. He therefore contented himself with stating: "I think that no one should rashly say or believe, as some have done or do, that until the time of Antichrist the Church will suffer no more than the ten persecutions she has already suffered" [XVIII, lii, 1–5].

Augustine may have felt toward quite a few other points of Orosius' philosophy of history what he felt concerning the parallels "drawn so nicely and ingeniously" between the ten plagues of Egypt and the ten persecutions: "I can see here no prophetic spirit, but mere human guess-work which sometimes hits the truth and sometimes misses it" [XVIII, lii, 17–20]. He did not choose, however, to give open voice to his criticism. But as far as his own work was concerned, he most definitely did *not* "avail himself" of *The Seven Books of Histories,* as Dante was to assume in *The Divine Comedy*. And as far as his personal attitude to Orosius is concerned, it is worth noting that we find but one mention of Orosius by name in any of the later writings and correspondence of Augustine, whereas he had praised him quite highly, as we have seen, in some letters written before the composition of *The Seven Books.* Only at the very end of his life did Augustine refer to Orosius, but, interestingly enough, in a noncommital, perhaps even rather slighting fashion. For in his *Retractationes* he said that he wrote his book *Against the Priscillianists* (415) in reply to an inquiry from "a certain Spanish priest, Orosius" [II, xliv].

Whether or not the condemnatory character of Augustine's silence was understood by his contemporaries, we do not know. But it is certain that later generations were completely unaware of it. They were bound to remember the close master-pupil relationship which had once existed between the two men, and above all they must have been deeply impressed by the words with which Orosius concluded his final address to Augustine at the end of his work: "If you publish it, you approve it; if you destroy it, you condemn it" [VII, 43, 20]. Since the work obviously had not been destroyed, it was logical to assume that it had met with Augustine's full approval and therefore to accept the interpretation of the course and the meaning of history which *The Seven Books* contained as an authoritative expression of Augustinian thought. There is no doubt that the practicing historians of the Middle Ages were more apt to read *The Seven Books of Histories* than *The City of God.* Consequently we find that most medieval universal histories set forth ideas and judgments and reflect a philosophy of history which cannot be called truly Augustinian. Rather they reflect a philosophy of history which rightly may be called Orosian.

Bibliography of the Writings of Theodor E. Mommsen

BOOKS

Studien zum Ideengehalt der deutschen Aussenpolitik im Zeitalter der Ottonen und Salier. Dissertation. Berlin, 1930.

Italienische Analekten zur Reichsgeschichte des 14. Jahrhunderts (1310–1378). (With the collaboration of Wolfgang Hagemann.) *Schriften der Monumenta Germaniae Historica,* XI. Stuttgart, 1952.

Petrarch's Testament. Ithaca, N.Y., 1957.

INTRODUCTIONS

Introduction to Petrarch's *Sonnets and Songs* (New York, 1946), pp. xv–xlii.

Introduction to Charles Homer Haskins' *Rise of the Universities* (Ithaca, N. Y., 1957), pp. v–ix.

ARTICLES

"Eine Niederaltaicher Privaturkunde aus dem 9. Jahrhundert," in *Festschrift Albert Brackmann,* ed. Leo Santifaller (Weimar, 1931), pp. 64–80.

"Zur Freisinger Urkunden-Ueberlieferung," *Zeitschrift für bayerische Landesgeschichte,* V (1932), 129–139, 416–428.

"Beiträge zur Reichsgeschichte von 1313–1349. Aus süddeutschen

Archiven," *Neues Archiv der Gesellschaft für ältere deutsche Geschichtskunde,* L (1933), 388–423.
"Eine Urkunde Kaiser Ludwigs des Bayern für die Stadt Eberbach," *Zeitschrift für die Geschichte des Oberrheins,* N.F. XLVII (1934), 385–387.
"Castruccio e l'Impero," in *Castruccio Castracani degli Antelminelli. Miscellanea di studi storici e letterari edita della Reale Accademia Lucchese, Atti della R. Accademia Lucchese,* N.S. III (1934), 33–45.
"Karl der Grosse–Kaiser der Franzosen?" *Deutsche Zukunft. Wochenzeitung für Politik, Wirtschaft und Kultur,* April 7, 1935, p. 5.
"Das Habsburgisch-Angiovinische Ehe-Bündnis von 1316," *Neues Archiv der Gesellschaft für ältere deutsche Geschichtskunde,* L (1935), 600–615.
"Die Landvogtei Ortenau und das Kloster Gengenbach unter Kaiser Ludwig dem Bayern. Eine urkundenkritische Untersuchung," *Zeitschrift für die Geschichte des Oberrheins,* N.F. XLIX (1936), 165–213.
"Die ältesten Rothenburger Königsurkunden. Ein Beitrag zur Geschichte des Landgerichts und der Landvogtei in Rothenburg von Rudolf I. bis zu Ludwig dem Bayern," *Zeitschrift für bayerische Landesgeschichte,* X (1937), 19–64.
"The Date of Petrarch's Canzone *Italia Mia,*" *Speculum,* XIV (1939), 28–37.
"Football in Renaissance Florence," *Yale University Library Gazette,* XVI (1941), 14–19.
"The Venetians in Athens and the Destruction of the Parthenon in 1687," *American Journal of Archaeology,* XLV (1941), 544–556.
"Petrarch's Conception of the 'Dark Ages' ," *Speculum,* XVII (1942), 226–242.
"The Accession of the Helvetian Federation to the Holy League: An Unpublished Bull of Pope Julius II of March 17, 1512," *Journal of Modern History,* XX (1948), 123–132.
"The *Monumenta Germaniae Historica:* Present Status and Plans" (with J. P. Elder), *Speculum,* XXIV (1949), 307–308.
"Un' antica raffigurazione del Petrarca poeta laureato," *Studi Petrarcheschi,* II (1949), 100–105.
"Un problema riguardante la topografia medioevale di Roma: S. Nicola in Carcere nell' anno 1400," *Rendiconti della Pontificia Accademia Romana d'Archeologia,* XXIII–XXIV (1947–1949), 309–315.

"A Bibliography of Books and Articles on Italian Renaissance Thought," *Philosophical Review,* LIX (1950), 237–239.

"St. Augustine and the Christian Idea of Progress. The Background of The City of God," *Journal of the History of Ideas,* XII (1951), 346–374.

"Petrarch and the Decoration of the Sala Virorum Illustrium in Padua," *Art Bulletin,* XXXIV (1952), 95–116.

"Rudolph Agricola's Life of Petrarch," *Traditio,* VIII (1952), 367–386.

"Petrarch and the Story of the Choice of Hercules," *Journal of the Warburg and Courtauld Institutes,* XVI (1953), 178–192.

"Augustus and Britain: A Fragment from Livy?," *American Journal of Philology,* LXXV (1954), 175–183.

"Aponius and Orosius on the Significance of the Epiphany," in *Late Classical and Mediaeval Studies in Honor of Albert Mathias Friend, Jr.,* ed. Kurt Weitzmann (Princeton, N.J., 1955), pp. 96–111.

REVIEW ARTICLES

G. B. Ladner, *Die Papstbildnisse des Altertums und des Mittelalters,* I. *Traditio,* V (1947), 351–359.

"Frederick Antal's Florentine Painting and Its Social Background," *Journal of the History of Ideas,* XI (1950), 369–379.

Otto of Freising, *The Deeds of Frederick Barbarossa,* ed. and tr. Charles Christopher Mierow, with the collaboration of Richard Emery. *Speculum,* XXIX (1954), 303–306.

REVIEWS

P. E. Schramm, *Kaiser, Rom und Renovatio. Neues Archiv,* XLIX (1932), 577–578.

E. Franzel, *König Heinrich VII. von Hohenstaufen. Studien zur Geschichte des "Staates" in Deutschland. Neues Archiv,* XLIX (1932), 588–589.

H. Fischer, *Die verfassungsrechtliche Stellung der Juden in den deutschen Städten während des 13. Jahrhunderts. Neues Archiv,* XLIX (1932), 675–676.

K. Schünemann, *Die Entstehung des Städtewesens in Südosteuropa. Neues Archiv,* XLIX (1932), 677–678.[1]

[1] Shorter notices among the *Nachrichten* of the *Neues Archiv* will be found in vol. XLIX (1932), pp. 575, 576, 577, 594, 605, 627–628, 660–661, 667, 677, 679, 706–707, 769 and in vol. L (1935), 649, 651, 652, 653–654, 736, 743, 755.

Franz Lerner, *Kardinal Hugo Candidus. Mitteilungen des österreichischen Instituts für Geschichtsforschung,* XLVII (1933), 365–366.

Ferdinand Scheville, *History of Florence from the Founding of the City through the Renaissance. Yale Review,* XXVI (1937), 628–630.

Wallace K. Ferguson, *The Renaissance. American Historical Review,* XLVI (1941), 365–367.

Jacob Burckhard, *Force and Freedom: Reflections on History,* ed. James Hastings Nichols. *Yale Review,* XXXIII (1943), 177–179.

Leonardo Olschki, *Machiavelli, the Scientist. American Historical Review,* LI (October 1945), 150.

Jacob Burckhard, *The Civilization of the Renaissance in Italy. Yale Review,* XXXV (1945), 182–183.

Leonhard von Muralt, *Machiavellis Staatsgedanke. American Historical Review,* LI (1946), 706–708.

H. W. Garrod, *Scholarship: Its Meaning and Value. American Historical Review,* LII (1947), 765–766.[2]

Eugenio Garin, *Der italienische Humanismus. Philosophical Review,* LVIII (1949), 627–630.

Honoré Bonet, *The Tree of Battles,* ed. and tr. G. W. Coopland. *American Historical Review,* LV (1950), 660–661.

Margaret Mann Phillips, *Erasmus and the Northern Renaissance. American Historical Review,* LVI (October 1950), 178.

H. Fichtenau, *Das karolingische Imperium. Traditio,* VII (1949–1951), 500–502.

George Bingham Fowler, *Intellectual Interests of Engelbert of Admont. Deutsches Archiv für Geschichte des Mittelalters,* VIII (1951), 633.

J. M. Patton, *Chapters on Mediaeval and Renaissance Visitors to Greek Lands. American Historical Review,* LVII (October 1951), 209–210.

Lauri Houvinen, *Das Bild vom Menschen im politischen Denken*

[2] Cf. Mommsen's letter to the Editor of the *William and Mary Quarterly* on the article by A. P. Adair, "The Mystery of the Horn Papers," *William and Mary Quarterly,* IV (1947), 409–445. He writes that the committee appointed to investigate the Horn Papers not only succeeded "in fully proving the spuriousness of the 'primary' material contained in *The Horn Papers,* but it solved this task with such methodological precision and completeness that its Report ought to be widely used in graduate Seminars on methods of historical research . . ." (*William and Mary Quarterly,* V [1948], 463).

Niccolò Machiavellis. American Historical Review, LVII (1952), 1012.

Craig R. Thompson, *Inquisitio de fide: A Colloquy by Erasmus. American Historical Review,* LIX (1954), 669.

Garrett Mattingly, *Renaissance Diplomacy. American Historical Review,* LXI (1956), 948–949.

Paul Oskar Kristeller, *The Classics and Renaissance Thought. American Historical Review,* LXI (1956), 997–998.

Syntagma Friburgense: Historische Studien Hermann Aubin dargebracht zum 70. Geburtstag am 23.12.1955. American Historical Review, LXIII (October 1957), 171–172.

Werner Kaegi, *Jacob Burckhardt: Eine Biographie.* Band III, *Die Zeit der klassischen Werke. American Historical Review,* LXIII (1958), 976–978.